www.wadsworth.com

About the Authors

George F. Cole (right) is Professor of Political Science at the University of Connecticut. A specialist in the administration of criminal justice, he has published extensively on such topics as prosecution, courts, and corrections. George Cole is also co-author with Christopher Smith of *Criminal Justice in America*, co-author with Todd Clear of *American Corrections*, and co-author with Marc Gertz of *The Criminal Justice System: Politics and Policy*. He developed and directed the graduate corrections program at the University of Connecticut and was a Fellow at the National Institute of Justice. Among his other accomplishments, he has been granted two awards under the Fulbright-Hays Program to conduct criminal justice research in England and the former Yugoslavia. In 1995 he was named a Fellow of the Academy of Criminal Justice Sciences for distinguished teaching and research.

Christopher E. Smith is Professor of Criminal Justice at Michigan State University. Trained as a lawyer and social scientist, he is the author of fifteen books and more than seventy scholarly articles on law, courts, and criminal justice policy. His most recent books include *Law and Contemporary Corrections* and *Courts, Politics, and the Judicial Process*. He is also the co-author, with George Cole, of *Criminal Justice in America*.

THE AMERICAN SYSTEM OF

Criminal Justice

NINTH EDITION

George F. Cole
UNIVERSITY OF CONNECTICUT

Christopher E. Smith
MICHIGAN STATE UNIVERSITY

Wadsworth
Thomson Learning

Australia • Canada • Mexico • Singapore • Spain • United Kingdom • United States

Criminal Justice Editor: Dan Alpert
Development Editor: Terri Edwards
Assistant Editor: Ann Tsai
Editorial Assistant: Cortney Bruggink
Marketing Manager: Jennifer Somerville
Project Editor: Jennie Redwitz
Print Buyer: Karen Hunt
Permissions Editor: Bobbie Broyer

Production Service: Greg Hubit Bookworks
Text Designer: Paul Uhl/Design Associates; rosa+wesley
Photo Researcher: Roberta Spieckerman Associates
Copy Editor: Colleen McGuiness
Cover Designer: Gladys Rosa-Mendoza, rosa+wesley
Cover Images: *Upper,* © Leeson Photography;
                lower, © Mark Richards/PhotoEdit
Compositor: rosa+wesley
Text and Cover Printer: Von Hoffmann Press, Inc.

Wadsworth/Thomson Learning
10 Davis Drive
Belmont, CA 94002-3098
USA

For more information about our products, contact us:
Thomson Learning Academic Resource Center
1-800-423-0563
http://www.wadsworth.com

International Headquarters
Thomson Learning
International Division
290 Harbor Drive, 2nd Floor
Stamford, CT 06902-7477
USA

UK/Europe/Middle East/South Africa
Thomson Learning
Berkshire House
168-173 High Holborn
London WC1V 7AA
United Kingdom

Asia
Thomson Learning
60 Albert Street, #15-01
Albert Complex
Singapore 189969

Canada
Nelson Thomson Learning
1120 Birchmount Road
Toronto, Ontario M1K 5G4
Canada

Library of Congress Cataloging-in-Publication Data
Cole, George F.
    The American system of criminal justice / George F.
Cole, Christopher E. Smith—9th ed.
        p. cm.
    Includes bibliographical references and index.
    ISBN 0-534-57555-2
    1. Criminal justice. Administration of—United States.
I. Title: Criminal justice. II. Smith, Christopher E.
III. Title.
KF9223.C648   2001
364.973—dc20   00-042645

 This book is printed on acid-free recycled paper.

Brief Contents

Contents

Chapter 3
Criminal Justice and the Rule of Law   82

Chapter 6
Policing: Issues and Trends   202

Preface

Most students come to the introductory course in criminal justice intrigued by the prospect of learning about crime and the operation of the criminal justice system. Many of them look forward to the roles they may one day fill in allocating justice, either as citizens or in careers with the police, courts, or corrections. All have been exposed to a great deal of information—and misinformation—about criminal justice through the news and entertainment media. Whatever their views, few are indifferent to the subject they are about to explore.

Like all newcomers to a field, however, introductory students in criminal justice need, first, a *solid foundation* of valid information about the subject and, second, a *way to think about* this information. They need conceptual tools that enable them not only to absorb a large body of factual content but also to process that information critically, reflect on it, and extend their learning beyond the classroom. Providing both the essential content and the critical tools is the dual aim of this text.

The Approach of This Text: Three Key Themes

When the first edition of *The American System of Criminal Justice* was published in 1975, it embodied three assumptions about the future direction of criminal justice as a discipline and the way the introductory course should be taught.

- *The field of criminal justice is interdisciplinary,* with research contributions from criminology, sociology, law, history, psychology, and political science.
- *Criminal justice involves public policies* that are developed within the political framework of the democratic process.
- *The concept of social system is an essential tool* for explaining and analyzing the way criminal justice is administered and practiced.

This book's approach has met with a degree of acceptance that has been gratifying and also challenging. Instructors at hundreds of colleges and universities throughout the nation have chosen this book, and over the years more than a half million of their students have used it. Yet no textbook author can afford to rest on his or her laurels, particularly in a field as dynamic as criminal justice. The social scene changes, research multiplies, theories are modified, and new policies are proposed and implemented while old ones become unpopular and fade away. Students and their needs change as well. Accordingly, we have made this ninth edition of "the Eagle" even more current, vital, cohesive, and appealing to students and instructors alike.

Highlights of the Ninth Edition

This edition is a revision in both content and presentation. A greater emphasis has been given to criminal justice policies and the role public opinion plays in the development of those policies. Care has been taken to streamline the entire book. The organization of each chapter has also been reexamined and improved.

In addition to these structural changes, the content, research sources, examples, and emphasis have been updated in every chapter. The text has been rewritten line by line to make descriptions succinct and clear and chapters and sections cohesive. The text's special features help the student see the significance of important issues and the context in which they occur. The text is also now more accessible to students at all levels. We hope that these changes make this ninth edition even more usable and "teachable" than its predecessors.

Content Mastery: Organization, Coverage, and Study Aids

While instructors who have used the book will find the basic plan of the text familiar, this edition embodies several important changes. Study and review aids have been revised and enhanced to coordinate with these changes.

Crime and Justice in a Multicultural Society

Disparities in the treatment of African Americans, Hispanic Americans, and other minorities are pervasive in the criminal justice system. This issue is addressed in Chapter 1 and reexamined in succeeding chapters in discussions of what minority-group members experience when they come in contact with the police, the courts, and corrections. The complex issue of attributing criminality to race is carefully examined. Special attention is given to the current controversy over racial profiling. New sections describe the role of Native American tribal police and trial courts and the difficulties some recent immigrants have had in adjusting to American law and customs.

Crime Control Policy

Recent years have seen a major shift to a greater emphasis on crime control. Legislatures, in response to public opinion, have toughened sentences, increased the number of police officers, and reduced funding for rehabilitative programs. We examine this shift in light of the decrease in crime rates and the increase in prison populations.

Policy issues are presented at the end of each part of the book. An issue is described, the pros and cons are outlined, and then students are asked to determine the policy the United States should adopt. The controversies of mandatory sentencing of drug offenders and the presence of a "prison-commercial" complex are new to this edition.

Improved Coverage of Policing

Major changes are occurring in American policing as the law enforcement/crime fighter emphasis is supplemented by a focus on community policing and problem solving. Part Two (Chapters 4, 5, and 6) has been reoriented to illustrate this shift in police operations, and the most up-to-date research has been incorporated into the text. Police tactics—aggressive public order enforcement, high-speed chase policies, profiling—are explored more deeply than in previous editions.

Study and Review Aids

To help students identify and master core concepts, the text provides several study and review aids.

- *Chapter outlines* preview the structure of each chapter.
- *Opening vignettes* introduce the chapter topic with a high-interest real-life episode.
- *Questions for Inquiry* highlight the chapter's key topics and themes.
- *Checkpoints* throughout each chapter allow students to test themselves on content.
- *Going Online* provides students with a set of exercises using the World Wide Web and InfoTrac College Edition.
- *Chapter Summaries* and *Questions for Review* reinforce key concepts and provide further checks on learning.
- *Key Terms* are defined throughout the text in the margins of each chapter and can also be located in the Glossary. *Key Cases* explain major issues decided by the courts.
- An appendix on *understanding statistical figures and tables* helps readers interpret the data presented in this text and research in other fields as well.

Enhanced Graphics

Today's students have been influenced by television all their lives. They are attuned to colorful images that convey values and emotions as well as information. For this edition, outstanding graphic artists and photo researchers have helped to develop an impressive array of full-color illustrations. Quantitative data are illuminated by conversion into bar graphs, pie charts, and other graphic forms; written summaries guide comprehension of the graphic presentations. Special care has been taken to place photographs and their captions so that the images are linked to the message of the text.

Promoting Critical Understanding

Aided by the features just described, diligent students can master the essential content of the introductory course. While such mastery is no small achievement, most instructors aim higher: they want students, whether future criminal justice professionals or simply citizens, to complete this course with the ability to take a more thoughtful and critical approach to issues of crime and justice than they did at the start of the course. The ninth edition provides several features that help students learn how to think about the field.

Thematic Emphases

A gratifying number of instructors have welcomed the key assumptions that have guided the writing of this book. These assumptions—that criminal justice is an interdisciplinary field, that crime and justice are public policy issues, and that criminal justice can best be seen as a social system—are introduced in Chapter 1 and reiterated in the chapters that follow.

The text is truly *interdisciplinary* in that it draws upon the research and writings of scholars from a range of academic and applied disciplines. In each chapter students are exposed to the contributions of historians, criminologists, legal scholars, psychologists, political scientists, and others. They will recognize, for example, that the penitentiary is an American invention and that its development in the 1830s was greatly influenced by the social and political ideas of that era. Likewise, the administrative sciences have contributed to the organization and tactics of the police.

The *role of public policy* in criminal justice is developed through examples and explicit discussions throughout the text. For example, we examine policies such as "three strikes and you're out," assistance to crime victims, community policing, and the death penalty for both their content and their potential impact on the system. Throughout the book, students are reminded that the definition of behaviors as criminal, the funding of criminal justice operations, and the election of judges and prosecutors all result from decisions that are politically influenced. In this edition greater attention is placed on the role of public opinion in the development of criminal justice policies.

The *system perspective,* which is developed in Chapter 1, is carried throughout the book as a concept that is useful in analyzing criminal justice operations. The idea of the system is reinforced graphically with illustrations that remind students of exchange relationships, the flow of decision making, and the way the criminal justice system is itself embedded in a larger governmental and societal context.

Close-Ups and Other Real-Life Examples

Understanding criminal justice in a purely theoretical way is not enough. In order to help students gain a balanced understanding, the wealth of illustrations in this book shows how theory plays out in practice and what the human implications of policies and procedures are. In addition to the many examples in the text, the *Close-Up* features in each chapter draw from newspapers, court decisions, first-person accounts, and other current sources. In this edition, the Close-Ups are smoothly integrated into the context so that students readily see their relevance.

A Question of Ethics

Criminal justice requires that decisions not only be made within the framework of law but also be consistent with the ethical norms of American society. In each chapter, *A Question of Ethics* scenarios place students in the context of decision makers faced with a problem involving ethics. Students become aware of the many ethical dilemmas that criminal justice personnel must deal with and the types of questions they may have to answer if they assume a role in the system.

What Americans Think

Public opinion plays an important role in the policy-making process in a democracy. The opinions of Americans, as collected through surveys, are presented alongside controversial criminal justice issues. Students are encouraged to compare their own opinion with the national perspective. This feature is linked to the text-specific Web site.

Comparative Perspectives

With the move toward more global thinking in academia and society at large, students are showing new interest in learning more about criminal justice in other parts of the world. Most chapters of this edition include a *Comparative Perspective* section that describes a component of the criminal justice system in another country. In addition to broadening students' conceptual horizons, these sections encourage a more critical appreciation of the system many Americans take for granted. By learning about others, students learn more about themselves.

Supplements

The most extensive package of supplemental aids for a criminal justice text accompanies this edition. A number of separate items have been developed to enhance the course and to assist instructors and students.

Annotated Instructor's Edition

A fully annotated instructor's edition will assist instructors in organizing their classroom presentations and reinforcing the themes of the course. Marginal notes tie all of the supplements, directly to the text topics, and also reference teaching suggestions from the *Instructor's Resource Manual*.

Instructor's Resource Manual and Computerized Test Bank

A full-fledged *Instructor's Resource Manual* has been developed by text author Christopher E. Smith. The manual includes resource lists, lecture outlines, and teaching suggestions that will help time-pressed teachers more effectively communicate with their students and also strengthen coverage of course material. Each chapter has multiple choice and true/false test items, as well as sample essay questions.

ExamView®

This computerized testing software helps instructors create and customize exams in minutes. Instructors can easily edit and import their own questions and graphics, change test layout, and reorganize questions. This software also offers the ability to test and grade online. It is available for both Windows and Macintosh.

CNN Today Video Series

Exclusively from Wadsworth/Thomson Learning, the *CNN Today Video Series* offers compelling videos that feature current news footage from the Cable News Network's comprehensive archives. *Criminal Justice in the News: Volume I* and *Criminal Justice in the News: Volume II* provide a collection of three- to five-minute clips on hot topics in criminal justice such as high-tech policing, registering sex offenders, cocaine/crack sentencing, juveniles behind bars, and much more. Available to qualified adopters, both videotapes are great lecture launchers as well as classroom discussion pieces.

The Wadsworth Criminal Justice Video Library

The Wadsworth Criminal Justice Video Library offers an exciting collection of videos to enrich lectures. Qualified adopters may select from a wide variety of professionally prepared videos covering various aspects of policing, corrections, and other areas of the criminal justice system. The selections include videos from *Films for Humanities*, Court TV videos that feature provocative one-hour court cases to illustrate seminal and high-profile cases in-depth, *A&E American Justice Series* videos, *National Institute of Justice: Crime File* videos, ABC News videos, and *MPI Home Videos*.

Web Site for *The American System of Criminal Justice,* Ninth Edition

Designed exclusively for this text, this is one of the best book-specific web sites on the Internet. In addition to participating in exciting online polls, students can use this site as a launching point for research, meet other students in cyberspace to discuss criminal justice topics, and improve test scores by using the online quizzes.

Transparencies

To bring the graphic portions of the text to the classroom, fifty full-color transparencies for overhead projection are available. These transparencies help instructors to fully discuss concepts and research findings with students.

PowerPoint Presentation Tool

The Introduction to Criminal Justice PowerPoint Presentation 2001 is an important tool that instructors can use to prepare for class lectures. The more than 450 color images will aid instructors in visually representing to students the main concepts and ideas contained in the text.

Student Study Guide

An extensive student guide has been developed for this edition by text author Christopher Smith. Because students learn in different ways, a variety of pedagogical aids is included in the guide to help them. Each chapter is outlined, major terms are defined, and summaries and sample questions are provided.

Web Tutor™

Designed specifically for *The American System of Criminal Justice,* Ninth Edition, Web Tutor is an online resource that gives both instructors and students a virtual environment that is rich with study and communication tools. For instructors, Web Tutor can provide virtual office hours, post syllabi, set up threaded discussions, and track student progress. Web Tutor can also be customized in a variety of ways, such as uploading images and other resources and adding web links to create customized practice materials. For students, Web Tutor offers real-time access to many study aids, including flash cards, practice quizzes, online tutorials, and Web links.

Careers in Criminal Justice Interactive CD-ROM

This engaging self-exploration CD-ROM provides an interactive discovery of the wide range of careers in criminal justice. The self-assessment helps steer students to suitable careers based on their personal profile. Students gather information on various careers from job descriptions, salaries, employment requirements, sample tests, and video profiles of criminal justice professionals.

Crime Scenes CD-ROM

The first CD-ROM developed specifically for the introductory criminal justice course, this highly visual and interactive program casts students as the decision makers in various roles as they explore all aspects of the criminal justice system. Exciting videos and supporting documents put students in the midst of a juvenile murder trial, a prostitution case that turns to manslaughter, and several other scenarios. This product received the gold medal in higher education and silver medal for video interface from *New Media Magazine's Invision Awards*.

Mind of a Killer CD-ROM

Based on Eric Hickey's book *Serial Murderers and Their Victims*, this award-winning CD-ROM offers viewers a look at the psyches of the world's most notorious killers. Students can view confessions of and interviews with serial killers, and they can examine famous cases through original video documentaries and news footage. Included are 3-D profiling simulations, which are extensive mapping systems that seek to find out what motivates these killers.

InfoTrac College Edition

Students receive four months of real-time access to InfoTrac College Edition's online database of continuously updated, full-length articles from hundreds of journals and periodicals. By doing a simple keyword search, users can quickly generate a list of related articles, then select relevant articles to explore and print out for reference or further study.

Criminal Justice Internet Investigator

This handy brochure lists the most useful criminal justice links on the World Wide Web. It includes the most popular criminal justice sites, listservs, online newsletters, grants and funding information, and more.

Seeking Employment in Criminal Justice

Written by J. Scott Harr and Kären Hess, this practical book, now in its third edition, helps students develop a search strategy to find employment in criminal justice and related fields. Each chapter includes "insiders' views," written by individuals in the field and addressing promotions and career planning.

Guide to the Internet for Criminal Justice

Developed by Daniel Kurland and Christina Polsenberg, this easy reference text helps newcomers as well as experienced Web-surfers use the Internet for criminal justice research.

Your Research: Data Analysis for Criminal Justice and Criminology

Written by criminal justice experts Michael Blankenship and Gennaro Vito, this book, in its second edition, is an easy-to-use data analysis and graphics program with an accompanying workbook replete with examples of criminological research projects. This software is available for PCs.

A Group Effort

It is not possible to be expert about every aspect of the criminal justice system. Authors need help in covering new developments and ensuring that research findings are correctly interpreted. This revision has greatly benefited from the advice of three sets of scholars. One group of almost twenty-five hundred participated in a national survey designed to reveal to us more about the way the introductory course is taught, the type of text that instructors and students want, and the pluses and minuses of *The American System of Criminal Justice* compared with other texts. A second group of criminal justice scholars was asked to comment on the entire manuscript, especially its organization and pedagogical usefulness. These reviewers were chosen from the wide range of colleges and universities throughout the country that have used previous editions, so their comments concerning presentation, levels of student abilities, and the requirements of introductory courses at their institutions were especially useful. Reviewers in the third group were nationally recognized experts in the field; they focused their attention on the areas in which they specialized. Their many comments helped us avoid errors and drew our attention to points in the literature that had been neglected.

The many criminal justice students and instructors who used the eighth edition also contributed abundantly to this edition. Several hundred readers returned the questionnaire included in that edition. Their comments provided crucial practical feedback. Others gave us their comments personally when we lectured in criminal justice classes around the country.

We have also been assisted in writing this edition by a diverse group of associates. Chief among them was Executive Editor Sabra Horne, who has always been supportive of our efforts. Our editor, Dan Alpert, also helped us shape the vision for this edition. The project has benefited much from the attention of our project editor, Jennie Redwitz, who helped keep the book on course. Copy editor Colleen McGuiness prevented us from committing egregious errors in the use of English. The interior of the book was designed by rosa+wesley. Assistant Editor Ann Tsai was invaluable in helping us develop the supplemental aids. And the following reviewers contributed valuable comments:

John Cochran
University of South Florida

Tom Dempsey
Christopher Newport University

Frank Morn
Illinois State University

Matthew Robinson
Appalachian State University

William Ruefle
University of South Carolina

Gary Uhrin
Westmoreland County Community College

John Wyant
Illinois Central College.

Ultimately, however, the full responsibility for the book is ours alone.

George F. Cole
gcole@uconnvm.uconn.edu

Christopher E. Smith
smithc28@msu.edu

What is the sequence of events in the criminal justice system?

This flowchart provides an overview of the criminal justice system as it will be described in this book. It is important to recognize that the system portrayed here is a social system. Each event depicted represents a complex interaction of people, politics, and procedures.

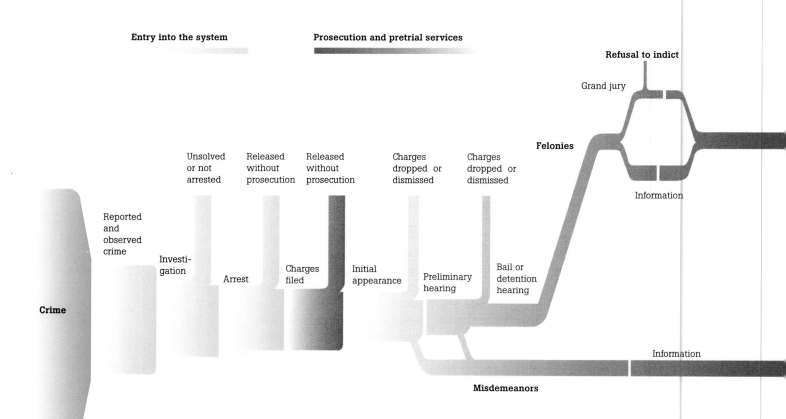

Originally published by the President's Commission on Law Enforcement and Administration of Justice in 1967, the flowchart was revised in 1997 by the Bureau of Justice Statistics.

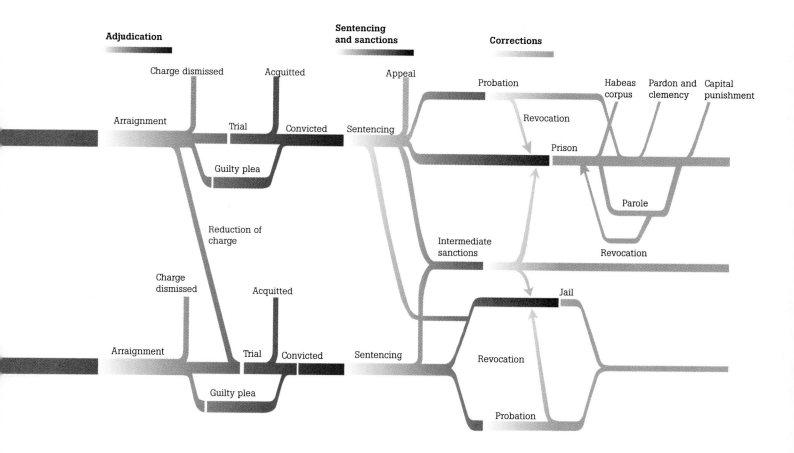

Adjudication

Charge dismissed   Acquitted

Arraignment

Trial   Convicted

Guilty plea

Reduction of charge

Charge dismissed   Acquitted

Arraignment

Trial   Convicted

Guilty plea

Sentencing and sanctions

Appeal

Sentencing

Intermediate sanctions

Sentencing

Revocation

Probation

Corrections

Probation   Habeas corpus   Pardon and clemency   Capital punishment

Revocation

Prison

Parole

Revocation

Jail

The Criminal Justice Process

The American system of criminal justice is a response to a problem that has required the attention of all societies from the beginning of time: crime. To understand how the system works and why crime persists in spite of efforts to control it, both the nature of criminal behavior and the functioning of the justice system itself must be examined. The reality of crime and justice involves much more than "cops and robbers," the details of legal codes, and the penalties for breaking laws. From defining what behavior counts as criminal to deciding the fate of offenders who are caught, the process of criminal justice is a *social* process subject to many influences other than written law.

Part One, in introducing the study of this process, provides a broad framework for analyzing how American society—through its police, courts, and corrections—tries to deal with the age-old problem of crime.

Crime and Justice in America

Newspaper headlines across the country proclaim: "Killings Soar in Big Cities across U.S.," "Shopowners Demand Foot Patrol," "Drug Turf War Yields Violence," "Neighbors Unite against Crime," "Prison Population Reaches New High." Television news programs depict urban neighborhoods ravaged by drugs and crime, small towns anxious about local shoot-outs, and citizens expressing fears about leaving their homes at night.

Meanwhile public opinion polls indicate people remain very fearful of crime, even though serious crime has declined since the record-setting years of the early 1980s. Crime continues to appear at or near the top of surveys asking Americans to name the most important issues facing the country (see What Americans Think).

They tell pollsters they are frightened by events such as schoolyard killings, the murder in New Jersey of 11-year-old Edward Werner as he sold candy door to door, the Texas railway serial killer, deaths of four women in Yosemite National Park, carjackings, the burning of

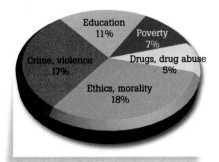
churches in Indiana, and the torture of women in New Mexico. Crime reporting has become such a staple of local television news coverage that it has acquired its own cliche: "If it bleeds, it leads" (*New York Times,* July 6, 1997:E4). Whatever else has happened, the story of someone having been murdered, raped, or assaulted will lead the newscast. No wonder Americans go to bed fearful.

Responding to these concerns, politicians have tried to outdo one another in being "tough on crime." This toughness has led to shifts in public policies: funding for 100,000 additional police officers, building more prisons, extending the death penalty to cover sixty additional federal offenses, mandating longer sentences, and requiring parolees to register with the police.

But is the concern about crime justified? As one reporter noted, "It is as though the country were confronting a devastating new wave of theft and violence" (*San Jose Mercury* News, October 23, 1993). However, there *is* no national crime wave. The news that crime is not rampant may surprise most Americans, but Federal Bureau of Investigation (FBI) data support this fact. For example, serious crime has fallen every year since 1993. The homicide rate is the lowest nationwide since 1969. In 1998 the number of violent crimes and property crimes each fell 7 percent, and the number of murders was down 8 percent. The biggest decrease occurred in robbery, which fell 11 percent, followed by motor vehicle theft, which declined 10 percent (Butterfield, 1999c). Yet despite this good news, Americans "are afraid of and obsessed with crime" (Donziger, 1996:1).

Themes of This Book

The study of criminal justice offers a fascinating view of a crucial social problem. Drawing from the perspectives of such academic disciplines as economics, history, law, political science, psychology, and sociology, the field of criminal justice aims to supply knowledge and develop policies to deal with criminality. But it is a challenge to a democracy to develop policies that deal with **crime** while preserving individual rights, the rule of law, and justice. Chapter 1 presents the two themes of this book: (1) crime and justice are public policy issues, and (2) criminal justice can best be seen as a social system. In this chapter we will look at the goals and organization of the criminal justice system and at the flow of decision making as a person is moved through the system. To guide your study, the following Questions for Inquiry will be addressed:

crime

A specific act of commission or omission in violation of the law, for which a punishment is prescribed.

QUESTIONS for Inquiry

- How are public policies on crime formed?
- How do the crime control and due process models of criminal justice help explain the system?
- What are the goals of the criminal justice system?
- How is criminal justice pursued in a federal system of government?
- What are the major features of criminal justice as a social system?
- What are the main agencies of criminal justice, and how do they interrelate?
- What is the flow of decision making from arrest to correction and release?

Crime and Justice as Public Policy Issues

Crime and justice are crucial public policy issues. In a democracy, striking a balance between maintaining public order and protecting individual freedom is a struggle. Policies could be imposed that make citizens feel safe from crime, such as placing a police officer on every street corner and executing suspected criminals. Such severe practices have been used elsewhere in the world. While they may reduce crime, they also fly in the face of democratic values. If law enforcement officers are given a free hand to work their will on the public, citizens in a democracy would be giving up individual freedom, due process, and their conception of justice.

Some critics of criminal justice, such as Jeffrey Reiman, argue that the U.S. system is designed "not to reduce crime or to achieve justice but to project to the American people a visible image of the threat of crime" (Reiman, 1996:1). This is done by maintaining a sizable population of criminals while at the same time failing to reduce crime. Reiman argues that a move needs to be made away from a system of *criminal* justice to one of criminal *justice*. He urges policies that

- end crime-producing poverty;
- criminalize the dangerous acts of the affluent and white-collar offenders;
- create a correctional system that promotes human dignity;
- make the exercise of police, prosecution, and judicial power more just; and
- establish economic and social justice.

If adopted, Reiman's thought-provoking critical perspective would revolutionize the criminal justice system as well as many of the attitudes and customs of American society.

Dealing with the crime problem concerns not only the arrest, conviction and punishment of offenders. Policies must also be developed to deal with a host of issues such as gun control, stalking, hate crimes, cybertheft, drugs, child abuse, and global criminal organizations. Many of these issues are controversial; policies must be hammered out in the political arenas of state legislatures and Congress.

The Role of Public Opinion

In a democracy, political leaders are greatly influenced by public opinion. They know that if policies are developed that are not in accord with what the public thinks, elections may be lost and the legitimacy of those policies may be diminished. But legislators also know that they can play to the American public's anxiety about crime and community safety. As a result, policies often appear to be enacted that are popular with the general public but that are thought by researchers to have little potential impact on the crime problem.

Throughout this book, you will find marginal notations labeled "What Americans Think." These present the results of public opinion surveys on issues concerning crime and the administration of justice. As you read each chapter, consider these expressions of public opinion. Do you agree with the majority of Americans on each issue? Does your understanding of criminal justice give you a different perspective on the policies that might better address these problems? Is your opinion different from the opinions of other criminal justice students?

http://cj.wadsworth.com/cole/

To find out the opinions of other criminal justice students, please go to the web site shown in the margin. Click on "Survey" and answer the questionnaire. Your responses will be collated with those of other students so that you can review

http://cj.wadsworth.com/cole/

the results by clicking on the web site again. You may want to download and print out your responses as well as those of your classmates throughout the country. Compare your opinion, student opinion, and the general public's opinion.

Contemporary Policies

Policies that have been adopted over the past decades to deal with crime have been promoted by those who can be classified as either conservative or liberal in their thinking about social issues.

Conservatives believe that the answer lies in stricter enforcement of the law through the expansion of police forces and the enactment of laws that require swift and certain punishment of criminals (Logan and DiIulio, 1993:486). Advocates of such policies have been politically dominant since the early 1980s. They argue that there must be stronger crime control, which they claim has been hindered by certain decisions of the United States Supreme Court and by programs that substitute government assistance for individual responsibility.

In contrast, liberals argue that stronger crime control measures endanger the values of due process and justice (Walker, 1993a:504). They claim that strict measures are ineffective because the answer lies in reshaping the lives of offenders and changing the social and economic conditions from which criminal behavior springs.

As you encounter these arguments, think about how they relate to crime trends. Crime increased in the 1960s when the liberal approach of rehabilitating offenders was taken. Does this mean that the approach does not work? Perhaps it was merely overwhelmed by the sheer number of people who were in their crime-prone years (between the ages of 16 and 24). Perhaps there would have been even more crime if not for the efforts to rehabilitate people. Crime rates decreased when tough policies were implemented in the 1980s. Was that because of the conservative policies in effect, or because fewer people were in the crime-prone age group? If conservative policies are effective, then why did violent crime rates rise in the early 1990s, when tough policies were still in force? Clearly, there are no easy answers, yet choices must be made about how to use the police, courts, and corrections system most effectively.

Crime and Justice in a Democracy

Americans agree that criminal justice policies should control crime by enforcing the law *and* should protect the rights of individuals. But these goals are difficult to achieve. They involve questions such as the amount of power police should have to search persons without a warrant, the rules judges must follow in deciding if certain types of evidence may be used, and the power of prison wardens to punish inmates. These questions are answered differently in a democracy than they would be in an authoritarian state.

The administration of justice in a democracy differs from that in an authoritarian state in the nature and extent of the protections provided for an accused person as guilt is determined and punishment imposed. The police, prosecutors, judges, and correctional officials are expected to act according to democratic values—especially respect for the rule of law and the maintenance of civil rights and liberties. But citizens must also view the criminal justice system as legitimate and have confidence in the actions taken (see What Americans Think).

What Americans Think

Question "I am going to read you a list of institutions in American society. Please tell me how much confidence you, yourself, have in each one—a great deal, quite a lot, some, or very little: the criminal justice system?"

Very little 34%

Some 40%

None 3%

Great deal/ quite a lot 23%

SOURCE U.S. Department of Justice, Bureau of Justice Statistics, *Sourcebook of Criminal Justice Statistics,* 1998 (Washington, D.C.: Government Printing Office, 1999), Table 2.17.

U.S. laws begin with the premise that all people—the guilty as well as the innocent—have rights. Moreover, unlike laws in some other countries, U.S. laws reflect the desire to avoid unnecessarily depriving people of liberty, either by permitting the police to arrest people at will or by punishing a person for a crime that he or she did not commit.

Although all Americans prize freedom and individual rights, they often disagree about policies to deal with crime. The greatest challenge as the twenty-first century dawns may be to find ways to remain true to the principles of fairness and justice while operating a system that can effectively protect, investigate, and punish.

① **What criminal justice policies are advocated by conservatives?**

② **What criminal justice policies are advocated by liberals?**

③ **What are the two criminal justice goals that Americans agree on?**

(Answers are at the end of the chapter.)

Crime Control versus Due Process

In one of the most important contributions to systematic thought about criminal justice, Herbert Packer (1968) described two competing models of the administration of criminal justice: the **crime control model** and the **due process model.** These are opposing ways of looking at the goals and procedures of the criminal justice system. The crime control model is much like an assembly line, while the due process model is like an obstacle course.

In reality, no one official or agency functions according to one model or the other. Elements of both models are found throughout the system. However, the two models reveal key tensions within the criminal justice process, as well as the gap between how the system is described and the way most cases are actually processed. Table 1.1 presents the major elements of each model.

Crime Control: Order as a Value

The crime control model assumes that every effort must be made to repress crime. It emphasizes efficiency and the capacity to catch, try, convict, and punish a high proportion of offenders; it also stresses speed and finality. This model places the goal of controlling crime uppermost, putting less emphasis on protecting

crime control model
A model of the criminal justice system that assumes that freedom is so important that every effort must be made to repress crime; it emphasizes efficiency, speed, finality, and the capacity to apprehend, try, convict, and dispose of a high proportion of offenders.

due process model
A model of the criminal justice system that assumes freedom is so important that every effort must be made to ensure that criminal justice decisions are based on reliable information; it emphasizes the adversarial process, the rights of defendants, and formal decision-making procedures.

TABLE 1.1   **Due process model and crime control model compared**

What other comparisons can be made between the two models?

	GOAL	VALUE	PROCESS	MAJOR DECISION POINT	BASIS OF DECISION MAKING
Due process model	Preserve individual liberties	Reliability	Adversarial	Courtroom	Law
Crime control model	Repress crime	Efficiency	Administrative	Police, pretrial processes	Discretion

individuals' rights. As Packer points out, to achieve liberty for all citizens, the crime control model calls for efficiency in screening suspects, determining guilt, and applying sanctions to the convicted. Because of high rates of crime and the limited resources of law enforcement, speed and finality are necessary. All of these elements depend on informality, uniformity, and few challenges by defense attorneys or defendants.

In this model, police and prosecutors decide early on how likely the suspect is to be found guilty. If a case probably will not end in conviction, the prosecutor may drop the charges. At each stage, from arrest to preliminary hearing, arraignment, and trial, established procedures are used to determine whether the accused should be passed on to the next stage. Instead of stressing the combative aspects of the courtroom, this model promotes bargaining between the state and the accused. Nearly all cases are disposed of through such bargaining, and they typically end with the defendant pleading guilty. Packer's description of this model as an assembly-line process conveys the idea of quick, efficient decisions by actors at fixed stations that turn out the intended product—guilty pleas and closed cases.

Due Process: Law as a Value

If the crime control model looks like an assembly line, the due process model looks more like an obstacle course. This model assumes that freedom is so important that every effort must be made to ensure that criminal justice decisions are based on reliable information. It stresses the adversarial process, the rights of defendants, and formal decision-making procedures. For example, because people are poor observers of disturbing events, police and prosecutors are likely to be wrong in presuming a defendant to be guilty. Thus, people should be labeled as criminals only on the basis of conclusive evidence. To reduce error, the government must be forced to prove beyond a reasonable doubt that the defendant is guilty of the crime. Therefore, the process must give the defense every opportunity to show that the evidence is not conclusive, and the outcome must be decided by an impartial judge and jury. According to Packer, the assumption that the defendant is innocent until proved guilty has a far-reaching impact on the criminal justice system.

In the due process model, the state must prove that the person is guilty of the crime as charged. Prosecutors must prove their cases while obeying rules dealing with such matters as the admissibility of evidence and respect for defendants' constitutional rights. Forcing the state to prove its case in a trial protects citizens from wrongful convictions. Thus, the due process model emphasizes particular aspects of the goal of doing justice. It protects the rights of individuals and reserves punishment for those who unquestionably deserve it. These values are stressed even though some guilty defendants may go free because the evidence against them is not conclusive enough. By contrast, the crime control model values efficient case processing and punishment over the possibility that innocent people might be swept up in the process.

CHECK POINT

④ What are the main features of the crime control model?

⑤ What are the main features of the due process model?

Crime and Justice in a Multicultural Society

African Americans, Hispanic Americans, and other minorities are subjected to the criminal justice system at much higher rates than the white majority (Hagan and Peterson, 1995:14). For example:

- African Americans account for one-third of all arrests and one-half of all incarcerations in the United States.
- Since 1980 the proportion of Hispanic Americans among all inmates in U.S. prisons has risen from 7.7 percent to 16.0 percent.
- About one-third of all black males in their twenties are under criminal justice supervision.
- The rate of unfounded arrests of Hispanics in California is double that of whites.
- Among 100,000 black males aged 15 to 19, 68 will die as the result of a homicide involving a gun, compared with about 6 among 100,000 white males in the same age group.
- The crime victimization rate is 260 per 1,000 Hispanic households versus 144 per 1,000 non-Hispanic households.
- The violent crime victimization rate for Native Americans is more than twice the rate for the nation as a whole.

A central question is whether racial and ethnic disparities such as those just listed are the result of discrimination (Mann, 1993:vii–xiv; Wilbanks, 1987). A **disparity** is a difference between groups that can be explained by legitimate factors. For example, the fact that 18- to 24-year-old men are arrested out of proportion to their numbers in the general population because they commit more crime. The high arrest rate is not thought to be the result of public policy to single out young males. **Discrimination** occurs when groups are differentially treated without regard to their behavior or qualifications; for example, if people of color are routinely sentenced to prison regardless of their criminal history.

Racial disparities in criminal justice are often explained in one of three ways: (1) people of color commit more crimes, (2) the criminal justice system is racist, with the result that people of color are treated more harshly, or (3) the criminal justice system expresses the racism found in society as a whole. Let us consider each of these views in turn.

disparity
The inequality of treatment of one group by the criminal justice system, compared with the treatment accorded other groups.

discrimination
Differential treatment of individuals or groups based on race, ethnicity, gender, sexual orientation, or economic status, instead of on their behavior or qualifications.

Explanation 1: People of Color Commit More Crimes

Nobody denies that the proportion of minorities arrested and placed under correctional supervision (probation, jail, prison, parole) is greater than their proportion of the general population. However, people disagree over whether bias is responsible for the disparity.

Disparities in arrests and sentences may stem from legitimate factors. For example, prosecutors and judges are supposed to take into account differences between serious and petty offenses and between repeat and first-time offenders. Thus, more people of color will end up in the courts and prisons if they are more likely to commit more serious crimes and have more serious prior records than do whites (Walker, Spohn, and DeLone, 1996:15–16).

The police often become targets for tensions arising in a multicultural society, such as this confrontation in Atlanta. How should the officers react in such situations?

But why do minorities commit more crimes? The most extreme answer is that they are more predisposed to criminality. This assumes that people of color are a "criminal class." Little evidence supports this view. For example, self-report studies, in which people are asked to report on their own criminal behavior, have shown that nearly everyone has committed a crime, although most are never caught. Furthermore, young adults, men, whites, and those with less than a high school education are more likely to use illicit drugs. As "drug czar" General Barry McCaffrey said, "The typical drug user is not poor and unemployed" (*New York Times,* September 9, 1999:A14).

The link between crime and economic disadvantage is significant. Minority groups suffer greatly from poverty. Nearly half (46 percent) of African American children and 39 percent of Hispanic American children are poor, compared with 16 percent of white children (Sherman, A., 1994). Unemployment rates are highest among people of color, and family income is lowest. It is only with the booming job market of the late 1990s that young black men with little education are working in greater numbers and committing fewer crimes (*New York Times,* May 23, 1999:A1). Thus, it would be reasonable to expect Native Americans, Hispanic Americans, and African Americans to engage in more crimes.

Related to the link between crime and disadvantage is that most crime in America is *intra*racial, not *inter*racial. Victimization rates, especially homicide and robbery, are higher for minorities than for whites. The lifetime risk for black males is 4.16 per 100, followed by Native American males (1.75), black females (1.02), white males (.64), Native American females (.46), and white females (.26) (Sampson and Lauritsen, 1997:319). As John DiIulio points out, "No group of Americans suffers more when violent and repeat criminals are permitted to prey upon decent, struggling, law-abiding inner city citizens and their children than…'black America's silent majority' " (DiIulio, 1994:3). The poor cannot move away from the social problems of the inner cities. As a result, victimization by one's neighbors is a tragedy faced by many African Americans.

One way to explain racial disparities in the criminal justice system, then, is to note that African Americans and Hispanic Americans are arrested more often and for more serious offenses than whites. Some analysts argue that the most effective crime control policies would be those that reduce the social problems contributing to higher crime rates among the poor (Tonry, 1995).

Explanation 2: The Criminal Justice System Is Racist

Racial disparities may result if people who commit similar offenses are treated differently by the criminal justice system because of their race or ethnicity. In this view, the fact that people of color are arrested more often than whites does not mean that they are more crime-prone. For example, although African Americans are 13 percent of monthly drug users, they represent 35 percent of those arrested for drug possession, 55 percent of convictions, and 74 percent of prison sentences (Butterfield, 1995b). One study found that the police make unfounded arrests of African Americans four times as often as of whites (Donziger, 1996:109). Racial profiling, as described in the Close-Up on p. 11, is an example of what many people believe is a racist activity by police.

The disparity between crime rates, arrest rates, and rates of incarceration is a key factor in the claim that the criminal justice system is biased against minority groups. The arrest rate of minority citizens is greater than even their higher offense rates would justify. For example, 29 percent of rape victims report that their assailant was African American, but 43 percent of persons arrested for rape

CLOSE up

Racial Stereotyping

Most people of all races and ethnic groups are never convicted of a crime, but stereotypes can work to brand all members of some groups with suspicion. These stereotypes are bad enough in the culture at large, but they work their way into law enforcement through the use of criminal profiles, putting an undue burden on innocent members of these groups.

A particularly clear example of this phenomenon is found in a study of Maryland state troopers and the searches they made of motorists on Interstate Highway 95. On this particular stretch of highway, motorists were found to be speeding equally across races.

Black motorists, for example, constituted 17 percent of the motorists and 17.5 percent of the speeders. But black motorists

were the subject of 77 percent of the automobile searches made by the police looking for contraband.

Why were black motorists searched so often? The police might justify such practices on the ground that blacks are more likely to carry contraband. And the statistics show this to be true: the police found contraband in 33 percent of the searches of black motorists and in 22 percent of the searches of white motorists. But the mischief in this practice is quickly exposed. Blacks had a 50 percent higher chance of being found with contraband but were searched 400 percent more often. The result is that 274 innocent black motorists were searched, while only 76 innocent white motorists were searched. The profiles apparently used by the Maryland state troopers make 17 percent of the motorists pay 76 percent of the price of the law enforcement strategy, solely because of their race.

SOURCE: Drawn from Christopher Stone, "Race, Crime, and the Administration of Justice," *National Institute of Justice Journal* (April 1999): 24–32.

---

are African American. Similarly, 22.6 percent of assault victims say the offender was African American, but 34 percent of those arrested for assault are African Americans. In sum, the odds of arrest are higher for African American offenders than for white offenders.

Higher arrest rates may also lead to higher incarceration rates. Some point to the fact that 50 percent of the prison population is African American as further evidence of a racist system. One study found that differences in incarceration rates of African Americans and whites reflected "significant disparities that could not be attributed to arrest charges [or] prior criminal charges" (New York, Office of Justice Systems Analysis, 1991:1).

Criminal justice officials need not act in racist ways to cause disparities in arrest and incarceration rates. At each stage of the process, the system may operate so that minority group members are put at a disadvantage. The number of minority arrests may be greater because police patrols are more heavily concentrated in areas where nonwhites live, where drug use is more open, and where users are more likely to be observed by police. Further, a study of 150,000 cases in Connecticut found that on average an African American or Hispanic American man must pay *double*

Four African Americans and their attorneys announce the filing of a civil suit against two New Jersey state troopers. The men were driving in a rented van along the New Jersey Turnpike when Troopers John Hogan and James Kenna pulled them over and then opened fire on the van, shooting three and critically injuring two. The plaintiffs charge they were stopped because of their race. The 1998 incident brought to national attention the issue of racial profiling.

the bail that would be paid by a white man for the same offense (Donziger, 1996:111). Most pretrial release practices take into account factors such as employment status, living arrangements, and prior criminal record. Poor offenders are less likely to be able to make bail and hire their own lawyer. Prosecutors may be less likely to dismiss charges against a poor, unemployed African American or Hispanic offender. These offender characteristics may further skew sentencing.

Is the criminal justice system racist? The result of the system's decisions cannot be disputed—African American and Hispanic American males end up in prison and jails in higher proportions than can be explained by their crime and arrest rates. A review of thirty-eight studies found more than two-thirds of the studies had uncovered biases in the system that were disadvantageous to African Americans. The authors concluded that "race is a consistent and frequently significant disadvantage when [imprisonment] decisions are considered . . . [but] race is much less of a disadvantage when it comes to sentence length" (Chiricos and Crawford, 1995).

Explanation 3: America Is a Racist Society

Some people claim that the criminal justice system is racist because it is embedded in a racist society. Some accuse the system of being a tool of a racist society. For example, as stated by Steven Barkan and Steven Cohn, "Recent research suggests that whites' approval of police use of force may derive partly from racial prejudice against African Americans" (1998:743).

Evidence of racism exists in the way society asks the criminal justice system to operate. For example, federal sentencing guidelines punish users of crack cocaine about one hundred times more harshly than users of powder cocaine, even though the drugs are almost identical. The only difference is that people of color in the inner cities tend to use crack cocaine, while whites tend to use cocaine in its powder form.

In addition, sentencing studies find a stronger link between unemployment rates and rates of imprisonment than between crime rates and rates of imprisonment. This suggests that prisons are used to confine people who cannot find jobs—and many of the unemployed are African American males (Chircos and Bales, 1991). Finally, according to Michael Tonry, the war on drugs was "foreordained to affect disadvantaged black youths disproportionately [and was based on] the willingness of the drug war's planners to sacrifice young black Americans" (Tonry, 1995:123). Others point out that enforcement of drug laws focuses "almost exclusively on low-level dealers in minority neighborhoods" (Donziger, 1996:115). Yet federal health statistics define the typical drug addict as a white male in his 20s who lives in a suburb where drug busts almost never happen (*New York Times*, May 10, 1999:A26).

Other evidence of racism in American society may be seen in the stereotyping of offenders. As Coramae Richey Mann points out, such stereotyping varies among racial and ethnic groups, depending on the crime and the section of the country. She suggests that white Americans view the rapist as a "black man," the opium user as a "yellow man," the knife wielder as a "brown man," the drunken Indian as a "red man," and people of color as the cause of the "crime problem" (Mann, 1993:vii). Conditioned to think of social ills as minority problems, readers of a *Hartford Courant* series on drug-addicted prostitutes were stunned to learn that 70 percent were white (*New York Times*, May 10, 1999:A26).

That racist stereotyping affects police actions can be seen in cases of African American and Hispanic American professionals who have been falsely arrested when the police were looking for a person of color and these individuals happened to be "out of place." Judge Claude Coleman was handcuffed and dragged through crowds of shoppers in Short Hills, New Jersey, while protesting his innocence; Harvard philosopher Cornel West was stopped on false cocaine charges while traveling to Williams College; and law student Brian Roberts was pulled over by the police as he drove in an affluent St. Louis neighborhood on his way to interview a judge for a class project (Tonry, 1995:51).

If people of color are overrepresented in the justice system because the larger society is racist, finding a solution may be a bit daunting. Nobody knows how to quickly rid a society of racist policies, practices, and attitudes.

⑥ **What is meant by racial or ethnic disparities in criminal justice?**

⑦ **What three explanations may account for such disparities?**

The Politics of Crime and Justice

Criminal justice policies are developed in national, state, and local political arenas. A risk always exists that politicians will simply do what they believe voters want to hear rather than think seriously about whether those policies will achieve their goals. For example, the crime bill passed by Congress in 1994 expanded the death penalty to cover sixty additional offenses, including the murder of members of Congress, the Supreme Court, and the president's staff. These are tough provisions, but will they accomplish anything? Many criminologists doubt it.

The political process often displays a knee-jerk quality. A problem occurs and gets much public attention. Calls are heard to "do something." Politicians respond with (1) outrage, (2) a study of the problem, and (3) a law—often poorly thought out and with little regard for unintended consequences.

Megan's Law is an example of good intentions gone awry. Though it varies from state to state, the legislation was passed in reaction to the rape and murder by a convicted sex offender of a New Jersey child, Megan Kanka. This well-meaning attempt to deal with dangerous sexual predators has been difficult to implement fairly. For example, under Connecticut's version of the law, sex offenders who have served their sentences must report their addresses for display on an Internet web site for the public to peruse. The law was so poorly written that hundreds are labeled dangerous sex offenders when only a small percentage on the list might fit that category (*Hartford Courant,* September 10, 1999:A22).

The clearest link between politics and criminal justice can be seen in the statements of Republicans and Democrats who try to outdo each other in showing how tough they can be on crime (Estrich, 1998). Just as important are the more "routine" links between politics and the justice system. Penal code provisions and the budgets of criminal justice agencies are decided by legislators who are responding to the demands of voters. Congress appropriates millions of dollars to help states and cities wage the "war on drugs" but limits spending for legal counsel for poor defendants. At the state and local levels, many criminal justice authorities—including sheriffs, prosecutors, and judges—are also elected officials. Their decisions will be influenced by the concerns and values of their communities (see What Americans Think).

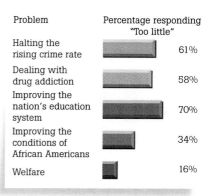

What Americans Think

Question: "We are faced with many problems in this country, none of which can be solved easily or inexpensively. I'm going to name some of the problems and for each one I'd like you to tell me whether you think we're spending too much money on it, too little money, or about the right amount."

Problem	Percentage responding "Too little"
Halting the rising crime rate	61%
Dealing with drug addiction	58%
Improving the nation's education system	70%
Improving the conditions of African Americans	34%
Welfare	16%

SOURCE: U.S. Department of Justice, Bureau of Justice Statistics, *Sourcebook of Criminal Justice Statistics,* 1998 (Washington, D.C.: Government Printing Office, 1999), Table 2.47.

As you learn about each part of the criminal justice system, keep in mind the ways decision makers and institutions are connected to politics and government. Criminal justice is closely linked to society and its institutions, and to fully understand it you must be aware of those links.

CHECK POINT

⑧ **At what level of government are most crime policies made?**
⑨ **How does politics influence criminal justice policies?**

The Goals of Criminal Justice

To begin our study of the criminal justice system, we must ask: What goals does the system serve? Although these goals may seem straightforward as ideas, it can be hard to say exactly what they mean in practice.

In 1967 the President's Commission on Law Enforcement and Administration of Justice described the criminal justice system as an apparatus that society uses to "enforce the standards of conduct necessary to protect individuals and the community" (President's Commission on Law Enforcement and Administration of Justice, 1967:7). This statement is the basis of our discussion of the goals of the system. Although the purposes of criminal justice are greatly debated, most people agree that the system has three goals: (1) doing justice, (2) controlling crime, and (3) preventing crime.

Doing Justice

Doing justice is the basis for the rules, procedures, and institutions of the criminal justice system. Without the principle of justice, little difference would be discerned between criminal justice in the United States and in authoritarian countries. Fairness is essential. Americans want to have fair laws. Americans want to investigate, judge, and punish fairly. Doing justice also requires upholding the rights of individuals and punishing those who violate the law. Thus, the goal of doing justice embodies three principles: (1) offenders will be held fully accountable for their actions, (2) the rights of persons who have contact with the system will be protected, and (3) like offenses will be treated alike and officials will take into account relevant differences among offenders and offenses (DiIulio, 1993a:10).

Successfully doing justice is a tall order, and it is easy to identify situations in which criminal justice agencies and processes fall short of this ideal. In authoritarian political systems, criminal justice clearly serves the interests of those in power, but in a democracy people can try to improve the capacity of their institutions to do justice. Thus, however imperfect they may be, criminal justice institutions and processes can enjoy public support. In a democracy, a system that makes doing justice a key goal is viewed as legitimate and thus is able to pursue the secondary goals of controlling and preventing crime.

The goals of the criminal justice system cannot be accomplished solely by the police, courts, and corrections. All citizens should take an interest, such as is exhibited by this demonstration against drug use and killings in East Los Angeles.

Controlling Crime

The criminal justice system is designed to control crime by arresting, prosecuting, convicting, and punishing those who disobey the law. A major constraint on the system, however, is that efforts to control crime must be carried out within the framework of law. The criminal law not only defines what is illegal but also outlines the rights of citizens and the procedures officials must use to achieve the system's goals.

In every city and town, the goal of crime control is being actively pursued: police officers walk a beat, patrol cars race down dark streets, lawyers speak before a judge, probation officers visit clients, or the wire fences of a prison stretch along a highway. Taking action against wrongdoers helps to control crime, but the system must also attempt to prevent crimes from happening.

Preventing Crime

Crime can be prevented in various ways. Perhaps most important is the deterrent effect of the actions of police, courts, and corrections. These not only punish those who violate the law, but also provide examples that are likely to keep others from committing wrongful acts. For example, a racing patrol car is responding to a crime situation while serving as a warning that law enforcement is at hand.

Crime prevention depends on the actions of criminal justice officials and citizens. Unfortunately, many people do not take the often simple steps necessary to protect themselves and their property. For example, they leave their homes and cars unlocked, do not use alarm systems, and walk in dangerous areas.

Citizens do not have the authority to enforce the law; society has assigned that responsibility to the criminal justice system. Thus, citizens must rely on the police to stop criminals; they cannot take the law into their own hands. Still, they can and must be actively engaged in preventing crime (see A Question of Ethics above).

The ways in which American institutions have evolved to achieve the goals of doing justice, controlling crime, and preventing crime lead to a series of choices. Decisions must be made that reflect legal, political, social, and moral values. As we study the system, we must be aware of the possible conflicts among these values and the implications of choosing one value over another. The tasks assigned to the criminal justice system could be much easier to perform if they were clearly defined so that citizens and officials could act with precise knowledge of their duties.

A Question of
Ethics

After his jewelry store had been burglarized for the third time in less than six months, Tom Henderson was frustrated. The police were of little help, merely telling him that they would have a patrol officer keep watch during nightly rounds. Tom added new locks and an electronic security system. After unlocking his shop one morning, he saw that he had been cleaned out again. He looked around the store to see how the thief had entered, as the door was locked and evidently the security alarm had not sounded. Suddenly he noticed that the glass in a skylight was broken.

"Damn, I'll fix him this time," he swore.

That evening, after replacing the glass, he stripped the insulation from an electric cord and strung it around and across the frame of the skylight. He pulled the cord into a socket, locked the store, and went home.

Two weeks later, when he entered the store and flipped the light switch, nothing happened. He walked toward the fuse box. It was then that he noticed the burned body lying on the floor below the skylight.

■ What are the limits to which one can go to "protect one's castle"? If the police are unable to solve a crime problem, is it ethical for individuals to take matters into their own hands?

CHECK POINT

⑩ **What are the three goals of the criminal justice system?**

⑪ **What is meant by "doing justice"?**

Criminal Justice in a Federal System

Criminal justice, like other aspects of American government, is based on the concept of **federalism,** in which power is divided between a central (national) government and regional (state) governments. States have a great deal of authority over their own affairs, but the federal government handles matters of national concern. Because of federalism, no single level of government is solely responsible for the administration of criminal justice.

The American governmental structure was created in 1789 with the ratification of the U.S. Constitution. The Constitution gives the national government certain powers—to raise an army, to coin money, to make treaties with foreign countries—but all other powers, including police power, were retained by the states. No national police force with broad powers may be established in the United States.

The Constitution does not include criminal justice among the federal government's powers. However, the government is involved in criminal justice in many ways. The Federal Bureau of Investigation is a national law enforcement agency. In addition, criminal cases are often tried in U.S. district courts, which are federal courts, and federal prisons are found throughout the nation. Most criminal justice activity, however, occurs at the state, not the national, level.

Two Justice Systems

Both the national and state systems of criminal justice enforce laws, try criminal cases, and punish offenders, but their activities differ in scope and purpose. The vast majority of criminal laws are written by state legislatures and enforced by state agencies. However, a variety of national criminal laws have been enacted by Congress and are enforced by the FBI, the Drug Enforcement Administration, the U.S. Secret Service, and other federal agencies.

Except in the case of federal drug offenses, relatively few offenders break federal criminal laws compared with the large numbers who break state criminal laws. For example, only small numbers of people violate the federal law against counterfeiting and espionage, while large numbers violate state laws against assault, larceny, and drunk driving. Even in the case of drug offenses, which during the 1980s and 1990s swept large numbers of offenders into federal prisons, many violators end up in state corrections systems because such crimes violate both state and federal laws.

The role of criminal justice agencies after the assassination of President John F. Kennedy in November 1963 illustrates the division of jurisdiction between federal and state agencies. Because Congress had not made killing the president a federal offense, the suspect, Lee Harvey Oswald, would have been charged under Texas laws had he lived (Oswald was shot to death by Jack Ruby shortly after his arrest). The Secret Service had the job of protecting the president, but apprehending the killer was the formal responsibility of the Dallas police and other Texas law enforcement agencies.

Expansion of Federal Involvement

Over time, federal involvement in the criminal justice system has slowly expanded. Because many crimes span state borders, some crimes are no longer thought of as being committed at a single location within a single state. For example, crime syndicates and gangs deal with drugs, pornography, and gambling on a national basis. Thus, Congress has expanded the powers of the FBI and other federal agencies to pursue criminal activities that formerly were the responsibility of the states.

Congress has also passed laws designed to allow the FBI to investigate situations in which local police forces are likely to be less effective. Under the National Stolen Property Act, for example, the FBI may investigate thefts of more than $5,000 in value when the stolen property is likely to have been transported across state lines. As a national agency, the FBI is better able than any state agency to pursue criminal investigations across state borders.

Disputes over jurisdiction may occur when an offense violates both state and federal laws. If the FBI and local agencies do not cooperate, each may seek to catch the same criminals. This can have major implications if the court to which the case is brought is determined by the agency that makes the arrest. Usually, however, law enforcement officials at all levels of government seek to cooperate and to coordinate their efforts.

Because of the existence of both state and federal systems, criminal justice in the United States is highly decentralized. As Figure 1.1 shows, about 60 percent of all criminal justice employees work for local government. The majority of workers in all of the subunits of the system—except corrections—are tied to local government. Likewise, the costs of criminal justice are distributed among the federal, state, and local governments.

Laws are enforced and offenders are brought to justice mainly in the states, counties, and cities. As a result, local traditions, values, and practices shape the way criminal justice agencies operate. Local leaders, whether members of the city

FIGURE 1.1 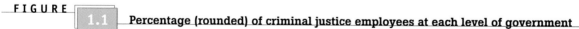 **Percentage (rounded) of criminal justice employees at each level of government**

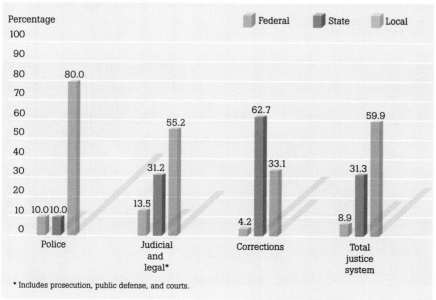

The administration of criminal justice in the United States is very much a local affair, as these employment figures show. It is only in corrections that states employ a greater percentage of workers than do municipalities.

* Includes prosecution, public defense, and courts.

SOURCE: U.S. Department of Justice, Bureau of Justice Statistics, *Sourcebook of Criminal Justice Statistics*, 1997 (Washington, D.C.: Government Printing Office, 1998), 18.

council or influential citizens, can help set law enforcement priorities by putting pressure on the police. Will the city's police officers crack down on illegal gambling? Will juvenile offenders be turned over to their parents with stern warnings, or will they be sent to state institutions? The answers to these and other important questions vary from city to city.

 CHECK POINT

⑫ **What are the key features of federalism?**

⑬ **What powers does the national government have in the area of crime and justice?**

⑭ **What factors have caused federal involvement in criminal justice to expand?**

Criminal Justice as a System

To achieve the goals of criminal justice, many kinds of organizations—police, prosecution, courts, corrections—have been formed. Each has its own functions and personnel. We might assume that criminal justice is an orderly process in which a variety of professionals act on each case on behalf of society. To know how the system really works, however, we must look beyond its formal organizational chart. In doing so, we can use the concept of a **system:** a complex whole made up of interdependent parts whose actions are directed toward goals and influenced by the environment in which they function.

system

A complex whole consisting of interdependent parts whose operations are directed toward goals and are influenced by the environment within which they function.

The System Perspective

Criminal justice is a system made up of a number of parts or subsystems. The subsystems—police, courts, corrections—have their own goals and needs but are also interdependent. When one unit changes its policies, practices, or resources, other units will be affected. An increase in the number of people arrested by the police,

Exchange relationships influence decision making throughout the criminal justice system. Here, Attorney Terry Gilbert, center, and Chief Assistant Cuyahoga County (Ohio) Prosecutor Carmen Marinoa, right, talk with Judge Ronald Suster. Suster is hearing a motion to have Dr. Sam Sheppard, who was convicted of murdering his wife in 1954, declared innocent and wrongly imprisoned, as indicated by DNA tests.

for example, will affect not only the judicial subsystem, but also the probation and correctional subsystems. For criminal justice to achieve its goals, each part must make its own contribution; each must also have at least minimal contact with at least one other part of the system.

Although understanding the nature of the entire criminal justice system and its subsystems is important, we must also see how individual actors play their roles. The criminal justice system is made up of a great many persons doing specific jobs. Some, such as police officers and judges, are well known to the public. Others, such as bail bondsmen and probation officers, are less well known. A key concept here is **exchange,** meaning the mutual transfer of resources among individual actors, each of whom has goals that he or she cannot accomplish alone. Each needs to gain the cooperation and assistance of other actors by helping those actors achieve their own goals. The concept of exchange allows interpersonal behavior to be seen as the result of individual decisions about the costs and benefits of different courses of action.

Many kinds of exchange relationships exist in the criminal justice system, some more visible than others. Probably the most obvious example is a **plea bargain,** in which the defense attorney and the prosecutor reach an agreement: The defendant agrees to plead guilty in exchange for a reduction of charges or a lighter sentence. As a result of this exchange, the prosecutor gains a quick, sure conviction; the defendant achieves a shorter sentence; and the defense attorney can move on to the next case. Thus, the cooperation underlying the exchange promotes the goals of each participant.

The concept of exchange serves as a reminder that decisions are the products of interactions among individuals and that the subsystems of the criminal justice system are tied together by the actions of individual decision makers. Figure 1.2 presents selected exchange relationships between a prosecutor and other individuals and agencies involved in the criminal justice process.

The concepts of system and exchange are closely linked, and they are useful tools for the analysis of criminal justice. In this book, these concepts serve as an organizing framework to describe individual subsystems and actors and help reveal how the justice process works. However, several other characteristics of the system shape the decisions that determine the fates of defendants.

exchange
A mutual transfer of resources; a balance of benefits and deficits that flow from behavior based on decisions about the values and costs of alternatives.

plea bargain
A defendant's plea of guilty to a criminal charge with the reasonable expectation of receiving some consideration from the state for doing so, usually a reduction of the charge. The defendant's ultimate goal is a penalty lighter than the one formally warranted by the charged offense.

FIGURE 1.2   **Exchange relationships between prosecutors and others**

The prosecutor's decisions are influenced by relationships with other agencies and members of the community.

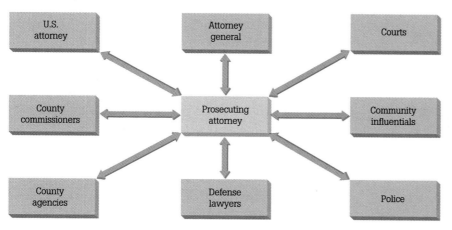

Characteristics of the Criminal Justice System

The workings of the criminal justice system have four major characteristics: (1) discretion, (2) resource dependence, (3) sequential tasks, and (4) filtering.

Discretion

discretion

The authority to make decisions without reference to specific rules or facts, using instead one's own judgment; allows for individualization and informality in the administration of justice.

At all levels of the justice process, there is a high degree of **discretion.** This term refers to officials' freedom to act according to their own judgment and conscience (see Table 1.2). For example, police officers decide how to handle a crime situation, prosecutors decide what charges to file, judges decide how long a sentence will be, and parole boards decide when an offender may be released from prison.

The extent of such discretion may seem odd, given that the United States is ruled by law and has created procedures to ensure that decisions are made in accordance with law. However, instead of a mechanical system in which decisions are dominated by law, criminal justice is a system in which actors may take many factors into account and exercise many options as they dispose of a case.

Two arguments are often used to justify discretion in the criminal justice system. First, discretion is needed because the system lacks the resources to treat every case the same way. If every violation of the law were pursued through trial, the costs would be immense. Second, many officials believe that discretion permits them to achieve greater justice than rigid rules would produce.

Resource Dependence

Criminal justice agencies do not generate their own resources but depend on other agencies for funding. Therefore, actors in the system must cultivate and maintain good relations with those who allocate resources; that is, political decision makers, such as legislators, mayors, and city council members. Some police departments gain revenue through traffic fines and property forfeitures, but these sources are not enough to sustain their budgets.

Because budget decisions are made by elected officials who seek to please the public, criminal justice officials must also maintain a positive image and good relations with voters. If the police have strong public support, for example, the mayor will be reluctant to reduce the law enforcement budget. Criminal justice officials also seek positive coverage from the news media. Because the media often provide a crucial link between government agencies and the public, criminal justice officials may announce notable achievements while trying to limit publicity about controversial cases and decisions.

Sequential Tasks

Decisions in the criminal justice system are made in a specific sequence. The police must make an arrest before a defendant is passed along to the prosecutor. The prosecutor's decisions determine the nature of the court's workload. Officials cannot achieve their goals by acting out of sequence. For example, prosecutors and judges cannot bypass the police by making arrests, and corrections officials cannot punish anyone who has not passed through the earlier stages of the process.

TABLE 1.2   Who exercises discretion?

Discretion is exercised by various actors throughout the criminal justice system.

THESE CRIMINAL JUSTICE OFFICIALS...	MUST OFTEN DECIDE WHETHER OR HOW TO:
Police	Enforce specific laws
	Investigate specific crimes
	Search people, vicinities, buildings
	Arrest or detain people
Prosecutors	File charges or petitions for adjudication
	Seek indictments
	Drop cases
	Reduce charges
Judges or magistrates	Set bail or conditions for release
	Accept pleas
	Determine delinquency
	Dismiss charges
	Impose sentence
	Revoke probation
Correctional officials	Assign to type of correctional facility
	Award privileges
	Punish for infractions of rules
	Determine date and conditions of parole
	Revoke parole

SOURCE: U.S. Department of Justice, Bureau of Justice Statistics, *Report to the Nation on Crime and Justice*, 2d ed. (Washington, D.C.: Government Printing Office, 1988), 59.

The sequential nature of the system is a key element in the exchange relationships among decision makers who depend on each other to achieve their goals. Thus, the system is highly interdependent.

Filtering

The criminal justice system may be viewed as a **filtering process.** At each stage some defendants are sent on to the next stage, while others are either released or processed under changed conditions. As shown in Figure 1.3, persons who have been arrested may be filtered out of the system at various points. Note that very

filtering process
A screening operation; a process by which criminal justice officials screen out some cases while advancing others to the next level of decision making.

FIGURE 1.3 **Criminal justice as a filtering process**

Decisions at each point in the system result in some cases being dropped while others are passed to the next point. Are you surprised by the small portion of cases that remain?

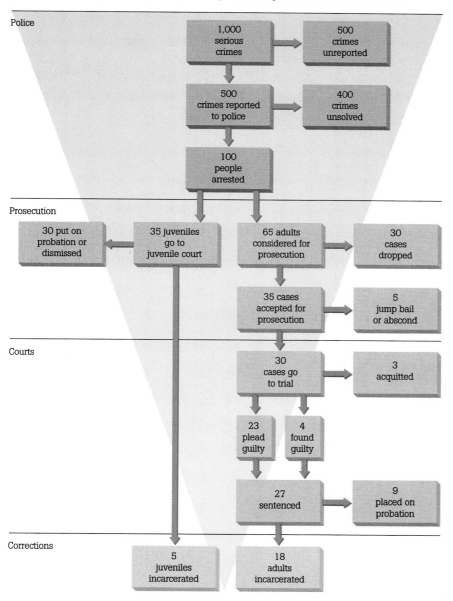

SOURCE: Data in this figure have been drawn from many sources including U.S. Department of Justice, Brueau of Justice Statistics, *Sourcebook of Criminal Justice Statistics, 1998* (Washington, D.C.: Government Printing Office, 1999); and U.S. Department of Justice, Bureau of Justice Statistics, *Bulletin* (February 1988).

few suspects who are arrested are then prosecuted, tried, and convicted. Some go free because the police decide that a crime has not been committed or that the evidence is not sound. The prosecutor may decide that justice would be better served by sending the suspect to a substance abuse clinic. Many defendants will plead guilty, the judge may dismiss charges against others, and the jury may acquit a few defendants. Most of the offenders who are tried, however, will be convicted. Thus, the criminal justice system is often described as a funnel—many cases enter it, but only a few result in conviction and punishment.

To summarize, the criminal justice system is composed of a set of interdependent parts (subsystems). This system has four key attributes: (1) discretion, (2) resource dependence, (3) sequential tasks, and (4) filtering. Using this framework, we look next at the operations of criminal justice agencies and then examine the flow of cases through the system.

CHECK POINT

⑮ **Define a system.**

⑯ **Give an example of an exchange relationship.**

⑰ **What are the major characteristics of the criminal justice system?**

Operations of Criminal Justice Agencies

The criminal justice system has been formed to deal with persons who are accused of violating the criminal law. Its subsystems consist of more than sixty thousand public and private agencies with an annual budget of more than $100 billion and almost two million employees. Here we review the main parts of the criminal justice system and their functions.

In emotionally charged situations, such as this protest sparked by an accident in which a Hasidic motorist struck and killed a black child in the Crown Heights section of New York City, the police must consider the circumstances of the incident before they act.

Police

The police are usually thought of as being on the "front line" in controlling crime. The term *police,* however, does not refer to a single agency or type of agency, but to many agencies at each level of government. The complexity of the criminal justice system can be seen in the large number of organizations engaged in law enforcement. There are 18,769 state and local law enforcement agencies in the United States but only 50 agencies of the federal government. Forty-nine are state agencies (Hawaii has no state police). The remaining 18,720 agencies are found in counties, cities, and towns, reflecting the fact that the police function is dominated by local governments. At the state and local levels, these agencies have more than 920,000 full-time employees and a total annual budget that exceeds $41 billion (BJS, 1998b).

Police agencies have four major duties:

❶ Keeping the peace. This broad and important mandate involves the protection of rights and persons in situations ranging from street-corner brawls to domestic quarrels.

❷ Apprehending violators and combating crime. This is the task that the public most often associates with police work, although it accounts for only a small proportion of police time and resources.

❸ Preventing crime. By educating the public about the threat of crime and by reducing the number of situations in which crimes are likely to be committed, the police can lower the rate of crime.

❹ Providing social services. Police officers recover stolen property, direct traffic, give emergency medical aid, help people who have locked themselves out of their homes, and provide other social services.

Courts

The United States has a **dual court system** that consists of a separate judicial system for each state in addition to a national system. Each system has its own series of courts; the U.S. Supreme Court is responsible for correcting certain errors made in all other court systems. Although the Supreme Court can review cases from both the state and federal courts, it will hear only cases involving federal law or constitutional rights.

With a dual court system, the law may be interpreted differently in different states. Although the wording of laws may be similar, none of the state courts interprets the law in the same way. To some extent, these variations reflect different social and political conditions. The dominant values of citizens and judges may differ from one region to another. Differences in interpretation may also stem from attempts by state courts to solve similar problems by different means. For example, before the Supreme Court ruled that evidence the police obtained in illegal ways should be excluded at trials, some states had already enacted rules barring the use of such evidence.

Courts are responsible for **adjudication**—determining the guilt or innocence of a defendant. In so doing, they must use fair procedures that will produce just, reliable decisions. Courts must also impose sentences that are appropriate to the behavior being punished.

dual court system
A system consisting of a separate judicial structure for each state in addition to a national structure. Each case is tried in a court of the same jurisdiction as that of the law or laws broken.

adjudication
The process of determining the guilt or innocence of a defendant.

Corrections

On any given day, about six million (one of every thirty-four) American adults are under the supervision of state and federal corrections systems. There is no "typical" corrections agency or official. Instead, a variety of agencies and programs are provided by private and public organizations—including federal, state, and local governments—and carried out in many different community and closed settings.

While the average citizen may equate corrections with prisons, less than 30 percent of convicted offenders are in prisons and jails; the rest are being supervised in the community. Probation and parole have long been important aspects of corrections, as have community-based halfway houses, work release programs, and supervised activities.

The federal government, all the states, most counties, and all but the smallest cities engage in corrections. Nonprofit private organizations such as the Young Men's Christian Association (YMCA) have also contracted with governments to perform correctional services. In recent years, for-profit businesses have also entered into contracts with governments to build and operate correctional institutions.

The police, courts, and corrections are the main agencies of criminal justice. Each is a part, or subsystem, of the criminal justice system. Each is linked to the other two subsystems, and the actions of each affect the others. These effects can be seen as we examine the flow of decision making within the criminal justice system.

CHECK POINT

⑱ **What are the four main duties of police?**

⑲ **What is a dual court system?**

⑳ **What are the major types of state and local corrections agencies?**

The Flow of Decision Making in the Criminal Justice System

The processing of cases in the criminal justice system involves a series of decisions by police officers, prosecutors, judges, probation officers, wardens, and parole board members. At each stage in the process, they decide whether a case will move on to the next stage or be dropped from the system. Although the flowchart shown in Figure 1.4 appears streamlined, with cases entering at the top and moving swiftly toward the bottom, the actual route taken may be long and may involve many detours. At each step, officials have the discretion to decide what happens next. Many cases are filtered out of the system, others are sent to the next decision maker, and still others are dealt with by informal means.

Moreover, the flowchart does not show the influences of social relations or the political environment. For example, in 1997 reports surfaced indicating that Michael Kennedy, then a 39-year-old lawyer and nephew of the late president John F. Kennedy, had carried on an affair with his children's baby sitter when she was 14 years old. If true, Kennedy would have been guilty of statutory rape, because having sexual relations with an underage girl is a felony, even if she willingly participates. Amid reports that Kennedy's lawyers were negotiating a quiet financial settlement with the girl and her family, the local prosecutor announced that no criminal charges would be filed because the girl—a college student at the time reports of the alleged affair became public—refused to provide any evidence against Kennedy.

In other cases, prosecutors and judges may pressure witnesses to testify, sometimes even jailing reluctant witnesses for contempt of court. Did the prosecutor decline to press charges because Kennedy was a member of a politically powerful family? No one knows for sure; political factors or behind-the-scenes negotiations could have influenced the prosecutor's discretionary decisions. Such factors may influence decisions in ways that are not reflected in a simple description of decision-making steps. As we follow the thirteen steps of the criminal justice process, bear in mind that the formal procedures do not hold in every case. Discretion, political pressure, and other factors may alter the outcome for different defendants.

Steps in the Decision-Making Process

The criminal justice system consists of thirteen steps that cover the stages of law enforcement, adjudication, and corrections. The system looks like an assembly line where decisions are made about defendants—the raw material of the process. As these steps are described, recall the concepts discussed earlier: system, discretion, sequential tasks, filtering, and exchange. Be aware that the terms used for different stages in the process may differ from state to state, and the sequence of the steps differs in some parts of the country, but the flow of decision making generally follows this pattern.

❶ **INVESTIGATION.** The process begins when the police believe that a crime has been committed. At this point an investigation is begun. The police normally depend on a member of the community to report the offense. Except for traffic and public order offenses, the police usually do not observe illegal behavior themselves. Because most crimes have already been committed and offenders have left the scene before the police arrive, the police are at a disadvantage in quickly finding and arresting the offenders.

❷ **ARREST.** If the police find enough evidence showing that a particular person has committed a crime, an **arrest** may be made. An arrest involves physically taking a person into custody pending a court proceeding. This action not only restricts the suspect's freedom, but it is also the first step toward prosecution.

Under some conditions, arrests may be made on the basis of a **warrant**—a court order issued by a judge authorizing police officers to take certain actions, such as arresting suspects or searching premises. In practice, most arrests are made without warrants. In some states, police officers may issue a summons or citation that orders a person to appear in court on a certain date. This avoids the need to hold the suspect physically until decisions are made about the case.

❸ **BOOKING.** After an arrest the suspect is usually transported to a police station for booking, in which a record is made of the arrest. When booked, the suspect may be fingerprinted, photographed, interrogated, and placed in a lineup to be identified by the victim or witnesses. All suspects must also be warned that they have the right to counsel, that they

arrest
The physical taking of a person into custody on the ground that probable cause exists to believe that he or she has committed a criminal offense. Police may use only reasonable physical force in making an arrest. The purpose of the arrest is to hold the accused for a court proceeding.

warrant
A court order authorizing police officials to take certain actions; for example, to arrest suspects or to search premises.

may remain silent, and that any statement they make may be used against them later. Bail may be set so that the suspect learns what amount of money must be paid or what other conditions must be met to gain release from custody until the case is processed.

❹ **CHARGING.** Prosecuting attorneys are the key link between the police and the courts. They must consider the facts of the case and decide whether there is reasonable cause to believe that an offense was committed and that the suspect committed the offense. The decision to charge is crucial because it sets in motion the adjudication of the case.

❺ **INITIAL APPEARANCE.** Within a reasonable time after arrest, the suspect must be brought before a judge. At this point, the suspect is given formal notice of the charge(s) for which he or she is being held, advised of his or her rights, and, if approved by the judge, given a chance to post bail. At this stage, the judge decides whether enough evidence has been gathered to hold the suspect for further criminal processing. If enough evidence has not been produced, the judge will dismiss the case.

The purpose of bail is to permit the accused to be released while awaiting trial and to ensure that he or she will show up in court at the appointed time. Bail requires the accused to provide or arrange a surety (or pledge), usually in the form of money or a bond. The amount of bail is based mainly on the judge's view of the seriousness of the crime and the defendant's prior criminal record. Suspects may also be released *on their own recognizance*—a promise to appear in court at a later date. In a few cases bail may be denied and the accused held because he or she is viewed as a threat to the community.

❻ **PRELIMINARY HEARING/GRAND JURY.** After a suspect has been arrested, booked, and brought to court to be informed of the charge and advised of his or her rights, a decision must be made as to whether there is enough evidence to proceed. The preliminary hearing, used in about half the states, allows a judge to decide whether probable cause exists to believe that a crime has been committed and that the accused person committed it. If the judge does not find probable cause, the case is dismissed. If there is enough evidence, the accused is bound over for arraignment on an **information**—a document charging a person with a specific crime.

In the federal system and in some states, the prosecutor appears before a grand jury, which decides whether enough evidence is available to file an **indictment** or "true bill" charging the suspect with a specific crime. The preliminary hearing and grand jury are designed to prevent hasty and malicious prosecutions, to protect persons from mistakenly being humiliated in public, and to decide whether there are grounds for prosecution.

❼ **INDICTMENT/INFORMATION.** If the preliminary hearing leads to an information or the grand jury vote leads to an indictment, the prosecutor prepares the formal charging document and presents it to the court.

❽ **ARRAIGNMENT.** The accused person appears in court to hear the indictment or information read by a judge and to enter a plea. Accused persons may plead guilty or not guilty or, in some states, stand mute. If the accused pleads guilty, the judge must decide whether the plea is made voluntarily and whether the person has full knowledge of the consequences. When a guilty plea is accepted as knowing and voluntary,

information

A document charging an individual with a specific crime. It is prepared by a prosecuting attorney and presented to a court at a preliminary hearing.

indictment

A document returned by a grand jury as a "true bill" charging an individual with a specific crime on the basis of a determination of probable cause as presented by a prosecuting attorney.

there is no need for a trial and the judge imposes a sentence. Plea bargaining may take place at any time in the criminal justice process, but it is likely to be completed before or after arraignment. Very few criminal cases proceed to trial. Most move from the entry of the guilty plea to the sentencing phase.

FIGURE 1.4   The flow of decision making in the criminal justice system

Each agency is responsible for a part of the decision-making system. Thus the police, prosecution, courts, and corrections are bound together through a series of exchange relationships.

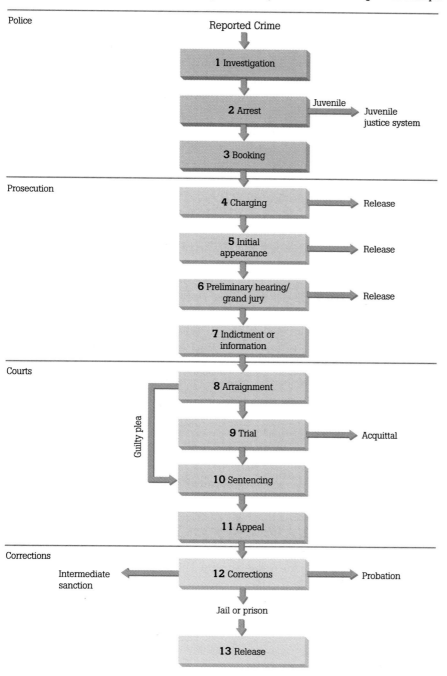

Police

Reported Crime

1 Investigation

2 Arrest — Juvenile → Juvenile justice system

3 Booking

Prosecution

4 Charging → Release

5 Initial appearance → Release

6 Preliminary hearing/ grand jury → Release

7 Indictment or information

Courts

8 Arraignment

9 Trial → Acquittal

Guilty plea

10 Sentencing

11 Appeal

Corrections

Intermediate sanction ← **12** Corrections → Probation

Jail or prison

13 Release

❾ TRIAL. For the small percentage of defendants who plead not guilty, the right to a trial by an impartial jury is guaranteed by the Sixth Amendment if the charges are serious enough to warrant a prison sentence of more than six months. In many jurisdictions, lesser charges do not entail a right to a jury trial. Most trials are summary or bench trials; that is, they are conducted without a jury. Because the defendant pleads guilty in most criminal cases, only about 10 to 15 percent of cases go to trial and only about 5 percent are heard by juries. Whether a criminal trial is held before a judge alone or before a judge and jury, the procedures are similar and are set out by state law and Supreme Court rulings. A defendant may be found guilty only if the evidence proves beyond a reasonable doubt that he or she committed the offense.

❿ SENTENCING. Judges are responsible for imposing sentences. The intent is to make the sentence suitable to the offender and the offense within the limits set by the law. Although criminal codes place limits on sentences, the judge still has leeway. Among the judge's options are a suspended sentence, probation, imprisonment, or other sanctions such as fines and community service.

⓫ APPEAL. Defendants who are found guilty may appeal convictions to a higher court. An appeal may be based on the claim that the trial court failed to follow the proper procedures or that the defendant's constitutional rights were violated by the actions of police, prosecutors, defense attorneys, or judges. The number of appeals is small compared with the total number of convictions, and in about 80 percent of appeals, trial judges and other officials are ruled to have acted properly. Even defendants who win appeals do not go free right away. Normally the defendant is given a second trial, which may result in an acquittal, a second conviction, or a plea bargain to lesser charges.

⓬ CORRECTIONS. The court's sentence is carried out by the correctional subsystem. Probation, intermediate sanctions such as fines and community service, and incarceration are the sanctions most often imposed. Probation allows offenders to serve their sentences in the community under supervision. Youthful offenders, first offenders, and those convicted of minor violations are most likely to be sentenced to probation instead of incarceration. The conditions of probation may require offenders to observe certain rules—to be employed, maintain an orderly life, or attend school—and to report to their supervising officer from time to time. If these requirements are not met, the judge may revoke the probation and impose a prison sentence.

Many new types of sanctions have been used in recent years. These intermediate sanctions are more restrictive than probation but less restrictive than incarceration. They include fines, intensive supervision probation, boot camp, home confinement, and community service.

Whatever the reasons used to justify them, prisons exist mainly to separate criminals from the rest of society. Those convicted of misdemeanors usually serve their time in city or county jails, while felons serve time in state prisons. Isolation from the community is one of the most painful aspects of incarceration. Not only are letters and visits restricted, but supervision and censorship are also ever present. To maintain security, prison officials make unannounced searches of inmates and subject them to strict discipline.

⑬ **RELEASE.** Release may occur when the offender has served the full sentence imposed by the court, but most offenders are returned to the community under the supervision of a parole officer. Parole continues for the duration of the sentence or for a period specified by law. Parole may be revoked and the offender returned to prison if the conditions of parole are not met or if the parolee commits another crime.

The case of Christopher Jones is described on p. 30. Jones, a 31-year-old man from Battle Creek, Michigan, was arrested, charged, and convicted of serious crimes arising from the police investigation of a series of robberies.

CHECK POINT

㉑ **List and define the steps of the criminal justice process.**

The Criminal Justice Wedding Cake

Although the flowchart shown in Figure 1.5 is helpful, keep in mind that not all cases are treated equally. The process applied to a given case, as well as its outcome, is shaped by the importance of the case to decision makers, the seriousness of the charge, and the defendant's resources.

Some cases are highly visible either because of the notoriety of the defendant or victim or because of the shocking nature of the crime. At the other extreme are run-of-the-mill cases involving unpublicized, minor crimes.

As shown in Figure 1.5, the criminal justice process can be compared with a wedding cake. This model shows clearly how different cases receive different kinds of treatment in the justice process.

Layer 1 of the cake consists of celebrated cases that are highly unusual, get great public attention, result in a jury trial, and often drag on through many appeals. These cases embody the ideal of an adversary system of justice in which each side actively fights against the other, either because the defendant faces a stiff sentence or because the defendant has the wealth to pay for a strong defense. The case of serial killer and cannibal Jeffrey Dahmer, the conviction of "Unabomber" Theodore Kaczynski, and the celebrated trial of O. J. Simpson on double murder charges are of this type. Not all cases in Layer 1 receive national attention. From time to time, local crimes, especially cases of murder and rape, are treated in this way.

These cases are like morality plays. The carefully crafted arguments of the prosecution and defense are seen as expressing key issues in society or tragic flaws in individuals. Too often, however, the public concludes that all criminal cases follow this model.

Layer 2 consists of **felonies** that are considered serious by officials: violent crimes committed by persons with long criminal records against victims

felonies
Serious crimes usually carrying a penalty of death or incarceration for more than one year.

FIGURE 1.5 The criminal justice wedding cake

This figure shows that different cases are treated in different ways. Only a very few cases are played out as high drama; most are handled through plea bargaining and dismissals.

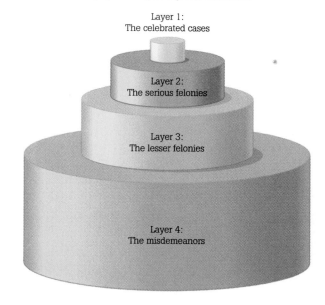

Layer 1: The celebrated cases
Layer 2: The serious felonies
Layer 3: The lesser felonies
Layer 4: The misdemeanors

SOURCE: Drawn from Samuel Walker, *Sense and Nonsense about Crime and Drugs*, 4th ed. (Belmont, Calif.: Wadsworth Publishing, 1998), 30–37.

The Criminal Justice Process: The State of Michigan versus Christopher Jones

In October 1998, police in Battle Creek, Michigan, investigated a string of six robberies that occurred in a ten-day period. People were assaulted during some of the robberies. One victim was beaten so badly with a power tool that he required extensive reconstructive surgery for his face and skull. The police received an anonymous tip on their Silent Observer hotline, which led them to put together a photo lineup—an array of photographs of local men who had criminal records. Based on the tip and photographs identified by the victims, the police began to search for two men who were well known to them, Christopher Jones and his cousin Fred Brown.

Arrest

Jones was a 31-year-old African American. A dozen years of struggles with cocaine addiction had cost him his marriage and several jobs. He had a criminal record stretching back several years from pleading guilty to charges of attempted larceny and attempted breaking and entering in separate incidents. Thus he had a record of stealing to support his drug habit. He had spent time on probation and done a short stretch in a minimum security prison and a boot camp. But he had never been caught with drugs or been accused of an act of violence.

Fearing that Jones would be injured or killed by the police if he tried to run or resist arrest, his parents called the police and told them he was holed-up in the bedroom of their home. At approximately 10 P.M. on October 28, as officers surrounded the house, the family opened the door and showed the officers the way to the bedroom. Jones surrendered peacefully and was led to the waiting police car in handcuffs.

At the police station, a detective with whom Jones was acquainted read him his *Miranda* rights, then informed him that he was looking at the possibility of a life sentence in prison unless he helped the police by providing information about Brown. Jones said that he did not want to talk to the police, and he asked to be given an attorney. The police thus ceased questioning Jones, and he was taken to the jail.

Booking

At the jail, Jones was strip searched, was given a bright orange jumpsuit to wear, was photographed and fingerprinted. He was told that he would be arraigned the next morning. That night he slept on the floor of the overcrowded holding cell—a large cell where people are placed immediately upon arrest.

Arraignment

The next morning, Jones was taken to a room for video arraignment. A two-way camera system permitted Jones to see the district courtroom in the neighboring courthouse. At the same time the judge and others could view him on a television screen. Jones was informed by the judge that he was being charged with breaking and entering, armed robbery, and assault with intent to commit murder. The final charge alone could draw a life sentence. Under Michigan law, these charges can be filed directly by the prose-

LOCAL Juvenile worker has charge dropped/3A

SPORTS Local football teams eye playoffs/1B

LIFESTYLE Program instills good values/1C

Battle Creek ENQUIRER

CITY EDITION

FRIDAY Oct. 30, 1998

Glenn relives space history

Hero is 'enjoying the show'

2 charged in violent robberies

Kellogg Co. earnings per share

Kellogg's earnings expected to be low

cutor without being presented to a grand jury for indictment as in federal courts and some other states. The judge set bond (bail) at $200,000.

At a second video arraignment several days later, Jones was informed that he faced seven additional counts of assault with intent to commit murder, armed robbery, unarmed robbery, and home invasion for four other robberies. Bond was set at $200,000 for each alleged robbery. Thus he faced ten felony charges for the five robberies and his total bail was $1 million.

Unable to make bail, Jones was held in the Calhoun County Jail to await his day in court. Eventually he would spend nine months in the jail before all of the charges against him were processed.

Preliminary Hearing

Under state court procedures, Jones was supposed to have a preliminary hearing within two weeks after his arraignment. At the preliminary hearing the district judge would determine whether enough evidence had been gathered to justify sending Jones's case up to the Calhoun County Circuit Court, which handled felony trials.

Jones received a letter informing him of the name of the private attorney appointed by the court to represent him, but he did not meet the attorney until he was taken to court for his preliminary hearing. Minutes before the hearing, the attorney, David Gilbert, introduced himself to Jones. Jones wanted to delay any preliminary hearing until a lineup could be held to test the victims' identifications of him as a robber. Gilbert said they must proceed with the preliminary hearing for the armed robbery case in which the victim was beaten with the power tool, because a witness had traveled from another state to testify. Preliminary hearings on the four additional robbery cases were postponed, but the out-of-town witness's testimony led the district judge to conclude that sufficient evidence existed to move that case to the circuit court on an armed robbery charge.

Lineup

Jones waited for weeks for the lineup to be scheduled. Finally, his attorney complained to the judge that the lineup had never been conducted. The judge ordered that the lineup be held as soon as possible.

At the lineup Jones and five other men stood in front of a one-way mirror. One by one, the victims of each of the six robberies looked at the men and attempted to determine if any were their assailant. At the end of each identification, one of the men was asked to step forward. Because he was asked to step forward only twice, Jones guessed that he was picked out by two of the victims.

Gilbert was unable to attend the lineup and another attorney went in his place. Jones was disappointed that the substitute attorney was not more active in objecting that the other men looked too short and too old to adequately test the victims' ability to make an identification. He later discovered that his substitute attorney had just entered private practice after serving as an assistant prosecutor at Jones' preliminary hearing for armed robbery.

Second Preliminary Hearing

At the next preliminary hearing, the victims of the four additional robberies testified. Because they focused mainly on Brown as the perpetrator of the assaults and robberies, the defense attorney argued that many of the charges against Jones should be dropped. However, the judge determined that the victims' testimony provided enough evidence to send most of the charges against Jones to the circuit court.

Plea Bargaining

Jones waited for weeks in jail without hearing much from his attorney. Although he did not know it, the prosecutor was formulating a plea agreement and communicating to the defense attorney the terms under which charges would be dropped in exchange for a guilty plea from Jones. A few minutes before a hearing on the proposed plea agreement,

Gilbert told Jones that the prosecutor had offered to drop all of the other charges if Jones would plead guilty to one count of unarmed robbery for the incident in which the victim was seriously injured by the power tool wielded by Brown and one count of home invasion for another robbery. Jones did not want to accept the deal because he was being asked to plead guilty for home invasion when he was not even present. The attorney insisted that this was an excellent deal compared with all of the other charges that the prosecutor could pursue. Jones still resisted.

In the courtroom, Judge James Kingsley read aloud the offer, but Jones refused to enter a guilty plea. Like the defense attorney, the judge told Jones that this was a favorable offer compared with the other more serious charges that the prosecutor could still pursue. Jones again declined.

As he sat in the holding area outside of the courtroom, Jones worried that he was making a mistake by turning down the plea offer. He wondered if he could end up with a life sentence if one of the victims identified him by mistake as having done a crime that was committed by Brown. When his attorney came to see him, he told Gilbert that he had changed his mind. They went right back into the courtroom and told the judge that he was ready to enter a guilty plea. As they prepared to plead guilty, the prosecutor said that as part of the agreement Jones would be expected to provide information about the other robberies and to testify against Brown. The defense attorney protested that this was not part of the plea agreement. Jones told the judge that he could not provide information about the home invasion to which he was about to plead guilty because he was not present at that robbery and had no knowledge of what occurred. Judge Kingsley declared that he would not accept a guilty plea when the defendant claimed to have no knowledge of the crime.

After the hearing, discussions about a plea agreement were renewed. Jones agreed to take a polygraph test so that the prosecutor could find out which robberies he knew about. Jones hoped to show prosecutors that his involvement with Brown was limited. No test was ever administered.

Trial and Plea Agreement

Jones waited in jail for several more weeks. When Gilbert next came to visit him, Jones was informed that the armed robbery trial was scheduled for the following day. In addition, the prosecutor's plea offer had changed. Brown had pleaded guilty to armed robbery and assault with intent less than murder and was facing twenty-five to fifty years in prison. No longer did the prosecutor need Jones' testimony in Brown's trial. Now he wanted Jones to plead to the same charges as Brown in exchange for dropping the other pending charges. According to Jones, Gilbert urged him to accept the new plea offer by saying that otherwise the prosecutor would pursue all of the other charges, which could bring a life sentence. Jones refused to plead guilty.

Prior to entering court the next day, Gilbert again encouraged Jones to accept the plea agreement. According to Jones, Gilbert said that the guilty plea could be withdrawn if the probation office's sentencing recommendation was too high. Because he did not want to risk a life sentence and he believed he could later withdraw the plea, Jones decided to accept the offer.

With his attorney's advice, he entered a plea of "no contest" to the two charges. A "no contest" plea is treated the same as a guilty plea for punishment purposes.

Before taking the plea, Judge Kingsley informed Jones that by entering the plea he would be waiving his right to a trial, including his right to question witnesses, and to have the prosecutor prove his guilt beyond a reasonable doubt. Judge Kingsley then read the charges of armed robbery and assault with intent to do great bodily harm and asked," What do you plead?" Jones replied: "No contest." Then the judge asked a series of questions:

Judge Kingsley: "Mr. Jones, has anyone promised you anything other than the plea bargain to get you to enter this plea?"

Jones: "No."

Judge Kingsley: "Has anyone threatened you or forced you or compelled you to enter the plea?"

Jones: "No."

Judge Kingsley: "Are you entering this plea of your own free will?"

Jones: "Yes."

The judge reminded Jones that no final agreement had been reached on his sentence and gave Jones one last opportunity to change his mind about pleading "no contest." Jones repeated his desire to enter the plea, so the plea was accepted.

Immediately after the hearing Jones had second thoughts. According to Jones, "I was feeling uneasy about being pressured [by my attorney] to take the plea offer . . . [so I decided] to write to the Judge and tell him about the pressures my attorney put upon me as well as [the attorney] telling me I had a right to withdraw my plea."

When Gilbert learned that Jones had written the letter, he asked the judge to permit him to withdraw as Jones's attorney. Judge Kingsley initially refused. However, when Jones spoke in open court at his sentencing hearing about his criticisms of Gilbert, as well as his complaints about the prosecutor's handling of the lineup and the failure to administer the polygraph test, the judge decided to appoint a new defense attorney, Virginia Cairns, to handle sentencing at a rescheduled hearing. But the judge would not permit the plea to be withdrawn.

Sentencing

Although arrested in October 1998, Jones was not sentenced until July 1999. At the hearing Judge Kingsley asked Jones if he would like to make a statement. Jones faced the judge as he spoke, glancing at his family and at the victim when he referred to them.

First and foremost, I would like to say what happened to the victim was a tragedy. I showed great remorse for that. He is in my prayers along with his family. Even though, your Honor, I'm not making any excuses for what I'm saying here today, the injuries the victim sustained were not at the hands of myself nor did I actually rob this victim. I was present, your Honor, as I told you once before, yes, I was. And it's a wrong. Again I'm not making any kind of excuse whatsoever...

Your Honor, I would just like to say that drugs has clouded my memory, and my choices in the past. I really made some wrong decisions. Only times I've gotten into trouble were because of my drug use . . . . One of the worst decisions I really made was my involvement of being around the co-defendant Fred Brown. That bothers me to this day because actually we didn't even get along. Because of my drug use again I chose to be around him.

Jones also talked about his positive record as a high school student and athlete, his work with the jail minister, and his desire to talk to young people about his experiences to steer them away from drugs.

Attorney Cairns spoke next. She called the court's attention to several errors in the pre-sentence report, which recommended Jones serve five to twenty-five years for armed robbery and four to seven years for assault. She emphasized letters of support from Jones' family, which she had encouraged them to write to the judge describing his positive qualities and prospects for successful rehabilitation. She argued that Jones should receive a less severe sentence than that imposed on Brown.

Next, the victim spoke about his injuries and how his $40,000 worth of medical bills had driven him to bankruptcy.

I went from having perfect vision to not being able to read out of my left eye. I got steel plates in my head . . . .

They left me to die that morning. He took the keys to my car . . . . So today it's true, I don't think Mr. Jones should be sentenced same as Brown. That's who I want—I want to see him sentenced to the maximum. He's the one that crushed my skull with a drill. But Jones did hit me several times while Mr. Brown held me there to begin with. It's true that I did hit him with a hammer to get them off me. But he still was there. He still had the chance of not leaving me without keys to my car so I could get to a hospital. He still had the choice to stop a—at least a phone on the way and say there's someone that could possibly be dead, but he didn't. . . . You don't treat a human being like that. And if you do you serve time and pretty much to the maximum. I don't ask the Court for 25 years. That's a pretty long time to serve. And I do ask the Court to look at 15 to 20. I'd be happy. Thank you.

Gary Brand, the assistant prosecutor, rose and recommended a twenty-year sentence and noted that Jones should be responsible for $35,000 in restitution to the victim and to the state for medical expenses and lost income.

Judge Kingsley then addressed Jones. He acknowledged that Jones's drug problem had led to his criminal activity. He also noted that Jones's family support was much stronger than that of most defendants. He chastised Jones for falling into drugs when life was tougher after enjoying a successful high school career. Judge Kingsley then proceeded to announce his sentencing decision.

You are not in my view as culpable as Mr. Brown. I agree with [the victim] that you were there. When I read your letter, Mr. Jones, I was a bit disturbed by your unwillingness to confront the reality of where you found yourself with Mr. Brown. You were not a passive observer to everything that went on in my view. You were not as active a participant as Mr. Brown...

What I'm going to do, Mr. Jones, is as follows: Taking everything into consideration as it relates to the armed robbery count, it is the sentence of the Court that you spend a term of not less than 12 years nor more than 25 years with the Michigan Department of Corrections. I will give you credit for the [261 days] you have already served.

The judge also ordered payment of $35,000 in restitution as a condition of parole. He concluded the hearing by informing Jones of his right to file an application for a leave to appeal.

Prison

After spending a few more weeks in jail awaiting transfer, Christopher Jones was sent to the state corrections classification center at Jackson for evaluation to determine to which of Michigan's forty prisons he would be sent. Prison security classifications range from Level I for minimum to Level VI for "super maximum," high security. Jones was assigned to a Level IV prison, St. Louis Correctional Facility, where he lives with a cellmate in a space designed to house one prisoner.

Because Jones is a high school graduate who had previously attended a community college, he works as a tutor for other prisoners and is head clerk of the prison library. He hopes that he can contribute to his own personal development while doing productive work that might help him eventually earn parole.

T. Christenson, "Two Charged in Violent Robberies," *Battle Creek Enquirer*, October 30, 1998, p.1A; interview with Christopher Jones, St. Louis Correctional Facility, St. Louis, Michigan, October 19, 1999; letters to Chistopher Smith from Christopher Jones, October and November 1999; and Calhoun County Circuit Court transcripts for plea hearing, May 20, 1999, and sentencing hearing, July 16, 1999.

Celebrated cases such as the Jasper, Texas, trials of John King, Lawrence Brewer, and Shawn Berry attract much public attention. The three were charged with first-degree murder in the death of James Byrd, Jr., who was tied to a truck and dragged to his death along a rural East Texas road.

unknown to them. Police and the prosecutors speak of these as "heavy" cases that should result in "tough" sentences. In such cases the defendant has little reason to plead guilty and the defense attorney must prepare for trial.

Layer 3 also consists of felonies, but the crimes and the offenders are seen as less important than those in Layer 2. The offenses may be the same as in Layer 2, but the offender may have no record, and the victim may have had a prior relationship with the accused. The main goal of criminal justice officials is to dispose of such cases quickly. For this reason, many are filtered out of the system, often through plea bargaining.

Layer 4 is made up of **misdemeanors.** About 90 percent of all cases fall into this category. They concern such offenses as public drunkenness, shoplifting, prostitution, disturbing the peace, and traffic violations. Looked upon as the garbage of the system, these cases are handled by the lower courts, where speed is essential. Prosecutors use their discretion to reduce charges or recommend probation as a way to encourage defendants to plead guilty quickly. Trials are rare, processes are informal, and fines, probation, or short jail sentences result.

The wedding cake model is a useful way of viewing the criminal justice system. Cases are not treated equally; some are seen as very important, others as merely part of a large number that must be processed. When one knows the nature of a case, one can predict fairly well how it will be handled and what its outcome will be.

misdemeanors

Offenses less serious than felonies and usually punishable by incarceration of no more than a year, probation, or intermediate sanction.

CHECK POINT

㉒ **What is the purpose of the wedding cake model?**

㉓ **Describe the types of cases found on each layer.**

Summary

- Crime and justice are high on the agenda of national priorities.
- Crime and justice are public policy issues.
- Criminal justice can best be seen as a social system.
- In a democracy there is a struggle to strike a balance between maintaining public order and protecting individual freedom.
- The crime control model and the due process model are two ways of looking at the goals and procedures of the criminal justice system.
- Racial disparities in criminal justice are explained in one of three ways: minorities commit more crimes; the criminal justice system is racist; the criminal justice system expresses the racism of society.
- Criminal justice policies are developed in national, state, and local political arenas.
- The three goals of the criminal justice system are doing justice, controlling crime, and preventing crime.
- Both the national and state systems of criminal justice enforce laws, try cases, and punish offenders.
- Criminal justice is a system made up of a number of parts or subsystems—police, courts, corrections.
- Exchange is a key concept for the analysis of criminal justice processes.
- Four major characteristics of the criminal justice system are discretion, resource dependence, sequential tasks, and filtering.
- The processing of cases in the criminal justice system involves a series of decisions by police officers, prosecutors, judges, probation officers, wardens, and parole board members.
- The criminal justice system consists of thirteen steps that cover the stages of law enforcement, adjudication, and corrections.
- The four-layered criminal justice wedding cake model indicates that not all cases are treated equally.

Questions for Review

1. What are the goals of criminal justice in a democracy?
2. What is the challenge of criminal justice in a multicultural society?
3. What are the major elements of Herbert Packer's due process model and crime control model?
4. What are the goals of the criminal justice system?
5. What is meant by the concept of system? How is the administration of criminal justice a system?
6. What are the thirteen steps in the criminal justice decision making process?
7. Why is the criminal justice wedding cake a better depiction of reality than a linear model of the system?

Key Terms

adjudication (p. 23)
arrest (p. 26)
crime (p. 4)
crime control model (p. 7)
discretion (p. 20)
discrimination (p. 9)
disparity (p. 9)

dual court system (23)
due process model (p. 7)
exchange (p. 19)
federalism (p. 16)
felony (p. 29)
filtering process (p. 21)
indictment (p. 27)

information (p. 27)
misdemeanor (p. 34)
plea bargain (p. 19)
system (p. 18)
warrant (p. 26)

For Further Reading

Cole, David. *No Equal Justice.* New York: The New Press, 1999. Argues that a double standard compromises the legitimacy of criminal justice and exacerbates racial divisions.

Friedman, Lawrence M. *Crime and Punishment in American History.* New York: Basic Books, 1993. A historical overview of criminal justice from colonial times. Argues that the evolution of criminal justice reflects transformations in America's character.

Parenti, Christian. *Lockdown America: Police and Prisons in the Age of Crisis.* New York: Verso, 1999. Argues that

beginning in the late 1960s American capitalism hit a dual social and economic crisis. In response was a buildup of the criminal justice system, which has led to state repression and surveillance.

Reiman, Jeffrey. *...And the Poor Get Prison: Economic Bias in American Criminal Justice.* Boston: Allyn & Bacon, 1996. A stinging critique of the system. Argues that the system serves the powerful by its failure to reduce crime.

Tonry, Michael. *Malign Neglect: Race, Crime and Punishment in America.*

New York: Oxford University Press, 1995. Impact of crime control policies on black communities.

Walker, Samuel. *Sense and Nonsense about Crime and Drug Policy,* 4th ed. Belmont, Calif.: Wadsworth Publishing, 1998. A provocative look at crime policies.

Walker, Samuel, Cassia Spohn, and Miriam DeLone. *The Color of Justice: Race, Ethnicity and Crime in America.* Belmont, Calif.: Wadsworth Publishing, 1996. An excellent overview of the links between crime, race, and ethnicity.

Going Online

1 Using the Internet, access a leading national or state newspaper. Count the number of crime and noncrime stories appearing on the front page for a typical week. What percentage of crime stories do you find? What types of crimes are described? Should readers be concerned about crime in their community?

2 Enter the title of the National Criminal Justice Commission's book, *The Real War on Crime*, in any search engine to access the site. Would you categorize the Commission's recommendations as "liberal" or "conservative"? Do data exist to support the "Five Crime Myths" cited by the Commission?

3 Using InfoTrac College Edition, enter the keywords *police* and *racial profiling*. Read the *New York Times Upfront* September 6, 1999, article. Summarize the two positions. Should race be used by the police when stopping, questioning, or searching individuals?

CHECK POINT ANSWERS

1 Stricter enforcement of the law through the expansion of police forces and the enactment of laws that require swift and certain punishment of offenders.

2 Stronger crime measures endanger the values of due process and justice. Focus on changing social conditions.

3 That criminal justice policies should control crime by enforcing the law and protecting the rights of individuals.

4 Every effort must be made to repress crime through efficiency, speed, and finality.

5 Every effort must be made to ensure that criminal justice decisions are based on reliable information. It stresses the adversarial process, the rights of defendants, and formal decision-making procedures.

6 That racial and ethnic minorities are subjected to the criminal justice system at much higher rates than the white majority.

7 Minorities commit more crime; the criminal justice system is racist; America is a racist society.

8 State and local levels of government.

9 Penal codes and budgets are passed by legislatures, many criminal justice officials are elected, and criminal justice policies are developed in political arenas.

10 Doing justice, controlling crime, preventing crime.

11 Offenders are held fully accountable for their actions; the rights of persons who have contact with the system will be protected; and like offenses will be treated alike and officials will take into account relevant differences among offenders and offenses.

⑫ A division of power between a central (national) government and regional (state) governments.

⑬ Enforcement of federal criminal laws.

⑭ The expansion of criminal activities across state borders.

⑮ A complex whole made up of interdependent parts whose actions are directed toward goals and influenced by the environment within which it functions.

⑯ Plea bargaining.

⑰ Discretion, resource dependence, sequential tasks, filtering.

⑱ Keeping the peace, apprehending violators and combating crime, preventing crime, providing social services.

⑲ A separate judicial system for each state in addition to a national system.

⑳ Prisons, jails, probation, parole, intermediate sanctions. Public, nonprofit, and for-profit agencies carry out these programs.

㉑ (1) Investigation, (2) arrest, (3) booking, (4) charging, (5) initial appearance, (6) preliminary hearing/grand jury, (7) indictment/information, (8) arraignment, (9) trial, (10) sentencing, (11) appeal, (12) corrections, (13) release.

㉒ To show that not all cases are treated equally.

㉓ Layer 1: celebrated cases in which the adversarial system is played out in full. Layer 2: serious felonies committed by persons with long criminal records against victims unknown to them. Layer 3: felonies in which the crimes and the offenders are viewed as less serious than in Layer 2. Layer 4: misdemeanors.

Crime, Victimization, and Criminal Behavior

Rape. The very harshness of the word conveys violence, fear, and disgust. A taboo since ancient times—when the purity of bloodlines and the theft of property (the value of the woman's virtue) were of concern—rape has evolved into a formal offense.

Forcible rape is sexual intercourse by a male with a female who is not his wife against her will and under conditions of threat or force. However, different countries have defined it in different ways and imposed different punishment on offenders. For example, in England the House of Lords ruled that "if a man believes that a woman is consenting to sex, he cannot be convicted of rape, no matter how unreasonable his belief may be" (Estrich, 1987:92). In some countries rape is not charged if the victim is a servant. Among the Gusii, a large tribe in Kenya, forcible rape by unmarried males is an accepted form of sexual relations (Levine, 1959; Erez and Thompson, 1990). In Western countries the law distinguishes among rape, forcible rape,

What Americans Think

"Do you think the use of marijuana should be made legal or not?"

Should   28%

Should Not   66%

"Do you think homosexual relations between consenting adults should be made legal or not?"

Should   50%

Should Not   43%

"When a person has a disease that cannot be cured, should doctors be allowed by law to assist the patient to commit suicide if the patient requests it?"

Should   53%

Should Not   39%

SOURCE U.S. Department of Justice, Bureau of Justice Statistics, *Sourcebook of Criminal Justice Statistics, 1998* (Washington, D.C.: Government Printing Office, 1999), Tables 2.72, 2.99, 2.100.

and statutory rape on the basis of such factors as age, level of force, and the nature of the sexual conduct.

In the United States, before the rise of the women's movement in the early 1970s, some states required that a rape victim's word be confirmed by some other person. This requirement was difficult to meet. Moreover, the defense could bring up the victim's past sexual conduct, even though it was not relevant.

The variety of definitions of rape and the kinds of evidence required to prove that rape took place are reminders that laws are written by humans. Laws emerge from human experience and are carried out by humans. Thus people often disagree about the exact nature of the act a law defines as criminal.

In this chapter we first look at how crime is defined and measured, and at crime victimization. Next we examine theories about the causes of crime. As we learn about what crime is and why it occurs, we will begin to see some of the reasons the "crime problem" is such a challenge.

QUESTIONS for Inquiry

What is a crime?

What are the major types of crimes in the United States?

How much crime is there, and how is crime measured?

Who are the victims of crime?

What theories have been proposed to explain criminal behavior?

Defining Crime

Why does the law label some types of behavior as criminal and not others? For example, a young person might ask, "Why can't I smoke marijuana if I'm old enough to consume alcohol?" If the answer is that marijuana might be addictive, could lead to the use of more potent drugs, and may have negative effects on health, then the questioner might point out that alcoholism is a major social problem, drinking beer may create a thirst for hard liquor, and overuse of alcohol leads to heart and liver disorders as well as many deaths in auto accidents. An argument-stopping response might be: "Because pot smoking is against the law, and that's that!"

The criminal law is defined by elected representatives in state legislatures and Congress who make choices about the behaviors that government will punish. Some of those choices reflect a broad consensus in society that certain actions, such as rape, assault, and murder, are so harmful that they must be punished. Such crimes have traditionally been called *mala in se*—wrong in themselves.

However, for other criminal laws, legislatures make decisions even though society may be conflicted about the harmfulness of certain acts. These crimes are referred to as *mala prohibita*—they are crimes because they are prohibited by the government and not because they are wrong in themselves. Everyone does not agree, for example, that gambling, prostitution, and drug use should be punished.

mala in se

Offenses that are wrong by their very nature.

mala prohibita

Offenses prohibited by law but not wrong in themselves.

Today, some people view these behaviors as free choices that adults should be able to make themselves (see What Americans Think). And in the past, these behaviors were not criminalized. However, note that the consumption of alcohol and performing a first-term abortion were once illegal.

Evidence from a national survey helps show the extent to which Americans agree about the behaviors that should be defined as crimes (BJS, 1988:16). In this survey, respondents were asked to rank the seriousness of 204 illegal events. The results showed wide agreement on the severity of certain crimes (see Table 2.1). However, crime victims scored those acts higher than did nonvictims. The ratings assigned by minority-group members tended to be lower than those assigned by whites. Thus disagreement exists about which behaviors to punish as crimes.

American laws are often in conflict with the religious and cultural practices of recent non-Western immigrants. In Maine, a refugee from Afghanistan was seen kissing the penis of his baby boy, a traditional expression of love by his father. To his neighbors this was child abuse and the boy was taken away (*New York Times,* March 6, 1999:A15). A court in Lincoln, Nebraska, gave four- to six-year prison terms to two Iraqi men, 28 and 34 years old, for sexual assault on a child. They had married the daughters, aged 13 and 14, of a fellow Iraqi immigrant in a Muslim ceremony. Their attorney argued that they were following Iraqi custom and did not know that the minimum age for marriage in Nebraska is 17 (*Kansas City Star,* September 24, 1997:A2). Sexual practices, puberty rites, animal sacrifices, and the

TABLE 2.1

How do people rank the severity of a crime?

Respondents to a survey were asked to rank 204 illegal events ranging from school truancy to planting a deadly bomb. A severity score of 40 indicates that people believe the crime is twice as bad as a severity score of 20.

SEVERITY SCORE	TEN MOST SERIOUS OFFENSES	SEVERITY SCORE	TEN LEAST SERIOUS OFFENSES
72.1	Planting a bomb in a public building. The bomb explodes and twenty people are killed.	1.3	Two persons willingly engage in a homosexual act.
52.8	A man forcibly rapes a woman. As a result of physical injuries, she dies.	1.1	Disturbing the neighborhood with loud, noisy behavior.
43.2	Robbing a victim at gunpoint. The victim struggles and is shot to death.	1.1	Taking bets on the numbers.
39.2	A man stabs his wife. As a result, she dies.	1.1	A group continues to hang around a corner after being told by a police officer to break up.
35.7	Stabbing a victim to death.	.9	A youngster under 16 runs away from home.
35.6	Intentionally injuring a victim. As a result, the victim dies.	.8	Being drunk in public.
33.8	Running a narcotics ring.	.7	A youngster under 16 breaks a curfew law by being on the street after the hour permitted by law.
27.9	A woman stabs her husband. As a result, he dies.	.6	Trespassing in the backyard of a private home.
26.3	An armed person skyjacks an airplane and demands to be flown to another country.	.3	A person is vagrant. That is, he has no home and no visible means of support.
25.8	A man forcibly rapes a woman. No other physical injury occurs.	.2	A youngster under 16 is truant from school.

SOURCE: U.S. Department of Justice, Bureau of Justice Statistics, *Report to the Nation on Crime and Justice,* 2d ed. (Washington, D.C.: Government Printing Office, 1988), 16.

use of narcotics have been portrayed as traditional rituals of particular cultures. But can ethnic groups claim that their practices should not conform to the law?

CHECK POINT

① **Who defines certain behaviors as criminal?**

② **What is meant by *mala in se* and by *mala prohibita*?**

(Answers are found at the end of the chapter.)

Types of Crime

Crimes can be classified in a number of ways. As we have seen, scholars often use the distinction between *mala in se* and *mala prohibita*. Crimes can also be classified as either felonies or misdemeanors. A third scheme classifies crimes by the nature of the act. This approach produces five types of crime: occupational crime, organized crime, visible crime, victimless crime, and political crime. Each type has its own level of risk and reward, each arouses varying degrees of public disapproval, and each is committed by a certain kind of offender. New types of crime emerge as society changes. Cybercrimes committed through the use of computers over the Internet are becoming a major global problem.

Occupational Crime

occupational crime

Criminal offenses committed through opportunities created in a legal business or occupation.

Occupational crimes are committed in the context of a legal business or profession. Often viewed as shrewd business practices rather than as illegal acts, they are crimes that, if "done right," are never discovered. The U.S. Department of Commerce estimates that occupational crimes cost businesses $40 billion annually (Dumaine, 1998:193).

Crimes committed in the course of business were first described by criminologist Edwin Sutherland in 1939, when he developed the concept of "white-collar crime." He noted that such crimes are committed by respectable people taking advantage of opportunities arising from their business dealings. He forced criminologists to recognize that criminal behavior was not confined to lower-class people (so-called blue-collar crime) but reached into the upper levels of society (Sutherland, 1949; Shover, 1998:133).

The distinction between white-collar and blue-collar crime has lost much of its meaning in modern society. Since the 1970s, research on white-collar crime has shifted from the individual to the organization (Friedrichs, 1996:38). Gary Green has described four types of occupational crimes (Green, 1990:10):

❶ Occupational crimes for the benefit of employing organizations. Employers, not employees, benefit directly from these crimes. They include price fixing, theft of trade secrets, and falsification of product tests. In these cases an employee may commit the offense but does not benefit personally, except perhaps through a bonus or promotion. It is the company that benefits. These crimes are "committed in the suites rather than in the streets." Well-known examples include charges that tobacco companies knew, but denied, the health dangers of smoking, Exxon

Corporation's overbilling of customers by amounts totaling $2 billion, and the admission by Prudential Securities that it had committed crimes in a $1.4-billion sale of limited partnerships.

❷ Occupational crimes through the exercise of government authority. In these crimes the offender has the legal power to enforce laws or command others to do so. Examples include removal of drugs from the evidence room by a police officer, acceptance of a bribe by a public official, or the falsification of a document by a notary public. In one scandal, senior Pentagon officials were accused of taking bribes from defense contractors such as Raytheon and Lockheed. When the crime was discovered, more than $1 billion in contracts were canceled.

❸ Occupational crimes committed by professionals in their capacity as professionals. Doctors, lawyers, and stockbrokers may take advantage of clients by, for instance, illegally dispensing drugs, using funds placed in escrow, or using "insider" stock trading information for personal gain.

The conviction of stockbroker Ivan Boesky on insider-trading charges is an example of this type of crime. Boesky made millions of dollars because he knew about certain corporate mergers in advance. Likewise, Michael Milken, the "junk-bond king," was sentenced to ten years in prison for committing securities fraud and filing false information with the Securities and Exchange Commission.

❹ Occupational crimes committed by individuals as individuals, where opportunities are not based on governmental power or professional position. Examples of this type of crime include thefts by employees from employers, filing of false expense claims, and embezzlement. Employee crime is believed to account for about 1 percent of the gross domestic product and causes consumer prices to be 10 to 15 percent higher than they would be otherwise. Employee theft is involved in about a third of business failures. The total loss caused by employee theft therefore is greater than all business losses from shoplifting, burglary, or robbery (Friedrichs, 1996:115).

Former Louisiana Governor Edwin Edwards waves as he leaves the federal courthouse in Baton Rouge. In May 2000, Edwards was convicted of racketeering, conspiracy, and extortion charges relating to the awarding of state riverboat casino licenses.

Although they are highly profitable, most types of occupational crime do not come to public attention. Regulatory agencies, such as the Federal Trade Commission and the Securities and Exchange Commission, often do not enforce the law effectively. Many business and professional organizations "police" themselves, dropping employees or members who commit offenses.

The low level of enforcement of occupational crimes may result from the general public's view that they are not serious. Such crimes usually do not involve violence or threats to public safety, although some may involve selling unsafe food or defective products. Many people may not realize, however, the huge costs of such crimes to society.

Organized Crime

The term **organized crime** refers to a *framework* within which criminal acts are committed, rather than referring to the acts themselves. This crime syndicate has an organizational structure, rules, a division of labor, and the capacity for ruthless violence and to corrupt law enforcement, labor and business leaders, and

organized crime
A framework for the perpetration of criminal acts—usually in fields such as gambling, drugs, and prostitution—providing illegal services that are in great demand.

money laundering
Moving the proceeds of criminal activities through a maze of businesses, banks, and brokerage accounts so as to disguise their origin.

politicians (Jacobs and Panarella,1998:160). Those in organized crime provide goods and services to millions of people. They will engage in any activity that provides a minimum of risk and a maximum of profit. Thus organized crime involves a network of activities, usually cutting across state and national borders, that range from legitimate businesses to shady deals with labor unions, to providing "goods"—such as drugs, sex, and pornography—that cannot be obtained legally. In recent years organized crime has been involved in new services such as commercial arson, illegal disposal of toxic wastes, and **money laundering.** Few in organized crime are arrested and prosecuted.

Investigations of the crime "families," which are known as the Mafia and Cosa Nostra, have yielded detailed accounts of their structure, membership, and activities. The FBI and the media give the impression that the Mafia is a unified syndicate, but scholars tend to believe that the "families" are fairly autonomous local groups (Abadinsky, 1994; Albanese, 1991).

Although the public often associates organized crime with Italian Americans, other ethnic groups have been dominant at various times. Thirty years ago, one scholar noted the strangeness of America's "ladder of social mobility," in which each new immigrant group uses organized crime as one of the first few rungs of the climb (Bell, 1967:150). However, there is debate about this notion, given that not all immigrant groups have engaged in organized crime (Kenney and Finckenauer, 1995:38).

Some believe that the pirates of the seventeenth century were an early form of organized crime in America. But in the 1820s, the "Forty Thieves," an Irish gang in New York City, were the first to organize on a large scale. They were followed by Jews who dominated gambling and labor rackets at the turn of the century. The Italians came next, but they did not climb very far up the ladder until the late 1930s (Ianni, 1973:1–2). Over the last few decades, the Mafia has been greatly weakened by law enforcement efforts. Beginning in 1978 the federal government mounted extraordinary efforts to eradicate the Mafia. Using electronic surveillance, undercover agents, and mob turncoats, the FBI, the federal Organized Crime Task Forces, and the U.S. attorneys' offices, investigations and prosecutions were launched. As James Jacobs notes, "The magnitude of the government's attack on Cosa Nostra is nothing short of incredible." By 1992, twenty-three bosses were convicted and the leadership and soldiers of five New York City families (Bonanno, Colombo, Gambino, Genovese, Lucchese) were decimated (Jacobs, Panarella, and Worthington, 1994:4). In addition, an aging leadership, lack of interest by younger family members, and pressures from new immigrant groups have contributed to the fall of the Mafia. As Vicki Agnelli, daughter of the famed godfather John Gotti, said, "My father is the last of the Mohicans. They don't make men like him anymore. They never will."

Today African Americans, Hispanics, Russians, and Asians have formed organized crime groups in some cities (see Close-Up on p. 45). Drug dealing has brought Colombian and Mexican crime groups to U.S. shores, and Vietnamese-, Chinese-, and Japanese-led groups have been formed in California. These new groups do not fit the Mafia pattern, and law enforcement agencies have had to find new ways to deal with them (Kleinknecht, 1996).

Just as multinational corporations have emerged during the past twenty years, organized crime has also developed global networks. Increasingly, transnational criminal groups "live and operate in a borderless world" (Zagaris,

CLOSE  up

The **Russian Mafiya** of **Brighton Beach**

Brighton Beach, an immigrant neighborhood in New York City, is famous in Russia and Eastern Europe as the hub of the Russian mafiya. Like other Russian crime organizations in Denver, Los Angeles, and Toronto, the mafiya is involved in heroin dealing, prostitution, money laundering, and toxic waste disposal.

The 1995 indictment of twenty-five Russian immigrants on tax fraud charges is evidence of the growing power of these groups in the New York metropolitan area. The charges described a scheme to cheat the government out of more than $140 million in taxes on more than $500 million in fuel sales.

The Russians had developed a clever scheme based on the fact that diesel fuel and one type of home heating oil are almost the same, but no taxes are imposed on home heating oil. Posing as a legitimate company, the group created Kings Motor Oils, which bought home heating oil. Through a series of dummy companies, this oil was transferred to Petro Plus as diesel fuel at the wholesale price plus 36 cents a gallon in taxes. When the Internal Revenue Service tried to collect the taxes, the dummy company disappeared.

A further aspect of this scam was that much of the diesel fuel contained hazardous wastes. For a fee, the mafiya would collect these wastes from businesses. An illegal "sludge runner" would blend the polluted oil with pure heating oil to create a "cocktailed fuel" that was sold as diesel. Engines burning "cocktailed" fuel cause a great deal of pollution and are soon destroyed. In addition, high levels of airborne particles have been found in the Greenpoint section of Brooklyn, and the Environmental Protection Agency believes that the polluted fuel is being used to heat many apartment buildings in this area.

SOURCE: Drawn from Clifford J. Levy, "Russian Emigres Are among Twenty-five Named in Tax Fraud in Newark," *New York Times*, August 8, 1995, p. A1; Bruce Frankel, "Extortion Now the Least of Its Illegal Activities," *USA Today*, September 14, 1995, p. A1; and Julienne Salzano, "The Sludge Runners," *Heavy Duty Trucking* (August 1993), 106–108.

1998:1402). In a recent book Senator John Kerry describes a "global criminal axis" involving the drug trade, money laundering, and terrorism (Kerry, 1997). In 1999 a federal grand jury indicted three Russian immigrants and three of their companies on money laundering charges. The indictment said that those charged had moved $7 billion through the Bank of New York over three and a half years. Investigators say the Russian funds may have involved corporate embezzlement, political graft, and organized crime. The FBI and their Russian counterparts have been investigating the source of the funds and the conduits through which they were moved (*New York Times*, October 6, 1999:A1).

Visible Crime

Visible crime, often called "street crime" or "ordinary crime," ranges from shoplifting to homicide. For offenders, these crimes are the least profitable and, because they are visible, the least protected. These are the acts that the public regards as criminal. Most law enforcement resources are used to deal with them. Visible crimes can be divided into three categories: violent crimes, property crimes, and public order crimes.

visible crime

Offenses against persons and property committed primarily by members of the lower class. Often referred to as "street crimes" or "ordinary crimes," these offenses are most upsetting to the public.

Violent Crimes

Acts against persons in which death or physical injury results are violent crimes. These include criminal homicide, assault, rape, and robbery. They are treated by the criminal justice system as the most serious offenses and are punished accordingly. Although the public is most fearful of violence by strangers, most of these offenses are committed by persons who know their victim.

Property Crimes

These are acts that threaten property held by private persons or by the state. Numerous types of crimes are in this category including theft, larceny, shoplifting, embezzlement, and burglary. Some property offenders are amateurs who occasionally commit these crimes because of situational factors such as financial need or peer pressure. In contrast professional criminals make a significant portion of their livelihood by committing property offenses.

Public Order Crimes

Acts that threaten the general well-being of society and challenge accepted moral principles are defined as public order crimes. They include public drunkenness, aggressive panhandling, vandalism, and disorderly conduct. Although the police tend to treat these behaviors as minor offenses, evidence increasingly shows that this type of disorderly behavior instills fear in citizens, leads to more serious crimes, and hastens urban decay (Kelling and Coles, 1996).

Those who commit visible crimes tend to be young, low-income, minority-group males. Some argue that this stems from the class bias of a society that has singled out visible crimes for priority enforcement. They note that occupational crimes are not focused upon to the same extent as street crimes.

Crimes without Victims

crimes without victims

Offenses involving a willing and private exchange of illegal goods or services that are in strong demand. Participants do not feel they are being harmed, but these crimes are prosecuted on the ground that society as a whole is being injured.

Crimes without victims involve a willing and private exchange of goods or services that are in strong demand but are illegal—in other words, offenses against morality. Examples include prostitution, gambling, and drug sales and use. These are called "victimless" crimes because those involved do not feel that they are being harmed. Prosecution for these offenses is justified on the grounds that society as a whole is harmed because the moral fabric of the community is threatened. However, using the law to enforce moral standards is costly. The system is swamped by these cases, which often require the use of police informers and thus open the door for payoffs and other kinds of corruption.

The "war on drugs" is the most obvious example of policies against one type of victimless crime. Possession and sale of drugs—marijuana, heroin, cocaine, opium, amphetamines—have been illegal in the United States for more than a hundred years. But especially during the past forty years, extensive government resources have been used to enforce these laws and punish offenders.

In "One Man's Journey Inside the Criminal Justice System" (see http://cj.wadsworth.com/cole/), Chuck Terry describes his love of heroin and the consequences as he traveled inside the criminal justice system.

Political Crime

Political crime refers to criminal acts either by the government or against the government that are carried out for ideological purposes (Hagan, 1997:2). Political criminals believe they are following a morality that is above the law. Examples include James Kopp, wanted for the murder of Dr. Barnett Slepian near Buffalo, New York, and other doctors who performed abortions, and Eric Rudolph, wanted for the bombing of abortion clinics in Atlanta and Birmingham and the pipe bomb explosion at the 1996 Atlanta Olympics.

In some authoritarian states, merely making statements that are critical of the government is a crime that may lead to prosecution and imprisonment. In Western democracies today there are few political crimes other than treason, which is rare. Many illegal acts, such as the World Trade Center and Oklahoma City bombings, can be traced to political motives. But they have been prosecuted as visible crimes under laws against bombing, arson, and murder.

The Iran-contra scandal is an example of political crime by government. During the Reagan presidency, arms were sold by the government to Iran in exchange for hostages. The more than $30 million obtained from the arms sale was then diverted to assist the contras, rebels opposing the Marxist Sandinista regime in Nicaragua. These actions violated U.S. policies of not selling arms to Iran and not trading arms for hostages. In addition, government officials violated the Boland Amendment passed by Congress to forbid aid to the contras. Discovery of the conspiracy led to indictments and convictions of officials including Marine Lt. Col. Oliver L. North of the White House National Security Council staff, National Security Adviser John Poindexter, retired Air Force Maj. Gen. Richard Secord, and Secretary of Defense Caspar W. Weinberger (Hagan, 1997:75).

Political crimes against government include activities such as treason, sedition (rebellion), and espionage. Since the nation's founding, many laws have been passed in response to perceived threats to the established order. The Sedition Act of 1789 made it a crime to utter or publish statements against the government. The Smith Act of 1940 made it a crime to call for the overthrow of the government by force or violence. During the Vietnam War, the federal government used charges of criminal conspiracy to deter those who opposed its military policies.

Cybercrime

As new technologies emerge, so, too, do people who take advantage of these advances for their own gain. One has only to think of the impact of the invention of the automobile to realize the extent to which the computer age will lead to new kinds of criminality. Today, the justice system is beginning to deal with the ramifications of cybercrimes on the criminal law. To illustrate the problems that may arise, FBI Special Agent Richard Bernes of San Jose points out, "Everything you touch sets a new precedent. Suppose someone accesses your computer and downloads files. What should she be charged with? Burglary or trespassing? Wire fraud or copyright violation?" (Gill, 1997:116).

Cybercrimes involve the use of the computer and the Internet to commit acts against persons, property, public order, or morality. Thus, cybercriminals have learned "new ways to do old tricks." Some use computers to steal information, resources, or funds.

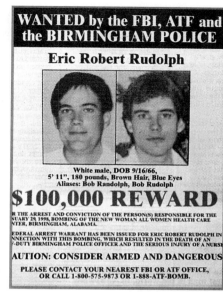

Eric Rudolph, political activist wanted in connection the bombing of abortion clinics and the Atlanta Olympics, is believed to be hiding in the mountains of North Carolina.

political crime
An act that constitutes a threat against the state (such as treason, sedition, or espionage).

cybercrime
An offense, committed through the use of one or more computers.

CLOSE up

You Could Get Raped

Randi Barber, a 28-year-old North Hollywood, California, woman started getting dirty solicitations on her answering machine. When a stranger knocked on her apartment door, she hid. When he later telephoned, she learned he was responding to her sexy ad on the Internet.

"What ad? What did it say?" Barber asked.

"Let me put it to you this way," the caller said. "You could get raped."

Barber, who does not own a computer, later discovered that a stalker had assumed her identity in cyberspace and had posted ads on the Internet seeking men to fulfill her kinky sexual desires. Under such log-ons as "playfulkitty4U," the sadomasochistic content of the messages were most disturbing. The stalker included directions to Barber's home, details of her social plans, and advice as to how to short-circuit her alarm system.

Months later, the Los Angeles County Sheriff's Department arrested an acquaintance of Barber's, Gary Dellapenta, a 50-year-old security guard. He was charged under a California law that criminalizes stalking and harassment on the Internet.

Others use the Internet to disseminate child pornography, to advertise sexual services, or to stalk the unsuspecting (see the Close-Up above). The more sophisticated "hackers" create and distribute viruses designed to destroy computer programs.

In April 1999, the country was confronted by the Melissa virus created by a New Jersey hacker. When people opened an innocent e-mail message labeled "Important," they found a message that read, "Here is that document you asked for . . . don't show it to anyone." The document was sent as an attachment that, when opened, revealed a list of passwords for pornography sites on the World Wide Web. As a reader pondered the list, Melissa automatically sent the message to the first fifty names in the user's address book.

Three California men in December 1999 were charged by the federal government with stock fraud, saying they used the Internet to manipulate the price of NEI Webworld stock, a tiny company going through bankruptcy liquidation. The men bought large blocks of shares in the company. They then sent a series of false messages over the Internet to three investment chat sites saying that the company would undergo a "reverse merger" with a private San Jose company, LGC Wireless, Inc. This sent the stock price skyrocketing from 13 cents to more than $15 in less than two trading days. The three unloaded the stock and reaped a profit of $364,000 (*Los Angeles Times*, December 16, 1999:C–1).

Officers Tom Harrington and Don Conden patrol cyberspace, looking for child predators. Florida's Computer Child Exploitation statute makes it a crime to download child pornography or solicit sex with minors online. When arresting offenders, these officers also seize the computer, using the hard drive as evidence.

The global nature of the Internet presents new challenges to the criminal justice system. For example, through electronic financial networks that link much of the world, money launderers in Moscow can simply tap on their computer keyboard and send their digital money to New York. A few more keystrokes and the money can be sent to a private account in Antigua where it will be shielded from the prying eyes of government agencies.

Congress and the states have been slow to develop legislation to deal with cybercrime. Congress passed the Counterfeit Active Device and Computer Fraud and Abuse Act in 1984, which made it a felony to illegally enter a computer for personal gain or to affect the national interest. This law has been updated in recent years. In 1994 it was amended to focus on such abuses as obtaining financial records or using a computer to defraud, obtain something of value, destroy data, or plant viruses.

Which of these main types of crime is of greatest concern to you? If you are like most people, it is visible crime. Thus, as a nation, the United States devotes most of its criminal justice resources to dealing with such crimes. To develop policies to address these crimes, more needs to be known about the amount of crime and types of crimes that occur. As seen in the Close-Up on p. 50, new types of crime are being added to the criminal law.

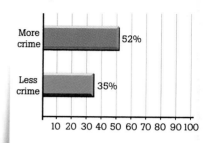

What Americans Think

Question "Is there more crime in the U.S. than there was a year ago, or less?"

More crime 52%

Less crime 35%

10 20 30 40 50 60 70 80 90 100

SOURCE: *The Gallup Poll* (July 20, 1999), at www.Gallup.com.

CHECK POINT

③ What are the five main types of crime?

④ Why is the term "occupational crime" more useful today than "white-collar crime"?

⑤ What is the function of organized crime?

⑥ Who commits "visible" or "street" crimes?

⑦ What is meant by the term "crimes without victims"?

⑧ What are political crimes?

The Crime Problem Today

Public opinion polls show that Americans rank crime among the nation's greatest problems. Many people believe that the crime rate is rising, even though it has declined (see What Americans Think). Is crime still at record levels? Is the United States the most crime-ridden nation of the world's industrial democracies? How is the amount of crime measured? What are the current and future trends? By trying to answer these questions, a better understanding is gained of the crime problem itself and the public's beliefs about it.

The Worst of Times?

There has always been too much crime, and ever since the nation's founding people have felt threatened by crime. Outbreaks of violence occurred after the Civil War, after World War I, during Prohibition, and during the Great Depression (Friedman, 1993). But extended periods, such as the 1950s, saw comparatively little crime. Thus, ours is neither the best nor the worst of times.

CLOSE up

Hate Crimes: A New Category of Personal Violence

Black churches are set afire in the Southeast; the home of the mayor of West Hartford, Connecticut, is defaced by swastikas and anti-Semitic graffiti; gay Wyoming student Matthew Shepard is murdered; a black woman in Maryland is beaten and doused with lighter fluid in a race-based attack. These are just a few of the more than seventy-five hundred hate crimes reported to the police each year.

Hate crimes have been added to the penal codes of forty-six states and the District of Columbia. They are violent acts aimed at individuals or groups of a particular race, ethnicity, religion, sexual orientation, or gender. The laws also make it a crime to vandalize religious buildings and cemeteries or to intimidate another person out of bias. Although the Ku Klux Klan, the World Church of the Creator, and Nazi-style "skinhead" groups are the most visible perpetrators, most hate crimes are committed by individuals acting alone.

Hate crime laws have been challenged on the ground that they violate the right of free speech. It is argued that racial and religious slurs must be allowed on this basis. Supporters of hate crime laws say that limits must be placed on freedom of speech and that some words are so hateful that they are outside the free speech protection of the First Amendment.

The U.S. Supreme Court has considered the constitutionality of such laws in two cases. In *R.A.V. v. City of St. Paul* (1992), the Court ruled unconstitutional a law that singled out only certain "race baiting" words. However, in *Wisconsin v. Mitchell* (1993), it upheld a law providing for a more severe sentence in cases in which the offender "intentionally selects the person against whom the crime [is committed] because of the race, religion, color, disability, sexual orientation, national origin or ancestry of that person." The defendant had incited a group of young black men who had just seen the film "Mississippi Burning" to assault a young white man by asking, "Do you all feel hyped up to move on some

Members of the white supremacist Aryan Nation and the Klu Klux Klan march in Coeur D'Alene, Idaho. What challenges do such group pose to the ideals of democracy?

white people?" and by calling out, "There goes a white boy; go get him." The Court said that the penalty was appropriate because the conduct was "thought to inflict greater individual and societal harm." It rejected the argument that the law would have a "chilling effect" on free speech.

In a society that is becoming more diverse, hate crimes hurt not only their victims but also the social fabric itself. Democracy depends upon people sharing common ideals and working together. When groups are pitted against one another, the entire community suffers. But is the criminal law the way to attack this problem?

SOURCE: Drawn from J. Jacobs, "Should Hate Be a Crime?" *The Public Interest* (Fall 1993):1–14.

FIGURE 2.1 A century of murder

The murder rate per 100,000 people in the United States has risen, fallen, and—since 1960—risen again. Data from the last few years show a decline from the peak in 1980. What causes these trends?

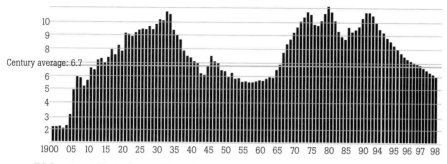

SOURCE: U.S. Department of Justice, Bureau of Justice Statistics, *Crime Data Brief* (January 1999); Federal Bureau of Investigation, *Crime in the United States—1998* (Washington, D.C.: Government Printing Office, 1999); and *New York Times*, January 28, 1996, p. E5.

Although crime is an old problem, the amount and types of crime have not always been the same. During the 1880s and 1930s pitched battles took place between strikers and company police. Race riots occurred in Atlanta in 1907 and in Chicago, Washington, D.C., and East St. Louis, Illinois, in 1919. Organized crime was rampant during the 1930s. The murder rate, which reached a high in 1933 and a low during the 1950s, rose to a new high in 1980 and has been falling since 1993 (see Figure 2.1).

The Most Crime-Ridden Nation?

How does the amount of crime in the United States compare with the amount in other countries? It is often said that the United States has more crime than other modern industrial nations. But as James Lynch argues, this belief is too simple to be useful (Lynch, 1995:11). He points out that comparing crime rates in different nations is difficult. First, one must choose nations that are similar to the United States—nations with democratic governments, similar levels of economic development, and the same kinds of legal systems (MacCoun, Saiger, Kahan, and Reuter, 1993). Second, one must get data from reliable sources. The two main sources of cross-national crime data are Interpol and the International Crime Survey.

Lynch compared crime rates in the United States and in Australia, Canada, England and Wales, West Germany, France, the Netherlands, Sweden, and Switzerland. Both police and victim data showed that the homicide rate in the United States was more than twice that in Canada, the next highest country, and many times that in the other countries. The same was generally true for robbery (see Table 2.2). However, the victim surveys showed that for other violent crimes, such as assault and robbery, rates of victimization were lower for Americans than for Canadians, Australians, and Spaniards (Donziger, 1996:10).

When it comes to property crimes, the data are surprising. The Interpol data for burglary and motor vehicle theft show a 40 percent higher rate in Australia than in the United States, a 12 percent higher rate in Canada, and a 30 percent higher rate in England and Wales. Even the Netherlands and Sweden, thought to have low crime rates, have burglary rates that are 35 and 85 percent higher, respectively, than those in the United States. The victim surveys show that rates of property crime are fairly similar in the United States and other common law

TABLE **2.2**   **Rates of crime reported by the police per 100,000 population, by nation and offense**

These data collected by Interpol show that the United States leads the countries surveyed in homicide and robbery, but not in burglary and motor vehicle theft.

NATION	HOMICIDE	ROBBERY	BURGLARY	AUTO THEFT
United States	7.9	205.4	1,263.7	437.1
Australia	3.4[a]	83.6	1,754.3	584.7
Canada	2.7	92.8	1,420.6	304.9
England and Wales[c]	1.1	44.6	1,639.7	656.6
France	2.3	105.6	809.8	483.4
Netherlands	1.2	52.9	2,328.7	155.9
Sweden	1.4	44.1	1,708.8	460.0
Switzerland	1.1	24.2	276.8	NA[b]
West Germany	1.5	45.8	1,554.1	118.0

[a] This figure includes attempted homicide as well as completed homicide.

[b] NA - not applicable. These data were not reported because they include bicycle theft as well as motor vehicle theft.

[c] These data are for 1983

SOURCE: U.S. Department of Justice, Bureau of Justice Statistics, *International Crime Rates* (Washington, D.C.: Government Printing Office, 1988), 3.

countries (Van Dijk and Mayhew, 1992:24). However, the European countries, which have higher rates of property crime than the United States according to police statistics, have substantially lower rates of property crime in victim surveys (Lynch, 1995:17).

A recent study of crime in England found that rates for serious crimes were higher than in the United States. The major exception was for homicide, which is six times higher in the United States than in England. Firearms also are much more involved in violent crimes in the United States, where they were used in 68 percent of murders and 41 percent of robberies compared with 7 and 5 percent, respectively, in England (BJS, 1998e).

In sum, the risk of lethal violence is much higher in the United States than in other industrial democracies. But the risk of minor violence is not greater than in other common law countries. In contrast, the United States has lower rates of serious property crime and even lower rates than many countries that are thought to be safer (Lynch, 1995:17).

Of interest is evidence that, like in the United States, crime rates in Western countries may have begun to decline (Tonry, 1998b:22–23). Crime in Canada fell 4.1 percent in 1998, the seventh consecutive drop in as many years—like the United States (*Halifax Chronicle Herald,* July 22, 1999:1). English and Dutch victimization data likewise show significant declines as do data from many of the eleven industrial countries in the International Crime Victimization Survey (Mayhew and van Dijk, 1997).

Insight into the nature and extent of crime in the United States can be gained by looking at countries, such as Iceland, where there is little crime. Some might say that because Iceland is small, homogeneous, and somewhat isolated, the two countries cannot be compared. But as we can see in the Comparative Perspective (p. 54), other factors help explain differences in the amount and types of crime in different countries.

Finding the amount of crime is not as easy as it may seem. Let us look more closely at the sources of crime data and ask what they say about crime trends.

Keeping Track of Crime

One of the frustrations in studying criminal justice is the lack of accurate means of knowing the amount of crime. Surveys reveal that much more crime occurs than is reported to the police. This is referred to as the **dark figure of crime.**

Most homicides and auto thefts are reported to the police. In the case of a homicide a body must be accounted for, and insurance companies require a police report before they will pay for a stolen car. But about 69 percent of rape or sexual assault victims do not report the attack; almost half of robbery victims and 61 percent of victims of simple assault do not do so. Figure 2.2 shows the percentage of victimizations not reported to the police.

Crimes go unreported for many reasons. Some victims of rape and assault do not wish to be embarrassed by public disclosure and police questioning. But the most common reason for not reporting a violent crime is that it was a personal, private matter. In the case of larceny, robbery, or burglary, the value of the property lost may not be worth the effort of calling the police. Many people do not report crimes because they do not want to become involved, fill out papers at the station house, perhaps go to court, or appear at a police lineup. As these examples suggest, many people feel the costs of reporting crimes outweigh the benefits.

Until 1972, the only crimes counted by government were those that were known to the police and that made their way into the Federal Bureau of Investigation's *Uniform Crime Reports* (UCR). Since then the Department of Justice has sponsored the National Crime Victimization Survey (NCVS), which queries the public to find out how much victimization has occurred. One might hope that the data from these two sources would provide a clear picture of the amount of crime, crime trends, and the characteristics of offenders. However, the picture is blurred, perhaps even distorted, because of differences in the way crime is measured by the UCR and the NCVS.

dark figure of crime
A metaphor that emphasizes the dangerous dimension of crime that is never reported to the police.

FIGURE 2.2 Percentage of victimizations *not* reported to the police

Why do some people not report crimes to the police? What can be done to encourage reporting?

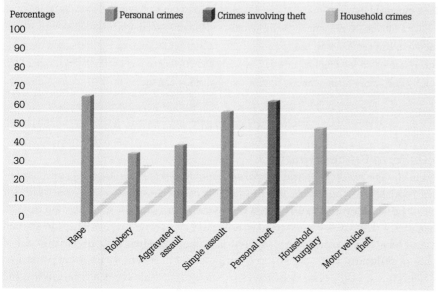

SOURCE: U.S. Department of Justice, Bureau of Justice Statistics, *Bulletin* (July 1999), 10.

Iceland:
A Country with
Little Crime

Iceland is a country where there is little crime. Why is it that Iceland should differ so much from its neighbors and other developed countries? Is it the size of the population? The homogeneity of the people? The physical isolation from the major centers of Europe? What is it like to live in a country where only two homicides are committed per year, and where the first bank robbery with a firearm occurred in 1984?

Iceland, with a population of 270,000, is an island republic the size of Virginia. It has strong cultural ties to Denmark, which ruled it from 1380 until 1944, and to the other countries of Scandinavia. The Icelandic population is ethnically homogeneous and policies have been instituted to restrict immigration. Relatively small differences are found along class lines, literacy is very high, and about 95 percent of the population belongs to the Evangelical Lutheran Church. The people enjoy a high standard of living, an extensive health and welfare system, and a low unemployment rate.

Even though 90 percent of the Icelandic people live in urban areas, the society is one where extended families, strong community ties, and a homogeneous culture seem to act as effective agents of social control. Iceland is also relatively equalitarian; slum areas are nonexistent, education and health care are provided to all—thus further reducing social disparities.

After centuries of isolation, Iceland came into extensive contact with European and North American countries only after the end of World War II. The result has been a cultural lag in the shift to industrialization and urbanization. Iceland has retained many aspects of an agrarian society.

When compared with the United States, Icelandic crime rates are extremely low. For example, the assault rate per 100,000 people is 14 in Iceland and 388 in the United States; the rate for homicide is .73 in Iceland and 7 in the United States; the rate for rape is 16.35 in Iceland and 36 in the United States. The homogeneous population, geographic isolation from other countries, and prohibition of handgun ownership all may contribute to the low level of violence in Iceland.

The Icelandic public has become most concerned by the increase in drug use during the past two decades, but it is minuscule compared with other Western countries. Marijuana use increased during the 1970s but has declined since then. Still, a study conducted in 1997 found a greater

The *Uniform Crime Reports*

Uniform Crime Reports (UCR)
An annually published statistical summary of crimes reported to the police, based on voluntary reports to the FBI by local, state, and federal law enforcement agencies.

Issued each year by the FBI, the *Uniform Crime Reports* is a statistical summary of crimes reported to the police. At the urging of the International Association of Chiefs of Police, Congress authorized this system for compiling crime data in 1930 (Rosen, 1995). The UCR comes from a voluntary national network of some sixteen thousand local, state, and federal law enforcement agencies, policing 98 percent of the U.S. population. With the sharp drop in crime in recent years, new pressures have been placed on police executives to show that their cities are following the national trend. Some agencies have allegedly falsified their crime statistics because percentage of Icelanders had used marijuana at least once than in the other Nordic nations with the exception of Denmark. However, only 1.6 percent admitted using marijuana during the last six months. This is similar to the other Nordic countries.

Although much concern has been raised about the use of "hard" drugs, the situation seems minor when compared with the United States. In 1984 about 4 percent of Icelanders aged 16 to 36 said they had consumed amphetamines. It was not until 1983 that police found cocaine for the first time; they first seized a significant amount (one kilo) in 1987. Yet scholars believe that drug use has increased considerably during the past five years.

Undoubtedly the size of Iceland's population and its isolation from the major drug supply routes account for the low level of drug abuse. However, special "drug police" were established in the 1970s. Today, the Reykjavik police allocate a greater portion of their budget to drug control than do the police in Copenhagen and Oslo. But containing the "drug problem" is enhanced by the ease with which the country may be "sealed," given that import routes are few and that drug users find hiding their habit difficult in such a tightly knit community.

There seem to be no organized drug rings in Iceland.

Whereas most Western countries are preoccupied with the war on drugs, this social problem is overshadowed in Iceland by concern over the abuse of alcohol. Alcohol abuse has a high correlation with the crime rate, particularly in the form of drunken driving. Total consumption of alcohol has increased during recent decades, and public drunkenness is the most common violation of the criminal law.

With the number of automobiles per capita the highest in the world, Iceland's drunk driving rules are strictly enforced with a resulting high arrest rate (1,400 per 100,000 people versus 386 per 100,000 in the United States). Most arrests occur as a result of intensive routine highway checks. When blood tests reveal a level of .5 to 1.2 per milliliter alcohol, drivers lose their licenses for one month. When tests show a level of more than 1.2 per milliliter, drivers lose their licenses for a year. A third offense means a prison sentence. With low levels of serious crime and a policy of treating alcohol offenses severely, 20 percent of prisoners in Iceland have been committed for drunk driving.

The number of crimes reported to the Icelandic police has reflected the rapid transformation of the society during the past thirty years. As in other countries, the crime rate increased after World War II but has leveled off during the past decade. The increases in crime compared with a generation ago can be accounted for by several factors. For example, the growth in economic crime seems to be a consequence of more complex business activities. Concern over the abuse of alcohol has resulted in proactive law enforcement policies that have contributed to the amount of crime as measured by arrests. But these increases must be viewed in the context of the very low levels of criminality in Iceland as compared with other developed countries. As with other Scandinavian countries, as well as such low-crime countries as Switzerland, there appear to be cultural, geographic, economic, and public policy factors that explain the relative absence of crime in Iceland.

SOURCE: Drawn from Omar H. Kristmundsson, "Crime and the Crime Control System of Iceland" (unpublished paper, University of Connecticut, 1999) and Helgi Gunnlaugsson, "Icelandic Sociology and the Social Production of Criminological Knowledge," *From a Doll's House to the Welfare State: Reflections on Nordic Sociology*, ed. Margareta Bertilsson and Goran Therborn (Montreal, Canada: International Sociological Association, 1998), 83–88.

promotions, pay raises, and department budgets are increasingly dependent on positive data (Butterfield, 1998b:A1).

The UCR uses standard definitions to ensure uniform data on the twenty-nine types of crimes listed in Table 2.3. For eight major crimes—Part I or "index offenses"—the data show factors such as age, race, and number of reported crimes solved. For the other twenty-one crimes, Part II or "other offenses," the data are less complete.

The UCR, the main publication of which is an annual volume, *Crime in the United States*, presents crime data in three ways: (1) as *aggregates* (a total of 446,625

TABLE 2.3 — *Uniform Crime Reports* offenses

The *Uniform Crime Reports* (UCR) present data on eight index offenses and twenty-one other crimes for which less information is available. A limitation of the UCR is that it tabulates only crimes that are reported to the police.

PART I (INDEX OFFENSES)	PART II (OTHER OFFENSES)
1. Criminal homicide	9. Simple assaults
2. Forcible rape	10. Forgery and counterfeiting
3. Robbery	11. Fraud
4. Aggravated assault	12. Embezzlement
5. Burglary	13. Buying, receiving, or possessing stolen property
6. Larceny-theft	14. Vandalism
7. Auto theft	15. Weapons (carrying, possession, etc.)
8. Arson	16. Prostitution and commercialized vice
	17. Sex offenses
	18. Violation of narcotic drug laws
	19. Gambling
	20. Offenses against the family and children
	21. Driving under the influence
	22. Violation of liquor laws
	23. Drunkenness
	24. Disorderly conduct
	25. Vagrancy
	26. All other offenses (excluding traffic)
	27. Suspicion
	28. Curfew and loitering (juvenile)
	29. Runaway (juvenile)

SOURCE: U.S. Department of Justice, Federal Bureau of Investigation, *Crime in the United States—1998* (Washington, D.C.: Government Printing Office, 1999).

robberies were reported to the police in 1998), (2) as *percentage changes* over different periods (a 10.0 percent decrease in robberies occurred from 1997 to 1998), and (3) as a *rate per 100,000 people* (the robbery rate in 1998 was 165.0) (FBI, 1999:4).

The UCR provides a useful, but incomplete, picture of crime levels. Because it covers only reported crimes, it does not include data on crimes for which people failed to call the police. Also, the UCR does not measure occupational crimes and other offenses that are not included in the twenty-nine types covered. And because reporting is voluntary, police departments may not take the time to make complete and careful reports.

In response to criticisms of the UCR, the FBI has made some changes in the program, which are now being implemented nationwide. Some offenses have been redefined, and police agencies are being asked to report more details about crime events. Using the **National Incident-Based Reporting System** (NIBRS), police agencies are to report all crimes committed during an incident, not just the most serious one, as well as data on offenders, victims, and the places where they interact. While the UCR now counts incidents and arrests for the eight index offenses and counts arrests for other crimes, NIBRS provides detailed incident data on forty-six offenses in twenty-two crime categories. The NIBRS, unlike the UCR, distinguishes between attempted and completed crimes.

The National Crime Victimization Surveys

A second source of crime data is the **National Crime Victimization Survey** (NCVS). Since 1972, the Census Bureau has done surveys to find out about the extent and nature of crime victimization. Thus, data have been gathered on unreported as well as reported crimes. Interviews are conducted with a national probability sample of about 100,000 people in fifty thousand households. The same people are interviewed twice a year for three years and asked if they have been victimized in the last six months.

Each person is asked a set of "screening" questions (for example, did anyone beat you up, attack you, or hit you with something such as a rock or a bottle?) to determine whether he or she has been victimized. The person is then asked questions designed to elicit specific facts about the event, the offender, and any financial losses or physical disabilities caused by the crime.

Besides the household interviews, surveys are carried out in the nation's twenty-six largest cities; separate studies are done to find out about victimization of businesses. As a result, estimates can be made of how many crimes have occurred, more can be learned about the offenders, and demographic patterns can be noted. The results show that for the crimes measured (rape, robbery, assault, burglary, theft) there are thirty-five million victimizations each year (down from forty-three million in 1973) (BJS, 1999e). This level is much higher than that indicated by the number of crimes reported to the police.

Although the NCVS provides a more complete picture of the nature and extent of crime, it, too, has flaws. Because the survey is done by government employees, the people interviewed are unlikely to report crimes in which they or members of their family took part. They also may not want to admit that a family member engages in crime, or they may be too embarrassed to admit that they have allowed themselves to be victimized more than once.

The NCVS is also imperfect because it depends on the victim's perception of an event. The theft of a child's lunch money by a bully may be reported as a crime by one person but not mentioned by another. People may say that their property was stolen when they lost it. Moreover, people's memories of dates may fade, and they may misreport the year in which a crime occurred even though they remember the event itself clearly. In 1993 the Bureau of Justice Statistics made some changes in the NCVS to improve its accuracy and detail.

Next time you hear or read about crime rates, take into account the source of the data and its possible limitations. Table 2.4 compares the *Uniform Crime Reports* and the National Crime Victimization Surveys.

National Incident-Based Reporting System (NIBRS)
A reporting system in which the police describe each offense in a crime incident, together with data describing the offender, victim, and property.

National Crime Victimization Survey (NCVS)
Interviews of samples of the U.S. population conducted by the Bureau of Justice Statistics to determine the number and types of criminal victimizations and thus the extent of unreported as well as reported crime.

TABLE 2.4   The UCR and the NCVS

Compare the data sources. Remember that the *Uniform Crime Reports* (UCR) tabulate only crimes reported to the police, while the National Crime Victimization Survey (NCVS) is based on interviews with victims.

	UNIFORM CRIME REPORTS	NATIONAL CRIME VICTIMIZATION SURVEY
Offenses measured	Homicide	
	Rape	Rape
	Robbery (personal and commercial)	Robbery (personal)
	Assault (aggravated)	Assault (aggravated and simple)
	Burglary (commercial and household)	Household burglary
	Larceny (commercial and household)	Larceny (personal and household)
	Motor vehicle theft	Motor vehicle theft
	Arson	
Scope	Crimes reported to the police in most jurisdictions; considerable flexibility in developing small-area data	Crimes both reported and not reported to police; all data are for the nation as a whole; some data are available for a few large geographic areas
Collection method	Police department reports to Federal Bureau of Investigation	Survey interviews: periodically measures the total number of crimes committed by asking a national sample of 49,000 households representing 101,000 people over the age of 12 about their experiences as victims of crime during a specific period
Kinds of information	In addition to offense counts, provides information on crime clearances, persons arrested, persons charged, law enforcement officers killed and assaulted, and characteristics of homicide victims	Provides details about victims (such as age, race, sex, education, income, and whether the victim and offender were related) and about crimes (such as time and place of occurrence, whether or not reported to police, use of weapons, occurrence of injury, and economic consequences)
Sponsor	Department of Justice's Federal Bureau of Investigation	Department of Justice's Bureau of Justice Statistics

Trends in Crime

Experts agree that, contrary to public opinion and the claims of politicians, crime rates have not been steadily rising. In fact, the rates for many crimes have dropped since the early 1980s.

The National Crime Victimization Surveys show that the victimization rate peaked in 1981 and has declined since then. The greatest declines are in property crimes, but crimes of violence have also dropped, especially since 1993. The *Uniform Crime Reports* show similar results. They reveal a rapid rise in crime rates beginning in 1964 and continuing until 1980, when the rates began to level off or decline. The overall crime rate has declined each year since 1991.

The most surprising trend has been the 27 percent decline in violent crime since 1993. That year tallied more than four million violent victimizations. In 1998 the figure had dropped to 2.8 million. During the 1993–1998 period, significant decreases were evident in every major type of violent and property crime, and every demographic group experienced substantial drops in violent victimization. For example, in 1998 rates for males and females were 32 percent lower than in 1993, and victimizations against African Americans decreased 42 percent (BJS, 1999e).

Figure 2.3 displays four measures of violent crime, adjusted for changes made in the NCVS in 1992. Total violent crime and victimizations reported to the police are based on the victimization survey, while crimes recorded by the police and arrests for violent crime are from the UCR. Remember that the differences in the trends indicated by the NCVS and the UCR are explained in part by the different data sources and different populations on which their tabulations are based. The UCR is based on crimes reported to the police, while the NCVS records crimes experienced by victims.

What explains the drop in both violent and property crime back to 1973 levels? Among the reasons given by analysts are the aging of the baby boom population, the increased use of security systems, the aggressive police efforts to keep handguns off the streets, and the dramatic decline in the use of crack cocaine. Other factors often cited are the booming economy of the 1990s and the quadrupling of the number of people incarcerated since 1970. Let us look at two of these factors—age and crack cocaine—as a means of assessing future crime levels.

FIGURE 2.3 Four measures of serious violent crimes

Data from both the *Uniform Crime Reports* and the National Crime Victimization Survey (NCVS) show that violent crime has declined in recent years. What might account for the decline?

NOTE: The violent crimes included are rape, robbery, aggravated assault, and homicide. The vertical white line at 1992 indicates that because of changes made to the victimization survey, data prior to 1992 are adjusted to make them comparable to data collected under the redesigned methodology.

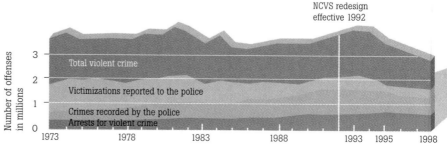

SOURCE: U.S. Department of Justice, Bureau of Justice Statistics (September 1999), at www.ojp.usdoj.gov/bjs/.

Age

Changes in the age makeup of the population are a key factor in the analysis of crime trends. It has long been known that males aged 16 to 24 are the most crime-prone group. The rise in crime in the 1970s has been blamed on the post-World War II baby boom. By the 1970s the "boomers" had entered the high-risk crime group of 16- to 24-year-olds. They made up a much larger portion of the U.S. population than had been true in the past. Between 40 and 50 percent of the total arrests during that decade could have been expected as a result of the growth in the total population and in the size of the crime-prone age group. Likewise, the decline in most crime rates that began during the 1980s has been attributed to the maturing of the post-World War II generation.

During the 1990s the 16- to 24-year age cohort was smaller than it had been at any time since the early 1960s, and many people believe that this contributed to the decline in crime. One controversial study argues that contributing to the small age cohort and the decline in crime in the 1990s was the Supreme Court's 1973 decision legalizing abortions (Samuelson, 1999:76).The study, by Steven D. Levitt and John J. Donohue III, suggests that those who would have been at greatest risk for criminal activity during their crime-prone years —"the unwanted offspring of teenage, poor and minority women—were aborted at disproportionately high rates." (Brandon, 1999:A5). Abortions reduced the size of the 1973–1989 age cohort by about 40 percent.

In 1994 a small, but influential, group of criminologists predicted that by the year 2000 a great increase would be evident in the number of males in the 14- to 24-year-old cohort. They argued that the decline in crime experienced in the 1990s was merely the "lull before the storm" (Steinberg, 1999:4WK). In the words of James Fox, "To prevent a blood bath in 2005, when we will have a flood of 15-year olds, we have to do something today with the 5-year olds" (Krauss, 1994:4). However, this link between increases in the juvenile population and a rise in violent crime has not occurred. In the years since the prognostication was made the homicide rate among teenaged offenders has been falling.

Crack Cocaine

The huge increase in violent crime, especially homicide, in the late 1980s and early 1990s is now generally attributed to killings by young people aged 24 and under. These killings were driven by the spread of crack cocaine and the greater use of high-powered semiautomatic handguns by young people in that market (Blumstein, 1996; Butterfield, 1998a). During this period hundreds of thousands of unskilled, unemployed, young men from poor urban neighborhoods became street vendors of crack. To protect themselves, because they were carrying valuable merchandise—drugs and money—they were armed. They felt they needed this protection because drug dealers cannot call for police assistance if threatened. As shootings increased among sellers engaged in turf battles over drug sales, others began to arm themselves and the resulting violence continued to skyrocket (Blumstein, 1996). The sharp drop in violent crime in the 1990s followed the sudden decline in the use of crack as more and more people saw the devastation that the drug brought (Egan, 1999a:A1).

Crime Trends: What Is Really Known?

It is hard to point to specific factors that cause an increase or decrease in crime rates. The thought once was that, with the proper tools, the crime problem could be analyzed and solved. However, crime is a very complex phenomenon.

Key questions remain: Do changes in crime rates occur because of demography, unemployment rates, housing conditions, and changes in family structure? Or are crime rates a result of interactions among these and other factors? How do law enforcement, sentencing, and corrections policies affect criminality? Until more is known about the causes of criminal behavior, governmental policies can neither be blamed or praised for shifts in crime rates.

CHECK POINT

⑨ **Has crime in the United States reached record levels?**

⑩ **For which crimes does the United States have the highest rates among industrial nations?**

⑪ **What are the two main sources of crime data?**

⑫ **What are key factors in crime trends?**

Crime Victimization

victimology

A field of criminology that examines the role the victim plays in precipitating a criminal incident.

Until the past few decades, researchers paid little attention to crime victims. The field of **victimology,** which emerged in the 1950s, focused attention on four questions: (1) Who is victimized? (2) What is the impact of crime? (3) What happens to victims in the criminal justice system? (4) What role do victims play in causing the crimes they suffer?

Who Is Victimized?

Everyone does not have an equal chance of being a crime victim. Research shows that certain groups are more likely to be victimized than others. As Andrew Karmen notes, "Vulnerability to crime is always a matter of degree." Victimologists have puzzled over this fact and come up with several answers (Karmen, 1996).

One answer is that demographic factors (age, gender, income) affect lifestyle—people's routine activities, such as work, home life, and recreation. Lifestyles, in turn, affect people's exposure to dangerous places, times, and people.

Nonwhite males aged 14–24 are the most criminally victimized group. What factors might account for this?

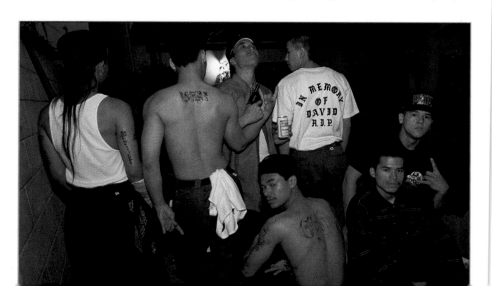

FIGURE 2.4 **Lifestyle-exposure model of victimization**

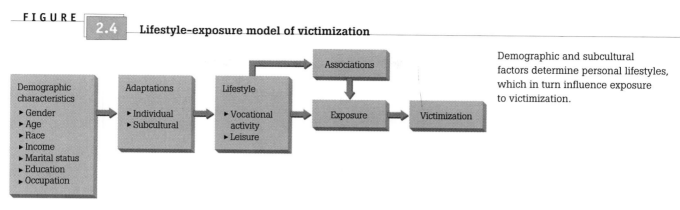

Demographic and subcultural factors determine personal lifestyles, which in turn influence exposure to victimization.

SOURCE: Adapted from Robert F. Meier and Terance D. Miethe, "Understanding Theories of Criminal Victimization," *Crime and Justice: A Review of Research*, ed. Michael Tonry (Chicago: University of Chicago Press, 1993), 467.

Thus, differences in lifestyles lead to varying degrees of exposure to risks (Meier and Miethe, 1993:466). Figure 2.4 shows the links among the factors used in the lifestyle-exposure model of personal victimization. Using this model, think of a person whose lifestyle includes going to night clubs in a "shady" part of town. Such a person runs the risk of being robbed if she walks alone through a dark high-crime area at two in the morning to her luxury car. By contrast, an older person who watches television at night in her small-town home has a very low chance of being robbed. But these cases do not tell the entire story. What other factors make victims more vulnerable than nonvictims?

Males, Youths, Nonwhites

The lifestyle-exposure model and survey data shed light on the links between personal characteristics and the chance that one will become a victim. Figure 2.5 shows the influence of gender, age, and race on the risk of being victimized by a violent crime, such as rape, robbery, or assault.

If these findings are applied to the lifestyle-exposure model, the suggestion might be that teenage black males are most likely to be victimized because of where they live (urban, high-crime areas), how they spend their leisure time (on the streets late at night), and the people with whom they associate (other violence-prone youths). Lifestyle factors may also explain why elderly white females are least likely to be victimized by a violent crime. Perhaps it is because they do not go out at night, do not associate with people who are prone to crime, carry few valuables, and take precautions such as locking their doors. Thus, lifestyle choices have a direct effect on the chances of victimization.

Race is a key factor in exposure to crime. African Americans and other minorities are more likely than whites to be raped, robbed, and assaulted. The rate of violent crime victimization for whites is 36 per 1,000 persons compared with 42 per 1,000 for African Americans (BJS, 1999e:4). White Americans are fearful of

FIGURE 2.5 **Victimization rates for violent crimes**

Black male teenagers have the highest victimization rate for violent crimes. Why are they more likely than other age, gender, and racial groups to be robbed or assaulted?

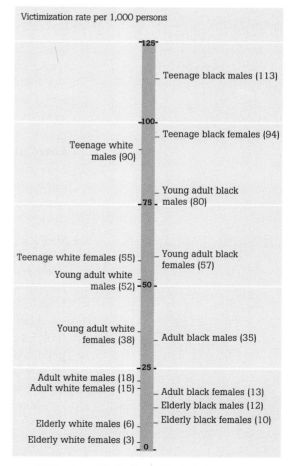

SOURCE: U.S. Department of Justice, Bureau of Justice Statistics, *Highlights from Twenty Years of Surveying Crime Victims* (Washington, D.C.: Government Printing Office, 1993), 20.

FIGURE 2.6   Victims and offenders are of the same race in three out of four violent crimes

Although whites seem most fearful of being victimized by blacks, most violent crime is intraracial. Why do people have such misperceptions?

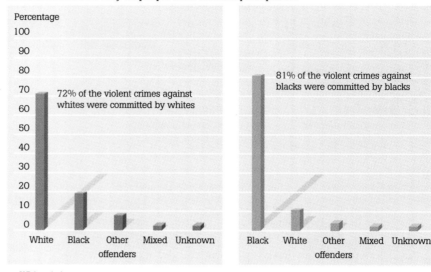

a   White victims

72% of the violent crimes against whites were committed by whites

b   Black victims

81% of the violent crimes against blacks were committed by blacks

SOURCE: U.S. Department of Justice, Bureau of Justice Statistics, *Report to the Nation on Crime and Justice*, 2d ed. (Washington, D.C.: Government Printing Office, 1988), 21.

being victimized by black strangers (Skogan, 1995:59). However, most violent crime is intraracial: three of every four victims are of the same race as the attacker (see Figure 2.6). The same is true of property crimes: most victims and offenders are of the same race and social class. Probably this is related to the fact that in modern America people come into contact mainly with others of the same race.

Low-Income City Dwellers

Income is also closely linked to exposure to crime. Economic factors largely determine where people live, work, and seek recreation. For low-income people these choices are limited. Some may have to live in crime-prone areas, may lack security devices to protect their homes, cannot avoid contact with people who are prone to crime, or cannot spend their leisure time in safe areas. Poor people and minorities have a greater risk of being victimized, because they are likely to live in inner cities with high rates of street crime. People with higher incomes have more lifestyle-exposure choices open to them and can avoid risky situations (Meier and Miethe, 1993:468).

Living in a city is a key factor in victimization. Violent crime occurs mainly in large cities where the victimization rate is 50 per 1,000 persons compared with 36 per 1,000 in suburbs and 28 per 1,000 in rural areas. Urban households are also more prone to property victimizations with a rate of 310 per 1,000 households compared with the suburban rate of 210 and the rural rate of 190 (BJS, 1998d:6).

Murder rates have risen the most in the inner cities, where drug dealing and drug use are rampant. Most of the victims, like their killers, tend to be young African Americans. The national homicide rate among African American males aged 18 to 24 is 143 for every 100,000 black males in that age group, about nine times that for white males in the same age bracket (BJS, 1999k:Table 3.139). But this does not tell the whole story, because homicide rates differ by city and state. One study found that Michigan was the most dangerous state for young black males, with a homicide rate of 232 per 100,000 black men aged 15 to 24, and California was next, with 155 young black males killed per 100,000 (*New York Times,* June 27, 1990:A10).

However, crime rates will not necessarily be high in any poor urban area. More crime occurs in some poor areas than in others. The crime rate in an area may be affected by other factors, such as the physical condition of the neighborhood, the residents' attitudes toward society and the law, the extent of opportunities for crime, and social control by families and government.

The lifestyle-exposure model explains some of the factors that increase or decrease the risk of being victimized, but what is the impact of crime on the nation and on individuals?

CHECK POINT

⑬ **What are the main elements of the lifestyle-exposure model?**

⑭ **What are the characteristics of the group that is most victimized by violent crime? Of the least victimized group?**

The Impact of Crime

Crime affects not only the victim but also all members of society. Everyone pays for crime through higher taxes, higher prices, and fear. However, estimating the precise impact of crime is hard.

Costs of Crime

Crime has many kinds of costs: (1) the economic costs—lost property, lower productivity, and the cost of medical care; (2) the psychological and emotional costs—pain, trauma, and lost quality of life; and (3) the costs of operating the criminal justice system.

A Justice Department study estimates the total annual cost of tangible losses from crime (medical expenses, damaged or lost property, work time) at $105 billion. The intangible costs (pain, trauma, lost quality of life) to victims are estimated at $450 billion (NIJ, 1996). Operating the criminal justice system costs taxpayers more than $70 billion a year. These figures do not include the costs of occupational and organized crime to consumers. In addition, there are the costs to citizens who install locks and alarms or employ guards and security patrols.

Fear of Crime

One impact of crime is fear. Fear limits freedom. Because they are fearful, many people limit their activities to "safe" areas at "safe" times. Fear also creates anxieties that affect physiological and psychological well-being. And the very persons who have the least chance of being victimized, such as women and the elderly, are often the most fearful (Miethe, 1995:14).

Media attention—such as that generated by serial killer Andrew Cunanan, who murdered fashion designer Gianni Versace and four others—instills in many a fear of crime.

What Americans Think

Question "Is there any area right
around here—that is, within a
mile—where you would be afraid
to walk alone at night?"

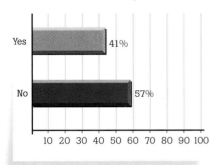

SOURCE: U.S. Department of Justice, Bureau of
Justice Statistics, *Sourcebook of Criminal Justice
Statistics, 1998* (Washington, D.C.: Government
Printing Office, 1999), 118.

Since 1965, public opinion polls have asked Americans whether they "feel more uneasy" or "fear to walk the streets at night" (see What Americans Think). Over time more than 40 percent of respondents say that fear of crime limits their freedom. Figure 2.7 shows the results of a twelve-city study of perceptions of community safety. The percentage of fearful residents differs not only by city but also by the extent to which they fear crime in their city or neighborhood or being a victim of street crime. In some large cities more than 60 percent of residents say they are afraid to walk through their neighborhoods at night, while in small towns and rural areas fewer than 30 percent express this concern.

High levels of fear are found among nonwhites and people with low incomes, the groups that are most likely to be victimized. However, women, the elderly, and upper-income suburban dwellers—groups with low rates of victimization—are also more fearful than the average citizen (Warr, 1993:25, BJS 1999k:Table 2.38).

A Seattle study found that the most feared crime was residential burglary, a crime that holds little risk of personal injury. Murder, the most serious offense, was ranked tenth. In explaining these findings, researchers suggest that the degree to which certain crimes are feared depends on two factors: the seriousness of the offense and the chances that it will occur. A Gallup poll supports this view. Thirty-five percent of those interviewed said they worried very frequently about being burglarized when they were not home, whereas 19 percent worried about being murdered (Warr, 1993:27).

Crime rates are down, yet Americans seem to be as fearful as ever. People do not have a clear picture of the actual risk of crime in their lives. Their views about crime seem to be shaped more by what they see on television, by talk at their workplace, and by what politicians are saying. Although fewer than 8 percent of victimizations result from violent crime, such crimes are the ones most frequently reported by the media. In the mid-1990s with violent crime in decline, television and newspaper coverage of violent crime increased more than 400 percent. One result was a jump in the percentage of Americans ranking crime as the nation's foremost problem from 9 percent to 49 percent (Chiricos, Escholz, and Gertz, 1997:342).

The amount of news coverage of crime, compared with coverage of the economy or government, can be startling (Chermak, 1995:48). Crime stories sell newspapers, build viewership, and appeal to certain types of audiences. Data from the Nation Opinion Survey on Crime and Justice revealed the regular viewers of television crime programs such as *Cops* and *America's Most Wanted* showed a higher degree of fear "about the probability of being sexually assaulted, beaten, knifed, and getting killed" (Haghighi and Sorensen, 1996:29).

Most people do not experience crime directly but instead learn about it indirectly (Skogan and Maxfield, 1981:157). Local television news has a major impact on attitudes about crime (Kurtz,1997). In addition, tabloid shows such as *Hard Copy* and *A Current Affair* present reports of heinous crimes almost daily (Kappeler, Blumberg, and Potter, 1996:47). Researchers believe that conversations with friends also tend to magnify the amount of local violence.

FIGURE 2.7   Fear of Crime in Twelve Cities

Percentage of residents who said they were fearful of crime in
their city or neighborhood or of being a victim of street crime.

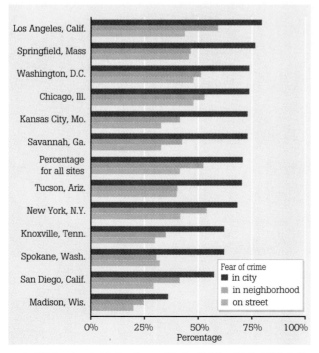

SOURCE: U.S. Department of Justice, Bureau of Justice Statistics, *Criminal Victimization
and Perceptions of Community Safety in Twelve Cities, 1998* (Washington, D.C.:
Government Printing Office, 1999), 10.

Such conversations often focus on crimes against women, the elderly, and children. Stories about defenseless victims create a feeling that violent crime lurks everywhere.

Evidence exists of a link between fear of crime and disorderly conditions in neighborhoods and communities (Wilson and Kelling, 1982; Skogan, 1990). As discussed by George Kelling and Catherine Coles, in urban areas, disorderly behavior—public drunkenness, urination, aggressive panhandling, and menacing behavior—offends citizens and instills fear. Unregulated disorderly behavior is a signal to citizens that an area is unsafe. Because of this fear they "will stay off the streets, avoid certain areas, and curtail their normal activities and associations" (Kelling and Coles, 1996:20). Avoidance by residents of "unsafe" business areas may lead to store closings, declines in real estate values, and flight to more orderly neighborhoods.

Among all groups, the fear of crime outstrips the reality. People do not assess the risk of crime in the same ways as other risks, such as those caused by nature or by accident (see Table 2.5).

Actions that might reduce the fear of crime are costly, and those who can best afford to protect themselves are those who are least threatened by crime. Some responses to the perceived risk of crime may not seem costly, such as staying at home after dark. Yet even such a simple measure is often far easier for the rich than for the poor. The rich are more likely to work during the day and to have some control over their hours of work. Poorer people are more likely to work evenings and nights as waitresses, security guards, or convenience store clerks. Other measures, such as moving to the suburbs, installing home security systems, and hiring private security companies, are also most available to the rich who are least at risk of becoming victims.

The Experience of Victims within the Criminal Justice System

After a crime has occurred, the victim is often forgotten. Victims may have suffered physical, psychological, and economic losses, yet the criminal justice system focuses on finding and prosecuting the offender.

Too often the system is not sensitive to the needs of victims. For example, defense attorneys may ask them hostile questions and attempt to paint them as guilty. Likewise, while victims are a key source of evidence, the police may question them closely—and in a hostile fashion—to find out if they are telling the truth. Often the victim never hears the outcome of a case. Sometimes a victim comes face to face with the assailant, who is out on bail or on probation. This can be a shock, especially if the victim had assumed that the offender was in prison.

Victims may be forced to miss work and lose pay to appear at judicial proceedings. They may be summoned to court again and again, only to learn that the arraignment or trial has been postponed. Any recovered property may be held by the court for months as the case winds its way through the system. In short, after cases have been completed, victims may feel that they have been victimized twice, once by the offender and once by the criminal justice system.

TABLE 2.5 Rates of crime compared with rates of other events

Crime is a major concern to many Americans, but what are the risks of victimization compared with other kinds of risks?

EVENTS	RATE PER 1,000 ADULTS PER YEAR
Accidental injury, all circumstances	220
Accidental injury at home	66
Personal theft	61
Accidental injury at work	47
Violent victimization	31
Assault (aggravated and simple)	25
Injury in motor vehicle accident	22
Death, all causes	11
Victimization with injury	11
Serious (aggravated) assault	8
Robbery	6
Heart disease death	5
Cancer death	3
Rape (women only)	1
Accidental death, all circumstances	0.4
Pneumonia/influenza death	0.4
Motor vehicle accident death	0.2
Suicide	0.2
HIV infection death	0.1
Homicide/legal intervention	0.1

SOURCE: U.S. Department of Justice, Bureau of Justice Statistics, *Highlights from Twenty Years of Surveying Crime Victims* (Washington, D.C.: Government Printing Office, 1993), 4.

During the past two decades, justice agencies have become more sensitive to the interests of crime victims. This has happened partly because victims often are the only witnesses to the crime and their help is needed. Many victims are not willing to provide such help if it involves economic and emotional costs.

A proposed federal "Crime Victims' Bill of Rights" would grant victims the right to be informed about plea bargains, to obtain restitution for losses, and to bar offenders from earning income from books and films about their crimes. At least twenty states have amended their constitutions to achieve these objectives.

Programs that give information, support, and compensation to victims have been started in many states. Information programs are designed (1) to sensitize justice officials to the need to treat crime victims courteously and (2) to let victims know what is happening at each stage of a case. In some states the investigating officer gives the victim a booklet listing the steps that will be taken and telephone numbers that can be called should questions arise.

Support is most important when the victim faces medical, emotional, or financial problems as a result of a crime. Such support is offered by rape crisis centers, victim assistance programs, and family shelters. In most states compensation programs help victims of violent crime by paying the medical expenses of those who cannot afford them. When property has been stolen or destroyed, compensation programs encourage judges to order restitution by the offender.

CHECK POINT

⑮ **What are some of the impacts of crime?**

⑯ **Why is fear of crime high among some groups?**

⑰ **What are the costs of crime?**

The Role of Victims in Crime

Victimologists study the role victims play in some crimes. Researchers have found that many victims behave in ways that invite the acts committed against them. This is not to say that the victim was at fault when a crime occurred. Rather, the victim's behavior may have led to the crime through consent, provocation, enticement, risk taking, or carelessness with property.

What do studies reveal about these situations? First, some people do not take proper precautions to protect themselves. For example, they may leave keys in their cars or enter unsafe areas. Using common sense may be part of the price of living in modern society. Second, some victims may provoke or entice another person to commit a crime. Third, victims of crimes of nonstrangers may not be willing to help with the investigation and prosecution. These behaviors do not excuse criminal acts, but they do encourage thinking about other aspects of the crime situation.

Karmen points out that the victim may be partly to blame for motor vehicle theft (Karmen, 1996:124). In some cases the victims are legally blameless, while in others they are posing as victims to commit insurance fraud. Karmen believes that about 20 percent of thefts result from *negligence* (leaving the keys in the vehicle), while 10 to 25 percent are caused by either *precipitation* (leaving the car in a vulnerable location so it will be stolen) or *provocation* (arranging to have a vehicle damaged or destroyed).

Violence against women is perpetrated mainly by those with whom they are intimate—husbands, boyfriends, lovers. What factors might explain this situation?

Victimologists now recognize that victims play a key role in dealing with crime. But this does not mean that criminologists are less interested in finding out what causes crime.

CHECK POINT

⑱ **What behaviors of victims can invite crime?**

Causes of Crime

Whenever news of a crime hits the headlines, whether the crime is a grisly murder or a complex bank fraud, the first question is, "Why did he (or she) do it?" Do people commit crimes because they are poor, greedy, mentally ill, or just stupid?

Criminology is concerned mainly with learning about criminal behavior, the nature of offenders, and how crime can be prevented. Research focuses mainly on the offender. Fewer questions are asked about how factors such as the economy, government policy, family, and education affect crime (Messner and Rosenfeld, 1994:45–47). In this section we look at the two major schools of criminological thought—classical and positivist. We then examine biological, psychological, and sociological theories of the causes of criminal behavior.

Classical and Positivist Theories

Two major schools of criminological thought are the classical and positivist schools. Each was pioneered by scholars who were influenced by the dominant intellectual ideas of their times.

The Classical School

Until the eighteenth century, most Europeans explained criminal behavior in supernatural terms: they saw it as the work of the devil. Those who did wrong were possessed by the devil. Some Christians believed that all humanity had fallen with Adam and has been in a state of total depravity ever since. Indictments often began, "[John Doe], not having the fear of God before his eyes but being moved and seduced by the instigation of the devil, did commit [a certain crime]." Even today the media report that some crimes are committed by members of "satanic cults." Alleged child-abuse victims have told gripping stories of ceremonies involving sex, blood, and animal sacrifice carried out in the name of the devil.

Not only did pre-eighteenth-century religious ideas guide thinking about crime, but defendants also had few rights. The accused had few chances to put forth a defense; confessions were obtained through torture; and the penalty for most offenses was physical punishment or death.

In 1764, Cesare Beccaria published his *Essays on Crime and Punishments.* This was the first attempt to explain crime in secular, or worldly, terms, as opposed to religious terms. The book also pointed to injustices in the administration of criminal laws. Beccaria's ideas prompted reformers to try to make criminal law and procedures more rational and consistent. From this movement came **classical criminology,** whose main principles are as follows:

classical criminology
A school of criminology that views behavior as stemming from free will, demands responsibility and accountability of all perpetrators, and stresses the need for punishments severe enough to deter others.

❶ Criminal behavior is rational, and most people have the potential to engage in such behavior.

❷ People may choose to commit a crime after weighing the costs and benefits of their actions.

❸ Fear of punishment keeps most people in check. Therefore, the severity, certainty, and speed of punishment affects the level of crime.

❹ The punishment should fit the crime, not the person who committed it.

❺ The criminal justice system must be predictable, with laws and punishments known to the public.

Classical ideas declined in the nineteenth century, partly because of the rise of science and partly because its principles did not take into account differences among individuals or the way the crime was committed.

Neoclassical Criminology

After remaining dormant for almost a hundred years, classical ideas took on new life in the 1980s. In a more conservative America, a renewed interest was seen in some aspects of classical theory. Some scholars argued that crimes may result from the rational choice of people who have weighed the benefits to be gained from the crime against the costs of being caught and punished. But they also recognize that the criminal law must take account of differences among individuals. To a large extent, sentencing reform, criticisms of rehabilitation, and greater use of incarceration stem from a renewed interest in classical ideas. However, the positivist school of thought dominated American criminology in the twentieth century.

Positivist Criminology

positivist criminology
A school of criminology that views behavior as stemming from social, biological, and psychological factors. It argues that punishment should be tailored to the individual needs of the offender.

By the middle of the nineteenth century, as the scientific method began to take hold, the ideas of the classical school seemed old-fashioned. Instead of stressing the classical idea that "bad laws made bad people," **positivist criminology** used science to study the body, mind, and environment of the offender. Science could help to reveal why offenders committed crimes and how they could be rehabilitated. Key features of this approach are as follows:

❶ Human behavior is controlled by physical, mental, and social factors, not by free will.

❷ Criminals are different from noncriminals.

❸ Science can be used to discover the causes of crime and to treat deviants.

Understanding the main theories of crime causation is important because they affect how laws are enforced, guilt or innocence is determined, and crimes are punished. As each of the theories is described, consider its implications for crime policies. For example, if biological theories are viewed as sound, then the authorities might try to identify potential offenders through genetic analysis and then segregate or supervise them. However, the acceptance of sociological theories might lead to efforts to end poverty, improve education, and provide job training.

⑲ **What were the main assumptions of the classical school?**

⑳ **What are the main assumptions of the positivist school?**

Biological Explanations

The medical training of Cesare Lombroso (1836–1909) led him to suppose that physical traits distinguish criminals from law-abiding citizens. He believed that some people are at a more primitive state of evolution and hence are *born* criminal. These "throwbacks" have trouble adjusting to modern society. Lombroso's ideas can be summarized as follows (Lombroso, 1968):

❶ Certain people are **criminogenic**; that is, they are born criminals.

❷ They have primitive physical traits such as strong canine teeth, huge jaws, and high cheekbones.

❸ These traits are acquired through heredity or through alcoholism, epilepsy, or syphilis.

criminogenic
Factors thought to bring about criminal behavior in an individual.

Around the beginning of the twentieth century, interest shifted from physical traits to inherited traits that affect intelligence. Some scholars believed that criminals commit crimes to alleviate pathological urges inherited from mentally defective ancestors. They studied genealogies to find the links between these traits and the criminal records of family members.

Two studies published in 1875 and 1902, of families with the fictitious names of Jukes and Kallikak, presented evidence that genetic defects passed on to offspring could condemn them to lives of crime. Richard Dugdale studied more than one thousand descendants of the woman he called Ada Jukes, whom he dubbed the "mother of criminals." Among them were 280 paupers, 60 thieves, 7 murderers, 140 criminals, 40 persons with venereal diseases, and 50 prostitutes (Dugdale, 1910).

Similar data collected by Henry H. Goddard supported the belief that the Kallikak family, whose members were all related to the illegitimate son of Martin Kallikak, contained more criminals than the descendants from Martin's later marriage into a "good" family (Goddard, 1902).

These early studies have drawn much criticism, but they were taken seriously in their time. Many states passed laws that required repeat offenders to be sterilized. The assumption was that crime could be controlled if criminal traits were not passed from parents to children. Not until 1942 did the U.S. Supreme Court declare required sterilization unconstitutional (*Skinner v. Oklahoma*).

biological explanations
Explanations of crime that emphasize physiological and neurological factors that may predispose a person to commit crimes.

Although **biological explanations** of crime were ignored or condemned as racist after World War II, they have attracted renewed interest. *Crime and Human Nature*, by James Q. Wilson and Richard J. Herrnstein, reviews the research on this subject (Wilson and Herrnstein, 1985). Unlike the early positivists, the authors do not claim that any one factor explains criminality. Instead, they argue that biological factors *predispose* some people to a crime. Genetic makeup, body type, and intelligence quotient (IQ) may outweigh social factors as predictors of criminality. The findings of research on nutrition, neurology, genetics, and endocrinology give some support to the view that these factors may be related to violent behavior in some people (Brennan, Mednick, and Volavka, 1995:65).

These findings have given biological explanations a renewed influence and reduced the dominance of sociological and psychological explanations in the twentieth century. Scientists are doing further research to see if they can find biological factors that make some people prone to violence and criminality (Fishbein, 1990:27).

Policy Implications of Biological Explanations

A policy based on biological theories of crime would attempt to identify persons with traits that make them prone to crime and then to treat or control those persons. This might lead to selective incarceration, intensive supervision, or drug therapies. Special education might be required for those with learning disabilities. Proposals calling for the castration of repeat sex offenders are erroneously based on biological explanations.

CHECK POINT

21 **What were the main elements of Lombroso's theory?**

Psychological Explanations

psychological explanations
Explanations of crime that emphasize mental processes and behavior.

Criminal behavior has often been viewed as having been caused by a mental condition, a personality disturbance, or limited intellect. These ideas are the focus of **psychological explanations** of crime. Before the eighteenth century, those who engaged in such behavior were thought to be possessed by demons. However, some scholars suggested that defects in the body and mind caused people to act "abnormally."

One early advocate of this idea was Henry Maudsley (1835–1918), an English psychologist who believed that criminals were "morally insane." Moral insanity, he argued, is an innate characteristic, and crime is a way of expressing it. Without crime as an outlet, criminals would become insane (Maudsley, 1974).

Sigmund Freud (1856–1939), now seen as one of the foremost thinkers of the twentieth century, proposed a *psychoanalytic theory* that crime is caused by unconscious forces and drives. Freud also claimed that early childhood experiences had major effects on development of the personality. Freud's followers expanded his theory, saying that the personality is made up of three parts: the id, ego, and

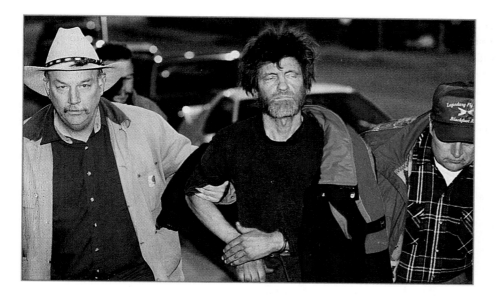

Theodore Kaczynski's attorneys believed his best hope of escaping a death sentence was to plead mental illness. The Unabomer refused and tried to fire his counsel. The case raised fundamental questions about a defendant's right to participate in his own defense and the role of psychiatry in the courtroom.

superego. The id controls drives that are primarily sexual, the ego relates desires to behavior, and the superego (often referred to as the conscience) judges actions as either right or wrong. Psychoanalytic theory explains criminal behavior as resulting from either an undeveloped superego or an overdeveloped superego. For example, a person who commits a violent sex crime is thought to have an undeveloped superego, because urges cannot be controlled. Alternatively, a person with an overdeveloped superego may suffer from guilt and anxiety. To reduce the guilt, the person may commit a crime knowing that punishment will follow. To ensure punishment, the offender will unconsciously leave clues at the crime scene. Psychoanalysts say this occurred in the famous Loeb-Leopold murder of Bobby Franks in 1924 (Regoli and Hewitt, 1994).

Psychiatrists have linked criminal behavior to such concepts as innate impulses, psychic conflict, and the repression of personality. These psychological explanations see crime as a behavior that takes the place of abnormal urges and desires. This approach takes many different forms, all of which are based on the idea that early personality development is a key factor in later behavior.

Psychopathology

The terms *psychopath, sociopath,* and *antisocial personality* refer to a person who is unable to control impulses, cannot learn from experience, and does not feel emotions, such as love. This kind of person is viewed as psychologically abnormal, as a crazed killer or sex fiend.

During the 1940s, after a number of widely publicized sex crimes, many state legislatures passed "sexual psychopath laws" designed to place "homicidal sex fiends" in treatment institutions. Such laws were later shown to be based on false assumptions. They reveal the political context within which the criminal law is fashioned (Sutherland, 1950).

Psychological theories have been widely criticized. Some critics point to the difficulty of measuring emotional factors and separating out persons thought to be prone to crime. Others note the wide range of theories—some contradicting one another—that take a psychological approach to crime.

Policy Implications of Psychological Explanations

Despite the criticisms, psychological explanations have played a major role in criminal justice policy during the twentieth century. The major implication of these theories is that people with personality disorders should receive treatment. Those whose illegal behaviors stem from learning should be punished so that they will learn that crime is not rewarded.

Policies that stress rehabilitation attempt to change the offender's personality and, hence, behavior. From the 1940s to the mid-1970s, psychotherapy, counseling, group therapy, behavioral modification, and moral development programs were used in efforts to rehabilitate criminals. However, in the past two decades there has been less reliance on these policies.

CHECK POINT

㉒ **What is a psychopath?**

Sociological Explanations

sociological explanations
Explanations of crime that emphasize the social conditions that bear on the individual as causes of criminal behavior.

In contrast to psychological approaches, **sociological explanations** stress that people are members of social groups that shape their behavior. Sociologists do not believe that criminality is inborn; instead, it is caused by external factors. Thus, sociological theories of crime assume that the offender's personality and actions are molded by contact with the social world and by such factors as race, age, gender, and income.

The social theorist Emile Durkheim argued that when a simple rural society develops into a complex urbanized one, traditional standards decline. Some people are unable to adjust to the new rules and will engage in criminal acts.

In the 1920s a group of researchers at the University of Chicago looked closely at aspects of urban life that seemed to be linked to crime: poverty, bad housing, broken families, and the problems faced by new immigrants. They found high levels of crime in those neighborhoods with many opportunities for delinquent behavior and few legitimate means of earning a living.

From a sociological perspective, criminals are made, not born. Among the many theories stressing the influence of societal forces on criminal behavior, three deserve special mention: social structure theory, social process theory, and social conflict theory.

Social Structure Theory

social structure theories
Theories that blame crime on the existence of a powerless lower class that lives with poverty and deprivation and often turns to crime in response.

Social structure theories suggest that criminal behavior is related to social class. People in different social classes have different amounts of wealth, status, and power. Those in the lower class suffer from poverty, poor education, bad housing, and lack of political power. Therefore, members of the lower class, especially the younger members, are more likely to engage in crime. Crime is thus created by the structure of society.

anomie
A breakdown in and disappearance of the rules of social behavior.

Sociologist Robert Merton extended Durkheim's ideas about the role of social change and urbanization on crime. He stressed that social change often leads to a state of **anomie,** in which the rules or norms that guide behavior have weakened or disappeared. People may become anomic when the rules are unclear or they are unable to achieve their goals. Under such conditions antisocial or deviant behavior may result.

For example, American society arguably puts a high value on success but makes achievement impossible for some of its members. It follows that those who are caught in this trap may use crime as a way out. Theorists believe that this type of situation has led some ethnic groups into organized crime. Others argue that social disorganization brings about conditions in which, among other things, family structure breaks down, alcohol or drug abuse becomes more common, and criminal behavior becomes more frequent. They assert that poverty must be ended and the social structures reformed if crime is to be reduced.

Policy Implications of Social Structure Theories

Because social structure theories are based on the premise that crime is caused by social conditions, then actions should be taken to reform the conditions that breed crime. Such actions include education and job training, urban redevelopment, better health care, and economic development.

Social Process Theory

The poor are not the only people who commit crimes. Many criminologists therefore believe that the social structure approach is inadequate. **Social process theories,** which date from the 1930s but did not gain recognition until the 1960s and 1970s, assume that any person, regardless of education, class, or upbringing, has the potential to become a criminal. However, some people are likely to commit criminal acts because of the circumstances of their lives. Thus, these theories try to explain the processes by which certain people become criminals.

There are three main types of social process theories: learning theories, control theories, and labeling theories.

Learning theories hold that criminal activity is learned behavior. Through social relations, some people learn how to be a criminal and acquire the values associated with that way of life. This view assumes that people imitate and learn from one another. Thus family members and peers are viewed as major influences on a person's development.

In 1939 Edwin Sutherland proposed the **theory of differential association,** which states that behavior is learned through interactions with others, especially family members (Sutherland, 1947). Criminal behavior occurs when a person encounters others who are more favorable to crime than opposed to it. If a boy grows up in a family, in which, say, an older brother is involved in crime, he is likely to learn criminal behavior. If people in the family, neighborhood, and gang believe that illegal activity is nothing to be ashamed of, chances are greater that the young person will engage in crime.

Control theory holds that social links keep people in line with accepted norms (Hirschi, 1969; Gottfredson and Hirsch, 1990). In other words, all members of society have the potential to commit crime, but most are restrained by their ties to the family, church, school, and peer groups. Thus, sensitivity to the opinion of others, commitment to a conventional lifestyle, and belief in the standards or values shared by friends are all factors that influence a person to abide by the law. A person for whom one or more of these influences is lacking may engage in crime.

The third type of social process theory, **labeling theory,** stresses the social process through which certain acts and people are labeled as deviant. As Howard Becker notes, society creates deviance—and, hence, criminality—"by making the rules whose infraction constitutes deviance, and by applying those rules to particular people and labeling them outsiders" (Becker, 1963).

social process theories
Theories that see criminality as normal behavior. Everyone has the potential to become a criminal, depending on the influences that impel one toward or away from crime and also how one is regarded by others.

learning theories
Theories that see criminal behavior as learned, just as legal behavior is learned.

theory of differential association
Theories that people become criminals because they encounter more influences that view criminal behavior as normal and acceptable than influences that are hostile to criminal behavior.

control theory
Theories holding that criminal behavior occurs when the bonds that tie an individual to society are broken or weakened.

labeling theory
Theories emphasizing that the causes of criminal behavior are not found in the individual but in the social process that labels certain acts as deviant or criminal.

Becker studied the process through which people become deviant. Social control agencies, such as the police, courts, and corrections, are created to label certain people as outside the normal, law-abiding community. When they have been labeled, those people come to believe that the label is true. They take on a deviant identity and start acting in deviant ways. Once labeled, these people are presumed by others to be deviant, and they react accordingly. This reinforces the deviant identity.

Labeling theory suggests that criminals are not very different from other people. It is only that the police or courts have labeled them as deviant. In this view, the justice system creates criminals by labeling people to serve its own bureaucratic and political ends. Those who support this view call for decriminalization of drug use, gambling, and prostitution.

Policy Implications of Social Process Theories

If crime is a learned behavior, it follows that people need to be treated in ways that build conventional bonds, develop positive role models, and avoid labeling. Policies to promote stable families and develop community agencies to help those in need are based on this view.

Social Conflict Theory

In the mid-1960s, the biological, psychological, and sociological explanations of criminal behavior were challenged by **social conflict theories.** These theories assume that criminal law and the justice system are designed mainly to control the poor. The rich commit as many crimes as the poor, it is argued, but the poor are more likely to be caught and punished.

Those in power use the law to impose their version of morality on society to protect their property and safety. They use their power to change the definitions of crime to cover acts they view as threatening.

There are different types of social conflict theories. One type, proposed by critical, radical, or Marxist criminologists, holds that the class structure causes certain groups to be labeled as deviant. In this view, "deviance is a status imputed to groups who share certain structural characteristics (e.g., powerlessness)" (Spitzer, 1975:639). Thus, the criminal law is aimed at the behavior of specific groups or classes. One result is that the poor are deeply hostile toward the social order, and this hostility is one factor in criminal behavior. Moreover, when the status quo is threatened, legal definitions of crime are changed to trap those who challenge the system. For example, vagrancy laws have been used to arrest labor union organizers, civil rights workers, and peace activists when those in power believed that their interests were threatened by these groups.

Policy Implications of Social Conflict Theories

Conflict theories require policies that would reduce class-based conflict and injustice. Policies to help women, the poor, and minorities deal with government agencies would follow. Criminal justice resources would need to focus on crimes committed by upper-class offenders, not just on those committed by lower-class offenders.

Like other theories about the causes of criminal behavior, sociological theories have been criticized. Their critics argue that these theories are imprecise, not supported by evidence, and based on ideology. Even so, sociological theories have served as the basis for many attempts to prevent crime and rehabilitate offenders.

---

social conflict theories

Theories that assume criminal law and the criminal justice system are primarily a means of controlling the poor and the have-nots.

23 **What is the main assumption of social structure theories?**

24 **What is the main assumption of social process theories?**

25 **What is the main assumption of social conflict theories?**

Women and Crime

Theories about causes of crime are almost all based on observations of males. This is understandable, given that males commit far more crimes than females. It also reflects the fact that until recently most criminologists were male. Only in the past few decades has research focused on women and crime. Although they have raised new questions, scholars in this field base their research on the theories just described (Daly, 1998:85–108).

Except in the case of so-called female crimes such as prostitution and shoplifting, before the 1970s little research was done on female offenders, who account for fewer than 10 percent of arrests. The assumption was that most women, because of their nurturant and dependent nature, were unable to commit serious crimes. Those who did commit crimes were deemed to be "bad" women. Unlike male criminals, female criminals were viewed as moral offenders—"fallen women." Today criminologists are looking more closely at female offenders (Daly and Chesney-Lind, 1988:497).

Two books published in 1975, Freda Adler's *Sisters in Crime: The Rise of the New Female Criminal* and Rita Simon's *Women and Crime,* led to a new view of gender and crime (Adler, 1975; Simon, 1975). Both books looked at increases in female crimes, but they reached different conclusions.

Adler stressed the impact of the women's movement. She believed that as the roles of women changed, their criminality would be more like that of men. As she noted, "When we did not permit women to swim at the beaches, the female drowning rate was quite low. When women were not permitted to work as bank tellers or presidents, the female embezzlement rate was low" (Adler, 1975:31). In other words, as women and men become more equal, gender differences will decrease.

According to Simon, because of recent changes, women now have greater freedom, are less likely to be victimized and oppressed by men, and are less likely to be dependent on them. Simon placed less emphasis than Adler on the women's movement and more on changes in the job market. She argued that with new opportunities for women, the number of business-related and property crimes committed by women is likely to rise (Simon, 1975:19).

University of California, Santa Cruz, student Emma Rose Freeman, 18, accused of pointing a .380-caliber Beretta semiautomatic handgun while robbing a hair salon and a Costco warehouse store with another student.

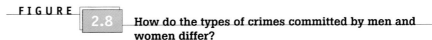

While most arrests are of men, arrests of women is highest for larceny-theft.

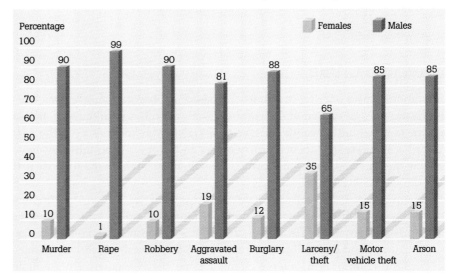

SOURCE: U.S. Department of Justice, *Crime in the United States—1998* (Washington, D.C.: Government Printing Office, 1999).

But has there really been a change in female criminality? Some scholars believe that arrest data do not suggest major shifts in the types of crimes committed by women. However, from 1960 to 1990 the female share of all arrests rose from 10 percent to 20 percent. This shift was most evident among women under 18 and older women. For both age groups the greatest increase was for larceny-theft and for older women fraud and forgery (Daly, 1998:88). Over the last decade, the total number of arrests have risen by 7 percent, arrests of males increased 2 percent, but arrests of females increased 28 percent (FBI, 1999). The data show an increase of 150 percent in the number of women arrested for property offenses and an increase of more than 270 percent in arrests of women for drug dealing and use. About 14 percent of all violent offenders are women. Three out of four female violent offenders commit simple assaults, and three out of four of these are against other women (BJS, 1999g).

The "war on drugs" has been a major factor in the astonishing 573 percent increase from 1980 to 1997 of women in prison (Mauer, Polter, and Wolf, 1999). Even with these increases, however, the amount of crime committed by women is small compared with the amount committed by men. As shown in Figure 2.8, women make up less than 19 percent of arrestees for all types of crime except larceny-theft. As Herrnstein notes, "As a rule, the more heinous the crime or more chronic the criminal, the greater the disproportion between males and females" (Herrnstein, 1995:57).

For most crimes women remain minor players. Yet one study found that many women play a leadership role when committing crimes with male partners. Many of the women "initiated criminal behavior, led others into crime, and took primary roles in committing numerous criminal offenses" (Alarid, Marquart, Burton, and Cuvelier, 1996:451).

TABLE 2.6 Major theories of criminality and their policy implications

Various types of policies are supported by scholars and by the public. Very little is known about the real causes of crime, but note how many people think they have the answers.

THEORY	MAJOR PREMISE	POLICY IMPLICATIONS	POLICY IMPLEMENTATION
Biological	Genetic, biochemical, or neurological defects cause some people to commit crime.	Identification and treatment or control of persons with crime-producing biological factors. Selective incapacitation, intensive supervision.	1 Use of drugs to inhibit biological urges of sex offenders. 2 Use of controlled diet to reduce levels of antisocial behavior caused by biochemical imbalances. 3 Identification of neurological defects through CAT scans. Use of drugs to suppress violent implulses. 4 Special education for those with learning disabilities.
Psychological	Personality and learning factors cause some people to commit crime.	Treatment of those with personality disorders to achieve mental health. Those whose illegal behavior stems from learning should have their behavior punished so they will realize that crime is not rewarded.	1 Psychotherapy and counseling to treat personality disorders. 2 Behavior modification strategies, such as electric shock and other negative impulses, to change learned behavior. 3 Counseling to enhance moral development. 4 Intensive individual and group therapies.
Social structure	Crime is the result of underlying social conditions such as poverty, inequality, and unemployment.	Actions should be taken to reform social conditions that breed crime.	1 Education and job training programs. 2 Urban redevelopment to improve housing, education, and health care. 3 Community development to provide economic opportunities.
Social process	Crime is normal learned behavior and is subject to either social control or labeling effects.	Individuals must be treated in groups, with emphasis on building conventional bonds and avoiding stigmatization.	1 Youth programs that emphasize positive role models. 2 Community organizing to establish neighborhood institutions and bonds that emphasize following society's norms. 3 Programs designed to promote family stability.
Social conflict	Criminal definitions and punishments are used by some groups to control other groups.	Fundamental changes in the political and social systems to reduce class conflict.	1 Development of programs to remove injustice in society. 2 Provision of resources to assist women, minorities, and the poor in dealing with the criminal justice system and other governmental agencies. 3 Modification of criminal justice to deal similarly with crimes committed by upper-class members and crimes committed by lower-class members.

As the status of women changes and as more women pursue careers in business and industry, some scholars believe that women will commit more economic and occupational crimes, such as embezzlement and fraud. However, research continues to show that arrested women, like male offenders, tend to come from poor families in which physical and substance abuse are present (Rosenbaum, J. L., 1989:31). Other researchers believe that the higher crime rates among women stem in part from the greater willingness of police and prosecutors to treat them like men. Thus far, the findings of research on gender differences in crime are not conclusive (Decker, Wright, Redfern, and Smith, 1993:142).

CHECK POINT

㉖ **What have Freda Adler and Rita Simon contributed to theories of female criminality?**

㉗ **For what crimes has the percentage of women offenders risen the most?**

Assessing Theories of Criminality

Undoubtedly all of the theories of crime described here contain a kernel of truth. However, none is powerful enough to predict criminality or establish a specific cause for an offender's behavior. The theories are limited in other ways as well. They tend to focus on visible crimes and the poor. They have little to say about upper-class or organized crime. Most of the theories also focus on the behavior of males. What is missing, and truly needed, is a theory that merges these disparate ideas about the causes of crime. Once a complete and testable account is devised of what causes crime, better policies can be developed to deal with it (see Table 2.6).

Summary

- Behavior that is defined as criminal varies from society to society and from one era to the next.
- There are five broad categories of crime: occupational crime, organized crime, visible crime, crimes without victims, and political crime.
- Each type has its own level of risk and profitabiity, each arouses varying degrees of public disapproval, and each has its own group of offenders with differing characteristics.
- Today's crime problem is not unique. Throughout the history of the United States, crime has reached high levels at different times.
- Violent crime is the only type that occurs at a higher rate in the United States than in similar countries.
- The amount of crime is difficult to measure. The *Uniform Crime Reports* and the National Crime Victimization Survey are the best sources of crime data.
- Only in recent decades have researchers directed their attention to the victims of crime. Research has focused on who is victimized, the impact of crime, the experiences of victims in the criminal justice system, and victim precipitation of crime.

- The classical school of criminology emphasized reform of the criminal law, procedures, and punishments.
- The rise of science led to the positivist school, which viewed behavior as stemming from social, biological, and psychological factors.
- Positivist criminology has dominated the study of criminal behavior in the twentieth century.
- The criminality of women has only recently been studied. It is argued that, as women become more equal with men in society, crimes committed by females will increase in number.

Questions for Review

❶ What are the five types of crimes?

❷ What are the positive and negative attributes of the two major sources of crime data?

❸ What are the four types of victimization studies?

❹ What are the major theories of criminality?

Key Terms

anomie (p. 72)
biological explanations (p. 70)
classical criminology (p. 68)
control theory (p. 73)
crimes without victims (p. 46)
criminogenic (p. 69)
cybercrime (p. 48)
dark figure of crime (p. 53)
labeling theory (p. 73)
learning theories (p. 73)

mala in se (p. 40)
mala prohibita (p. 41)
money laundering (p. 44)
National Crime Victimization Survey (NCVS) (p. 57)
National Incident-Based Reporting System (NIBRS) (p. 57)
occupational crime (p. 42)
organized crime (p. 43)
political crime (p. 47)

positivist criminology (p. 68)
psychological explanations (p. 70)
social conflict theories (p. 74)
social process theories (p. 73)
social structure theories (p. 72)
sociological explanations (p. 72)
theory of differential association (p. 73)
Uniform Crime Reports (UCR) (p. 54)
victimology (p. 60)
visible crime (p. 45)

For Further Reading

Butterfield, Fox. *All God's Children: The Bosket Family and the American Tradition of Violence.* New York: Avon, 1996. A detailed account of the transmission of a culture of violence through multiple generations of one family.

Erikson, Kai T. *Wayward Puritans.* New York: Wiley, 1966. A classic analysis of three "crime waves" in Puritan New England.

Friedrichs, David O. *Trusted Criminals: White-Collar Crime in Contemporary Society.* Belmont, Calif.: Wadsworth Publishing, 1996. Overview of the many facets of white-collar crime and the challenge of responding to that criminality.

Heidensohn, Frances M. *Women and Crime.* New York: New York University Press, 1985. An account and critique of criminological and sociological writings on women and criminality.

Katz, Jack. *Seductions of Crime: Moral and Sensual Attractions of Doing Evil.* New York: Basic Books, 1988. A challenge to positivist criminology that argues there is an emotional appeal to "being bad" and "being hard."

Messner, Steven F., and Richard Rosenfeld. *Crime and the American Dream.* Belmont, Calif.: Wadsworth Publishing, 1994. Argues that high levels of serious crime result from the normal functioning of the American social system.

Rhodes, Richard. *Why They Kill: The Discoveries of a Maverick Criminologist.* New York: Knopf, 1999. Exploration of the ideas of criminologist Lonnie Athens who challenges the theory that violent behavior is impulsive, unconsciously motivated and predetermined.

Going Online

❶ Access the Racketeer Influenced and Corrupt Organizations Act (Title 18 U.S.C., Chapter 96) at www4.law. Cornell.edu/USCode/18. Examine the act's definition of "racketeering activity." What activities are listed?

❷ Access the *Uniform Crime Reports* at www.fbi.gov. What is the crime rate for the eight index offenses?

❸ Go to the web site of the University of Dayton School of Law at www.cybercrimes.net. List the types of cybercrimes described there.

❹ Using **InfoTrac College Edition**, enter the keywords *aged crime victims.* Read the article, "Police Practice: Assisting Senior Victims," *FBI Law Enforcement Bulletin* (February/ March 1996). How does the Senior Victims Assistance Team of the Colorado Springs police department work? What assistance to elderly crime victims does it provide?

1. Elected representatives in state legislatures and Congress.

2. *Mala in se*—offenses that are wrong in themselves (murder, rape, assault). *Mala prohibita*—acts that are crimes because they are prohibited (vagrancy, gambling, drug use).

3. Occupational crime, organized crime, visible crime, crimes without victims, political crime.

4. Occupational crimes are committed in a variety of employment contexts other than those involving the traditonal view of white-collar workers' criminality.

5. To provide goods and services that are in high demand but are illegal.

6. Poor people.

7. These are crimes against morality in which the people involved do not believe they have been victimized.

8. Crimes such as treason committed for a political purpose.

9. No, there have been other eras when crime was high.

10. Only violent crimes.

11. *Uniform Crime Reports,* National Crime Victimization Survey.

12. Demography, unemployment, housing conditions, family structure.

13. Demographic characteristics, adaptations, lifestyle, associations, exposure.

14. Most victimized: young black males. Least victimized: elderly white women.

15. Fear, financial costs, emotional costs, lifestyle restrictions.

16. Because they learn about crime through the media and conversations that emphasize the most shocking crimes.

17. Financial costs (lost property, medical care); psychological and emotional costs; costs of the criminal justice system.

18. Failing to take precautions; taking actions that may provoke or entice; not assisting police with investigations.

19. Criminal behavior is rational, and the fear of punishment keeps people from committing crimes.

20. Criminal behavior is the product of social, biological, and psychological factors.

21. Offenders are born criminals and have traits that mark them.

22. A person who is unable to control impulses, cannot learn from experience, and does not have normal human emotions.

23. Crime is a creation of lower-class culture based on poverty and deprivation and the response of the poor to this situation.

24. Everyone has the potential of becoming a criminal, depending on the influences that impel one toward or away from crime and on how one is regarded by others.

25. Criminal law and the criminal justice system are primarily a means of controlling the poor and the have-nots.

26. The idea that women would commit more crimes as they became liberated.

27. Larceny-theft and drug offenses.

Criminal Justice and the Rule of Law

In 1998, 25-year-old Timothy Boomer went canoeing down the Rifle River in rural

Arenac County, Michigan, 130 miles north of Detroit. Boomer and several friends drank beer

and enjoyed themselves as they floated down the river. Along the way, Boomer's canoe hit a

rock and he was thrown into the water. He reacted to the unexpected dunking by venting his

surprise and frustration with a few choice words. When the event was later described in

court testimony, both the county prosecutor and Boomer's friends agreed that his words

included profanity. Disagreement arose, however, about exactly what Boomer said and how

he said it. Boomer's friends testified that he said the "f-word" a few times but did not yell.

By contrast, the prosecution's witnesses claimed that Boomer screamed the "f-word" at

least twenty-five times. In American society, hearing profanity is not always surprising,

such as when angry drivers yell at each other while bickering over a parking space

or even in movies available for rent at any video store. Despite the regular use of such language in certain contexts, Boomer's use of profanity sent him to criminal court. Arenac County prosecutor Richard Vollbach charged Boomer for violating a Michigan law enacted in 1897 that made it a crime to curse in front of women and children. Because women and children were present on the river when Boomer used profanity, he faced the possibility of ninety days in jail and a $100 fine if convicted of the offense. After a brief trial ended on June 11, 1999, a jury composed of Arenac County citizens deliberated for less than hour before finding Boomer guilty of the crime.

Boomer's case raises many interesting and important questions. Was Boomer's action truly a "crime"? Didn't his right to freedom of speech permit him to say whatever he wanted? Why should it be a crime to swear in front of women and children, but not in front of men? More importantly, in a society that faces problems with murder, rape, drug trafficking, robbery, and other harmful criminal acts, is it worthwhile for prosecutors and judges to spend their time focusing on someone accused of using profanity? Does it make sense to use scarce jail space to punish someone for uttering offensive words? Moving closer to home, have you ever heard someone use profanity in front of women and children? If so, do you believe that person deserves to be sent to jail? Although these issues are worthy of debate, the reality for Timothy Boomer was that he faced the prospect of spending time in jail for doing something that millions of other people have done (and continue to do every day) with no punishment more severe than looks of disapproval from those who feel offended by profanity.

How can the use of profanity possibly be a crime? Easily. It can be a crime for the same reason that any other human action becomes a crime: a legislature enacts a law declaring a particular behavior to be deserving of criminal punishment. One of the primary functions of criminal law is to define those behaviors that are labeled criminal and, thus, worthy of punishment. Legislatures bear primary responsibility for defining crimes, but judges frequently interpret what legislators meant in establishing criminal offenses. A second primary function of criminal law is to describe the procedures to be followed under the U.S. adversarial system by those responsible for law enforcement, adjudication, and corrections. Legislatures enact statutes to establish procedures, but these procedures are frequently modified as judges determine if any processes violate the rights of criminal defendants. Criminal law must also address other important issues, such as who may be held responsible for various crimes. Could Boomer have been convicted of his crime if he had been 11 years old and used profanity in front of other children? What if Boomer had been mentally ill? In defining crimes, a person's mental status and intentions are often considered. Thus, for example, the use of the insanity defense is permitted. Furthermore, intentional acts are punished more harshly than inadvertent actions. Intentional crimes, such as premeditated murder, are more serious than negligent harmful acts, such as involuntarily manslaughter. The definitions of crimes and people eligible for punishment are spelled out in **substantive criminal law.** By contrast, **procedural criminal law** concerns the processes followed by police, prosecutors, and judges as well as the rights possessed by suspects and defendants, such as the right to trial by jury.

In previous chapters, we saw how criminal justice operates as a system influenced by political and social forces; now we turn to the third ingredient of our analysis—law. This chapter explores the two main aspects of criminal law: substantive criminal law and the law of criminal procedure.

substantive criminal law
Law defining the acts that are subject to punishment, and specifying the punishments for such offenses.

procedural criminal law
Law defining the procedures that criminal justice officials must follow in enforcement, adjudication, and correction.

QUESTIONS
for Inquiry

- What are the bases and sources of American criminal law?
- How does substantive criminal law define a crime and the legal responsibility of the accused?
- How does procedural criminal law define the rights of the accused and the processes for dealing with a case?
- How has the United States Supreme Court interpreted the criminal justice amendments to the Constitution?

Foundations of Criminal Law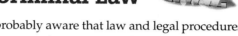

Like most Americans, you are probably aware that law and legal procedures are key elements of the criminal justice system. Americans are fond of saying that "we have a government of laws, not of men (and women)." The United States does not have a system based on the decisions of a king or dictator. Presidents, governors, and mayors cannot simply choose to punish people they dislike. Instead, even America's most powerful leaders must make decisions within limits imposed by law.

Laws tell citizens what they can and cannot do. Laws also tell government officials when they can seek to punish citizens for violations and how they must go about it. Government officials may not do whatever they want. They must follow and enforce the law. Thus, in a democracy, laws are a major tool to prevent government officials from seizing too much power or using power improperly.

Substantive Law and Procedural Law

Criminal law is only one category of law. Peoples' lives and actions are also affected by **civil law,** which governs business deals, contracts, real estate, and the like. For example, if you damage other people's property or harm them in an accident, they may sue you to pay for the damage or harm. By contrast, the key feature of criminal law is the government's power to punish people for harm they have done to society.

Criminal law is divided into two categories, substantive and procedural. Substantive criminal law defines actions that may be punished by the government. It also defines the punishments for such offenses. Often called the "penal code," substantive law answers the question "*What* is illegal?" Elected officials in Congress, state legislatures, and city councils write the substantive criminal laws. These legislators decide which kinds of behaviors are so harmful that they deserve to be punished. They also decide whether each violation should be punished by imprisonment, a fine, probation, or in another way. When questions arise about the meaning of substantive criminal laws, judges interpret the laws by seeking to fulfill the legislators' intentions.

By contrast, procedural criminal law defines the rules that govern *how* the laws will be enforced. It protects the constitutional rights of defendants and provides the rules that officials must follow in all areas of the criminal justice system. Many aspects of procedural criminal law are defined by legislatures, such as how

civil law
Law regulating the relationships between or among individuals, usually involving property, contract, or business disputes.

bail will be set and which kind of preliminary hearing will take place before a trial. However, the U.S. Supreme Court and state supreme courts also play a key role in defining procedural criminal law. These courts define the meaning of constitutional rights in the U.S. Constitution and in state constitutions. Their interpretations of constitutional provisions create rules on such issues as when and how police officers can question suspects and when defendants can receive advice from their attorneys. Procedural criminal law answers the question "*How* is the law enforced?"

CHECK POINT

① **What is contained in a state's penal code?**

② **What is the purpose of procedural criminal law?**

(Answers are at the end of the chapter.)

Sources of Criminal Law

The earliest known codes of law appeared in the Sumerian law of Mesopotamia (3100 B.C.) and the Code of Hammurabi (1750 B.C.). These written codes were divided into sections to cover different types of offenses. Other important ancestors of Western law are the Draconian Code, produced in the seventh century B.C. in Greece and the Law of the Twelve Tables, created by the Romans (450 B.C.). However, the main source of American law is the **common law** of England.

The Draconian Code, promulgated in classical Greece in the seventh century B.C., is one of the earliest foundations of Western law.

Common Law

Common law was based on custom and tradition as interpreted by judges. In continental Europe, a system of civil law developed in which the rules were set down in detailed codes produced by legislatures or other governing authorities. By contrast, the common law of England was not written down as a list of rules. Instead, it took its form from the collected opinions of the judges, who looked to custom in making their decisions. The judges created law when they ruled on specific cases. These rulings, also known as *precedents,* established legal principles to be used in making decisions on similar cases. When such cases arose, judges looked to the principles arising from earlier rulings to find the ones that applied to the type of case they were deciding. Over time, as new kinds of situations emerged, judges had to create new legal principles to address them. As more rulings on various kinds of legal issues were written down, they grew into a body of law—composed of principles and reasoning—that other judges could use in deciding their own cases. The use of a common set of precedents made the application of law more stable and consistent. Moreover, the judges' ability to adjust legal principles when new kinds of situations arose made the common law flexible enough to respond to changes in society.

The English precedents and procedures were maintained in the American colonies, but after independence the states began to make some changes in the law. For example, the definitions of crimes and punishments in the English common law were often enacted into penal codes by state legislatures. Although these legislative actions altered the nature and force of common law, they did not eliminate the common law process. American courts still create precedents when they interpret laws passed by legislatures and the provisions of federal and state constitutions. These judicial rulings guide the decisions of American courts on issues concerning both substantive and procedural criminal law.

Written Law

Having a document that clearly stated the criminal law, both substantive and procedural, would be helpful. It would allow citizens to know when they might be in danger of committing an illegal act and to be aware of their rights if official action were taken against them. If such a document could be written in simple language, society would probably need fewer lawyers. However, writing such a document is not possible. U.S. criminal laws and procedures are too complex to be reduced to simple terms. The scope and complexity of criminal law are constantly expanding. In defining new illegal acts—such as pirating of videotaped films or fraud in electronic filing of tax returns—the law must be able to respond to unfamiliar, complex problems. Moreover, any effort to reduce rules to words on a page creates opportunities for those words to be interpreted in different ways. If a crime is called "negligent homicide," for example, how will "negligence" be defined? The need for interpretation means that lawyers and judges will always have a role in shaping—and changing—the meaning of both substantive and procedural law.

Because a single, complete document that provides the details of criminal law cannot be compiled, society will continue to rely on four sources of law: constitutions, statutes, court decisions (also known as case law), and administrative regulations.

Constitutions contain basic principles and procedural safeguards. The Constitution of the United States was written in Philadelphia in 1787 and went into effect in 1789 after it had been ratified by the required number of states. It sets forth the country's governing system and describes the institutions (legislature, courts, and president) that make and execute its laws. The first ten amendments to the Constitution, together known as the Bill of Rights, were added in 1791. Most of these amendments provide protections against governmental actions that would violate basic rights and liberties. Several have a direct bearing on the criminal law, because they guarantee the rights of due process, jury trial, and representation by counsel, as well as protection against unreasonable searches and cruel and unusual punishments. Most state constitutions also contain protections against actions by state and local governments. During the early 1960s the U.S. Supreme Court decided to require state and local governments to respect most of the rights listed in the Bill of Rights. (Before that time the Bill of Rights protected citizens only against actions by the federal government.) As a result of Supreme Court decisions, the power of police officers, prosecutors, and judges is limited by the U.S. Constitution and state constitutions.

Statutes are laws passed by legislative bodies; the substantive and procedural rules of most states are found in their statutes. Although criminal law is written mainly by state legislatures, Congress and local governments also play a role in shaping the law. As discussed in Chapter 1, federal criminal laws passed by Congress deal mainly with violations that occur on the property of the U.S.

common law
The Anglo-American system of uncodified law, in which judges follow precedents set by earlier decisions when they decide new but similar cases. The substantive and procedural criminal law was originally developed in this manner but was later codified—set down in codes—by state legislatures.

constitutions
The basic laws of a country defining the structure of government and the relationship of citizens to that government.

statutes
Laws passed by legislatures. Statutory definitions of criminal offenses are found in penal codes.

government or with acts that involve the national interest (counterfeiting money) or more than one state (taking a kidnap victim across state lines). The states give cities and towns some authority to pass laws dealing with local problems. Some overlap exists among national, state, and local rules governing certain kinds of criminal conduct. Possession or sale of drugs, for example, may violate criminal laws at all three levels of government. In such situations, law enforcement agencies need to decide which one will prosecute the offender.

To find the definition of a crime covered by a statute, one should consult a state's penal code. The acts that constitute a crime and the penalty to be imposed are clearly specified. Although the laws of most states are similar, there are some differences. To make state laws more uniform, the American Law Institute has developed a Model Penal Code that it urges legislatures to adopt.

Court decisions, often called **case law,** are a third source of criminal law. The major principle of the common law system is that judges look to earlier decisions to guide their rulings. Although much of the common law has been replaced by statutes, precedent is still an important aid to lawyers and judges in interpreting penal codes.

Administrative regulations are laws and rules made by federal, state, and local agencies. The legislature, president, or governor has given those agencies the power to make rules governing specific policy areas such as health, safety, and the environment. Most such rules have been produced in the twentieth century to deal with modern problems, such as wages and work hours, pollution, traffic, workplace safety, and pure food and drugs. Many of the rules are part of the criminal law, and violations are processed through the criminal justice system.

As you can see, the criminal law is more than just a penal code written by a state legislature or Congress. The sources of criminal law are summarized in Figure 3.1.

case law

Court decisions that have the status of law and serve as precedents for later decisions.

administrative regulations

Rules made by governmental agencies to implement specific public policies in areas such as public health, environmental protection, and workplace safety.

CHECK POINT

③ **How does the common law shape criminal law?**

④ **What are the forms of written law?**

Felony and Misdemeanor

Crimes are classified by how serious they are. The distinction between a felony and a misdemeanor is one of the oldest in the criminal law. Most laws define felonies and misdemeanors in light of the punishment that may be imposed. Conviction on a felony charge usually means that the offender may be given a prison sentence of more than a year. The most severe felonies may draw the death penalty. Those who commit misdemeanors are dealt with more leniently; the sentence might be a fine, probation, or a prison sentence of less than a year. Some states define the seriousness of the offense according to the place of punishment: prison for felonies, jail for misdemeanors.

Whether a defendant is charged with a felony or a misdemeanor determines not only how the person is punished, but also how the criminal justice system will process the defendant. Certain rights and penalties follow from this distinction. For example, the conditions under which the police may make an arrest and the trial level where the charges will be heard are based on the seriousness of the charge. In 1996, the U.S. Supreme Court declared that people who face less than

FIGURE 3.1   Sources of criminal law

Although codes of law existed in ancient times, American criminal law is derived mainly from the common law of England. The common law distinguishes English-speaking systems from the civil law systems of the rest of the world.

CONSTITUTIONAL LAW

The Constitution of the United States and the state constitutions define the structure of government and the rights of citizens.

STATUTORY LAW

The substantive and procedural criminal laws are found in laws passed by legislative bodies such as the U.S. Congress and state legislatures.

CASE LAW

Consistent with the common law heritage, legal opinions by judges in individual cases have the status of law.

ADMINISTRATIVE LAW

Also having the status of law are some decisions of federal and state governmental agencies that have been given the power to regulate such areas as health, safety, and the environment in the public interest.

six months in prison for a charge are not entitled to a jury trial. The Constitution requires only that they be tried in front of a judge (*Lewis v. United States*).

The distinction between types of crimes also can affect a person's future. People with felony convictions may be barred from certain professions, such as law and medicine, and in many states they are also barred from certain other occupations (bartender, police officer, barber). Felony convictions may also keep people from ever voting, serving on juries, or running for election to public office (Olivares, Burton, and Cullen, 1996).

Criminal versus Civil Law

The legal system makes basic distinctions between criminal and civil law. A violation of criminal law is an offense against society as a whole, while civil law regulates relations between individuals. The focus of the criminal law is on the intent of the wrongdoer. Intentional acts are most deserving of punishment, and the prosecutor may decide to press criminal charges when a harmful event was "an accident." In some cases, both criminal and civil proceedings may arise from the

Although he was found not guilty of murdering Nicole Brown Simpson and Ron Goldman, O. J. Simpson lost a civil suit brought by their families. To satisfy that judgment his golf equipment and other personal property, including the 1968 Heisman Trophy, were sold at auction.

civil forfeiture

The confiscation of property by the state as punishment for a crime. In recent years the police have used civil forfeiture to seize property that they believe was purchased with drug profits.

same event. If you are hunting and you carelessly fire a shot that crashes through the window of a home and wounds the homeowner, the homeowner may bring a civil suit against you to recover the cost of the damage you caused. The damage could include paying for medical bills and the cost of fixing the window. This legal action falls within the area of civil law known as *torts,* which deals with compensation for injured individuals. In a separate action the state may charge you with a violation of the criminal law because your actions violated society's rules for the lawful use of firearms.

Although criminal and civil law are distinct, both attempt to control human behavior by steering people to act in a desired manner and imposing costs on those who violate social rules. Increasingly, civil suits are being brought against offenders who previously were subject only to criminal charges. For example, some rape victims have brought civil suits against their attackers, and some department stores are suing shoplifters for large amounts. Rape victims have successfully sued apartment complexes for failing to maintain secure conditions that would prevent criminal attacks. Victims could even win civil lawsuits against defendants who have been acquitted of criminal charges. Such was the case when the families of murder victims Nicole Brown Simpson and Ronald Goldman won a wrongful death lawsuit worth millions of dollars against O. J. Simpson, despite the retired football star's acquittal on criminal charges of murder. To gain a criminal conviction, prosecutors must persuade the jury or judge of the existence of proof showing the defendant's guilt "beyond a reasonable doubt." The Simpson jury in the criminal case did not believe that the evidence met this high standard of proof. In the later civil trial, however, a jury believed that the evidence satisfied the lower civil law standard of showing by a "preponderance of evidence" that Simpson was most likely responsible for the two deaths.

Another example of a link between criminal and civil law is **civil forfeiture.** This concept, derived from English common law, allows for the taking of property and has increasingly been applied in drug law enforcement (Stahl, 1992).

U.S. courts have distinguished between forfeiture actions *in personam* (against a person) and those in *rem* (against a thing). A case brought against a person is treated as criminal, and forfeiture may result if the offender is convicted. Actions in *rem* are civil cases based on the idea that the issue is the guilt or innocence of the property itself. As Supreme Court Justice Stephen J. Field explained in *Miller v. United States* (1871), "The thing is the instrument of wrong, and is forfeited by reason of the unlawful use made of it. . . . [P]roceedings in *rem* [are] wholly independent of, and unaffected by, the criminal proceedings against the person." Thus, one finds court dockets that include cases titled *United States v. One Assortment of 89 Firearms* or *United States v. One 1986 Chevrolet Van.* Forfeiture can even affect property owners who are not guilty of any crime. In 1996 the U.S. Supreme Court decided that, despite her innocence, a wife lost her ownership rights in a car when her husband used the vehicle to pick up a prostitute (*Bennis v. Michigan*). The use of forfeiture by law enforcement agencies has generated controversy, especially when applied against people who have never been convicted of any crime. In 1999, the U.S. House of Representatives voted overwhelmingly to limit the government's authority to seize property through forfeiture, but it was unclear whether the Senate would approve the legislation (Labaton, 1999).

The bases of the American criminal law are complex. The English common law and the laws found in such written sources as constitutions, statutes, case law, and administrative regulations all contribute to what most people call "the criminal law." Within this body of law, a major division exists between the substantive criminal law and procedural criminal law.

POINT

⑤ **What is the difference between a felony and a misdemeanor?**

⑥ **What types of legal issues arise in civil law cases?**

Substantive Criminal Law

The substantive criminal law defines acts that are subject to punishment and specifies the punishments. It is based on the doctrine that no one may be convicted of or punished for an offense unless the offense has been defined by the law. In short, people must know in advance what is required of them. Thus, no act can be regarded as illegal until it has been defined as punishable under the criminal law. While this sounds like a simple notion, the language of law is often confusing and ambiguous. As a result, judges must become involved in interpreting the law so that the meaning intended by the legislature can be understood.

Seven Principles of Criminal Law

Legal scholar Jerome Hall (1947) has developed a seven-point formalization of the major principles of Western law. For a behavior to be defined as criminal and subject to the penalties of the law, a prosecutor must prove that all seven principles have been fulfilled (see Figure 3.2).

❶ *Legality.* A law must define the specific action as a crime. Offensive and harmful behavior is not illegal unless it has been prohibited by law before it was committed. The U.S. Constitution forbids ex post facto laws, or laws written and applied after the fact. Thus, when the legislature defines a new crime, people can be prosecuted only for violations that occur after the new law has been passed.

❷ *Actus reus.* Criminal laws are aimed at human acts, including acts that a person failed to undertake. The U.S. Supreme Court has ruled that people may not be convicted of a crime simply because of their status. Under this *actus reus* requirement, for a crime to occur an act of either commission or omission must have been committed by the accused. In *Robinson v. California* (1962), for example, the Supreme Court struck down a California law that made it a crime to be addicted to drugs. States can prosecute people for using, possessing, selling, or transporting drugs when they catch them performing these acts, but states cannot prosecute them for the mere status of being addicted to drugs.

FIGURE

3.2 **The seven principles of criminal law**

These principles of Western law are the basis for defining acts as criminal and the conditions required for successful prosecution.

A crime is	
1 legally proscribed	(legality)
2 human conduct	(*actus reus*)
3 causative	(causation)
4 of a given harm	(harm)
5 which conduct coincides	(concurrence)
6 with a blameworthy frame of mind	(*mens rea*)
7 and is subject to punishment	(punishment)

❸ *Causation.* For a crime to have been committed, a causal relationship must be evident between an act and the harm suffered. In Ohio, for example, a prosecutor tried to convict a burglary suspect on a manslaughter charge when a victim, asleep in his house, was killed by a stray bullet as officers fired at the unarmed, fleeing suspect. The burglar was acquitted on the homicide charge because his actions in committing the burglary and running away from the police were not the direct cause of the victim's death (Bandy, 1991).

❹ *Harm.* To be a crime, an act must cause harm to some legally protected value. The harm can be to a person, property, or some other object that a legislature deems valuable enough to deserve protection through the government's power to punish. This principle is often questioned by those who feel that they are not committing a crime because they may be causing harm only to themselves. Laws that require motorcyclists to wear helmets have been challenged on this ground. Such laws, however, have been written because legislatures see enough forms of harm to require protective laws. In the motorcyclists example, these forms of harm include injuries to helmetless riders, tragedy and loss for families of injured cyclists, and the medical costs imposed on society for head injuries that could have been prevented.

An act can be deemed criminal if it could do harm that the law seeks to prevent; this is called an **inchoate offense.** Thus, the criminal law includes conspiracies and attempted criminal actions, even when the lawbreaker does not complete the intended crime. For example, people can be prosecuted for planning to murder someone or hiring a "hit man" to kill someone. The potential for grave harm from such acts justifies the application of the government's power to punish.

❺ *Concurrence.* For an act to be considered a crime, the intent and the act must be present at the same time (Hall, 1947:85). Let's imagine that Joe is planning to murder his archenemy, Bill. He spends days planning how he will abduct Bill and carry out the murder. While driving home from work one day, Joe accidentally hits and kills a jogger who suddenly—and foolishly—ran across the busy street without looking. The jogger turns out to be Bill. Although Joe had planned to kill Bill, he is not guilty of murder because the accidental killing was not connected to Joe's intent to carry out a killing.

❻ *Mens rea.* The commission of an act is not a crime unless it is accompanied by a guilty state of mind. This concept is related to intent. It seeks to distinguish between harm-causing accidents, which generally are not subject to criminal punishment, and harm-causing *crimes,* in which some level of intent is present. Certain crimes require a specific level of intent; examples include first-degree murder, which is normally a planned, intentional killing, and larceny, which involves the intent to permanently and unlawfully deprive an owner of his or her property. Several defenses, such as necessity and insanity, can be used to assert that a person did not have *mens rea*—a "guilty mind" or blameworthy state of mind—and hence should not be held responsible for a criminal offense. The element of *mens rea* becomes problematic when questions arise about an offender's capability of understanding or planning harmful activities, as when the perpetrator is mentally ill or a child.

---

inchoate offense

Conduct that is criminal even though the harm that the law seeks to prevent has not been done but merely planned or attempted.

---

mens rea

"Guilty mind" or blameworthy state of mind, necessary for legal responsibility for a criminal offense; criminal intent, as distinguished from innocent intent.

Exceptions to the concept of *mens rea* are strict liability offenses involving health and safety, in which showing intent is not necessary. Legislatures have criminalized certain kinds of offenses to protect the public. For example, a business owner may be held responsible for violations of a toxic waste law whether or not the owner knew that his employees were dumping polluting substances into a river. Other laws may apply strict liability to the sale of alcoholic beverages to minors. The purpose of such laws is to put pressure on business owners to make sure that their employees obey regulations designed to protect the health and safety of the public. Courts often limit the application of such laws to situations in which recklessness or indifference is present.

❼ *Punishment*. A provision in the law must call for punishment of those found guilty of violating the law. The punishment is enforced by the government and may carry with it loss of freedom, social stigma, a criminal record, and loss of rights.

The seven principles of substantive criminal law allow authorities to define certain acts as being against the law and provide the accused with a basis for mounting a defense against the charges. During a criminal trial, defense attorneys will often try to show that one of the seven elements either is unproven or can be explained in a way that is acceptable under the law.

Not all societies and cultures base their criminal law on the same principles. As can be seen in the Comparative Perspective (p. 94), other countries base their laws on different principles (Souryal, Potts, and Alobied, 1994). Laws typically reflect the values and traditions of a society. Criminal law may be based on religious tenets instead of laws enacted by legislatures. The values protected by the law may also differ. In the United States, *defamation*—slander or libel by making false statements that harm someone else's reputation—is addressed by civil tort law. A person can sue to gain compensation from someone who harms his or her reputation. By contrast, under Islamic law certain kinds of defamation may be punished by society as criminal offenses.

Although it is important to remember that the nature and content of criminal law differ according to the traditions, values, and social structures of various countries, differences can also be seen among the laws of various states within the United States. As indicated in the description of Islamic law, alcoholic beverages are forbidden. While American law is generally thought of as permitting drinking, differences exist among states' laws and these differences, as with the Islamic example, may be influenced by religious values. Most notably, Utah has significant restrictions on the availability of alcoholic beverages. Liquor is served only at clubs with dues-paying members and at a limited number of restaurants that are not allowed to advertise that they have a liquor license. Grocery stores can sell only low-alcoholic-content beer. Moreover, it is a crime for anyone other than a licensed dealer to bring alcoholic beverages into the state. The restrictions on drinking in Utah are usually attributed to the political dominance of Mormons, members of a religion that forbids drinking (Foy, 1999). In learning about Islamic law and its differences from criminal law in the United States, think about differences in the definitions of crimes and punishments in the United States that also reflect the way in which law is shaped by values and traditions.

CHECK POINT

❼ **What are the seven principles of criminal law?**

COMPARATIVE

perspective

Islamic Criminal Law

The rise of fundamentalist Islamic thought throughout the world has made Americans aware of great cultural differences between Westerners and people elsewhere in the world. Islamic criminal law, in particular, appears to be at odds with justice as it is administered in the West. What are some of the major differences that exist between the two systems of law? How is Islamic criminal law a reflection of a nation's culture?

Americans were shocked to read in November 1996 the graphic description of the stoning of two adulterers in Afghanistan before thousands of witnesses. The condemned woman was lowered into a pit dug into the earth so that only her chest and head were above ground. Her lover was blindfolded and taken to a spot about twenty paces away and stood before the Muslim cleric who was the judge. Between the condemned were two piles of stones. The judge threw the first stone at the woman. Quickly stones thrown by military men hailed down on the condemned. Death came after ten minutes to the male, but longer to the female. Her son stepped forward and told the judge she was still alive. At this point one of the men picked up a large rock and dropped it on her head, killing her.

To the West, justice in Islamic states—such as Iran, Afghanistan, Pakistan, and Sudan—seems harsh and unforgiving. The practices of stoning for adultery and amputation for theft are often given as examples of the ferocity of Islamic law. What most Americans do not realize is that the *Shari'a,*

An Afghanistani reenacts his role in the stoning execution of a couple for adultery under Islamic law.

Islamic *Hudud* offenses, required proofs, and punishments

CRIME	PROOF	PUNISHMENT
Adultery	Four witnesses or confessions	Married persons: stoning to death. Convict is taken to a barren site. Stones are thrown first by witnesses, then by the *qadi*, and finally by the rest of the community. For a woman, a grave is dug to receive the body. Unmarried person: 100 lashes. *Maliki* school also punishes unmarried males with one year in prison or exile.
Defamation	Unsupported accusation of adultery	Free: 80 lashes. Slave: 40 lashes. Convict is lightly attired when whipped.
Apostasy	Two witnesses or confessions	Male: death by beheading. Female: imprisonment until repentance.
Highway robbery	Two witnesses or confessions	With homicide: death by beheading. The body is then displayed in a crucifixion-like form. Without homicide: amputation of right hand and left foot. If arrested before commission: imprisonment until repentance.
Use of alcohol	Two witnesses or confessions	Free: 80 lashes (*Shafi'i*, 40). Slave: 40 lashes. Public whipping is applied with a stick, using moderate force without raising the hand above the head so as not to lacerate the skin. Blows are spread over the body and are not to be applied to the face and head. A male stands, and a female is seated. A doctor is present. Flogging is inflicted by scholars well versed in Islamic law, so that it is justly meted out.
Theft	Two witnesses or confessions	First offense: amputation of hand at wrist, by an authorized doctor. Second offense: amputation of second hand at wrist, by an authorized doctor. Third offense: amputation of foot at ankle, by an authorized doctor, or imprisonment until repentance.
Rebellion	Two witnesses or confessions	If captured: death. If surrendered or arrested: *Ta'azir* punishment.

SOURCE: From "Hudud Crimes," by A. A. Mansour, in M. C. Bassiouni (ed.), *The Islamic Criminal Justice System*, 195. Copyright © 1982 by Oceana Publications. *The New York Times*, November 3, 1996, p. A18.

the law of Islam, provides judicial and evidentiary safeguards. Islamic criminal law is concerned with (1) the safety of the public from physical attack, insult, and humiliation, (2) the stability of the family, (3) the protection of property against theft, destruction, or unauthorized interference, and (4) the protection of the government and the Islamic faith against subversion.

Criminal acts are divided into three categories. *Hudud* offenses are crimes against God, and punishment is specified in the Koran and the Sunna, a compilation of Muhammad's statements. *Quesas* are crimes of physical assault and murder, which are punishable by retaliation—"the return of

life for a life in case of murder." As shown below for the seven *Hudud* offenses, the Koran defines the crime, specifies the elements of proof required, and sets the punishment.

THEFT

Theft is the taking of property belonging to another, the value of which is equal to or exceeds a prescribed amount, usually set at ten dirhams or about seventy-five cents. The property must be taken from the custody of another person in a secret manner, and the thief must obtain full possession of the property. "Custody" requires that the

property should have been under guard or in a place of safekeeping.

By contrast, American criminal law focuses on ownership, not custody, so that stealing something left in the open, including items sitting unattended in public places, clearly fall under laws against theft if the offender intends to take items known to be owned by others.

EXTRAMARITAL SEXUAL ACTIVITY

Sexual relations outside marriage are believed to undermine marriage and lead to family conflict, jealousy, divorce, litigation, and the spread of disease.

Some American states continue to criminalize adultery and premarital cohabitation through old laws that remain on the books. However, these laws are rarely enforced and many prosecutors doubt whether juries will convict people of such offenses because society has become more tolerant of such commonplace behavior.

DEFAMATION

In addition to false accusations of fornication, this offense includes impugning the legitimacy of a woman's child. Defamation by a husband of his wife leads to divorce and is not subject to punishment.

Defamation under American law can lead to civil lawsuits concerning harmful falsehoods spoken or written about a person that significantly harm that person's reputation.

HIGHWAY ROBBERY

This crime interferes with commerce and creates fear among travelers and is therefore subject to punishment.

American robbery statutes typically apply in all contexts and are not focused on travelers. The primary exception is "carjacking" statutes that were enacted by Congress and state legislatures in response to highly publicized incidents of drivers being killed and injured by robbers who forcibly stole their vehicles as they sat at traffic lights or stop signs.

USE OF ALCOHOL

Drinking wine and other intoxicating beverages is prohibited because it brings about indolence and inattention to religious duties.

By contrast, alcoholic beverages are legal in the United States, subject to regulations concerning the legal drinking age and criminal statutes concerning the operation of vehicles while under the influence of alcohol.

APOSTASY

This is the voluntary renunciation of Islam. The offense is committed by any Muslim who converts to another faith, worships idols, or rejects any of the tenets of Islam.

In the United States, the First Amendment protections for freedom of religion and freedom of speech permit people to change religions and to criticize the religions of others without fear of criminal prosecution.

REBELLION

The intentional, forceful overthrow or attempted overthrow of the legitimate leader of the Islamic state constitutes rebellion.

In the United States, the government can change only through the process of democratic elections. Any effort to use force as the means to overthrow the government will result in criminal prosecutions.

SOURCE: From *Islamic Criminal Law and Procedure: An Introduction,* by M. Lippman, S. McConville, and M. Yerushalmi, 42–43. Copyright © 1988 by Praeger Publishers. Reprinted by permission of Greenwood Publishing Group, Inc., Westport, Conn. From "Hudud Crimes," by A. A. Mansour, in M. C. Bassiouni (ed.), *The Islamic Criminal Justice System,* 195. Copyright © 1982 by Oceana Publications. *New York Times,* November 3, 1996, p. A18.

Elements of a Crime

Legislatures define certain acts as crimes when they fulfill the seven principles under certain "attendant circumstances" while the offender has a certain state of mind. These three factors—the act (*actus reus*), the attendant circumstances, and the state of mind (*mens rea*)—are together called the elements of a crime. They can be seen in the following section from a state penal code:

> Section 3502. Burglary
>
> 1 **Offense defined:** A person is guilty of burglary if he enters a building or occupied structure, or separately secured or occupied portion thereof, with intent to commit a crime therein, unless the premises are at the time open to the public or the actor is licensed or privileged to enter.

The elements of burglary are, therefore, entering a building or occupied structure (*actus reus*) with the intent to commit a crime therein (*mens rea*) at a time when the premises are not open to the public and the actor is not invited or otherwise entitled to enter (attendant circumstances). For an act to be a burglary, all three elements must be present.

Even if the accused appears to have committed a crime, prosecution will be successful only if the elements match the court's interpretations of the law. For example, Pennsylvania judges have interpreted the *actus reus* of burglary to include entering a building that is open to the public, such as a store or tavern, so long as the entry was "willful and malicious—that is, made with the intent to commit a felony therein." Thus, in Pennsylvania one can be convicted of burglary for entering a store with the intent to steal even though the entry was made during business hours and without force.

Statutory Definitions of Crimes

Federal and state penal codes often define criminal acts somewhat differently. To find out how a state defines an offense, one must read its penal code; this will give a general idea of which acts are illegal. To understand the court's interpretations of the code, one must analyze the judicial opinions that have sought to clarify the law.

In the following discussion we focus on two of the eight index crimes of the *Uniform Crime Reports* (UCR), homicide and rape. The elements of these crimes are interpreted differently in different states.

Murder and Non-negligent Manslaughter

The common law definition of criminal homicide has been subdivided into degrees of murder and voluntary and involuntary manslaughter. In addition, some states have created new categories, such as reckless homicide, negligent homicide, and vehicular homicide. Each of these definitions involves slight variations in the *actus reus* and the *mens rea*. Table 3.1 defines these offenses according to the *Uniform Crime Reports,* which counts murder and non-negligent manslaughter as index offenses.

In legal language, the phrase *malice aforethought* is used to distinguish murder from manslaughter. This phrase indicates that the crime of murder is a deliberate, premeditated, and willful killing of another human being. Most states extend the definition of murder to these two circumstances: (1) defendants knew their behavior had a strong chance of causing death, showed indifference to life, and thus recklessly engaged in conduct that caused death, or (2) defendants' behavior caused death while they were committing a felony. Mitigating circumstances, such as "the heat of passion" or extreme provocation, would reduce the offense to manslaughter because the requirement of malice aforethought would be absent or reduced. Likewise, manslaughter would include a death resulting from an attempt to defend oneself that was not fully excused as self-defense. It might also include a death resulting from recklessness or negligence.

Rape

In recent years mounting pressure has been exerted, especially by women's groups, for stricter enforcement of laws against rape and for greater sensitivity toward victims. Successful prosecution of suspected rapists is difficult because proving *actus reus* and *mens rea* may not be possible (Hickey, 1993). Because the act usually takes place in private, prosecutors may have difficulty showing that sexual intercourse took place without consent. Some states have required evidence from someone other than the victim. Force is a necessary element in the definition of rape. In some courts, the absence of injury to the victim's body has been taken to show that there was no resistance, which may imply that consent was given. Since the 1970s, many

TABLE 3.1   **Definitions of offenses in the *Uniform Crime Reports* (Part 1)**

The exact descriptions of offenses differ from one state to another, but these *Uniform Crime Reports* definitions provide a national standard that distinguishes among criminal acts.

1 **Criminal homicide:**

a. Murder and nonnegligent manslaughter: the willful (nonnegligent) killing of one human being by another. Deaths caused by negligence, attempts to kill, assaults to kill, suicides, accidental deaths and justifiable homicides are excluded. Justifiable homicides are limited to: (1) the killing of a felon by a law enforcement officer in the line of duty; and (2) the killing of a felon by a private citizen.

b. Manslaughter by negligence: the killing of another person through gross negligence. Excludes traffic fatalities. While manslaughter by negligence is a Part I crime, it is not included in the Crime Index.

2 **Forcible rape:**

The carnal knowledge of a female forcibly and against her will. Included are rapes by force and attempts or assaults to rape. Statutory offenses (no force used—victim under age of consent) are excluded.

3 **Robbery:**

The taking or attempting to take anything of value from the care, custody, or control of a person or persons by force or threat of force of violence and/or by putting the victim in fear.

4 **Aggravated assault:**

An unlawful attack by one person upon another for the purpose of inflicting severe or aggravated bodily injury. This type of assault usually is accompanied by the use of a weapon or by means likely to produce death or great bodily harm. Simple assaults are excluded.

5 **Burglary—breaking or entering:**

The unlawful entry of a structure to commit a felony or a theft. Attempted forcible entry is included.

6 **Larceny-theft (except motor vehicle theft):**

The unlawful taking, carrying, leading, or riding away of property from the possession or constructive possession of another. Examples are thefts of bicycles or automobile accessories, shoplifting, pocket-picking, or the stealing of any property or article which is not taken by force and violence or by fraud. Attempted larcenies are included. Embezzlement, "con" games, forgery, worthless checks, and so on, are excluded.

7 **Motor vehicle theft:**

The theft or attempted theft of a motor vehicle. A motor vehicle is self-propelled and runs on the surface and not on rails. Specifically excluded from this category are motorboats, construction equipment, airplanes, and farming equipment.

8 **Arson:**

Any willful or malicious burning or attempt to burn, with or without intent to defraud, a dwelling house, public building, motor vehicle or aircraft, personal property of another, and so on.

SOURCE: U.S. Department of Justice, Federal Bureau of Investigation, *Uniform Crime Reports, 1992* (Washington, D.C.: Government Printing Office, 1993).

jurisdictions have either eliminated the traditional requirements of corroborating evidence and resistance by the victim or interpreted those requirements as demanding only minimal substantiation (Horney and Spohn, 1991).

Another problem in prosecuting rape is that rape victims often feel humiliated when their identities are revealed and they are questioned in court about actions that could indicate consent to engage in sex. Many victims therefore are reluctant to press charges (Bast, 1995). Some are unwilling even to report rape because of the insensitive way victims have been treated. In recent decades many states have enacted laws that limit the kinds of questions that can be asked of rape victims in courts, especially questions concerning the victim's reputation or sexual history.

Unlike murder, rape is not usually divided into degrees; but under some circumstances offenders are charged with other offenses, such as "deviate sexual intercourse," "sexual assault," "statutory rape," or "aggravated assault." These charges may be used to designate sexual offenses that do not contain all the elements necessary to prove rape.

From this review of the crimes of murder and rape, we can see that the substantive criminal law defines the conditions that must be met before a person can be convicted of an offense. The seven principles of Western law categorize these doctrines, and the penal code of each of the states and the laws of the United States define offenses in precise terms. But as the Close-Up shows (see p. 99), individual perceptions of what constitutes a crime also come into play. Does an

C L O S E up

Acquaintance Rape

He was her friend. So the 26-year-old real estate agent agreed when he asked to come over after work one night. Around midnight, she unlocked the door to her one-room apartment overlooking Connecticut Avenue. She listened indulgently to her friend, a former lover, complain about his job managing a local restaurant. Finally, she asked him to leave. He seemed to ignore her, so she decided to lie on her bed, fully clothed. She dozed off as her friend droned on. At one point, she slipped under the comforter of her bed and wriggled out of her jeans. Sometime in the next hour, she was aware that he was sitting on the bed. Suddenly she awoke with a start, as she realized he had climbed on top of her.

She screamed and tried to push him off the bed. He shoved her back, wrenching her neck and pinning her down. She began to cry. He placed his hand tightly over her mouth and penetrated her. Sobbing and unable to breathe, she began to choke. Blood vessels around her eyes popped from lack of oxygen.

Then she stopped fighting and went limp, psychologically retreating to a place where he could not hurt her. His hand slipped off her mouth; she gasped, "Just get it over with." With that he stopped. He rolled off her. He apologized. He swore at himself. He said he had made a mistake and threatened to kill himself. Then he ran out of her apartment carrying his clothes.

SOURCE: Chris Spolar and Angela Walker, "Rape," *Washington Post*, September 4, 1990, Health section, p. 4. © 1990, *The Washington Post*. Reprinted with permission.

acquaintance rape or date rape, such as the one described, fit the legal definition of rape? If the defendant claimed that the victim had consented, how would the victim show that an assault took place, especially in light of the late hour at which she permitted him to visit her apartment? Would the prior relationship between the defendant and the victim lead people to believe that the victim had consented?

⑧ **What kinds of reforms have been made in criminal law concerning rape?**

Responsibility for Criminal Acts

Thus far the elements of crime and the legal definition of offenses have been described; we now need to look at the question of responsibility. Of the seven principles of criminal law, *mens rea* is crucial in establishing responsibility for the act. To obtain a conviction, the prosecution must show that the offender not only committed the illegal act but also did so in a state of mind that makes it appropriate to hold him or her responsible for the act. In April 1999, 11-year-old twin boys in rural Vance County, North Carolina, killed their father and shot their mother and sister in a shooting rampage that left authorities perplexed (Griffin and Rhee, 1999). Were these young boys old enough to plan their crime and understand the consequences of their actions? Is a child capable of forming the same intent to commit a crime as an adult? The analysis of *mens rea* is difficult because the court must inquire into the defendant's mental state at the time the offense was

A Vance County, North Carolina, deputy sheriff and an unidentified woman try to shield one of the 11-year-old identical twins charged with killing their father and wounding their mother and sister. Should 11-year-olds be held responsible for criminal acts?

strict liability

An obligation or duty that when broken is an offense that can be judged criminal without a showing of mens rea, *or criminal intent; usually applied to regulatory offenses involving health and safety.*

committed. It is not easy to know what someone was thinking when he or she performed an act.

Although many defendants admit that they committed the harmful act, they may still plead not guilty. They do so not only because they know that the state must prove them guilty but also because they—or their attorneys—may believe that *mens rea* was not present. Accidents are the clearest examples of such situations: the defendant argues that it was an accident that the gun went off and the neighbor was killed, or that the pedestrian suddenly crossed into the path of the car. As Justice Oliver Wendell Holmes once said, "Even a dog distinguishes between being stumbled over and being kicked" (Holmes, 1881:3).

The courts label events accidents when responsibility is not fixed; *mens rea* is not present because the event was not intentional. But a court may not accept the claim that an event was an accident. In some cases the offender is so negligent or reckless that the court may hold him or her responsible for some degree of the resulting harm. If a passing pedestrian was killed as the result of a game of throwing a loaded gun into the air and watching it fire when it hit the ground, the reckless gun-tossers could be held responsible. If a pedestrian was killed by a car in which the driver was preoccupied with speaking on a cellular phone, the reckless driver could be charged with a crime. The law holds people accountable for irresponsible actions that cause serious harms and such actions are not easily justified as being merely "accidents" for which no one should be punished.

Note that *mens rea*, or criminal responsibility, may be fixed without showing that the defendant intended to cause harm. In other words, it is not the quality of one's motives that establishes *mens rea* but the nature and level of one's intent. The *Model Penal Code* lists four mental states that can be used to meet the requirement of *mens rea:* the act must have been performed intentionally, knowingly, recklessly, or negligently. Some offenses require a high degree of intent. For example, the crime of larceny requires a finding that the defendant intentionally took property to which she knew she was not entitled, intending to deprive the rightful owner of it permanently.

A major exception to the *mens rea* principle has to do with public welfare offenses or **strict liability** offenses—criminal acts that require no showing of intent. Most of these offenses are defined in a type of law first enacted in England and the United States in the late 1800s. These laws dealt with issues arising from urban industrialization, such as sanitation, pure food, decent housing, and public safety. Often the language of the law did not refer to *mens rea*. Some courts ruled that employers were not responsible for the carelessness of their workers because they had no knowledge of the criminal offenses being committed by them. An employer who did not know that the food being canned by his employees was contaminated, for example, was not held responsible for a violation of pure food laws even if people who ate the food died. Other courts, however, ruled that such owners were responsible to the public to ensure the quality of their products, and therefore they could be found criminally liable if they failed to meet the standards set forth in the law.

The concept of strict liability was best described by Justice Robert Jackson in *Morissette v. United States* (1952), in which he upheld the power of legislatures to make certain acts criminal even if *mens rea* was absent. He recognized that such laws were needed to protect people's welfare and maintain social order. He wrote, "In this respect, whatever the intent of the violator, the injury is the same... Hence, legislation applicable to such offenses does not specify intent as a necessary element."

The reasoning used by Justice Jackson to uphold the principle of strict liability has not been followed in all cases. Some experts believe that the principle should be applied only to violations of health and safety regulations that carry no prison sentence or stigma. In practice, in such cases the penalty is usually imposed on business owners only after many failed attempts to persuade them to obey the law.

In a complex society, such as in the United States, the concept of strict liability presumably will be applied to a range of other acts in which a guilty mind is not present. However, courts likely will apply the concept only in situations with evidence of recklessness or indifference.

The absence of *mens rea*, then, does not guarantee a verdict of not guilty in every case. In most cases, however, it relieves defendants of responsibility for acts that would be labeled criminal if they had been intentional. Besides the defense of accidents, there are eight defenses based on lack of criminal intent: entrapment, self-defense, necessity, duress, immaturity, mistake of fact, intoxication, and insanity.

Entrapment

Entrapment is a defense that may be used to show lack of intent. The law excuses a defendant when government agents have been shown to have induced the person to commit the offense. That does not mean the police may not use undercover agents to set a trap for criminals, nor does it mean the police may not provide ordinary opportunities for the commission of a crime. But the entrapment defense may be used when the police have acted so as to *encourage* the criminal act.

The defense of entrapment has evolved through a series of court decisions in the twentieth century. In earlier times judges were less concerned with whether the police had baited a citizen into committing an illegal act and were more concerned with whether or not the citizen had taken the bait. Now when the police investigate a crime or implant the idea for a crime in the mind of a person who then commits the offense, entrapment may have occurred. Entrapment raises tough questions for judges who must decide whether the police went too far toward making a crime occur that otherwise would not have happened (Camp, 1993).

The key question is the predisposition of the defendant. In 1992 the Supreme Court stressed that the prosecutor must show beyond a reasonable doubt that a defendant was predisposed to break the law before he or she was approached by government agents. The case involved Keith Jacobson, a Nebraska farmer who had ordered from a California bookstore magazines containing photographs of nude boys. The material did not violate the law at that time, but a few months later Congress passed the Child Protection Act, and the U.S. Postal Service and the Customs Service began enforcing it. These agencies set up five fictional organizations with names such as the American Hedonist Society and sent letters to Jacobson and others whose names were on the California bookstore's mailing list. The letters urged Jacobson to fight the new law by ordering items that "we believe you will find to be both interesting and stimulating." One postal inspector, using a pseudonym, even became Jacobson's "pen pal." Jacobson ordered the material and was arrested by federal agents. No other pornographic material was found in his home.

___entrapment___
The defense that the individual was induced by the police to commit the criminal act.

In the majority opinion, Justice Byron R. White wrote that government officials may not "originate a criminal design, implant in an innocent person's mind the disposition to commit a criminal act, and then induce commission of the crime so that the government may prosecute."

Self-Defense

A person who feels that he or she is in immediate danger of being harmed by another person may ward off the attack in *self-defense*. The laws of most states also recognize the right to defend others from attack, to protect property, and to prevent a crime.

The level of force used in self-defense cannot exceed the person's reasonable perception of the threat. Thus, a person may be justified in shooting a robber who is holding a gun to her head and threatening to kill her, but homeowners generally are not justified in shooting an unarmed burglar who has left the house and is running across the lawn.

Bernhard Goetz, New York City's "subway vigilante," argued successfully that he was justified in shooting four youths who approached him in a threatening manner and asked for money. The focus of the case was not on whether the youth brandished lethal weapons (they did not) but on whether Goetz's belief in the need to use deadly force was reasonable. Goetz was not convicted on the most serious charges against him (attempted murder and assault), but he was convicted on a weapons-possession charge.

Necessity

Unlike self-defense, in which a defendant feels that he or she must harm an aggressor to ward off an attack, the necessity defense is used when people break the law to save themselves or prevent some greater harm. A person who speeds through a red light to get an injured child to the hospital or breaks into a building to seek refuge from a hurricane could claim to be violating the law out of necessity.

The English case *The Queen v. Dudley and Stephens* (1884) is a famous example of necessity. After their ship sank, four sailors were adrift in the ocean without food or water. Twenty days later, two of the sailors, Thomas Dudley and Edwin Stephens, killed the youngest sailor, the cabin boy, and ate his flesh. Four days later they were rescued by a passing ship. When they returned to England, they were tried for murder. The court found that:

> if the men had not fed upon the body of the boy they... within the four days have died of famine. That the boy, being in a much weaker condition, was likely to have died before them. That at the time of the act there was no sail in sight, nor any reasonable prospect of relief. That under these circumstances there appeared to the prisoners that unless they then fed or very soon fed upon the boy or one of themselves they would die of starvation. That there was no appreciable chance of saving life except by killing some one for the others to eat.

Despite these findings, the court did not accept their defense of necessity. Lord Coleridge, the chief justice, argued that regardless of the degree of need, standards had to be maintained and the law not weakened. Dudley and Stephens were convicted and sentenced to death, but the Crown later reduced the sentence to six months' imprisonment.

Duress (Coercion)

The defense of *duress* arises when someone commits a crime because he or she is coerced by another person. During a bank robbery, for instance, if an armed robber forces one of the bank's customers at gunpoint to drive the getaway car, the customer would be able to claim duress. However, courts generally are not willing to accept this defense if people do not try to escape from the situation. After heiress Patty Hearst was kidnapped by a radical political group and held for many months, she took part in some of the group's armed robberies. She could not use the defense of duress because she took part in the crimes without being directly coerced by her captors.

In another case, John Charles Green escaped from the Missouri prison to which he had been sentenced for three years. He was caught the next day by a state highway patrol officer some distance from the prison. Green claimed that his escape was justified because he had been subject to homosexual assaults in prison. He thus had to escape to protect himself from assault or bodily harm. However, the Missouri Supreme Court did not accept the defense, saying that Green was not being closely pursued by his assailants when he escaped and that he could have avoided harm if he had given prison officials the names of those who were threatening him.

Immaturity

Anglo-American law excuses criminal acts by children under age 7 on the grounds of their immaturity and lack of responsibility for their actions—*mens rea* is not present. Common law has presumed that children aged 7 to 14 are not liable for their criminal acts; however, prosecutors have been able to present evidence of a child's mental capacity to form *mens rea*. Juries can assume the presence of a guilty mind if it can be shown, for example, that the child hid evidence or tried to bribe a witness. As a child grows older, the assumption of immaturity has weakened. Since the development of juvenile courts in the 1890s, children above age 7 generally have not been tried by the same rules as adults. In some situations, however, children may be tried as adults—if, for example, they are repeat offenders or are charged with a particularly heinous crime. Because of the public's concerns about violent crimes by young people, in the 1990s prosecutors increasingly sought to hold children responsible for serious crimes in the same manner that adults are held responsible. For example, prosecutors in Pontiac, Michigan, charged an 11-year-old boy with first-degree murder and succeeded in having a court permit them to try the boy as adult, even though experts concluded that the defendant had the abstract reasoning abilities of a 6-year-old (Loof, 1999).

Mistake

The courts have generally upheld the view that ignorance of the law is no excuse for committing an illegal act. But what if there is a *mistake* of fact? If an accused person has made a mistake on some crucial fact, that may serve as a defense (Christopher, 1994). For example, suppose some teenagers ask your permission to grow sunflowers in a vacant lot behind your home. You help them weed the garden and water the plants. Then it turns out that they are growing marijuana. You were not aware of this because you have no idea what a marijuana plant looks like. Should you be convicted for growing an illegal drug on your property? The answer depends on the specific degree of knowledge and intent that the prosecution must prove for that offense. The success of such a defense may also depend on the extent to which jurors understand and sympathize with your mistake.

Multimillionaire John E. du Pont was found guilty but mentally ill in the shooting of Olympic wrestler David Schultz. Under Pennsylvania law, the verdict means that the jury found du Pont was sane enough to substantially understand right from wrong.

Intoxication

The law does not relieve an individual of responsibility for acts performed while voluntarily intoxicated. In some cases, however, *intoxication* can be used as a defense, as when a person has been tricked into consuming a substance without knowing that it may cause intoxication. More complex are cases in which the defendant must be shown to have had a specific, rather than a general, intent to commit a crime. For example, someone may claim that they were too drunk to realize that they had left a restaurant without paying the bill. Drunkenness can also be used as a mitigating factor to reduce the seriousness of a charge. In 1996 the U.S. Supreme Court narrowly let stand a Montana law that barred the use of evidence of intoxication, even for defendants who claimed that their condition prevented them from forming the specific intent necessary to be guilty of a crime (*Montana v. Egelhoff*). Thus states may enact laws that prevent the use of an intoxication defense.

Insanity

The defense of *insanity* has been a subject of heated debate. The public believes that many criminals "escape" punishment through the skillful use of psychiatric testimony. Yet only about 1 percent of incarcerated offenders are held in mental hospitals because they had been found "not guilty by reason of insanity." The insanity defense is rare and is generally used only in serious cases or where there is no other valid defense.

Over time American courts have used five tests of criminal responsibility involving insanity: the M'Naghten Rule, the Irresistible Impulse Test, the Durham Rule, the *Model Penal Code*'s Substantial Capacity Test, and the test defined in the federal Comprehensive Crime Control Act of 1984. These tests are summarized in Table 3.2, and the tests used in the various states are shown in Figure 3.3.

Before 1843 the insanity defense could be used only by those who were so lacking in understanding that they could not know what they were doing. In that year Daniel M'Naghten was acquitted of killing Edward Drummond, a man he had thought was Sir Robert Peel, the prime minister of Great Britain. M'Naghten

TABLE 3.2   Insanity defense standards

The standards for the insanity defense have evolved over time.

TEST	LEGAL STANDARD BECAUSE OF MENTAL ILLNESS	FINAL BURDEN OF PROOF	WHO BEARS BURDEN OF PROOF
M'Naghten (1843)	"Didn't know what he was doing or didn't know it was wrong"	Varies from proof by a balance of probabilities on the defense to proof beyond a reasonable doubt on the prosecutor	
Irresistible Impulse (1897)	"Could not control his conduct"		
Durham (1954)	"The criminal act was caused by his mental illness"	Beyond a reasonable doubt	Prosecutor
Model Penal Code (1972)	"Lacks substantial capacity to appreciate the wrongfulness of his conduct or to control it"	Beyond a reasonble doubt	Prosecutor
Present federal law	"Lacks capacity to appreciate the wrongfulness of his conduct"	Clear and convincing evidence	Defense

SOURCE: U.S. Department of Justice, National Institute of Justice, *Crime File*, "Insanity Defense," a film prepared by Norval Morris (Washington, D.C.: Government Printing Office, n.d.).

FIGURE 3.3   Standards for insanity used by the states

State laws differ in the standards used to determine insanity.

SOURCE: Adapted from Ingo Keilitz and Junikus Fulton, *The Insanity Defense and Its Alternatives: A Guide for Policy Makers* (Williamsburg, Va.: National Center for State Courts, 1984), 15, 88–89; and U.S. Department of Justice, Bureau of Justice Statistics, *Report to the Nation on Crime and Justice*, 2d ed. (Washington, D.C.: Government Printing Office, 1988), 87.

claimed that he had been delusional at the time of the killing, but the public outcry against his acquittal caused the House of Lords to ask the court to define the law with regard to delusional persons. The judges of the Queen's Bench answered by saying that a finding of guilty cannot be made if, "at the time of the committing of the act, the party accused was laboring under such a defect of reason, from disease of the mind, as not to know the nature and quality of the act he was doing, or if he did know it that he did not know he was doing what was wrong." This test, often referred to as the "right-from-wrong test," is accepted by many states today.

Over the years the M'Naghten Rule has often been criticized as not in keeping with modern concepts of mental disorder. Some argued that people may be able to distinguish right from wrong and still be insane in the psychiatric sense and that terms such as "disease of the mind," "know," and "nature and quality of the act" have not been defined adequately. Some states allow defendants to plead that, while they knew what they were doing was wrong, they were unable to control an urge to commit the crime. The Irresistible Impulse Test excuses defendants when a mental disease was controlling their behavior even though they knew that what they were doing was wrong. Four states use this test along with the M'Naghten Rule.

The Durham Rule, originally developed in New Hampshire in 1871, was adopted by the Circuit Court of Appeals for the District of Columbia in 1954 in the case of *Durham v. United States.* Monte Durham had a long history of criminal activity and mental illness. When he was 26, he and two companions broke into a house. He was found guilty. However, the appeal judge, David Bazelon,

CLOSE up

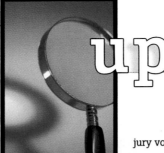

The **Insanity** Defense and Its **Aftermath**

Defendants who are judged not guilty by reason of insanity are typically committed to mental hospitals. If medical experts subsequently determine that they are not a danger to themselves or the community, they may be released. New York law provides the opportunity for a jury trial if a person acquitted through the insanity defense wants to challenge a judge's decision to extend the length of confinement in a mental hospital. In April 1999 Albert Fentress, a former schoolteacher, sought such a jury trial. Twenty years earlier, he had tortured, killed, and cannibalized a teenager but had been found not guilty by reason of insanity. The jurors listened to four expert witnesses presented by the prosecution who asserted that Fentress had not changed during two decades in the hospital. They also listened to four expert witnesses, including doctors from the state's psychiatric facility, who said that Fentress no longer posed a danger to society. How can jurors drawn from among average citizens in the general public know which set of experts presented the most accurate diagnosis? In the end, the jury voted 5-to-1 that, although Fentress was still mentally ill, he no longer needed to be confined to the hospital.

Undoubtedly, many members of the public would be shocked to think that someone such as Fentress who has committed an outrageous, gruesome murder could be released to walk freely among the rest of society. Many members of the public were probably equally shocked in 1999 when John Hinckley Jr., the man who shot President Ronald Reagan in 1981, was granted permission to take supervised outings away from the mental hospital where he had been confined after successfully presenting an insanity defense. Some states have sought to prevent the release of mentally ill, violent offenders by enacting statutes that permit the state to hold such people in mental hospitals after they have finished serving prison sentences. In 1997 the U.S. Supreme Court approved the use of such laws for people diagnosed as "sexually violent predators" (*Kansas v. Hendricks*). However, such laws apply only to people who are convicted of crimes, not to those found not guilty by reason of insanity.

The jury's decision in the Fentress case led the governor of New York to complain that "individuals like Albert Fentress can

overturned the guilty verdict and rejected the M'Naghten Rule, stating that an accused person is not criminally responsible "if an unlawful act is the product of mental disease or mental defect." The Durham Rule assumes that insanity is caused by many factors, not all of which may be present in every case.

The Durham Rule aroused controversy. Some argued that the rule offered no useful definition of "mental disease or defect." By 1972 (*United States v. Brawner*) the federal courts had overturned the Durham Rule in favor of a modified version of a test proposed in the *Model Penal Code*. By 1982 all federal courts and about half of the state courts had adopted the *Model Penal Code*'s Substantial Capacity Test, which states that a person is not responsible for criminal conduct "if at the time of such conduct as a result of mental disease or defect he lacks substantial capacity either to appreciate the criminality [wrongfulness] of his conduct or to conform his conduct to the requirements of law." The Substantial Capacity Test broadens and modifies the M'Naghten and Irresistible Impulse rules. Key terms have been changed to conform better with modern psychological concepts, and the standards lacking in *Durham* have been supplied. By stressing "substantial capacity," the test does not require that a defendant be unable to distinguish right from wrong.

hide behind an insanity plea to avoid the prison time they deserve." However, an insanity acquittal does not always lead to more lenient treatment for people committed to mental hospitals. In Virginia, for example, one-quarter of the 239 people confined to mental hospitals after asserting the insanity defense were only accused of misdemeanors. Thus, if they had been convicted, they would have served a jail sentence of one year or less. Instead, some of them may serve much longer commitments in the hospital. A man named Leroy Turner has spent more than thirteen years in Virginia's Central State Hospital after having been found not guilty by reason of insanity for the misdemeanor charge of breaking a window. His doctors say that his substance abuse problems are in remission and he is not psychotic. Even though some mental health experts estimate that as many as 40 percent of Virginia's defendants acquitted for reasons of insanity no longer need to be hospitalized, the state's Forensic Review Panel approves relatively few petitions for release. Is it fair for people to lose their liberty for long periods of time when they have been acquitted of minor crimes?

As the foregoing examples show, the insanity defense presents significant problems. How can the tradition continue of reserving criminal convictions for those people with sufficient mental capacity while also protecting society from dangerous people and avoiding unduly long hospital commitments for those acquitted on the insanity defense charged with minor offenses? These problems may be especially difficult when decision-making responsibilities are placed in the hands of jurors who lack knowledge about psychiatry and mental illness. In 1999 a jury in Sault Ste. Marie, Michigan, convicted Nathan Hanna of murdering a friend at work and sentenced him to life in prison, even though one of the state's psychiatrists, who usually testifies for the prosecution in insanity defense cases, concluded that Hanna's mental illness led Hanna to believe that the victim was "the Antichrist" whom God ordered him to kill. Did the jurors follow the proper test for the insanity defense or were they worried that Hanna might someday be released if they found him not guilty by reason of insanity? It is impossible to know. Clearly, however, judges, politicians, and the public periodically show great concern about how the insanity defense works in practice. In the aftermath of public outcry about the impending release of Albert Fentress in New York, a state judge overturned the jury's release decision and kept Fentress in the mental hospital. Do these examples raise questions about society's commitment to the insanity defense? If there are so many problems, then why keep the insanity defense? What would you do about this issue?

SOURCE: Drawn from John Flesher, "Testimony: Defendant Thought Victim Was Antichrist," *Lansing State Journal*, June 25, 1999, p. 3D; David M. Halbfinger, "Verdict in Cannibalism Case Is Set Aside," *New York Times*, June 11, 1999; "In Virginia, Insanity Plea Can Bring Long Incarceration," *Washington Post*, June 21, 1999, p. B3; Charlie LeDuff, "Jury Decides Hospitalized Killer in Cannibalism Case Can Go Free," *New York Times*, April 22, 1999; "Man Gets Life Sentence in Killing," *Lansing State Journal*, August 4, 1999, p. 3B; and Bill Miller, "Judges Let Stand Hinckley Ruling; St. Elizabeths Officials Have Right to Decide on Day Trips," *Washington Post*, April 28, 1999, p. A7.

All of the insanity tests are difficult to apply. Moreover, as the Close-Up shows (see above), significant difficulties arise in deciding what to do with someone who has been found not guilty by reason of insanity. Jurors' fears about seeing the offender turned loose might affect their decisions about whether the person was legally insane at the time of the crime.

John Hinckley's attempt to assassinate President Ronald Reagan in 1981 reopened the debate on the insanity defense. Television news footage showed that Hinckley had shot the president. Yet, with the help of psychiatrists, Hinckley's lawyers were able to counteract the prosecution's efforts to persuade the jury that Hinckley was sane. When Hinckley was acquitted the public was outraged, and several states acted to limit or abolish the insanity defense. Twelve states introduced the defense of "guilty but mentally ill" (Klofas and Yandrasits, 1989). This defense allows a jury to find the accused guilty but requires that he or she be given psychiatric treatment while in prison (Callahan, McGreevy, Cirincione, and Steadman, 1992). Hinckley gained permission to take supervised day trips away from the hospital in 1999. The idea that the man who shot the president of the United States could walk freely among other members of the public aroused new debates about the insanity defense.

In 1997 a Pennsylvania jury found multimillionaire John du Pont guilty of third-degree murder but mentally ill in the shooting of Olympic wrestler David Schultz. Under Pennsylvania law, a verdict of guilty but mentally ill means the defendant was sane enough to understand right from wrong. Third-degree murder is defined as killing without premeditation. Psychiatrists had testified that du Pont was a paranoid schizophrenic and that this mental illness contributed to the murder. The verdict means that du Pont will first go to a mental institution and then, if medical authorities say he is well enough, to prison to serve his sentence.

Norval Morris suggests that the defendant's condition after the crime should be taken into account in deciding whether he or she should be confined in a hospital or a prison (Morris, 1982). Illness at the time of the crime should also be considered in deciding the charge on which the defendant may be convicted. For example, a defendant found to have diminished mental capacity would be convicted of manslaughter, not murder.

The Comprehensive Crime Control Act of 1984 changed the federal rules on the insanity defense by limiting it to those who are unable to understand the nature or the wrongfulness of their acts as a result of severe mental disease or defect. This change means that the Irresistible Impulse Test cannot be used in the federal courts. It also shifts the burden of proof from the prosecutor, who in some federal courts had to prove beyond a reasonable doubt that the defendant was not insane, to the defendant, who has to prove his or her insanity. The act also creates a new procedure whereby a person who is found not guilty only by reason of insanity must be committed to a mental hospital until he or she no longer poses a danger to society. These rules apply only to federal courts, but they are spreading to a number of states.

The movement away from the insanity defense reduces the importance of *mens rea*. Many reform efforts have aimed at punishing crimes without regard for the knowledge and intentions of the offender.

The U.S. Supreme Court has reminded states that they cannot do away with considerations of mental competence in all cases. In the past, people who lacked the mental competence to understand the charges against them and to assist in their own defense were committed to mental hospitals until they were able to stand trial (Ho, 1998; Winick, 1995). In 1996 the justices unanimously declared that states cannot require defendants to meet an excessively high standard in proving incompetence to stand trial. Such standards would result in too many trials of people who lack the necessary mental competence to face charges (*Cooper v. Oklahoma*).

In practice, the outcomes of the various insanity tests frequently depend on jurors' reactions to the opinions of psychiatrists presented as expert witnesses by the prosecution and defense. For example, the prosecution's psychiatrist will testify that the defendant does not meet the standard for insanity, while the defendant's psychiatrist will testify that the defendant does meet that standard. The psychiatrists themselves do not decide whether the defendant is responsible for the crime. Instead the jurors decide, based on the psychiatrists' testimony and other factors. They may take into account the seriousness of the crime and their own beliefs about the insanity defense. The rules for proving insanity thus clearly favor wealthy defendants who can afford to hire psychiatrists as expert witnesses.

There is nothing automatic about the insanity defense, even for defendants who engage in highly abnormal behavior (Steury, 1993). Successfully presenting an insanity defense is rare. In 1991, for example, Jeffrey Dahmer was arrested for drugging and killing more than a dozen men and boys whom he had lured to his Milwaukee apartment. He had had sex with the corpses, cut up and eaten the bodies, and saved body parts in his refrigerator. Despite his shocking behavior, a Wisconsin jury rejected his insanity defense, perhaps because they feared that he might be released someday if he were not held fully responsible for the crimes.

Even when defendants are acquitted by reason of insanity, they are nearly always committed to a mental hospital (Robinson, 1993). Although the criminal justice system does not consider hospitalization to be "punishment," commitment to a psychiatric ward results in loss of liberty and often a longer period of confinement than if the person had been sentenced to prison. A robber may have faced only ten years in prison, yet an acquittal by reason of insanity may lead to a lifetime of hospital confinement if the psychiatrists never find that he has recovered enough to be released. Thus the notion that those acquitted by reason of insanity have somehow "beaten the rap" may not reflect reality.

CHECK POINT

⑨ **What kind of offense has no *mens rea* requirement?**

⑩ **What are the defenses in substantive criminal law?**

⑪ **What are the tests of criminal responsibility used for the insanity defense?**

---

procedural due process
The constitutional requirement that all persons be treated fairly and justly by government officials. An accused person can be arrested, prosecuted, tried, and punished only in accordance with procedures prescribed by law.

Procedural Criminal Law   **WWW.**

Procedural law defines how the state must process cases. According to **procedural due process,** accused persons must be tried in accordance with legal procedures. The procedures include providing the rights granted by the Constitution to criminal defendants. As we saw in Chapter 1, the due process model is based on the premise that freedom is so valuable that efforts must be made to prevent erroneous decisions that would deprive an innocent person of his or her freedom. Rights are not only intended to prevent the innocent from being wrongly convicted. They also seek to prevent unfair police and prosecution practices aimed at guilty people, such as conducting improper searches, using violence to pressure people to confess, and denying defendants a fair trial.

The concept of due process dates from the thirteenth century, when King John of England issued the Magna Carta, promising that "no free man shall be arrested, or imprisoned, or disseized, or outlawed, or exiled, or in any way molested; nor will we proceed against him unless by the lawful judgment of his peers or by the law of the land." This rule, that persons must be tried not by arbitrary procedures but according to the process outlined in the law, became a basic principle of procedural law.

The importance of procedural law has been evident throughout history. American history contains many examples of police officers and prosecutors harassing and victimizing those who lack political power, including poor people, racial and ethnic minorities, and unpopular religious groups. The development of procedural safeguards through the decisions of the U.S. Supreme Court

The Magna Carta, signed by England's King John in 1215, is the first written guarantee of due process. It established the principle that persons must be arrested and tried according to the processes outlined in the law.

What Americans Think

Percentage of college freshman who agree with the statement "There is too much concern in the courts for the rights of criminals."

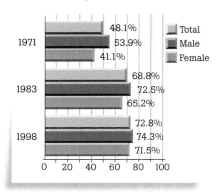

1971
48.1% Total
53.9% Male
41.1% Female

1983
68.8%
72.5%
65.2%

1998
72.8%
74.3%
71.5%

0 20 40 60 80 100

SOURCE: U.S. Department of Justice, Bureau of Justice Statistics, *Sourcebook of Criminal Justice Statistics 1998* (Washington, D.C.: Bureau of Justice Statistics, 1999), Table 2.93.

self-incrimination

The act of exposing oneself to prosecution by being forced to respond to questions whose answers may reveal that one has committed a crime. The Fifth Amendment protects defendants against self-incrimination. In any criminal proceeding the prosecution must prove the charges by means of evidence other than the testimony of the accused.

has helped protect citizens from such actions. In these decisions, the Supreme Court may favor guilty people by ordering new trials or may even release them from custody because of the weight it places on protecting procedural rights and preventing police misconduct.

Public opinion does not always support the decisions by the Supreme Court and other courts that uphold the rights of criminal defendants and convicted offenders. Many Americans would prefer if other goals for society, such as stopping drugs and ensuring that guilty people are punished, took a higher priority over the protection of rights. Such opinions raise questions about Americans' commitment to the rights described in the Bill of Rights. Public opinion data indicate that most college freshman believe that courts have placed too much emphasis on the rights of criminal defendants. Moreover, this sentiment has grown over the past thirty years. In addition, although male and female students' support for rights differed in 1971, little difference is evident between the two groups today. Do you agree that there are too many rights? Can you identify specific rights that give too much protection to criminal defendants? Would there be any risks from reducing the rights available in the criminal justice process?

Unlike substantive criminal law, which is defined by legislatures through statutes, procedural criminal law is defined by courts through judicial rulings. Judges interpret the provisions of the U.S. Constitution and state constitutions, and those interpretations establish the procedures that government officials must follow. Because it has the authority to review cases from state supreme courts as well as from federal courts, the U.S. Supreme Court has played a major role in defining procedural criminal law. The Supreme Court's influence stems from its power to define the meaning of the U.S. Constitution, especially the Bill of Rights—the first ten amendments to the Constitution, which list legal protections against actions of the government. Although public opinion may clash with Supreme Court rulings, the Supreme Court can make independent decisions because its members cannot be removed from office by the voters. Because justices of the Supreme Court can be removed from office only through impeachment for misconduct, they can define the rights in the Bill of Rights as they see fit, even if the public disagrees with their decisions.

The Bill of Rights

The U.S. Constitution contained few references to criminal justice when it was ratified in 1789. Because many people were concerned that the document did not set forth the rights of individuals in enough detail, ten amendments were added in 1791. Four of those amendments bear on criminal justice issues. The Fourth Amendment bars unreasonable searches and seizures. The Fifth Amendment outlines basic due process rights in criminal cases. For example, consistent with the assumption that the state must prove the defendant's guilt, protection against **self-incrimination** means that persons cannot be forced to respond to questions whose answers may reveal that they have committed a crime. The protection against **double jeopardy** means that a person may be subjected to only one prosecution or punishment for a single offense within the same jurisdiction. The Sixth Amendment provides for the right to a speedy, fair, and public trial by an impartial jury, as well as the right to counsel. The Eighth Amendment bars excessive bail, excessive fines, and cruel and unusual punishment.

For most of American history the Bill of Rights did not apply to most criminal cases because it was designed to protect people from abusive actions by the *federal* government. It did not seek to protect people from state and local officials, who handled nearly all criminal cases. This view was upheld by the U.S. Supreme Court in the 1833 case of **Barron v. Baltimore.** However, this view gradually changed in the late nineteenth and early twentieth centuries.

The Fourteenth Amendment and Due Process

After the Civil War, three amendments were added to the Constitution. These amendments were designed to protect individuals' rights against infringement by state and local government officials. Two of the amendments had little impact on criminal justice. The Thirteenth Amendment abolished slavery, and the Fifteenth Amendment attempted to prohibit racial discrimination in voting. The other amendment, however, had a profound impact on criminal justice. The Fourteenth Amendment, ratified in 1868, barred states from violating a person's right to due process of law. It states that "no State shall ... deprive any person of life, liberty, or property without due process of law; nor deny to any person within its jurisdiction the equal protection of the laws." These rights to due process and equal protection served as a basis for protecting individuals from abusive actions by local criminal justice officials. However, the terms *due process* and *equal protection* are so vague that it was left to the U.S. Supreme Court to decide if and how these new rights applied to the criminal justice process.

The effort to convince the Supreme Court to declare that the Fourteenth Amendment provided specific protections for individuals spanned several decades and met with limited success. Not until the 1920s did the Supreme Court begin to name specific personal rights that were protected by the Fourteenth Amendment.

At first, the Supreme Court ruled against convictions gained by prosecutors under conditions that were clearly unfair. In 1923 it overturned the convictions of five African American men who had been sentenced to death after a forty-five-minute trial featuring a howling lynch mob outside the courthouse (*Moore v. Dempsey*).

A few years later, in **Powell v. Alabama** (1932), the Supreme Court ruled that the due process clause required courts to provide attorneys for poor defendants facing the death penalty. This decision stemmed from a notorious case in Alabama in which nine African American men, known as the "Scottsboro boys," were quickly convicted and condemned to death for allegedly raping two white women, even though one of the alleged victims later admitted that she had lied about the rape (Goodman, 1994).

The Supreme Court also overturned convictions of African American defendants in Mississippi who had been hung from trees and beaten with metal-studded belts until they confessed (*Brown v. Mississippi,* 1936). The Supreme Court's description of the actions of the Mississippi sheriff's deputies shows why the justices believed that such brutality violated the right to due process of law:

> [The deputies] hanged [the defendant] by a rope to the limb of a tree, and having let him down, they hung him again, and when he . . . still protested his innocence, he was tied to a tree and whipped. ... [S]igns of the rope on his neck were plainly visible. . . . [Other defendants] were made to strip and they were laid over chairs and their backs were cut to pieces with a leather strap with buckles on it.

double jeopardy
The subjecting of a person to prosecution more than once in the same jurisdiction for the same offense; prohibited by the Fifth Amendment.

Barron v. Baltimore (1833)
The protections of the Bill of Rights apply only to actions of the federal government.

Powell v. Alabama (1932)
An attorney must be provided to a defendant facing the death penalty.

In these early cases, the justices had not developed clear rules for deciding which specific rights applied to the state and local officials as components of the due process clause of the Fourteenth Amendment. They implied that procedures must meet a basic standard of **fundamental fairness.** In essence, the justices simply reacted against brutal situations that shocked their consciences. In doing so, they showed the importance of procedural criminal law in protecting individuals from abusive and unjust actions by government officials.

fundamental fairness

A legal doctrine supporting the idea that so long as a state's conduct maintains basic standards of fairness, the Constitution has not been violated.

The Due Process Revolution

From the 1930s to the 1960s, the fundamental fairness doctrine was supported by a majority of the Supreme Court justices. It was applied on a case-by-case basis, not always in a consistent way. Throughout this period, Justice Hugo L. Black argued that all the provisions of the Bill of Rights should be incorporated into the due process clause of the Fourteenth Amendment and hence applied to state and local governments. He sought to instantly nationalize the Bill of Rights by making it protect people from unfair actions of state and local officials the same way that it protected them from unfair actions by federal officials. Black's arguments received a boost in 1953 when Republican president Dwight D. Eisenhower named former California governor Earl Warren chief justice of the United States, and a new liberal majority began to form on the Court.

Warren led the Supreme Court in a revolution that changed the meaning and scope of constitutional rights. Instead of requiring state and local officials merely to uphold fundamental fairness, the Court began to require them to abide by the specific provisions of the Bill of Rights. Previously states could design their own procedures so long as those procedures passed the fairness test. Under Warren's leadership, however, the Supreme Court's new approach imposed detailed procedural standards on the police and courts. As it applied more and more constitutional rights against the states, the Court made decisions that favored the interests of many criminal defendants. These defendants had their convictions overturned and received new trials because the Court believed that protecting the values underlying criminal procedure was more important than single-mindedly seeking convictions of criminal offenders.

Warren and the other justices were strongly criticized by politicians, police chiefs, and members of the public. Critics believed that the Warren Court was rewriting constitutional law in a manner that gave too many legal protections to criminals who harm society. In addition, Warren and his colleagues were criticized for ignoring established precedents that defined rights in a limited fashion. Some alleged that the justices were advancing their own political views rather than following the true meaning of the Constitution.

Mapp v. Ohio (1961)

The Fourth Amendment protects citizens from unreasonable searches and seizures by state officials.

In 1961 the Supreme Court ruled in the case of *Mapp v. Ohio* that the Fourth Amendment protections against unreasonable searches and seizures applied to the states exactly as they applied against the federal government. Thus improperly obtained evidence, even if it demonstrated the defendant's guilt, had to be excluded from use at trials. Through this decision, the Supreme Court imposed a new rule that affected police practices in every city and county across the nation. The Court moved beyond the Fourth Amendment to issue decisions concerning the Fifth, with its protection against self-incrimination, the Sixth, which guarantees the right to counsel, and the Eighth, which prohibits excessive fines and cruel and unusual punishment. By applying all four of these amendments against the states—incorporating them as part of the Fourteenth Amendment's due process clause—the Court ensured that almost all activities in the criminal justice system would come under the detailed supervision of the federal judiciary.

From 1962 to 1972 the Supreme Court, under the chief justiceships of both Earl Warren (1953–1969) and Warren Burger (1969–1986), applied most criminal justice safeguards to the states. By the end of this period, the process of **incorporation** was nearly complete. Criminal justice officials at all levels—federal, state, and local—were obligated to respect the constitutional rights of suspects and defendants.

incorporation
The extension of the due process clause of the Fourteenth Amendment to make binding on state governments the rights guaranteed in the first ten amendments to the U.S. Constitution (the Bill of Rights).

CHECK POINT

⑫ **What is "incorporation"?**

⑬ **What test was used by the Supreme Court to decide which rights applied to the states prior to incorporation?**

⑭ **Which Supreme Court era (named for the chief justice) expanded the definitions of constitutional rights for criminal defendants?**

The Fourth Amendment: Protection against Unreasonable Searches and Seizures

The right of the people to be secure in their persons, houses, papers, and effects, against unreasonable searches and seizures, shall not be violated, and no Warrants shall issue, but upon probable cause, supported by Oath or affirmation, and particularly describing the place to be searched, and the persons or things to be seized.

The Fourth Amendment limits the ability of law enforcement officers to search a person or property to obtain evidence of criminal activity. It also limits the ability of the police to detain a person without justification (Perkins and Jamieson, 1995).

Before going through this Broward County, Florida, crack house, the police had to obtain a search warrant (unless the situation had fitted one of the exceptions specified by the U.S. Supreme Court).

The Fourth Amendment does not prevent the police from conducting searches; it merely protects people's privacy by barring "unreasonable" searches. The Supreme Court must define the situations in which a search is "reasonable" or "unreasonable." Because different Supreme Court justices do not always agree on the Constitution's meaning, the definitions of these words and the rules for police searches can change as the makeup of the Court changes.

The wording of the Fourth Amendment makes clear that the authors of the Bill of Rights did not believe that law enforcement officials should have the power to pursue criminals at all costs. The Fourth Amendment's protections apply to suspects as well as law-abiding citizens. Police officers are supposed to follow the rules for obtaining search warrants, and they may not conduct unreasonable searches even when they are trying to catch dangerous criminals.

In 1914 the Supreme Court declared, in *Weeks v. United States*, that federal courts must exclude any evidence that was obtained through an improper search by federal law enforcement agents. With this **exclusionary rule,** the Court created the principle that such evidence must be excluded from a trial; it was assumed that this would cause law enforcement officers to follow the dictates of the Fourth Amendment. The Supreme Court expanded this rule to include searches by state and local law enforcement officers in *Mapp v. Ohio* (1961) by incorporating the Fourth Amendment exclusionary rule into the due process clause of the Fourteenth Amendment.

President Richard M. Nixon (1969–1974) was one of the Warren Court's critics who believed that the Supreme Court had expanded defendants' rights too far and therefore prevented law enforcement officers from accomplishing their mission of catching criminals. Subsequent Republican presidents Gerald R. Ford (1974–1977), Ronald Reagan (1981–1989), and George Bush (1989–1993) shared Nixon's view. Thus, when justices retired from the Supreme Court after Nixon's election in 1968, Republican presidents appointed replacements who were less likely to interpret the Constitution as providing broad rights for suspects and defendants.

After being broadened during the Warren Court era (1953–1969), Fourth Amendment rights were narrowed during the chief justiceships of Warren Burger (1969–1986) and William H. Rehnquist (1986–present). For example, in *United States v. Leon* (1984) the Court created a "good-faith" exception to the exclusionary rule. In this case police officers had used outdated information from an unreliable informant to obtain a warrant to conduct a search for narcotics. Using that warrant, the police found illegal drugs in the course of their search. Under the rule established in *Mapp v. Ohio*, the drugs should have been excluded because the search warrant was defective. However, the justices created an exception to the exclusionary rule. Because the police had tried to follow proper procedures, and a judge, not the police, had made the error in issuing the improper warrant, the Supreme Court ruled that the evidence could be used against the defendant. Justice Byron White explained the ruling, writing that the social costs of excluding evidence outweighed the social benefits of deterring improper searches. White's claim is subject to debate because evidence is excluded in very few cases, and the police often have other evidence to support a conviction even when some evidence is barred (Nardulli, 1983; Uchida and Bynum, 1991).

This decision and others have made it easier for law enforcement officials to use evidence obtained through improper searches, but they have also made the exclusionary rule less clear (Crocker, 1993). The creation of exceptions makes it

---

exclusionary rule

The principle that illegally obtained evidence must be excluded from a trial.

harder for police to know beforehand whether evidence obtained from an improper search can be used in a trial.

The Burger and Rehnquist Courts did not abolish the exclusionary rule, but they limited its applicability and gave police greater flexibility to conduct searches without obtaining a search warrant (Vaughn and del Carmen, 1997). For example, the Rehnquist Court made it much easier for police to conduct warrantless searches of cars and closed containers found inside cars. Such searches are often used in efforts to combat drug trafficking. In 1999, for example, the Supreme Court decided that when a police officer saw a syringe sticking out of the pocket of a car's driver, he could search the purse of a car passenger, even though the officer had no specific reason to suspect that the passenger had any drugs (*Wyoming v. Houghton*). Officers have also used other approaches, such as stopping people who fit the profiles of suspected drug couriers. When the courts give police more flexibility in search and seizure actions, innocent citizens are more likely to feel that their rights have been infringed (Robin, 1993; Janikowski and Giacopassi, 1993).

CHECK POINT

⑮ **What controversial principle was applied against the states in *Mapp v. Ohio*?**

The Supreme Court will undoubtedly continue to face new cases that force it to interpret the "reasonableness" of searches and the Fourth Amendment's warrant requirements. In recent years technological advances and new situations have led the Court to consider, for example, whether helicopter surveillance of property constitutes a search that requires a warrant (the justices said no) and whether the Fourth Amendment applies to the search and seizure of a noncitizen outside the United States by government agents (again, the justices said no). Other new issues will likely include electronic surveillance and prosecutors' efforts to gain access to computer files. Because of its composition, the Court probably will continue to tilt in favor of law enforcement officials and will not establish broader Fourth Amendment rights for criminal defendants. Despite its conservative orientation, however, the Court regularly demonstrates that it will not let police officers conduct any kind of search that they may wish to make. For example, in 1999, the Supreme Court struck down an Iowa law that permitted police officers to conduct warrantless automobile searches whenever they issued traffic citations (*Knowles v. Iowa*). The justices unanimously agreed that officers need a reason, such as arresting the driver for committing a crime or a reasonable suspicion that the vehicle contains weapons, before they can conduct a search.

The Fifth Amendment: Protection against Self-Incrimination and Double Jeopardy

No person shall be held to answer for a capital, or otherwise infamous crime, unless on a presentment or indictment of a Grand Jury, except in cases arising in the land or naval forces, or in the Militia, when in actual service in time of war or public danger; nor shall any person be subject for the same offense to be twice put in jeopardy of life or limb; nor shall be compelled in any criminal case to be a witness against himself, nor be deprived of life, liberty, or property, without due process of law; nor shall private property be taken for public use, without just compensation.

The Fifth Amendment clearly states some key rights related to the investigation and prosecution of criminal suspects. Here we explore two of them: the protections against compelled self-incrimination and against double jeopardy.

Self-Incrimination

One of the most important due process rights is the protection against compelled self-incrimination—that is, people cannot be pressured to act as witnesses against themselves (Gardner, 1993). This right is consistent with the assumption that the state must prove the defendant's guilt. It is connected to other protections, especially the Sixth Amendment right to counsel, because representation by a defense attorney is seen as a means of preventing self-incrimination during questioning by police or prosecutors (Richardson, 1993).

In the past the validity of confessions hinged on their being voluntary, because a confession involves self-incrimination. Under the doctrine of fundamental fairness, which was applied before the 1960s, the Supreme Court was unwilling to allow confessions that were beaten out of suspects, that emerged after extended questioning, or that resulted from the use of other physical tactics. Such tactics can impose inhumane treatment on suspects and create risks that innocent people will be wrongly convicted. In the cases of *Escobedo v. Illinois* (1964) and *Miranda v. Arizona* (1966), the Warren Court outraged politicians, law enforcement officials, and members of the public by placing limits on the ability of police to question suspects without an attorney present. The justices ruled that, prior to questioning, the police must inform suspects of their right to remain silent and their right to have an attorney present. In response, many police officers argued that they depended on interrogations and confessions as a major means of solving crimes. However, nearly four decades later many suspects continue to confess for a number of reasons, such as feelings of guilt, inability to understand their rights, and the desire to gain a favorable plea bargain (Leo, 1996a).

The justices were not seeking to limit police officers' ability to investigate crimes when they required them to read the "*Miranda* warnings" to suspects. They were trying to satisfy the Fifth Amendment prohibition of compelled self-incrimination. They also knew that confessions can be unreliable, especially if no limits are set on questioning by the police. The justices knew that law enforcement officials often "solve" crimes when they are allowed to badger, intimidate, or coerce suspects into confessing. This may mean that the crime is "solved," but whether the person who confessed is the one who committed the crime remains uncertain.

The Warren Court made the exclusionary rule applicable to violations of Fifth Amendment as well as Fourth Amendment rights. If police questioned suspects without giving them proper warnings and access to an attorney, incriminating statements and confessions by those suspects could not be used against them. However, just as the Burger Court created the "good-faith" exception in a Fourth Amendment case, other exceptions to the exclusionary rule were created in the Fifth Amendment context. For example, the Court created an "inevitable discovery rule" that allows police to use evidence that they would have discovered even without improper questioning of the suspect (*Nix v. Williams*). In the case in question, police learned the location of a murder victim's body by improperly questioning the suspect without his attorney present. The body was later admitted into evidence because the police convinced the Court that search parties would have inevitably found the body even without the suspect's confession. In another example, the Court ruled that evidence obtained from improper questioning could be

---

Escobedo v. Illinois (1964)

An attorney must be provided to suspects when they are taken into police custody.

Miranda v. Arizona (1966)

Confessions made by suspects who were not notified of their due process rights cannot be admitted as evidence.

used if the situation posed an immediate threat to public safety, such as seeking information about a gun that the police knew to be hidden somewhere nearby (*New York v. Quarles*).

In 1999 new debates emerged about *Miranda* warnings that may eventually lead the Supreme Court to reconsider the famous Warren Court precedent (Carelli, 1999). Some scholars claim that *Miranda* warnings permit thousands of guilty criminals to escape conviction (Cassell and Fowles, 1998). One federal appeals court ruled that *Miranda* warnings are not required by the Constitution and that a congressional statute can relieve federal law enforcement officers of any obligation to provide *Miranda* warnings to suspects before questioning (*U.S. v. Dickerson*, 4th Circuit, U.S. Court of Appeals). The stage is set for the Supreme Court to reexamine the necessity of *Miranda* warnings if it so chooses.

Double Jeopardy

Because of the limit imposed by the Fifth Amendment, a person charged with a criminal act may be subjected to only one prosecution or punishment for that offense in the same jurisdiction. As interpreted by the Supreme Court, however, the right against double jeopardy does not prevent a person from facing two trials or receiving two sanctions from the government (Hickey, 1995; Lear, 1995; Henning, 1993). Because a single criminal act may violate both state and federal laws, for example, a person may be tried in both courts. Thus, even though Los Angeles police officers were acquitted of assault charges in a state court after they had been videotaped beating motorist Rodney King, they later stood trial again and were convicted in a federal court for violating King's civil rights. The Supreme Court further refined the meaning of double jeopardy in 1996 by ruling that prosecutors could employ both property forfeiture *and* criminal charges against someone who grew marijuana at his home. The Court did not apply the double jeopardy right in the case because the property forfeiture was not a "punishment" (*United States v. Ursery*)

The Sixth Amendment:
The Right to Counsel and a Fair Trial

In all criminal prosecutions, the accused shall enjoy the right to a speedy and public trial, by an impartial jury of the State and district wherein the crime shall have been committed, which district shall have been previously ascertained by law, and to be informed of the nature and cause of the accusation; to be confronted with the witnesses against him; to have compulsory process for obtaining witnesses in his favor, and to have the assistance of counsel for his defense.

The Sixth Amendment includes a number of provisions dealing with fairness in a criminal prosecution. These include the right to counsel, to a speedy and public trial, and to an impartial jury.

The Right to Counsel

Although the right to counsel in a criminal case had prevailed in federal courts since 1938, not until the Supreme Court's landmark decision in ***Gideon v. Wainwright*** (1963) was this requirement made binding on the states. Many states already provided attorneys, but the Court forced all of the states to meet Sixth Amendment standards. In previous cases, the Court, applying the

Gideon v. Wainwright **(1963)**
Defendants have a right to counsel in felony cases. States must provide defense counsel in felony cases for those who cannot pay for it themselves.

doctrine of fundamental fairness, had ruled that states must provide poor people with counsel only when required by the special circumstances of the case. A defense attorney had to be provided when conviction could lead to the death penalty, when the issues were complex, or when a poor defendant was either very young or mentally handicapped.

Although the *Gideon* ruling directly affected only states that did not provide poor defendants with attorneys, it set in motion a series of cases that affected all the states by deciding how the right to counsel would be applied in various situations. Beginning in 1963, the Court extended the right to counsel to preliminary hearings, initial appeals, post-indictment identification lineups, and children in juvenile court proceedings. Later, however, the Burger Court declared that attorneys need not be provided for discretionary appeals or for trials in which the only punishment is a fine (*Ross v. Moffitt; Scott v. Illinois*).

The Right to a Speedy and Public Trial

The nation's founders were aware that in other countries accused people often might languish in jail awaiting trial and often were convicted in secret proceedings. At the time of the American Revolution, the right to a speedy and public trial was recognized in the common law and included in the constitutions of six of the original states. But the word *speedy* is vague, and the Supreme Court has recognized that the interest of quick processes may conflict with other interests of society (such as the need to collect evidence) as well as with interests of the defendant (such as the need for time to prepare a defense).

The right to a public trial is intended to protect the accused against arbitrary conviction. The Constitution assumes that judges and juries will act in accordance with the law if they must listen to evidence and announce their decisions in public. Again, the Supreme Court has recognized that cases may arise in which the need for a public trial must be balanced against other interests. For example, the right to a public trial does not mean that all members of the public have the right to attend the trial. The courtroom's seating capacity and the interests of a fair trial, free of outbursts from the audience, may be considered. In hearings on sex crimes when the victim or witness is a minor, courts have barred the public to spare the child embarrassment. In some states, trials have become even more public than the authors of the Sixth Amendment ever imagined because court proceedings are televised, and some are even carried on national cable systems through COURT-TV.

The Right to an Impartial Jury

The right to a jury trial was well established in the American colonies at the time of the Revolution. In their charters, most of the colonies guaranteed trial by jury, and it was referred to in the First Continental Congress's debates in 1774, the Declaration of Independence, the constitutions of the thirteen original states, and the Sixth Amendment to the U.S. Constitution. Juries allow citizens to play a role in courts' decision making and to prevent prosecutions in cases in which there is not enough evidence.

Several Supreme Court decisions have dealt with the composition of juries. The Magna Carta required that juries be drawn from "peers" of the accused person living in the area where the crime was committed. However, the Sixth Amendment does not refer to a jury of one's peers. Instead, the Supreme Court has held that the amendment requires selection procedures that create a jury pool made up of a cross section of the community. Most scholars believe that an impartial jury can best be achieved by drawing jurors at random from the broadest possible base (Hans and Vidmar, 1986; Levine, 1992). The jury is expected to represent the community, and the extent to which it does so is a central concern of jury administration (Smith, 1994). Prospective jurors are usually summoned randomly from voter registration lists or drivers' license records. After the jury pool has been formed, attorneys for each side may ask potential jurors questions and seek to exclude specific jurors (Smith and Ochoa, 1996). Thus the final group of jurors may not, in fact, reflect the diversity of a particular city or county's residents (King, 1994).

The Eighth Amendment: Protection against Excessive Bail, Excessive Fines, and Cruel and Unusual Punishment

> Excessive bail shall not be required, nor excessive fines imposed, nor cruel and unusual punishment inflicted.

The briefest of the amendments, the Eighth Amendment deals with the rights of defendants during the pretrial (bail) and corrections (fines, punishment) phases of the criminal justice system.

Release on Bail

The purpose of bail is to allow for the release of the accused while he or she is awaiting trial. The Eighth Amendment does not require that all defendants be released on bail, only that the amount of bail not be excessive. Despite these provisions, many states do not allow bail for those charged with some offenses, such as murder, and few limits are imposed on the amounts that can be required. In 1987 the Supreme Court, in *United States v. Salerno and Cafero,* upheld provisions of the Bail Reform Act of 1984 that allow federal judges to detain without bail suspects who are considered dangerous to the public.

Excessive Fines

The Supreme Court ruled in 1993 that the forfeiture of property related to a criminal case can be analyzed for possible violation of the excessive fines clause (*Austin v. United States*). In 1998 the Court declared for the first time that a forfeiture constituted an impermissible excessive fine. In that case, a man failed to comply with the federal law requiring that travelers report if they are taking $10,000 or more in cash outside the country (Smith, 1999a). There is no law against transporting any amount of cash. The law only concerns filing a report to the government concerning the transport of money. When one traveler at the Los Angeles airport failed to report the money detected in his suitcase by a cash-sniffing dog trained to identify people who might be transporting money for drug dealers, he was forced to forfeit all $357,000 that he carried in his luggage. Because no evidence was produced that the money was obtained illegally and because the usual punishment for the offense would be only a fine of $5,000, a slim five-member majority on the Supreme Court ruled that the forfeiture of all the traveler's money constituted an excessive fine (*United States v. Bajakajian*). It remains to be seen whether the Court's recent interest in violations of the excessive fines clause will limit law enforcement agencies' practices in forcing criminal defendants to forfeit cash and property.

Ethics

At a June 1998 sentencing hearing in Long Beach, California, Ronnie Hawkins, a petty thief, served as his own attorney as he faced a possible sentence of twenty-five years to life under the state's three-strikes law. He sat in the courtroom wearing chains and shackles to prevent him from escaping. He also wore a stun belt designed to deliver a high voltage electric shock if he disobeyed law enforcement officers. When Hawkins interrupted Judge Joan Comparet-Cassani, she warned him not to interrupt again or he would receive an electric shock. When he repeatedly interrupted the judge, she ordered the bailiff to activate the belt. Hawkins was zapped with a painful eight-second jolt of fifty-thousand volts of electricity.

Is the use of electric shock devices proper under the Supreme Court's test that applies contemporary community standards to define cruel and unusual punishment? Do electric shocks constitute the sort of torture that the framers of the Eighth Amendment intended to ban? Technically, the Supreme Court applies the Eighth Amendment only to punishments inflicted on convicted offenders. Defendants who have not yet been convicted of a crime are protected against abuses by the due process clause, but the courts apply the Eighth Amendment test to determine if pretrial detainees' due process rights have been violated. Stun belts are placed on both pretrial detainees and convicted offenders, especially when they are being transported and there are fears that they might try to escape, so the belts might be regarded as violating both the Eighth Amendment and the due process clause. The threat of painful electric shocks may be frightening for prisoners because the belt's manufacturer claims that fewer than three dozen people have been subjected to the shock in the fifty thousand times that the belt has been used. The human rights group, Amnesty International, argues that electroshock stun belts are inhumane. Should such devices be used on offenders such as Hawkins who, chained and shackled in a courtroom chair, were not attempting to escape or threatening public safety? Even if it does not violate the Eighth Amendment to use such stun belts (the courts have not yet decided the issue), is it ethical to use such painful techniques to force defendants and offenders to cooperate?

SOURCE: Drawn from Minerva Canto, "Federal Government Investigates Use of Stun Belt," *Lansing State Journal,* August 7, 1998, p. 4A; "Commission Investigating Judge Who Shocked Inmate," *Lansing State Journal,* August 27, 1998, p. 4A; and "Noisy Defendant Shocks Judge with Security Belt," *National Law Journal,* July 27, 1998.

Cruel and Unusual Punishment

The nation's founders were concerned about the barbaric punishments that had been inflicted in seventeenth- and eighteenth-century Europe, where offenders were sometimes burned alive or stoned to death. Hence the ban on "cruel and unusual punishment." The Warren Court set the standard for judging issues of cruel and punishment in a case dealing with a former soldier who was deprived of U.S. citizenship for deserting his post during World War II (*Trop v. Dulles,* 1958). Chief Justice Earl Warren declared that judges must use the values of contemporary society to determine whether a specific punishment is cruel and unusual. This test has been used in death penalty cases, but the justices have strongly disagreed over the values of American society on this issue. For example, only Justices William Brennan, Thurgood Marshall, and later, Harry A. Blackmun felt that the death penalty violates the Eighth Amendment's ban on cruel and unusual punishments. Examine the Question of Ethics and consider whether the use of new technologies may raise issues concerning cruel and unusual punishment.

In 1972 a majority of justices decided that the death penalty was being used in an arbitrary and discriminatory way (*Furman v. Georgia*). After many state legislatures passed new laws that required more careful decision-making procedures in death penalty cases, a majority of justices in **Gregg v. Georgia** allowed the states to reactivate the death penalty. The new procedures require a trial to determine the defendant's guilt and a separate hearing to consider whether he or she deserves the death penalty. In the sentencing hearing, the jury or judge must examine any factors that make the offender especially deserving of the most severe punishment—for example, "aggravating factors" such as an especially gruesome killing. They must also examine any "mitigating factors" that make the offender less deserving of the death penalty, such as youth or mental retardation (Acker and Lanier, 1995; Acker and Lanier, 1994; Blankenship, Luginbuhl, Cullen, and Redick, 1997).

In the 1980s, lawyers brought new cases to the Supreme Court in an unsuccessful effort to persuade the justices to declare the death penalty a cruel and unusual punishment. *McCleskey v. Kemp* (1987) presented the Court with statistics showing that the process in Georgia to decide who will receive the death penalty discriminated against African Americans. African American defendants charged with killing white victims are much more likely to be sentenced to death than white killers of African Americans (Baldus, Woodworth, and Pulaski, 1994; Keil and Vito, 1992). A narrow majority of the justices rejected the use of statistics to prove such discrimination and stated that defendants must show clear evidence of racial bias in specific cases—not in the Georgia criminal justice system generally—to challenge a conviction.

By 2000 the number of offenders sentenced to death in the United States had topped thirty-six hundred. The pace of executions, however, remained slow. During the early 1990s an average of thirty death row inmates in the United States were executed each year, but the pace of executions increased later in the decade with sixty-eight and ninety-eight executions in 1998 and 1999, respectively (Death Penalty Information Center, 2000). The Supreme Court has consistently declared that capital punishment does not violate the Eighth Amendment, but the justices must still deal with cases that raise questions about whether proper procedures were followed in death penalty cases.

Since the 1950s, the rights of defendants in state criminal trials have greatly expanded. The Supreme Court has incorporated most portions of the Fourth, Fifth, Sixth, and Eighth Amendments, as shown in Figure 3.4. Figure 3.5 shows the amendments that protect defendants at various stages of the criminal justice process.

Gregg v. Georgia (1976)
Capital punishment statutes are permissible if they provide careful procedures to guide decision making by judges and juries.

FIGURE 3.4 — **Relationship of the Bill of Rights and the Fourteenth Amendment to the rights of the accused**

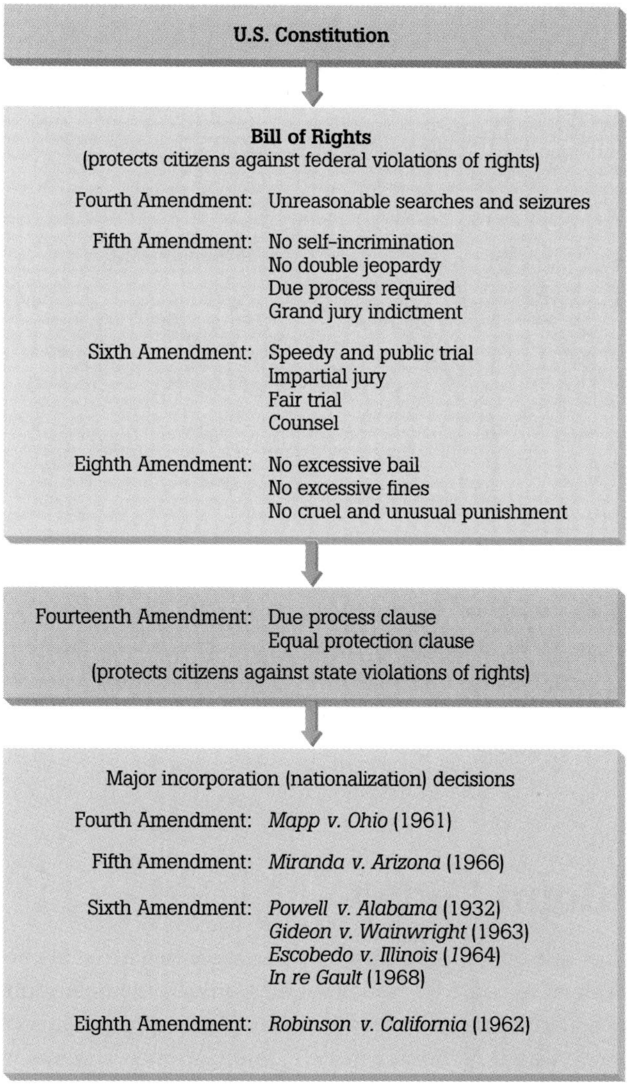

For most of U.S. history, the Bill of Rights protected citizens only against violations by officials of the federal government. The Warren Court pursued the process of incorporation, in which portions of the Fourteenth Amendment were interpreted as protecting citizens from unlawful actions by state officials.

U.S. Constitution

Bill of Rights
(protects citizens against federal violations of rights)

Fourth Amendment: Unreasonable searches and seizures

Fifth Amendment: No self-incrimination
No double jeopardy
Due process required
Grand jury indictment

Sixth Amendment: Speedy and public trial
Impartial jury
Fair trial
Counsel

Eighth Amendment: No excessive bail
No excessive fines
No cruel and unusual punishment

Fourteenth Amendment: Due process clause
Equal protection clause
(protects citizens against state violations of rights)

Major incorporation (nationalization) decisions

Fourth Amendment: *Mapp v. Ohio* (1961)

Fifth Amendment: *Miranda v. Arizona* (1966)

Sixth Amendment: *Powell v. Alabama* (1932)
Gideon v. Wainwright (1963)
Escobedo v. Illinois (1964)
In re Gault (1968)

Eighth Amendment: *Robinson v. California* (1962)

FIGURE **3.5** Protections of the Bill of Rights

The Bill of Rights protects defendants during various phases of the criminal justice process.

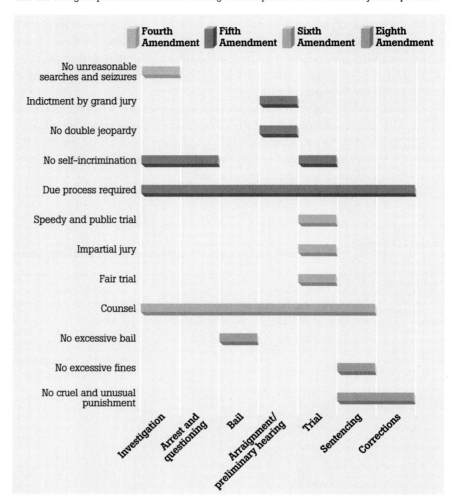

CHECK POINT

⑯ **What are the main criminal justice rights set forth in the Fifth Amendment?**

⑰ **What are the main criminal justice rights set forth in the Sixth Amendment?**

⑱ **What are the main criminal justice rights set forth in the Eighth Amendment?**

The Supreme Court Today

When William Rehnquist became chief justice in 1986, a new conservative majority on the Supreme Court began to consider issues such as preventive detention, unreasonable searches and seizures, and the death penalty. The appointments of Anthony M. Kennedy in 1988, David H. Souter in 1990, and Clarence Thomas in

1991 added more conservative justices to the Court. Even with the seating of Ruth Bader Ginsburg in 1993 to fill the vacancy left by Byron White and of Stephen G. Breyer in 1994 to fill the vacancy left by Harry Blackmun, two appointees placed on the high court by Democratic president Bill Clinton, the Court continues to lean in a conservative direction on criminal justice issues.

Despite its conservative reputation, the Rehnquist Court has not been as conservative as many of its critics believe (Hensley and Smith, 1995). It has maintained the landmark precedents dealing with the right to counsel (*Gideon v. Wainwright*), the exclusionary rule (*Mapp v. Ohio*), warnings to suspects (*Miranda v. Arizona*), and other rights. Although the Court has reduced the rights of defendants and given more flexibility to criminal justice officials, it still requires the authorities to be aware of the Bill of Rights in carrying out their responsibilities.

Some civil libertarians argue that state supreme courts have replaced the U.S. Supreme Court as the primary protectors of citizens' rights. State supreme courts are empowered to interpret their own states' constitutions to provide broader rights than those defined by the U.S. Supreme Court under the U.S. Constitution. For example, the U.S. Supreme Court decided that the Michigan State Police could set up random roadblocks that stopped all drivers, without any basis for suspicion, to look for drunk drivers (*Michigan Department of State Police v. Sitz*). Later, the Michigan Supreme Court barred such roadblocks as a violation of the state constitution (*Sitz v. Michigan Department of State Police*). States cannot provide less protection of individual rights than does the U.S. Constitution, but they can provide more. During the new era of conservatism on the Supreme Court, state judges might take the lead in providing broad protection for defendants in the criminal justice process.

Summary

- Criminal law focuses on prosecution and punishment by the state of people who violate specific laws enacted by legislatures, while civil law concerns disputes between private citizens or businesses.
- Criminal law is divided into two parts: substantive law that defines offenses and penalties, and procedural law that defines individuals' rights and the processes that criminal justice officials must follow in handling cases.
- The common law tradition, which was inherited from England, involves judges' shaping law through their decisions.
- Criminal law is found in written constitutions, statutes, judicial decisions, and administrative regulations.
- Substantive criminal law involves seven important elements that must exist and be demonstrated by the prosecution to obtain a conviction: legality, *actus reus*, causation, harm, concurrence, *mens rea*, punishment.
- The *mens rea* element, concerning intent or state of mind, can vary with different offenses, such as various degrees of murder or sexual assault. The element may also be disregarded for strict liability offenses that punish actions without considering intent.

■ Criminal law provides opportunities to present several defenses based on lack of criminal intent: entrapment, self-defense, necessity, duress (coercion), immaturity, mistake, intoxication, and insanity.

■ Standards for the insanity defense vary by jurisdiction with various state and federal courts using several different tests: M'Naghten Rule, Irresistible Impulse Test, Durham Rule, Comprehensive Crime Control Act Rule, the Model Penal Code rule.

■ The provisions of the Bill of Rights were not made applicable to state and local officials by the U.S. Supreme Court until the mid-twentieth century, when the Court incorporated most of the Bill of Rights' specific provisions into the due process clause of the Fourteenth Amendment.

■ The Fourth Amendment prohibition on unreasonable searches and seizures has produced many cases questioning the application of the exclusionary rule. Decisions by the Burger and Rehnquist Courts during the 1970s, 1980s, and 1990s have created several exceptions to the exclusionary rule and given greater flexibility to law enforcement officials.

■ The Fifth Amendment provides protections against compelled self-incrimination and double jeopardy. As part of the right against compelled self-incrimination, the Supreme Court created *Miranda* warnings that must be given to suspects before they are questioned.

■ The Sixth Amendment includes the right to counsel, the right to a speedy and public trial, and the right to an impartial jury.

■ The Eighth Amendment includes protections against excessive bail, excessive fines, and cruel and unusual punishments. Many of the Supreme Court's most well-known Eighth Amendment cases concern the death penalty, which the Court has endorsed, provided that states employ careful decision-making procedures that consider aggravating and mitigating factors.

Questions for Review

❶ What two functions does law perform? What are the two major divisions of the law?

❷ What are the sources of the criminal law? Where would you find it?

❸ List the seven principles of criminal law theory.

❹ What is meant by *mens rea*? Give examples of defenses that may be used by defendants in which they deny that *mens rea* existed when the crime was committed.

❺ What is meant by the "incorporation" of the Fourteenth Amendment to the U.S. Constitution?

Key Terms and Cases

administrative regulations (p. 86)

case law (p. 86)

civil forfeiture (p. 88)

civil law (p. 83)

common law (p. 85)

constitutions (p. 85)

double jeopardy (p. 109)

entrapment (p. 99)

exclusionary rule (p. 112)

fundamental fairness (p. 110)

inchoate offense (p. 90)

incorporation (p. 111)

mens rea (p. 90)

procedural criminal law (p. 82)

procedural due process (p. 107)

self-incrimination (p. 108)

statutes (p. 85)

strict liability (p. 98)

substantive criminal law (p. 82)

Barron v. Baltimore (p. 109)

Escobedo v. Illinois (p. 114)

Gideon v. Wainwright (p. 115)

Gregg v. Georgia (p. 119)

Mapp v. Ohio (p. 110)

Miranda v. Arizona (p. 114)

Powell v. Alabama (p. 109)

For Further Reading

Fletcher, George P. *A Crime of Self-Defense: Bernhard Goetz and the Law on Trial.* New York: Free Press, 1988. An insightful examination of the legal issues involved in the Goetz case.

Katz, Leo. *Bad Acts and Guilty Minds.* Chicago: University of Chicago Press, 1987. Exploration of questions raised by the insanity defense.

Lewis, Anthony. *Gideon's Trumpet.* New York: Vintage Books, 1964. A classic examination of the case of *Gideon v. Wainwright* showing the process by which the issues came to the U.S. Supreme Court.

Morris, Norval. *Madness and the Criminal Law.* Chicago: University of Chicago Press, 1982. A stimulating and controversial examination of the insanity defense by a leading criminal justice scholar.

Simpson, Alfred W. Bain. *Cannibalism and the Common Law.* Chicago: University of Chicago Press, 1984. Exciting study of the case of *The Queen v. Dudley and Stephens* showing that many such incidents occurred during the age of sail in which punishment did not follow.

Going Online

❶ Look at the criminal laws of your state (or another state). Are there any laws that some people might claim are out of step with current society, such as Michigan's law against using profanity in front of women and children? (www.findlaw.com)

❷ Find a U.S. Supreme Court decision from the past few years that has clarified or changed the rights possessed by suspects and defendants. How will this decision affect the behavior of police officers, prosecutors, and other officials in the criminal justice system? (www.law.cornell.edu)

❸ **Using InfoTrac College Edition,** find and read an article on the use of the insanity defense in criminal cases. Did the information or perspective provided by the article's author change your views about how the insanity defense ought to be defined and applied?

CHECK POINT ANSWERS

❶ Penal codes contain substantive criminal law that defines crimes and also punishments for those crimes.

❷ Procedural criminal law specifies the defendants' rights and tells justice system officials how they can investigate and process cases.

❸ Based on English tradition, judges make decisions relying on the precedents of earlier cases.

❹ Constitutions, statutes, case law, and administrative regulations.

❺ A felony usually involves a potential punishment of one year or more in prison; a misdemeanor carries a shorter term of incarceration, probation, fines, or community service.

❻ Civil law includes tort lawsuits (for example, personal injury cases), property law, contracts, and other disputes between two private parties.

❼ Legality, *actus reus*, causation, harm, concurrence, *mens rea*, punishment.

❽ New definitions of graded sex offenses that do not contain all the elements necessary to prove rape; new protections for victims with respect to questions asked in court.

❾ Strict liability offenses.

❿ Entrapment, self-defense, necessity, duress (coercion), immaturity, mistake, intoxication, insanity.

⓫ M'Naghten Rule (right-from-wrong test), Irresistible Impulse Test, Durham Rule, Model Penal Code, federal (Crime Control Act).

⓬ Taking a right from the Bill of Rights and applying it against state and local officials by making it a component of the due process clause of the Fourteenth Amendment.

⓭ Fundamental fairness.

⓮ Warren Court.

⓯ Exclusionary rule.

⓰ The right against compelled self-incrimination and against double jeopardy (also due process).

⓱ The right to counsel, to a speedy and fair trial, to a jury trial (also confrontation and compulsory process).

⓲ The right to protection against excessive bail, excessive fines, and cruel and unusual punishments.

Have Tough Crime Control Policies Caused a Decline in Crime?

There's good news and there's bad news. The good news is that by all measures, the amount of crime in the United States, especially violent crime, has been decreasing in recent years. In 1999 the FBI reported that serious crime had decreased for the seventh year in a row, the longest decline in twenty-five years. Two months later the Bureau of Justice Statistics announced that, during the 1993–1998 period, significant decreases were seen in every type of violent and property crime, and virtually every demographic group experienced drops in violent victimization.

Any reduction in crime is welcome, but the bad news is that, as criminologist Franklin Zimring has noted, it is "doubtful whether any experts really understand the causes for the decline in crime" (*New York Times*, January 5, 1997). Have the tough crime control policies of the past twenty years been successful in reducing crime? Or have crime rates declined because of factors unrelated to anything police, prosecution, courts, and corrections have done?

Is the drop in crime because of the tough crime control policies of federal and state governments over the past twenty years? Some experts say yes. They point to the 1994 Violent Crime Control and Law Enforcement Act, which proposed putting 100,000 extra police officers on the streets, extended the death penalty for sixty additional offenses, and funded more prisons. They say the police have been more aggressive in dealing with public order offenses, the waiting period for handgun purchases required by the Brady Law has been effective,

sentencing laws are tougher, and more than a million Americans are already in prison and off the streets. In other words, the police and other agencies of criminal justice do make a difference.

But have these policies been that important in reducing crime? Other experts point out that unemployment is low, the economy is good, and, most important, the number of males in the "crime-prone" age group is low. Many also say that the tough crime policies, instead of reducing crime, have devastated minority communities and diverted resources from dealing with the underlying causes of crime—unemployment, homelessness, and poverty. They urge policies that "put justice back in criminal justice."

Although crime rates have been falling, fear of crime is rising. A Gallup survey in 1998 found that 20 percent of Americans saw crime as the country's most important problem, the highest cited among the twenty-seven problems mentioned. Crime has been ranked number one since 1994, yet arguably it should rank much lower given the fall in victimizations. Because views of crime are shaped more by television news than by statistics, Americans have an unrealistic picture of the crime problem. A grisly picture of a murder scene on the evening news sticks in the mind like the results of crime studies never do.

Drugs and crime are popular issues in American politics, especially at a peaceful time when the country is less concerned about foreign enemies. Legislators respond easily to pressures to "do something about crime." Who can argue with that? They usually act by coming up with new laws mandating stiffer sentences and allocating more money for police and corrections. But is this the best direction for public policy to go?

For Tough Crime Control

Supporters of the tough crime control policies of the past two decades say crime, especially violent crime, is a serious problem. Even though rates have declined, they argue, violence is still many times higher than in other developed democracies. The United States must continue to pursue criminals through strict law enforcement, aggressive prosecutions, and the sentencing of career criminals to long prison terms. To take the pressure off because of recent declines in crime rates will open the way for more problems in the future.

To summarize the arguments for tough crime control policies:

- The United States has a serious crime problem. It must ensure that offenders receive strict and certain penalties.
- Crime is not caused by poverty, unemployment, and other socioeconomic factors. Instead, crime causes poverty.
- The expansion of the prison population has taken hardened criminals out of the community, thus contributing to the drop in crime.
- The police must have the resources and legal backing to pursue criminals.

Against Tough Crime Control

Opponents of the "get tough on crime" approach agree that crime is a problem, but they believe better ways are available to deal with the issue. They argue that crime is no more effectively controlled today than it was in the early 1970s and that in many respects the crime problem has worsened, because the gravest crisis is in the poorest, most crime-ridden and drug-dominated neighborhoods. Neither the "war on crime" nor the "war on drugs" has failed to stop the downward spiral of livability in these neighborhoods. Another price of the tough crime control policies has been an erosion of civil rights and liberties—especially for racial and ethnic minorities. What is needed is an infusion of justice into the system.

To summarize the arguments against tough crime control policies:

- The get-tough policies have not significantly reduced crime.
- Resources should be diverted from the criminal justice system to get to the underlying causes of criminal behavior—poor housing, unemployment, and racial injustice.
- Tough incarceration policies have devastated poor communities. With large numbers of young males in prison, families live in poverty, and children grow up without guidance from their fathers and older brothers.
- Crime policies emphasizing community policing, alternatives to incarceration, and community assistance programs will do more to promote justice than the failed get-tough policies of the past.

What Should U.S. Policy Be?

Operating the criminal justice system costs about $100 billion a year. Advocates of tough crime control policies say that the high cost is worth the price—cutting back would cost much more to crime victims and society as a whole. The crime rate is lower because of the more aggressive and punitive policies of the past two decades.

Opponents of these policies respond that law enforcement and the administration of justice have had little impact on crime levels. Other factors—the smaller number of males in the "crime-prone" age cohort and a booming economy, for instance—have been responsible for the reduction. The diversion of resources—in both money and people—to fighting crime has limited government programs that could improve conditions in poor neighborhoods where crime flourishes.

Even though they are told crime has gone down, Americans remain fearful. Their opinions translate into support for politicians who advocate the tough approach. No candidate for public office wants to be labeled "soft on crime." What would be the costs—economic and human—of continuing the get-tough policies? Would that same fearful public be affected?

Police

Most Americans have an image of the police that they get from movies and television, but the reality differs greatly from the dramatic exploits of the cops in *Law & Order* or *NYPD Blue.* Although the police

are the most visible agents of the criminal justice system, images of them come mainly from fiction.

In Part Two the police are examined as the key unit of the criminal justice system: the one that confronts crime in the community. Chapter 4 traces the history of policing and looks at its functions and organization. Chapter 5 explores the daily operations of the police, and Chapter 6 analyzes current issues and trends in policing. As we will see, police work is often done in a hostile environment in which life and death, honor and dishonor may be at stake. Police officers are given discretion to deal with many situations; how they use it has an important effect on the way society views policing.

Police

At 9:02 A.M. on April 19, 1995, a bomb blast ripped through the Alfred P. Murrah Federal Building in Oklahoma City, collapsing nine floors and piling debris on almost two hundred of the five hundred people in the building. When the dust and smoke had cleared 168 bodies, 19 of them children, were found at the site. This was the deadliest act of terrorism in the history of the United States.

While public safety agencies rushed to the bomb site, Timothy McVeigh was sixty miles north of Oklahoma City, tooling along I–35 in his yellow 1977 Mercury Marquis. He was pulled over by a state trooper who noticed that the car did not have license tags. McVeigh was arrested on a firearms charge after the traffic stop and held pending bail. On April 21, as he was about to make bail, federal authorities arrested McVeigh because he resembled the bombing suspect labeled "John Doe No. 1." This arrest, and the investigation and trial that followed, led to McVeigh's death sentence by a Denver jury in June 1997.

The events at Oklahoma City gave Americans a lesson in the complex nature of law enforcement in the United States. Within hours of the blast, units from the Federal Bureau of Investigation, Drug Enforcement Administration, Bureau of Alcohol, Tobacco and Firearms, Department of Defense, Oklahoma National Guard, Oklahoma Department of Public Safety, and the Oklahoma City Police were on the scene to rescue survivors, remove the dead, and track down the people responsible for the bombing.

Before the destruction of the Murrah Building, few Americans had ever heard of the Bureau of Alcohol, Tobacco, and Firearms of the U.S. Treasury Department—or had known that it might act in such circumstances. The fact that so many different law enforcement agencies were involved was further evidence of the network of relationships among national, state, and local police forces. This complexity may have surprised and confused those who think only of their local police when they think of law enforcement.

The men and women in blue are the most visible presence of government in U.S. society. Whether they are members of the local or state police, sheriff's departments, or federal agencies, the more than 700,000 sworn officers in the country play key roles in American society. Citizens look to them to perform a wide range of functions: crime prevention, law enforcement, order maintenance, and community services. However, the public's expectations of the police are not always clear. Citizens also form judgments about the police, and those judgments have a strong impact on the way the police function.

In a free society the police are required to maintain order. In performing this task, police officers are given a great deal of authority. Using their powers to arrest, search, detain, and use force, they can interfere with the freedom of any citizen. If they are excessive in the use of such powers, they can threaten the basic values of a stable, democratic society.

In this chapter we examine several aspects of policing. A brief history of the police is followed by discussions of how police officers carry out their duties and how law enforcement decisions are made.

QUESTIONS
for Inquiry

- How has policing evolved in the United States?
- What are the main types of police agencies, and how are they organized?
- What influences police policy and styles of policing?
- What are the functions of the police?
- How do police officers balance action, decision making, and discretion?

 ## The Development of Police in the United States

Law and order is not a new concept; it has been a subject of debate since the first police force was formed in London in 1829. Looking back even further, to the Magna Carta of 1215, limits were placed on constables and bailiffs. Reading between the lines of that historic document reveals that the problems of police abuse, maintenance of order, and the rule of law in thirteenth-century England were those faced by modern societies. The same remedies— recruiting better-qualified people to serve as police, stiffening the penalties for official misconduct, creating a civilian board of control— were suggested even then to ensure that order was kept in accordance with the rule of law.

The English Roots of the American Police

The roots of American policing lie in the English legal tradition. Three major aspects of American policing evolved from that tradition: (1) limited authority, (2) local control, and (3) fragmented organization. Like the British police, but unlike police in continental Europe, the police in the United States have limited authority; their powers and duties are specifically defined by law. England, like the United States, has no national police force; instead, forty-three regional authorities are headed by elected commissioners who appoint the local chief constable. Above the local authorities is the home secretary of the national government who provides funding and may intervene in cases of police corruption, mismanagement, and discipline. In the United States policing is fragmented: there are many types of agencies— constable, county sheriff, city police, FBI—each with its own special jurisdiction and responsibilities.

English "bobbies" began serving the London public after passage of the Metropolitan Police Act of 1829.

Systems for protecting citizens and property existed before the thirteenth century. The **frankpledge** system required that groups of ten families, called tithings, agree to uphold the law, keep order, and bring violators to a court. By custom, every male above the age of 12 was part of the system. When a man became aware that a crime had occurred, he was obliged to raise a "hue and cry" and to join others in his tithing to track down the offender. The tithing was fined if members did not perform its duties.

Over time England developed a system in which individuals were chosen within each community to take charge of catching criminals. The Statute of Winchester, enacted in 1285, set up a parish constable-watch system. Members of the community were still required to pursue criminals, just as they had been under the frankpledge system, but now a constable supervised those efforts. The constable was a man chosen from the parish to serve without pay as its law enforcement officer for one year. The constable had the power to call the entire community into action if a serious disturbance arose. Watchmen, who were appointed to help the constable, spent most of their time patrolling the town at night to ensure that "all's well" and enforcing the criminal law. They were also responsible for lighting street lamps and putting out fires.

Not until the eighteenth century did an organized police force evolve in England. With the growth of commerce and industry, cities expanded while farming declined as the main source of employment and the focus of community life. In the larger cities these changes produced social disorder.

In the mid-eighteenth century, the novelist Henry Fielding and his brother, Sir John Fielding, led efforts to improve law enforcement in London. They wrote newspaper articles to inform the public about crime and published flyers describing known offenders. After Henry Fielding became a magistrate in 1748, he organized a small group of "thief takers" to pursue and arrest lawbreakers. The government was so impressed with Fielding's Bow Street Amateur Volunteer Force

frankpledge

A system in old English law in which members of a tithing, a group of ten families, pledged to be responsible for keeping order and bringing violators of the law to court.

(known as the "Bow Street Runners") that it paid the participants and attempted to form similar groups in other parts of London.

After Henry Fielding's death in 1754, these efforts declined. As time went by, many saw that the government needed to assert itself in enforcing laws and maintaining order. London, with its unruly mobs, had become an especially dangerous place.

In the early 1800s several attempts were made to create a centralized police force for London. While people saw the need for social order, some feared that a police force would threaten the freedom of citizens and lead to tyranny. Finally, in 1829, Sir Robert Peel, home secretary in the British Cabinet, pushed Parliament to pass the Metropolitan Police Act, which created the London police force.

This agency was organized like a military unit, with a one-thousand-man force commanded by two magistrates, later called "commissioners." The officers were called "bobbies" after Sir Robert Peel. In the British system, Cabinet members who oversee government departments are chosen from the elected members of Parliament. Thus, because it was supervised by Peel, the first police force was under the control of democratically elected officials.

Under Peel's direction the police had a four-part mandate:

❶ To prevent crime without using repressive force and to avoid having to call upon the military to control riots and other disturbances.
❷ To maintain public order by nonviolent means, using force to obtain compliance only as a last resort.
❸ To reduce conflict between the police and the public.
❹ To show efficiency through the absence of crime and disorder rather than through visible police actions. (Manning, 1977:82)

In effect, this meant keeping a low profile while maintaining order. Because of fears that a national force would threaten civil liberties, political leaders made every effort to focus police activities at the local level. These concerns were transported to the United States.

CHECK POINT

① **What are the three main features of American policing that were inherited from England?**

② **What was the frankpledge and how did it work?**

③ **What did the Statute of Winchester (1285) establish?**

④ **What did the Metropolitan Police Act (1829) establish?**

⑤ **What were the four mandates of the English police in the nineteenth century?**
(Answers are at the end of the chapter.)

Policing in the United States

Before the Revolution, Americans shared the English belief that members of a community had a duty to help maintain order; therefore they adopted the offices of constable, sheriff, and night watchman. The watch system was the main means of keeping order and catching criminals. Each citizen was required to be a member of the watch, but paid watchmen could be hired as replacements. Over time cities began to hire paid, uniformed watchmen to deal with crime.

After the formation of the federal government in 1789, police power remained with the states, again in response to fear of centralized law enforcement. However, the American police developed under conditions that were different from those in England. Unlike the British, police in the United States had to deal with ethnic diversity, local political control, regional differences, the exploration and settling of the West, and a generally more violent society.

American policing is often described in terms of three historical periods: the political era (1840–1920), the professional model era (1920–1970), and the community model era (1970–present) (Kelling and Moore, 1988). This description has been criticized because it applies only to the urban areas of the Northeast and does not take into account the very different development of the police in rural areas of the South and West. Still, it is useful as a framework for exploring the organization of the police, the focus of police work, and the strategies employed by police (Williams and Murphy, 1990).

During the Political Era, the officer on a neighborhood beat dealt with crime and disorder as it arose. Police also performed various social services, such as providing beds and food for the homeless.

The Political Era: 1840–1920

The period from 1840 to 1920 is called the political era because of the close ties that were formed between the police and local political leaders. In many cities the police seemed to work for the mayor's political party rather than for the citizens. This relationship served both groups in that the political "machines" recruited and maintained the police while the police helped the machine leaders get out the vote for favored candidates. Ranks in the police force were often for sale to the highest bidder, and many officers took payoffs for not enforcing laws on drinking, gambling, and prostitution (Walker, 1999:26).

In the United States as in England, the growth of cities led to pressures to modernize law enforcement. Social relations in cities were different from those in the towns and countryside. From 1830 to 1870 the large cities experienced much civil disorder. Ethnic conflict, hostility toward nonslave blacks and abolitionists, mob actions against banks during economic declines, and violence in settling questions of morality, such as the use of alcohol—all these factors contributed to fears that a stable democracy would not survive.

Around 1840 the large cities began to create police forces. In 1845 New York City established the first full-time, paid police force. Boston and Philadelphia were the first to add a daytime police force to supplement the night watchmen; other cities—Chicago, Cincinnati, New Orleans—quickly followed.

By 1850 most major cities had created police departments organized on the English model. Departments were headed by a chief appointed by the mayor and council. The city was divided into precincts, and full-time, paid patrolmen were assigned to each. Early police forces sought to prevent crimes and keep order through the use of foot patrols. The officer on the beat dealt with crime, disorder, and other problems as they arose.

In addition to foot patrols, the police performed a number of service functions, such as caring for derelicts, operating soup kitchens, regulating public health, and handling medical and social emergencies. In cities across the country, the police provided beds and food for homeless people. In station houses, overnight "lodgers" might sleep on the floor or sometimes in clean bunkrooms (Monkkonen, 1981:127). Because they were the only governmental agency that had close contact with life on the streets of the city, the police became general public servants as well as crime control officers. Because of these close links with and their service to the community, they had the support of citizens (Monkkonen, 1992:554).

Police developed differently in the South because of the existence of slavery and the agrarian nature of that region. Historians note that the first organized police agencies with full-time officers developed in cities with large numbers of slaves (Charleston, New Orleans, Richmond, and Savannah), where white owners feared slave uprisings (Rousey, 1984:41). The owners created "slave patrols" to deal with runaways. The patrols had full power to break into the homes of slaves who were suspected of keeping arms, to physically punish those who did not obey their orders, and to arrest runaways and return them to their masters.

Westward expansion in the United States produced conditions different from those in either the urban East or the agricultural South. The frontier was settled before order could be established. Thus, those who wanted to maintain law and order often had to take matters into their own hands by forming vigilante groups.

One of the first official positions created in rural areas was that of sheriff. Although the sheriff had duties similar to those of the "shire reeves" of seventeenth-century England, the American sheriff was elected and had broad powers to enforce the law. As elected officers, sheriffs had close ties to local politics. They also depended on the men of the community for assistance. This is how the *posse comitatus* (Latin for "power of the county"), borrowed from fifteenth-century Europe, came into being. Local men above the age of 15 were required to respond to the sheriff's call for assistance, forming a body known as a *posse.*

After the Civil War the federal government appointed U.S. marshals to help enforce the law in the western territories. Some of the best-known folk heroes of American policing were U.S. Marshals Wyatt Earp, Bat Masterson, and Wild Bill Hickok, who tried to bring law and order to the "Wild West" (Calhoun, 1990). While some marshals did extensive law enforcement work, most had mainly judicial duties, such as keeping order in the courtroom and holding prisoners for trial.

During the twentieth century all parts of the country became increasingly urban. This change blurred some of the regional differences that had helped define policing in the past. In addition, growing criticism of the influence of politics on the police led to efforts to reform the nature and organization of the police. Reformers sought to make police more professional and to reduce their ties to local politics.

The Professional Model Era: 1920–1970

American policing was greatly influenced by the Progressive movement. The Progressives were mainly upper-middle-class, educated Americans with two goals: more efficient government and more governmental services to assist the less fortunate. A related goal was to reduce the influence of party politics and patronage (favoritism in handing out jobs) on government. The Progressives saw a need for professional law enforcement officials who would use modern technology to benefit society as a whole, not just local politicians.

The key to the Progressives' concept of professional law enforcement is found in their slogan, "The police have to get out of politics, and politics has to get out of

During the Professional Era, the police saw themselves as crime fighters. Yet many inner-city residents saw them as a well-armed, occupying force rather than as public servants who might be looked to for help.

the police." August Vollmer, chief of police of Berkeley, California, from 1909 to 1932, was one of the leading advocates of professional policing. He initiated the use of motorcycle units, handwriting analysis, and fingerprinting. With other police reformers, such as Leonhard Fuld, Raymond Fosdic, Bruce Smith, and O. W. Wilson, he urged that the police be made into a professional force, a nonpartisan agency of government committed to public service. This model of professional policing has six elements:

❶ The force should stay out of politics.
❷ Members should be well trained, well disciplined, and tightly organized.
❸ Laws should be enforced equally.
❹ The force should use new technology.
❺ Personnel procedures should be based on merit.
❻ The main task of the police should be fighting crime.

Refocusing attention on crime control and away from maintaining order probably did more than anything else to change the nature of American policing. The narrow focus on crime fighting broke many of the ties that the police had formed with the communities they served. By the end of World War I, police departments had greatly reduced their involvement in social services. Instead, for the most part, cops became crime fighters.

O. W. Wilson, a student of Vollmer, was a leading advocate of professionalism. He earned a degree in criminology at the University of California in 1924 and became chief of police in Wichita, Kansas, in 1928. He came to national attention by reorganizing the department and fighting police corruption. He promoted the use of motorized patrols, efficient radio communication, and rapid response. He believed that one-officer patrols were the best way to use personnel and that the two-way radio, which allowed for supervision by commanders, made officers more efficient (Reiss, 1992:51). He rotated assignments so that officers on patrol would not become too familiar with people in the community (and thus prone to corruption). In 1960 Wilson became superintendent of the Chicago Police Department with a mandate to end corruption there.

The new emphasis on professionalism spurred the formation of the International Association of Chiefs of Police (IACP) in 1902 and the Fraternal Order of Police (FOP) in 1915. Both organizations promoted the use of new technologies, training standards, and a code of ethics.

Advocates of professionalism urged that the police be made aware of the need to act lawfully and to protect the rights of all citizens, including those suspected of crimes. They sought to instill a strong—some would even say rigid ("Just the facts, ma'am")—commitment to the law and to equal treatment (Goldstein, 1990:7).

By the 1930s, the police were using new technologies and methods to combat serious crimes. They became more effective against crimes such as murder, rape, and robbery—an important factor in gaining citizen support. By contrast, efforts to control victimless offenses and to strictly maintain order often aroused citizen opposition. As Mark Moore and George Kelling have noted, "The clean, bureaucratic model of policing put forth by the reformers could be sustained only if the scope of police responsibility was narrowed to 'crime fighting' " (Moore and Kelling, 1983:55).

In the 1960s the civil rights and antiwar movements, urban riots, and rising crime rates challenged many of the assumptions of the professional model. In their attempts to maintain order during public demonstrations, the police in many cities seemed to be concerned mainly with maintaining the status quo. Thus, police officers found themselves enforcing laws that tended to discriminate against African Americans and the poor. With America's growing numbers of low-income racial minorities living in the inner cities, the professional style isolated the police from the communities they served. In the eyes of many inner-city residents, the police were an occupying army keeping them at the bottom of society, not public servants helping all citizens.

Although the police continued to portray themselves as crime fighters, citizens became aware that the police often were not effective in this role. Crime rates rose for many offenses, and the police were unable to change the perception that the quality of urban life was declining.

The Community Policing Era: 1970–Present

Beginning in the 1970s, calls were heard for a move away from the crime-fighting focus and toward greater emphasis on keeping order and providing services to the community. Research studies revealed the complex nature of police work and the extent to which day-to-day practices deviated from the professional ideal. The research also questioned the effectiveness of the police in catching and deterring criminals.

Three findings of this research are especially noteworthy:

❶ Increasing the number of patrol officers in a neighborhood was found to have little effect on the crime rate.

❷ Rapid response to calls for service did not greatly increase the arrest rate.

❸ Improving the percentage of crimes solved is difficult.

Such findings undermined acceptance of the professional crime-fighter model (Moore, 1992:99). Critics argued that the professional style isolated the police from the community and reduced their knowledge about the neighborhoods they served, especially when police patrolled in cars. Use of the patrol car prevented personal contacts with citizens. Instead, it was argued, police should get out of their cars and spend more time meeting and helping residents. This would permit the police to help people with a range of problems and in some cases to prevent problems from arising or growing worse. For example, if the police know about conflicts between people in a neighborhood, they can try to mediate and perhaps prevent the conflict from growing into a criminal assault or other serious problem. It was hoped that closer contact with citizens would not only permit the police to help them in new ways but also make them feel safer, knowing that the police were available and interested in their problems.

In a provocative article titled "Broken Windows: The Police and Neighborhood Safety," James Q. Wilson and George L. Kelling argued that policing should work more on "little problems" such as maintaining order, providing services to those in need, and adopting strategies to reduce the fear of crime (Wilson and Kelling, 1982:29). They based their approach on three assumptions:

❶ Neighborhood disorder creates fear. Areas with street people, youth gangs, prostitution, and drunks are high-crime areas.

❷ Just as broken windows are a signal that nobody cares and can lead to more serious vandalism, untended disorderly behavior is a signal that the community does not care. This also leads to more serious disorder and crime.

❸ If the police are to deal with disorder and thus reduce fear and crime, they must rely on citizens for assistance.

Advocates of the community policing approach urge greater use of foot patrols so that officers will become known to citizens, who in turn will cooperate with the police. They believe that through attention to little problems, the police may not only reduce disorder and fear but also improve public attitudes toward policing. When citizens respond positively to police efforts, the police will have "improved bases of community and political support, which in turn can be exploited to gain further cooperation from citizens in a wide variety of activities" (Kelling, 1985:299).

Closely related to the community policing concept is *problem-oriented policing.* Herman Goldstein, the originator of this approach, argued that instead of focusing on crime and disorder the police should identify the underlying causes of such problems as noisy teenagers, spouse batterers, and abandoned buildings used as drug houses. In so doing they could reduce disorder and fear of crime (Goldstein, 1979:236). Closer contacts between the police and the community might then reduce the hostility that has developed between officers and residents in many urban neighborhoods (Sparrow, Moore, and Kennedy, 1990).

In *Fixing Broken Windows,* a book written in response to the Wilson and Kelling article, George L. Kelling and Catherine Coles (1996) call for strategies to restore order and reduce crime in public spaces in U.S. communities. In Baltimore, New York, San Francisco, and Seattle, police are paying greater attention to "quality-of-life crimes"—by arresting subway fare-beaters, rousting loiterers and panhandlers from parks, and aggressively dealing with those obstructing sidewalks, harassing, and soliciting. By handling these "little crimes," the police not only help restore order but also often prevent more serious crimes. In New York, for example, searching fare-beaters often yielded weapons, questioning a street vendor selling hot merchandise led to a fence specializing in

Community policing encourages personal contact between officers and citizens. How does such contact affect citizens' expectations about relationships with police?

stolen weapons, and arresting a person for urinating in a park resulted in discovery of a cache of weapons.

Although reformers argue for a greater focus on order maintenance and service, they do not call for an end to the crime-fighting role. Instead, they want a shift of emphasis. The police should pay more attention to community needs and seek to understand the problems underlying crime, disorder, and incivility. These proposals have been adopted by police executives in many cities and by influential organizations such as the Police Foundation and the Police Executive Research Forum.

Can—and should—community policing be implemented throughout the nation? The populations of some cities, especially in the West, are too dispersed to permit a switch to foot patrols. In many cities foot patrols and community police stations have been set up in public housing projects. Time will tell if this new approach will become as widespread as the focus on professionalism was in the first half of the twentieth century. The call for a new focus for the police has not gone unchallenged (Reichers and Roberg, 1990:105). Critics question whether the professional model really isolated police from community residents (Walker, 1984:88). Taking another view, Carl Klockars doubts that the police will give higher priority to maintaining order and wonders whether Americans want their police to be something other than crime fighters (Klockars, 1985:300).

Whichever approach the police take—professional, crime fighting, or community policing—it must be carried out through a bureaucratic structure. We therefore turn to a discussion of police organization in the United States.

CHECK POINT

(6) **What are the three historical periods of American policing?**

(7) **What was the main feature of the political era?**

(8) **What were the major recommendations of the Progressive reformers?**

(9) **What are the main criticisms of the professional era?**

(10) **What is community policing?**

Organization of the Police

As discussed in Chapter 1, the United States has a federal system of government with separate national and state structures, each with authority over certain functions. Most of the nineteen thousand police agencies at the national, state, county, and municipal levels are responsible for carrying out four functions: (1) enforcing the law, (2) maintaining order, (3) preventing crime, and (4) providing services to the community. They employ a total of more than one million people, sworn and unsworn. The agencies include the following:

- 13,578 municipal police departments,
- 3,088 sheriffs' departments,
- 1,316 special police agencies (jurisdictions limited to transit systems, parks, schools, and so on),
- 49 state police departments (all states except Hawaii),
- 135 Native American tribal police agencies, and
- 50 federal law enforcement agencies (BJS, 1998b).

This list shows both the fragmentation and the local orientation of American police. The local nature of law enforcement is also revealed by the fact that only 17 percent of funds for police work are spent by the national government, and only 11 percent by state governments. The other 72 percent are spent by municipal and county governments. Each level of the system has different responsibilities, either for different kinds of crimes, such as the federal authority over counterfeiting, or for different geographic areas, such as state police authority over major highways (see Figure 4.1). Local units exercise the broadest authority.

Federal Agencies

Federal law enforcement agencies are part of the executive branch of the national government. They investigate a specific set of crimes defined by Congress. Recent federal efforts against drug trafficking, organized crime, insider stock trading, and environmental pollution have attracted attention to these agencies even though they employ only seventy-five thousand full-time officers authorized to make arrests and handle relatively few crimes.

The Federal Bureau of Investigation is an investigative agency within the U.S. Justice Department with the power to investigate all federal crimes not placed under the jurisdiction of other agencies. Established as the Bureau of Investigation in 1908, it came to national prominence under J. Edgar Hoover, its director from 1924 until his death in 1972. Hoover made major changes in the Bureau (renamed the Federal Bureau of Investigation in 1935) to increase its professionalism. He sought to remove political factors from the selection of agents, established the national fingerprint filing system, and oversaw the development of the Uniform Crime Reporting System. Although Hoover has been criticized for many aspects of his career, such as FBI spying on civil rights and antiwar activists during the 1960s, his role in improving police work and the FBI's effectiveness is widely recognized.

FIGURE 4.1 — **The organization of police in the United States**

Policing is found at all levels of government and involves many types of work.

FEDERAL

The fifty police agencies of the federal government are primarily concerned with violations of federal law, especially those criminal acts that cross state boundaries.

STATE

All states except Hawaii have a law enforcement agency with statewide jurisdiction, yet only two-thirds of state forces have general police powers.

COUNTY

In rural areas the county sheriff is responsible for law enforcement.

LOCAL

Most police officers work for local governments and are responsible for order maintenance, law enforcement, and service.

With about eleven thousand agents and an annual budget of $3 billion, the FBI now places greater emphasis on five areas: white-collar crime, organized crime, terrorism, foreign intelligence operations in the United States, and political corruption (Proveda, 1990). The Bureau provides valuable assistance to state and local law enforcement through its crime laboratory, training programs, and databases on fingerprints, stolen vehicles, and missing persons.

As noted by Samuel Walker, since Hoover's death the FBI has been more responsive to the law enforcement policies of each presidential administration (Walker, 1999:57). An indication that the bureau is no longer above criticism, as it was during Hoover's reign, is the congressional investigation of the FBI's 1993 attack and resulting explosion of the Branch Davidian compound in Waco, Texas.

Specialization in Federal Law Enforcement

Other federal agencies are concerned with specific kinds of crimes. Within the FBI is the semiautonomous Drug Enforcement Administration (DEA). As part of the Treasury Department, the Internal Revenue Service (IRS) pursues violations of tax laws; the Bureau of Alcohol, Tobacco, and Firearms deals with alcohol, tobacco, and gun control; and the Customs Service enforces customs regulations. Other federal law enforcement agencies include the Secret Service Division of the Treasury Department (counterfeiting, forgery, and protection of the president), the Bureau of Postal Inspection of the Postal Service (mail offenses), and the Border Patrol of the Department of Justice's Immigration and Naturalization Service (INS). Some other departments of the executive branch, such as the U.S. Coast Guard and the National Parks Service, have police powers related to their specific duties.

Internationalization of U.S. Law Enforcement

The general public is not aware that law enforcement agencies of the U.S. government have increasingly stationed officers overseas (Nadelmann, 1993). Agents of the Customs Service, the Immigration and Naturalization Service, and the Postal Inspection Service have worked with foreign governments since the nation's founding. In recent years, however, the FBI, IRS, and DEA have also established offices overseas. In a shrinking world with a global economy,

Agents of the Bureau of Alcohol, Tobacco, and Firearms of the U.S. Treasury Department use force to enter a residence suspected of harboring illegal weapons.

electronic communications, and jet aircraft, much crime is transnational, giving rise to a host of international criminal law enforcement tasks. American law enforcement is being "exported" in response to increased international terrorism, drug trafficking, smuggling of illegal immigrants, violations of U.S. securities laws, money laundering, and the potential theft of nuclear materials. Global crime is not new, but international criminality is increasingly seen as a national security issue (*New York Times*, April 17, 1995:1).

To meet these challenges, U.S. agencies have dramatically increased the number of officers stationed in foreign countries. For example, "between 1967 and 1991 the number of U.S. drug agents stationed abroad rose from 12 in eight foreign cities to about 300 in more than seventy foreign locations" (Nadelmann, 1993:3). Similar increases can be cited for FBI, Customs, Secret Service, INS, and Commerce Department officers. More than fifteen hundred law enforcement personnel are now assigned to more than fifty countries.

With a growing concern about Russian organized crime, the FBI has opened a full-fledged office in Budapest. The Hungarian capital is home to many of Russia's mob leaders, who use the city as a portal to Western Europe and the United States. The Hungarian government requested help from the United States and has given FBI agents the right to carry weapons and, in conjunction with their Hungarian counterparts, make arrests (*New York Times*, Febuary 21, 2000:3).

Agencies operating overseas seek to enforce U.S. laws and protect the American people; however, they are limited by the sovereignty of the host countries. Although U.S. law may permit U.S. police to investigate, seize evidence, and make arrests abroad, foreign laws may forbid law enforcement activities by foreign agents on their territory. To deal with these issues, efforts have been made to work jointly with foreign governments on common problems.

U.S. operatives have been able to track down a number of wanted criminals with the cooperation of the host country. In February 1995 Ramzi Ahmed Yousef, the suspected ringleader of the World Trade Center bombing in New York, was captured as a result of FBI efforts in Japan, Pakistan, and the Philippines. And three foreigners have been added to the FBI's "Ten Most Wanted Fugitives": Juan Garcia Abrego, chief of the Mexican drug cartel, and Abdel Basset Ali Al-Megrahi and Lamen Kahlifa Fhimah, the two Libyans wanted for the bombing of Pan Am flight 103, which killed 279 people over Lockerbie, Scotland.

The complexities—and risks—of working with law enforcement agencies of several countries are seen in the DEA's efforts to gain the cooperation of Mexico to stop the flow of Colombian cocaine shipped to the United States through Mexico. In February 1997 those efforts were compromised when the head of Mexico's national drug agency, General Gutierrez Rebollo, was dismissed and detained following charges that he had protected and accepted huge payments from one of Mexico's most notorious drug barons (*New York Times*, February 20, 1997:1).

Interpol, the International Criminal Police Organization, now based in Lyon, France, was created in 1946 to foster cooperation among the world's police forces (Anderson, 1989). Interpol maintains an intelligence databank and serves as a clearinghouse for information gathered by agencies of its 177 member nations. Long criticized by law enforcement experts for its outdated technology, complex bureaucracy, the unreliable protection of sensitive intelligence information, Interpol has undergone major reforms to become a "formidable instrument for combating global crime" (*Los Angeles Times*, January 4, 1998:1).

The U.S. Interpol unit, the U.S. National Central Bureau based in Washington, D.C., facilitates communication with foreign police agencies. It has a permanent staff of eighty-five, plus officers assigned by thirteen federal agencies including the FBI, the Secret Service, and the DEA. In recent years Interpol has formed links with state and local police forces in the United States (Geller and Morris, 1992:297). With criminals increasingly viewing their activities on a global scale and taking advantage of technological advances, cooperation among law enforcement agencies around the world is essential.

Since the end of the cold war, American police organizations have assisted United Nations peacekeeping operations in Bosnia, Cyprus, Haiti, Kosovo, Panama, and Somalia. In these countries more than three thousand police officers from around the world "have engaged in monitoring, mentoring, training, and generally assisting their local counterparts" (Perito, 1999:9). American involvement has emphasized the need for policing to be conducted by civilian police forces whose officers are trained in basic law enforcement skills and display respect for the law and for human rights.

State Agencies

Every state except Hawaii has its own law enforcement agency with statewide jurisdiction. In about half, state police agencies carry out a wide range of law enforcement tasks. The others have state highway patrols with limited authority, primarily the task of enforcing traffic laws. The American reluctance to centralize police power has generally kept state police forces from replacing local ones.

Before 1900 only Texas had a state police force. The Texas Rangers, a quasi-military force, had been formed to protect residents from bandits and Indian raids. It had already been established by 1836, when Texas declared its independence from Mexico. But the modern state police forces were organized after the turn of the century, mainly as a wing of the executive branch that would enforce the law when local officials did not. The Pennsylvania State Constabulary, formed in 1905, was the first such force. By 1925 almost all of the states had police forces.

All state forces regulate traffic on main highways, and two-thirds of the states have also given them general police powers. In only about a dozen populous states are these forces able to perform law enforcement tasks outside the cities. Where the state police are well established—as in Massachusetts, Michigan, New Jersey, New York, and Pennsylvania—they also enforce the law in rural areas. For the most part, however, they operate only in areas where no other form of police protection exists or where local officers ask for their help. In many states, for example, the crime lab is run by the state police as a means of assisting local law enforcement agencies.

County Agencies

Sheriffs are found in almost every one (except Alaska) of the thirty-one hundred counties in the United States, employing 263,000 sworn and unsworn officers. Sheriffs' departments are responsible for policing rural areas, but over time, especially in the Northeast, many of their criminal justice functions have been assumed by the state or local police. In parts of the South and West, however, the sheriff's department is a well-organized force. In thirty-three states sheriffs are elected and hold the position of chief law enforcement officer in the county. Even when the sheriff's office is well organized, however, it may lack jurisdiction over cities and towns. In these situations, the sheriff and his or her deputies patrol unincorporated parts of the county or small towns that do not have police forces of their own.

In addition to performing law enforcement tasks, the sheriff is often an officer of the court; sheriffs may operate jails, serve court orders, and provide the bailiffs who maintain order in courtrooms. In many counties, politics mixes with law enforcement: sheriffs may be able to appoint their political supporters as deputies and bailiffs. In other places, such as Los Angeles County and Oregon's Multnomah County, the sheriff's department is staffed by professionals.

Native American Tribal Police

Through treaties with the United States, Native American tribes are separate, sovereign nations and have a significant degree of legal autonomy. They have the power to enforce tribal criminal laws against members and non-Indians on tribal lands (Mentzer, 1996:24–29). The last national census found 1.9 million Native Americans belonging to approximately five hundred tribes. However, many tribes are not recognized by the federal government, and many Native Americans do not live on reservations.

Traditionally Native American reservations have been policed either by federal officers of the Bureau of Indian Affairs (BIA) or by their own tribal police. The Bureau of Justice Statistics identified 135 tribal law enforcement agencies with a total of 1,731 full-time sworn officers. An additional 339 full-time sworn officers of the BIA provide law enforcement services on other reservations (BJS, 1999a:32). As the number of non-Native Americans entering reservations for recreational purposes (especially to gamble) increases, criminal jurisdiction disputes have risen.

Municipal Agencies

The police departments of cities and towns have general law enforcement authority. City police forces range in size from more than thirty-seven thousand sworn officers in the New York City Police Department to only one sworn officer in 1,657 small towns. Slightly more than half of municipal police departments employ fewer than ten sworn officers. There are an estimated 531,496 full-time employees of police departments, almost 80 percent sworn personnel (officers with arrest powers) (BJS, 1999f).

Nearly 90 percent of local police agencies serve populations of 25,000 or less, but half of all sworn officers are employed in cities of at least 100,000 (BJS, 1998b:5). The six largest departments—New York City, Chicago, Los Angeles, Houston, Philadelphia, Detroit—

Referred to as the "militarization of Mayberry," police SWAT teams became part of the "war on drugs" during the 1980s. But does a city such as Meriden, Connecticut (population 40,000), really need such a team today?

provide law enforcement services to less than 8 percent of the U.S. population, yet face 23 percent of all violent crime. These big-city departments employ 13 percent of all sworn officers (Pate and Hamilton, 1991:34–35).

In a metropolitan area composed of a central city and a number of suburbs, policing is usually divided among agencies at all levels of government, giving rise to conflicts between jurisdictions that may interfere with efficient use of police resources. The city and each suburb buys its own equipment and deploys its officers without coordinating with those of nearby jurisdictions. In some areas with large populations, agreements have been made to enhance cooperation between jurisdictions.

COMPARATIVE
perspective

France has a population of about 52 million and a unitary form of government. Political power and decision making are highly centralized in bureaucracies located in Paris. The entire country has a single criminal code and standardized criminal justice procedures. The country is divided into ninety-six territories known as departments and further divided into districts and municipalities. In each district, a commissaire of the republic represents the central government and exercises supervision over the local mayors.

Organization of the Police in France

Police functions are divided between two separate forces under the direction of two ministries of the central government. With more than 200,000 personnel employed in police duties, France has a

ratio of law enforcement officers to the general population that is greater than that of the United States or England.

The older police force, the Gendarmerie Nationale, with more than eighty thousand officers, is under the military and is responsible for policing about 95 percent of the country's territory. The gendarmerie patrols the highways, rural areas, and those communities with populations of less than ten thousand. Members are organized into brigades or squads collectively known as the Departmental Gendarmerie. They operate from fixed points, reside in their duty area, and constitute the largest component of the force. A second agency, the Mobile Gendarmerie, may be deployed anywhere in the country. These are essentially riot police; their forces are motorized, have tanks, and even light aircraft. The

In essence, the United States is a nation of small police forces, each of which is authorized, funded, and operated within the limits of its own jurisdiction. This is in direct contrast to the centralized police forces found in many other countries. For example, in France the police are a national force divided between the Ministry of Interior and the Ministry of Defense. All police officers report to these national departments, as can be seen in the Comparative Perspective above.

Because of the fragmentation of police agencies in the United States, each jurisdiction develops its own enforcement goals and policies. Each agency must make choices about how to organize itself and use its resources to achieve its goals.

CHECK POINT

11. What is the jurisdiction of federal law enforcement agencies?
12. Why are some law enforcement agencies of the U.S. government located overseas?
13. What are the functions of most state police agencies?
14. Besides law enforcement, what functions do sheriffs perform?
15. What are the main features of the organization of the police in the United States?

Republican Guard, the third component of the Gendarmerie, is stationed in Paris, protects the president, and performs ceremonial functions.

The Police Nationale is under the Ministry of the Interior and operates mainly in urban centers with populations greater than ten thousand. The Police Nationale is divided into the Directorate of Urban Police, which is responsible for policing the cities with patrol and investigative functions, and the Directorate of Criminal Investigation, which provides regional detective services and pursues cases beyond the scope of the city police or the gendarmerie. Another division, the Air and Frontier Police, is responsible for border protection. The Republican Security Companies are the urban version of the Mobile Gendarmerie but without the heavy armament.

In addition to traditional patrol and investigative functions, the Police Nationale also contains units responsible for the collection of intelligence information and for the countering of foreign subversion. The Directorate of General Intelligence and Gambling has twenty-five hundred officers and gathers "intelligence of a political, social, and economic nature necessary for the information of government." This includes data from public opinion surveys, mass media, periodicals, and information gathered through the infiltration of various political, labor, and social groups. The Directorate of Counterespionage has the mission of countering the efforts of foreign agents on French soil intent on impairing the security of the country.

The police system of the central government of France is powerful; the number,

armament, legal powers, and links to the military are most impressive. The turbulent history of France before and after the revolution of 1789 gave rise to the need for the government to be able to assert authority. Since the 1930s France has had to deal not only with crime but also with political instability—the Nazi invasion of 1940, weak governments following World War II, the Algerian crisis in 1958, and student rioting in 1968 all brought conditions that nearly toppled the existing regime. The need to maintain order in the streets would seem to be a major concern of the government.

SOURCE: Adapted from Philip John Stead, *The Police of France* (New York: Macmillan, 1983), 1–12. Copyright © 1983 by Macmillan Publishing Company, a division of Macmillan, Inc. Reprinted by permission of the Gale Group.

Police Policy

The police cannot enforce every law and catch every lawbreaker. Legal rules limit the ways officers can investigate and pursue lawbreakers. For example, the constitutional ban on unreasonable searches and seizures prevents police from investigating many crimes without a search warrant.

Because the police have limited resources, they cannot have officers on every street at all times of the day and night. This means that they must make choices about how to deploy their resources. They must decide which offenses will receive the most attention and which tactics will be used. Police executives must decide, for example, whether to have officers patrol neighborhoods in cars or on foot. Changes in policy—such as increasing the size of the night patrol or tolerating prostitution and other public offenses—affect the amount of crime that gets official attention and the system's ability to deal with offenders. Policies with regard to the high-speed pursuit are discussed in the Close-Up (see p. 148).

For most of the past half-century, the police have emphasized their role as crime fighters. As a result, police in most communities focus on the crimes covered by the FBI's *Uniform Crime Reports*. These crimes make headlines, and politicians point to them when they call for increases in the police budget. They are also the crimes that tend to be committed by the poor. White-collar crimes such as

CLOSE

High-Speed Pursuit

The suspect's pickup truck barreled across the Bridgeport, Connecticut, city line with a Trumbull police cruiser in hot pursuit. When the driver of the truck lost control, it slammed into a parked station wagon with two women inside. One, a mother of three, later died and her sister was hospitalized for seven months. The truck continued on its way. Instead of stopping to assist the injured, the officer continued the pursuit.

Trumbull police say the pursuing officer followed departmental procedures. The suspect had broken into a house and stolen a microwave oven and other household goods. Critics say that the officer was so intent on making his collar that he never noticed others on the street.

National Highway and Traffic Safety Administration data show that about four hundred people die annually in police chases nationwide. About 1 to 3 percent of pursuits result in death. In Metro-Dade County, Florida, researchers found that 20 percent of pursuits resulted in injuries and 41 percent in accidents. Of interest is that only 35 percent of pursuits were initiated to catch suspected felons, nearly half for traffic violators.

Critics have called for strict rules banning high-speed chases, arguing that the risk to public safety is too great. Police organizations say that officers cannot be constrained too tightly or they will not be able to catch suspects. They argue that if fugitives know they will not be pursued they will get away. However, public pressure to restrict high-speed chases has come from accident victims and their families who, since 1980, have filed an increasing number of civil lawsuits.

Many states now require police departments to have written policies governing high-speed chases. Some departments have banned them completely. Others have guidelines requiring officers to consider such factors as driving conditions, seriousness of the crime, and the danger the suspect poses to the community before pursuing a suspect. Courts have considered the liability of officers for damages resulting from high-speed chases in light of departmental policies.

As in so much of police work, guidelines may exist but it is still the officer, acting alone, who must analyze the situation and exercise discretion in a highly emotional environment.

SOURCE: *Hartford Courant*, September 12, 1997, p. 1; and Geoffrey P. Alpert, "Pursuit Driving: Planning Policies and Action from Agency, Officer, and Public Information," *Police Forum 7* (January 1997), 3.

forgery, embezzlement, or tax fraud are viewed as less threatening by the public and thus get less attention from the police. Voters pressure politicians and the police to enforce laws that help them feel safe and secure in their daily lives.

Decisions about how police resources will be used affect the types of people who are arrested and passed through the criminal justice system. Think of the hard choices you would have to make if you were a police chief. Should more officers be sent into high-crime areas? Should more officers be assigned to the central business district during shopping hours? What should be the mix between traffic control and crime fighting? These questions have no easy answers. Police officials must answer them according to their goals and values.

American cities differ in governmental, economic, and racial and ethnic characteristics as well as in their degree of urbanization. These factors can affect the style of policing expected by the community. In a classic study, James Q. Wilson found that citizen expectations regarding police behavior are brought to bear through the political process in the choice of the top police executive. Chiefs who run their departments in ways that antagonize the community are not likely to stay in office long. Wilson's key finding was that a city's political culture, which reflects its socioeconomic characteristics and its governmental organization, had a major impact on the style of policing found there. Wilson described three different styles of policing—the watchman, legalistic, and service styles (Wilson, 1968). Table 4.1 documents these styles of policing and the types of communities in which they are found.

Departments with a *watchman* style stress order maintenance. Patrol officers may ignore minor violations of the law, especially those involving traffic and juveniles, as long as there is order. The police exercise discretion and deal with many infractions in an informal way. Officers make arrests only for flagrant violations and when order cannot be maintained. The broad discretion exercised by officers can produce discrimination when officers do not treat members of different racial and ethnic groups in the same way. The beating of Rodney King by Los Angeles police officers is an example of an abuse resulting from the watchman style.

In departments with a *legalistic* style, police work is marked by professionalism and emphasis on law enforcement. Officers are expected to detain a high proportion of juvenile offenders, act vigorously against illicit enterprises, issue traffic tickets, and make a large number of misdemeanor arrests. They act as if there is a single standard of community conduct—that prescribed by the law—rather than different standards for juveniles, minorities, drunks, and other groups. Thus, while officers may not discriminate in making arrests and issuing citations, the strict enforcement of laws, including traffic laws, can seem overly harsh to some groups in the community.

Suburban middle-class communities often experience a *service* style. Residents expect the police to provide service and feel that they deserve individual treatment. Burglaries and assaults are taken seriously, while minor infractions tend to be dealt with by informal means such as stern warnings. The police are expected to deal with the misdeeds of local residents in a personal, nonpublic way so as to avoid embarrassment.

Regardless of the style of policing being used, even before officers investigate crimes or make arrests, each police chief decides on policies that will govern the level and type of enforcement in the community. Given that the police are the entry point to the criminal justice system, all segments of the system are affected by the decisions made by police officials. Just as community expectations shape decisions about enforcement goals and the allocation of police resources, they also shape the cases that will be handled by prosecutors and corrections officials.

TABLE 4.1 Styles of policing

James Q. Wilson found three distinct styles of policing in the communities he studied. Each style emphasizes different police functions, and each is linked with the specific characteristics of the community.

STYLE	DEFINING CHARACTERISICS	COMMUNITY TYPE
Watchman	Emphasis on maintaining order	Declining idustrial city, mixed racial/ethnic composition, blue collar
Legalistic	Emphasis on law enforcement	Reform-minded city government, mixed socioeconomic composition
Service	Emphasis on service with balance between law enforcement and order maintenance	Middle-class suburban community

SOURCE: Drawn from James Q. Wilson, *Varieties of Police Behavior* (Cambridge, Mass.: Harvard University Press, 1968).

CHECK POINT

⑯ **What are the characteristics of the watchman style of policing?**

⑰ **What is the key feature of the legalistic style of policing?**

⑱ **Where are you likely to find the service style of policing?**

Police Functions

The police are expected to maintain order, enforce the law, prevent crime, and serve the community. However, they perform other tasks as well, many of them having little to do with crime and justice. They direct traffic, handle accidents and illnesses, stop noisy parties, find missing persons, enforce licensing regulations, provide ambulance services, take disturbed people into protective custody, and so on. The list is long and varies from place to place. Some researchers have suggested that the police have more in common with social service agencies than with the criminal justice system.

The American Bar Association has published a list of police goals and functions that includes the following:

❶ Prevent and control conduct considered threatening to life and property (serious crime).

❷ Aid people who are in danger of harm, such as the victim of a criminal attack.

❸ Protect constitutional rights, such as the right of free speech and assembly.

❹ Facilitate the movement of people and vehicles.

❺ Aid those who cannot care for themselves: the drunk or the addicted, the mentally ill, the disabled, the old, and the young.

❻ Resolve conflict, whether between individuals, groups of individuals, or individuals and government.

❼ Identify problems that could become more serious for the citizen, for the police, or for government.

❽ Create a feeling of security in the community. (Goldstein, 1977:5)

How did the police gain such broad responsibilities? In many places the police are the only public agency that is available seven days a week and twenty-four hours a day to respond to calls for help. They are also best able to investigate many kinds of problems. Moreover, the power to use force when necessary allows them to intervene in problem situations.

The functions of the police can be classified into three groups: (1) order maintenance, (2) law enforcement, and (3) service. Police agencies divide their resources among these groups on the basis of community need, citizen requests, and department policy (see Figure 4.2).

Order Maintenance

order maintenance

The police function of preventing behavior that disturbs or threatens to disturb the public peace or that involves face-to-face conflict among two or more persons. In such situations the police exercise discretion in deciding whether a law has been broken.

The **order maintenance** function is a broad mandate to prevent behavior that either disturbs or threatens to disturb the peace or involves face-to-face conflict among two or more persons. A domestic quarrel, a noisy drunk, loud music in the night, a beggar on the street, a tavern brawl—all are forms of disorder that may require action by the police.

Unlike most laws that define specific acts as illegal, laws regulating disorderly conduct deal with ambiguous situations that may be viewed in different ways by different police officers. For many crimes, determining when the law has been broken is easy. Order maintenance requires officers to decide not only whether a law has been broken, but also whether any action should be taken, and if so, who

FIGURE

4.2 Police functions

The police are given a wide range of responsibilities, from directing traffic to solving homicides, but the work can be divided into three categories: order maintenance, law enforcement, and service. Departments will emphasize one or more of these functions according to the community's government structure and socioeconomic characteristics.

ORDER MAINTENANCE

Preventing behavior that disturbs or threatens to disturb the peace. In these situations the police exercise discretion to determine if the law has been broken.

LAW ENFORCEMENT

Controlling crime by intervening in situations where the law has been broken and the identity of the guilty person must be established.

SERVICE

Providing help to the public, ranging from checking door locks to providing medical assistance to finding missing persons.

should be blamed. In a bar fight, for example, the officer must decide who started the fight, whether an arrest should be made for assault, and whether to arrest other people besides those who started the conflict.

Patrol officers deal mainly with behavior that either disturbs or threatens to disturb the peace. They confront the public in ambiguous situations and have wide discretion in matters that affect people's lives. If an officer decides to arrest someone for disorderly conduct, that person may spend time in jail and could lose his or her job even without being convicted of the crime.

Officers often must make judgments in order maintenance situations. They may be required to help persons in trouble, manage crowds, supervise various kinds of services, and help people who are not fully accountable for what they do. The officers have a high degree of discretion and control over how such situations will develop. Patrol officers are not subject to direct control. They have the power to arrest, but they may also decide not to make an arrest. The order maintenance function is made more complex by the fact that the patrol officer is normally expected to "handle" a situation rather than to enforce the law, usually in an emotionally charged atmosphere. In controlling a crowd outside a rock concert, for example, the arrest of an unruly person may restore order by removing a troublemaker and also serving as a warning to others that they could be arrested if they do not cooperate. However, an arrest may cause the crowd to become hostile toward the officers, making things worse. Officers cannot always predict precisely how their discretionary decisions may promote or hinder order maintenance.

Law Enforcement

law enforcement

The police function of controlling crime by intervening in situations in which the law has clearly been violated and the police need to identify and apprehend the guilty person.

The **law enforcement** function applies to situations in which the law has been violated, the offender needs to be identified or located, and the suspect must be apprehended. Police officers who focus on law enforcement are in specialized branches such as the vice squad and the burglary detail. Although the patrol officer may be the first officer at the scene of a crime, in serious cases a detective usually prepares the case for prosecution by bringing together all the evidence for the prosecuting attorney. When the offender is identified but not located, the detective conducts the search. If the offender is not identified, the detective must analyze clues to find out who committed the crime.

Although the police often portray themselves as enforcers of the law, one can ask how effective they are in this function. For example, when a property crime is committed, the perpetrator usually has a time advantage over the police. This limits the ability of the police to identify, locate, and arrest the suspect. Burglaries, for instance, usually occur when people are away from home. The crime may not be discovered until hours or days later. The effectiveness of the police is also reduced when assault or robbery victims are unable to identify the offender. Victims often delay in calling the police, reducing the chances that a suspect will be apprehended.

Service

service

The police function of providing assistance to the public, usually in matters unrelated to crime.

Police perform a broad range of services, especially for lower-income citizens, that are not related to crime. This **service** function—providing first aid, rescuing animals, helping the disoriented, and so on—has become a major police function. Crime prevention has became a major component of police services to the community. Through education and community organizing the police can assist the public in taking steps to prevent crime.

Research has shown how important the service function is to the community. Analysis of more than twenty-six thousand calls to twenty-one police departments found that about 80 percent of requests for police assistance do not involve crimes; the largest percentage of calls, 21 percent, were requests for information (Scott, 1981). Because the police are available twenty-four hours a day, people turn to them in times of trouble. Many departments provide information, operate ambulance services, locate missing persons, check locks on vacationers' homes, and intervene in suicide attempts.

It may appear that valuable resources are being diverted from law enforcement to services. However, performing service functions can help police control crime. Through the service function, officers gain knowledge about the community, and citizens come to trust the police. Checking the security of buildings clearly helps prevent crime, but other activities—dealing with runaways, drunks, and public quarrels—may help solve problems before they lead to criminal behavior.

Implementing the Mandate

While the public may depend most heavily on the order maintenance and service functions of the police, it acts as though law enforcement—the catching of lawbreakers—is the most important function. According to public opinion polls, the crime-fighter image of the police is firmly rooted in citizens' minds and is the main reason given by recruits for joining the force.

Public support for budgets is greatest when the crime-fighting function is stressed. This emphasis can be seen in the organization of big-city departments. The officers who perform this function, such as detectives, have high status. The focus on crime leads to the creation of special units to deal with homicide, burglary, and auto theft. All other tasks presumably will be handled by the patrol division. In some departments, this pattern may create morale problems because extra resources are allocated and prestige devoted to a function that is concerned with a small percentage of the problems brought to the police. In essence, police are public servants who keep the peace, but their organization reinforces their own law enforcement image and the public's focus on crime fighting.

But do the police prevent crime? David Bayley claims that they do not. He says that "the experts know it, the police know it, but the public does not know it" (Bayley, 1994:3). He bases this claim on two facts. First, no link has been found between the number of police officers and crime rates. For example, among cities with populations greater than a million in 1987, Dallas had the highest crime rate (16,282 per 100,000) and Kansas City, Missouri, the lowest (3,789 per 100,000), yet they had the same number of police per capita. Chicago, with the highest number of police per capita—4.1 per 1,000—had a crime rate only slightly above that of San Diego, where there were only 1.5 officers per 1,000 residents.

Second, the main strategies used by modern police have little or no effect on crime. Those strategies are street patrolling by uniformed officers, rapid response to emergency calls, and expert investigation of crime by detectives. Bayley says that the police believe these strategies are essential to protect public safety, yet no evidence exists that they achieve this goal (Bayley, 1994:5).

Peter Manning's observation of many years ago remains valid today: the police have an "impossible mandate":

> To much of the public the police are seen as alertly ready to respond to citizen demands, as crime-fighters, as an efficient, bureaucratic, highly organized force that keeps society from falling into chaos. The policeman himself considers the essence of his role to be the dangerous and heroic enterprise of crook-catching and the watchful prevention of crimes. . . . They do engage in chases, in gunfights, in careful sleuthing. But these are rare events. (Manning, 1971:157)

CHECK POINT

⑲ **Define the order maintenance function. What are officers expected to do in these situations?**

⑳ **Compare law enforcement situations with order maintenance situations.**

Police Actions

We have seen how the police are organized and how the three functions of policing—law enforcement, order maintenance, and service—operate. Now let us look at the everyday actions of the police as they deal with citizens in often highly discretionary ways. We will then discuss domestic violence as an example of the way police respond to one of many serious problems.

Police and National Guard personnel used tear gas, pepper spray, and mass arrests to end the protests and riots at the World Trade Organization meeting in Seattle.

Encounters between Police and Citizens

Public confidence is essential if the police are to carry out their mission because they depend on the public to help them identify crime and carry out investigations (see What Americans Think). Each year one in five Americans have some sort of face-to-face contact with law enforcement officers. A third of these contacts involve people seeking help or offering assistance. Another third witness or report a crime. A little less than a third say that the police initiated the contact. Males in their twenties are the most likely to have contacts while Hispanics and blacks are 70 percent more likely than whites (*Los Angeles Times,* 1997; BJS, 1997d).

Although most people are willing to help the police, fear, self-interest, and other factors keep some from cooperating. Many people fail to call the police because they think it is not worth the effort and cost. They do not want to spend time filling out forms at the station, appearing as a witness, or confronting a neighbor or relative in court. In some low-income neighborhoods, citizens are reluctant to assist the police because their past experience has shown that contact with law enforcement "only brings trouble." Without information about a crime, the police may decide not to pursue an investigation. Clearly, then, citizens have some control over the work of the police through their decisions to call or not to call them.

Officers know that developing and maintaining effective communications with people is a key to doing their job. As Officer Marcus Laffey of the New York Police Department has written, "If you can talk a good game as a cop, you're halfway there." He says that police use of "confrontation and force, of roundhouse punches and high speed chases" makes the movies and the news, but "what you say and how you say it come into play far more than anything you do with your stick or your gun, and can even prevent the need for them" (Laffey, 1998:38).

Citizens expect the police to act both effectively and fairly. In encounters between citizens and police, fairness is often affected by department policy. When should the patrol officer frisk a suspect? When should a deal be made with the addict-informer? Which disputes should be mediated on the spot and which left

What Americans Think

Question "I am going to read you a list of institutions in American society. Please tell me how much confidence you, yourself, have in each one—a great deal, quite a lot, some or very little: the police?"

Great deal/ quite a lot 57%

Very little 10%

Some 33%

SOURCE: U.S. Department of Justice, Bureau of Justice Statistics, *Sourcebook of Criminal Justice Statistics, 1998* (Washington, D.C.: Government Printing Office, 1999), Table 2.18.

to more formal procedures? Surprisingly, these conflicts between the demands of fairness and policy are seldom decided by heads of departments but are left largely to the discretion of the officer on the scene. In many areas the department has little control over the actions of individual officers.

Police Discretion

The judgments of police officers determine which crimes will be targeted and which suspects will be arrested. Patrol officers—the most numerous, the lowest ranking, the newest to police work—have the most discretion. This is necessary because they are out on the streets dealing with ambiguous situations. If they chase a young thief into an alley, they can decide, outside of the view of the public, whether to make an arrest or just recover the stolen goods and give the offender a stern warning.

Patrol officers' primary task is to maintain order and enforce ambiguous laws such as those dealing with disorderly conduct, public drunkenness, breach of the peace, and other situations in which it is unclear if a law has been broken, who committed the offense, and whether an arrest should be made. Wilson describes the patrol officer's role as "unlike that of any other occupation . . . one in which subprofessionals, working alone, exercise wide discretion in matters of utmost importance (life and death, honor and dishonor) in an environment that is apprehensive and perhaps hostile" (Wilson, 1968:30).

In the final analysis, the officer on the scene must define the situation, decide how to handle it, and determine whether and how the law should be applied. Four factors are especially important:

❶ The nature of the crime. The less serious a crime is to the public, the more freedom officers have to ignore it.

❷ The relationship between the alleged criminal and the victim. The closer the personal relationship, the more variable the use of discretion. Family squabbles may not be as grave as they appear, and police are wary of making arrests, because a spouse may later decide not to press charges.

❸ The relationship between the police and the criminal or victim. A polite complainant will be taken more seriously than a hostile one. Likewise, a suspect who shows respect to an officer is less likely to be arrested.

❹ Department policy. The policies of the police chief and city officials will promote more or less discretion.

Although some people call for detailed guidelines for police officers, such guidelines would probably be useless. No matter how detailed they were, the officer would still have to make judgments about how to apply them in each situation. At best, police administrators can develop guidelines and training that, one hopes, will give officers shared values and make their judgments more consistent.

Domestic Violence

How the police deal with domestic violence can show the links between police-citizen encounters, the exercise of discretion, and actions taken (or not taken) by officers. Domestic violence, also called "battering" and "spouse abuse," has been defined as assaultive behavior involving adults who are married or who have a prior or an ongoing intimate relationship. Violence by an intimate (husband, ex-husband, boyfriend, or ex-boyfriend) accounts for about 21 percent of all

CLOSE

Battered Women, Reluctant Police

As Joanne Tremins was moving some belongings out of her ramshackle house on South Main Street [Torrington, Connecticut], her 350-pound husband ran over, grabbed the family cat and strangled it in front of Tremins and her children.

For more than three years, Tremins said, she had complained to Torrington police about beatings and threats from her husband. Instead of arresting him, she said, the police acted "like marriage counselors."

The cat attack finally prompted police to arrest Jeffrey Tremins on a minor charge of cruelty to animals. But four days later, outside a local cafe, he repeatedly punched his wife in the face and smashed her against a wall, fracturing her nose and causing lacerations and contusions to her face and left arm.

That Joanne Tremins is suing this New England town of 34,000 is not without historical irony. For it was here that Tracey Thurman . . . won a $2 million judgment against the police department in a federal civil rights case that has revolutionized law enforcement attitudes toward domestic violence.

The Thurman case marked the first time that a battered woman was allowed to sue police in federal court for failing to protect her from her husband. The ruling held that such a failure amounts to sex discrimination and violates the Fourteenth Amendment.

The resulting spate of lawsuits has prompted police departments nationwide to reexamine their longstanding reluctance to make arrests in domestic assault cases, particularly when the wife refuses to press charges. State and local lawmakers, facing soaring municipal insurance costs, are also taking notice.

Here in hilly Torrington . . . Police Chief Mahlon C. Sabo said [the Thurman case] had a "devastating" effect on the town and his seventy-member force. "The police somehow, over the years, became the mediators," said Sabo. "There was a feeling that it's between husband and wife. In most cases, after the officer left, the wife usually got battered around for calling the police in the first place."

Although the law now requires them to make arrests, police officers here said, the courts toss out many domestic cases for the same reason that long hampered police.

"Unfortunately, many women just want the case dropped and fail to recognize they're in a dangerous situation," said Anthony

violence experienced by female victims, compared with 2 percent for male victims. The highest rates of nonlethal violence by an intimate are among African American women, women aged 16 to 24, women in households in the lowest income categories (less than $10,000), and women residing in urban areas. A National Crime Victimization Survey estimated that during any one year 960,000 women aged 12 or older had been victims of violence by an intimate. The survey also found that 28 percent of all female murder victims were killed by an intimate (BJS, 1998i:5, 11).

Despite (or perhaps because of) the high level of domestic violence in American society, in the past not much was done about it. Before 1970 most citizens and criminal justice agencies viewed domestic violence as a "private" affair best settled within the family. It was thought that police involvement might make the situation worse for the victim because she faced the possibility of reprisal (Buzawa and Buzawa, 1990). Yet today even though the largest number of calls to the police involve family disturbances about half go unreported.

From the viewpoint of most police departments, domestic violence was thought to be a "no-win" situation in which officers responding to calls for help

J. Salius, director of the family division of Connecticut Superior Court. "If she really doesn't want to prosecute, it's very difficult to have a trial because we don't have a witness."

Nearly five years after the attack by her estranged husband, Tracey Thurman remains scarred and partially paralyzed from multiple stab wounds to the chest, neck and face. Charles Thurman was sentenced to fourteen years in prison.

For eight months before the stabbing, Thurman repeatedly threatened his wife and their young son. He worked at Skee's Diner, a few blocks from police headquarters, and repeatedly boasted to policemen he was serving that he intended to kill his wife, according to the lawsuit.

In their defense, police said they arrested Thurman twice before the stabbing. The first charges were dropped, and a suspended sentence was imposed the second time. Tracey Thurman later obtained a court order barring her husband from harassing or assaulting her.

On June 10, 1983, Tracey Thurman called police and said her husband was menacing her. An officer did not arrive for twenty-five minutes and, although he found Charles Thurman holding a bloody knife, he delayed several minutes before making an arrest, giving Thurman enough time to kick his wife in the head repeatedly.

Less than a year after police were found liable in the attack on Thurman, Joanne Tremins also found that a restraining order obtained against her husband was worthless. . . . Tremins recounted how she made about sixty calls to police to complain about her husband, a cook. But she acknowledges that, on most of the occasions, when the police asked if she wanted him arrested, she said no.

"How could I say that?" she asked. "He's threatening to kill me if I have him arrested. He's threatening to kill my kids if I have him arrested. He'd stand behind the cops and pound his fist into the palm of his hand."

Hours before Tremins strangled the cat, . . . he beat and kicked his wife and her son, Stanley Andrews, fourteen. When an officer arrived, Joanne Tremins said, he told her that he could not make an arrest unless she filed a complaint at the police station.

"My son was all black and blue," Tremins said. "But [the officer] refused to come into my room and look at the blood all over the walls and the floor."

After Tremins was taken into custody for the cat incident, police did charge him with assaulting the son. He was released on bond, and his wife was issued a restraining order.

When her husband approached Tremins days later at a cafe in nearby Winsted, police refused to arrest him, despite the order. After the beating, Jeffrey Tremins was charged with assault and sentenced to two years in prison.

SOURCE: Howard Kurtz, "Battered Women, Reluctant Police," *Washington Post,* February 28, 1988, p. A1. Copyright © 1988, The Washington Post. Reprinted with permission.

were often set upon by one or both disputants. If an arrest was made, the police found that the victim often refused to cooperate with a prosecution. In addition, entering a home to deal with an emotion-laden incident was thought to be more dangerous than investigating "real" crimes. Many officers believed that trying to deal with family disputes was a leading cause of officer deaths and injury (Hirschel, Hutchinson, Dean, and Mills, 1992:247). However, this belief has been challenged by researchers who have found that domestic violence cases are no more dangerous to officers than other incidents (Garner and Clemmer, 1986; Stanford and Mowry, 1990:244–249).

Police response to domestic violence is a highly charged, uncertain, and possibly dangerous encounter with citizens in which officers must exercise discretion. In such a situation, how does an officer maintain order and enforce the law in accordance with the criminal law, department policies, and the needs of the victim? This question is addressed in the Close-Up above, which presents the stories of Joanne Tremins and Tracey Thurman—two women who suffered years of abuse by their husbands without any action by the police.

Until the 1970s, most citizens and criminal justice agencies viewed domestic violence as a "private" matter best settled within the family. Today, the largest number of calls to the police involve family disturbances.

CHECK POINT

21 **Why do patrol officers have so much discretion?**

22 **Why have police in the past failed to arrest in domestic violence situations?**

In the past, most police departments advised officers to try to calm the parties and refer them to social service agencies rather than arrest the attacker. This policy of leniency toward male spouse abusers was studied in Chester, Pennsylvania. Researchers found that the police were less likely to arrest a male who attacked a female intimate than they would males who had committed similar violent acts (Fyfe, Klinger, and Flavin, 1997:455–473).

Departments, prodded by the women's movement, began to rethink this policy of leniency when research in Minneapolis found that abusive spouses who are arrested and jailed briefly are much less likely to commit acts of domestic violence again (Sherman and Berk, 1984:261). Although studies in other cities (Charlotte, Milwaukee, and Omaha) did not produce similar results, the research led some departments to order officers to make an arrest in every case in which evidence existed of an assault (Sherman, Schmidt, Rogan, Gartin, Cohn, Collins, and Bacich, 1991:821). Police officers may have supported the arrest policy because it gave them a clear directive as to what to do (Friday, Metzger, and Walters, 1991:198–213). But officers in Minneapolis told researchers they preferred to retain the discretion to do what was necessary (Steinman, 1988:1–5).

If arrest will stem domestic violence in some cases, it has been suggested that arrest followed by prosecution will have a greater impact. However, a study of prosecutorial discretion in domestic violence cases in Milwaukee showed that factors such as the victim's injuries and the defendant's arrest record influenced the decision to charge, not just the fact of spouse abuse (Schmidt and Steury, 1989:487).

In many states policies have been changed as a result of lawsuits by injured women who claimed that the police ignored evidence of assaults and in effect allowed the spouse to inflict serious injuries. In addition, there is a growing sense that domestic violence can no longer be left to the discretion of individual patrol officers. Today, twenty-three states and the District of Columbia now require the arrest of suspects in violent incidents without a warrant, even if the officer did not witness the crime but has probable cause to believe that one was committed by the suspect (Hoctor, 1997:643). Most large departments and police academies have programs to educate officers about the problem.

Even though a number of policy changes have been imposed to deal with domestic violence, the fact remains that the officer in the field must handle these situations. As with most law enforcement situations, laws, guidelines, and training can help; but, as is often true in police work, in the end the discretion of the officer inevitably determines what actions will be taken.

Summary

- The police in the United States owe their roots to early nineteenth-century developments in policing in England.
- Like their English counterparts, the American police have limited authority, are under local control, and are organizationally fragmented.
- Three eras of American policing are: the political era (1840–1920), the professional era (1920–1970), and the community policing era (1970–present).
- In the U.S. federal system of government, police agencies are found at the national, state, county, and municipal levels.
- Police executives develop policies on how they will allocate their resources according to one of three styles: the watchman, legalistic, or service styles.
- The functions of the police are order maintenance, law enforcement, and service.
- Discretion is a major factor in police actions and decisions. Patrol officers exercise the greatest amount of discretion.
- The problem of domestic violence illustrates the links between police encounters with citizens, their exercise of discretion, and the actions they take.

Questions for Review

1. What principles borrowed from England still underlie policing in the United States?

2. What are the three eras of policing in the United States and what are the characteristics of each?

3. What are the functions of the police?

4. How do communities influence police policy and police styles?

5. How does the problem of domestic violence illustrate basic elements of police action?

Key Terms

frankpledge (p. 133)

order maintenance (p. 150)

law enforcement (p. 152)

service (p. 152)

For Further Reading

Goldstein, Herman. *Problem-Oriented Policing.* New York: McGraw Hill, 1990. Examination of the move toward problem-oriented, or community, policing. Argues for a shift to this focus.

Greene, Jack R., and Steven Mastrofski, eds. *Community Policing: Rhetoric or Reality?* New York: Praeger, 1988. An excellent collection of essays on community policing.

Nadelmann, Ethan. *Cops across Borders: The Internationalization of U.S. Criminal Law Enforcement.* University Park, Pa.: Pennsylvania State University Press, 1993. A major work describing the increased presence of American law enforcement agencies in foreign countries.

Skolnick, Jerome H. *Justice without Trial: Law Enforcement in a Democratic Society.* New York: Wiley, 1966. One of the first books to examine the subculture of the police and the exercise of discretion.

Tonry, Michael, and Norval Morris, eds. *Modern Policing.* Chicago: University of Chicago Press, 1992. An outstanding collection of essays by leading scholars examining the history, organization, and operational tactics of the police.

Wilson, James Q. *Varieties of Police Behavior.* Cambridge, Mass.: Harvard University Press, 1968. A classic study of the styles of policing in different types of communities. Shows the impact of politics on the operations of the force.

Going Online

❶ **Using InfoTrac College Edition,** access the article "The Comprehensive Care Model" in *FBI Law Enforcement Bulletin* (May 1998). After you read the article list the reasons that the author believes citizen participation is so important for crime prevention. Give examples of things citizens can do to prevent crime and help the police.

❷ Go to www.FBI.gov and obtain information on entry requirements and the application process for becoming a special agent. What types of people is the FBI seeking? Do you qualify?

❸ **Using InfoTrac College Edition,** access the article "DVERTing Domestic Violence: The Domestic Violence Enhanced Response Team," *FBI Law Enforcement Bulletin* (June 1998).

Describe the Colorado Springs DVERT approach to domestic violence. What actions are police officers expected to take when investigating a domestic violence situation? What has been the impact of the DVERT program?

1 Limited authority, local control, organizational fragmentation.

2 Required groups of ten families to uphold the law and maintain order.

3 Established a parish constable system. Citizens were required to pursue criminals.

4 Established the first organized police force in London.

5 To prevent crime without the use of repressive force, to manage public order nonviolently, to minimize and reduce conflict between citizens and the police, to demonstrate efficiency by the absence of crime.

6 Political era, professional era, community policing era.

7 Close ties between the police and local politicians, leading to corruption.

8 The police should be removed from politics, police should be well trained, the law should be enforced equally, technology should be used, merit should be the basis of personnel procedures, the crime-fighting role should be prominent.

9 The professional, crime-fighting role isolated the police from the community. The police should try to solve the problems underlying crime.

10 The police should be close to the community, should provide services and deal with the "little problems."

11 Enforce the laws of the federal government.

12 Because of the increase in international criminality in a shrinking world.

13 All state police agencies have traffic law enforcement responsibilities and in two-thirds of the states they have general police powers.

14 In addition to law enforcement functions, sheriffs operate jails, move prisoners, and provide court bailiffs.

15 Local control, fragmentation.

16 Emphasis on order maintenance, extensive use of discretion, and differential treatment of racial and ethnic groups.

17 Professionalism and using a single standard of law enforcement throughout the community.

18 Suburban middle-class communities.

19 Police have a broad mandate to prevent behavior that either disturbs or threatens to disturb the peace or involves face-to-face conflict among two or more people. Officers are expected to "handle" the situation.

20 The police in order maintenance situations must first determine if a law has been broken, but in law enforcement situations that fact is already known. Thus officers must only find and apprehend the offender.

21 They deal with citizens, often in private, and are charged with maintaining order and enforcing laws. Many of these laws are ambiguous and deal with situations in which the participants' conduct is in dispute.

22 Officers are often set upon by both parties, the victim is often uncooperative, and intervention is thought to be dangerous.

Police Operations

"O fficer Down!" burst over the radios of patrol cars in Bristol, Connecticut, a city of sixty thousand, on a Saturday evening in May 1996. As police sped to 10 Addison Street, 26-year-old Officer John Reilly lay sprawled on a driveway, bleeding from eight gunshot wounds to his arm, shoulder, abdomen, and legs.

Earlier that day Reilly had responded to a domestic disturbance call at the Addison Street address, where he found that the male suspect had already left. He returned that evening to arrest the suspect when he came home. Reilly was sitting in his patrol car across from the house when a car drove into the driveway. Assuming that he had found his man, Reilly pulled his car behind the one in the driveway. As he approached, the driver ran behind a garage. Reilly followed, but as he turned the corner the suspect fired, hitting him twice. The suspect then made a full circle around the garage, approached Reilly, and shot him six more times. Even as he lay on the ground, Reilly was able to return the fire and radio for help as the suspect fled.

Four hours later the suspect, Brent McCall, was spotted limping on his wounded leg, as he tried to make his way to his sister's house. When McCall saw the police, he started shooting again. He was finally subdued by the officers' bullets. But McCall, wanted for a series of armed robberies, was not the suspect that Reilly had been seeking.

The shoot-out on Addison Street is the type of incident that gets attention. In much of America, law enforcement agencies face tough situations as they deal with crime, violence, racial tensions, and drugs. Handling such situations, often without warning or with incomplete information, is a tall order for patrol officers—especially because they must try to do so within the limits of the law.

In this chapter, we focus on the actual work of the police as they pursue suspects and prevent crimes. The police must be organized so that patrol efforts can be coordinated, investigations carried out, arrests made, evidence gathered, crimes solved, and violators prosecuted.

QUESTIONS
for Inquiry

- How are the police organized?
- What three factors affect police response?
- What are the main functions of police patrol, investigation, and special operations units?
- What are the legal mandates that guide police actions?

Organization of the Police

Most police agencies are organized in a military manner. A structure of ranks—patrol officer, sergeant, lieutenant, captain, and on up to chief—makes clear the powers and duties of officers at each level. Relationships between superiors and subordinates emphasize discipline, control, and accountability. These values are important in efficiently mobilizing police resources and ensuring that civil liberties are protected. If police officers are accountable to their superiors, they are less likely to abuse their authority by needlessly interfering with the freedom and rights of citizens.

The structure of a well-organized police department, such as the one shown in Figure 5.1, is designed to fulfill five functions:

❶ Divide the workload among members and units according to a logical plan.
❷ Make sure lines of authority and responsibility are as clear and direct as possible.
❸ Provide unity of command so that no question arises as to which orders should be followed.
❹ Link duties with the appropriate amount of authority and accountability.
❺ Coordinate the efforts of members and units so that all will work together to achieve their goals.

Urban police departments divide the city into districts or precincts. This allows them to allocate resources and supervise personnel, taking into account the needs and problems of each district. Although specialized units are often located at headquarters, patrol and traffic units may be located in district stations.

Large police departments assign officers to special units that focus on specific functions: patrol, investigation, traffic, vice, and juvenile. These units perform the basic tasks of crime prevention and control. The patrol and investigation (detective) units are the core of the modern department. The patrol unit handles a wide

FIGURE 5.1 — **Organization of the Phoenix, Arizona, Police Department**

This is a typical structure. Note the major divisions of management and support services, investigations, field operations (patrol), and special operations. The internal affairs bureau reports directly to the chief.

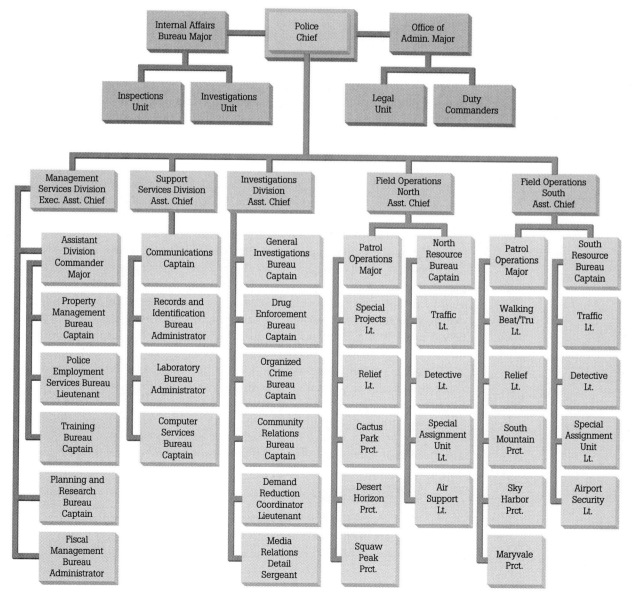

SOURCE: City of Phoenix, Arizona, Police Department, *Annual Report* (1990).

range of functions, including preventing crime, catching suspects, mediating quarrels, helping the ill, and giving aid at accidents. The investigation unit identifies, apprehends, and collects evidence against lawbreakers who commit serious crimes. The separation of patrol and investigation can cause problems because of their overlapping responsibilities. While the investigation unit usually focuses on murder, rape, and major robberies, the patrol unit has joint responsibility for investigating those crimes and the more numerous lesser crimes.

The extent to which departments create specialized units may depend on the size of the city and its police force. While many departments have traffic units, only those in mid-sized to large cities also have vice and juvenile units. As a result of the "war on drugs," some cities have special units working only on this problem. Large departments usually have an internal affairs section to investigate charges of corruption against officers and other problems associated with the staff and officers. The juvenile unit works with young people, focusing mainly on crime prevention. All special units depend on the patrol officers for information and assistance.

The police play an important role as a bureaucracy within the broader criminal justice system. Three issues arise in the organizational context within which the police operate. First, the police are the gateway through which information and individuals enter the justice system to be processed. Police have the discretion to determine which suspects will be arrested and moved into the system. Cases that are sent to the prosecutor for charging and then to the courts for adjudication begin with an officer's decision that probable cause exists for an arrest. The care taken by the officer in making the arrest and collecting evidence has a major impact on the ultimate success of the prosecution. The outcome of the case, whether through plea bargaining by lawyers or through a trial with a judge and jury, hinges on the officer's judgment and evidence-gathering activities.

Second, police administration is influenced by the fact that the outcome of a case is largely in the hands of others. The police bring suspects into the criminal justice process, but they cannot control the decisions of prosecutors and judges. In some cases, the police officers may feel that their efforts have been wasted if the prosecutor agrees to a plea bargain that does not, in the eyes of the officer, adequately punish the offender. The potential for conflict between police and other decision makers in the system is increased by the difference in social status between lawyers and judges, who have graduate degrees, and police officers, many of whom do not have college degrees.

Third, as part of a bureaucracy, police officers are expected to observe rules and follow the orders of superiors while at the same time making independent, discretionary judgments. They must stay within the chain of command, yet they also make choices in response to events that occur on the streets. To understand the impact of these factors on the behavior of the police, let us examine two aspects of their daily work—organizational response and productivity.

CHECK POINT

① **What are the five functions of a well-organized police department?**

② **What are the five main divisions of a large urban department?**

(Answers are at the end of the chapter.)

Police Response and Action

In a free society people do not want police on every street corner asking them what they are doing. Thus, the police are mainly **reactive** (responding to citizen calls for service) rather than **proactive** (initiating actions in the absence of citizen requests). Studies of police work show that 81 percent of actions result from citizen telephone calls, 5 percent are initiated by citizens who approach an officer, and only 14 percent are initiated in the field by an officer. These facts affect the way departments are organized and the way the police respond to a case.

Because they are mainly reactive, the police usually can arrive at the scene only after the crime has been committed and the perpetrator has fled. This means that the police are hampered by the time lapse and sometimes by inaccurate information given by witnesses. For example, a mugging may happen so quickly that victims and witnesses cannot accurately describe what transpired. In about a third of cases in which police are called, no one is present when the police arrive on the scene.

Citizens have come to expect that the police will respond quickly to every call, whether it requires immediate attention or can be handled in a more routine manner. The result is **incident-driven policing,** in which calls for service are the primary instigators of action. But studies have shown that less than 30 percent of calls to the police involve criminal law enforcement; most calls concern order maintenance and service (Walker, 1999:80). To a large extent, then, reports by victims and observers define the boundaries of policing.

The police do use proactive strategies such as surveillance and undercover work to combat some crimes. When addressing crimes without victims, they must rely on informers, stakeouts, wiretapping, stings, and raids. Because of the current focus on drug offenses, police resources in many cities have been assigned to proactive efforts to apprehend people who use or sell illegal drugs. Because drug users and sellers do not call the police, crime rates for such offenses are nearly always rates of arrest instead of rates of known criminal acts. The result is a direct link between the crime rate for these proactive efforts and the assignment of police personnel.

reactive
Occurring in response, such as police activity in response to notification that a crime has been committed.

proactive
Acting in anticipation, such as an active search for offenders initiated by the police without waiting for a crime to be reported. Arrests for crimes without victims are usually proactive.

incident-driven policing
A reactive approach to policing emphasizing a quick response to calls for service.

Organizational Response

How the police respond to citizens' calls is influenced by how the police bureaucracy is organized. Factors that affect the response process include the separation of police into various functional groups (patrol, vice, investigation, and so on), the quasi-military command system, and the techniques used to induce patrol officers to respond in desired ways.

Police departments are being reshaped by new communications technology, which has tended to centralize decision making. The core of the department is the communications center, where commands are given to send officers into action. Patrol officers are expected to be in constant touch with headquarters and must report each of their actions. Two-way radios, cell phones, and computers are the primary means by which administrators monitor the decisions of officers in the field. In the past, patrol

Aggressive take-back-the-streets tactics have made a big dent in urban crime. But in some cities a tough question is being raised: Does that style of policing come at an unacceptable price?

officers might have administered on-the-spot justice to a mischievous juvenile, but now they must file a report, take the youth into custody, and start formal proceedings. Because officers must contact headquarters by radio or computer with reports about each incident, headquarters is better able to guide officers' discretion and ensure that they comply with department policies.

Most residents in urban and suburban areas can now call 911 to report a crime or obtain help or information. The 911 system has brought a flood of calls to police departments—many not directly related to police responsibilities. In Baltimore, a "311 system" has been implemented to help reduce the number of nonemergency calls, estimated as 40 percent of the total calls. Residents have been urged to call 311 when they need assistance that does not require the immediate dispatch of an officer. A recent study found that this innovation reduced calls to 911 by almost 25 percent and resulted in extremely high public support (*New York Times,* October 10, 1997:A12). The Close-Up (opposite) shows how emotionally draining is the work of a 911 operator.

differential response

A patrol strategy that assigns priorities to calls for service and chooses the appropriate response.

To improve efficiency, police departments use a **differential response** system that assigns priorities to calls for service. This system assumes that rushing a patrol car to the scene is not always necessary. The appropriate response depends on several factors—such as whether the incident is in progress, has just occurred, or occurred some time ago; and whether anyone is or could be hurt. A dispatcher receives the calls and asks for certain facts. The dispatcher may: (1) send a sworn officer to the scene right away, (2) give the call a lower rank so that the response by an officer is delayed, (3) send someone other than a sworn officer, or (4) refer the caller to another agency.

Evaluations of differential response policies have found them to be successful. In Greensboro, North Carolina, only about half of the calls received warranted an immediate response by an officer, 26.9 percent received a delayed response by an officer, and no officer was dispatched in 19.5 percent—most of which concerned cold burglaries. Both officers and residents were satisfied with the procedures (Cohen and McEwen, 1984). Research in Lansing, Michigan, found differential response both efficient and equitable. Low-priority calls received a response in an average of sixteen minutes and calls not requiring the presence of an officer were dealt with by a report given over the telephone. People across racial and income lines in Lansing were satisfied with police response (Worden, 1993:1–32).

The policy of differential response saves police resources but has other payoffs. For example, with trained officers manning "911," (1) more detailed information is received from callers, (2) callers have a better sense of when to expect a response, and (3) patrol officers have more information about the case when they respond.

Some experts are critical of centralized communications and decision making. Many advocates of community policing believe that certain technologies tend to isolate the police from citizens. As discussed in Chapter 4, widespread use of motorized patrols has meant that residents get only a glimpse of officers as they cruise through their neighborhoods. Community-oriented policing attempts to overcome some of the negative aspects of centralized response.

Productivity

Following the lead of New York's Compstat program, police departments in Baltimore, Indianapolis, New Orleans, and others now emphasize accountability at the precinct level for crime reduction. Through twice-weekly briefings before

C L O S E up

Holding the 911 Line

It's a new day. I walk down to the basement of the public safety building, pass through a secured entrance and walk slowly down a long, quiet corridor. My stomach tightens a bit as I approach a final locked door. . . . I'm in the Phoenix Police Communications Center, known as "911."…

It's 0800 hours. I take a deep breath, say a little prayer and hope that I don't make any mistakes that might get me on the 6 o'clock news. This will be my not happy home for the next 10 hours.

"911, what is your emergency?" It's my first call of the day. The woman is crying but calm. She has tried to wake her elderly husband. With the push of a button I connect her to the fire department. They ask if she wants to attempt CPR [cardiopulmonary resuscitation], but she says, "No, he's cold and blue…. I'm sure he's dead." I leave the sobbing widow in the hands of the fire dispatcher. I'm feeling sad, but I just move on. I have more incoming calls to take. It's busy this morning. The orange lights in each corner of the room are shining brightly, a constant reminder that nonemergency calls have been holding more than 90 seconds. My phone console appears to be glowing, covered with blinking red lights. It's almost hypnotic, like when you sit in the dark and stare at a lit Christmas tree, or gaze into a flickering fireplace. But then I remember that each light represents a person—a person with a problem, someone in crisis.

A loud bell is ringing. It means an emergency call is trying to get through but the lines are jammed. All operators are already on a call. I quickly put my caller on hold. He's just reporting a burglary that occurred over the weekend.…

"911, what is your emergency?" This one's serious. A bad traffic accident, head-on collision. "Yes, sir, we'll get right out there." I get officers started and advise the fire department. Now everyone in the vicinity of the accident is calling. "Yes, ma'am, we're on the way." "We'll be out shortly, sir, thanks for calling." My supervisor comes out of his office to advise us of something. He always looks serious, but this time it's different. He looks worried and upset. He tells us that two of our detectives were involved in the collision. He doesn't know who they are or how badly they're injured. My heart stops momentarily because my husband is a detective. I quickly call the office and confirm that he is safe. I'm relieved but still stunned…. But there's not much time for sentiment. There are more calls to take, more decisions to make and more pressures needing attention.…

"911, what is your emergency?" It's just a boy on a phone getting his kicks by calling me vulgar names. He hangs up before I have a chance to educate him on correct 911 usage. We get a lot of trivial calls, pranksters, hang-ups, citizens complaining to us about a noncrime situation, something they should handle themselves. People call us because they don't know where to turn. Everyone must be treated fairly and with respect. It's a difficult balance to maintain.

My supervisor again comes out to advise us. His face shows a sadness I've never seen in him. "The officers were killed in the accident." A quietness descends over the room. I suppose the bells are still ringing and the lights flashing but I don't hear or see them. The typing stops; talking ceases. I just want to get out of here and cry, but I have to stay and do my job. I have to keep going. I can break down on my long drive home tonight; for now I have phones to answer, people to help.

their peers and senior executives, precinct commanders must explain the results of their efforts to reduce crime. Essential to this management strategy is timely, accurate information. Computer systems have been developed to put up-to-date crime data into the hands of managers at all levels. This allows discussion of department-wide strategies and puts pressure on low producers (Sherman, 1998:430;

clearance rate

The percentage of crimes known to the police that they believe they have solved through an arrest; a statistic used to measure a police department's productivity.

What Americans Think

Question "I would like to ask you about the police in your community: How much confidence do you have in the ability of the police to protect you from crime? To solve crime? To prevent crime? A great deal, some, little, none at all?"

Crime protection

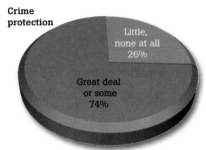

Little, none at all 26%

Great deal or some 74%

Crime solving

Little, none at all 26%

Great deal or some 74%

Crime prevention

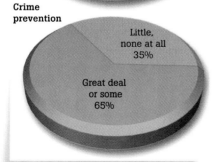

Little, none at all 35%

Great deal or some 65%

SOURCE: W. Wilson Huang and Michael S. Vaughn, "Support and Confidence: Public Attitudes toward the Police," in *Americans View Crime and Justice*, ed. Timothy J. Flanagan and Dennis R. Longmire (Thousand Oaks, Calif.: Sage Publications, 1996), 38.

Silverman, 1999). This innovation has brought major changes to police operations and raised questions as to how police work should be measured.

Quantifying police work is difficult in part, because of the wide range of duties and day-to-day tasks of officers. In the past, the crime rate and the clearance rate have been used as measures of "good" policing. A lower crime rate might be cited as evidence of an effective department, but critics note that this measure is affected by other factors beside policing.

The **clearance rate**—the percentage of crimes known to police that they believe they have solved through an arrest—is a basic measure of police performance. The clearance rate varies by type of offense. In reactive situations—for example, burglary—the police may learn about the crime hours or even days later; the clearance rate is only about 14 percent.

Police have much more success in handling violent crimes (46 percent), in which victims tend to know their assailants (FBI, 1999:182). In proactive situations the police are not responding to the call of a crime victim; instead they seek out crimes. Hence, at least in theory, arrests for prostitution, gambling, and drug selling have a clearance rate of 100 percent, because every crime known to the police is matched with an arrest.

The arrest of a person often results in the clearance of other reported offenses because the police can link some arrested persons with similar, unsolved crimes. Interrogation and lineups are standard procedures, as is the lesser-known operation of simply assigning unsolved crimes to the suspect. When an offender enters a guilty plea, part of the bargain may be an admission that he or she committed prior crimes. Professional thieves know that they can gain favors from the police in exchange for "confessing" to unsolved crimes that they may not have committed.

These measures of police productivity may be supplemented by other data, such as the numbers of traffic citations issued, illegally parked cars ticketed, and suspects stopped for questioning as well as the value of stolen goods recovered. These additional ways of counting work done reflect the fact that an officer may work hard for many hours yet have no arrests to show for his or her efforts (Kelling, 1992:23). Yet society may benefit more when officers spend their time in activities that are hard to measure, such as calming disputes, becoming acquainted with people in the neighborhood, and providing services to those in need.

One might think that police effectiveness would depend upon a city's population, crime level, and size of the police force. But, as seen in Figure 5.2, these variables are not always related. For example, the Dallas police force is small relative to the population, but its rates of index offenses are high. In contrast, index offenses in Washington, D.C., rank in the middle range of the cities studied, but its force is the largest. The issue is even more complicated: police productivity is governed in part by population density, the number of nonresidents who spend part of their day working or visiting in the area, local politics, and other factors. In sum, like other public agencies, the police have trouble gauging the quantity and quality of their work. Perhaps greater attention should be paid to the attitudes of the consumers of police services, the public (see What Americans Think).

CHECK POINT

③ What is "incident-driven policing"?

④ What is "differential response"?

⑤ What is the basic measure of police productivity?

FIGURE
5.2 **Sworn officers and index offenses per 1,000 population in fifteen U.S. cities**

These major cities have varying numbers of police officers and crimes for every 1,000 residents. The amount of crime and numbers of police do not always correlate.

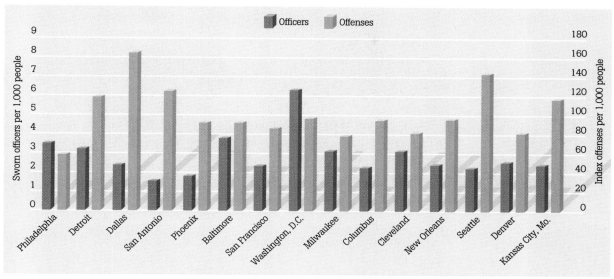

SOURCE: *Issues Paper: Metropolitan Police Department Resource Allocation* (Washington, D.C.: Police Executive Research Forum, 1990).

Delivery of Police Services

In service bureaucracies such as the police, a distinction is often made between line and staff functions. **Line functions** are those that directly involve field operations such as patrol, investigation, traffic control, vice and juvenile crimes, and so on. By contrast, *staff functions* supplement or support the line functions. Staff functions are based in the chief's office and the support or services bureau, as well as in the staff inspection bureau (see Figure 5.1). An efficient department has an appropriate balance between line and staff duties. A department such as the one in Phoenix would be about 16 percent staff and 84 percent line. Figure 5.3 shows the allocation of line personnel in the nation's six largest departments.

Patrol Functions

Patrol is often called the backbone of police operations. The word *patrol* is thought to be derived from a French word, *patrouiller,* which once meant "to tramp about in the mud." This is an apt description of a function that one expert has described as "arduous, tiring, difficult, and performed in conditions other than ideal" (Chapman, 1970:ix). For most Americans the familiar sight of a uniformed and armed patrol officer, on call twenty-four hours a day, is *policing.*

Every police department has a patrol unit. Even in large departments, patrol officers account for up to two-thirds of all **sworn officers**—those who have taken an oath and been given the powers to make arrests and use necessary force

line functions
Police components that directly perform field operations and carry out the basic functions of patrol, investigation, traffic, vice, juvenile, and so on.

sworn officers
Police employees who have taken an oath and been given powers by the state to make arrests and use necessary force, in accordance with their duties.

FIGURE 5.3 **Distribution of sworn police personnel in the nation's six largest departments**

What does the distribution of officers reveal about the role of the police in urban areas? How might smaller departments differ from these large urban departments?

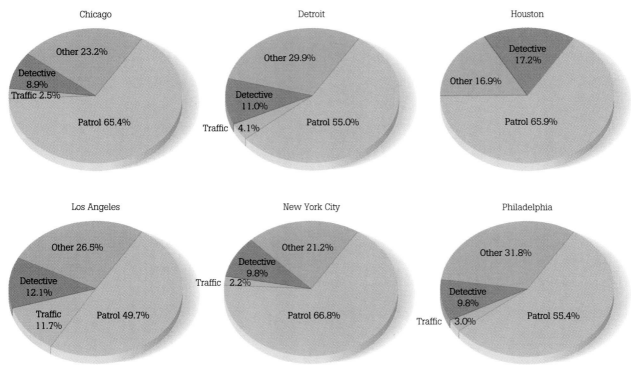

NOTE: *Other* refers to specialized units such as communications, antiterrorism, administration, and personnel.
SOURCE: Adapted from Anthony Pate and Edwin Hamilton, *The Big Six: Policing America's Largest Departments* (Washington, D.C.: Police Foundation, 1990), 60.

in accordance with their duties. In small communities, police operations are not specialized, and the patrol force is the department. The patrol officer must be prepared for any imaginable situation and must perform many duties.

Television portrays patrol officers as always on the go—rushing from one incident to another and making a number of arrests in a single shift. A patrol officer may be called to deal with a robbery in progress or to help rescue people from a burning building. However, while such activities are important, the patrol officer's life is not always so exciting. The officer may perform some challenging tasks, but he or she may also handle routine and even boring tasks such as directing traffic at accident scenes and road construction sites.

Most officers, on most shifts, do not make even one arrest (Bayley, 1994:20). To better understand patrol work, note how the police of Wilmington, Delaware, allocate time to various activities, as shown in Figure 5.4.

The patrol function has three parts: answering calls for help, maintaining a police presence, and probing suspicious circumstances. Patrol officers are well suited to answering calls because they usually are near the scene and can move quickly to provide help or catch a suspect. At other times, they engage in **preventive patrol**—that is, making the police presence known in an effort to deter crime and to make officers available to respond quickly to calls. Whether walking

preventive patrol

Making the police presence known, to deter crime and to make officers available to respond quickly to calls.

The time spent on each activity was calculated from records for each police car unit. Note the range of activities and the time spent on each.

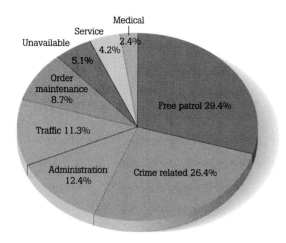

Free patrol: park and walk

Crime related: officer in trouble, suspicious person/vehicle, crime in progress, alarm, investigate crime not in progress, service warrant/subpoena, assist other police

Administration: meal break, report writing, firearms training, police vehicle maintenance, at headquarters, court related

Traffic: accident investigation, parking problems, motor vehicle driving problems, traffic control, fire emergency

Order maintenance: order maintenance in progress, animal complaint, noise complaint

Service: service related

Medical: medical emergency, at local hospital

SOURCE: Jack R. Greene and Carl B. Klockars, "What Police Do," in *Thinking about Police*, 2d ed., ed. Carl B. Klockars and Stephen D. Mastrofski (New York: McGraw-Hill, 1991), 279.

the streets or cruising in a car, the patrol officer is on the lookout for suspicious people and behavior. With experience, officers come to trust in their own ability to spot signs of suspicious activity that merit stopping people on the street for questioning.

Patrol officers also help maintain smooth relations between the police and the community. As the most visible members of the criminal justice system, they can have a profound effect on the willingness of citizens to cooperate. When officers earn the trust and respect of the residents of the neighborhoods they patrol, people are much more willing to provide information about crimes and suspicious activities. Effective work by patrol officers can also help reduce citizens' fear of crime and foster a sense of security.

Patrol officers' duties sound fairly straightforward, yet these officers often find themselves in complex situations requiring sound judgments and careful actions. As the first to arrive at a crime scene, the officer must comfort and give aid to victims, identify and question witnesses, control crowds, and gather evidence. This calls for creativity and good communication skills.

Because the patrol officer has the most direct contact with the public, the image of the police and their relations with the community are based on patrol officers' actions. Moreover, successful investigations and prosecutions often depend on patrol officers' actions in questioning witnesses and gathering evidence after a crime. As you read the continuation of Chuck Terry's journey inside the criminal justice system at the book-specific web site shown in the margin, consider the role of patrol officers in his arrest and pretrial processing.

http://cj.wadsworth.com/cole/

Because the patrol officer's job involves the most contact with the public, it should be done by the best-qualified officers. However, because of the low status of patrol assignments, many officers seek higher-status positions such as that of detective. A key challenge facing policing is to grant to patrol officers a status that reflects their importance to society and the criminal justice system.

CHECK POINT

⑥ **What is the difference between line and staff functions?**

⑦ **What are the three parts of the patrol function?**

Issues in Patrolling

In the last thirty years, much research has been done on police methods of assigning tasks to patrol officers, transporting them, and communicating with them. Although the conclusions of these studies have been mixed, they have caused experts to rethink some aspects of patrolling. Yet even when researchers agree on the patrol practices that would be most effective, those practices often run counter to the desires of departmental personnel. For example, foot patrol may be a key to community policing, but many officers would rather be in their squad cars than beating the pavement. Police administrators therefore must deal with many issues, including (1) assignment of patrol personnel, (2) preventive patrol, (3) hot spots, (4) response time, (5) foot patrol versus motorized patrol, (6) one-person versus two-person patrol units, (7) aggressive patrol, (8) community-oriented policing, and (9) special populations.

Assignment of Patrol Personnel

In the past it has been assumed that patrol officers should be assigned where and when they will be most effective in preventing crime, keeping order, and serving the public. For the police administrator, the question has been: Where should the officers be sent, when, and in what numbers? There are no guidelines to answer this question, and most assignments seem to be based on the notion that patrols should be concentrated in areas where crime rates and calls for service are high or in "problem" neighborhoods. Thus, the assignment of officers is based on factors such as crime statistics, 911 calls, degree of urbanization, pressures from business and community groups, ethnic composition, and socioeconomic conditions.

Patrol officers are assigned to shifts and to geographic areas. Demands on the police differ according to the time of day, day of the week, and even season of the year. Most serious crimes occur during the evening hours, and crime is lowest in the early morning. Police executives try to allocate their patrol resources according to these variables.

Preventive Patrol

Preventive patrol has long been thought to help deter crime. Since the days of Sir Robert Peel, it has been argued that a patrol officer's moving through an area will keep criminals from carrying out illegal acts. In 1974 this assumption was tested in Kansas City, Missouri. The results were surprising and shook the theoretical foundations of American policing (Sherman and Weisburd, 1995).

In the Kansas City Preventive Patrol Experiment, a fifteen-beat area was divided into three sections, each with similar crime rates, population characteristics, income levels, and numbers of calls to the police. In one area, labeled "reactive," all preventive patrol was withdrawn, and the police entered only in response to citizens' calls for service. In another section, labeled "proactive," preventive patrol was raised to as much as four times the normal level: all other services were provided at the same levels as before. The third section was used as a control, and the usual level of services, including preventive patrol, was maintained. After observing events in the three sections for a year, the researchers concluded that the changes in patrol strategies had had no major effects on the amount of crime reported, the amount of crime as measured by citizen surveys, or citizens' fear of crime (Kelling, Pate, Dieckman, and Brown,1974). Neither a decrease nor an increase in patrol activity had any apparent effect on crime.

Despite contradictory findings of other studies using similar research methods, the Kansas City finding "remains the most influential test of the general deterrent effects of patrol on crime" (Sherman and Weisburd, 1995:626). Because of this study, many departments have shifted their focus from law enforcement to maintaining order and serving the public. Some have argued that if the police cannot prevent crime by changing their patrol tactics, they may serve society better by focusing patrol activities on other functions while fighting crime as best they can.

Those who support the professional crime-fighting model of policing have criticized this and other studies that question the effectiveness of preventive patrol. They claim that the research attacks the heart of police work. But the research simply calls into question the inflexible aspects of preventive patrol.

Hot Spots

In the past, patrols were organized by "beats." The assumption was that crime can happen anywhere, and the entire beat must be patrolled at all times. Research shows, however, that crime is not spread evenly over all times and places. Instead, direct-contact predatory crimes, such as muggings and robberies, occur when three elements converge: motivated offenders, suitable targets, and the absence of anyone who could prevent the violation. This means that resources should be focused on "hot spots," places where crimes are likely to occur (Cohen and Felson, 1979:589).

In a study of crime in Minneapolis, researchers found that a small number of hot spots—3 percent of streets and intersections—produced 50 percent of calls to the police. By analyzing the places from which calls were made, they could identify those that produced the most crime (Sherman, Gartin, and Buerger, 1989:27).

With this knowledge, officers can be assigned to **directed patrol**—a proactive strategy designed to direct resources to known high-crime areas. A risk always exists, however, that the extra police pressure will simply cause lawbreakers to move to another neighborhood. The premise of this argument is that "there are only so many criminals seeking outlets for the fixed number of crimes they are predestined to commit" (Sherman and Weisburd, 1995:629). Although this shifting of "the action" may be a factor in some public drug markets, it does not fit all crime or even all vice—such as prostitution (Sherman, 1990; Weisburd and Green, 1995).

Police administrators are aware that the amount of crime varies by season and time. Rates of predatory crimes such as robbery and rape increase in the summer months, when people are outdoors. By contrast, domestic violence is more frequent in winter, when intimates spend more time indoors in close proximity to each other.

directed patrol

A proactive form of patrolling that directs resources to known high-crime areas.

There are also "hot times," generally between 7 P.M. and 3 A.M. A one-year study done in Minneapolis found that 51.9 percent of crime calls to the police came during this period, while the fewest calls were made between 3 A.M. and 11 A.M. With this knowledge, the department increased patrol presence in hot spots and at hot times (Koper, 1995). Although the result was less crime, many officers disliked the new tactics. Being a "presence" in a hot spot might deter criminals, but the officers were bored. Preventing crime is not as glamorous as catching criminals (Sherman and Weisburd, 1995:646).

Response Time

Most departments are organized so that calls for help come to a central section that dispatches the nearest officers by radio to the site of the incident. Because most citizens have access to phones, most cities have 911 systems; and because most officers are in squad cars linked to headquarters by two-way radios, police can respond quickly to calls. But are response times short enough to catch the offender?

Several studies have measured the impact of police response time on the ability of officers to intercept a crime in progress and arrest the criminal. In a classic study, William G. Spelman and Dale K. Brown found that the police were successful in only twenty-nine of one thousand cases. It made little difference whether they arrived two minutes or twenty minutes after the call. What did matter, however, was how soon the police were called (Spelman and Brown, 1984). Figure 5.5 presents these findings.

Although delayed arrival of the police is often caused by slowness in calling, arrest rates probably would not be improved merely by educating the public about their key role in stopping crime. As Spelman and Brown point out, three *decision-making* delays slow the process of calling the police:

FIGURE 5.5 **Probability of arrest as a function of elapsed time after crime**

The probability of arrest declines sharply when the police are not called within seconds. What does this imply for patrol policies?

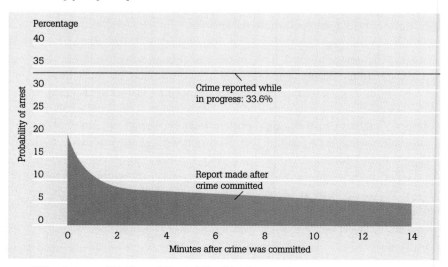

SOURCE: William Spelman and Dale Brown, *Calling the Police: Citizen Reporting of Serious Crime* (Washington, D.C.: Police Executive Research Forum, 1984), 64. Reprinted by permission.

❶ Ambiguity delays. Some people find the situation *ambiguous* and are not sure whether the police should be called. They might see an event but not know whether it is a robbery or two young men "horsing around."

❷ Coping delays. Other people are so busy *coping*—taking care of the victim or directing traffic—that they cannot leave the scene to call the police.

❸ Conflict delays. Still other people must first resolve *conflicts* before they call the police. For example, they may call someone else for advice about whether to call the police.

Besides these delays, communication problems can slow response. For example, a telephone may not be available, the emergency number may have to be looked up, or the dispatcher may not be able to handle the incoming call because she or he is dealing with other problems. The 911 system was designed to deal with communication delays.

Although delay is a major problem, reducing delay would only slightly increase arrest rates. In about three-quarters of crime calls, the police are reactive, in that the crimes (burglary, larceny, and the like) are "discovered" long after have they have occurred. A much smaller portion are "involvement" crimes (robbery, rape, assault) that victims know about right away and for which they can call the police right away (Spelman and Brown, 1984:4).

In theory, rapid police response should prevent injury, increase arrests, and deter crime. However, as Lawrence Sherman says, "In practice, it seems to do none of these things." He notes that injuries occur during the first seconds of the event, and the chances of catching a criminal after a five-minute delay are not great. Rapid response time is valuable for only a small fraction of all calls. In sum, the costs of police resources and the danger created by high-speed response may outweigh any increase in effectiveness owing to faster response times (Sherman, 1995:334).

CHECK POINT

⑧ **What factors affect patrol assignments?**

⑨ **What did the Kansas City study show about preventive patrol?**

⑩ **What is a "hot spot"?**

⑪ **What is directed patrol?**

⑫ **What types of delays reduce response time?**

Foot versus Motorized Patrol

One of the most frequent citizen requests is for officers to be put back on the beat. This was the main form of police patrol until the 1930s, when motorized patrol came to be viewed as more effective. A recent study found that in large cities almost 94 percent of patrol time is used in motorized patrol (Reaves, 1992). Squad cars increase the amount of territory that officers can patrol. With advances in communication technologies and onboard computers, patrol officers have direct links to headquarters and to criminal information databases. Now they can be quickly sent where needed with crucial information in their possession.

However, many citizens and some researchers claim that patrol officers in squad cars have become remote from the people they protect and less aware of their needs and problems. As Sherman points out, motorized patrols and telephone dispatching have caused a shift from "watching to prevent crime" to "waiting to respond to crime" (Sherman, 1983:149). Because officers rarely leave the patrol car, citizens have few chances to tell them what is going on in the community: "who is angry at whom about what, whose children are running wild, what threats have been made, and who is suddenly living above his apparent means" (Sherman, 1984). If they do not know about problems and suspicious activities within neighborhoods, patrol officers cannot mediate disputes, investigate suspected criminal activity, and make residents feel the police care about their well-being. When officers are distant and aloof from the people they serve, citizens may be less inclined to call for help or provide information (Moore, 1992:113).

By contrast, officers on foot are close to the daily life of the neighborhood. They are better able to detect criminal activity and apprehend those who have broken the law. Further, patrol officers who are known to citizens are less likely to be viewed as symbols of oppression by poor or minority residents. In large cities, personal contact may help reduce racial tensions and conflict.

The past decade has seen a revived interest in foot patrol because of citizens' demands for a familiar figure walking through the neighborhood. The cost and impact of foot patrol have been studied in a number of cities (Brown and Wycoff, 1987). These studies have shown that foot patrols are costly and do not greatly reduce crime, but that they make citizens less fearful of crime. In addition, citizen satisfaction with the police increases and the officers have a greater appreciation of neighborhood values (Cohen, Miller, and Rossman, 1990; Kelling, 1991). In terms of the cost and benefit, foot patrols are effective in high-density urban neighborhoods and business districts.

One-Person versus Two-Person Patrol Units

The debate over one-person versus two-person patrol units has raged in police circles for years. Patrolling is costly and two one-officer units can cover twice as much territory and respond to twice as many calls as a two-officer unit. A 1991 study of large cities found that 70 percent of patrol cars are staffed by one officer, but this pattern varies. For example, Los Angeles uses one-person cars for about half of its units during the day, but only 9 percent at night. Philadelphia, however, uses only one-officer cars (Pate and Hamilton, 1991).

Officers and their union leaders support the two-person squad car. They claim that police are safer and more effective when two officers work together in dangerous or difficult situations. However, police administrators contend that the one-person squad car is much more cost-effective and permits them to deploy more cars on each shift. With more cars to deploy, each can be assigned to a smaller area and response time can be decreased. They also contend that an officer working alone is more alert and attentive because he or she cannot be distracted by idle conversation with a colleague.

Aggressive Patrol

aggressive patrol

A patrol strategy designed to maximize the number of police interventions and observations in the community.

Aggressive patrol is a proactive strategy designed to maximize police activity in the community. It takes many forms, such as "sting" operations, firearms confiscation, raids on crack houses, programs that encourage citizens to list their valuables, and the tracking of high-risk parolees. James Q. Wilson and Barbara Boland have shown that patrol tactics that increase the risk of arrest are linked with lower crime rates. They argue that the effect of the police on crime depends less on how many officers are deployed in an area than on what they do while they are there (Wilson and Boland, 1979).

Officers in an "anticrime patrol" in New York worked the streets of high-crime areas in civilian clothes. Although they accounted for only 5 percent of the officers assigned to each precinct, during one year they made more than 18 percent of the felony arrests, including more than half of the arrests for robbery and about 40 percent of the arrests for burglary and auto theft .

The zero-tolerance policing of the 1990s in New York City is an example of aggressive patrol linked to the "broken windows" theory. As discussed in Chapter 4, this theory holds "that if not firmly suppressed, disorderly behavior in public will frighten citizens and attract predatory criminals, thus leading to more serious crime problems" (Greene, 1999:172). Thus, the police should focus on minor, public order crimes such as aggressive panhandling, graffiti, prostitution, and urinating in public. By putting more police on the streets, decentralizing authority to the precinct level, and instituting officer accountability, the zero-tolerance policy was judged to be a major factor in reducing New York City's crime rate (Silverman, 1999). However, by the end of the decade increasing cries of outrage were heard from citizens, especially those living in low-income, minority neighborhoods, that the police were being too aggressive (Reibstein, 1997:66).

Handguns are the leading risk factor for criminal harm. Studies show a strong link between the number of guns in a community and rates of gun injury. James Q. Wilson argues that the police should focus their gun-control efforts on guns being carried in high-risk places, by high-risk people, at high-risk times (Wilson, 1994:47). The police may legally seize firearms when they are carried without a permit, when they are concealed, and when the person carrying one is on probation or parole.

In the 1990s some police departments began to seize illegally possessed firearms as a way of getting guns off the street. In Kansas City, Missouri, aggressive traffic enforcement was used as a way to seize firearms in a beat with a high homicide rate. The police seized one gun for every twenty-eight traffic stops (Sherman and Rogan, 1995a:673). Aggressive patrol tactics were also used in raids on crack houses to seize firearms (Sherman and Rogan, 1995b:755). The result was a doubling of the gun recovery rate and a major reduction in gun violence (Sherman, 1995:340).

Release of violent felons from prison also poses a risk to community safety. The use of repeat offender squads to track high-risk parolees has proven successful in several cities. Using proactive tactics, the Washington, D.C., Repeat Offender Program targeted offenders with long records who were believed to be engaged in criminal activity. One squad, the "Hunter" squad, focused on warrant targets, especially those sought for violent crimes; the "Trapper" squad carried out long-term investigations designed to close unsolved cases and recover stolen property; "Fisherman" squads followed up on tips, made warrant arrests, and "cruised" targeted areas to spot crimes as they occurred. The program succeeded in removing repeat offenders from the streets, but it was costly because it moved officers away from other duties (Martin and Sherman, 1986).

Antifencing efforts, often called "stings," are a widely used law enforcement technique. Typically police set up a storefront operation, then they pose as fences and buy stolen property from thieves. Large amounts of property are recovered and thieves are arrested and successfully prosecuted.

The impact of these programs has been questioned. Robert Langworthy studied an auto theft sting conducted by police in Birmingham. He claims that, with respect to the goal of increased publicity and public support, the sting went well

(Langworthy, 1989:27). With respect to crime prevention, however, an apparent increase in auto theft may have resulted from the sting. He notes that stings may cause police to engage in illegal behavior, a risk that may not be worth taking.

The most cost-effective of the aggressive patrol strategies seem to be those that encourage officers to carry out more field questioning and traffic stops. To implement such a strategy, the department must recruit certain kinds of officers, train them, and devise requirements and reward systems (traffic ticket quotas, required numbers of field interrogations, chances for promotion) that will encourage them to carry out the intended strategy.

Although aggressive patrol strategies reduce crime, they may also lead to citizen hostility. In Charlotte, New York, Pittsburgh, Washington, D.C., and other cities, polls show support for the strategy. However, in some neighborhoods there are rumblings that aggressive patrol has gone too far and is straining police relations with young African Americans and Hispanics. This issue pits the need to balance the rights of individuals against the community's interest in order. "Put another way, it's whose son is being hassled" (Reibstein, 1997:66; Kolbert, 1999:50).

Community Policing

As discussed in Chapter 4, the concept of community policing has taken hold in many cities. To a great extent community policing has been seen as the solution to problems with the crime-fighter stance that prevailed during the professional era (Murphy, 1992). Community policing consists of attempts by the police to involve residents in making their own neighborhoods safer. Based on the belief that citizens may be concerned about local disorder as well as crime in general, this strategy emphasizes cooperation between the police and citizens in identifying community needs and determining the best ways to meet them (Moore, 1992).

Community policing has four components:
1. Community-based crime prevention.
2. Changing the focus of patrol activities to nonemergency services.
3. Making the police more accountable to the public.
4. Decentralizing decision making to include residents. (Skolnick and Bayley, 1988)

Agnes Brooks, a police volunteer, helped devise a plan that stopped burglaries at this storage center. Involving residents in fighting crime is part of San Diego's Neighborhood Policing Philosophy.

Community policing may be carried out by patrol officers assigned to walk neighborhood beats so that they can get to know residents better. It may entail creating police ministations in the community and police-sponsored programs for youth and the elderly. Police departments may also survey citizens to find out about their problems and needs.

Associated with community policing, a method called **problem-oriented policing** tries to find out what is causing citizen calls for help (Goldstein, 1990). The police seek to identify, analyze, and respond to the conditions underlying the events that prompt people to call the police. Knowing those conditions, officers can enlist community agencies and residents to help resolve them. Police using this approach do not just fight crime; they address a broad array of problems that affect the quality of life in the community.

Regardless of whether the police focus their resources on order maintenance, law enforcement, or service, they tend to respond to specific incidents. In most cases, a citizen's call or an officer's field observation triggers a police response. The police are often asked to respond to a rash of incidents in the same location. Because the police traditionally focus on *incidents*, they do not try to identify the roots of these incidents. By contrast, those engaged in problem-oriented policing seek to address the underlying causes.

The police departments of Newport News, Virginia, and Baltimore County, Maryland, have gained national recognition for their problem-oriented policing (Cordner, 1988). Although their procedures and organization differ, both departments involve officers and community residents in finding ways to reduce crime, disorder, and fear.

The problem-oriented approach asks officers to look beyond the department for information. They talk to residents, businesspeople, offenders, and public officials—anyone who might offer information. They may find that incidents will cease if street lighting is improved, aggressive measures are taken against streetwalkers, or the closing hours of a local bar are enforced. Whatever the solution, it usually means getting help from other agencies (Spelman and Eck, 1987).

Community policing has spread across the country and gained a great deal of support from citizens, legislators, and Congress (Bayley, 1994). This support can be seen in the emphasis on community policing in the Violent Crime Control and Law Enforcement Act passed by Congress in 1994. Portions of the act call for increases in the numbers of officers assigned to community policing and for the development of new community policing programs.

San Diego has adopted a Neighborhood Policing Philosophy that emphasizes two concepts: (1) police and citizens share responsibility for identifying and solving crime problems, and (2) law enforcement is but one tool for addressing crime (Mears, 1998). As Jerry Sanders, the police chief has said, community policing begins with a practical consideration, "Listen to the community and let them tell us what their priorities are" (Butterfield, 1999b:4). The police learned that what the people wanted them to work on were not serious crimes, but mainly abandoned cars or houses, which attract other problems, and—in the worst areas—drug houses.

Through this approach San Diego police have fostered connections with the community to share information, working with citizens to address crime and disorder, and tap other public and private agency resources to help solve them. Examples of the neighborhood policing strategy in San Diego include:

problem-oriented policing
An approach to policing in which officers routinely seek to identify, analyze, and respond to the circumstances underlying the incidents that prompt citizens to call the police.

COMPARATIVE
perspective

Patrol in Japan

Many community policing strategies now being used in the United States have been the tradition in Japan for many years. Patrol officers walking through their assigned neighborhoods and working out of local offices are a hallmark of Japanese policing.

Japanese policemen are addressed by the public as Omawari san— Mr. Walkabout. This is an accurate reflection of what the public sees the police doing most of the time. Foot patrolling is done out of *kobans* [mini police stations in urban neighborhoods], usually for periods of an hour. Patrols are more common at night, when officers work in pairs. . . . Patrolmen amble at a ruminative pace that allows thorough observation. . . . Patrolling by automobile, which is much less common than foot patrolling, can be frustrating too. Due to the narrow congested streets of Japanese cities . . . patrol cars are forced to move at a snail's pace. . . .

Patrolling is by no means a matter of high adventure. For the most part it consists of watching and occasionally answering questions. Patrolmen rarely discover genuine emergencies; the chance of coincidence between patrolmen and sudden need are simply too great. Patrolling does not reduce reaction time or particularly enhance availability. What patrolling does

is to demonstrate the existence of authority, correct minor inconveniences . . . such as illegally parked cars . . . and generate trust through the establishment of familiar personal relations with a neighborhood's inhabitants. On patrol, policemen are alert for different kinds of problems in different places. In a residential area they watch for people who appear out of place or furtive. In public parks they give attention to loitering males. Around major railroad stations they look for runaway adolescents, lured by the glamour of a big city, who could be victimized by criminal elements. They also watch for *teyhaishi*... labor contractors . . . who pick up and sell unskilled laborers to construction companies. In a neighborhood of bars and cabarets, patrolmen stare suspiciously at stylishly dressed women standing unescorted on street corners. They determine whether wheeled carts piled with food or cheap souvenirs are blocking pedestrian thoroughfares. Throughout every city they pay particular attention to illegally parked cars and cars that have been left with their doors unlocked. . . .

When a Japanese policeman is out on patrol he makes a special point of talking to people about themselves, their purposes, and their behavior. These conversations may be innocent or investigatory. The law provides that policemen may stop and question people only if there is reasonable ground for suspecting they have committed

- Support for "neighborhood watch" and citizen patrols that look for suspicious activity, identify community problems, and work on crime prevention.
- Use of civil remedies and strict building code enforcement to abate nuisance properties and close down "drug houses."

In Japanese cities each neighborhood has its own koban, or police box, staffed by an officer 24 hours a day. Officers leave the koban to "walkabout," meeting residents, solving problems, and dealing with disturbances and occasionally crimes.

or are about to commit a crime or have information about a crime. Nevertheless, standard procedure on patrol is to stop and question anyone whenever the policeman thinks it may be useful. One reason for doing so is to discover wanted persons. And the tactic has proved very effective; 40 percent of criminals wanted by the police have been discovered by patrolmen on the street. Not only do officers learn to question people adroitly on the street, they become adept at getting people to agree to come to the *koban* so that more extended, less public inquiries can be made. People are under no

obligation to do so, any more than they are to stop and answer questions. The key to success with these tactics is to be compelling without being coercive. This in turn depends on two factors: the manner of the police officer and a thorough knowledge of minor laws. The first reduces hostility, the second provides pretexts for opening conversations justifiably. People who park illegally, ride bicycles without a light, or fail to wear helmets when riding a motorcycle are inviting officers to stop them and ask probing questions. The importance with which the police view on-street interrogation is

indicated by the fact that prefectural and national contests are held each year to give recognition to officers who are best at it. . . . Senior officers continually impress upon new recruits the importance of learning to ask questions in inoffensive ways so that innocent people are not affronted and unpleasant scenes can be avoided. . . .

The most striking aspect of the variety of situations confronted by policemen is their compelling, unforced naturalness. The police see masses of utterly ordinary people who have been enmeshed in situations that are tediously complex and meaningful only to the persons immediately involved. The outcomes are of no interest to the community at large; the newspapers will not notice if matters are sorted out or not; superior officers have no way of recording the effort patrolmen expend in trying to be helpful; and the people themselves are incapable by and large of permanently escaping their predicaments. Policemen are responsible for tending these individuals, for showing that they appreciate—even when they are tired, hurried, bored, and preoccupied—the minute ways in which each person is unique. It is perhaps, the greatest service they render.

SOURCE: David H. Bayley, *Forces of Order: Police Behavior in Japan and the United States* (Berkeley: University of California Press, 1979), 33, 34, 37, 41, 51–52. Copyright © 1976 The Regents of the University of California. Reprinted by permission.

■ Collaborate with community organizations and businesses to clear up, close down, or redesign specific locations and properties that repeatedly attract prostitution, drugs, and gang problems (Greene, 1999:183).

Assisting the San Diego police are twelve hundred volunteers who have received police training, wear police-like uniforms, and use police cars. They watch their neighborhoods so that officers can patrol (Butterfield, 1999b:4).

Although community policing has won support from police executives, the Police Foundation, the Police Executive Research Forum, and police researchers, it may be difficult to put into effect. As with any reform, change may not come easily. Police are used to dealing with problems according to established procedures and may feel that their authority is decreased when responsibility is given instead to precinct commanders (Kelling and Bratton, 1993). Another problem with implementing community policing is that it does not reduce costs; it requires either additional funds or redistribution of existing budgets. Measuring the success of this approach in reducing fear of crime, solving underlying problems, maintaining order, and serving the community is also difficult. Finally, the question arises of how far the police should extend their role beyond crime fighting to remedying other social problems. As New York City mayor Rudolph Giuliani has said, community policing has "resulted in officers doing too much social work and making too few arrests" (*Criminal Justice Newsletter*, 1994:1).

Special Populations

Urban police forces must deal with a complex population. City streets contain growing numbers of mentally ill, homeless, runaways, public drunkards, drug addicts, and people with acquired immune deficiency syndrome (AIDS). Crowded jails, the release of mental health patients from institutions, the decriminalization of public drunkenness, and cutbacks in public assistance—all have increased the number of "problem" people on city streets. Most of these people do not commit crimes, but their presence is disturbing to residents, and they may contribute to disorder and fear of crime.

Patrol officers cooperate with social service agencies in helping individuals and responding to requests for order maintenance. The police must walk a fine line when requiring a person to enter a homeless shelter, obtain medical assistance, or be taken to a mental health unit (McCoy, 1986; Melekian, 1990). Police departments have developed various techniques for dealing with special populations. In Los Angeles, New York City, and Philadelphia, mobile units are equipped with restraining devices, mace, and medical equipment to handle disturbed people. Madison, Wisconsin, has educated officers about special populations and ways of dealing with them. Birmingham, Alabama, uses social workers to deal with the mentally ill, freeing the police to respond to other problems (NIJ, 1988).

Clearly, dealing with special populations is a major problem for police in most cities. Each community must develop policies so that officers will know when and how they are to intervene when a person may not have broken the law but is upsetting residents.

The Future of Patrol

Preventive patrol and rapid response to calls for help have been the hallmarks of policing in the United States for the past half-century. However, research done in the past thirty years has raised many questions about patrol strategies that police should employ. The rise of community policing has shifted law enforcement toward problems that affect the quality of life of residents. Police forces need to use patrol tactics that fit the needs of the neighborhood. Neighborhoods with crime hot spots may require different strategies than neighborhoods where residents are concerned mainly with order maintenance. Many researchers believe that traditional patrol efforts have focused too narrowly on crime control, neglecting the order maintenance and service activities for which police departments were originally formed. Critics have urged that the police become more community oriented and return to the first principle of policing: "to remain in close and frequent contact with citizens" (Williams and Pate, 1987). To see this policy in action, look at Japan, where most patrolling is done on foot, as described in the Comparative Perspective (pp. 182–183).

⑬ **What are the advantages and disadvantages of foot patrol? Of motorized patrol?**

⑭ **What are the advantages and disadvantages of one-person versus two-person patrol units?**

⑮ **What is aggressive patrol?**

⑯ **What are the major elements of community policing?**

Investigation

All cities with a population of more than 250,000, and 90 percent of smaller cities, have officers (detectives) assigned to investigative duties. Detectives make up 15 percent of police personnel. They have a higher status in the department: their pay is higher, their hours are more flexible, and they are supervised less closely than patrol officers. Detectives do not wear uniforms, and their work is considered more interesting than that of patrol officers. In addition, they are engaged solely in law enforcement and do no order maintenance or service work; hence, their activities conform more closely to the image of the police as crime fighters.

Detectives in small departments are generalists who investigate whatever crimes occur. But in large departments they are assigned to special units such as homicide, robbery, auto theft, forgery, and burglary. In recent years, because of public pressures, some departments have set up new special units to deal with bias crimes, child abuse, sexual assault, and computer crime (Bayley, 1994:26).

Most investigative units are separated from the patrol chain of command. Many argue that this results in duplication of effort and lack of continuity in handling cases. It often means that vital information known by one branch is not known by the other.

Like patrol, criminal investigation is largely reactive. Detectives become involved after a crime has been reported and a preliminary investigation has been done by a patrol officer. The job of detectives is mainly to find out what happened by talking to people—victims, suspects, witnesses. On the basis of this information, detectives develop theories about who committed the crime and then set out to gather the evidence that will lead to arrest and prosecution. Bayley notes that detectives do not maintain an open mind about the identity of the offender. They know that if the suspect cannot be identified by people on the scene, they are not likely to find him or her on their own. Detectives collect physical evidence to support testimony that identifies a suspect, not to find the suspect (Bayley, 1994:26).

Goldstein (1977:55) has outlined the process of investigation as follows:

- When a serious crime occurs and the suspect is identified and caught right away, the detective prepares the case to be presented to the prosecuting attorney.
- When the suspect is identified but not caught, the detective tries to locate him or her.
- When the offender is not identified but there is more than one suspect, the detective conducts investigations to determine which one committed the crime.
- When there is no suspect, the detective starts from scratch to find out who committed the crime.

In performing an investigation, detectives depend not only on their own experience but also on technical experts. Much of the information they need will come from criminal files, lab technicians, and forensic scientists. Many small departments turn to the state crime laboratory or the FBI for such information. Detectives are often pictured as working alone, but they are part of a team.

Although detectives focus on serious crimes, they are not the only ones who investigate crimes. Patrol, traffic, vice, and juvenile units may also be involved. In small towns and rural areas, patrol officers must conduct investigations because police departments are too small to have separate detective bureaus. In urban areas, because they are likely to be the first police to arrive at the scene of a crime, patrol officers must do much of the initial investigative work. The patrol unit's investigation can be crucial. Successful prosecution of many kinds of cases, including robbery, larceny, and burglary, is closely linked to the speed with which a suspect is arrested. If patrol officers cannot obtain information from victims and witnesses right away, they have less chance of arresting and prosecuting the suspect.

Apprehension

The discovery that a crime has been committed sets off a chain of events leading to the capture of a suspect and the gathering of the evidence needed to convict that person. It may also lead to a number of dead ends, such as a lack of clues pointing to a suspect or a lack of evidence to link the suspect to the crime.

The process of catching a suspect has three stages: detection of a crime, preliminary investigation, and follow-up investigation. Depending on the outcome of the investigation, these three steps may be followed by a fourth: clearance and arrest. As shown in Figure 5.6, these actions are designed to use criminal justice resources to arrest a suspect and assemble enough evidence to support a charge.

❶ DETECTION OF A CRIME Information that a crime has been committed usually comes in a call to the police. The patrol officer on the beat may also come upon a crime, but usually the police are alerted by others. The police may be informed of a crime on business premises by automatic alarms linked to police headquarters. Such direct communications help shorten response time and increase the chances of catching the suspect.

❷ PRELIMINARY INVESTIGATION The first law enforcement official on the scene is usually a patrol officer who has been dispatched by radio. The officer must give aid to the victim, secure the crime scene for investigation, and document the facts of the crime. If a suspect is present or nearby, the officer conducts a "hot" search and may apprehend the suspect. This initial work is crucial. The officer must gather the basic facts, including the name of the victim, a description of the suspect, and the names of witnesses. After the information is collected, it is sent to the investigation unit.

❸ FOLLOW-UP INVESTIGATION After a crime has been brought to the attention of the police and a preliminary investigation has been made, the detective will decide what course of action to pursue. In the big-city departments, incident reports from each day are analyzed the next morning. Investigators receive assignments based on their specialties. They study the information, weigh each factor, and decide whether there is a good chance the crime can be solved.

Some departments have guidelines for making these decisions so that resources will be used efficiently. If the detectives decide little chance exists of solving the crime quickly, the case may be dropped. Steven Brandl found that in burglary and robbery follow-up investigations the value of the lost property and the detective's belief that the case could be resolved through an arrest were the main factors affecting how much time and effort were spent in solving the crime (Brandl, 1993:141).

When detectives decide that a full-scale investigation is warranted, a wider search—known as a "cold" search—for evidence or weapons is carried out. Witnesses may be questioned again, informants contacted, and evidence gathered. Because of the pressure of new cases, however, an investigation may be shelved so that resources may be directed toward "warmer" cases.

FIGURE 5.6 **The apprehension process**

Apprehension of a felony suspect may result from a sequence of actions by patrol officers and detectives. Coordination of these efforts is a key factor in solving major crimes.

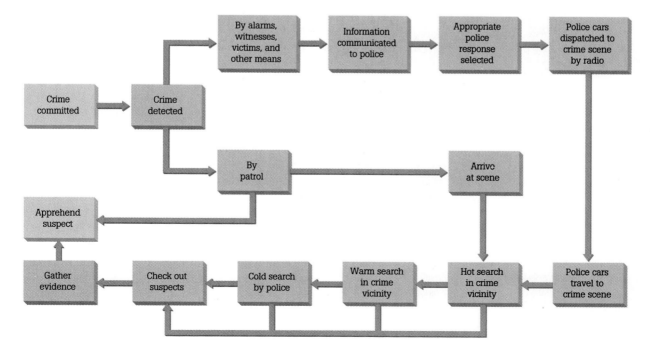

④ CLEARANCE AND ARREST   The decision to arrest is a key part of the apprehension process. In some cases, further evidence or links between suspects and others are not discovered if arrests are made too soon. A crime is considered cleared when the evidence supports the arrest of a suspect. If a suspect admits having committed other unsolved crimes, those crimes are also "cleared." When a crime is cleared in police files, it does not always mean that the suspect will be found guilty.

Forensic Techniques

American police have long relied on science in gathering, identifying, and analyzing evidence. Scientific analysis of fingerprints, blood, semen, hair, textiles, and weapons has helped the police identify criminals (see Table 5.1). It has also helped prosecutors convince jurors of the guilt of defendants. Forensic labs can be found in all states and many large cities.

DNA "fingerprinting" is the latest weapon to be employed in investigating many kinds of crimes. This technique is used to identify people through their distinctive gene patterns (also called "genotypic features"). DNA, or deoxyribonucleic acid, is the basic component of all chromosomes and is the same for all the cells in a person's body, including skin, blood, organs, and semen. The characteristics of certain segments of DNA vary from person to person and thus form a genetic "fingerprint." Therefore, DNA from, say, samples of hair can be analyzed and compared with those of suspects.

Use of the DNA technique has been hampered by the fact that few labs are equipped to perform DNA analysis. Moreover, many detectives and prosecutors do not make full use of these resources, and some people argue that the method does not yet have a sound scientific foundation. Courts in most states now accept DNA results as evidence, but in some states, defense attorneys have successfully challenged the use of DNA evidence (Neufeld and Colman, 1990:46).

Since 1989 DNA testing has aided in more than twenty thousand convictions, particularly in sexual contact and abuse cases. (Burns and Smith, 1999:1). But it has also been responsible for the release from prison of an increasing number of persons after testing has shown that they could not have committed the crimes for which they were imprisoned (Connors, Lundregan, Miller, and McEwan, 1996:2). In 1998 the FBI announced creation of a national DNA database made up of data from all fifty states unified by common test procedures. A DNA sample from a suspect or crime scene in one state can now be compared with all others in the system.

An example of the use of the DNA database to solve crimes comes from Florida. A Ft. Lauderdale detective searching old cases noticed in an unsolved 1986 murder case a trail of blood leading away from the victim indicated the attacker had been wounded. A single droplet from a floor tile, stored for more than a decade, matched the DNA of a convicted sex offender Scott Edward Williams. Williams was in

Forensic scientist Henry Lee and members of the Connecticut State Police crime team mark a mannequin to indicate where 14-year-old Aquan Salmon was shot by Hartford Police Officer Robert Allen. Salmon was fleeing from a car and Allen thought Salmon was reaching for a gun.

TABLE 5.1 **The frontiers of forensics**

Analyses of fingerprints, blood, hair, and DNA (deoxyribonucleic acid) are four of the major forensic tools used by the police.

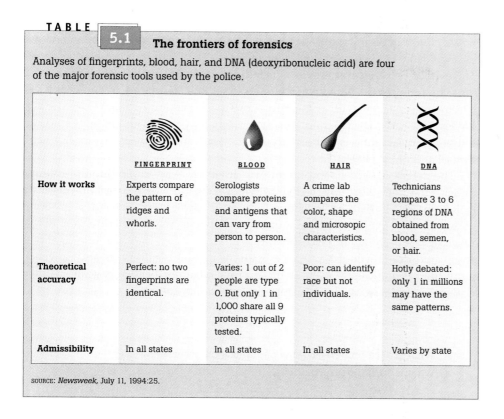

	FINGERPRINT	BLOOD	HAIR	DNA
How it works	Experts compare the pattern of ridges and whorls.	Serologists compare proteins and antigens that can vary from person to person.	A crime lab compares the color, shape and microsopic characteristics.	Technicians compare 3 to 6 regions of DNA obtained from blood, semen, or hair.
Theoretical accuracy	Perfect: no two fingerprints are identical.	Varies: 1 out of 2 people are type O. But only 1 in 1,000 share all 9 proteins typically tested.	Poor: can identify race but not individuals.	Hotly debated: only 1 in millions may have the same patterns.
Admissibility	In all states	In all states	In all states	Varies by state

SOURCE: *Newsweek*, July 11, 1994:25.

custody but was scheduled to be released. When confronted with the evidence he confessed and committed suicide a week later (*Newsweek*, November 16, 1998:69).

Research on Investigation

The results of several studies raise questions about the value of investigations and the role detectives play in apprehension. This research suggests that the police have attached too much importance to investigation as a means of solving crimes and shows that most crimes are cleared because of arrests made by the patrol force at or near the scene. Response time is a key factor in apprehension, as is the information given by the victim or witnesses.

A classic study of 153 large police departments found that a key factor in solving crimes was identification of the perpetrator by the victim or witnesses. Of those cases that were not solved right away but were cleared later, most were cleared by routine procedures such as fingerprint searches, tips from informants, and mug-shot "show-ups." The report found that actions by the investigative staff were important in very few cases. In sum, about 30 percent of the crimes were cleared by on-scene arrest and another 50 percent through identification by victims or witnesses when the police arrived. Thus, only about 20 percent could have been solved by detective work. Even among this group, however, the study found that most crimes "were also solved by patrol officers, members of the public who spontaneously provide further information, or routine investigative practices" (Greenwood, Chaiken, and Petersilia, 1977:227).

In some cities, the amount of serious crime has gone down during the past decade, but the number of unsolved cases has remained relatively stable. In part this may be accounted for by the lack of resources allocated to pursuing "cold cases." Detectives emphasize that although forensic tools are important, solving crimes "the old-fashioned way" through much street work is still effective.

Does this research show that detectives are not important? No. If cases are divided into categories, some are weak with little evidence, some are strong with a lot of evidence. Police need not devote a great deal of effort in these polar cases. However, in between are cases in which the strength of the evidence is moderate. These do require additional effort by detectives, and, as John Eck found, this "is extremely important with respect to subsequent making of follow-up arrests" (Bayley, 1998:149). The Eck finding was confirmed by Brandl and Frank's study of follow-up investigations of burglary and robbery in a Midwestern department (Brandl and Frank, 1994:163).

The detective's role is important in at least two ways in addition to solving crimes. First, the status of detective provides a goal to which patrol officers may aspire and gives them an incentive to excel in their work. Second, the public expects the police to conduct investigations. Citizens may have more trust in the police or feel more willing to cooperate with them when they see investigations being conducted, even if those investigations may not lead to arrests. However many high-profile cases, such as the murder of junior beauty pageant winner JonBenet Ramsey (see Close-Up, opposite), remain unsolved.

CHECK POINT

(17) **What are the four steps of the apprehension process?**

(18) **What is "DNA fingerprinting"?**

Special Operations

Patrol and investigation are the two largest and most important units in a police department. In metropolitan areas, however, special units are set up to deal with specific types of problems. The most common such units are for traffic, vice, and juveniles. Some cities also have units to deal with organized crime and drugs. The existence of special units should not overshadow the fact that patrol officers and investigators must also deal with the same problems.

Although the Boulder police continue to place them under an "umbrella of suspicion," John and Patsy Ramsey contend that JonBenet was killed by a pedophile intruder who disabled the little girl with a stun gun.

Traffic

Traffic regulation is a major job of the police. On average 7 percent of officers are assigned to traffic units (Bayley, 1994:94). The police regulate the flow of vehicles, investigate accidents, and enforce traffic laws. This work may not seem to have much to do with crime fighting or order maintenance, but it does. Besides helping to maintain order, enforcement of traffic laws educates the public in safe driving habits and provides a visible service to the community.

Traffic duty can also help the police catch criminals. In enforcing traffic laws, patrol officers can stop cars and question drivers. Stolen property and suspects linked to other criminal acts are often found in this way. Most departments can now automatically check license numbers against lists of wanted vehicles and suspects.

CLOSE

up

Who Killed JonBenet Ramsey?

At 5:52 A.M., December 26, 1996, the Boulder, Colorado, police received a 911 call from a frantic mother, Patsy Ramsey, saying that her 6-year-old daughter, JonBenet, had been kidnapped. When Officer Rick French arrived eight minutes later he was shown a ransom note demanding $118,000. He made a quick search of the Ramsey house, finding neither JonBenet nor a forced entry. Detectives and a forensic team soon arrived as did friends of the Ramseys. Later, a group of victims' advocates, trained to help families through traumatic situations, brought in bagels and coffee. Throughout this period no attempt was made by the police to limit access to interior parts of the house.

Seven hours after the first call to the police, Detective Linda Arndt asked Mr. Ramsey to search his house. He did this without a police escort. Within minutes he emerged from the basement carrying his daughter's body. Detective Arndt moved the body to the living room near the Christmas tree and lay a blanket over it. Moving the body contaminated the crime scene and may have disturbed critical evidence.

With the crime now a homicide, attention shifted to the Ramseys. The police found that JonBenet has been garroted with a paintbrush from the house and a nylon cord. The two and a half page ransom note, written with pen and paper from the house and identified by handwriting expert's as similar in style to that of Patsy Ramsey's, contained details that few outside of the family would have known. FBI statistics indicate a 12-to-1 probability that when a child is murdered it is a family member or caregiver. The Ramseys maintained their innocence and refused to speak to the police. Instead they hired a defense team of eight lawyers, four publicists, three private investigators, two handwriting analysts, and a retired FBI profiler.

Investigation of the murder was hampered by conflicts between the Boulder police and the office of District Attorney Alex Hunter. These tensions were heightened by erroneous reports given to the media (by the police, say the Ramseys) as to crucial elements of the case. Steve Thomas, the lead investigator, publicly denounced the district attorney's office as "thoroughly compromised." Lou Smit, a detective for thirty-two years, accused the police department of "going in the wrong direction." The squabbling, accusations, and contravening orders about the sharing of evidence contributed to public dismay as to the ability of criminal justice officials to solve the case. By December 1997 John Eller, the lead investigator, and Chief Tom Koby had resigned from the Boulder police. Finally, admitting defeat in March 1998 District Attorney Hunter was forced to request a grand jury investigation.

On September 15, 1998, 628 days after JonBenet was murdered, a twelve-member grand jury convened. The jury heard from police investigators, handwriting experts, nationally known forensic expert Dr. Henry Lee, and JonBenet's brother, Burke, but not John and Patsy Ramsey. Under the rules of grand jury secrecy, it is not known how the testimony was conducted and how each juror voted. On October 13, 1999, District Attorney Hunter announced that the grand jury had completed its work and that no charges had been filed. He admitted that there was not "sufficient evidence to warrant filing charges against anyone who has been investigated at this time." The Ramseys said: "We take no satisfaction from this result because a child killer remains free and undetected."

SOURCE: Marc Peyer and Sherry Keene-Osborn, "A Body in the Basement," *Newsweek*, January 13, 1997:38; Daniel Click and Sherry Keene-Osborn, "Complications in the Case," *Newsweek*, June 23, 1997:46; Sherry Keene-Osborn and Daniel Glick, "A Case Forever Unraveling," *Newsweek*, September 15, 1997:78; Daniel Glick, Sherry Keene-Osborn, and Andrew Murr, "The Door the Cops Never Opened," *Newsweek*, July 13, 1998:32; Lawrence Shiller, "A Death in Paradise," *Newsweek*, February 22, 1999:58; Daniel Glick and Sherry Keene-Osborn, "No Justice for JonBenet," *Newsweek*, October 25, 1999:36; James Brooke, "Bungled JonBenet Case Bursts a City's Majesty," *New York Times*, December 5, 1997, p. A14; Michael Janofsky, "No Charges in Death of Child Beauty Queen," *New York Times*, October 14, 1999, p. 14; and Joyce Carol Oates, "The Mystery of JonBenet Ramsey," *New York Review of Books* (June 24, 1999):31.

Enforcement of traffic laws is a good example of police discretion. Bayley (1986) has shown that when officers stop drivers for traffic violations they choose among five options:

1. Issue a citation (43 percent of stops).
2. Release the driver with a warning (20.7 percent).
3. Arrest the driver for intoxication or for another crime (14 percent).
4. Let the driver go (13.4 percent).
5. Issue a citation while also giving a stern lecture (12 percent).

Traffic work is mostly proactive, and the level of enforcement is linked to department policies. Guided by these policies, officers target certain kinds of violations or certain highways. Some departments expect officers to issue a certain number of citations during each shift. Although these norms may be informal, they are a way of gauging the productivity of traffic officers. For the most part, selective enforcement is the general policy, because the police have neither the desire nor the resources to enforce all traffic laws.

Vice

Enforcement of vice laws depends on proactive police work, which often involves the use of undercover agents and informers. Most large city police departments have a vice unit. Strict enforcement of these laws requires that officers be given wide discretion. They must often engage in degrading activities, such as posing as prostitutes or drug dealers, to catch lawbreakers. The special nature of vice work requires members of the unit to be well trained in the legal procedures that must be followed if arrests are to lead to convictions.

The potential for corruption in this type of police work presents some administrative dilemmas. Undercover officers are in a position to blackmail gamblers and drug dealers and may also be offered bribes. In addition, officers must be transferred when their identities become known.

The growth of undercover work and electronic surveillance troubles critics who favor more open policing. They fear that the use of these tactics violates civil liberties and increases government intrusion into the private lives of citizens, whether or not those citizens commit crimes.

Posing as a drug dealer, a South Florida officer tips his hat to signal officers hidden nearby. Proactive police work is necessary for the enforcement of laws against vice. What are some of the problems associated with this approach?

Drug Law Enforcement

Many large cities have a bureau to enforce drug laws. Within these agencies, task forces may deal with organized crime or gangs involved in drug dealing. Other groups may use sting operations to arrest drug sellers on the street or to provide drug education in the community.

Drug enforcement may reflect the goal of "aggressive patrol," assigning resources so as to get the largest number of arrests and stop street dealing. Police executives believe that it is important to show dealers and the community that drug laws are enforced.

Various strategies have been used to attack drug dealing. One of these is building inspections of houses and buildings used by drug dealers. Those that do not meet city standards can be boarded up to rid the neighborhood of dealers. Streets where drugs are dealt openly may be flooded with officers who engage in proactive stops and questioning.

Another strategy is to disrupt the drug market. In Phoenix, Arizona, and other cities, police placed signs warning motorists entering "drug neighborhoods" that they may be stopped and questioned. In New York City's "Operation Pressure Point," one thousand police officers were moved into the Lower East Side to shut down the area's "drug supermarket." The police made thousands of arrests, abandoned buildings were torn down, and storefronts used by dealers were padlocked (Zimmer, 1987). This approach has been used in other parts of New York, in Los Angeles, and in other cities. But how effective is this approach? Do these efforts simply shift the drug market to another area, or do they reduce the availability of drugs?

The "war on drugs" consumes much of the resources of many urban police departments. While some officers might prefer patrolling a regular beat than being a drug cop, other officers like the work. As Officer Marcus Laffey of the New York Police Department explained, moving to narcotics from being a beat cop was refreshing.

> For one thing, you deal only with criminals. No more domestic disputes, barricaded schizo-phrenics, or D.O.A.s [dead on arrivals], the morass of negotiable and nonnegotiable difficul-ties people have with their neighbors or boyfriends or stepchildren. (Laffey, 1999:29)

Laffey says that patrol cops deal with the "fluid whole of people's lives, but usually when the tide's going out." People who call the cops are not having a good time, and the suspect is not happy to see the police. "Now all I do is catch sellers of crack and heroin, and catch their customers to show that they sold it. Patrol is politics, but narcotics is pure technique" (Laffey, 1999:29).

Although arrests for drug sale or possession have increased dramatically, some observers believe that this is not the best way to deal with the problem. Many public officials argue that drugs should be viewed as a public health problem instead of a crime problem. Critics of current policies believe society would benefit more if more resources were devoted to drug treatment programs, which can get some people to stop using drugs, than from police actions that fill prisons without doing much to reduce drug use.

Police Actions and the Rule of Law

As discussed in Chapter 3, the police must work within the framework of the law; they are not free to use any means to fight crime. The law requires that the police investigate crimes by gathering information required to successfully prosecute a suspect and to free the innocent. To secure a conviction, the police must provide prosecutors with evidence that is admissible in court. **Admissible evidence** is evidence that has been gathered according to the rules specified in the Constitution, as interpreted by the courts. Three police practices—search and seizure, arrest, and interrogation—are structured to ensure that the rule of law is upheld and the rights of citizens protected.

Two rules that have been devised by the Supreme Court make sure that police respect the rights of suspects. First, the exclusionary rule states that evidence seized by illegal means and confessions obtained in improper ways cannot be used in trials. Second, the Court has ruled that the Sixth Amendment right to

admissible evidence
Evidence that has been gathered by the police according to the law as specified in the Constitution, court decisions, and statutes.

counsel means that the defendant may have a lawyer present when he or she is questioned by police. Police departments have policies and procedures for searches, arrests, and interrogations that officers learn during training. Officers are keenly aware that prosecution of a case may be jeopardized if they do not follow proper procedures.

Search and Seizure

In *Mapp v. Ohio* (1961), the Supreme Court applied the exclusionary rule to all searches conducted by state and local police departments. Before that case, the rule had applied only to federal law enforcement officials and to the police in states that had their own rules about exclusion of improperly obtained evidence. Now all police officers must conduct investigations and arrests in accordance with the Fourth Amendment's rules against unreasonable searches and seizures. However, in some situations searches are reasonable, and evidence obtained from them can be used in court even if a judge did not authorize the search.

Search Warrant

search warrant

An order of a judge that allows a police officer to search a designated place for specific persons or items to be seized.

When a judge has issued a **search warrant,** the police may search a designated place for specific persons or items to be seized. To obtain the warrant, the officer must do two things:

❶ Provide reliable information showing that there is probable cause to believe that a crime has been or is being committed.

❷ Identify the premises and pieces of property to be seized. (The officer must swear under oath that the facts given are correct.)

Warrantless Searches

In day-to-day police work, the majority of searches take place without a warrant. It is in this area that the courts have been most active in defining the term *unreasonable*. Five kinds of searches may be legally conducted without a warrant and still be in accord with the Fourth Amendment: (1) searches incident to a lawful arrest, (2) searches during field interrogation, (3) searches of automobiles under special conditions, (4) seizures of evidence in "plain view," and (5) searches when consent is given. Warrantless searches raise a number of ethical concerns (see A Question of Ethics, opposite).

Warrantless searches of automobiles may be conducted when there is probable cause to believe that a vehicle contains criminal evidence. Lieutenant Tim Laun checks the inside and under a car seat after he and his colleagues arrested a suspect; they found marijuana in the vehicle on Midland Avenue in Syracuse, New York.

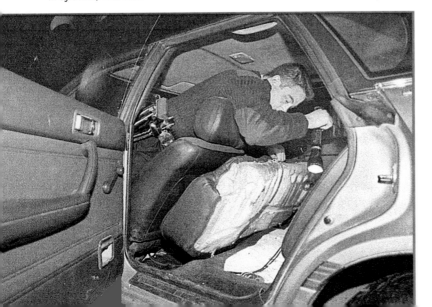

❶ **SEARCHES INCIDENT TO A LAWFUL ARREST** When an officer has observed a crime or believes that one has been committed, an arrest may be made and a search conducted without a warrant. Such searches are justified when they meet three requirements: (1) the officer has probable cause to arrest the suspect, (2) there is a need to prevent the loss of evidence or to protect officers and bystanders, and (3) the search is limited to that necessary to seize weapons or evidence.

In *Chimel v. California* (1969), the Supreme Court ruled that such a search is limited to the person of the arrestee and the area within the arrestee's "immediate control," defined as that area "from within which he might [obtain] a weapon or something that could have been used as evidence against him" to destroy it. Thus, if the police are holding a person in one room of a house, they may not search and seize property in another part of the house.

2 FIELD INTERROGATION The police often stop, frisk, and interrogate persons without knowing any facts that might justify an arrest. As a society, Americans want police to investigate people who behave in suspicious ways as well as those who disrupt public order. Thus, officers often stop people on the street to ask them who they are and what they are doing. Officers must have a *reasonable suspicion* that the person may have committed or be about to commit a crime. These field interrogations, often called "threshold inquiries," allow for brief questioning and frisking—patting down the outside of the suspect's clothing to find out whether he or she has a concealed weapon.

In the case of ***Terry v. Ohio*** (1968), the Supreme Court upheld the stop-frisk procedure when a police officer stopped and patted down three men who had been looking into store windows in a suspicious way. The officer found handguns during the patdown, and the Court ruled that such a search could be conducted if the officer reasonably believed that the person might be dangerous.

On the basis of this and later decisions, a police officer now may stop and question a person if he or she can reasonably assume that a crime is being committed, is about to be committed, or has been committed. The person may be frisked if the officer fears for his or her life and believes that the person has a weapon. The courts have concluded that an officer may conduct this kind of search to investigate suspicious persons without first showing probable cause. All that is required of the police officer is that he or she have a reasonable suspicion that the suspect may be armed and was considering criminal activity.

In the recent case of *Illinois v. Wardlow* (2000) a divided Court agreed that flight at the mere sight of a police officer, in the context of other factors, could justify the police in conducting a stop-and-frisk search. Sam Wardlow was walking in a Chicago neighborhood when he bolted at the sight of a convoy of police cars. He was chased into an alley, where officers found he was carrying a loaded gun. For the majority, Chief Justice William H. Rehnquist held that Wardlow's presence in an area known for heavy narcotics trafficking, combined with his unprovoked flight, justified the search.

A Question of Ethics

Officer Mike Groton knocked on the apartment door. He and fellow officer Howard Reece had gone to this rundown part of town to arrest Richard Watson on the basis of evidence from an informer that Watson was a major drug seller. "Police officers, open up," said Groton. The door opened slowly, and a small, tense woman peered into the hallway.

"Ma'am, we have a warrant for the arrest of Richard Watson. Is he here?"

"No. I don't know any Watson," was the answer.

"Well, let us in so that we can see for ourselves."

Groton and Reece entered the apartment. Reece quickly went to a back bedroom. The window leading to a fire escape was open and the bed looked as though someone had left it in a rush. Reece poked around the room, opening drawers and searching the closet. In the back of the closet he saw a woman's purse hanging on a hook. He opened it and found three glassine packages of a white powder.

"Hey Mike, look what I found," he called. Groton came into the bedroom. "Looks like heroin to me," said Reece. "Too bad we can't use it."

"Why can't we use it? This is the place."

"But the warrant specifies the arrest of Watson. It doesn't say anything about searching his closet."

"Let's just keep those packets. When we catch him we can 'find' it in his pocket."

■ What are the issues here? Can the officers keep the heroin packets? Is bending the rules acceptable in some cases? If so, are they acceptable in the one just described? What should the officers do?

Terry v. Ohio (1968)
A police officer may stop and frisk an individual if it is reasonable to suspect that a crime has been committed.

❸ AUTOMOBILES Warrantless searches may be conducted when there is probable cause to believe that a vehicle contains criminal evidence. The Supreme Court permits officers to search cars more freely than houses because cars are mobile and evidence may be lost if officers must seek a warrant before conducting a search.

The Supreme Court has struggled to define the conditions under which a vehicle may be searched. It has concluded that the search of a car without a warrant may include items within the car if there is probable cause to believe that they contain evidence of a crime (*United States v. Ross*, 1982).

The police cannot randomly stop vehicles to search for evidence of illegal activity (*Delaware v. Prouse*, 1979). However, stopping motorists at roadblocks to check licenses or safety equipment is legal if it is done in a systematic way (*Michigan Department of State Police v. Sitz*, 1990). Passengers may be asked to step out of the car when the driver has been stopped for an ordinary traffic violation (*Maryland v. Wilson*, 1997).

Because of the importance of the automobile in American society, there will undoubtedly be further interpretation of the Fourth Amendment with regard to unreasonable search and seizure, including cases dealing with searches of passengers and drivers.

❹ PLAIN VIEW Items that are in "plain view" may be searched and seized without a warrant when officers have reason to believe that they are linked to a crime. If an officer has a warrant to search a house for cocaine and finds guns in the course of the search, the guns may also be seized. For the plain-view doctrine to apply, the officer must be legally entitled to be at the location, such as inside a house, and the item must be plainly visible. Moreover, the value of the item as evidence must be apparent.

Two decisions have further defined the plain-view doctrine. In *New York v. Class* (1986), the Supreme Court ruled that a gun protruding from under a seat, seen by an officer when he entered the car to look for the vehicle identification number, was within the bounds of the doctrine. However, in *Arizona v. Hicks* (1987), the Court ruled that an officer who moved a stereo system to find its identification number during a legal search for weapons had violated the Fourth Amendment ban on unreasonable search and seizure. The serial number was not in plain view, and the police did not have probable cause to believe that the stereo had been stolen.

❺ CONSENT A person may waive the rights granted by the Fourth Amendment and allow the police to conduct a search or seize items without a warrant. The prosecution must be able to prove, however, that the consent was given voluntarily. Officers do not have to inform the person that he or she is not required to give consent. In some cases, as when passengers' belongings are searched by security employees before they board a plane and by customs agents at international borders, consent is implied.

Sometimes questions arise about who may give consent to search a location. May consent be given, for example, by a landlord or parent of the defendant? In *Illinois v. Rodriguez* (1990), the Supreme Court allowed police to use evidence obtained when officers reasonably, but mistakenly, believed that a defendant's girlfriend lived at his apartment and therefore could grant permission for a search of the premises.

Arrest

Arrest is the seizure of a person by a government official with the authority to take him or her into custody. Because the suspect is taken to the station house, an arrest is more intrusive than a street stop or field questioning. The law of arrest mixes the Fourth Amendment protections with local procedures. This means that the arresting officer must be able to show that there is probable cause to believe that a crime has been committed and that the person taken into custody is the perpetrator. Although courts prefer that officers seek warrants before making felony arrests, such warrants have not been required. Officers often make arrests without a warrant even when they had time to get one.

arrest
The physical taking of a person into custody on the ground that there is probable cause to believe that he or she has committed a criminal offense. Police may use only reasonable physical force in making an arrest. The purpose of arrest is to hold the accused for a court proceeding.

Interrogation

Protection against self-incrimination is one of the most important rights contained in the Fifth Amendment. People may not be forced to be witnesses against themselves. In the U.S. adversarial system, the government must prove the defendant's guilt. The prosecutor and police are not supposed to seek that proof by putting pressure on defendants to provide evidence of their own guilt. Courts will exclude from evidence any confession obtained through undue pressure. In addition, the Sixth Amendment right to counsel protects suspects by allowing them to have the advice and assistance of an attorney during questioning.

As discussed in Chapter 3, the Supreme Court ruled that as soon as the investigation of a crime begins to focus on a particular suspect and he or she is taken into custody, the so-called *Miranda* warnings must be read aloud before questioning can begin (*Escobedo v. Illinois,* 1964; *Miranda v. Arizona,* 1966). Suspects must be told four things:

❶ They have the right to remain silent.
❷ If they decide to make a statement, it can and will be used against them in court.
❸ They have the right to have an attorney present during interrogation or to have an opportunity to consult with an attorney.
❹ If they cannot afford an attorney, the state will provide one.

The Controversy over Exclusion of Evidence

The Supreme Court's *Mapp* and *Miranda* rulings gave rise to much controversy. It was argued that (1) confessions are needed to apprehend and convict violators, (2) informing suspects of their rights would greatly reduce the ability of the police to obtain confessions, (3) few police would give the required warnings, (4) remedies other than exclusion of evidence could be used to punish officers who failed to observe rules, and (5) instead of deterring police misconduct, exclusion of evidence would punish society by letting guilty people go free.

All of these arguments were challenged both by law enforcement officials and by social scientists studying the impact of the rulings. The most extensive of these studies found that fewer than 1 percent of the felony cases that reached the courts had been dismissed because of the exclusionary rule. Upon reviewing the findings of a number of studies Peter E. Nardulli was able to say that the exclusionary rule has had only a slight impact on the criminal court system (Nardulli, 1983:585). However, the controversy has continued with some scholars still calling for the Supreme Court to reverse *Miranda* (Cassell, 1995).

After more than three decades of experience with the warnings, are officers able to obtain confessions in spite of *Miranda*? Evidence from a number of states shows that in many instances the warnings are merely a "speed bump" in the interrogation process. In some departments interrogations are video taped so that defense attorneys cannot claim their clients were coerced into confessing. Observers say that with the increasingly savvy tactics of investigators, the vast majority of suspects waive their rights (*New York Times,* March 29, 1998:1; *New York Times,* March 30, 1998:1). The courts have also chipped away at *Miranda* so that once a suspect enters the interrogation room, officers are able "to use tricks, deceptions, and lies—anything short of threats of violence or promises of lenience—to extract confessions" (*New York Times,* March 30, 1998:1).

Drawing on more than five hundred hours of observations in three departments, Richard Leo argues that police interrogations can best be understood as a confidence game. He says that in many situations officers will develop a rapport so as to get the suspect to voluntarily waive his or her *Miranda* rights. Once this has been negotiated and the suspect has indicated a willingness to speak, "the detective presses the suspect to respond" to questions truthfully. This may be followed by factual or emotional appeals for the suspect to confess to wrongdoing. The detective may portray himself as being an ally who will relay to superiors and prosecutors the suspect's story in the best possible light. With a confession, the interrogation enters a cooling-out phase during which the detective congratulates the suspect for owning up to wrongdoing, a fact that will be weighed favorably when the prosecutor, judge, and jury evaluate the case (Leo, 1996b:259).

In most cities the police solve crimes either by catching the suspect in the act or by finding witnesses who will testify. Because most departments have limited resources for investigation, suspects are not usually arrested until the crime is solved and conviction is assured. In these cases, interrogation is less essential than many critics of the *Miranda* rule believed. Instead of decreasing officers' ability to catch lawbreakers, rulings such as *Miranda* and *Mapp* seem to have made officers more conscious of the legal rules that govern their decisions and actions.

Modifications of the Exclusionary Rule

In the 1980s the composition of the Supreme Court changed as some of the justices retired and Republican presidents Ronald Reagan and George Bush named their successors. However, the new conservative majority on the Court has not overturned the liberal rules established by the *Mapp* and *Miranda* decisions. Instead, the Court has created exceptions to these rules or narrowed their application. Three of the most important exceptions to the exclusionary rule are the "public safety" exception, the inevitable discovery rule, and the "good-faith" exception

In the case of *New York v. Quarles* (1984), a public safety exception to the *Miranda* warnings was established. Officers may ask arrested suspects questions before reading the *Miranda* warnings if the questions deal with an urgent situation affecting public safety. The suspect in the *Quarles* case had hidden a gun in a store as the police chased him, and when he was handcuffed, the police asked him where the gun was. The police were concerned that someone else might find the gun if they did not question the suspect as soon as possible.

The inevitable discovery exception was established by the Court in *Nix v. Williams* (1984). During the investigation of the murder of a 10-year-old girl, the police asked Robert Williams, the prime suspect, to show them where she was buried. Although officers had promised that they would not question Williams outside of his lawyer's presence, they did point out that the girl's parents had a right to hold a funeral for the little girl, who had been snatched from them on Christmas and murdered. In response Williams led the police to the burial site. Williams was convicted, but he appealed the ruling on the ground that he had been improperly questioned because his lawyer was not present. The Supreme Court accepted the prosecution's argument that the body would have been located inevitably even without the improper questioning of the defendant.

Under the good-faith exception to the exclusionary rule, the Supreme Court has ruled that evidence may be used even though it was obtained under a search warrant that later proved to be technically invalid. In ***United States v. Leon*** (1984), police presented evidence to a judge concerning an informant's tip about drug activity at a certain house. The judge made an error in issuing a search warrant. The Supreme Court approved the search, despite the defective warrant, because the real error had been made by the judge. The police followed proper procedures by presenting evidence to the judge that they believed supported their request for a warrant. The Court ruled that the costs of enforcing the exclusionary rule, namely overturning the conviction, outweighed the benefits of seeking to deter police misconduct.

United States v. Leon **(1984)**
Evidence seized using a warrant that is later found to be defective is valid if the officer was acting in good faith.

In large part, the Supreme Court decisions affecting the exclusionary rule reflect a continuing debate in American society. Supporters of the Warren Court's decisions argue that constitutional rights must protect all Americans, including criminal defendants, against excessive use of power by police and prosecutors. Critics say that the Supreme Court has gone too far and that too many guilty people have avoided prosecution and punishment. This debate will probably continue, and the relationship of police actions to the rule of law will always be a subject of controversy.

CHECK POINT

⑲ **What are the five kinds of searches that may be conducted without a warrant and still be in accord with the Fourth Amendment?**

⑳ **What is the exclusionary rule?**

㉑ **What are the three exceptions that the Supreme Court has made to the *Mapp* and *Miranda* decisions?**

Summary

■ Police operations are shaped by their formal organizational structures and also influenced by social and political processes both within and outside the department.

■ The police are organized along military lines so that authority and responsibility can be located at appropriate levels.

■ Police services are delivered through the work of the patrol, investigation, and specialized operations units.

■ The patrol function has three components: answering calls for assistance, maintaining a police presence, and probing suspicious circumstances.

- Discussions of the future of policing are dominated by issues concerning the allocation of personnel, response time, foot versus motorized patrol, and community-oriented policing.
- The investigation function is the responsibility of detectives in close coordination with patrol officers.
- The felony apprehension process is a sequence of actions that includes crime detection, preliminary investigation, follow-up investigation, clearance, and arrest.
- Specialized units dealing with traffic, drug, and vice are found in large departments.
- The police must work within the law so as not to violate the rights of citizens.
- Decisions by the Supreme Court over the past quarter-century have interpreted the Bill of Rights with regard to search and seizure, arrest, and interrogation.

Questions for Review

1 What are some of the issues that influence police administrators in their allocation of resources?

2 What is the purpose of patrol? How is it carried out?

3 What has research shown about the effectiveness of patrol?

4 Why do detectives have so much prestige on the force?

5 How do various amendments to the Bill of Rights affect police operations?

Key Terms and Cases

admissible evidence (p. 193)

aggressive patrol (p. 178)

arrest (p. 197)

clearance rate (p. 170)

differential response (p. 168)

directed patrol (p. 175)

incident-driven policing (p. 167)

line functions (p. 171)

preventive patrol (p. 172)

proactive (p. 167)

problem-oriented policing (p. 181)

reactive (p. 167)

search warrant (p. 194)

sworn officers (p. 171)

Terry v. Ohio (1968) (p. 195)

United States v. Leon (1984) (p. 199)

For Further Reading

Bayley, David H. *Police for the Future.* New York: Oxford University Press, 1994. Examination of policing in five countries—Australia, Canada, Great Britain, Japan, and the United States. Includes a suggested blueprint for the future.

Bratton, William. *Turnaround: How America's Top Cop Reversed the Crime Epidemic.* New York: Random House, 1998. Description by former police commissioner William Bratton of the efforts he took to reduce crime in New York City.

Brown, Michael K. *Working the Street.* New York: Russell Sage Foundation, 1981. A classic study of patrol work by officers of the San Diego Police Force.

Geller, William A., ed. *Police Leadership in America.* New York: Praeger, 1985. A collection of essays written by some of the most progressive police executives.

Manning, Peter K. *Police Work.* Cambridge, Mass.: MIT Press, 1977. A look at police work. Manning argues that the police have an "impossible mandate." They have emphasized their crime-fighting

stance, a role that they do not play successfully.

Skogan, Wesley G. *Disorder and Decline: Crime and the Spiral of Decay in American Neighborhoods.* New York: Free Press, 1990. Support for community policing on the basis of studies spawned by the Wilson-Kelling thesis that police should work more on "little problems."

Skolnick, Jerome H., and David H. Bayley. *The New Blue Line.* New York: Free Press, 1986. A look at modern policing by two major criminal justice scholars.

Going Online

❶ Go to www.Theatlantic.com/ politics/crime/windows.htm and read the classic article by James Q. Wilson and George L. Kelling, "Broken Windows: The Police and Neighborhood Safety." Summarize the major points in the article. How does the "broken windows" concept relate to community policing? To aggressive enforcement of public order?

❷ Why is protecting the criminal scene of primary importance in an investigation? Find the reasons given by George Scheio at the "Crime Scene Investigation Site," http://police2.ucr.edu/csi.html

❸ What are the steps a police officer should take when responding to a hate crime? Find out by accessing the web site of the International Association of Chiefs of Police (www.theiacp.org). Under "Information/Publications," access the manual *Responding to Hate Crimes: A Police Officer's Guide to Investigation and Prevention.*

CHECK POINT ANSWERS

❶ (1) Apportion the workload among members and units according to a logical plan. (2) Ensure that lines of authority and responsibility are as definite and direct as possible. (3) Specify a unity of command throughout so that no question arises as to which orders should be followed. (4) Link duties with the appropriate amount of authority and accountability. (5) Coordinate the efforts of members and units so that all will work harmoniously to accomplish the mission.

❷ Patrol, investigation, traffic, vice, juvenile.

❸ Citizen expectation that the police will respond quickly to every call.

❹ Policy that gives priority to calls according to whether an immediate or delayed response is warranted.

❺ Clearance rate—the percentage of crimes known to the police that they believe they have solved through an arrest.

❻ Personnel assigned to line functions are directly involved in field operations. Personnel assigned to staff functions supplement and support the line function.

❼ Answering calls for assistance, maintaining a police presence, and probing suspicious circumstances.

❽ Crime rates, "problem neighborhoods," degree of urbanization, pressures from businesspeople and community groups, socioeconomic conditions.

❾ Crime rates do not seem to be affected by changes in patrolling strategies, such as assigning more officers.

❿ A hot spot is a location where there is evidence of a high number of calls for police response.

⓫ A proactive patrol strategy designed to direct resources to known high-crime areas.

⓬ Decision-making delays caused by ambiguity, coping activities, and conflicts.

⓭ Officers on foot patrol have greater contact with residents of a neighborhood, thus gaining their confidence and assistance. Officers on motorized patrol have a greater range of activity and can respond speedily to calls.

⓮ One-person patrols are more cost-efficient; two-person patrols are thought to be safer.

⓯ Aggressive patrol is a proactive strategy to maximize the number of police interventions and observations in the community.

⓰ Community policing emphasizes order maintenance and service. It attempts to involve members of the community in making their neighborhood safe. Foot patrol and the decentralization of command are usually part of community policing efforts.

⓱ The four steps in apprehension are detection of crime, preliminary investigation, follow-up investigation, clearance and arrest.

⓲ A process of identifying individuals based on their distinctive gene patterns.

⓳ Incident to a lawful arrest, field interrogation, automobiles, "plain view," consent.

⓴ That evidence illegally seized by the police must be excluded from the prosecution's case and the trial.

㉑ Public safety, inevitable discovery, and good-faith exceptions.

Policing
Issues and Trends

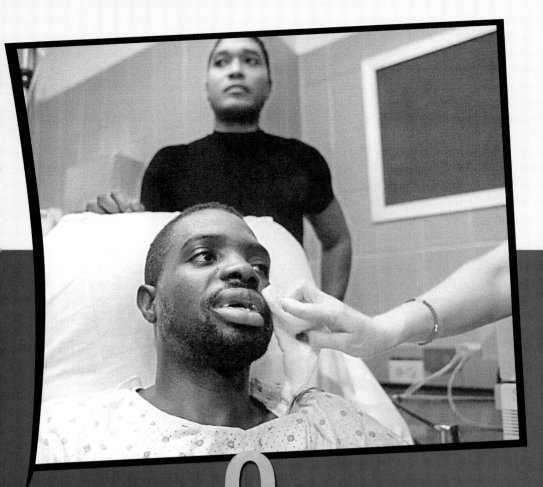

On the night of August 9, 1997, Abner Louima, a 32-year-old Haitian immigrant, was arrested for disorderly conduct following a melee outside of the Club Rendez-Vous in Brooklyn. As he was hustled to a patrol car, Louima was struck by Officer Justin Volpe. The beatings continued in the police car as Volpe and Officers Charles Schwarz, Thomas Wiese, and Thomas Bruder drove to the Seventieth Precinct station house. There, Louima was taken into the restroom where Volpe rammed a broken broomstick into his rectum and threated to kill him if he ever told anyone about the assault. Volpe paraded around the station house brandishing the feces-covered stick. Later, Louima was taken to the hospital with broken teeth and a pierced bladder.

In the aftermath of the brutal assaults on Louima, five officers were brought to trial on a number of federal civil rights and criminal charges. After trial testimony by a fellow officer that Volpe had bragged about torturing Louima with the handle, Volpe suddenly changed his plea to guilty to six of the charges with the expectation that he would escape a life sentence. On December 13, 1999, Volpe was sentenced to thirty years in federal prison plus five years of probation.

The brutal attack on Abner Louima illustrates a frequent problem in law enforcement. How can society make sure that those with authority do not misuse their power? Police officers have sworn an oath to protect society against crime; thus, it is shocking when they, of all people, violate the public trust. The bonds between the police and the community are often fragile, especially when racial, gender, or class bias comes into play.

In this chapter we consider a number of issues concerning the police and their relationship to society. First, we look at recruitment and training. Second, we examine the unique subculture of police officers. Third, we consider the link between the police and the community. Fourth, we discuss the problem of abuse of power by the police and what is being done to make police more accountable. Finally, we look at private policing, a trend that is affecting police operations today.

QUESTIONS for Inquiry

- Why do some people choose policing as a career?
- How does the police subculture influence the behavior of officers?
- What role does the link between the police and the community play in preventing crime?
- In what ways do the police abuse their power, and how can they be controlled?
- What methods can be used to make police more accountable to citizens?
- What is the future of private policing?

Who Are the Police?

If you or someone you know plans a career in law enforcement, ask yourself what aspects of the job make it more appealing than other kinds of work. Some people might want the adventure and excitement of investigating crimes and catching suspects. Others might be drawn to the satisfactions that come from being a public servant. Still other people may be attracted to a civil service job with good benefits. Table 6.1 presents the reasons people give for choosing police work as a career.

Recruitment

How can departments recruit well-rounded, dedicated public servants who will represent the diversity of contemporary America? If pay scales are low, educational requirements minimal, and physical standards unrealistically rigid, police work will attract only those who are unable to enter other occupations. This was a problem in the past. Most departments now offer entrance salaries of more than $29,000 plus a great deal of overtime pay (BJS, 1999k:48). While many departments now expect at least two years of college, most require new members to have only a high school education. Good physical condition and lack of a criminal

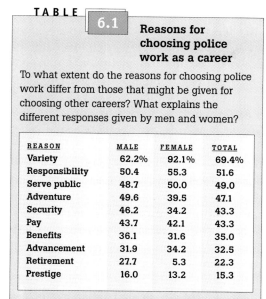

TABLE 6.1

Reasons for choosing police work as a career

To what extent do the reasons for choosing police work differ from those that might be given for choosing other careers? What explains the different responses given by men and women?

REASON	MALE	FEMALE	TOTAL
Variety	62.2%	92.1%	69.4%
Responsibility	50.4	55.3	51.6
Serve public	48.7	50.0	49.0
Adventure	49.6	39.5	47.1
Security	46.2	34.2	43.3
Pay	43.7	42.1	43.3
Benefits	36.1	31.6	35.0
Advancement	31.9	34.2	32.5
Retirement	27.7	5.3	22.3
Prestige	16.0	13.2	15.3

SOURCE: Harold P. Slater and Martin Reiser, "A Comparative Study of Factors Influencing Police Recruitment," *Journal of Police Science and Administration* 16 (1988):170.

FIGURE 6.1

The changing profile of the American police officer

Today about 1 in 10 officers is female and 1 in 5 is a racial or ethnic minority.

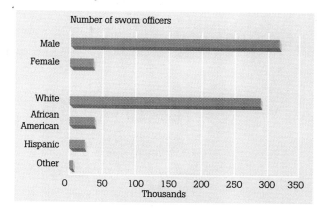

NOTE: Data from law enforcement agencies employing one hundred or more sworn officers. This constitutes about half of the total number of officers.

SOURCE: U.S. Department of Justice, Office of Justice Programs, *Bureau of Justice Statistics Fiscal Year 1996: At a Glance* (Washington, D.C.: Government Printing Office, 1996), 25.

record are required by all departments. To widen the pool of recruits and avoid discriminating against women and some ethnic groups, height and weight requirements have been changed, and many departments even overlook a minor criminal record if it was acquired when the applicant was under 18. Most big-city departments now require written tests, a psychological interview, and polygraph—as well as physical fitness tests—to identify the best candidates (Langworth, Hughes, and Sanders, 1995:26).

The profile of the American police officer has changed dramatically during the past thirty years. Compared with the 1970s, today's officer is better educated with more than 23 percent holding college degrees. The percentage of minority group members and women has doubled. Figure 6.1. shows some of the characteristics of the American police officer.

In 1994 Congress provided money for six states to develop pilot Police Corps, modeled after the military's Reserve Officers Training Corps. The programs would reimburse as much as $30,000 in educational costs to college graduates who agree to serve four years on a participating police force. Maryland was the first state to establish a Police Corps, with Baltimore being the first major city to adopt the approach (*New York Times,* March 30, 1997:12).

While recruiting efforts and entry requirements affect the pool of potential officers, their training affects their attitudes.

Training

The performance of the police is not based solely on the types of people recruited; it is also shaped by their training. Most states require preservice training for all recruits. This is often a formal course at a police academy, but in some states candidates for police jobs must complete a basic training program, at their own expense, before being considered for employment. Large departments generally run their own programs, while state police academies train recruits from rural and

Although most new officers are formally trained, it is on the job that they really "learn the ropes."

socialization

The process by which the rules, symbols, and values of a group or subculture are learned by its members.

small-town units. The courses range from two-week sessions that stress the handling of weapons to more academic four-month programs followed by fieldwork. Recruits hear lectures on social relations, receive foreign language training, and learn emergency medical treatment.

Formal training is needed to gain an understanding of legal rules, weapons use, and other aspects of the job. However, the police officer's job also demands skills in dealing with people that cannot be learned from a lecture or a book. Much of the most important training of police officers takes place during a probationary period when new officers work with and learn from experienced officers. When new officers finish their classroom training and arrive for their first day of patrol duty, they may be told by experienced officers, "Now, I want you to forget all that stuff you learned at the academy. You really learn your job on the streets."

The process of **socialization**—in which members learn the symbols, beliefs, and values of a group or subculture—includes learning the informal rather than the rule-book ways of law enforcement. New officers must learn how to look "productive," how to take shortcuts in filling out forms, how to keep themselves safe in dangerous situations, how to analyze conflicts so as to maintain order, and a host of other bits of wisdom, norms, and folklore that define the subculture of a particular department. Recruits learn that loyalty to fellow officers, esprit de corps, and respect for police authority are highly valued.

In police work, the success of the group depends on the cooperation of its members. All patrol officers are under direct supervision, and their performance is measured by their contribution to the group's work. Supervisors are not the only people who evaluate the officers' contribution. Officers are also influenced by their colleagues. Officers within a department may develop strong, shared views on the best way to "handle" various situations. How officers use their personal skills and judgment can mean the difference between defusing a conflict and making it worse so that it endangers citizens and other officers. In tackling their "impossible mandate," new recruits must learn the ways of the world from the other officers, who depend on them and on whom they depend.

The Changing Profile of the Police

For most of the nation's history, almost all police officers were white men. Today, women and minorities are a growing percentage of police departments in many areas. There are several reasons for this. In 1968 the National Advisory Commission on Civil Disorders found that police-minority relations were a major factor in ghetto riots of the 1960s. The Equal Employment Opportunity Act of 1972 bars state and local governments from discriminating in their hiring practices. Pressured by state and federal agencies as well as by lawsuits, most city police forces have mounted campaigns to recruit more minority and female officers (Martin, 1991).

Minority Police Officers

Before the 1970s, many police departments did not hire nonwhites. As this practice declined, the makeup of police departments changed, especially in large cities. A study of the nation's fifty largest cities found that, from 1983 to 1992, 29 percent of the departments reported an increase of 50 percent or more in the number of African American officers, and 20 percent reported a similar increase in the number of Hispanic officers (Walker and Turner, 1992). A 1993 Bureau of Justice Statistics study found that minority police officers made up about 20 percent of all local departments (BJS, 1993a).

As political power shifts toward minorities in some American cities, the makeup of their police forces is changing to reflect the change. But the election of an African American or Hispanic American mayor does not always produce an immediate change in the composition of the police force. However, three-quarters of Detroit's population is now African American as is about half of the city's police officers (Walker and Turner, 1992). A survey of Detroit residents found that African Americans held more favorable attitudes toward the police than did whites. As the researchers note, "In Detroit, the people who perform the police function are not alien to African-Americans; instead they represent an indigenous force" (Frank, Brandl, Cullen, and Stichman, 1996:332). Surprisingly, in the melting pot city of New York the police are among the most racially imbalanced in the United States, with white officers comprising 67 percent of the force but only 43 percent of the population (*New York Times,* March 8, 1999:A14).

An increasing number of women have become officers. What are some of the problems they face? With the public? With their colleagues?

Women on the Force

Women have been police officers since 1905, when Lola Baldwin was made an officer in Portland, Oregon. However, the number of women officers remained small for most of the twentieth century because of the belief that policing was "men's work." As this attitude changed, the percentage of female officers rose from 1.5 percent of sworn officers in 1970 to about 9 percent in the late 1990s (*New York Times* August 7, 1997:A35). The larger the department, the higher the proportion of women as sworn officers. In cities of more than 250,000, the proportion is more than 14 percent (FBI, 1999:76). In some police departments, such as Detroit, more than 20 percent of officers are women (Walker and Turner, 1992). Despite the changes, about half of U.S. police agencies still employ no women.

Although some male police officers still question whether women can handle dangerous situations and physical confrontations, most policewomen have easily met the expectations of their superiors. Studies done by the Police Foundation and other researchers have found that, in general, male and female officers perform in similar ways. Alissa Worden's research found that there were few differences in the ways male and female officers viewed "their role, their clientele, or their departments" (Worden, 1993). Research has also found that most citizens have positive things to say about the work of policewomen (Bloch and Anderson, 1974; Sichel, 1978; Worden, 1993).

CLOSE  up

Patrol Officer Cristina Murphy

Jim Dyer was drunk out of his mind when he called the Rochester [New York] Police Department [P.D.] on a recent Saturday night. He wanted to make a harassment complaint; a neighbor, he claimed, was trying to kill him with a chair. Officer Cristina Murphy, 27, a petite, dark-haired, soft-spoken three-year veteran of the Rochester P.D., took the call.

"What's the problem here?" she asked when she arrived at the scene. A crowd had gathered. Dyer's rage was good local fun.

"You're a woman!" Dyer complained as Murphy stepped from her squad car. "All they send me is women. I called earlier and they sent me a Puerto Rican and she didn't do nothing either."

"Mr. Dyer, what exactly is the problem?"

"Dickie Burroughs is the problem. He tried to kill me." Through a drunken haze, Dyer made certain things clear: He wanted Dickie Burroughs locked up. He wanted him sent to Attica for life. He wanted it done that night. Short of all that, Dyer hoped that the police might oblige him by roughing up his foe, just a little.

"We don't do that sort of thing," Murphy explained in the voice she uses with drunks and children. "Mr. Dyer, I can do one of two things for you. I can go find Mr. Burroughs and get his side of the story; I can talk to him. The other thing I can do is take a report from you and advise you how to take out a warrant. You'll have to go downtown for that."

Later, in her squad car, Murphy would say that she isn't usually so curt to complaining citizens. "But it's important not to take crap about being a female. Most of the stuff I get, I just let slip by. This guy, though, he really did not want service on his complaint, he wanted retribution. When he saw a woman taking his call, he figured that I wouldn't give it to him; it never struck him that no male officer would either. You know, everyone has an opinion about women being police officers—even drunks. Some people are very threatened by it. They just can't stand getting orders from a woman. White males, I think, are the most threatened. Black males seem the least—they look at me and they just see blue. Now women, they sometimes just can't stand the idea that a woman exists who can have power over them. They feel powerless and expect all women to feel that way too. As I said, everyone has an opinion."

SOURCE: Claudia Driefus, "People Are Always Asking Me What I'm Trying to Prove," *Police Magazine* (March 1980). Reprinted by permission of the Edna McConnell Clark Foundation.

Despite these findings, women still have trouble breaking into police work. Cultural expectations of women often conflict with ideas about the proper behavior of officers, as the Close-Up above reveals.

Many people do not think women are tough enough to confront dangerous suspects. Also, women often find it hard to gain promotions and must contend with prejudice from their male colleagues. Especially with regard to patrol duty, questions such as the following are often raised:

- Can women handle situations that involve force and violence?
- What changes must be made in training and equipment to accommodate women?
- Should women and men have equal opportunities to be promoted?
- Does assigning men and women as patrol partners tend to create tensions with their spouses?

As these questions reveal, women have to overcome resistance from their fellow officers and some citizens. In particular, they encounter resistance when they assert their authority. They are often subjected to sexist remarks and more overt forms of sexual harassment. Many male officers are upset by the entry of women into what they view as a male world. They complain that if their patrol partner is a woman, they cannot be sure of her ability to help them in times of danger—that she simply lacks the physical stature to act effectively when the going gets tough.

Proving herself as an effective police officer came to Letitia Cook one night in 1987 when she and her partner broke up a fight in a barroom. She was 21 and new to the Montville, New Jersey, department and the town's first female officer. She was "anxious to prove her moxie to the male officers who showed up minutes later." As she said ten years later, "I got right down on the ground with everyone else. That's when they stepped back and said: 'All right, she can handle herself. She can help us' " (*New York Times*, August 7, 1997:A35).

Few women have been promoted to supervisory jobs, so they are not yet able to combat the remaining barriers to the recruitment, retention, and promotion of female officers (Walker and Turner, 1992). However, the role of women in police work will undoubtedly evolve along with changes in the nature of policing, in cultural values, and in the organization of law enforcement. As citizens become used to women on patrol, women officers will have an easier time gaining their cooperation. Finally, there are signs that more and more citizens and policemen are beginning to take it for granted that women will be found on patrol along with men.

CHECK POINT

① **What are the main requirements for becoming a police officer?**

② **What type of training is required of police recruits?**

③ **Where does socialization to police work take place?**

④ **How has the profile of American police officers changed?**

The Police Subculture

A **subculture** is made up of the symbols, beliefs, values, and attitudes shared by members of a subgroup within the larger society. The subculture of the police helps define the "cop's world" and each officer's role in it. Like the subculture of any occupational group that sees itself as distinctive, police develop shared values that affect their view of human behavior and their role in society. But the characteristics of a subculture are not static, they change as new members join the group and as the surrounding environment changes. For example, the racial, gender, and educational composition of the police has changed dramatically during the past thirty years. These "new officers" likely will bring different attitudes and cultural values to the police subculture (Walker, 1999:332).

There are four key issues regarding the police subculture: the concept of the "working personality," the role of police morality, the isolation of the police, and the stressful nature of much police work.

subculture
The symbols, beliefs, and values shared by members of a subgroup within the larger society.

The occupational environment and working personality of officers are so interlocked that they greatly influence the daily experience of the police. How would you handle this situation?

working personality

A set of emotional and behavioral characteristics developed by a member of an occupational group in response to the work situation and environmental influences.

The Working Personality

Social scientists have demonstrated that a relationship exists between one's occupational environment and the way one interprets events. The police subculture produces a **working personality**—that is, a set of emotional and behavioral characteristics developed by members of an occupational group in response to the work situation and environmental influences. The police working personality thus influences the way officers view and interpret their occupational world.

The working personality of the police is defined by two elements of police work: (1) the threat of danger and (2) the need to establish and maintain one's authority (Skolnick, 1966:44).

Danger

Because they are often in dangerous situations, officers are keenly aware of clues in people's behavior or in specific situations that indicate that violence and lawbreaking may be about to happen. As they drive the streets, they notice things that seem amiss—a broken window, a person hiding something under a coat, anything that looks suspicious. As sworn officers, they are never off duty. People who know that they are officers will call on them for help at any time, day or night.

Throughout the socialization process, experienced officers warn recruits to be suspicious and cautious. Rookies are told about officers who were killed while trying to settle a family squabble or writing a traffic ticket. The message is clear: Even minor offenses can escalate into extreme danger. Constantly pressured to recognize signs of crime and be alert to potential violence, officers may become suspicious of everyone, everywhere. Thus, police officers are in a constant state of "high alert," always on the lookout and never letting down their guard.

The sense that they are surrounded by risks creates tension in officers' lives. They may feel constantly on edge and worried about possible attack. This concern with danger may affect their interactions with citizens and suspects. Their caution and suspicion may be seen as hostile by citizens who come into contact with them and may generate hostile reactions from suspects. As a result, on-street interrogations and arrests may lead to confrontations.

Authority

The second aspect of the working personality is the need to exert authority. Unlike many professionals, such as doctors, psychiatrists, and lawyers, whose clients recognize and defer to their authority, a police officer must *establish* authority through his or her actions. The officer's uniform, badge, gun, and nightstick are symbols of his or her position and power, but the officer's demeanor and behavior determine whether people will defer to him or her.

Victims are glad to see the police when they are performing their law enforcement function, but the order maintenance function puts pressure on officers' authority. If they try too hard to exert authority in the face of hostile reactions, they may cross the line and use excessive force. For example, when officers are sent to investigate a report of a fight, drunken neighbor, or domestic quarrel, they usually do not find a cooperative complainant. Instead, they must contend not only with the perpetrators, but also with onlookers who may escalate the conflict. In such circumstances they must "handle the situation" by asserting authority without getting emotionally involved. Even when citizens challenge their conduct and their right to enforce the law, the police are expected to react in a detached or neutral manner. For officers who feel burdened with the twin pressures of danger and authority, this may not be easy. Thus, in the daily work of policing, the rules and procedures taught at the academy may have less impact on officers' actions than the need to exert authority in the face of danger.

At times, officers must give orders to people with higher status. Professionals, businesspeople, and others may respond to the officer not as a person working for the benefit of the community but as a public servant whom they do not respect. Given the blue-collar background of many cops, maintaining self-respect and refusing to accept disrespectful attitudes may be important ways of resolving this problem.

In sum, working personality and occupational environment are so closely linked that they have a major impact on the daily work of the police. Procedural rules and the structure of policing are overshadowed by the need to exert authority in the face of danger.

Police Morality

In his field observations of Los Angeles patrol officers, Steve Herbert found a high sense of morality in the law enforcement subculture. He believes that three aspects of modern policing create dilemmas that their morality helps overcome. These dilemmas are the contradiction between the goal of preventing crime and their inability to do so; the fact that they must use their discretion to "handle" situations in ways that do not strictly follow procedures; and "the fact that they invariably act against at least one citizen's interest, often with recourse to coercive force that can maim or kill" (Herbert, 1996:799).

Herbert believes that justifying their actions in moral terms, such as upholding the law, protecting society, and chasing "bad guys," helps officers lessen the dilemmas of their work. Thus use of force may be condoned as necessary to rid "evil from otherwise peaceable streets." It is the price one pays to cleanse society of the "punks," "crazies," or "terrorists." But police morality can also be applauded: officers work long hours and are genuinely motivated to help people and improve their lives, often placing themselves at risk. Yet to the extent that police morality crudely categorizes individuals and justifies insensitive treatment of some community members, it contributes to police-minority tensions.

Police Isolation

Police officers' suspicion and isolation from the public may be increased by their belief that the public is hostile to them. Many officers feel that they are looked upon with suspicion, in part because they have the authority to use force to gain compliance. Some scholars argue that this attitude increases officers' desire to use force on citizens (Regoli, Crank, and Culbertson, 1987). Public opinion polls have found that a majority of people have a high opinion of the police. However, as shown in What Americans Think, differences of opinion emerge regarding the

What Americans Think

Honesty and ethical standards

Question "Please tell me how you would rate the honesty and ethical standards of the police—very high, high, average, low or very low?"

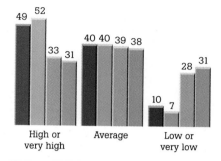

Confidence in the police

Question "Please tell me how much confidence you, yourself, have in the police. A great deal, quite a lot, some, or very little."

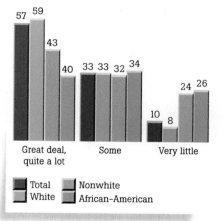

■ Total   ■ Nonwhite
■ White   ■ African-American

NOTE: Graph does not include "don't know" and "not sure/refused" responses. Nonwhite includes African American respondents.

SOURCE: U.S. Department of Justice, Bureau of Justice Statistics, *Sourcebook of Criminal Justice—1998* (Washington, D.C.: Government Printing Office, 1999), 105, 109.

honesty, ethical standards, and confidence in law enforcement that follow racial lines.

Police officers' isolation from the public is made more severe by the fact that many officers interact with the public mainly in moments of conflict, emotion, and crisis. Victims of crimes and accidents are often too hurt or distraught to thank the police. Citizens who are told to stop some activity when the police are trying to keep order may be angry at the police. Even something as minor as telling someone to turn down the volume on a stereo may make the police the "bad guy" in the eyes of people who believe that the officers' authority limits their own freedom. Ironically, these problems may be at their worst in ghetto neighborhoods where effective policing is needed most. Citizens in those areas may fail to report crimes and refuse to cooperate with investigations because of pervasive mistrust of the police.

Because they believe that the public is hostile to them and that the nature of their work makes the situation worse, the police tend to separate themselves from the public and to form strong in-group ties. The police culture also encourages the bonding that often occurs among people who deal with violence. This solidarity "permits fallible men to perform an arduous and difficult task, and . . . places the highest value upon the obligation to back up and support a fellow officer" (Brown, 1981:82).

One result of the demands placed on the police is that officers are often unable to separate their job from other aspects of their lives. From the time they are given badges and guns, they must always carry these symbols of the position—the tools of the trade—and be prepared to use them. Their obligation to remain vigilant even when off duty and to work at odd hours reinforces the values shared with other officers. Strengthening this bond is officers' tendency to socialize mainly with their families and other officers; they have little social contact with people other than fellow officers. As James Ahern, formerly chief of police of New Haven, Connecticut, has noted:

> When he gets off duty on the swing shift, there is little to do but go drinking and few people to do it with but other cops. He finds himself going bowling with them, going fishing, helping them paint their house or fix their cars. His family gets to know their families, and a kind of mutual protection society develops which turns out to be the only group in which the policeman is automatically entitled to respect. (Ahern, 1972:14)

Also important is that wherever they go, the police are recognized by people who want to talk shop; others harangue them about what is wrong with police service. This also adds to the stress and isolation felt by the police.

Job Stress

The work environment and police subculture can increase the stress felt by officers. This stress, stemming from the elements of danger and authority, may affect not only the way officers treat the citizens they encounter but also their own health.

Police officers are always on alert, sometimes face grave danger, and feel unappreciated by a public they perceive to be hostile, so it is

The threat of violence contributes to the high degree of stress that police officers experience. Here, Buffalo (N.Y.) Police Officer Michael Martinez, in wheelchair, is hugged by a fellow officer as he leaves the funeral service of his former partner, Charles E. McDougald, who was shot in the line of action.

not surprising that their physical and mental health may suffer. The American Institute of Stress has stated that policing is one of the ten most stress-producing jobs (*Newsweek,* April 25, 1988:43). The stress of police work may help explain why five times as many cops die by their own hands—about three hundred per year—as are killed in the line of duty (*Newsweek,* September 26, 1994:58; *New York Times,* January 1, 1997:12).

Newspaper and magazine articles with such titles as "Time Bombs in Blue" discuss the effects of the pent-up emotions, confrontations with violence and human tragedy, and physical demands of the job. However, only since the late 1970s have law enforcement officials been fully aware of these hazards. Researchers have noted that a higher proportion of police officers have marital, health, alcohol, and drug problems than in the general population. A long-held belief is that the police have higher suicide rates than people in other occupations. However, the evidence is mixed. A study of the Los Angeles police concluded that the suicide rate was lower for police than for the average adult (Josephsen and Reiser, 1990). But a study of the Buffalo department found that officers were three times more likely to take their own lives than were members of the general public (*Hartford Courant,* December 27, 1998:A1).

Psychologists have identified four kinds of stress to which officers are subject and the factors that cause each:

❶ **EXTERNAL STRESS.** This is produced by real threats and dangers, such as the need to enter a dark and unfamiliar building, respond to "man with a gun" alarms, and chase lawbreakers at high speeds.

❷ **ORGANIZATIONAL STRESS.** This is produced by the nature of work in a paramilitary structure: constant adjustment to changing schedules, irregular work hours, and detailed rules and procedures.

❸ **PERSONAL STRESS.** This may be caused by an officer's racial or gender status among peers, which may create problems in getting along with other officers and adjusting to group-held values that differ from one's own, as well as perceptions of bias and social isolation.

❹ **OPERATIONAL STRESS.** This reflects the total effect of dealing with thieves, derelicts, and the mentally ill; being lied to so often that all citizens become suspect; being required to face danger to protect a public that seems hostile; and always knowing that one may be held legally liable for one's actions (Cullen, Leming, Link, and Wozniak, 1985).

Police executives have been slow to deal with the problems of stress, but psychological and medical counseling has become more available. Some departments now have stress prevention, group counseling, liability insurance, and family involvement programs. Many states have more liberal disability and retirement rules for police than for other public employees because their jobs are more stressful (Goolkasian, Geddes, and DeJong, 1989).

Police officers face special pressures that can affect their interactions with the public and even harm their physical and mental health. How would you react to the prospect of facing danger and being on the lookout for crime at every moment even when you were not working? It seems understandable that police officers become a close-knit group, yet their isolation from society may decrease their understanding of other people. It may also strengthen their belief that the public is ungrateful and hostile. As a result, officers' actions toward members of the public may be hostile, gruff, and sometimes violent.

In sum, the effects of the police subculture on the behavior of officers are stronger in situations that produce conflict between the police and society. To endure their work, the police find they must relate to the public in ways that protect their own self-esteem. If the police view the public as hostile and police work as adding to that hostility, they will isolate themselves by developing strong values and norms to which all officers conform.

CHECK POINT

⑤ **What are the two key aspects of the police officer's working personality?**

⑥ **What are the four types of stress felt by the police?**

(Answers are at the end of the chapter.)

Police and the Community

The work of a police officer in an American city can be very hard. Hours of boring, routine work can be interrupted by short spurts of dangerous crime fighting. Although police work has always been frustrating and dangerous, officers today must deal with situations ranging from helping the homeless to dealing with domestic violence to confronting shoot-outs at drug deals gone sour. Yet police actions are often mishandled or misinterpreted, with the result that some people are critical of the police.

Policing in a Multicultural Society

Carrying out the complex tasks of policing efficiently and according to the law is a tough assignment even when the police have the support and cooperation of the public. But policing in a multicultural society such as the United States presents further challenges.

In the last quarter-century the racial and ethnic composition of the United States has changed. Many African Americans moved from the South to big cities elsewhere, and some upwardly mobile African Americans began to move from cities to suburbs. Hispanic immigrants from Cuba, Mexico, Puerto Rico, and South America have become the fastest growing minority population. Immigrants from Asia, Eastern Europe, the Middle East, and Russia have entered the country in greater numbers. Since 1980 the United States has witnessed a huge increase in immigration, rivaling the stream of foreigners that arrived in the early 1900s. People of color from Asia, Latin America, Caribbean countries, and other non-European locales make up most of this increase.

Policing requires trust, understanding, and cooperation between officers and the public. People must be willing to call for help and provide information about wrongdoing. But in a multicultural society, relations between the police and minorities are complicated by stereotypes, cultural differences, and language differences.

Officers may attribute undesirable traits to members of minority groups: "Asian Americans are shifty," "Arab Americans are terrorists," "African Americans are lazy," "Polish Americans are stubborn." But minorities may also stereotype the police as "fascist," "dumb," or "pigs." Treating people according to stereotypes, rather than as individuals, creates tensions that harden negative attitudes.

New immigrants often bring with them religious and cultural practices that differ from those of the dominant culture. Many times these practices, while accepted in the home country, are viewed as deviant or even against the law in this country. As discussed in Chapter 1, the police often must walk a fine line between upholding American law and respecting the customs of new residents.

Very few officers can speak a language other than English, and only in large urban departments do officers speak any of the many languages used by new immigrants. Limited English speakers who report crimes, are arrested, or are victimized may not be understood. Language can be a barrier for the police in responding to calls for help and dealing with organized crime. The language and cultural diversity barriers make it harder for the FBI or local police to infiltrate the Chinese, Russian, and Vietnamese organized crime groups now found in East and West Coast cities.

Public opinion surveys have shown that race and ethnicity are key factors shaping attitudes toward the police. As seen in What Americans Think, questions of fair treatment by the police differs among racial groups.

Surveys have also shown that when income, education, and victimization are taken into account, African Americans are less favorably disposed toward the police than whites (Gallup Poll, 1999). Even so, most African Americans and Hispanic Americans are similar to most white Americans in their attitudes toward the police. It is young, low-income racial-minority males who have the most negative attitudes toward the police (Walker, Spohn, and DeLone, 1996:87, 89). As discussed in the Close-Up (see p. 216), these attitudes help to explain why African Americans believed O. J. Simpson and not the police.

In inner-city neighborhoods—the areas that need and want effective policing—there is much distrust of the police; citizens therefore fail to report crimes and refuse to cooperate with the police. Encounters between officers and members of these communities are often hostile and sometimes lead to large-scale disorders.

Some argue that same-race policing may lead to a greater willingness of residents of minority neighborhoods to report crimes and to assist investigations. Some also believe that same-race policing will reduce the number of unjustified arrests, misuse of force, and police harassment. In the only research on this question John J. Donohue III and Steven D. Levitt found that same-race policing lead to a greater reduction of property crime. They argue that a given number of officers will have a greater impact on crime while requiring fewer arrests, if deployed in a same-race setting (Donohue and Levitt, 1998).

However, race is not the only factor in attitudes toward the police. Race and personal experience with the police interact. Attitudes toward the police may be tied to discontent with the quality of life in some neighborhoods. Thus police actions and policies clearly have a significant effect on the attitudes some citizens have about the fairness of the political community.

Why do some urban residents resent the police? John J. DiIulio argues that this resentment stems from permissive law enforcement and police abuse of power (DiIulio, 1993a:3). The police are charged with failing to provide protection and services to minority neighborhoods and with abusing residents physically or verbally.

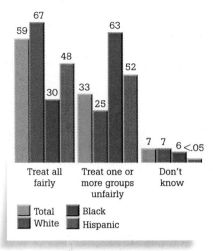

What Americans Think

Question "Do you think the police in your community treat all races fairly or do they tend to treat one or more of these groups unfairly?"

Treat all fairly: 59, 67, 48, 30

Treat one or more groups unfairly: 33, 25, 63, 52

Don't know: 7, 7, 6, <.05

Total, White, Black, Hispanic

SOURCE: U.S. Department of Justice, Bureau of Justice Statistics, *Sourcebook of Criminal Justice Statistics—1998* (Washington,D.C.: Government Printing Office, 1999), 111.

CLOSE  up

Living under Suspicion

If you're white and confused about why so many blacks think O. J. Simpson is innocent of murder, try a simple exercise. Take a few minutes to sit down with an African-American, preferably a male, and ask whether he has ever been hassled by the police. Chances are you'll get an education. . . .

He may have been pulled over for the offense of driving after dark through a white neighborhood, for the misdemeanor of driving with a white woman or for the felony of driving too fancy a car. He may have been questioned for making a suspicious late-night call from a public phone in a suburban mall or, as a boy, for flagrantly riding his new bike on his own street.

He may have been a student or a lawyer—even an off-duty policeman, threatened with drawn guns before he could pull out his badge. Some black parents warn their children never to run out of a store or a bank: Better to be late than shot dead.

When you grow up in vulnerability and live at the margins of society, the world looks different. That difference, starkly displayed after Mr. [O. J.] Simpson's acquittal in the criminal trial, has been less passionate but no less definitive since he was found liable in his civil trial. . . .

For many African-Americans, Mr. Simpson has become more symbol than individual. He is every black man who dared to marry a white women, who rose from deprivation to achievement, who got "uppity" and faced destruction by the white establishment that elevated him. He is every black man who has been pulled over by a white cop, beaten to the ground, jailed without evidence, framed for a crime he didn't commit.

Given that legacy, it is difficult for blacks not to doubt the police, and the doubts undermine law enforcement. In 1995 five Philadelphia policemen were indicted and pleaded guilty after years of fabricating evidence against poor blacks, calling into question some 1,500 prosecutions. One victim was Betty Patterson, a grandmother who spent three years in prison on a phony charge of selling crack; she later won a settlement of nearly $1 million from the city.

The indictments came as the Simpson jurors were hearing tapes of anti-black remarks by Detective Mark Fuhrman that reflected the endemic racism of the Los Angeles Police Department. As documented by the Christopher Commission, which investigated the department after the Rodney King beating in 1991, officers felt so comfortable in their bigotry that they typed racist computer messages to one another, apparently confident that they would face no punishment.

This is precisely the lesson of the black-white reactions to the Simpson case. Most policemen are not racist or corrupt, but most departments do not combat racism as vigorously as they do corruption. Many blacks have come to see the police as just another gang. Alarm bells should be going off, for the judicial system cannot function without credibility.

Of the country's institutions, police departments are probably furthest behind in addressing racism in their ranks. Some corporations are learning that a diverse work force enhances profits. The military knows that attracting volunteers and maintaining cohesion requires racial harmony. Police departments ought to understand that their bottom line is measured in legitimate convictions. They need to retrain officers and screen applicants for subtle bigotry. If morality is not argument enough, try pragmatism.

SOURCE: David K. Shipler, "Living under Suspicion," *New York Times*, February 7, 1997, p. A33.

The police are seen as permissive when an officer treats an offense against a person of the same ethnic group as the offender more lightly than a similar incident in which the offender and victim are members of different groups. The police say that such differences occur because they are working in a hostile environment. The white patrol officer may fear that breaking up a street fight among members of a minority group will provoke the wrath of onlookers, while community residents may view inaction as a sign that the police do not care about their neighborhood. The police are accused of not working effectively on crimes such as drug sales, gambling, petty theft, and in-group assault, although these crimes are most common in the urban neighborhoods and create the greatest insecurity and fear among residents.

Almost all studies reveal the prejudices of the police toward the poor and racial minorities. These attitudes lead many officers to see all African Americans or Hispanic Americans as potential criminals, and as a result police tend to exaggerate the extent of minority crime. If both police and citizens view each other with hostility, then their encounters will be strained and the potential for conflict great. As shown in What Americans Think, black males between the ages of 18 and 34 have very different attitudes toward the police than either whites or the population as a whole.

Racial profiling—the use by the police of race and ethnicity as clues to criminality—has recently become a highly charged public issue. As shown in What Americans Think (see p. 219), a majority of whites, as well as blacks, believe that the practice is widespread. Almost three-quarters of young black men interviewed by the Gallup Poll reported having been stopped by the police because of their race. As discussed in the Close-Up (p. 218), minority group members see racial profiling as one more example of police bias.

It is little wonder, therefore, that urban ghetto dwellers think of the police as an army of occupation and that the police think of themselves as combat soldiers. As noted by Jerome Skolnick and James Fyfe (1993:160), the military organization of the police and the "war on crime" can lead to violence against inner-city residents, who are viewed by the police as the enemy.

Community Crime Prevention

There is a growing awareness that the control of crime and disorder cannot be achieved solely by the police. Social control requires involvement by all members of the community. Community crime prevention can be enhanced if government agencies and neighborhood organizations cooperate. As one expert has said, "Voluntary local efforts must support official action if order is to be preserved within realistic budgetary limits and without sacrificing our civil liberties" (Skogan, 1990:125). Across the country, community programs to help the police have increased greatly.

Citizen crime-watch groups have been formed in many communities. More than six million Americans are now estimated to be members of such groups, which often have direct ties to police departments. In Detroit, Neighborhood Watch is organized on four thousand of the city's twelve thousand blocks; in New York, the Blockwatchers are seventy thousand strong and are trained at precinct houses to watch, listen, and report accurately; in Dade County, Florida, the 175,000-member Citizens Crime Watch has extended its operations into schools in an effort to reduce drug use (Garofalo and McLeod, 1989:326).

The Crime Stoppers Program is designed to enlist public help in solving crimes. Founded in Albuquerque, New Mexico, in 1975, it has spread across the country. Television and radio stations present the "unsolved crime of the week," and cash rewards are given for information that leads to conviction of the offender. Although these programs help solve some crimes, the numbers of solved crimes are still small compared with the total number of crimes committed.

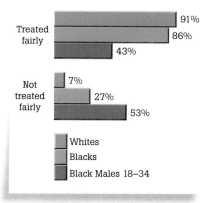

What Americans Think

Question "Do you feel you have been treated fairly or not by the local police in your area?"

Treated fairly
- 91%
- 86%
- 43%

Not treated fairly
- 7%
- 27%
- 53%

■ Whites
■ Blacks
■ Black Males 18–34

SOURCE: The Gallup Poll, December 11, 1999, at www.Gallup.com.

CLOSE  up

D.W.B.—Driving While **Black**

Dr. Elmo Randolph's commute to his office near Newark, New Jersey, usually takes only forty minutes, but the African American dentist is often late. Since 1991, Randolph has been stopped by state troopers on the New Jersey Turnpike more than fifty times. After stopping his gold BMW by the side of the road, he says the officer approaches and asks him the same question: "Do you have any drugs or weapons in your car?" One time when he refused to let police search his car, they seized his license and made him wait on the side of the highway for twenty minutes. Randolph asks, "Would they pull over a white middle-class person and ask the same question?" He has sold the BMW.

Racial profiling has become a highly charged issue after a rising number of complaints that minority drivers are being pulled over by the police in disproportionate numbers. Often the police have justified these stops on the grounds that the drivers fit a profile of a drug runner. Studies give credence to the complaints of African Americans and Hispanics that they are so frequently stopped on highways and frisked on city streets that only their race can explain the pattern. Their leaders have called the use of the tactic blatantly racist and a violation of civil rights. In Congress and a number of states, calls have been heard for legislation to end the practice. In some states (Connecticut, Maryland, New Jersey, North Carolina), the police are now required to record the reason for a motor vehicle stop and the race of the driver. The U.S. Department of Justice appointed a monitor in December 1999 to oversee the New Jersey State Police and to ensure that it enacts policy changes to end discrimination against minority motorists.

The police argue that race is only one characteristic used to determine if a person should be stopped for questioning. They say they are trained to develop a "sixth sense," the instinctive ability to sniff out situations or isolate individuals who seem potentially unsafe. From this viewpoint the police often act against individuals who seem "out of place"—a shabbily dressed youth in an upscale part of town or a man in a pinstriped suit prowling a gritty ghetto. Often, however, officers may have a vague sense that something is not right because of a furtive look or an uneasy gait.

One of the core principles of the Fourth Amendment is that the police cannot stop and detain an individual unless there is probable cause or at least reasonable suspicion that he or she is involved in criminal activity. However, in recent years the Supreme Court has weakened this protection. *Whren v. United States* (1996) allows the police to use traffic stops—whether minor or serious, real or alleged—as a reason to investigate a vehicle and its passengers. *Maryland v. Wilson* (1997) gave the police the power to order passengers out of a car, whether or not there is any basis to suspect they are dangerous. The American Civil Liberties Union has argued that these decisions have given the police virtually unlimited authority to stop and search any vehicle they want.

Determining when and how the police should use race to assess suspects and situations is a complicated balancing act of public safety and civil liberties. Law enforcement experts insist that effective police work depends upon quick analysis and that skin color is one factor among many—such as dress or demeanor—that officers must consider. But minority leaders say that racial profiling is based on the presumption that African Americans and Hispanics are linked to crime. This has led to the humiliation and physical abuse of innocent citizens.

SOURCE: Drawn from Jodi Wilgoren, "Police Profiling Debate: Acting on Experience, or on Bias," *New York Times,* April 9, 1999, p. A21; David Kocieniewski, "U.S. Will Monitor New Jersey Police on Race Profiling," *New York Times,* December 23, 1999, p. A1; American Civil Liberties Union, "Driving While Black: Racial Profiling on Our Nation's Highways" (June 1999, online edition); and Mark Hosenball, " 'It Is Not the Act of a Few Bad Apples,' " *Newsweek,* May 17, 1999:34.

To what extent can such programs be relied upon to reduce crime and maintain social order? The results are mixed. Research on forty neighborhoods in six cities shows that while crime prevention efforts and voluntary community groups have had some success in more affluent neighborhoods, they are less likely to be found in poor neighborhoods with high levels of disorder. In such areas, "residents typically are deeply suspicious of one another, report only a weak sense of community, perceive they have low levels of personal influence on neighborhood events, and feel that it is their neighbors, not 'outsiders,' whom they must watch with care" (Skogan, 1990:130; McGabey, 1986:230).

However, George Kelling and Catherine Coles have documented successful community-based crime prevention programs in Baltimore, Boston, New York, San Francisco, and Seattle (Kelling and Coles, 1996). In each city, community-based groups worked with the police and other governmental agencies to restore order and control crime. They explain that the citizens of a community must take responsibility for maintaining civil and safe social conditions. Experience has shown that "while police might be able to *retake* a neighborhood from aggressive drug dealers, police could not *hold* a neighborhood without significant commitment and actual assistance from private citizens" (Kelling and Coles, 1996:248).

The residents of the Boyd Booth neighborhood of Baltimore show how citizens working together can "take back" their community from drug dealers. Before their successful efforts, many residents had "retreated into their homes, afraid to report the violence to the police, afraid that drug dealers would burn them out, or worse" (Kelling and Coles, 1996:197). Assisted by a task force of city agencies, police, the Baltimore Law Center, and community associations, the Boyd Booth residents set out to deal with the problem of abandoned housing as a way of turning back urban decay. State money was provided to board up vacant houses, improve street lighting, and erect fences. Community members cleaned up trash, closed walkways, conducted vigils and street demonstrations, and held neighborhood picnics. The police increased their use of aggressive foot patrol and of special antidrug units. The results were a 56 percent decrease in violent crime from 1993 to 1995 and an 80 percent drop in narcotics calls to police and drug arrests (Kelling and Coles, 1996:198).

Law enforcement agencies need the support and help of the community for effective crime prevention and control. They need support when they take actions designed to maintain order. They need information about wrongdoing and cooperation with investigations. However, such support will not be forthcoming if the police abuse their power.

CHECK POINT

⑦ **What three factors make policing in a multicultural society difficult?**

⑧ **What are the characteristics of people who have the most negative attitudes toward the police?**

⑨ **What are the two basic reasons that urban residents resent the police?**

⑩ **How are citizen watch groups and similar programs helpful to the police?**

What Americans Think

Question "It has been reported that some police officers stop motorists of certain racial or ethnic groups because the officers believe that these groups are more likely than others to commit certain types of crimes. Do you believe that this practice, known as 'racial profiling,' is widespread or not?"

All respondents

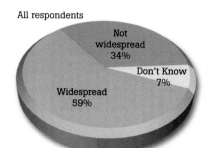

Not widespread 34%
Don't Know 7%
Widespread 59%

Whites

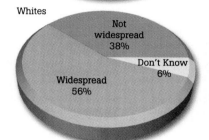

Not widespread 38%
Don't Know 6%
Widespread 56%

Blacks

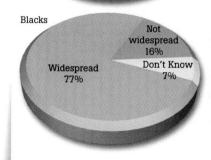

Not widespread 16%
Don't Know 7%
Widespread 77%

SOURCE: The Gallup Organization, "Racial Profiling Is Seen as Widespread, Particularly among Young Black Men," press release, December 9, 1999.

Police Abuse of Power

The misconduct of the New York City police officer described at the beginning of this chapter is not unique. The beating of Rodney King by Los Angeles police officers drew worldwide attention, as did the revenge killing by New Orleans police of Adolph Archer, who had shot an officer. The many recent police corruption scandals have made abuse of police power a major issue on the public agenda (Skolnick and Fyfe, 1993). Although such scandals have occurred throughout American history, only in the past quarter-century has the public been aware of the problems of police misconduct, especially illegal use of violence by law enforcement officers and criminal activities associated with police corruption. Most officers do not engage in misconduct, yet these problems deserve study because they raise questions about how much the public can control and trust the police.

Use of Force

Most people cooperate with the police, yet officers at times must use force to arrest, control disturbances, and deal with the drunken or mentally ill. As noted by Skolnick and Fyfe,

> As long as some members of society do not comply with law and resist the police, force will remain an inevitable part of policing. Cops, especially, understand that. Indeed, anybody who fails to understand the centrality of force in police work has no business in a police uniform. (1993:37)

Thus police may use *legitimate* force to do their job. When they use *excessive* force, they violate the law. But what is excessive force? This is a question that neither officers nor experts can easily answer.

In cities where racial tensions are high, conflicts between police and residents often result when officers are accused of acting in unprofessional ways. Citizens use the term *police brutality* to describe a wide range of practices, from the use of profane or abusive language to physical force and violence. As shown in What

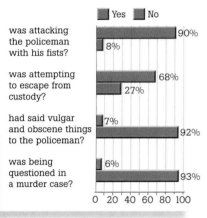

What Americans Think

Question "Would you approve of a policeman striking a citizen who . . .?"

Yes ■ No ■

was attacking the policeman with his fists?
90%
8%

was attempting to escape from custody?
68%
27%

had said vulgar and obscene things to the policeman?
7%
92%

was being questioned in a murder case?
6%
93%

0 20 40 60 80 100

SOURCE: U.S. Department of Justice, Bureau of Justice Statistics, *Sourcebook of Criminal Justice Statistics, 1998* (Washington, D.C.: Government Printing Office, 1999), 115.

On the witness stand, Officer Sean Carroll testifies how he led his three partners into the shooting of Amadou Diallo. Upon realizing he was unarmed, Carroll said he held Diallo and cried, "Don't die. Don't die. Keep breathing."

Americans Think, most people approve a police officer striking a citizen under certain circumstances.

Stories of police brutality are not new. However, unlike the untrained officers of the early 1900s, today's officers are supposed to be professionals who know the rules and understand the need for proper conduct. Thus, the beating of Rodney King and other incidents of brutality are disturbing (Ogletree, Schade, Hepburn, and Buchanan, 1995). Moreover, when abusive behavior by police comes to light, the public has no way of knowing how often police engage in such actions because most violence is hidden from public view. If a person looking on from a nearby window had not videotaped the beating of Rodney King, the officers could have claimed that they did not use excessive force and King would have had no way to prove that they did. How can such incidents be prevented, especially when they occur without witnesses?

The concept "use of force" takes many forms in practice. The various types of force can be arranged on a continuum ranging from most severe (civilians shot and killed) to least severe (come-alongs). Table 6.2 lists many of these forms of force according to their frequency of use. How often must force be used? Most research has shown that in police contacts with suspects, force is used infrequently and the type of force used is usually at the low end of the continuum—toward the less severe. Research in Phoenix found that the single largest predictor of police use of force was use of force by the suspect to which the police then responded (Garner, Schade, Hepburn, and Buchanan, 1995). Excessive use of force, in violation of department policies and state laws, constitutes abuse of police power.

By law, the police have the right to use force if necessary to make an arrest, keep the peace, or maintain public order. But just how much force is necessary and under what conditions it may be used are complex and debatable questions. In particular, the use of deadly force in the apprehending of suspects has become a deeply emotional issue with a direct connection to race relations. Research has shown that the greatest use of deadly force by the police is found in communities with high levels of economic inequality and large minority populations (Sorensen, Marquart, and Brock, 1993:493).

When the police kill a suspect or bystander while trying to make an arrest, their actions may produce public outrage and hostility. This was the case in November 1996 when a white officer in St. Petersburg, Florida, killed a black motorist who had refused to lower his window and appeared to be trying to drive away after a routine traffic stop. The riot that followed left more than a dozen people injured and caused $5 million in property damage. A second round of rioting was sparked after a predominantly white grand jury cleared the officer of wrongdoing (*USA Today*, November 11, 1996:electronic edition).

New Yorkers were outraged by the killing of Amadou Diallo, an unarmed West African immigrant, who died in a fuselage of forty-one bullets fired by four members of New York City's Street Crime Unit. Unarmed and standing alone, Diallo was killed in the vestibule of his apartment building. The officers were

TABLE 6.2

Reported uses of force by big-city police

Police have the legal right to use force to make an arrest, keep the peace, and maintain order. Of the many types of force available to police, the less severe types are used most often.

TYPE OF FORCE	RATE PER THOUSAND SWORN OFFICERS
Handcuff/leg restraint	490.4
Bodily force (arm, foot, or leg)	272.2
Come-alongs	226.8
Unholstering weapon	129.9
Swarm	126.7
Twist locks/wrist locks	80.9
Firm grip	57.7
Chemical agents (Mace or Cap-Stun)	36.2
Batons	36.0
Flashlights	21.7
Dog attacks or bites	6.5
Electrical devices (TASER)	5.4
Civilians shot at but not hit	3.0
Other impact devices	2.4
Neck restraints/unconsciousness-rendering holds	1.4
Vehicle rammings	1.0
Civilians shot and killed	0.9
Civilians shot and wounded but not killed	0.2

SOURCE: Drawn from U.S. Department of Justice, Bureau of Justice Statistics, *National Data Collection on Police Use of Force* (Washington, D.C.: Government Printing Office, 1996), 43.

looking for a rapist-murderer when they came upon Diallo. As they approached him, they said they thought he was reaching for a gun. The killing resulted in massive protests and the indictment of the officers on second-degree murder charges.

On February 25, 2000, officers Kenneth Boss, Sean Carroll, Edward McMellon, and Richard Murphy were acquitted of all charges related to Diallo's death. During the trial the officers said that they "reasonably believed" that Diallo was about to use deadly force against them. Despite a passionate prosecution summation that argued that Diallo was doomed from the time he was spotted by the officers, the jury's decision seemed to focus on the first shot fired and the officers' belief that Diallo had a gun—and not the duration of the firing or the number of bullets (*New York Times,* Febuary 26, 2000:A13).

The Diallo killing raised new questions about New York's "zero tolerance" policies and the aggressive tactics used by special street-crime units in other cities. As James J. Fyfe, an expert on police training and tactics, had said, "If officers are encouraged to engage in high-risk encounters, the possibility of these 'train wrecks' grows exponentially" (*Newsweek,* March 6, 2000:24).

No accurate data have been collected on the number of people shot by the police. The police shoot an estimated thirty-six hundred people each year, with fatal results in as many as one thousand of these incidents (Cullen, Cao, Frank, Langworthy, Browning, Kopache, and Stevenson, 1996:449). Although these numbers are alarming, keep in mind that force (hit, held, choked, threatened) is used against 500,000 people each year (BJS, 1997c:12). The number of police killings should not obscure the fact that most of those killed are young black men. However, the ratio of blacks to whites killed has declined, in part because of new police policies (Sherman and Cohn, 1986; Walker, Spohn, and DeLone, 1996:93).

Until the 1980s, the police had broad authority to use deadly force in pursuing suspected felons. Police in about half the states were guided by the common law principle that allowed the use of whatever force was necessary to arrest a fleeing felon. In 1985 the Supreme Court set a new standard in **Tennessee v. Garner,** ruling that the police may not use deadly force in apprehending fleeing felons "unless it is necessary to prevent the escape and the officer has probable cause to believe that the suspect poses a significant threat of death or serious physical injury to the officer or others."

The case dealt with the killing of Edward Garner, a 15-year-old eighth grader who was shot by a member of the Memphis Police Department. Officers Elton Hymon and Leslie Wright were sent to answer a "prowler inside" call. When they arrived at the scene, they saw a woman standing on her porch and gesturing toward the adjacent house. She told them she had heard glass breaking and someone was inside. While Wright radioed for help, Hymon went to the back of the house, heard a door slam, and saw someone run across the backyard toward a six-foot chain-link fence. With his flashlight, Hymon was able to see that Garner was unarmed. He called out, "Police! Halt!" but Garner began to climb the fence. Convinced that Garner would escape if he made it over the fence, Hymon fired, hitting him in the back of the head. Garner died in the operating room, the $10 he had stolen still in his pocket. Hymon had acted under Tennessee law and Memphis Police Department policy.

The standard set by *Tennessee v. Garner* presents problems given that judging how dangerous a suspect is can be hard. Because officers must make quick decisions in stressful situations, creating rules that will guide them in every case is impossible. The Court tried to clarify its ruling in the case of *Graham v. Connor* (1989). Here the justices established the standard of "objective reasonableness,"

Tennessee v. Garner **(1985)**
Deadly force may not be used against a fleeing suspect unless necessary to prevent the escape and unless the officer has probable cause to believe that the suspect poses a significant threat of death or serious injury to the officers or others.

saying that the officer's use of deadly force should be judged in terms of the "reasonableness at the moment." This means that the use of the deadly force should be judged from the point of view of the officer on the scene. The Court's decision says that it must be recognized that "officers are often forced to make split-second judgments—in circumstances that are tense, uncertain, and rapidly evolving—about the amount of force that is necessary in a particular situation."

The risk of lawsuits by victims of improper police shootings looms over police departments and creates a further incentive for administrators to set and enforce standards for the use of force. However, as long as officers carry weapons, some improper shootings will occur. Training, internal review of incidents, and disciplining or firing trigger-happy officers may help reduce the use of unnecessary force (Fyfe, 1993:128; Blumberg, 1989:442).

Although progress has been made in reducing police brutality and misuse of deadly force, corruption is still a major problem.

Corruption

Police corruption has a long history in America. Early in the twentieth century, city officials organized liquor and gambling businesses for their personal gain. In many cities ties were maintained between politicians and police officials so that favored clients would be protected and competitors harassed. Much of the Progressive movement to reform the police was designed to combat such corrupt arrangements. Although these political ties have been reduced in most cities, corruption still exists.

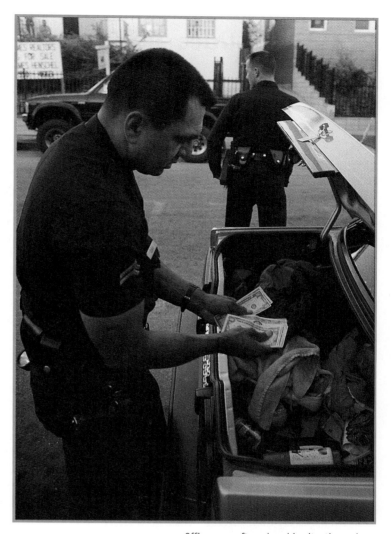

Officers are often placed in situations where they can be tempted to violate the law.

Sometimes corruption is defined so broadly that it ranges from accepting a free cup of coffee (see A Question of Ethics on p. 224) to robbing businesses or beating suspects. *Corruption* is not easily defined, and disagreements exist about what it includes. As a useful starting point, a distinction can be made between corrupt officers who are "grass eaters" and those who are "meat eaters."

Grass Eaters and Meat Eaters

"Grass eaters" are officers who accept payoffs that the routines of police work bring their way. "Meat eaters" are officers who actively use their power for personal gain. Although meat eaters are few in number, their actions make headlines when they are discovered. By contrast, because grass eaters are numerous, they make corruption seem acceptable and promote a code of secrecy that brands any officer who exposes corruption as a traitor. Grass eaters are the heart of the problem and are often harder to detect.

A Question of
Ethics

Bianco's Restaurant is a popular, noisy place in a tough section of town. Open from 6:30 A.M. until midnight, it is usually crowded with regulars enjoying the low prices and ample portions, teenagers planning their next exploit, and people grabbing a quick bite to eat.

Officer John Buchanan has just finished his late-night "lunch" before going back on duty. As he walks toward the cash register, Cheryl Bianco, the manager, takes the bill from his hand and says, "This one's on me, John. It's nice to have you with us."

Officer Buchanan protests, "Thanks, but I'd better pay for my own meal."

"Why do you say that? The other cops don't object to getting a free meal now and then."

"Well, they may feel that way, but I don't want anyone to get the idea that I'm giving you special treatment," Buchanan replies.

"Come off it. Who's going to think that? I don't expect special treatment; we just want you to know we appreciate your work."

■ What issues are involved here? If Buchanan refuses to accept Bianco's generosity, what is he saying about his role as a police officer? If he accepts the offer, what does that say? Might people who overhear the conversation draw other meanings from it? Is turning down a free $6.50 meal that important?

In the past, low salaries, politics, and poor hiring practices have been cited as factors contributing to corruption. While some claim that a few "rotten apples" should not taint an entire police force, corruption in some departments has been so rampant that the rotten-apple theory does not fully explain the situation. Some explanations are based on the structure and organization of police work. Much police work involves enforcement of laws in situations in which there is no complainant or it is unclear whether a law has been broken. Moreover, most police work is carried out at the officer's own discretion, without direct supervision. Thus, police officers may have many opportunities to gain benefits by using their discretion to protect people who engage in illegal conduct.

Examples of meat eaters among the police of Cleveland, Ohio, came to light in January 1998 as a result of an FBI sting operation. Forty-one officers were charged with protecting cocaine trafficking. The Cleveland case was one of a series of police corruption investigations that have struck cities across the country in recent years. In New Orleans ten officers were convicted for their role in protecting a warehouse containing 286 pounds of cocaine. In Chicago, in two unrelated cases, ten officers were charged with robbing and extorting money and narcotics from drug dealers. From 1994 to 1997, 508 officers in forty-seven cities have been convicted in federal corruption cases (*New York Times*, January 1, 1998:A16).

The most serious recent corruption case occurred in the Los Angeles Police Department, where by March 2000, twenty officers were fired or suspended, forty convictions were overturned, and several hundred were under review, following testimony by former officer Rafael Perez. Perez pled guilty to stealing cocaine from an evidence locker but gained a lighter, five-year sentence by telling investigators about misconduct by fellow officers. He contended that they beat, framed, stole from, and shot innocent people in the city's crime-ridden Ramparts area. Perez, a member of the department's elite anti-gang unit, said that in their zeal to bust suspected gang members, officers carried stashes of drugs to make a frame-up quick and easy. Police Chief Bernard C. Parks has told the city council that settling lawsuits could cost $125 million (*Washington Post*, February 12, 2000:A01).

If police administrators judge success merely by the maintenance of order on the streets and a steady flow of arrests and traffic citations, they may not have any idea what their officers do while on patrol. Officers therefore may learn that they can engage in improper conduct without worrying about investigations by supervisors as long as there is order on the streets and they keep their activities out of the public spotlight.

Opportunities for corruption will always arise when police administrators do not monitor the activities of officers. In 1993, New York's Mollen Commission found that department norms may shield corrupt cops from detection. Former police officer Kevin Hembury told the commission that at the police academy and in the locker room of the Seventy-third Precinct he had learned the "us against them" mentality and the "blue wall of silence"—that "cops never rat on other cops, that ratting on corrupt cops is worse than corruption itself." When he was exposed to the drug dealing and violence in his precinct, Hembury learned that "opportunities for money, drugs, power, and thrills were plentiful, and opportunities for friendly, productive contact with the thousands of good people who lived there were few." What startled the commission was his statement that "no commanding officer ever asked how he and his colleagues were spending their days . . . or how well they were serving the residents they were supposed to protect" (*New York Times*, November 1, 1992:A12).

Enforcement of vice laws, especially drug laws, creates major problems for police agencies. In many cities the rewards for vice offenders are so high that they can easily afford to make large payments to unethical officers to protect themselves against prosecution. Making the problem worse is that police operations against victimless crimes are proactive. Unless drugs are being sold openly, upsetting the residents of a neighborhood, no victims complain if officers ignore or even profit from the activities of drug dealers.

Over time, illegal activity may become accepted as normal. Ellwyn Stoddard, who studied "blue-coat crime," has said that it can become part of an "identifiable informal 'code.' " He suggests that officers are socialized to the code early in their careers. Those who "snitch" on their fellow officers may be ostracized. When corruption comes to official attention, officers protect the code by distancing themselves from the known offender instead of stopping their own improper conduct. Activities under this blue-coat code may include the following (Stoddard, 1968:205):

- Mooching: Accepting free coffee, cigarettes, meals, liquor, groceries, or other items, which are thought of as compensation either for being underpaid or for future favoritism to the donor.
- Bribery: Receiving cash or a "gift" in exchange for past or future help in avoiding prosecution. The officer may claim to be unable to identify a criminal, may take care to be in the wrong place when a crime is to occur, or may take some other action that can be viewed as mere carelessness.
- Chiseling: Demanding discounts or free admission to places of entertainment, whether on duty or not.
- Extortion: Demanding payment for an ad in a police magazine or purchase of tickets to a police function; holding a "street court" in which minor traffic tickets can be avoided by the payment of cash "bail" to the arresting officer, with no receipt given.
- Shopping: Picking up small items such as candy bars, gum, and cigarettes at a store where the door has been left unlocked at the close of business hours.
- Shakedown: Taking expensive items for personal use during an investigation of a break-in or burglary. Shakedown is distinguished from shopping by the value of the items taken and the ease with which former ownership of items may be determined if the officer is caught.
- Premeditated theft: Using tools, keys, or other devices to force entry and steal property. Premeditated theft is distinguished from shakedown by the fact that it is planned, not by the value of the items taken.
- Favoritism: Issuing license tabs, window stickers, or courtesy cards that exempt users from arrest or citation for traffic offenses (sometimes extended to family members and friends of recipients).
- Perjury: Lying to provide an alibi for fellow officers engaged in unlawful activity or otherwise failing to tell the truth so as to avoid sanctions.

■ Prejudice: Treating members of minority groups in a biased fashion, especially members of groups that lack political influence in City Hall to cause the arresting officer trouble.

Police corruption has three major effects on law enforcement: (1) suspects are left free to engage in further crime, (2) morale is damaged and supervision becomes lax, and (3) the image of the police suffers. The image of the police agency is very important in light of the need for citizen cooperation. When the police are seen as not much different from the "crooks," effective crime control is even further out of reach.

What is startling is that many people do not equate police corruption with other forms of crime. Some believe that police corruption is tolerable as long as the streets are safe. This attitude ignores the fact that corrupt officers are serving only themselves and are not committed to serving the public.

Controlling Corruption

The public has a role to play in stopping police corruption. Scandals attract the attention of politicians and the news media, but citizens must file complaints about improper actions. Once a citizen files a complaint, however, questions remain about how best to respond. All departments have policies about proper police behavior and ways of dealing with complaints, but some departments tend to sweep corruption complaints under the rug. The most effective departments often have strong leaders who make it clear to the public and to officers that corruption will not be tolerated and that complaints will be investigated and pursued seriously.

CHECK POINT

⑪ **What kinds of practices do citizens view as police brutality?**

⑫ **When may the police use force?**

⑬ **How did the Supreme Court rule in *Tennessee v. Garner*?**

⑭ **What is the difference between "grass eaters" and "meat eaters"?**

⑮ **List five of the ten practices cited by Ellwyn Stoddard as activities of "blue-coat crime."**

 # Civic Accountability

Relations between citizens and the police depend greatly on citizen confidence that officers will behave in accordance with the law and with department guidelines. Rapport with the community is enhanced when citizens feel sure that the police will protect their persons and property and the rights guaranteed by the Constitution. Striking a balance between making the police responsive to citizen complaints and burdening them with a flood of citizen complaints is hard. The main challenge in making the police more accountable is to use citizen input to force police to follow the law and department guidelines without placing too many limits on their ability to carry out their primary functions. At present, four less-than-perfect techniques are used in efforts to control the police: (1) internal affairs units, (2) civilian review boards, (3) standards and accreditation, and (4) civil liability lawsuits.

Internal Affairs Units

Controlling the police is mainly an internal matter that must be given top priority by administrators. The community must be confident that the department has procedures to ensure that officers will protect the rights of citizens. Many departments have no formal complaint procedures, and when such procedures do exist, they often seem to be designed to discourage citizen input (see Figure 6.2). Rumor has it, for example, that several years ago the Internal Affairs Bureau of the San Francisco Police Department posted a sign that said "Write your complaints here." Under the sign was a pile of one-inch-square scraps of paper.

Depending on the size of the department, a single officer or an entire section may serve as an **internal affairs unit** that receives and investigates complaints against officers. An officer charged with misconduct can face criminal prosecution or disciplinary action that can lead to resignation, dismissal, or suspension. Officers assigned to the internal affairs unit have duties similar to those of the inspector general's staff in the military. They must investigate complaints against their fellow officers. Hollywood films and television dramas depict dramatic investigations of drug dealing and murder, but investigations of sexual harassment, alcohol or drug problems, misuse of force, and violations of department policies are more common.

The internal affairs unit must be given enough resources to carry out its mission, as well as direct access to the chief. Some internal investigators may assume that a citizen complaint is an attack on the police as a whole and will shield officers against such complaints. When this happens, administrators do not get the information they need to correct a problem. The public, in turn, may come to believe that the department condones the practices they complain of and that filing a complaint is pointless. Moreover, even when the top administrator seeks to attack misconduct, it may be hard to persuade police to testify against fellow officers.

Internal affairs investigators find the work stressful because their status prevents them from maintaining close relationships with their fellow officers. A wall of silence rises around them. Such problems can be especially severe in smaller departments where all the officers know each other well and regularly socialize together.

Civilian Review Boards

If a police department cannot show the public that it effectively combats corruption among officers, the public is likely to demand that the department be investigated by a civilian review board. These boards are organized so that complaints can be channeled through a committee of persons who are not sworn police officers. The organization and powers of civilian review boards vary, but all oversee and review how police departments handle citizen complaints. The boards may also recommend remedial action. They do not have the power to investigate or discipline individual officers (Walker and Wright, 1995).

During the 1980s, as minorities gained more political power in large cities, civilian review boards experienced a revival. A survey of the fifty largest cities found that thirty-six had civilian review boards, as did thirteen of the fifty next largest cities (Walker and Wright, 1995).

internal affairs unit
A branch of a police department that receives and investigates complaints against officers alleging violation of rules and policies.

PART TWO

FIGURE 6.2 Path of citizen complaints

Compare the actions taken when a citizen is assaulted by a police officer in the course of dealing with a traffic violation and when a citizen is assaulted by a neighbor.

Left path:

An officer stops a citizen for a traffic violation. An argument ensues and the officer breaks the citizen's nose as his son looks on.

Victim is charged with breach of peace and resisting arrest.

Victim calls police to report assault.

Victim is told to come to station to file complaint but is warned he could be arrested for filing a false complaint.

Victim gives complaint to internal affairs, where victim is again warned he could be charged with filing a false complaint.

Investigators question victim and son, submit written questions to officer.

Review board hears testimony from victim and son, reads internal affairs report, finds there is not enough evidence to prove the charge; nothing happens to the officer.

If review board agrees that excessive force was used, recommendation is forwarded to chief.

If chief agrees, chief either reprimands or suspends officer. Breach of peace and resisting arrest charges against victim are dropped.

Right path:

A neighbor hits the victim, breaking nose, as victim's son looks on.

Victim calls police. Officers are sent to the home to take complaint and interview son.

Police arrest neighbor, who is booked on third-degree assault charge.

Neighbor goes to court, where he is arraigned and enters not guilty plea. Prosecutor, defense attorney, and judge are involved at this point.

Prosecutor offers a deal. But the neighbor rejects the deal and the victim's case goes to a pretrial hearing, where a judge determines that there is enough evidence to proceed. Prosecutor's investigators interview victim and son.

A prosecutor is assigned to case. He offers another deal.

Neighbor refuses, requesting a jury trial.

A six-member jury is selected and the victim tells how his neighbor hit him without provocation. Son testifies. Doctor testifies.

Neighbor convicted and sentenced to $1,000 fine and/or up to one year in prison.

SOURCE: *Hartford Courant*, September 30, 1991, p.A6.

The main argument made by the police against civilian review boards is that people outside law enforcement do not understand the problems of policing. The police contend that civilian oversight lowers morale and hinders performance and that officers will be less effective if they are worried about possible disciplinary actions. In reality, however, the boards have not been harsh.

Review of police actions occurs some time after the incident has taken place and usually comes down to the officer's word against that of the complainant. Given the low visibility of the incidents that lead to complaints, a great many complaints are not substantiated (Skolnick and Fyfe, 1993:229). The effectiveness of civilian review boards has not been tested; their presence may improve police-citizen relations. Even so, filing a complaint against the police may be frustrating, as shown in Figure 6.2.

Standards and Accreditation

One way to increase police accountability is to require that police actions meet nationally recognized standards. The movement to accredit departments that meet these standards has gained momentum during the past decade. It has the support of the Commission on Accreditation for Law Enforcement Agencies (CALEA), a private nonprofit corporation formed by four professional associations: the International Association of Chiefs of Police (IACP), the National Organization of Black Law Enforcement Executives (NOBLE), the National Sheriffs Association (NSA), and the Police Executive Research Forum (PERF).

The *Standards*, first published by CALEA in 1983, have been updated from time to time. The third edition, published in 1994, has 436 specific standards. Each standard is a statement, with a brief explanation, that sets forth clear requirements. For example, under "Limits of Authority," Standard 1.2.2 requires that "a written directive governs the use of discretion by sworn officers." The explanation states: "In many agencies, the exercise of discretion is defined by a combination of written enforcement policies, training and supervision. The written directive should define the limits of individual discretion and provide guidelines for exercising discretion within those limits" (Commission on Accreditation for Law Enforcement Accreditation, 1989:1). Because police departments have said almost nothing about their use of discretion, this is a major shift. However, the standard still is not specific enough. For example, does it cover stop-and-frisk actions, the handling of drunks, and the use of informants?

Police accreditation is voluntary. Departments contact CALEA, which helps them in their efforts to meet the standards. This process involves self-evaluation by department executives, the development of policies that meet the standards, and training of officers. CALEA personnel act like a military inspector general, visiting the department, examining its policies, and seeing if the standards are met in its daily operations. Certification is given to departments that meet the standards. The standards can be used as a management tool, with officers trained to know the standards and be accountable for their actions. By 1998, more than 460 agencies had been accredited (Walker, 1999:285).

The standards do not guarantee that police officers in an accredited department will not engage in misconduct. However, they are a major step toward providing clear guidelines to officers about proper behavior. Accreditation can also show the public that the department is committed to making sure officers carry out their duties in an ethical, professional manner.

Civil Liability Suits

Civil lawsuits against departments for police misconduct can increase civic accountability. Only recently has it been possible for citizens to sue public officials. In 1961, the U.S. Supreme Court ruled that Section 1983 of the Civil Rights Act of 1871 allows citizens to sue public officials for violations of their civil rights. This right was extended in 1978 when the Supreme Court ruled that individual officials and the agency may be sued when a person's civil rights are violated by the agency's "customs and usages." If an individual can show that harm was caused by employees whose wrongful acts were the result of these "customs, practices, and policies, including poor training and supervision," then he or she can sue (*Monell v. Department of Social Services for the City of New York*, 1978).

Lawsuits charging brutality, false arrest, and negligence are being brought in both state and federal courts. Damage awards in the millions of dollars have been granted in a number of states. For example, a Michigan court awarded $5.7 million to the heirs of a man who had been mistakenly shot by a Detroit officer, and Boston paid $500,000 to the parents of a teenager who was shot to death. The total amount paid by city governments in a year can be high. In 1997, for example, New York paid $27.3 million to settle 521 cases of police misconduct (*New York Times*, September 17, 1997:A33).

Civil liability rulings by the courts tend to be simple and severe: officials and municipalities are ordered to pay a sum of money, and that judgment can be enforced by the courts. With the potential for costly judgments, police departments have an incentive to improve the training and supervision of officers. Christopher E. Smith and John Hurst asked a sample of police executives to rank the policy issues most likely to be affected by civil liability decisions. The top-ranked issues were use of force, pursuit driving, and improper arrests (Smith and Hurst, 1996). Most departments have liability insurance, and many officers have their own insurance policies.

The courts have ruled that police work must follow generally accepted professional practices and standards. The potential for civil suits seems to have led to some changes in policy. For instance, a $2 million judgment won by Tracey Thurman against the Torrington, Connecticut, police had a profound impact (see the Close-Up, "Battered Women, Reluctant Police," in Chapter 4). Plaintiffs' victories in civil suits have spurred accreditation efforts because police executives believe that liability can be avoided or reduced if it can be shown their officers are meeting the highest professional standards. Insurance companies that provide civil liability protection now offer discounts to departments that are accredited.

CHECK POINT

⑯ **What are the four methods used to increase the civic accountability of the police?**

⑰ **What is an internal affairs unit?**

⑱ **Why are civilian review boards not more common?**

⑲ **What is the importance of the decision in *Monell v. Department of Social Services for the City of New York*?**

Private security is assuming an increasingly large role in American society. Tim Hitt, security guard at the Poughkeepsie (N.Y.) Galleria mall, says he patrols so as to provide a "certain level of calmness" in the shopping center.

Private Policing

Private policing is a new player in the quest for security. This is another trend that is changing the law enforcement landscape. Private policing existed in Europe and the United States before the formation of public police forces. Examples include Henry Fielding's Bow Street Runners in England and the bounty hunters of the American West. In the late nineteenth century, the Pinkerton National Detective Agency provided industrial spies and strikebreakers to thwart labor union activities, and Wells, Fargo and Company was formed to provide security for banks and other businesses.

In recent years, more and more firms have employed private security forces to deal with shoplifting, employee pilfering, robbery, and airplane hijacking. Today, retail and industrial firms spend nearly as much for private protection as all localities spend for police protection. Many private groups, such as residents of wealthy suburbs, have hired private police to patrol their neighborhoods.

Today, an estimated sixty thousand private agencies employ a total of 1.9 million people in security operations (Carlson, 1995:67). Each year an estimated $100 billion is spent on private security by businesses, organizations, and individuals. Private security companies now employ three times as many officers as all public police. Figure 6.3 compares this dramatic increase in private police to the numbers of public police.

The rise of private agencies has occurred for a number of reasons, including (1) an increase in crimes in the workplace, (2) an increase in fear (real or perceived) of crime, (3) the fiscal crises of the states, which have limited public protection, and (4) increased public and business awareness and use of more cost-effective private security services (Cunningham, Strauchs, and Van Meter, 1990:236).

6.3   Employment in private and public protection, 1970–2010 (projected)

The number of people employed by private security firms has surpassed the number employed by the public police and is growing. Such a large private force presents questions for the criminal justice system.

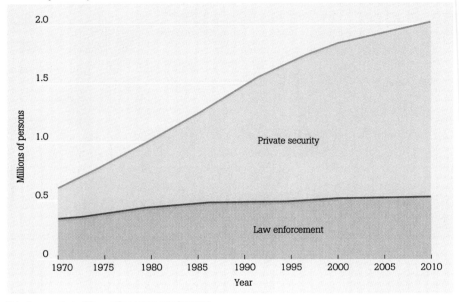

Private security and law enforcement employment

SOURCE: Adapted from William Cunningham, John Strauchs, and Clifford Van Meter, *Private Security: Patterns and Trends* (Washington, D.C.: National Institute of Justice, 1991), 3. Trend line projection to 2010 by the authors.

Functions of Private Police

The activities of private security personnel vary greatly: some act as guards and call the police at the first sign of trouble; others have the power to carry out patrol and investigative duties similar to those of police officers; and still others rely on their presence, and the ability to make a "citizen's arrest," to deter lawbreakers. In most cases, private persons are authorized by law to make an arrest only when a felony has been committed in their presence. Thus private security companies risk being held liable for false arrest and violation of civil rights.

Some states have passed laws that give civil immunity to store personnel who reasonably but mistakenly detain people suspected of shoplifting. More ambiguous is the search of the person or property of a suspect by a private guard. The suspect may resist the search and file a civil suit against the guard. If such a search yields evidence of a crime, the evidence may not be admitted in court. Yet the Supreme Court has not applied the *Miranda* ruling to private police. Federal law bars private individuals from engaging in wiretapping, and information so gathered cannot be entered as evidence at trial.

Security managers are willing to accept increased responsibility for minor criminal incidents that occur within their jurisdictions. They might perform such tasks as responding to burglar alarms, investigating misdemeanors, and carrying out preliminary investigations of other crimes. Law enforcement administrators indicated that they might be willing to transfer some of these tasks to private security firms. They cite a number of police tasks that are potentially more cost-effective if performed by private security, such as providing security in public buildings and enforcing parking regulations. In some parts of the country, these tasks are already being performed by personnel from private firms.

Private Employment of Public Police

Private firms are often eager to hire public police officers on a part-time basis. These officers retain their full powers and status as police personnel even when they work for a private firm while off duty. Although 20 percent of departments forbid "moonlighting," great numbers of police officers still work part time for private firms. While the use of off-duty officers expands the number and visibility of law enforcement officers, it also raises questions.

Conflict of Interest

Police officers must avoid any appearance of conflict of interest when they accept private employment. They are barred from jobs that conflict with their public duties. For example, they may not work as process servers, bill collectors, repossessors, or pre-employment investigators for private firms. They are also barred from working as investigators for criminal defense attorneys or as bail bondsmen. They may not work in places that profit from gambling, and many departments do not allow officers to work in bars or other places where regulated goods, such as alcohol, are sold. It is hard to know the full range of situations in which private employment of an officer might harm the image of the police or create a conflict with police responsibilities. Thus, departments need to be aware of new situations that might require that they refine their regulations for private employment of off-duty officers.

Management Prerogatives

Another issue concerns the impact of private employment on the capabilities of the local police department. Private employment cannot be allowed to tire officers and impair their ability to protect the public when they are on duty. Late-night duties as a private security officer, for example, may reduce an officer's ability to police effectively the next morning.

Departments require that officers request permission for outside work. Such permission may be denied for a number of reasons. Officers may not be allowed to perform work that lowers the dignity of the police, is too risky or dangerous, is not in the "home" jurisdiction, requires more than eight hours of off-duty service, or interferes with department schedules.

Several models have been designed to manage off-duty employment of officers. The *department contract model* permits close control of off-duty work, because firms must apply to the department to have officers assigned to them. Officers chosen for off-duty work are paid by the police department, which is reimbursed by the private firm, along with an overhead fee. Departments usually screen employers to make sure that the proposed use of officers will not conflict with the department's needs. When the private demand for police services exceeds the supply—and that is often the case—the department contract model provides a way of assigning staff so as to ensure that public needs are met.

The *officer contract model* allows each officer to find off-duty employment and to enter into a direct relationship with the private firm. Officers must apply to the department for permission, which is granted if the employment standards listed above are met. Problems may arise when an officer acts as an employment "agent" for fellow officers. This can lead to charges of favoritism and nepotism, with serious effects on discipline and morale.

In the *union brokerage model,* the police union or association finds off-duty employment for its members. The union sets the standards for the work and bargains with the department over pay, status, and conditions of the off-duty employment.

Each of these models has its backers. Albert Reiss notes another complication: the more closely a department controls off-duty employment, the more liability it assumes for officers' actions when they work for private firms (Reiss, 1988).

What is not known is the impact of uniformed off-duty patrol on crime prevention and the public's perception of safety. Public fears may be reduced because of the greater visibility of officers who citizens believe to be acting in their official capacity.

The Public–Private Interface

The relationship between public and private law enforcement is a concern for police officials. Private agents work for the people who employ them, and their goals may not always serve the public interest. Questions have been raised about the power of private security agents to make arrests, conduct searches, and take part in undercover investigations. A key issue is the boundary between the work of the police and that of private agencies. Lack of coordination and communication between public and private agencies has led to botched investigations, destruction of evidence, and overzealousness.

Growing awareness of this problem has led to efforts to have private security agents work more closely with the police. However, many security managers in private firms tend to treat crimes by employees as internal matters that do not concern the police. They report *Uniform Crime Reports* index crimes to the police, but employee theft, insurance fraud, industrial espionage, commercial bribery, and computer crime tend not to be reported to public authorities. In such cases the chief concern of private firms is to prevent losses and protect assets. Although some such incidents are reported, most are resolved through internal procedures ("private justice"). When such crimes are discovered, the offender may be "convicted" and punished within the firm by forced restitution, loss of the job, and the spreading of information about the incident throughout the industry.

Private firms often bypass the criminal justice system so they do not have to deal with prosecution policies, administrative delays, rules that would open the firms' internal affairs to public scrutiny, and bad publicity. Thus, the question arises: To what extent does a parallel system of private justice exist with regard to some offenders and some crimes (Davis, Lundman, and Martinez, 1991)?

Recruitment and Training

A major concern of law enforcement officials and civil libertarians is the recruitment and training of private security personnel. Studies have shown that such personnel often have little education and training; because the pay is low, the work often attracts people who cannot find other jobs or who seek temporary work. This portrait has been challenged by William Walsh, who argues that differences between private and public police are not that striking (Walsh, 1989).

The growth of private policing has brought calls for the screening and licensing of its personnel. Less than half of the states have such requirements. Several national organizations, such as the National Council on Crime and Delinquency, have offered model licensing statutes that specify periods of training and orientation, uniforms that permit citizens to distinguish between public and private police, and a ban on employment of persons with criminal records. In some states, security firms are licensed by the attorney general, while in others this is done by the local police. In general, however, such firms are subject to little regulation. The regulations that do exist tend to focus on contractual, as opposed to proprietary, private policing. Contractual security services are provided for a fee by locksmiths, alarm specialists, polygraph examiners, and firms such as Brink's, Burns, and Wackenhut, which provide guards and detectives. States and cities often require contract personnel to be licensed and bonded. Similar services are sometimes provided by *proprietary security* personnel, who are employed directly by the organization they protect—for example, retail stores, industrial plants, and hospitals. Except for those who carry weapons, proprietary security personnel are not regulated by the state or city.

Private policing has grown in response to a perceived need. The need may stem from the higher crime rates, but it may also come from a belief that the police cannot effectively carry out certain tasks. It is important to distinguish between public and private policing and to ensure that private policing does not hamper the work of law enforcement or create new problems by recruiting unqualified personnel, misusing off-duty police officers, or failing to communicate with police departments.

CHECK POINT

⑳ What are some early examples of private policing in the United States?

㉑ What is the significance of the growth of private policing?

㉒ When may a private person make an arrest?

㉓ What are the three models for private employment of police officers?

㉔ What are the differences between contractual and proprietary private policing services?

Summary

- To meet current and future challenges, the police must recruit and train individuals who will uphold the law and receive citizen support.
- Improvements have been made during the past quarter-century in recruiting more officers who are women, racial and ethnic minorities, and well-educated applicants.
- The police work in an environment greatly influenced by their subculture.
- The concept of the working personality helps explain the influence of the police subculture on how individual officers see their world.
- The isolation of the police strengthens bonds among officers but may also add to job stress.
- For the police to be effective they must maintain their connection with the community.

- Policing in a multicultural society requires an appreciation of the attitudes, customs, and languages of minority-group members.
- The problems of police misuse of force and corruption cause erosions of community support.
- Internal affairs units, civilian review boards, standards and accreditation, and civil liability suits are four approaches designed to increase police accountability to citizens.
- The expansion of private policing adds a new dimension to how order is maintained and laws are enforced.

Questions for Review

1. How do recruitment and training practices affect policing?
2. What is meant by the police subculture, and how does it influence an officer's work?
3. What factors in the police officer's "working personality" influence an officer's work?
4. What are the pros and cons of the major approaches to making the police accountable to citizens?
5. What has the Supreme Court ruled regarding police use of deadly force?
6. What are the problems associated with private policing?

Key Terms and Cases

internal affairs unit (p. 227)
socialization (p. 206)
subculture (p. 209)
working personality (p. 209)
Tennessee v. Garner (1985) (p. 222)

For Further Reading

Murano, Vincent. *Cop Hunter.* New York: Simon and Schuster, 1990. The story of an undercover cop who for ten years worked for the Internal Affairs Division of the New York City Police Department. Emphasizes the moral dilemmas of policing fellow officers.

Reiss, Albert J., Jr. *The Police and the Public.* New Haven, Conn.: Yale University Press, 1971. A classic study of the relationship of police officers to the public they serve.

Shearing, Clifford, and Philip C. Stenning, eds. *Private Policing.* Newbury Park, Calif.: Sage Publications, 1987. An excellent volume that explores various aspects of the private security industry.

Skolnick, Jerome H., and James J. Fyfe. *Above the Law: Police and the Excessive Use of Force.* New York: Free Press, 1993. Written in light of the Rodney King beating and the riots that followed. The authors believe that only by recruiting and supporting police chiefs who will uphold a policy of strict accountability can brutality be eliminated.

Going Online

❶ **Using InfoTrac College Edition**, access the article "Improving Deadly Force Decision Making" by Dean T. Olson in *FBI Law Enforcement Bulletin* (February 1998). The subject words are *police use of force*. What are the key elements of the deadly force triangle? How do they improve deadly force decision making?

❷ Access the web site of the Commission on Accreditation for Law Enforcement Agencies (CALEA) at www.calea.org. Using information presented on the web site, write a short paper on the history of CALEA noting the major accomplishments over the last twenty years.

❸ Review the career opportunities in the private security field by accessing the web site www.wackenhut.com. For what types of positions are you qualified? What training is given on the job? Is there a job opening in an area where you would like to live?

CHECK POINT ANSWERS

❶ High school diploma, good physical condition, absence of a criminal record.

❷ Preservice training, usually in a police academy.

❸ On the job.

❹ Better educated, more women and minority officers.

❺ Danger, authority.

❻ External stress, organizational stress, personal stress, operational stress.

❼ Stereotyping, cultural differences, language differences.

❽ Young, low-income, racial-minority males.

❾ Permissive law enforcement and police abuse of power.

❿ Assist the police by reporting incidents and providing information.

⓫ Profanity, abusive language, physical force, violence.

⓬ The police may use force if necessary to make an arrest, to keep the peace, or to maintain public order.

⓭ Deadly force may not be used in apprehending a fleeing felon unless it is necessary to prevent the escape and unless the officer has probable cause to believe that the suspect poses a significant threat of death or serious physical injury to the officer or to others.

⓮ Grass eaters are officers who accept payoffs that police work brings their way. Meat eaters are officers who aggressively misuse their power for personal gain.

⓯ Mooching, bribery, chiseling, extortion, shopping, shakedown, premeditated theft, favoritism, perjury, prejudice.

⓰ Internal affairs units, civilian review boards, standards and accreditation, civil liability suits.

⓱ A unit within the police department designated to receive and investigate complaints against officers alleging violation of rules and policies.

⓲ Opposition by the police.

⓳ Allows citizens to sue individual officers and the agency when an individual's civil rights are violated by the agency's "customs and usages."

⓴ Bounty hunters in the West; Pinkerton National Detective Agency; Wells Fargo and Company.

㉑ Public concern for order.

㉒ When a felony has been committed in his or her presence.

㉓ Department contract model, officer contract model, union brokerage model.

㉔ Contractual services are provided for a fee by private practitioners, such as locksmiths, alarm specialists, and organizations such as Brink's. Proprietary services are employed directly by the organizations, such as retail stores and industries, that they protect.

Should the Police Aggressively Enforce Public Order Offenses?

In "Broken Windows: The Police and Neighborhood Safety," James Q. Wilson and George L. Kelling argue that disorderly behavior that is unregulated and unchecked is a signal to residents that the area is unsafe (Wilson and Kelling, 1982:21). Disorder makes residents become fearful. They then stay off the streets, avoid certain areas, and withdraw to their homes. This retreat of fearful citizens undermines the fabric of urban life, increasing a neighborhood's vulnerability to an influx of disorderly behavior, serious crime, and urban decay.

Wilson and Kelling urge the police and the community to pay attention to public order offenses: aggressive panhandling, public drunkenness, soliciting by prostitutes, urinating in public, rowdiness, and blocking of sidewalks. These "little crimes," they say, can lead to more serious offenses. They believe the police must deal with public order offenses in an aggressive, proactive manner to prevent crime.

The connection between disorderly behavior, fear, and crime has long been recognized. Research has shown that (1) residents of a community generally agree on what constitutes disorder; (2) high levels of disorder are linked to high levels of crime, no matter how poor a community is, what its racial mix is, or how economically unstable the times are; and (3) disorder plays an important role in community decline, as fearful residents move, property values drop, and businesses close (Biderman, Johnson, McIntyre, and Weit, 1967; Skogan, 1990).

These links have been largely ignored until recently. Researchers, policy makers, and the police have instead been focusing on "serious crime," primarily the *Uniform Crime Reports* index offenses of murder, rape, robbery, assault, and burglary. The professional crime-fighter role that has dominated policing in America since the 1920s has meant that the order maintenance and service functions have been considered less important.

But the rise of the community policing movement has brought a shift in many cities to more targeting of public order offenses. Patrol officers assigned to "walk the beat" become acquainted with their neighborhoods, learn about local problems, and become known to residents. Officers also are able to use their discretion to establish informal rules defining what is accepted behavior in a particular neighborhood. They then enforce these rules by telling violators to stop, ordering panhandlers to move along, or making arrests.

How have the police responded to the findings that suggest they should shift to an order maintenance role? Many police executives are skeptical. They argue that the public expects them to control serious crime. They fear that law enforcement would get less political support, and therefore fewer resources, with a shift of emphasis to "little crimes." Police officers say they joined the police to fight crime, not to "do social work."

Although most departments have continued to emphasize the crime-fighting role, some—for example, Baltimore, New York City, San Francisco, and Seattle—are giving greater attention to enforcement of public order offenses to improve the quality of life in their communities. But to be effective, this focus requires the combined efforts of neighborhood groups, citizens, public officials, businesses, and the police. Community crime-fighting initiatives can reduce disorderly behavior, fear, and urban decay. And the lives of citizens are improved.

For Aggressively Enforcing Public Order Offenses

Supporters of a new focus on public order offenses argue that dealing with these "little crimes" is necessary to reduce residents' fears and prevent more serious crimes. Research has shown, they say, that preventive patrol in squad cars, rapid response, and centralized decision making isolate officers from the community. The use of community policing to deal effectively with public order offenses is a better way to control crime and make urban areas more livable. Through aggressive foot patrol, order can be restored and maintained.

To summarize arguments for aggressively enforcing public order offenses:

- Enforcing public order offenses reduces residents' fear, serious crime, and urban decay.
- When the police deal with low-level offenders, they learn about and are put in contact with those who have committed serious offenses.
- The police have a duty to improve the quality of life so residents do not have to deal with "street people" who impede pedestrian traffic and aggressively panhandle.
- Officers walking through a neighborhood become familiar with the residents and will gain their cooperation and assistance when serious crime erupts.
- Police action on public order offenses encourages citizens to uphold neighborhood standards for behavior in public spaces.

Against Aggressively Enforcing Public Order Offenses

Enforcing the law and improving the quality of urban life may seem to be positive goals for any community; however, opinion is divided on this shift in policy. Some police officers say they have enough to do just dealing with the "bad guys," and they should not divert resources to lesser offenses. Many doubt that disorder and fear are linked to serious crime. Civil libertarians and advocates for the homeless have opposed many attempts to enforce laws against people's using public areas to panhandle, sell goods, and sleep. They say the new policies targeting public order offenses are designed to harass the poor, the homeless, and the mentally ill—the people society has pushed into the streets. They also emphasize that some officers misuse force in enforcing these policies.

To summarize the arguments against aggressive enforcement of public order offenses:

- Police resources and tactics should be focused on fighting serious crime.
- The link between disorder, fear, and crime is uncertain and requires further research.
- Aggressive police tactics against people using public spaces are attacks upon the poor. Resources could be better spent on helping the poor, the mentally ill, the homeless, and other social outcasts.
- The civil liberties of the poor are infringed when the police aggressively enforce public order offenses.

What Should U.S. Policy Be?

How would the American people react if greater police resources were allocated to deal with public order offenses? Some researchers have argued that by aggressively dealing with disorder, the police reduce residents' fear and prevent more serious crimes. They believe that ignoring these issues sends a community on a downward spiral that ends in serious crime and urban decay. However, others see this new emphasis as targeting primarily the weak—the poor and the outcasts of society. Civil liberties are trampled in the process.

Courts

In a democracy, the arrest of a person is only the first part of a complex process designed to separate the guilty from the innocent. Part Three examines the process by which guilt is determined in accordance with the law's requirements, as well as the processes and underlying philosophies of

the punishment that further separates the convicted from the acquitted. Here we look at the work of prosecutors, defense attorneys, bondsmen, probation officers, and judges to understand the contribution each makes toward the ultimate decisions. In the adjudicatory stage, the goals of an administrative system blunt the force of the adversarial process prescribed by law. Although courtroom activities get more attention in the media, much of the action does not occur in court. Most decisions relating to the disposition of a case are made in less public surroundings. And after the sentencing, the case recedes even further from the public eye. After studying these chapters, think about whether justice is served by processes that are more like bargaining than like the adversarial combat between two lawyers that is expected. Also consider whether the punishments American courts hand out are doing the job they are supposed to do in punishing offenders.

Court

Behind the U.S. Capitol in Washington, D.C., stands an impressive marble building.

Sixteen columns, each nearly fifty feet tall, support the span upon which are carved the

words, "Equal Justice Under Law." At the entrance are brass doors, twenty feet high and

weighing more than six tons, which are decorated with scenes from ancient Greece and

Rome. This grand building is a court, the workplace of the nine justices of the U.S. Supreme

Court. Although the Supreme Court's marble temple fits the image of the grand surroundings

in which judges meet to decide legal cases, many courts are less awe-inspiring.

Far from Washington in a Midwestern city, a black-robed judge sits at a table in a confer-

ence room in a municipal office building. This, too, is a court. Even without the marble

columns, bronze doors, and high ceilings, this modest setting produces rulings that decide

the fates of people who have been drawn into the legal system. Elsewhere, an off-duty fire-

fighter, teacher, or accountant may face citizens across a card table in a room at the town hall.

Another court? Yes, American courts can meet in many kinds of locations under the direction of judges ranging from the legal scholars on the U.S. Supreme Court to neighbors elected to the office of part-time justice of the peace.

The word *court* means the place where legal cases are processed and decided. Basic principles of American law are applied in each setting, although each courtroom may look different.

Just as there are many possible court settings, there are many kinds of courts. The number and variety of courts in the United States can be bewildering to someone who wants to know how the criminal justice system functions. One way to sort out the different kinds of courts is to recognize that courts have differing responsibilities. For example, neither the part-time justice of the peace nor the U.S. Supreme Court justice conducts trials in serious criminal cases. The lowest courts handle traffic violations and petty offenses, while the highest courts handle appeals of rulings of other courts.

To understand how courts decide criminal cases, a picture of the entire court system must be rendered. How are courts organized? What are the responsibilities of each kind of court? After answering these questions, the courts that handle criminal cases should be examined to see how guilt is determined and sentences imposed.

As the design and operation of American courts are discussed, notice the role of judges in handling criminal cases. Judges do not work by themselves. They rely on prosecutors, defense attorneys, court clerks, and others. No single person decides what will happen to defendants.

Because courts are a central part of a larger criminal justice system, such factors as discretion and exchange relations, discussed in earlier chapters, are important for the work of courts, just as they are for police, corrections, and other parts of the system. As you read about courts and their operations, imagine how you would act and what decisions you would make if you were a judge or a prosecutor or a defense attorney. As you look at each aspect of court design and operations, ask yourself: is this a system that can achieve justice?

QUESTIONS

- What is the structure of the American court system?
- What are some of the management problems of trial courts?
- What qualities are desired in a judge, and how are judges chosen?
- What is the courtroom workgroup, and how does this concept help explain court actions?

 # The Structure of American Courts

The United States has a dual court system. Separate federal and state court systems handle matters from throughout the nation. Other countries have a single national court system, but American rules and traditions permit states to create their own court systems to handle most legal matters, including most crimes.

Frequently, state and federal courts sit virtually side-by-side in American cities. Each court has authority to handle matters that arise within that state, but each has responsibility over different kinds of legal cases. The federal courts oversee a limited range of criminal cases. For example, they deal with people accused of violating the criminal laws of the national government. Counterfeiting, kidnapping, smuggling, and drug trafficking are examples of federal crimes. But such cases account for only a small portion of the criminal cases that pass through American courts each year. For every felony conviction in federal courts, there are twenty-two felony convictions in state courts, because most crimes are defined by state laws (BJS, 1998g). The gap is even greater for misdemeanors because state courts bear primary responsibility for processing the lesser offenses, such as disorderly conduct, that arise on a daily basis. State supreme courts monitor the decisions of lower courts within their own states by interpreting state constitutions and statutes. The U.S. Supreme Court oversees both court systems by interpreting the U.S. Constitution, which protects the rights of defendants in federal and state criminal cases.

A third court system operates in several states, which adds to the complexity and coordination issues that face the country's decentralized courts. Native Americans have tribal courts, whose authority is endorsed by congressional statutes and Supreme Court decisions, with jurisdiction over their own people on tribal land. The existence of tribal courts permits Native American judges to apply their people's cultural values in resolving civil lawsuits and processing certain criminal offenses (Vicenti, 1995). Although tribal courts have jurisdiction over misdemeanors committed by Native Americans on tribal land, federal courts typically have jurisdiction over many felonies and crimes committed on tribal land involving non-Native Americans as defendants or victims. Tribal courts must work with state and federal officials to ensure that laws are enforced. However, because federal courts are often located many miles from Native American lands, there are complaints that federal court officials do not vigorously prosecute crimes committed by outsiders against Native Americans on tribal lands (Reno, 1995).

Both the federal and state court systems have trial and appellate courts. Cases begin in a trial court. In some states, the lower trial courts handle minor matters and traffic offenses, while upper trial courts handle felony cases and lawsuits. In other states, a single trial court handles all legal matters. After a guilty plea is entered or a guilty verdict is rendered in criminal cases, defendants may appeal the decision. Then a higher state or federal court, usually called a court of appeals, may review the case for errors. Further appeals may be filed with a state supreme court or the U.S. Supreme Court, depending on which court system the case is in and what kind of legal argument is being made.

American trial courts are highly decentralized. To be close to the people and responsive to their values, courts operate in local communities. Local judges not only decide the cases that pass through the courts, but also administer the court by hiring staff and developing local ties. Thus local political influences and community values are brought to bear on the courts: local officials determine their resources, residents make up the staff, and operations are managed so as to fit community needs. Only in a few small states is the court system organized on a statewide basis, with a central administration and state funding. In most of the country, the criminal courts operate under the state penal code but are staffed, managed, and financed by county or city government. The federal courts, by contrast, have central administration and funding, although judges in each district help to shape their own courts' practices and procedures.

CHECK POINT

① **What is the dual court system?**

② **What does it mean for courts to be decentralized?**

(Answers are at the end of the chapter.)

Federal Courts

The federal court system is shown on the left side of Figure 7.1 as a hierarchy, with the district courts at the bottom, the circuit courts of appeals above them, and the Supreme Court at the top. The United States is divided into ninety-four districts, each containing a *United States District Court.* District courts are found throughout the country, with at least one in each state, one in the District of Columbia, and four in the U.S. territories. Many districts have more than one federal courthouse and more than a dozen judges. For example, the U.S. District Court for the Eastern District of Michigan has courthouses in Ann Arbor, Bay City, Detroit, and Flint. These trial courts are the courts of original jurisdiction, where federal cases are first heard. Cases arising under federal law begin in district courts. These courts make the first decisions in each case, either through settlements (in civil cases), plea bargains (in criminal cases), or trials (in civil and criminal cases).

After decisions are reached in the U.S. District Courts, cases may be appealed to a *United States Circuit Court of Appeals.* Each of the eleven U.S. Circuit Courts of Appeals has jurisdiction over a portion of the country consisting of neighboring states. For example, the U.S. Court of Appeals for the Fifth Circuit handles federal

The Supreme Court of the United States has the final word on questions concerning interpretations of the Constitution.

FIGURE 7.1 The dual court system of the United States and routes of appeal

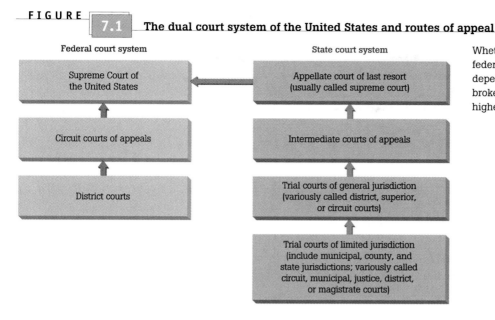

Federal court system

State court system

Supreme Court of the United States

Appellate court of last resort (usually called supreme court)

Circuit courts of appeals

Intermediate courts of appeals

District courts

Trial courts of general jurisdiction (variously called district, superior, or circuit courts)

Trial courts of limited jurisdiction (include municipal, county, and state jurisdictions; variously called circuit, municipal, justice, district, or magistrate courts)

Whether a case enters through the federal or the state court system depends on which law has been broken. The right of appeal to a higher court exists in either system.

appeals that arise from district court rulings in Louisiana, Mississippi, and Texas, while the Seventh Circuit covers Illinois, Indiana, and Wisconsin. The twelfth court, called the District of Columbia Circuit, handles appeals from the nation's capital and those that involve the federal government. Although the number of judges assigned to each circuit court can range from a half-dozen to nearly thirty, these courts can hear many cases at a time by forming three-judge panels. Thus, fifteen judges in the Sixth Circuit covering Kentucky, Michigan, Ohio, and Tennessee can hear five cases at once with three judges working as a team in each courtroom in a federal courthouse in Cincinnati.

The *United States Supreme Court* sits atop the federal court system and hears cases in Washington, D.C. The main task of the nation's highest court is to hear appeals from decisions by the U.S. Circuit Courts of Appeals, as well as those by state supreme courts for cases that raise issues concerning the U.S. Constitution. Like other federal judges, the Supreme Court's nine justices are appointed by the president and confirmed by a vote of the U.S. Senate (Maltese, 1998). They may stay in office for life, unless they commit crimes or other serious misconduct, in which case Congress may remove them by impeachment.

As the nation's highest court, the Supreme Court has the power to select which cases it will hear. The justices generally choose to hear cases that will have a broad, national impact or will resolve disputes among district and circuit judges about interpretations of the Constitution and federal statutes. The vast majority of cases filed in the Supreme Court are rejected. In the 1998–1999 term, for example, nearly seven thousand cases were filed in the Supreme Court, but the justices held oral arguments and issued full written opinions in only seventy-five cases (Greenhouse, 1999). Among these seventy-five cases, only twenty-two concerned criminal justice issues. Twelve of these criminal law decisions involved rights under the U.S. Constitution and ten focused on interpreting federal criminal statutes enacted by Congress (Smith, 2000).

CHECK POINT

③ **What kinds of cases are heard by the U.S. Supreme Court?**

State Courts

In the past the basic structure and organization of American state courts were designed to ensure that the courts would be responsive to the local community. Legislatures created court systems that were decentralized, linked to the local political system, and dependent for resources on the other branches of government. Judges, for example, were selected from the community, and their decisions reflected local values.

The growth of commerce and population during the nineteenth century produced new types of disputes for courts to handle. States and localities responded by creating new courts with specific **jurisdictions.** Small claims courts, juvenile courts, and family relations courts were added in many states. In most states these changes produced a confusing structure of courts with varying jurisdictions and overlapping duties. Court procedures could differ from one county to the next within the same state.

There are three levels of state courts: **appellate courts, trial courts of general jurisdiction,** and **trial courts of limited jurisdiction.** Among the appellate courts, all states have courts of last resort (usually called state supreme courts) and all but a few have an intermediate level (state courts of appeals). Although the basic, three-tier structure is found throughout the United States, the number of courts, their names, and their specific functions vary widely. Some states have reformed their court systems by simplifying the number and types of courts, while others still have a confusing assortment of lower courts. Figure 7.2 contrasts the court structure of Alaska, a reformed state, with that of Georgia, where the court structure has not been reformed. Both follow the three-tier model, but Georgia has more courts and a more complex system—and potential confusion—for determining which court will handle which kind of case.

In criminal cases, the thirteen thousand trial courts of *limited jurisdiction,* often called the "inferior" or "lower" trial courts, process cases concerning minor offenses and also decide preliminary matters in more serious cases. In these courts, the formal charges may be read to the defendant and a preliminary plea entered. These courts may also hold preliminary hearings to decide whether enough evidence has been gathered to send a felony case to a higher trial court. For minor offenses, the court's jurisdiction is based on the maximum sentence that may be imposed. In most states a maximum fine of $1,000 and up to twelve

jurisdiction
The geographic territory or legal boundaries within which control may be exercised; the range of a court's authority.

appellate courts
Courts that do not try criminal cases but hear appeals of decisions of lower courts.

trial courts of general jurisdiction
Criminal courts with jurisdiction over all offenses, including felonies. In some states these courts may also hear appeals.

trial courts of limited jurisdiction
Criminal courts with trial jurisdiction over misdemeanor cases and preliminary matters in felony cases. Sometimes these courts hold felony trials that may result in penalties below a specified limit.

FIGURE 7.2   Court structures of Alaska (reformed) and Georgia (unreformed)

Reformers have called upon states to reduce the number of courts, standardize their names, and clarify their jurisdictions.

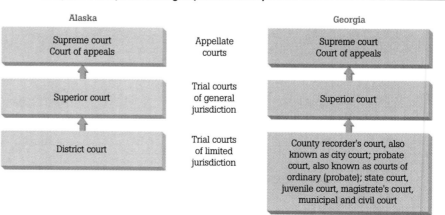

SOURCE: National Center for State Courts, *State Court Caseload Statistics: Annual Report* (Williamsburg, Va.: National Center for State Courts, 1989), 185, 194.

months in jail is the greatest penalty these courts may impose. About 90 percent of all criminal cases pass through these lower courts. In most places, such courts are organized and funded by county government, yet they operate under state law.

These courts do not always display the dignity and formal procedures of higher courts. They are not necessarily courts of record where a detailed account of proceedings is kept. Instead, they may function in an informal manner. In most urban areas, seemingly endless numbers of people are processed by these courts, and each defendant's "day in court" usually lasts only a few minutes. Americans expect their local courts to adhere to the standards that reflect democratic values of justice. Many are critical when the courts do not meet these ideals (see What Americans Think).

State laws give the *trial courts of general jurisdiction* the power to try all cases, both civil and criminal. With regard to criminal cases, they are often called felony courts. They are courts of record in that the proceedings are recorded, and they follow formal procedures specified by law. Although each county often has a separate felony court, these courts are organized and funded by the state.

The *appellate courts* do not hear evidence or decide defendants' guilt. Instead, they hear only appeals from the lower courts. These appeals focus on issues of law or procedure, such as claims that a police officer, prosecutor, or judge made an error during investigation, prosecution, or trial. In a dozen states only the state supreme court—an appellate court of last resort—is found at this level; in all other states, an intermediate court of appeals can be found as well.

Intermediate appellate courts (IACs) have become more common in the last thirty years. These courts are designed to receive all appeals from the trial courts so that the state supreme court (the court of last resort) can save its attention for a small number of select appeals that have broad implications for law and policy. Although the IAC's rulings may be reviewed by the state supreme court, they are final for most cases because so few are chosen for subsequent review (Chapper and Hanson, 1990).

State supreme courts normally sit *en banc* (as a whole), with all justices taking part in each case. Most of these courts have either five or seven justices. By contrast, IACs, which may have twenty or more judges, are usually divided into panels of three judges so the court can handle more cases simultaneously.

What Americans Think

Americans' views about courts in their community on equality and fairness issues

Question "Do you think each of the following is a problem or not?"

Percentage responding "It is a problem"

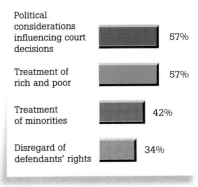

Political considerations influencing court decisions	57%
Treatment of rich and poor	57%
Treatment of minorities	42%
Disregard of defendants' rights	34%

SOURCE: Laura B. Myers, "Bringing the Offender to Heal: Views of the Criminal Courts," in *Americans View Crime and Justice*, ed. Timothy J. Flanagan and Dennis R. Longmire (Thousand Oaks, Calif.: Sage Publications, 1996), 52.

CHECK POINT

④ How do state trial courts of limited jurisdiction differ from state trial courts of general jurisdiction?

⑤ How do state courts of last resort differ from intermediate appellate courts?

Effective Management of the State Courts

Throughout the twentieth century, efforts have been made to reform the structure, administration, and financing of the state courts so they can deal more effectively with their huge caseloads. Concerns about effective judicial administration can be traced to a famous speech delivered in 1906 by Roscoe Pound, who was dean of Harvard Law School and one of the nation's greatest legal scholars.

Pound's speech focused on the organizational problems in the judicial system. Pound argued that there were too many courts, which caused duplication and inefficiency, and that there was a great waste of judicial power, because of rigid jurisdictional boundaries, poor use of resources, and frequent granting of new trials (Wigmore, 1937).

Although reformers still point to various problems in courts, such as lack of resources and the uneven quality of both elected and politically appointed judges, the fragmented structure of state courts is often viewed as the biggest barrier to effective justice. Proposed solutions include the creation of a unified court system with four goals:

❶ Eliminating overlapping and conflicting jurisdictional boundaries.

❷ Creating a hierarchical and centralized court structure with administrative responsibility held by a chief justice and a court of last resort.

❸ Having the courts funded by state government instead of local counties and cities.

❹ Creating a separate civil service personnel system run by a state court administrator.

These goals are at the forefront of the movement to make the state courts more efficient and able to dispense justice more effectively.

Court Structure

At the heart of reform efforts is the desire to consolidate and simplify court structures. A simple court structure is appealing because it creates an impression of efficiency and clarity of purpose. However, changing court structures is not always easy. Decentralized courts may become enduring components of the local political system. People from the community serve as the judges, bailiffs, clerks, and other court personnel. Their close ties to the community give citizens a sense of access to and influence over the operations of the courts. Any movement toward centralization can alter local political connections and influences. Fewer local lawyers may become judges in a reformed system, and they may in turn hire fewer local political supporters as court personnel. Thus structural changes that look good on paper may meet resistance when reformers try to carry them out.

Centralization of Administration

Who should run the courts? In the past judges have been in charge of their own courthouses (Wice, 1995). While judges may enjoy having the power to oversee all aspects of court operations, they do not always have the skills needed to manage well. Law school trains lawyers and judges to understand law, but it does not give them knowledge about the management, budget, and personnel issues that arise in running courts. Because judges focus attention on their own courthouses, no central authority may exist to monitor political events that affect the statewide court system. Thus, in decentralized court systems, no overall authority ensures continuity in procedures, provides supervision, or protects the judiciary from budget cuts or hiring limitations imposed by the legislative and executive branches.

Because state court systems have grown and become more complex, new kinds of issues and problems affect their day-to-day administration. Some person or committee must handle matters such as assignment of judges and cases, record keeping, personnel, and financing. Those who favor a unified court system argue that either the state supreme court or its chief justice should be given the power to assign judges, set rules, and decide on procedures for the system as a whole.

State Funding

Control of funds is a key source of power in any organization. People who are aware of the needs and operations of courts are in the best position to decide how money should be spent. However, because state courts have been funded by county government, their financial resources and freedom to make budget decisions have varied widely, even within the same state. Reformers insist that state government should fund all courts and that a state court administrator, under the direction of the chief justice, should prepare a budget for the whole system. Such a centralized system would ensure that the courts have adequate funds and that those funds are distributed fairly and used wisely.

In a study of judicial funding, Marcia Lim (1987) found that, while the state share of funding varied from 13 to 100 percent, the court systems of only twenty-one states received substantial or full support of their budget from the state. Sixty-two percent of funds for the judiciary come from county government and only 38 percent from state governments. Even more striking is that the larger a state's population, the lower the portion of court funds that come from the state government.

The past few years have seen a slow but significant move toward increased funding by a number of states. Because court costs have been rising along with the number of lawsuits filed, local political leaders seem more willing to let the state fund and manage the judiciary.

Separate Court Personnel System

Local political parties and judges often retain a great deal of influence over courts by using court jobs to reward campaign workers and other supporters. Without a separate civil service system for judicial employees, an effective statewide, unified court system cannot exist because the courts are beholden to local political leaders. To remedy that situation, the American Bar Association (ABA) in 1974 proposed a system of position classification, levels of compensation, and procedures for personnel evaluation. By seeking to standardize and professionalize the hiring and evaluation of judicial employees, reformers hope to increase the effectiveness and efficiency of court operations.

Toward Unified Court Systems

In recent years, problems in the administration of justice have drawn much attention from state and federal governments. Increases in certain kinds of crime, especially drug cases, and the huge caseloads of the courts have led to greater funding as a means of improving the administration of justice. Judicial spending in the states more than doubled during the past fifteen years. In addition, some populous states have moved toward a unified court system, and employment in state and local courts has grown.

Although many approve of these changes, questions are being raised about the basic assumptions of the unified court system model. Perhaps centralized management of state court systems will not automatically lead to greater efficiency and effectiveness. A tidy organization chart does not necessarily reflect how the courts really work. The interactions of the major players—judge, prosecutor, defense attorney, clerk, and bailiff—must be examined to see how the court functions. Only by gaining a clear picture of how courts work can an evaluation be made of whether proposed reforms are likely to improve court operations and the quality of justice (Flango, 1994a).

CHECK POINT

⑥ **What are the main goals of advocates of judicial reform?**

To Be a Judge

People tend to see judges as the most powerful actors in the criminal justice process. Their rulings and sentencing decisions influence the actions of police, defense attorneys, and prosecutors. If judges treat certain crimes lightly, for example, police and prosecutors may be less inclined to arrest and prosecute people who commit those offenses. Although judges are thought of primarily in connection with trials, some of their work—signing warrants, setting bail, arraigning defendants, accepting guilty pleas, scheduling cases—is done outside the formal trial process.

More than any other person in the system, the judge is expected to embody justice, ensuring that the right to due process is upheld and that the defendant is treated fairly. The prosecutor and the defense attorney each represent a "side" in a criminal case. By contrast, the judge's black robe and gavel are symbols of impartiality. Both within and outside the courthouse the judge is supposed to act according to a well-defined role. Judges are expected to make careful, consistent decisions that uphold the ideal of equal justice for all citizens. However, the neutrality of the judiciary cannot always be taken for granted in the United States. For example, prior to the 1970s, when state policies and practices discriminated against African Americans, many judges' decisions clearly showed their commitment to prejudice and discrimination (Friedman, 1993). Although openly biased practices may still occur (Kennedy, 1997), they are relatively rare in American courts today. However, certain factors continue to influence the work of judges and prevent them from making careful, impartial decisions in each case. For example, the need to handle a heavy flow of cases may force them to emphasize quick, efficient disposal of cases. They may lack the time to ensure that they can make consistent, thoughtful, and fair decisions in each case.

The traditional image of the courtroom stresses the individuality, aloofness, and loneliness of the black-robed judge, who sits above the courtroom battle and makes sure that the trial produces a just and fair result. While lawyers and jurors are concerned mainly with fact finding, judges function as lawgivers. They interpret laws, including legislative statutes and decisions in prior cases, and apply their interpretations to the specific circumstances of each case. Judges are expected to be isolated from the other participants in the trial and

Like all judges, the Honorable Sandra Townes, Syracuse City Court, is expected to "embody justice," ensuring that the right to due process is respected and that defendants are treated fairly.

to base their decisions on their own interpretation of the law after thoughtful consideration of the issues.

The image and role of judges are shaped by an adherence to an **adversary system** of justice. Under the American system, each side—the prosecution and defense—is represented by an attorney who is obligated to provide vigorous advocacy. Within the rules of court procedure, each side presents evidence and makes arguments to convince the judge and jury of the defendant's guilt (prosecutor) or the lack of sufficient evidence to prove guilt beyond a reasonable doubt (defense attorney). Ideally, the clash of skilled advocates will provide the court with complete information from which the truth will emerge. Thus the judge serves as a kind of "referee" who is responsible for ensuring that each attorney's presentation of evidence and arguments does not violate any court rules by presenting excessively biased or otherwise improper information.

The ideal of the adversary system depends on the attorneys in each case making the best possible presentation for the opposing sides. Unfortunately, prosecutors and defense attorneys who face each other in court do not always have equal skill, knowledge, and experience. Moreover, prosecutors often enjoy advantages from using the police to gather evidence on their behalf while defense attorneys, especially those appointed to represent poor defendants, often lack the resources to obtain all of the available evidence that might support the defendant. In addition, sometimes questions arise about whether defense attorneys are fully committed to advancing their clients' best interests.

Many other countries employ an alternative role for judges, which may avoid some of the problems presented by weaknesses in the adversary system. Under the **inquisitorial system,** the judge is an active participant in the case. In France, for example, a special judge—the examining magistrate—is responsible for investigating criminal cases. This judge submits a report to the chief trial judge who asks or approves all questions of witnesses and also questions the defendant in open court. At the conclusion of the trial, the chief judge and two associate judges join nine citizen-jurors in determining guilt and the sentence. Prior to the judges and jurors voting by secret ballot on the defendant's fate, the chief judge can actively seek to persuade the jurors about the defendant's guilt (Jacob, Blankenburg, Kritzer, Provine, and Sanders, 1996:177–248). In Germany, the judge actively asks questions based on the case investigation report prepared by the prosecutor and made available to both the judge and the defense attorney. The prosecutor and defense attorney are expected to present objective facts and arguments to assist the judge in finding the truth, rather than arguing on behalf of a particular side as in the American system (Jacob, Blankenburg, Kritzer, Provine, and Sanders, 1996:249–314). Although the inquisitorial system may appear committed to finding the truth, citizens and criminal suspects typically have fewer rights and legal protections than in the United States. In France, for example, claims have been made that police and examining magistrates can intrude too freely on citizens' lives while conducting criminal investigations. This criticism has been applied to Argentina where the judge investigates the case and then renders a decision as the defendant sits in jail during the lengthy process in which the judge writes a report on the case (O'Reilly, 1997). Criminal defendants in Germany are less likely than those in the United States to be represented by defense attorneys (Jacob, Blankenburg, Kritzer, Provine, and Sanders, 1996:177–314).

The image of the adversary system in the United States does not accurately represent what occurs in most cases. American judges do not devote themselves to careful and thoughtful decisions in all cases. Consistent with the crime control

---

adversary system
Basis for the American legal system in which a passive judge and jury seek to find the truth by listening to opposing attorneys who vigorously advocate on behalf of their respective sides.

inquisitorial system
Basis for legal systems in Europe in which the judge takes an active role in investigating the case and asking questions of witnesses in court.

model described in Chapter 1, lower court judges can face large caseloads that require them to quickly exercise discretion in disposing and punishing of minor offenses with little supervision from any higher court. Although judges are often portrayed as being forced to decide complex legal issues, in reality their tasks are routine. Because of the unending flow of cases, the criminal courtroom is frequently like an assembly line; many judges, like assembly-line workers, soon tire of the repetition.

CHECK POINT

⑦ **What is the image of the judge in the eyes of the public?**

⑧ **How do the adversary and inquisitorial systems differ?**

Who Becomes a Judge?

In American society the position of judge, even at the lowest level of the judicial hierarchy, has high status. People often seek judgeships even though they could obtain other jobs that would give them more wealth. Public service, political power, and prestige in the community may be more important than wealth to those who aspire to the judiciary. Many judges took a significant cut in pay to assume a position on the bench. Unlike private practice attorneys, who often work in excess of forty hours per week preparing cases and counseling clients, judges are typically better able to control their own working hours and schedules. Although judges are burdened with heavy caseloads, they frequently decide for themselves when to go home at the end of the workday. The ability to control one's own work schedule is an additional attraction for lawyers interested in becoming judges.

Historically, the vast majority of judges were white males with strong political connections. Women and members of minority groups had few opportunities to enter the legal profession prior to the 1960s and thus were seldom considered for judgeships. By the late twentieth century, political factors in many cities dictated that judges be drawn from specific racial, religious, and ethnic groups. In Philadelphia, Paul Wice found that almost every judge he interviewed was either Jewish, Irish, or Italian (Wice, 1995). Racial minorities are underrepresented on the bench. One study found that 3.6 percent of state court judges were black, most of them serving in the lower criminal courts (Graham, 1995:219). Comparing the racial and ethnic makeup of the judiciary with the race and ethnicity of many defendants in urban courts raises many questions. Is there a risk that people will think punishment is being imposed on behalf of a privileged segment of society rather than on behalf of the entire, diverse U.S. society? Might people believe that decisions about guilt and punishment are being made in an unfair manner if middle-aged white males have nearly all the power to make judgments about people from other segments of society?

In most cities criminal court judges hold the lowest rank in the judicial hierarchy. Neither lawyers nor citizens give them the degree of respect and prestige enjoyed by judges in civil and appellate courts. As with other professions, the status of criminal trial judges may be linked to that of the people they serve. Criminal court judges deal with the most despised segment of society—an endless flow of tragic stories, poor people, and substance abusers—and their work is often done in the busiest, noisiest, and least attractive courtrooms. This is a far cry from the solemn atmosphere and wood-paneled, velvet-curtained decor of higher courts. As a result, many criminal trial judges dream of moving to civil or appellate courts while they deal with the heavy caseloads and tough working conditions of the criminal court.

CHECK POINT

⑨ **Why might it be important for judges to be drawn from different segments of society?**

Functions of the Judge

Knowing that the criminal courts are clogged with a vast number of cases, you may be surprised to find the bench empty and the staff absent when you visit a local courtroom. Where are the judges? What do they do with their time? A study of the criminal courts in New York City found that, on average, judges were on the bench only three hours and three minutes a day. Although judges in other parts of the country typically spend more time on the bench, the New York example makes one wonder how judges spend their working hours.

While the job of a judge is usually thought of as presiding at trials, in reality the work of most judges extends to all aspects of the judicial process. Defendants see a judge whenever decisions about their future are being made: when bail is set, pretrial motions are made, guilty pleas are accepted, a trial is conducted, a sentence is pronounced, and appeals are filed (see Figure 7.3). However, judges' duties are not limited to making such decisions in the courtroom about criminal defendants. Judges also perform administrative tasks outside the courtroom. Judges have three major roles: adjudicator, negotiator, and administrator.

Although we think of the judiciary primarily in terms of activities in the courtroom, much of a judge's work takes place in chambers and extends to the administration of the judicial system.

PART THREE
COURTS

FIGURE 7.3 Actions of a trial court judge in processing a felony case

Throughout the process the judge ensures that legal standards are upheld; he or she maintains courtroom decorum, protects the rights of the accused, meets the requirement of a speedy trial, and ensures that case records are maintained properly.

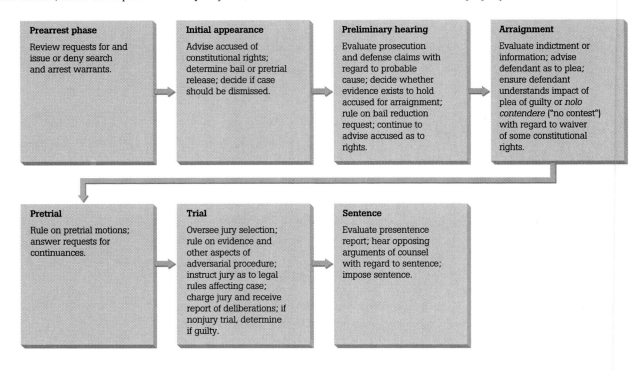

Prearrest phase

Review requests for and issue or deny search and arrest warrants.

Initial appearance

Advise accused of constitutional rights; determine bail or pretrial release; decide if case should be dismissed.

Preliminary hearing

Evaluate prosecution and defense claims with regard to probable cause; decide whether evidence exists to hold accused for arraignment; rule on bail reduction request; continue to advise accused as to rights.

Arraignment

Evaluate indictment or information; advise defendant as to plea; ensure defendant understands impact of plea of guilty or *nolo contendere* ("no contest") with regard to waiver of some constitutional rights.

Pretrial

Rule on pretrial motions; answer requests for continuances.

Trial

Oversee jury selection; rule on evidence and other aspects of adversarial procedure; instruct jury as to legal rules affecting case; charge jury and receive report of deliberations; if nonjury trial, determine if guilty.

Sentence

Evaluate presentence report; hear opposing arguments of counsel with regard to sentence; impose sentence.

Adjudicator

Judges must assume a neutral stance in overseeing the contest between the prosecution and the defense. They must apply the law so that the rights of the accused are upheld in decisions about detention, plea, trial, and sentence. Judges are given a certain amount of discretion in performing these tasks—for example, in setting bail—but they must do so according to law. In applying the law, judges are the final decision makers unless they are overruled by a higher court when a defendant files an appeal. If a nonjury trial is held, the judge not only rules on the issues of law but also decides issues of fact and whether the defendant is guilty— decisions that are made by jurors in a jury trial. Judges may exercise discretion in the sentencing of convicted persons if permitted by their state's laws. In doing so, they must not only decide fairly, but also give the appearance of fairness. They must avoid any conduct that may give an appearance or impression of bias. Judges are supposed to disqualify themselves from deciding cases involving their family, friends, and close acquaintances. This ethical rule can be difficult to fulfill in small towns and rural areas where townspeople, including the judge, are well known to each other and few other judges are available to take over cases (Goldschmidt and Shaman, 1996).

Negotiator

Many decisions that determine the fates of defendants are made outside of public view in the judge's private chambers. These decisions are reached through negotiations between prosecutors and defense attorneys about plea bargains, sentencing, and bail conditions. Judges spend much of their time in their chambers talking with prosecutors and defense attorneys. They often encourage the parties to work out a guilty plea or agree to proceed in a certain way. The judge may act as referee, keeping both sides on track in accordance with the law. Sometimes the judge takes a more active part in the negotiations, suggesting terms for an agreement or even pressuring one side to accept an agreement.

Administrator

A seldom-recognized function of most judges is managing the courthouse. In urban areas a professional court administrator may direct the people who keep records, schedule cases, and do the many other jobs that keep a system functioning. But even in cities, judges are in charge of their own courtroom and staff. In rural areas, where professional court administrators are not usually employed, the judges' administrative tasks may be more burdensome. The judge may be required to manage labor relations, budgeting, and maintenance of the courthouse building. As administrator, the judge must deal with political actors such as county commissioners, legislators, and members of the state executive bureaucracy. Chief judges in large courts may also use their administrative powers to push other judges to cooperate in advancing the court's goals of processing cases in a timely manner (Jacob, 1973). For judges whose training as lawyers focused on learning law and courtroom advocacy skills, managing a complex organization with a sizable budget and many employees can be a major challenge.

CHECK POINT

⑩ **What are judges' main functions?**

How to Become a Judge

The quality of justice depends to a great extent on the quality of those who make decisions about guilt and punishment. As the American jurist Benjamin Cardozo once said, "In the long run, there is no guarantee of justice except the personality of the judge" (1921:149). Because judges have the power to deprive a citizen of his or her liberty through a prison sentence, judges should be thoughtful, fair, and impartial. The character and experience of those appointed to federal courts and state appellate courts are examined closely (Goldman and Slotnick, 1999). Less attention has been focused on trial judges in state criminal courts. Yet, in these lower courts, citizens most often have contact with the judiciary, and the public image of the criminal justice system is shaped to a great extent by the trial judge's behavior in the courtroom. When a judge is rude or hasty or allows the courtroom to become noisy and crowded, the public may lose confidence in the fairness and effectiveness of the criminal justice process. In A Question of Ethics (see p. 258), the behavior of judges may raise concerns that the public will lose respect for the courts.

All judges are addressed as "Your Honor," and one must stand in deference whenever they enter or leave the courtroom. This does not mean that all judges are highly qualified and fair. Judges often are chosen for reasons that have little to do with either their legal qualifications or their judicial manner. Instead, they may be chosen because of their political ties, friendships with influential officials, or contributions to political parties.

A strong reform movement is afoot to place higher-quality judges on the bench. Reformers urge that judges be experienced experts in law. Many people believe that a nonpolitical selection process will produce higher-caliber judges who are more efficient, impartial, and fair. Others, however, argue that in a democracy the voters should elect those who carry out public policies, including judges. They contend that people chosen by their fellow citizens are better able to deal with the steady stream of human problems that judges confront every day.

Methods of Selection

Six methods are used to select state trial court judges: gubernatorial appointment, legislative selection, merit selection, **nonpartisan election, partisan election,** and a mixture of methods. Table 7.1 shows the method used in each of the states. All the methods bring up persistent concerns about the desired qualities of judges. The type of selection process used presumably will lead to a particular judicial style. On the one hand is the view that judges should be concerned only with the law; on the other is the view that they must feel the pulse of the people to render justice. Each selection method makes it easier for certain kinds of people to become judges and makes it less likely that other kinds of people will gain judgeships.

Selection by public voting occurs in more than half the states and has long been part of this nation's tradition (DuBois, 1980). One result is that judges must learn on the job. This method seems to counter the notion that judges are trained to "find the law" and apply neutral judgments (Hall, 1995). In Europe, by contrast, prospective judges are given special training in law school to become professional judges. These trained judges must serve as assistant judges and lower court judges before they can become judges in general trial and appellate courts.

Election campaigns for lower court judgeships tend to be low-key contests marked by little controversy. Usually only a small portion of the voters participate, judgeships are not prominent on the ballot, and candidates are constrained by ethical considerations from discussing controversial issues. The situation was summarized well by Judge Samuel Rosenman of New York (1964: 86):

> I learned at first hand what it meant for a judicial candidate to have
> to seek votes in political clubhouses, to ask for support of political
> district leaders, to receive financial contributions for his campaign
> from lawyers and others, and to make nonpolitical speeches about
> his own qualifications to audiences who could not care less—
> audiences who had little interest in any of the judicial candidates,
> of whom they had never heard, and whom they would never
> remember.

Although popular election of trial judges may be part of America's political heritage, these elections rarely get much attention from voters. In many cities judgeships are the fuel for the party machine. Because of the honors and material rewards of a place on the bench, political parties get support—in the

nonpartisan election
An election in which candidates who are not endorsed by political parties are presented to voters for selection.

partisan election
An election in which candidates endorsed by political parties are presented to voters for selection.

A Q u e s t i o n o f
Ethics

During an arraignment in New York for a defendant charged with assaulting his wife, the judge reportedly said, "What's wrong with that? You've got to keep them in line once in a while." When authorities acted to remove the judge from office, the judge's lawyer said that the judge makes lighthearted comments from the bench but does not misuse his position.

In California, a judge reportedly indicated to a good-looking defendant that other inmates at the prison would find him attractive. The judge also allegedly called a prosecutor in a drunk-driving case a "hypocrite" who was in all probability guilty of the same offense as the defendant. The judge's attorney claimed that the comments were taken out of context when a complaint was filed with the state's Commission on Judicial Performance.

■ Do the statements reportedly made by these judges harm the image of the courts? If so, how? If these statements are improper, what should happen to judges who say such things? If the judges apologize should they be forgiven and given another opportunity to behave in a proper manner? Is there any way to make sure that judges act at all times in accordance with the proper image of their judicial office?

SOURCE: Drawn from "Court Upholds Removal of Rockland Judge," *New York Times,* March 31, 1999 (Metro News); and Richard Marosi, "Hard-line Judge Is Being Judged Herself," *Los Angeles Times,* May 7, 1999, p. B–1.

TABLE **7.1** **Methods used by states to select judges**

States use different methods to select judges. Note that many judges are initially appointed to fill a vacancy, giving them an advantage if they must run for election at a later date.

PARTISAN ELECTION	NONPARTISAN ELECTION	GUBERNATORIAL APPOINTMENT	LEGISLATIVE SELECTION	MERIT SELECTION
Alabama	Arizona (some trial courts)	Connecticut	Rhode Island (appellate)	Alaska
Arkansas	California (trial)	Delaware	South Carolina	Arizona (appellate)
Illinois	Florida (trial)	Maine	Virginia	California (appellate)
Indiana (trial)	Georgia	Massachusetts		Colorado
Mississippi	Idaho	New Hampshire		Florida (appellate)
New Mexico (retention)	Kentucky	New Jersey		Hawaii
New York (trial)	Louisiana	New York (appellate)		Indiana (appellate)
North Carolina	Michigan	Rhode Island (trial)		Iowa
Pennsylvania (initial)	Minnesota			Kansas
Tennessee (supreme and trial)	Montana			Maryland
Texas	Nevada			Missouri
West Virginia	North Dakota			Nebraska
	Ohio			New Mexico (initial)
	Oklahoma (trial)			Oklahoma (appellate)
	Oregon			South Dakota (appellate)
	Pennsylvania (retention)			Tennessee (intermediate appellate)
	South Dakota (trial)			Utah
	Washington			Vermont
	Wisconsin			Wyoming

SOURCE: *The Book of the States, 1998–1999 Edition* (Lexington, Ky.: Council of State Governments, 1998), 135–137.

form of donated time and money—from attorneys seeking a judgeship. Parties also want judgeships to be elected posts because they can use courthouse staff positions to reward party loyalists. When a party member wins a judgeship, courthouse jobs may become available for campaign workers because clerks, bailiffs, and secretaries are chosen by the judge.

By contrast, elections for seats on state supreme courts may receive statewide media attention. Because of the importance of state supreme courts as policy-making institutions, political parties and interest groups may devote substantial energy to organizing and funding the election campaigns of their preferred candidates. When organized interests contribute tens of thousands of dollars to judicial campaigns, questions sometimes arise about whether the successful candidates who received those contributions will favor the interests of their donors when they begin to decide court cases (Reid, 1996; Champagne and Cheek, 1996).

Some states have tried to reduce the influence of political parties in the selection of judges while still allowing voters to select judges. These states hold nonpartisan elections in which only the names of candidates, and not their party affiliations, are on the ballot. However, political parties are often strongly involved in such elections. In Ohio, for example, the Republican and Democratic political parties hold their own primary elections to choose the judicial candidates whose names will go on the nonpartisan ballot for the general election (Felice and Kilwein, 1992). In other states, party organizations raise and spend money on behalf of candidates in nonpartisan elections. When candidates' party affiliations are not listed on the ballot, voters may be unaware of which party is supporting which candidate, especially in low-visibility elections for local trial judgeships. These judgeships do not receive the same level of media attention as elections for state supreme court seats (Lovrich and Sheldon, 1994).

Public opinion data show that Americans express concern about the influence of politics on judges, especially with respect to elected judges (see What Americans Think). If so many Americans are concerned about judges' involvement in political campaigns, why do so many states still rely on elections to select judges?

Merit selection, which combines appointment and election, was first used in Missouri in 1940 and has since spread to other states. When a judgeship becomes vacant, a nominating commission made up of citizens and attorneys evaluates potential appointees and sends the governor the names of three candidates, from which the replacement is chosen. After one year, a referendum is held to decide whether the judge will stay on the bench. The ballot asks, "Shall Judge X remain in office?" The judge who wins a majority vote serves out the term and can then be listed on the ballot at the next election. Merit selection is designed to remove politics from the selection of judges and is also supposed to allow the voters to unseat judges. However, most judges selected by this means remain in office. Studies have shown that relatively few judges have been removed by the voters in merit selection states (Hall and Aspin, 1987). However, after one member of the Tennessee Supreme Court lost a retention election in 1996 based on a vote she cast in a single death penalty case, observers around the country began to worry that political parties and interest groups were using retention elections to mount campaigns against political opponents (Bright, 1997). Indications are that judges in some states are increasingly inclined to mount campaigns on their own behalf to avoid losing their jobs in retention elections (Aspin and Hall, 1996).

Despite the support of bar associations, merit selection has not gone unchallenged. Although party politics may have been removed, some argue that it has been replaced by politics within the legal profession. Many lawyers see the system as favoring "blue bloods" (high-status attorneys with ties to corporations) over the "little guy" (Watson and Downing, 1969).

Results of Selection Methods

What are the effects of using one selection method instead of another? Does each function so that only judges from a certain social background reach the bench? Do some methods favor politically oriented judges over legally oriented ones? If each method has built-in biases, do these biases find their way into judges' decisions? Does one method favor judges who issue light sentences while another method favors judges who issue stiffer penalties?

These questions have been hotly debated. The selection method clearly may influence the type of judge chosen. Some appointed judges probably would not have reached the bench if they had had to win a partisan election (Fried, 1994). Others who ran and won probably would not have been selected by a governor (Cannon, 1991). In states where the legislature makes the decision, the evidence shows that former legislators are preferred. But most research seems to show that although judges have some differences in training and experience, these differences are not solely the result of the selection method used.

---

merit selection

A reform plan by which judges are nominated by a commission and appointed by the governor for a given period. When the term expires, the voters are asked to approve or disapprove the judge for a succeeding term. If the judge is disapproved, the committee nominates a successor for the governor's appointment.

The key point in this debate concerns the impact of selection methods on the behavior of judges. Here, too, the limited number of research studies are inconclusive. Martin Levin's early comparison of the criminal courts of Pittsburgh and Minneapolis remains the major study of the link between selection methods and judicial decisions (Levin, 1998). In Pittsburgh, judges were chosen in an extremely political manner by a city controlled by the Democratic machine, which needs to maintain ethnic and religious balance even on a judicial ticket. In the nonpartisan system in Minneapolis, the parties have almost no role in choosing judges, but the bar association does. When vacancies occur, Minnesota governors consider the association's preferences. The Minneapolis system produces judicial candidates who have usually been members of large, business-oriented law firms and who have not been active in partisan politics. Levin believes that the differing selection methods and political settings of these two cities produce judges with opposing judicial philosophies and therefore contrasting sentencing decisions. In general, Levin found that judges in Pittsburgh were more lenient than those in Minneapolis. Not only did white and black defendants receive more sentences of probation and shorter terms of incarceration in Pittsburgh, but also the pattern was maintained when the defendants' prior records, pleas, and ages were held constant.

The background of judges and the way they are chosen seem to influence their decisions. An elimination process may be operating here. In each system only certain types of people who have had certain kinds of experiences are available for selection. But it seems that any link between judges' backgrounds and their decisions is indirect. A key factor is the city's political culture and its influence on judicial selection methods.

Are there other approaches to judicial selection that could be employed in the United States? As evident in the Comparative Perspective (see p. 262), the United States is highly unusual in using elections to choose judges or to end their tenure in office. The use of judicial selection and retention elections helps to make American judges accountable to the voters. While accountability is usually considered desirable in a democratic system of government, observers fear that state judges lack the independence necessary to make courageous and correct decisions because they may fear that an unpopular decision will lead voters to remove them from office (White, 1997). By contrast, other countries use different means to select their judges. Could these alternative approaches be applied in the United States and, if so, what impact would they have on American courts?

⑪ **Why do political parties often prefer that judges be elected?**

⑫ **What are the steps in the merit selection process?**

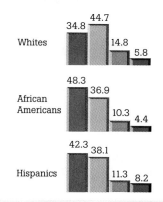

What Americans Think

Question 1. "Do you agree or disagree with the statement 'Judges' decisions are influenced by political considerations'?"

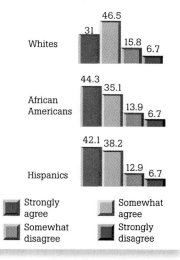

Whites — 34.8, 44.7, 14.8, 5.8

African Americans — 48.3, 36.9, 10.3, 4.4

Hispanics — 42.3, 38.1, 11.3, 8.2

Question 2. "Do you agree or disagree with the statement 'Elected judges are influenced by having to raise campaign funds'?"

Whites — 31, 46.5, 15.8, 6.7

African Americans — 44.3, 35.1, 13.9, 6.7

Hispanics — 42.1, 38.2, 12.9, 6.7

- Strongly agree
- Somewhat agree
- Somewhat disagree
- Strongly disagree

SOURCE: National Center for State Courts, *How the Public Views the State Courts: A 1999 National Survey*, report presented at the National Conference on Public Trust and Confidence in the Justice System, Washington, D.C., May 14, 1999.

The Courtroom: How It Functions

Justice is allocated in fairly similar ways throughout this large and diverse nation. States differ in the structure and organization of courts, in the methods used to select judges, and in the rules of criminal procedure. However, values are shared

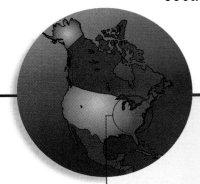

perspective

U.S. Judges versus **Their** Foreign Counterparts

In the United States, judges are selected through political processes that result in election to judicial office or appointment to the bench by the president, a governor, or a state legislature. A lawyer can become a judge without any specialized knowledge or experience in criminal law if he or she can win an election or has a close relationship with important political figures. In other countries, by contrast, the path to a judgeship may require special training or experience. Why does the United States differ? What does this say about its political and cultural ideals?

I n France, law school graduates must take a special competitive exam to gain entry into the national training school for judicial officers. Students study law and psychology and also undertake internships in local courts. Graduates of the school are placed in judicial positions based on their examination scores. Over the course of their careers, French judges can be promoted

to higher courts after long and impressive service in the lower courts.

The French approach, which employs specialized training and makes judgeships a career civil service position, appears to emphasize the knowledge and qualifications of persons selected to serve on the bench. However, the selection process clashes with the American tradition of permitting citizens to influence the selection and removal of local judges. Do you think that different influences may shape the decision making of American judges and French judges? Might these judges reach different decisions when confronted with a highly publicized case? Does the French system provide a desirable approach for selecting American judges?

Most criminal proceedings in England are decided by lay magistrates, nonlawyer citizens appointed to serve as part-time, unpaid judges. Sitting in panels of two or three and advised by a lawyer, the lay magistrates accept guilty pleas or try cases without a jury before imposing a sentence upon those who are found guilty. Very few offenders convicted in Magistrates' Courts are sentenced to prison. Most are fined or

concerning how those accused of crimes should be treated. These values are contained in the laws and constitutions of the states and of the United States. Thus, if a person lives in New Jersey but is arrested in Idaho, he or she will find that the processes and rules to determine guilt are about the same in both states.

Although similar rules and processes are used in criminal cases throughout the nation, courts differ in the precise ways they apply these rules and procedures. A study of criminal courts in nine communities in three states showed that similar laws and procedures can have different results in the treatment of defendants (Eisenstein, Flemming, and Nardulli, 1988). Some courts sentence offenders to longer terms than do others. In some places, court delays and tough bail policies keep many accused persons in jail awaiting trial, while in other places defendants are more likely to be released before trial or have their cases resolved quickly.

placed on probation. Cases that are likely to result in imprisonment are referred to the Crown Courts, which are staffed by professional, appointed judges with life tenure.

How would Americans feel about having criminal cases decided by nonlawyers? Lay judges serve in some places within the United States, but they typically sit in rural areas and handle only petty offenses that may result in fines. It would be a very different matter for the United States to rely on lay magistrates to decide the majority of criminal cases. How would you feel if you were charged with larceny and your case was heard by an insurance agent, a dentist, and an auto mechanic? On the one hand, Americans may feel uncomfortable at the thought that people who lack legal training are making important decisions in court. What if they do not understand the legal issues in the case? What if they have biases that keep them from being open-minded in making decisions? On the other hand, the English system could also be viewed as employing a kind of "mini-jury," because Americans are accustomed to thinking of verdicts regarding serious criminal offenses being decided by a panel of citizens drawn from the community. Using regular citizens

instead of law-trained professionals may help to keep court proceedings closely tied to local values and ensure that the "justice" produced in each case reflects community sentiments.

The use of elected state judges stands as the most striking difference between courts in the United States and courts in other countries. Many people throughout the world cannot imagine how a system can rely on elected judges because of concerns that judges' decisions will not be independent but instead will be calculated to gain reelection. Under Bulgaria's constitution, judges receive life tenure appointments from the Supreme Judicial Council, a body composed of representatives selected by the National Assembly and the judiciary. By gaining office through appointment instead of election and by having job security, these judges are supposed to have sufficient protection from political pressure to enable them to make independent decisions.

Are criminal cases affected by the use of elected judges instead of life-tenured appointed judges? It is possible. For example, comparisons of criminal cases in the United States and Canada provide indications that American defendants are more

likely to request jury trials than their Canadian counterparts who usually have bench trials before a judge alone. Because service as a prosecutor is a traditional stepping stone to election as a judge in the United States and judges facing reelection may wish to avoid any decisions that make them appear soft on crime, American defendants may be concerned about the neutrality of some judges. By contrast, Canadian judges are regularly appointed from among both former prosecutors and former defense attorneys and their job security may give defendants greater confidence about their ability to make fair decisions.

Do comparisons between the United States and other countries give you any ideas about how the American system of justice could be improved? What changes would you suggest?

SOURCE: Drawn from John C. Freeman, "England," in *Major Criminal Justice Systems: A Comparative Survey*, 2nd ed., ed. George F. Cole, Stanislaw J. Frankowski, and Marc G. Gertz (Newbury Park, Calif.: Sage, 1987), 48–70; Martin L. Friedland and Kent Roach, "Borderline Justice: Choosing Juries in the Two Niagaras," *Israel Law Review* 31 (1997):120–158; Albert P. Melone, "Judicial Independence and Constitutional Politics in Bulgaria," *Judicature* 80 (1997):280–285; and Herbert Jacob, Erhard Blankenburg, Herbert M. Kritzer, Doris Marie Provine, and Joseph Sanders, *Courts, Law, and Politics in Comparative Perspective* (New Haven, Conn.: Yale University Press, 1996), 177–248.

Guilty pleas may make up 90 percent of dispositions in some communities but only 60 percent in others. How can differences among courts be explained—differences that are found even in the same city?

Social scientists are aware that the culture of a community has a great influence on how its members behave. Culture implies shared beliefs about proper behavior. These beliefs can span entire nations or exist in smaller communities, including organizations such as corporations, churches, or neighborhoods. In any community, large or small, the culture can exert a strong effect on people's decisions and behavior.

Researchers have identified a **local legal culture**—values and norms shared by members of a particular court community (judges, attorneys, clerks, bailiffs, and others)—that determines how cases should be handled and the way court

local legal culture

Norms shared by members of a court community as to how cases should be handled and how a participant should behave in the judicial process.

officials should behave (Church, 1985). The local legal culture influences court operations in three ways:

❶ Norms (shared values and expectations) help participants distinguish between "our" court and other courts. Often a judge or prosecutor will proudly describe how "we" do the job differently and better than officials in a nearby county or city.

❷ Norms tell members of a court community how they should treat each other. For example, mounting a strong adversarial defense may be viewed as not in keeping with the norms of one court, but it may be expected in another. An attorney in Montgomery County, Pennsylvania, said that "suits challenging the operation of the criminal system 'upset' the bar, and that 'upsetting the bar would be rocking the boat' " (Eisenstein, Flemming, and Nardulli, 1988: 300).

❸ Norms describe how cases should be processed. The best example of such a norm is the **going rate,** the local view of the proper sentence, considering the offense, the defendant's prior record, and other factors. The local legal culture also includes attitudes on such issues as whether a judge should take part in plea negotiations, when continuances—lawyers' requests for delays in court proceedings—should be granted, and which defendants qualify for a public defender.

going rate
Local view of the appropriate sentence for the offense, the defendant's prior record, and other characteristics.

Differences among local legal cultures help explain why court decisions may differ, even though the formal rules of criminal procedure are basically the same. For example, while judges play a key role in sentencing, the "going rate" concept reveals that sentences are also a product of shared understandings among the prosecutor, defense attorney, and judge. In one court, shared understandings may mean a court imposes probation on a first-time thief; in other courts, different shared values may send first offenders to jail or prison for the same offense.

Informal rules and practices arise in particular settings, and "the way things are done" differs from place to place. As one might expect, the local legal culture of San Francisco inevitably differs from that of Burlington, Vermont, or Baltimore, Maryland. The norms and customs of each jurisdiction vary because local practices are influenced by factors such as size, politics, and demographics. Among these, differences between urban and rural areas are a major factor.

In small-town and rural settings, the local legal culture and the "going rate" have strong impacts on the allocation of justice. How may sentences in a small-town court differ from those in a city court?

CHECK POINT

⑬ **How does the local legal culture affect criminal cases?**

Differences between Urban and Rural Courts

People treat each other differently in a city than they do in a rural area; these differences are reflected in the operation of criminal courts. In their nine-county study, James Eisenstein, Roy Flemming, and Peter Nardulli (1988:261) found that community size was a major factor determining the local legal culture. In rural areas people know and interact with each other on personal terms. A small-town judge is likely to know the accused and the victim and the family circumstances of both. The prosecutor and defense attorney are likely to share that knowledge. The amount of crime is probably low, and few officials are involved in any given case. By contrast, in cities, offenders are known only by their case record, many courtrooms are used, the courthouse has a large staff, and caseloads are heavy.

A study of criminal courts in a rural Pennsylvania county found little crime and a desire to avoid trials; the judge, prosecutor, and public defender worked part time. "Everyone was thoroughly familiar with the principal [actors] in each case—the arresting officer, the defendant and his or her family, the victim, witnesses, and the attorneys" (Klinger, 1988). This knowledge made the actions of the judge, the opposing attorneys, and the defendant highly visible to others in the community. Because many people in small communities know each other, they have a strong desire to avoid conflict. One result is that most cases are disposed of through guilty pleas. Also, going rates may be less well established if not enough cases are processed to produce shared understandings about sentencing. Furthermore, with a low caseload, there is less routine handling of cases. Instead, each case is treated as a unique situation. All these factors increase the give-and-take among participants in small jurisdictions and thus raise the percentage of guilty pleas.

Different decision patterns may emerge in other rural settings. However, less is known about rural courts than about urban courts because most research studies focus on urban felony courts in which the court community is large, there are many cases, and bureaucratic practices guide decisions. Defendants may be treated more routinely in urban courts, where cases involving similar crimes are processed quickly and produce similar sentences.

CHECK **POINT**

⑭ **How do urban and rural courts differ?**

The Courtroom Workgroup

The image of an American courtroom may be based on those seen in television dramas such as *The Practice* or *Law & Order*. In these settings prosecutors and defense attorneys lock horns in verbal combat, each side trying to persuade a judge or jury to either convict or acquit the defendant. However, this image of adversarial proceedings does not reflect the actual scene in most American courtrooms. A more realistic portrayal would stress the interactions among the actors, who are guided by the norms and expectations of the local legal culture. Many of these interactions take the form of calm cooperation among the prosecutor, defense attorney, and judge, rather than the battle of adversaries portrayed in fictional accounts (Flemming, Nardulli, and Eisenstein, 1992).

Decision making in criminal cases is influenced by the fact that participants are organized in **workgroups.** The relationships among the judge, prosecutor, and defense attorney, along with those of the support staff (clerk, reporter, and bailiff), are required if the group is to carry out its task of disposing of cases. The workgroup concept is especially important in analyzing urban courts, where there are many courtrooms; large numbers of lawyers, judges, and other court personnel; and a heavy caseload.

workgroup

A collection of individuals who interact in the workplace on a continuing basis, share goals, develop norms regarding how activities should be carried out, and eventually establish a network of roles that differentiates the group from others.

Even in the most adversarial cases, courtroom participants form a workgroup that requires constant interaction, cooperation, and negotiation.

grouping

A collection of individuals who interact in the workplace, but because of shifting membership they do not develop into a workgroup.

Merely placing the major actors in the courtroom does not make them into a workgroup that can apply shared norms in a smooth, cooperative fashion. A judge, prosecutor, and defense attorney who are assigned to the same case might be called a **grouping.** They are simply a set of persons placed together to make decisions about the defendant's guilt and punishment. Only when the following conditions are met does a workgroup exist:

❶ The members interact.

❷ The members share (that is, have the same attitudes about) one or more motives or goals that determine the direction in which the group will move.

❸ The members develop a set of norms about how they will interact, treat each other, and make decisions.

❹ If interaction continues, a set of roles becomes established and guides cooperation among members of the group.

❺ A network of relationships is formed on the basis of the members' feelings toward each other.

The closer a set of people come to meeting these conditions, the closer they are to being a workgroup. The members in Courtroom A may meet only some conditions and thus be closer to a grouping, while the members of Courtroom B may meet all the conditions and thus form a closely knit workgroup as shown in Figure 7.4.

In light of the factors that define the workgroup, differences can be expected in groupings and workgroups from courthouse to courthouse, depending on the strength of these factors in each setting. For example, a rotation system that moves judges among courtrooms in a large courthouse may limit the development of workgroup norms and roles. Although the same prosecutors and defense attorneys may be present every day, the arrival of a new judge every week or month will require them to learn and adapt to new ideas about how cases should be negotiated or tried. When shared norms cannot develop, cases are likely to proceed in a more formal manner. The actors in such a courtroom have fewer chances to follow agreed-upon routines than a workgroup with a well-developed pattern of interactions.

However, if the same actors are in the courtroom on a continuing basis, the relationships among the judge, prosecutor, and defense attorney, as well as the staff, may shape the way decisions are made. The defendant, a person from outside the workgroup, will face "an organized network of relationships, in which each person who acts on his case is reacting to or anticipating the actions of others" (Neubauer, 1996: 73). When there are shared expectations and consistent relationships, the business of the courtroom proceeds in a regular but informal manner, with many shared understandings among members easing much of the work (Worden, 1995). Through cooperation, each member can achieve his or her goals as well as those of the group. The prosecutor wants to gain quick convictions, the defense attorney wants fair and prompt resolution of the defendant's case, and the judge wants cooperative agreements on guilt and sentencing. All of these actors want efficient processing of the steady flow of cases that burden their working lives.

FIGURE 7.4   The courtroom social system as a continuum

How might the interactions of the actors in Courtroom A differ from those of the actors in Courtroom B?

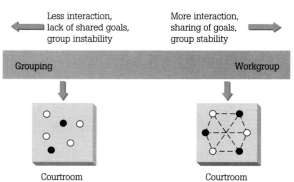

Less interaction, lack of shared goals, group instability

More interaction, sharing of goals, group stability

Grouping

Workgroup

Courtroom A

Courtroom B

Although the members of the courtroom workgroup share norms, goals, and expectations, they do not share roles and responsibilities. Each actor—judge, prosecutor, and defense attorney—has a specific role. Each has unique duties and responsibilities. If a lawyer moves from the public defender's office to the prosecutor's office and later to a judgeship, each new position calls for a different role in the workgroup because each represents a different sponsoring organization (Eisenstein and Jacob, 1977:43). One organization, loosely called the court, sends judges; the prosecuting attorney's office sends assistant prosecutors; the public defender's office sends counsel for indigents.

Sponsoring organizations provide the resources for the courtroom workgroup and—perhaps more important—regulate the behavior of their representatives in the courtroom. The policies of a sponsoring organization may stipulate rules to be followed, encourage or discourage plea bargaining, or insist that police evidence conform strictly to formal requirements. Thus the judge, prosecutor, or public defender must meet the needs and goals of the workgroup and at the same time must satisfy superiors in his or her sponsoring organization. The degree to which the chief judge, prosecuting attorney, and chief public defender oversee the work of those reporting to them strongly affects the degree to which members of the workgroup can adjust their actions to meet the group's goals.

Other people play supporting roles in the courtroom drama. Members of the judge's staff, such as clerks and court reporters, have access to vast amounts of confidential information. They may use this resource, as well as their access to the judge, to enhance their power within the group. Bailiffs, who keep order in the courtroom and escort prisoners, are supplied by the sheriff. Probation officers, who provide presentence reports and are often present in the courtroom, work closely with the judge. Although not directly tied to the close interactions of the judge, prosecutor, and defense attorney, probation officers provide information and perform duties in support of the major actors. Finally, all courtroom actors must keep in mind others with whom they have ties. Prosecutors must not endanger their relationship with the police; defense attorneys know that accused persons and their families expect to be represented in a competent way; judges must be alert to reactions to their decisions by the news media, appellate courts, and in some cases the voters.

These pressures may have two effects. First, they may require that actors give "performances" to satisfy their clients—performances that must have the support of other members of the courtroom "cast." Judges and prosecutors, for example, may have to show patience in letting a defense attorney make vocal arguments and loud objections in court, even though they all know that they have already agreed on a plea bargain and sentence. The defense attorney may need to perform publicly in this way to maintain the confidence and cooperation of the defendant and his or her family. Second, by cooperating in keeping the nature of their performances secret, the workgroup members may increase the strength of their own relationships and the cohesiveness of the group.

The elements of the courtroom workgroup and the influences that bear on decision making are shown in Figure 7.5. Note that the workgroup operates in an environment in which decision making is influenced by the local legal culture, recruitment and selection processes, nature of the cases, and the socioeconomic, political, and legal structures of the broader community.

Physical Setting

The work site of the courtroom group strengthens the patterns of interaction among its members. Each workgroup is physically separated from other courtrooms, sponsoring organizations, and officials. One result is that communications with persons outside the workgroup are limited.

The low visibility of courtroom activities to both the public and government officials is an important feature of the judicial system. Judges have little supervision because few people are watching. Higher courts may supervise the administration of justice, but only a small portion of criminal cases is appealed. Thus trial judges are the final decision makers for most issues, and judges' actions are seldom under public scrutiny. Although the general public may attend court proceedings, few people do so.

The bench is usually elevated to symbolize the judge's authority. Because it faces the lawyers' table, the spectators—and sometimes even the defendant—cannot see exchanges between the judge and the attorneys. In some courts the attorneys for both sides sit toward either end of a long table; the table does not define them as adversaries. Throughout the proceedings, lawyers from both sides periodically engage in muffled conversations with the judge out of the hearing of the defendant and spectators. When judges call attorneys into their chambers for private discussion, defendants remain in the courtroom. In most settings,

---

FIGURE 7.5   Model of criminal court decision making

This model ties together the elements of the courtroom workgroup, sponsoring organizations, and local legal culture. Note the effects on decision making. Are there other factors that should be taken into account?

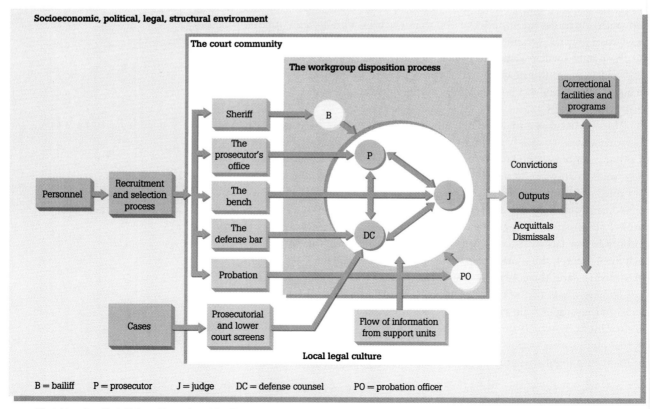

SOURCE: Adapted from Peter Nardulli, James Eisenstein, and Roy Flemming, *Tenor of Justice: Criminal Courts and the Guilty Plea Process* (Urbana: University of Illinois Press, 1988). Copyright © 1988 by the Board of Trustees of the University of Illinois. Reprinted by permission of the University of Illinois Press.

defendants sit alone either in the "dock" or in a chair behind their counsel. This defines their status as silent observers with no power to negotiate their own fate.

Given that public defenders may represent as many as 90 percent of the court's clients, they have a "permanent" place in the courtroom. Only on a few cases do they give up their desks to the private lawyers. While the courtroom encounters of private attorneys are brief and businesslike, public defenders view the courtroom as their regular workplace and thus give the impression that they are members of the courtroom workgroup.

The Role of the Judge

In the view of some defendants, the judge does not play a major part in deciding their cases; in their eyes, the defense attorney and prosecutor play much greater roles. These defendants feel that due process ideals have given way to bureaucratic goals. When the symbolic leader of the courtroom, who has formal decision-making power, does not determine the outcome of a case, the justice system does not appear to function as it should.

Yet judges are the leaders of the courtroom team. They ensure that procedures are followed correctly. Even if prosecutors and defense attorneys appear to make the key decisions, those decisions must be approved by the judge. Judges are responsible for coordinating the processing of cases. Even so, each judge can perform this role somewhat differently. Judges who run a loose administrative ship see themselves as somewhat above the battle. They give other members of the team a great deal of freedom in carrying out their duties and will usually approve group decisions—especially when the members of the group have shared beliefs about the court's goals and the community's values. Judges who exert tighter control over the process play a more active role. They anticipate problems, provide cues for other actors, threaten, cajole, and move the group toward efficient achievement of its goals. Such judges command respect and participate fully in the ongoing courtroom drama.

Because of their position in the justice system, judges can define the level of their involvement in the processing of criminal cases. How they define their role has a strong effect on interpersonal relations in the courtroom and the way the group performs its task, as measured by the way it disposes of cases. Judges' actions can, for example, pressure defense attorneys to encourage their clients to plead guilty instead of insisting on a trial (Lynch, 1999). Whether the judge actively participates in courtroom interactions or supervises from a distance will help define the speed, efficiency, and degree of cooperation involved in disposing of cases. The Close-Up describing Judge Stanley M. Goldstein of Miami's drug court shows the ability of a judge to be actively involved in the problems of defendants (see p. 270). Drug courts are an innovative effort to address the problems of substance abusers in efficient, focused proceedings (Brown, 1999).

Roles in the Workgroup

The courtroom is a meeting place for professionals (lawyers, probation officers, and social workers) who say they work on behalf of accused persons. They are supposed to meet the needs of their clients and thus serve society's interests in treating troubled people in an appropriate and fair manner. In part, their efforts are focused on teaching defendants how to cooperate in a manner that will help the proceedings move smoothly. They may encourage them to accept a plea bargain, be repentant, and accept the sentence without disruption. These

CLOSE  up

Miami's Drug Court, Judge Stanley M. Goldstein, Presiding

Standing in front of the judge in a special legal arena known as drug court, the defendant was on his own to explain why he had been arrested again for drug possession. He said he had picked up a hitchhiker who had been carrying drugs.

"I didn't do anything," the defendant said.

But in drug court, a national program for drug offenders that operates under unorthodox rules, the judge has a computer that tells him exactly what the defendant has been up to, how many urine tests have been "dirty" and how many treatment sessions have been missed. The judge also hears no prosecution or defense arguments to cloud his or her judicial instincts.

In the case involving the hitchhiker, Judge Stanley M. Goldstein's instincts told him that the defendant was playing games. "He just happened to give somebody a ride," the judge repeated, smiling, before sending the man to jail.

But the same judge looked joyous when another defendant, a woman, showed up for her last courtroom appearance. The woman, Michelle Ford, 32, had been in and out of treatment for six years and had finally quit crack.

"You get a hug and a kiss, and it's all over," he said as he beckoned Ms. Ford to the bench.

"Thank you, thank you judge," she said in his embrace, dissolving in tears.

The drama of addiction, and its intersection with crime, unfolds in courtrooms like Judge Goldstein's every workday in an experiment that has gained enthusiastic acceptance among judges and prosecutors and that criminal justice experts say offers hope amid the bleakness of rising drug use. . . .

Drug courts are small beachheads on a vast battleground. About 28,000 defendants are participating in 109 courts around the country or have graduated from them, a fraction of the more than 700,000 offenders arrested on drug possession charges each year.

In drug courts, defendants who have been charged with drug possession or related crimes in effect make a plea bargain. Judges set aside a formal trial, criminal charges, and sentences while defendants undergo treatment and court-monitored supervision. The judge can jail defendants if they violate the terms of the treatment plan. If they complete the treatment and become free of drugs, drug charges may be dismissed or sentences may be reduced.

Participants volunteer to submit to rigorous monitoring and counseling until they are classified as rehabilitated, and they receive help with searching for work and job training. . . .

Drug courts work, judges say, because they turn the judges into motivators with the power to praise, cajole and coerce defendants. . . .

But the addicts also credit their recoveries to the opportunity to talk over problems with the judge, a parental figure whom some defendants call "Daddy."

"You have moral support from an authority figure," said Kelvin Mobley, 34, a gardener who was buying cocaine on the street in June 1995 and is about to complete his treatment from Judge Goldstein. "That's a big boost."

Judge Goldstein's courtroom bustles like many others, but a visitor quickly notices differences. The prosecutor and the public defender work in agreement, tears flow easily among defendants, and the judge often says, "I love you."

But the compassion can turn into rage, as when he warned a man who was holding a yarmulke in one hand and his young son's hand in the other that if he showed cocaine in his urine in his next appointment he had better "pack a toothbrush."

"Want that kid to be a junkie?" he boomed as the man made a hasty exit. "You are the role models to your children. Don't push it off to ballplayers. You!"

Later addressing a new group of defendants, the judge made clear what they were up against if they wanted his court to dispense not punishment but a fresh start.

"There's nothing easy about this," he said. "But I know you all can do it. I also know not all of you will do it. No guts."

SOURCE: Mireya Navarro, "Special Courts Use New Tactics in Battle against Drug Addiction," *New York Times*, October 17, 1996, p. A1.

agent-mediators help people redefine themselves—from accused to defendant to convict—and prepare them for the next phase of their life.

Dress sometimes reveals the role each actor plays. Group members wear appropriate "uniforms": the judge wears robes, the attorneys are in conservative suits. Prosecutors tend to dress in more somber colors, perhaps to link their role with that of the judge or to convey the seriousness of their role. By contrast, some defense attorneys tend toward more expensive or flamboyant outfits, perhaps to show their clients that they are "successful" as defense attorneys or as a dramatic way to get attention and persuade the judge or jurors. Defendants may be dressed in jail clothes if they are detained for lack of bail, especially for preliminary hearings, but they cannot be forced to wear jail clothes during a trial. Even when defendants wear their own clothes, because most defendants are poor, their clothes tends to be different from that of the lawyers and others in the courtroom.

The behavior of defendants has a strong effect on how they are treated. They are expected to act remorseful, repentant, silent, and submissive. When the defendant admits guilt in public and states that he or she is entering a guilty plea voluntarily, acceptance of the plea can be followed by a brief lecture from the judge about the seriousness of the crime or the harm the defendant has caused to the victim, as well as to his or her own family. The defendant's contrite demeanor allows the judge to justify the lesser sentence negotiated by the prosecutor and the defense lawyer. The judge can "give a break" to the defendant for having cooperated. A defendant who pleads not guilty or whose behavior is inappropriate in other ways may be given a more severe sentence. In one study, Maureen Mileski (1971) found that the judge's harsh manner was not related to the seriousness of the charge. Instead, a minor disruption in the courtroom or a show of disrespect for its personnel led to reprimands from the judge or to sentences that were more severe than usual. But Mileski noted few cases in which the defendant's behavior was improper; only 5 percent evoked a harsh response from the judge. Most conformed to the norms of a routine bureaucratic encounter.

⑱ **How does a courtroom workgroup form and operate?**

The Impact of Courtroom Workgroups

The classic research of James Eisenstein and Herbert Jacob (1977) on the felony disposition process in Baltimore, Chicago, and Detroit offers important insights into the workgroup's impact on decisions in felony cases and reveals differences in the criminal justice systems of three cities. The researchers found that the same type of felony case was handled differently in each city, yet the outcomes of the dispositions were remarkably similar. Differences did not stem from the law, rules of procedure, or crime rate. Instead, they emerged from the structure of the courtroom workgroups, the influence of the sponsoring organizations, and sociopolitical factors.

Many felony defendants never reach a trial court because their cases are dismissed or the charges against them are reduced to a misdemeanor at a preliminary hearing. Eisenstein and Jacob found that preliminary hearings in the three cities had very different outcomes. In Chicago almost two-thirds of the cases were dismissed. By contrast, in Baltimore and Detroit about three-fifths and four-fifths of the cases, respectively, moved to the trial court after probable cause was found. Although these differences are striking, they do not tell the entire story. About half of the Baltimore defendants remained in jail before trial, compared with two-fifths in Chicago and Detroit. Baltimore released 21 percent on recognizance but set high bail amounts for the rest; almost no one was released on recognizance in Chicago, but money bail was kept low; in Detroit, almost half were released on recognizance (on a promise to return to court), and when money bail was required it was fairly low. Pretrial motions concerning the state's evidence were also treated differently in each city. Because most Baltimore defendants went directly to a trial court without a preliminary hearing, defense attorneys had few chances to present pretrial motions to suppress evidence. The preliminary hearing was carried out in an adversarial fashion in Detroit, less so in Chicago.

What impact did the courtroom workgroups have on these preliminary hearings? Eisenstein and Jacob found that the stable courtroom workgroups in Chicago had informal procedures for screening cases. Because of the groups' close links to the trial courtrooms, they felt pressure to screen out many cases and thus spare the resources of the judges and the courts. This led to a very high dismissal rate. In Detroit, also a city with stable workgroups, the prosecutors had discretion to screen cases before they reached the courtroom; hence most of the defendants who appeared at preliminary hearings were sent to trial. Baltimore had less stable workgroups, in part because members were rotated, and sponsoring organizations did not closely supervise assistant prosecutors and defense attorneys. The unstable workgroups lacked close working relationships, shared values, and reasons to cooperate. As a result, there were fewer guilty pleas and most defendants were sent on to the grand jury and thence to the trial courts.

Findings at the trial court stage were similar. As shown in Table 7.2, the conviction rates were similar in the three cities, but the methods used to dispose of cases differed greatly. Bear in mind, however, that in Baltimore cases were not screened, whereas 40 percent of felony arrests in Detroit and 85 percent in Chicago had been dropped at the preliminary hearing. The data also show that each city arrived at the results in different ways. Detroit operated at a pace three times faster than that of Baltimore and Chicago. Chicago and Detroit relied mainly on guilty pleas, while Baltimore processed more cases through trials than through plea bargaining. But in all three cities the workgroups shunned the jury trial: fewer than 10 percent of the cases were disposed of in this way.

Differences in case dispositions among the cities reflected, among other things, the structure of the courtroom workgroups. How workgroups dealt with cases was also influenced by defendants' characteristics, the strength of the

TABLE 7.2

Trial court dispositions of felony cases in three cities

While other factors were similar, the cities used different methods to dispose of cases. What might account for the lesser use of the guilty plea in Baltimore?

	BALTIMORE	CHICAGO	DETROIT
Defendants sent to trial whom court convicted	68.0%	75.5%	72.2%
Median number of days between grand jury indictment or information and trial courtroom disposition	178.0	151.5	56.0
Median number of days between arrest and trial courtroom disposition	226.0	267.5	71.2
Disposition methods			
Guilty pleas	34.7%	61.7%	63.9%
Bench trials	33.9%	19.9%	6.8%
Jury trials	9.4%	6.7%	7.3%
Dismissals	22.0%	11.7%	22.0%
	100.0%	100.0%	100.0%
	(N=549)	(N=519)	(N=1,208)

SOURCE: James Eisenstein and Herbert Jacob, *Felony Justice: An Organizational Analysis of Criminal Courts* (Boston: Little, Brown, 1977), 233. Copyright © 1977 by James Eisenstein and Herbert Jacob. Reprinted by permission of the authors.

evidence, and the nature of the offense—factors that entered into the ongoing social system of the courtroom. If defendants had been convicted of crimes in the past, if the evidence of guilt was clear and strong, or if the defendant was accused of a serious crime, the workgroup's processes were likely to produce a harsher punishment and show less flexibility in plea bargaining.

The disposition of felony cases results from the interaction of members of the courtroom workgroup. The decisions made by each member are influenced by the policies of their sponsoring organizations. These interactions and policies may vary from courthouse to courthouse. The stability of workgroup interactions can be upset by changes such as a new docket system or changes in the policies and practices of sponsoring organizations. For example, a public defender office may shift from making each attorney responsible for all aspects of a case to making each attorney responsible for a single stage in each case (for example, arraignment or preliminary hearing). Such a shift might make one public defender solely responsible for plea bargaining after the preliminary hearing and thus lead to formation of a new courtroom workgroup. The change would require courtroom actors to get to know a new defense attorney, and it would take some time for a strong sense of shared values and norms to develop. Similarly, a decision by the prosecutor to institute policies in which only cases that are expected to result in a conviction are brought to trial might change the dynamics of case processing. It would create new opportunities for plea bargaining in cases that previously would have gone to trial but would now be subject to negotiations because of doubts about key evidence. Courtroom actors must adapt to such changes, and the pattern of disposition of cases will change as a result.

⑯ **Why are courtroom workgroups different in different cities?**

Summary

- The United States has a dual court system consisting of state and federal courts that are organized into separate hierarchies.
- Trial courts and appellate courts have different jurisdictions and functions.
- Despite resistance from local judges and political interests, reformers have sought to improve state court systems through centralized administration, state funding, and a separate personnel system.
- The judge, a key figure in the criminal justice process, assumes the roles of adjudicator, negotiator, and administrator.
- State judges are selected through various methods, including partisan elections, nonpartisan elections, gubernatorial appointment, and merit selection.
- Merit selection methods for choosing judges have gradually spread to many states. Such methods normally use a screening committee to make recommendations of potential appointees who will, if placed on the

bench by the governor, go before the voters for approval or disapproval of their performance in office.

■ The outcomes in criminal cases are significantly influenced by a court's local legal culture, which defines the "going rates" of punishment for various offenses.

■ Courtroom workgroups made up of judges, prosecutors, and defense attorneys who work together can smoothly and efficiently handle cases through cooperative plea bargaining processes.

■ The cohesion of a workgroup is enhanced by the physical setting of the courtroom, the different roles performed by each actor—judge, prosecutor, and defense attorney—in the group, and the exchange relationships that develop between these actors.

Questions for Review

❶ Discuss the effects that partisan election of judges may have on the administration of justice. Which system of judicial selection do you think is most appropriate? Explain your reasons.

❷ The judge plays several roles. What are they? In your opinion, do any of them conflict with one another?

❸ What is the courtroom workgroup? What is necessary for its formation?

❹ If you are being prosecuted on a drug charge, what tactics might your attorney use to get you a light sentence? How would these tactics influence court operations?

Key Terms

adversary system (p. 253)
appellate courts (p. 248)
going rate (p. 264)
grouping (p. 266)
inquisitorial system (p. 253)

jurisdiction (p. 248)
local legal culture (p. 263)
merit selection (p. 260)
nonpartisan election (p. 258)
partisan election (p. 258)

trial courts of general jurisdiction (p. 248)
trial courts of limited jurisdiction (p. 248)
workgroup (p. 265)

For Further Reading

Blumberg, Abraham S. *Criminal Justice.* Chicago: Quadrangle Books, 1967. A classic examination of the criminal courts as organizations.

Eisenstein, James, Roy Flemming, and Peter Nardulli. *The Contours of Justice: Communities and Their Courts.* Boston: Little, Brown, 1988. A study of nine felony courts in three states. Emphasizes the impact of the local legal culture on court operations.

Eisenstein, James, and Herbert Jacob. *Felony Justice: An Organizational Analysis of Criminal Courts.* Boston: Little, Brown, 1977. Felony courts in three cities. Develops the concept of the courtroom workgroup and its impact on decision making.

Feeley, Malcolm M. *Court Reform on Trial.* New York: Basic Books, 1983. Study of court reform efforts such as diversion, speedy trial, bail reform, and sentencing reform. Notes the difficulties of bringing about change.

Satter, Robert. *Doing Justice: A Trial Judge at Work.* New York: Simon and Schuster, 1990. A judge's view of the cases that he faces daily and the factors that influence his decisions.

Wice, Paul. *Judges and Lawyers: The Human Side of Justice.* New York: Harper Collins, 1991. Provides detailed descriptions of the training, socialization, and work environments of lawyers and judges, including coverage of each profession's special pressures and ethical issues.

Going Online

❶ Using the Internet, go to the web page for the judiciary of Iowa: www.judicial.state.ia.us. Read the section entitled "About Our Courts." What are the differences between the various kinds of judges in Iowa, including judicial magistrates, associate juvenile judges, associate probate judges, district associate judges, and district court judges?

❷ Using the Internet, go to the web page for the U.S. District Court for the Southern District of Texas: www.txs.uscourts.gov. What is the fee to file a civil lawsuit in the federal courts? Do you think the fee prevents people from making use of the courts?

❸ **Using InfoTrac College Edition,** look for articles under the subject "judicial selection." What kinds of judges has President Bill Clinton appointed to the federal court? How have his appointments affected diversity among judges?

CHECK POINT ANSWERS

❶ Separate federal and state court systems handle cases from throughout the land.

❷ Most state and county courts are decentralized because they are operated and controlled by the local communities, instead of being run by a statewide administration.

❸ Primarily appeals from lower federal and state courts.

❹ Trial courts of limited jurisdiction have jurisdiction over misdemeanor cases and preliminary matters in felony cases. Sometimes they handle felony trials that may result in penalties below a specified limit. Trial courts of general jurisdiction have jurisdiction over all offenses, including felonies. In some states they may also hear appeals.

❺ Both are appellate courts, but the court of last resort usually only hears appeals after they have been heard by the intermediate appellate court and cases that may have wide policy implications.

❻ To create a unified court system with consolidated and simplified structures, that has centralized management, full funding by the state, and a central personnel system.

❼ That judges carefully and deliberately weigh the issues in a case before making a decision. Judges embody justice and dispense it impartially.

❽ In the American adversary system, the judge acts as a neutral referee during the trial, while the judge in the inquisitorial system used in Europe and elsewhere actively investigates the facts of the case and questions witnesses.

❾ So that all segments of society will view the decisions as legitimate and fair.

❿ Adjudicator, negotiator, administrator.

⓫ To secure the support of attorneys who aspire to become judges and to ensure that courthouse positions are allocated to party workers.

⓬ When a vacancy occurs, a nominating commission is appointed that sends the governor the names of approved candidates. The governor must fill the vacancy from this list. After a year's term, a referendum is held to ask the voters whether the judge should be retained.

⓭ The local legal culture consists of norms that distinguish between "our" court and other jurisdictions, that stipulate how members should treat one another, and that describe how cases should be processed.

⓮ In rural areas court participants know each other, the number of criminal offenses is low, and few officials are involved in the disposition process. Urban courts make decisions in a bureaucratic context—offenders are known only by their case record, multiple courtrooms are used, the courthouse has a large staff, and caseload pressures are great.

⓯ The courtroom workgroup is made up of judge, prosecutor, defense counsel, and support staff assigned to a specific courtroom. Through interaction of these members, goals and norms are shared and a set of roles becomes stabilized.

⓰ Several factors can vary in different cities: the structure of the courtroom workgroups, the influence of the sponsoring organizations, and the sociopolitical environment of the city.

Prosecution and Defense

On April 15, 1999, three men entered the New York office of Steven Stoute, a rap music producer. The men beat Stoute with several objects, including a chair and a champagne bottle. Stoute suffered a broken arm, a broken jaw, and cuts to his head. According to the police, the attack was recorded by security video cameras.

The following day, the police arrested Sean "Puff Daddy" Combs, a multimillionaire rap performer and producer. The other two men involved in the attack were reportedly Combs's bodyguards. Combs was charged with second-degree assault and criminal mischief. Under New York law, Combs faced the possibility of seven years in prison for the assault charge. Combs reportedly was angry at Stoute because of a disagreement about the content of a music video. This was not Puff Daddy's first brush with the law. Combs had a prior criminal conviction for criminal mischief from 1996 for threatening someone with a gun (MacFarquhar, 1999).

What should happen to a repeat offender who seriously injures a victim during an assault? The answer depends on the decisions of the prosecutor and the strategies of the defense attorney. Prosecutors must determine which charges to apply against the accused and decide if a negotiated plea is appropriate. The defense attorney must represent the defendant zealously and seek to advance the client's best interests, whether that be a plea bargain or a fight to the finish in a trial.

In June, Combs reconciled with Stoute and publicly apologized for his actions. Stoute told the prosecutor's office that he did not want criminal charges pressed against Combs. Although Combs said he did not pay Stoute any money as part of their reconciliation, sources told the news media that Combs's deal with Stoute included the promise of a future payment of $1 million (Phillips, 1999).

By September 1999, it became clear that Combs's attorney had been involved in negotiations with the prosecutor's office. On September 8th, Combs pleaded guilty to the charge of harassment (*Lansing State Journal,* September 9, 1999:8B). Instead of facing the possibility of seven years in prison, as he had under the original felony assault charge, Combs was ordered to attend a one-day class in anger management. His sentence did not include any jail time, fines, or community service. By pleading guilty to a harassment "violation" instead of a felony or misdemeanor under New York law, the charge did not even leave him with a criminal record for his actions against Stoute. After the sentence was announced, Combs's attorney, Harvey Slovis, declared that it was a "clear victory" for his client (Phillips, 1999).

Although Assistant District Attorney Ina Scherl declined to comment on the case, Slovis acknowledged that the prosecutor had threatened to reinstate felony assault charges if Combs declined to enter a guilty plea to the harassment charge. This acknowledgement made it clear that the defense attorney and the prosecutor had been negotiating in the weeks leading up to the plea and sentence. Did Combs's punishment fit his crime? Did the prosecutor fulfill society's interest in punishing people who commit crimes of violence? Did the defense attorney achieve a brilliant victory by outmaneuvering the prosecution? The answers to such questions are not clear. It is difficult to know the extent to which the crime victim's wishes influenced the prosecutor's decision to drop the felony charges. It is also difficult to know if the prosecutor's decision was affected by a pressing caseload of other, more serious cases. And because the prosecutor—like all prosecutors—was under no obligation to explain her decision, there is no way to know why she dropped the serious felony charges, even though Combs was apparently videotaped committing the violent crime.

When celebrities and the wealthy escape conviction and punishment for serious charges, concerns often arise that fame and money affected the outcomes. The rich and famous can afford to hire better legal representation than the typical attorney appointed to represent a poor person. In addition, gifts and favors given to the victim by the defendant could undercut the prosecutor's case by diminishing the victim's willingness to cooperate. The advantages enjoyed by Combs are apparent when his sentence is compared with that of other offenders. For example, several female students at Michigan State University in 1999 lifted their shirts to flash their bare breasts at a rowdy crowd filling the streets after a basketball game. They subsequently were convicted of indecent exposure and received jail sentences ranging from five to seventeen days plus months of probation and thousands of dollars in fines (DeJong and Smith, 2000). Some of the women were not represented by attorneys because they waived their right to counsel in the hope that their cases could be resolved quickly with a simple fine or probation. However, the prosecutor was not willing to drop or reduce charges as part of any plea agreement. Although the women committed no acts of violence, the prosecutor and judge treated them as if they were responsible for acts of arson and vandalism committed by people wandering the streets that evening. How did their actions compare with that of Combs? Was there equal treatment in the two cases? These are important questions. However, the power of prosecutors in each locality is so significant and the strategies of defense attorneys vary so much from case to case that comparable or equitable results cannot be expected in criminal cases.

The primary lesson demonstrated by both of these examples is that the prosecutor and defense attorney are the most influential figures in determining the outcomes of criminal cases. The American system places great power and responsibility in the hands of attorneys for each side in a criminal case. As a result, the justice system's ability to handle cases and produce fair results depends on the dedication, skill, and enthusiasm that these lawyers bring to the decisions they make in the private meetings that determine the fates of most criminal defendants.

QUESTIONS for Inquiry

- What are the roles of the prosecuting attorney?
- What is the process by which criminal charges are filed, and what role does the prosecutor's discretion play in that process?
- With whom does the prosecutor interact in decision making?
- What is the day-to-day reality of criminal defense work in the United States?
- Who becomes a defense attorney?
- How is counsel provided for defendants who cannot afford a private attorney?
- What role does the defense attorney play in the system, and what is the nature of the attorney-client relationship?

The Prosecutorial System

Prosecuting attorneys make discretionary decisions about whether to pursue criminal charges, which charges to make, and what sentence to recommend. They represent the government in pursuing criminal charges against the accused. Except in a few states, no higher authority second-guesses or changes these decisions. Thus prosecutors are more independent than most other public officials. As with other aspects of American government, prosecution is mainly a task of state and local governments. Because most crimes are violations of state laws, county prosecutors usually bring charges against suspects in court.

For cases that involve violation of federal criminal laws, prosecutions are handled in federal court by **United States attorneys.** These attorneys are responsible for a large number of drug-related and white-collar crime cases. They are appointed by the president and are part of the Department of Justice. One U.S. attorney and a staff of assistant U.S. attorneys prosecute cases in each of the ninety-four U.S. district courts.

United States attorney
Officials responsible for the prosecution of crimes that violate the laws of the United States. Appointed by the president and assigned to a U.S. district court jurisdiction.

attorney general

Chief legal officer of a state responsible for both civil and criminal cases.

prosecuting attorney

A legal representative of the state with sole responsibility for bringing criminal charges. In some states referred to as district attorney, state's attorney, or county attorney.

Each state has an elected **attorney general,** who usually has the power to bring prosecutions in certain cases. An attorney general may, for example, handle a statewide consumer fraud case if a chain of auto repair shops is suspected of overcharging customers. In Alaska, Delaware, and Rhode Island, the state attorney general also directs all local prosecutions.

However, the vast majority of criminal cases are handled in the 2,343 county-level offices of the **prosecuting attorney**—known in various states as the district attorney, state's attorney, commonwealth attorney, or county attorney—who pursues cases that violate state law. The number of prosecutors who work in these offices increased significantly during the 1990s as the nation devoted more resources to the criminal justice system. A total of seventy-one thousand attorneys worked as prosecutors in 1996, a number that constituted a 25 percent increase in prosecuting attorneys nationwide since 1992 (DeFrances and Steadman, 1998). Prosecutors have the power to make independent decisions about which cases to pursue and what charges to file. They also have the power to drop charges and to negotiate arrangements for guilty pleas.

In rural areas the prosecutor's office may be composed solely of the prosecuting attorney and a part-time assistant. By contrast, in some urban jurisdictions—such as Los Angeles, with five hundred assistant prosecutors and numerous legal assistants and investigators—the office is organized according to various types of crimes. Many assistant prosecutors use the trial experience gained in the prosecutor's office as a means of moving on to a more highly paid position in a private law firm.

Politics and Prosecution

In all states except Connecticut and New Jersey, prosecutors are elected, usually for a four-year term; the office thus is heavily involved in local politics. By seeking to please voters, many prosecutors have tried to use their local office as a springboard to higher office—such as state legislator, governor, or member of Congress.

The power of prosecutors flows directly from their legal duties, but the process of prosecution is strongly influenced by politics. Prosecutors often are able to mesh their own ambitions with the needs of a political party. The appointment of assistant prosecutors offers a chance to recruit bright young lawyers for the party. Prosecutors may choose certain cases for prosecution to gain the favor of voters or investigate charges against political opponents and public officials to get the attention of the public. Political factors may also cause prosecutors to apply their powers unevenly within a community.

Prosecutors' discretionary power can create the impression that some groups or individuals may receive harsher treatment, while others may receive protection. When famed horror writer Stephen King was seriously injured in 1999 after being struck by a minivan while he was walking along a road in Maine, the driver claimed that he was charged with aggravated assault only because a celebrity had been injured in the accident (*Lansing State Journal,* October 3, 1999:6B).

The existence of discretionary decision making creates the risk that discrimination will result. For example, some scholars see prosecutors' decisions as reflecting biases based on race, social class, and gender (Frohmann, 1997). However, other researchers believe the nature and extent of discrimination by prosecutors has not yet been fully established by research studies (Walker, Spohn, and

DeLeone, 1996). Some studies do raise questions about discrimination in specific situations, such as prosecutors' decisions to seek the death penalty (Sorensen and Wallace, 1999).

CHECK POINT

① **What are the titles of the officials responsible for criminal prosecution at the federal, state, and local levels of government?**

(Answers are at the end of the chapter.)

The Prosecutor's Influence

Prosecutors have great influence because they are concerned with all aspects of the criminal justice process (Jacoby, 1995). By contrast, other decision makers are involved in only part of the process. From arrest to final disposition of a case, prosecutors can make decisions that will largely determine the defendant's fate. The prosecutor chooses the cases to be prosecuted, selects the charges to be brought, recommends the bail amount, approves agreements with the defendant, and urges the judge to impose a particular sentence.

Throughout the justice process, prosecutors' links with the other actors in the system—police, defense attorneys, judges—shape the prosecutors' decisions. Prosecutors may, for example, recommend bail amounts and sentences that match the preferences of particular judges. They may make "tough" recommendations in front of "tough" judges but tone down their arguments before judges who favor leniency or rehabilitation. Likewise, the other actors in the system may adjust their decisions and actions to match the preferences of the prosecutor. For example, police officers' investigation and arrest practices are likely to reflect the prosecutor's priorities. Thus, prosecutors influence the decisions of others while also shaping their own actions in ways that reinforce their relationships with police, defense attorneys, and judges.

Prosecutors gain additional power from the fact that their decisions and actions are hidden from public view. For example, a prosecutor and a defense attorney may strike a bargain whereby the prosecutor reduces a charge in exchange for a guilty plea or drops a charge if the defendant agrees to seek psychiatric help. In such instances a decision on a case is reached in a way that is nearly invisible to the public. In the case against Sean "Puff Daddy" Combs, for example, the public has no way to know what discussions and considerations produced the plea agreement that involved a significant reduction in charges and a minimal sentence.

State laws do little to limit or guide prosecutors' decisions. Most laws describe the prosecutor's duties in such vague terms as "prosecuting all crimes and civil actions to which state or county may be party." Such laws do not tell the prosecutor which cases must be prosecuted and which ones dismissed. The prosecutor has significant discretion to make such decisions without direct interference from either the law or other actors in the justice system (Caulfield, 1994). When prosecutors' decisions are challenged, judges generally reject the claim.

Because most local prosecutors are elected, their decisions are influenced by public opinion. If they feel that the community no longer considers a particular act to be criminal, they may refuse to prosecute or try to convince the complainant not to press charges. Public influence over prosecutors can take two forms. First, because most prosecutors are elected, they must keep their decisions consistent with community values to increase their chances of gaining reelection. Second, because jurors are drawn from the local community, prosecutors do not want to waste their time and resources pursuing charges about which local jurors are unsympathetic or unconcerned. In some communities, for example, prostitution may be prosecuted actively, while in others it is ignored. About three-fourths of American prosecutors serve counties with populations of fewer than 100,000. The community often has only one prosecutor, and he or she may be subject to strong local pressures, especially with regard to victimless crimes such as marijuana smoking, petty gambling, and prostitution. Prosecutors therefore develop policies that reflect community attitudes. As a New York prosecutor has remarked, "We are pledged to enforcement of the law, but we have to use our heads in the process."

CHECK POINT

② **What are the powers of the prosecuting attorney?**

The Prosecutor's Roles

As "lawyers for the state," prosecutors face conflicting pressures to vigorously press charges against lawbreakers while also upholding justice and the rights of the accused. These pressures are often called "the prosecutor's dilemma." In the adversary system, prosecutors must do everything they can to win a conviction, yet as members of the legal profession they must see that justice is done even if it means that the accused is not convicted. The Canon of Ethics of the New York State Bar Association states, "The primary duty of a lawyer engaged in public prosecution is not to convict, but to see that justice is done. The suppression of facts and the secreting of witnesses capable of establishing the innocence of the accused is highly reprehensible" (Smith and Pollack, 1972:165). Even so, there is always a risk of "prosecutor's bias," sometimes called a "prosecution complex." Although they are supposed to represent all the people, including the accused, prosecutors may view themselves as instruments of law enforcement. Thus, as advocates on behalf of the state, their strong desire to close each case with a conviction may keep them from recognizing unfair procedures or evidence of innocence. A comparison of prosecutors in the United States and Japan, for example, found that American prosecutors often proceed with the assumption that the facts weigh against the defendant while Japanese prosecutors are more concerned with investigating the case to discover all available facts before making any decisions (Johnson, 1998).

What happens in the United States if prosecutors make a mistake and it appears that an innocent person may have been convicted? After a trial and the completion of the appellate process, sometimes no avenue is available for a defendant to gain reconsideration of the conviction (Tucker, 1997). A national commission appointed by U.S. Attorney General Janet Reno recommended in 1999 that prosecutors drop their

As lawyers for the state, prosecutors are expected to do everything to win each case, but they are also expected to see that justice is done.

adversarial posture and cooperate in permitting DNA testing of evidence saved from old cases that produced convictions before sophisticated scientific tests were developed (Lewis, 1999). Even though dozens of convicted offenders have been proved innocent in rape and murder cases through after-the-fact DNA testing, some prosecutors have resisted the reexamination of old evidence.

Prosecutors are seldom punished for mistakes they made in convicting innocent people. Prosecutors are generally immune from civil lawsuits for their official actions. Moreover, even in rare circumstances when prosecutors face criminal misconduct charges for excessive actions in seeking to convict an innocent person, juries may not convict the prosecutors of crimes. In June 1999, an Illinois jury acquitted seven prosecutors and law enforcement officers of conspiracy and obstruction of justice charges that stemmed from their efforts to convict Rolando Cruz of a gruesome child murder. Although Cruz was eventually released from prison when someone else confessed to crime, Cruz was not a model citizen and he gave inconsistent testimony about his treatment at the hands of police and prosecutors. Thus jurors were apparently reluctant to convict the prosecutors of crimes for the mistakes that they made in investigating Cruz's case (Possley and Gregory, 1999).

Although all prosecutors must uphold the law and pursue charges against lawbreakers, they may perform these tasks in different ways. Because of their personal values and professional goals, and the political climate of their city or county, they may define the prosecutor's role differently than prosecutors in other places. For example, a prosecutor who believes that young offenders can be rehabilitated may define the role differently than one who believes that young offenders should receive the same punishments as adults. One might send juveniles to counseling programs while the other seeks to process them though the adult system of courts and corrections. A prosecutor with no assistants and few resources for conducting full-blown jury trials may be forced to stress effective plea bargaining, while a prosecutor in a wealthier county may have more options when deciding whether to take cases to trial. Role definition is complicated by the relationships prosecutors must maintain with many other actors—police officers, judges, defense attorneys, political party leaders, and so forth—who may have conflicting ideas about what the prosecutor should do. The prosecutor's decisions will affect the ability of the others to perform their duties and achieve their goals. If the prosecutor decides not to prosecute, the judge and jury will not be called upon to decide the case and police officers may feel that their efforts have been wasted. If the prosecutor decides to launch a campaign against drugs or pornography, this decision will have effects in both the political and criminal justice arenas. Police may feel that they must redirect their time and energy toward the crimes emphasized by the prosecutor. However, they may also pressure the prosecutor to set new priorities by declining to devote their efforts to the kinds of crimes the prosecutor wants to concentrate on. Excessive attention to victimless crimes, such as gambling and prostitution, may produce a public backlash if citizens feel that the prosecutor should focus on more serious crimes.

When prosecutors are asked about their roles, they mention four distinct role conceptions:

❶ Trial counsel for the police. Prosecutors should reflect the views of law enforcement in the courtroom and take a crime-fighter stance in public.

❷ House counsel for the police. Prosecutors' main function is to give legal advice so that arrests will stand up in court.

❸ Representative of the court. Prosecutors' main function is to enforce the rules of due process to ensure that the police act according to the law and uphold the rights of defendants.

❹ Elected official. Prosecutors may be most responsive to public opinion. The political impact of their decisions is one of their major concerns.

Each of these roles involves a different view of the prosecutor's "clients" as well as his or her own responsibilities. In the first two roles, prosecutors appear to believe that the police are the clients of their legal practice. Take a moment to think about who might be the clients of prosecutors who view themselves as representatives of the court or as elected officials.

CHECK POINT

③ **What are the roles of the prosecutor?**

Discretion of the Prosecutor

Because they have such broad discretion, prosecutors can shape their decisions to fit different interests. Their decisions might be based on a desire to impress voters through tough "throw-the-book-at-them" charges in a highly publicized case (Maschke, 1995). Their decisions might stem from their personal values, such as an emphasis on leniency and rehabilitation for young offenders. Prosecutors may also shape their decisions to please local judges by, for example, accepting plea agreements that will keep the judges from being burdened by too many time-consuming trials. Any or all of these motives may shape prosecutors' decisions because no higher authority tells prosecutors how they must do their jobs. From the time the police turn a case over to the prosecutor, the prosecutor has almost complete control over decisions about charges and plea agreements. The discretion of American prosecutors sharply contrasts with the situation of prosecutors in European countries such as Germany (see the Comparative Perspective on p. 286). In Germany, the prosecutors face fewer pressures to win cases and instead bear greater responsibilities for evaluating the evidence and guilt of defendants before deciding whether to drop or pursue charges (Feeney, 1998). By contrast, American prosecutors who have doubts about whether the available evidence proves the defendant's guilt may just shrug their shoulders and say, "I'll just let the jury decide" rather than face public criticism for dropping charges. In Japan, prosecutors throughout the country work for a single, nationwide agency and are not elected officials. As such, they must gain approval from superiors for many of their decisions rather than make independent decisions the way local prosecutors in the United States do (Johnson, 1998).

While the rate of such dismissals varies from place to place, in most cities up to half of all arrests do not lead to formal charges. Prosecutors may decide not to press charges because of factors related to a particular case or because they have a policy of not bringing charges for certain offenses. For example, the U.S. Department of Justice gives its prosecutors guidelines for deciding whether a case should be dismissed or pursued (U.S. Department of Justice, 1980). They include the following:

❶ Federal law enforcement priorities.

❷ The nature and seriousness of the offense.

❸ The deterrent effect of prosecution.

❹ The person's culpability (blameworthiness) in connection with the offense.

❺ The person's history with respect to criminal activity.

❻ The person's willingness to cooperate in the investigation or prosecution of others.

❼ The probable sentence or other consequences if the person is convicted.

In addition to these formal considerations, decisions to pursue felony charges may be affected by the staffing levels of individual prosecutor's offices (Walker, 1998). If offices lack sufficient resources to pursue all possible cases, prosecutors may establish priorities and then reduce or dismiss charges in cases deemed less important.

If you were a prosecutor, what would you consider the most important factors in deciding whether to pursue a case? Would you have any concerns about the possibility of prosecuting an innocent person? Is it ethical for a prosecutor to pursue a case against someone whom the prosecutor does not believe is guilty of a crime? As you read A Question of Ethics, consider what you would do if you were the prosecutor assigned to the case.

Even after deciding that a case should be prosecuted, the prosecutor has great freedom in deciding what charges to file. Criminal incidents may involve a number of laws, so the prosecutor can bring a single charge or more than one. Suppose that Smith, who is armed, breaks into a grocery store, assaults the proprietor, and robs the cash drawer. What charges may the prosecutor file? By virtue of having committed the robbery, the accused can be charged with at least four crimes: breaking and entering, assault, armed robbery, and carrying a dangerous weapon. Other charges or **counts** may be added, depending on the nature of the incident. A forger, for instance, may be charged with one count for each act of forgery committed. By filing as many charges as possible, the prosecutor strengthens his or her position in plea negotiations. In effect, the prosecutor can use discretion in deciding the number of charges and thus increase the prosecution's supply of "bargaining chips."

The discretionary power to set charges does not give the prosecutor complete control over plea bargaining. Defense attorneys strengthen their position in the **discovery** process, in which information from the prosecutor's case file must be made available to the defense. For example, the defense has the right to see any statements made by the accused during interrogation by the police, as well as the results of any physical or psychological tests. This information tells the defense attorney about the strengths and weaknesses of the prosecution's case. The defense attorney may use it to decide whether a case is hopeless or whether it is worthwhile to engage in tough negotiations.

A Question of Ethics

Ethics

Assistant County Prosecutor Adam Dow entered the office of his boss, County Prosecutor Susan Graham. "You wanted to see me?" he said as he closed the door.

"Yes, I do," Graham replied with a flash of anger. "I don't agree with your recommendation to dismiss charges in the Richardson case."

"But the victim was so uncertain in making the identification at the lineup, and the security video from the ATM machine is so grainy that you can't really tell if Richardson committed the robbery," said Dow.

"Look. We've had six people robbed while withdrawing money at ATM machines in the past month. The community is upset. The banks are upset. The newspapers keep playing up these unsolved crimes. I want to put an end to this public hysteria. Richardson has a prior record for a robbery and the victim picked him out of the lineup eventually." Graham stared at him coldly. "I'm not going to dismiss the charges."

Dow shifted his feet and stared at the floor. "I'm not comfortable with this case. Richardson may be innocent. The evidence just isn't very strong."

"Don't worry about the strength of the evidence. That's not your problem," said Graham. "We have enough evidence to take the case to trial. The judge said so at the preliminary hearing. So we'll just let the jury decide. Whatever happens, the community will know that we took action against this crime problem."

"But what if he's innocent? The jury could make a mistake in thinking that he's the robber in the grainy videotape. I wouldn't want that on my conscience," replied Dow.

◼ Should Assistant Prosecutor Dow act as if he is the judge and jury by deciding on the certainty of the defendant's guilt before agreeing to take a case forward? Should Prosecutor Graham take the community's feelings into consideration in deciding whether to pursue charges against Richardson? Could an innocent person be convicted in a jury trial under such circumstances if the prosecutor is reluctant to dismiss questionable charges?

count
Each separate offense of which a person is accused in an indictment or an information.

perspective

Prosecution
in Germany

Unlike prosecutors in the United States, German prosecutors are not parties in an adversarial system; instead, they are required to act not only against but also in favor of the suspect at any stage of the proceedings. German prosecutors are not elected. They are civil servants and thus are immune from public opinion.

German prosecutors are expected to be objective above all, and thus one-third of all fraud cases studied were dismissed because of lack of sufficient evidence even though the suspect had made a confession in the course of police investigation. Another consequence of the rule of objectivity is that prosecutors need not concern themselves with winning every case. In up to 20 percent of all cases studied, the accused was acquitted by the trial judge, usually at the request of the prosecutor.

THE PROSECUTOR'S OFFICE AS AN INVESTIGATING AGENCY

In Germany the prosecutor controls the police investigations of each reported criminal case. Therefore, the prosecutor is often called "head of the preliminary proceedings." However, except in a few sensational cases such as murder, big commercial crimes, and, recently, terrorism, prosecutors seldom are truly in a supervisory role. Instead, a typical investigatory situation progresses as follows.

An offense will usually be reported to the police, who will then open and register a file. The police lack any discretionary power in deciding whether or not to file a case. They must follow up every suspicion and present all registered offenses—however vague the evidence may be—to the prosecutor, who alone makes the final decision. The police carry out all necessary investigations. If the police feel a case has been thoroughly investigated, they will forward it to the prosecutor, who must decide whether further investigation is necessary. The prosecutor can take over the investigation or can return the case to the police for further inquiries. The law requires the prosecutor to do everything to solve the case—regardless of its seriousness. It does not permit him or her to "filter" out cases, as American prosecutors are authorized to do.

discovery
A prosecutor's pretrial disclosure to the defense of facts and evidence to be introduced at trial.

nolle prosequi
An entry made by a prosecutor on the record of a case and announced in court to indicate that the charges specified will not be prosecuted. In effect, the charges are thereby dismissed.

The prosecutor's discretion does not end with the decision to file a certain charge. After the charge has been made, the prosecutor may reduce it in exchange for a guilty plea or enter a notation of **nolle prosequi** (*nol. pros.*). The latter is a freely made decision to drop the charge, either as a whole or as to one or more count. When a prosecutor decides to drop charges, no higher authorities can force him or her to reinstate them. When guilty pleas are entered, the prosecutor uses discretion in recommending a sentence.

> **CHECK POINT**

④ **How does a prosecutor use discretion to decide how to treat each defendant?**

THE PROSECUTOR'S OFFICE AS A CHARGING AGENCY

Calling the prosecutor's office a "charging agency" is something of a misnomer because on the average three out of four cases are dropped. The label refers to the main task of the prosecutor as it is the prosecutor's decision whether to charge or not. The charging decision involves two distinct considerations: evaluation of evidence and evaluation of guilt.

When prosecutors are *evaluating evidence,* they are more or less free in this decision. Some outside control is possible, however, because victims can file a formal complaint against the dismissal of a case. If the complaint is rejected by the attorney general (chief prosecutor of the state), the victim can file a motion for a judicial decision, which would, if successful, force the prosecutor to file a charge. Although this procedure is very seldom used, it is nonetheless feared by prosecutors. As a result, the status of victims may influence prosecutors' decisions. When the prosecutor is *evaluating guilt,* there are significant possibilities of hierarchical control over the decision. According to administrative rules issued by some of the ministries of justice of the states, deputy attorneys must present to their superiors for approval each case they want to dismiss based on minor guilt (mitigation). "In-house" instructions may also attempt to standardize the criteria by which "minor guilt" is defined.

The main task of prosecutors is to determine whether the evidence in a case is sufficient for conviction. As a result, they have large practical discretionary power when they describe whether "probable cause" exists in any given case. The prosecutor's "evaluation of evidence" was examined in two types of cases: petty and serious crimes. It was found that if the damage (monetary value or physical injuries) was considerable or if the suspect had previously been convicted, the prosecutor was less inclined to drop the charge even if the evidence was weak. This situation might be explained by the possibility that the more serious the crime the more likely the accused is to retain defense counsel, which may hinder police investigation.

The relationship between the suspect and the victim also markedly affects the prosecutor's evaluation of the evidence. Cases involving acquaintances or relatives of the victim instead of stranger-to-stranger cases are more likely to be dismissed if they involve the crimes of theft, robbery, or rape.

However, the opposite is true if the crime is fraud or embezzlement because of the special breach of trust connected with these types of acts.

In summary, then, it seems the prosecutor uses stricter evidentiary rules in *minor offenses* than in *serious offenses*. It may be that even though the evidence might not support a conviction in the more serious cases, the prosecutor still charges the case to use the charge itself as a sanction. The latter assumption is supported by the fact that prosecutors tend to regard prior criminal record as an element of proof and therefore charge recidivists more than first offenders. This tendency is in part counterbalanced by the judge, who—stressing the problem of proof more than the prosecutor—acquits more recidivists than first offenders.

Americans may wonder how the German system, with its requirement of compulsory prosecution, can be efficient. In Germany, caseloads are reduced by decriminalizing some acts, making prosecution contingent on the victim's formal request, turning felonies into misdemeanors, and extending the discretionary power of the prosecutor.

SOURCE: Adapted from Klaus Sessar, "Prosecutorial Discretion in Germany," in *The Prosecutor,* ed. William F. McDonald (Beverly Hills, Calif.: Sage, 1979), 255–273.

Key Relationships of the Prosecutor

Prosecutors' decisions are not based solely on formal policies and role conceptions (Fridell, 1990). They are also influenced by relationships with other actors in the justice system. Despite their independent authority, prosecutors must consider how police, judges, and others will react. They depend on these other officials to prosecute cases successfully. In turn, the success of police, judges, and corrections officials depends on prosecutors' effectiveness in identifying and convicting lawbreakers. Thus these officials build exchange relationships in which they cooperate with each other.

Prosecutors' decisions are influenced by their knowledge and relationships with judges. For example, knowing that a judge imposes exceptionally lenient sentences for particular offenses may discourage the prosecutor from pursuing such cases.

Police

Prosecutors depend on the police to provide both the suspects and the evidence needed to convict lawbreakers. Most crimes occur before the police arrive at the scene; therefore officers must reconstruct the crime on the basis of physical evidence and witness reports. Police must use their training, experience, and work routines to decide whether arrest and prosecution would be worthwhile. Prosecutors cannot control the types of cases brought to them because they cannot investigate crimes on their own. Thus the police control the initiation of the criminal justice process through their actions in investigating crimes and arresting suspects. These actions may be influenced by various factors, such as pressure on police to establish an impressive crime-clearance record. As a result, police actions may create problems for prosecutors if, for example, the police make many arrests without gathering enough evidence to ensure conviction.

Prosecutors depend on the police, but they can still influence the actions of the police. For example, prosecutors can return cases for further investigation and refuse to approve arrest warrants. Prosecutors and police have an exchange relationship in which the success of each depends on cooperation with the other.

Police requests for prosecution may be refused for reasons unrelated to the facts of the case. First, prosecutors regulate the workload of the justice system. They must make sure that a backlog of cases does not keep the court from meeting legal time limits for processing criminal cases. To keep cases from being dismissed by the judge for taking too long, prosecutors may themselves dismiss less important or weaker cases and focus on more serious charges or on cases in which clear proof exists of the defendant's guilt. Second, prosecutors may reject police requests for prosecution because they do not want to pursue poorly developed cases that would place them in an embarrassing position in the courtroom. Judges often scold prosecutors if weak cases are allowed to take up scarce courtroom time. Finally, prosecutors may return cases to make sure that police provide high-quality investigations and evidence.

Coordination between police and prosecutors has been a concern of criminal justice officials in recent decades (Buchanan, 1989). Lack of coordination causes cases to be dismissed or lost. Part of the problem is that lawyers and police have different views of crime and work for different sponsoring organizations. The police often claim that they have made a valid arrest and that the offender should be indicted and tried. But prosecutors look at cases to see if the evidence will result in a conviction. These different perspectives often lead to conflicts. In response to the need for greater coordination, many jurisdictions have formed police-prosecution teams to work together on cases. This approach is often used for drug or organized crime investigations and cases in which detailed information and evidence are required for conviction. Cooperation between the police and prosecutors is necessary in drug cases because without a network of informers, drug traffickers cannot be caught with evidence that can lead to convictions. Prosecutors can help police gain cooperation from informants by approving agreements to reduce charges or even to *nol. pros.* a case. The accused person may then return to the community to gather information for the police (see the Close-Up on p. 289).

CLOSE up

Drug Arrests: An Example of Exchange

Lt. Roger Cirella of the drug task force of the Seattle police entered the office of Chief Deputy Prosecutor Michael Ryan. Cirella reported that during questioning a well-known drug dealer intimated that he could provide evidence against a pharmacist suspected of illegally selling drugs. The officer wanted to transfer the case to the friendlier hands of a certain deputy prosecutor and to arrange for a reduction of charges and bail.

Cirella: Yesterday we got a break in the pharmacy case. We had arrested Sam Hanson after an undercover buy on First Avenue. He says that a druggist at the Green Cross Pharmacy is selling out the back door. We thought that something like that was happening because we had seen these guys standing around there, but we haven't been able to prove it. Hanson says he will cooperate if we'll go easy on him. Now, I'd like to get this case moved to Wadsworth. He's worked with us before and that new guy who's on it just doesn't understand our problems.

Ryan: Okay, but what's that going to accomplish?

Cirella: We also need to be able to fix it so Hanson gets out on bail without letting the druggies know he has become an informer. If we can get Judge Griffin to reduce bail he can probably put up the bond. Now we also need to reduce the charges yet keep him on the string so that we can bring him right back if he doesn't play ball.

Ryan: I want to cooperate with you guys, but I can't let the boss get a lot of heat for letting a pusher out on the street. How are we going to know that he's not going to screw up?

Cirella: Believe me, we will keep tabs on him.

Ryan: Okay, but don't come here telling me we're going to get splashed with mud in the *Times*.

Victims and Witnesses

Prosecutors depend on the cooperation of victims and witnesses. Although a case can be prosecuted whether or not a victim wishes to press charges, many prosecutors will not pursue cases in which the key testimony and other necessary evidence must be provided by a victim who is unwilling to cooperate. Prosecutors need the cooperation of people who have witnessed crimes.

The decision to prosecute is often based on an assessment of the victim's role in his or her own victimization and the victim's credibility as a witness. If a victim has a criminal record, the prosecutor may choose not to pursue the case in the belief that a jury would not consider the victim a credible witness—even though the jury will never learn that the victim has a criminal record. The decision not to prosecute may reflect the prosecutor's belief that someone with a criminal record is untrustworthy or does not deserve the protection of the law. In other words, the prosecutor's own biases in sizing up victims may affect which cases he or she pursues. If a victim is poorly dressed, uneducated, or a poor communicator, the prosecutor may be inclined to dismiss charges out of fear that a jury would find the victim unpersuasive (Stanko, 1988).

Other characteristics of victims may play a role. For example, prosecutors may not pursue cases in which victims are prostitutes who are raped, drug abusers who are assaulted by drug dealers, and children who cannot stand up to the pressure of testifying in court. Research indicates that victim characteristics, such as moral character, behavior at time of incident, and age, have greater influence over decisions to prosecute sexual assault cases than the strength of the evidence against the suspect (Spears and Spohn, 1997). Prosecutors may also base their decision on whether or not the victim and defendant had a prior relationship. Studies have shown that prosecutions are most successful when aimed at defendants accused of committing crimes against strangers (Boland, Brady, Tyson, and Bassler, 1983). When the victim is an acquaintance, a friend, or a relative of the defendant, he or she may refuse to act as a witness, and prosecutors and juries may view the offense as less serious. Even if police make an arrest on the scene, a fight between spouses may strike a prosecutor as a weak case, especially if the complaining spouse has second thoughts about cooperating. A high percentage of victims of violent crimes are acquainted with their assailants. That some victims would rather endure victimization than see a friend or relative punished in the justice system creates problems for the prosecution's case.

Based on the findings of a classic study, Figure 8.1 shows the outcomes of stranger and nonstranger robberies and burglaries in New York City. Note that 88 percent of arrests for robberies by strangers led to conviction, with 68 percent on a felony charge. Of those arrested, 65 percent were incarcerated, 32 percent for a year or more. In contrast, when the robbery victim knew the accused person, only 37 percent of those arrested were convicted, only 23 percent incarcerated, and none served more than a year. The same pattern can be seen in burglaries, although the punishments were less severe. Most of the burglars who were strangers were convicted, but only 8 percent on a felony charge. Prosecutors probably bargained these cases down to misdemeanors because the evidence was not strong. As with robberies of acquaintances, the burglars who knew their victims were treated more leniently by the prosecution (Vera Institute of Justice, 1981).

In recent years, many people have called for measures that would force prosecutors to make victims more central to the prosecution. Because in criminal cases

FIGURE 8.1 Outcomes of stranger and nonstranger robberies and burglaries in New York City

Victims of burglaries and robberies are less likely to pressure for conviction when the offender is known to them. If conviction is successful, the penalties tend to be less when the offender is not a stranger.

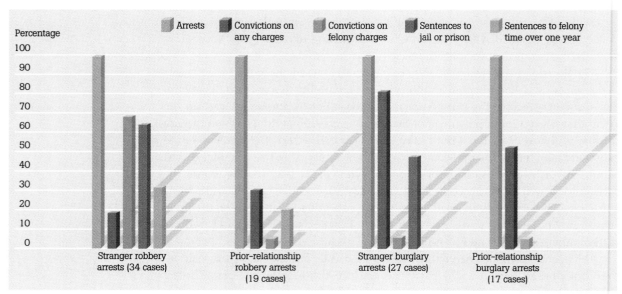

SOURCE: Vera Institute of Justice, *Felony Arrests: Their Prosecution and Disposition in New York City's Courts* (New York: Longman, 1981), 58, 86. Copyright © 1981 by Longman Publishing Group. Reprinted by permission of Vera Institute of Justice.

the state pursues charges against the accused, the victim is often forgotten in the process. The victims' rights movement has brought the proposal that victims be given a chance to comment on plea bargains, sentences, and parole decisions. In June 1996 President Bill Clinton endorsed a proposed constitutional amendment that, if ratified, would require prosecutors to keep victims informed on the progress of criminal cases and allow them to have some input in decisions on bail, plea bargains, and sentencing.

Judges and Courts

The sentencing history of each judge gives prosecutors an idea of how a case may be treated in the courtroom. Prosecutors may decide to drop a case if they believe that the judge assigned to it will not impose a serious punishment. Because prosecutors' offices have limited resources, they cannot afford to waste time pursuing charges in front of a specific judge if that judge shows a pattern of dismissing those particular cases.

Prosecutors depend on plea bargaining to keep cases moving through the courts. Prosecutors have difficulty persuading defendants and their attorneys to accept plea agreements unless judges' sentencing patterns are predictable. If the defendants and their lawyers are to accept a lesser charge or a promise of a lighter sentence in exchange for a guilty plea, some basis must exist to believe that the judge will support the agreement. Although some judges will informally approve plea agreements before the plea is entered, other judges believe taking part in plea bargaining is improper. Because these judges are unable to state their agreement with the details of any bargain, the prosecutor and defense attorney use the judges' past performance as a guide in arranging a plea that will be accepted in court.

In most jurisdictions, a person arrested on felony charges must be given a preliminary hearing within ten days. For prosecutors, this hearing is a chance to evaluate the testimony of witnesses, assess the strength of the evidence, and try to predict the outcome of the case should it go to trial. After that, prosecutors have several options: recommend that the case be held for trial, seek to reduce the charge to a misdemeanor, or conclude that they have no case and drop the charges. These decisions are greatly influenced by the prosecutor's perception of the court's caseload and the attitudes of the judges. If courts are overwhelmed with cases or if judges do not share the prosecutor's view about the seriousness of certain charges, the prosecutor may drop cases or reduce charges to keep the heavy flow of cases moving.

The Community

As a part of the wider political system, the criminal justice system responds to its environment. Public opinion and the media can play a crucial role in creating an environment that is either supportive or critical of the prosecutor. County prosecutors, like police chiefs and school superintendents, will not remain in office long if they are out of step with community values. They are likely to lose at the next election to an opponent who has a better sense of the community's priorities.

Public influence is especially important with respect to crimes that are not always fully enforced. Laws on the books may ban prostitution, gambling, and pornography, but public opinion in a community may tolerate them. In such a community the prosecutor will focus on other crimes rather than risk irritating citizens who believe that victimless crimes should not be strongly enforced. Other communities, however, may pressure the prosecutor to enforce morality laws and prosecute those who do not comply with local ordinances and state statutes. As elected officials, prosecutors must be sensitive to voters' attitudes.

Prosecutors' relationships and interactions with police, victims, defense attorneys, judges, and the community form the core of the exchange relations that shape decision-making in criminal cases. Prosecutors' decisions are also influenced by other relationships, such as those with news media, federal and state officials, legislators, and political party officials. This long list of actors illustrates that prosecutors' decisions are not based solely on whether a law was broken. The occurrence of a crime is only the first step in a decision-making process that may vary from one case to the next. Sometimes charges are dropped or reduced. Sometimes plea bargains are negotiated quickly. Sometimes cases move through the system to a complete jury trial. In every instance, prosecutors' discretionary decisions are shaped by relationships and interactions with a variety of actors both within and outside the justice system.

Studies have shown that the public's level of attention on the criminal justice system is low. Still, the community remains a potential source of pressure that leaders may activate against the prosecutor. The prosecutor's office generally keeps the public in mind when it makes its decisions.

CHECK POINT

⑤ **What are the prosecutor's key exchange relationships?**

Decision-Making Policies

Despite the many factors that may affect prosecutors' decisions in each case some general conclusions can be drawn about how prosecutors approach their office. Prosecutors develop their own policies on how cases will be handled. These policies shape the decisions made by the assistant prosecutors and thus have a major impact on the administration of justice. In different counties, prosecutors may pursue different goals in forming policies on which cases to pursue, which ones to drop, and which to ones to plea bargain. For example, some prosecutors may wish to maintain a high conviction rate and therefore will drop cases with weak evidence. Others may be concerned about using limited resources effectively. They will focus most of their time and energy on the most serious crimes.

The data in Figure 8.2 show how prosecutors handle felony cases in two different jurisdictions. Some make extensive use of screening and are less inclined to press charges. Guilty pleas are the main method of processing cases in some offices, while pleas of not guilty strain the courts' trial resources in others. Some offices remove cases—by diverting or referring them to other agencies—soon after they are brought to the prosecutor's attention by the police; in others, disposition occurs as late as the first day of trial. The period from the receipt of the police report to the start of the trial thus is a time of review in which the prosecutor uses discretion to decide what actions should be taken.

Prosecution policies are created within the context of political and community pressures. During a shoot-out in Ruby Ridge, Idaho, between the FBI and separatist Randy Weaver, Agent Lon Horiuchi shot Weaver's wife. The U.S. Justice Department concluded that Horiuchi had committed no federal crime. However, Boundary County Prosecutor Denise Woodbury, with Sheriff Greg Sprungl at her side, announced that she has filed state manslaughter charges against the FBI sharpshooter.

FIGURE 8.2 **Differences in how prosecutors handle felony cases in two jurisdictions**

The discretion of the prosecutor is evident in these two flowcharts. Note that different screening policies seem to be in operation: cases are referred earlier in the process in Utah and later in Colorado.

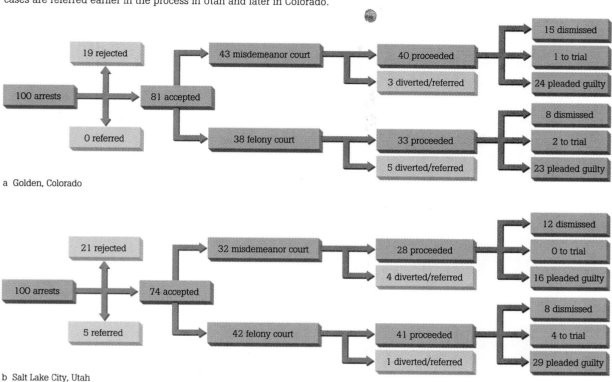

a Golden, Colorado

b Salt Lake City, Utah

SOURCE: U.S. Department of Justice, Bureau of Justice Statistics, *Report to the Nation on Crime and Justice*, 2d ed. (Washington, D.C.: Government Printing Office, 1988), 71.

Implementing Prosecution Policy

Joan Jacoby analyzed the management policies that prosecutors use during the pretrial process and how they staff their offices to achieve their goals. On the basis of data from more than three thousand prosecutors, she described three policy models: legal sufficiency, system efficiency, and trial sufficiency. The choice of a policy model is shaped by personal aspects of the prosecutor (such as role conception), external factors such as crime levels, and the relationship of prosecution to the other parts of the criminal justice system (Jacoby, 1979).

The policy model adopted by a prosecutor's office affects the screening and disposing of cases. As shown in Figure 8.3, the policy models dictate that prosecutors select certain points in the process to dispose of most of the cases brought to them by the police. Each model identifies the point in the process at which cases are filtered out of the system. A particular model may be chosen to advance specific goals, such as saving the prosecutor's time and energy for the most clear-cut or serious cases. Each model also affects how and when prosecutors interact with defense attorneys in exchanging information or discussing plea bargain options.

In the **legal sufficiency model,** prosecutors are merely asking whether enough evidence has been gathered to serve as a basis for prosecution. Some prosecutors believe they should pursue any case for which they think they can prove that the minimum legal elements of the charge are met. Prosecutors who use this policy may decide to prosecute a great many cases. As a result, they must have strategies to avoid overloading the system and draining their own resources.

legal sufficiency model
The presence of the minimum legal elements necessary for prosecution of a case. When a prosecutor's decision to prosecute a case is customarily based on legal sufficiency, a great many cases are accepted for prosecution, but the majority of them are disposed of by plea bargaining or dismissal.

FIGURE 8.3   Three policy models of prosecutorial case management

Prosecutors develop policies to guide the way their offices will manage cases. These models all assume that a portion of arrests will be dropped at some point in the system so that few cases reach trial.

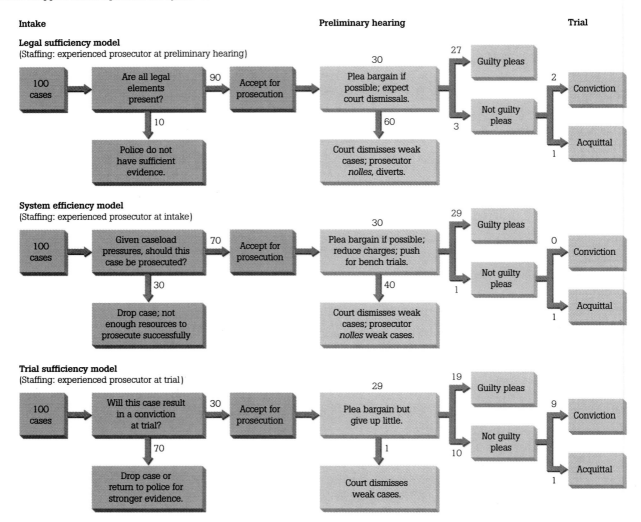

Thus, assistant prosecutors, especially those assigned to misdemeanor courts, make extensive use of plea bargains to keep cases flowing through the courts. In this model judges may dismiss many cases after determining that not enough evidence exists for prosecution to continue.

The **system efficiency model** aims at speedy and early disposition of a case. Each case is evaluated in light of the current caseload pressures. To close cases quickly, the prosecutor might charge the defendant with a felony but agree to reduce the charge to a misdemeanor in exchange for a guilty plea. According to Jacoby's research, this model is usually followed when the trial court is backlogged and the prosecutor has limited resources.

In the **trial sufficiency model,** a case is accepted and charges are made only when there is enough evidence to ensure conviction. For each case the prosecutor asks, "Will this case result in a conviction?" The prosecutor's prediction about the likelihood of conviction may not be correct in every case. However, the prosecutor

system efficiency model

Policy of the prosecutor's office that encourages speedy and early disposition of cases in response to caseload pressures. Weak cases are screened out at intake, and other nontrial alternatives are used as primary means of disposition.

will make every effort to win a conviction when he or she believes the evidence proves that all necessary legal elements for a crime are present. This model requires good police work, a prosecution staff with trial experience, and—because there is less plea bargaining—courts that are not too crowded to handle trials on a regular basis.

These three models lead to different results. While a suspect's case may be dismissed for lack of evidence in a trial sufficiency court, the same case may be prosecuted and the defendant pressured to enter a guilty plea in a legal sufficiency court.

Case Evaluation

The **accusatory process** is the series of activities that take place from the moment a suspect is arrested and booked by the police to the moment the formal charge—in the form of an indictment or information—is filed with the court. In an indictment, evidence is presented to a grand jury made up of citizens who determine whether to issue a formal charge. In an information, the prosecutor files the charge. Although these two charging processes seem clear-cut (see Figure 8.4), in practice, variations can mix the roles of the police, prosecutor, and court. In some places the prosecutor has full control of the charging decision; in others, the police informally make the decision, which is then approved by the prosecutor; in still others, the prosecutor not only controls the charging process but also is involved in functions such as setting the court calendar, appointing defense counsel for indigents, and sentencing.

Throughout the accusatory process, the prosecutor must evaluate various factors to decide whether to press charges and what charges to file. He or she must decide whether the reported crime will appear credible and meet legal standards in the eyes of judge and jury. Problems with evidence and witnesses were the main reasons for rejecting cases in most of the prosecution offices studied (see Figure 8.5).

A prosecutor's decision will be influenced by the policy model his or her office uses. The models of case management cannot, however, be applied automatically. Each requires an evaluation of the quality and quantity of evidence for a particular case. Each model may also include assessments of the resources of the prosecutor's office and trial court. For example, if the court is overcrowded and the prosecutor does not have enough lawyers, the prosecutor may be forced to use the system efficiency model even if he or she would prefer to use another approach.

In some cases prosecutors may decide that the accused and society would benefit from a certain course of action. For example, a young first-time offender or a minor offender with drug abuse problems may be placed in a diversion program instead of prosecuted in the criminal justice system. In applying their own values in making such judgments, prosecutors may make decisions that run counter to the ideals of law. Prosecutors are, after all, human beings who must respond to some of the most troubling problems in American society. In evaluating cases, they may knowingly or unknowingly permit their personal biases to affect their decisions. A study in Los Angeles County found that men were more likely to be prosecuted than women and that Hispanics were prosecuted more often than African Americans, who were prosecuted more often than Anglos. The researchers believed that in borderline cases—those that could either be pursued or dismissed—the scale was often tipped against minorities (Spohn, Gruhl, and Welch, 1987).

---

trial sufficiency model
The presence of sufficient legal elements to ensure successful prosecution of a case. When a prosecutor's decision to prosecute a case is customarily based on trial sufficiency, only cases that seem certain to result in conviction at trial are accepted for prosecution. Use of plea bargaining is minimal; good police work and court capacity to go to trial are required.

---

accusatory process
The series of events from the arrest of a suspect to the filing of a formal charge (through an indictment or information) with the court.

FIGURE 8.4

Two models of the accusatory process

Indictment and information are the two methods used in the United States to accuse a person of a crime. Note the role of the grand jury in the case of an indictment and the preliminary hearing in the case of an information. According to the ideal of due process, each method is designed to spare an innocent person the psychological, monetary, and other costs of prosecution.

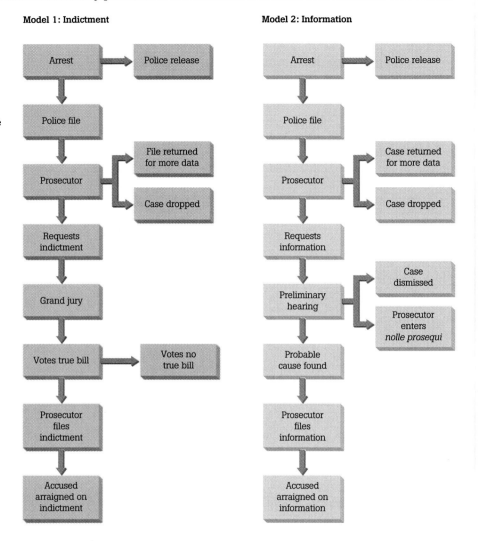

The prosecutor's established policies and decisions play a key role in determining whether charges will be filed against a defendant. Keep in mind, though, that the prosecutor's decision-making power is not limited to decisions about charges. As shown in Figure 8.6, the prosecutor makes important decisions at each stage, both before and after a defendant's guilt is determined. Because the prosecutor's involvement and influence span the justice process, from seeking search warrants during early investigations to arguing against post-conviction appeals, the prosecutor is a highly influential actor in criminal cases. No other participant in the system is involved in so many different stages of the criminal process.

CHECK POINT

⑥ **What are the three models of prosecution policy and how do they differ?**

FIGURE 8.5 Reasons for declining to prosecute felony cases in four cities

Insufficient evidence was the main reason for declining to prosecute in the four cities studied, but note that the proportions vary.

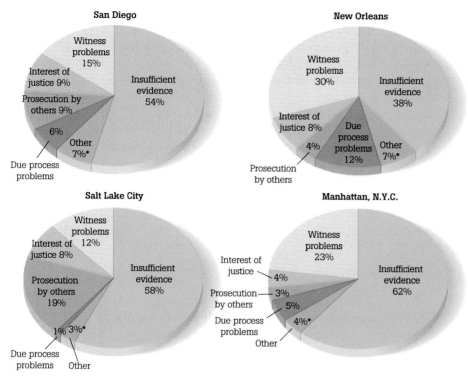

NOTE: Figures may not add up to 100 percent because of rounding.
*Includes diversion and plea to include another case.
SOURCE: Adapted from U.S. Department of Justice, Bureau of Justice Statistics, *Report to the Nation on Crime and Justice,* 2d ed. (Washington, D.C.: Government Printing Office, 1988), 73.

FIGURE 8.6 Typical actions of a prosecuting attorney in processing a felony case

The prosecutor has certain responsibilities at various points in the process. At each point the prosecutor is an advocate for the state's case against the accused.

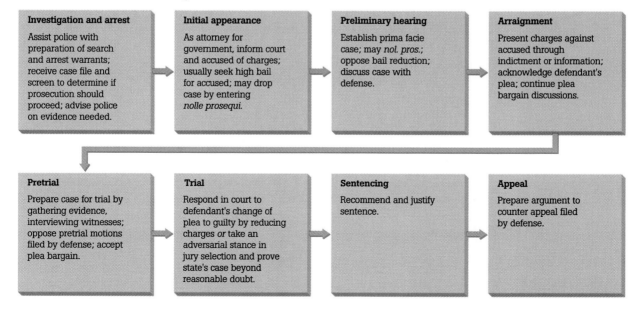

The Defense Attorney: Image and Reality

In an adversarial system, the **defense attorney** is the lawyer who represents accused and convicted persons in their dealings with the criminal justice system. Most Americans have seen defense attorneys in action on television dramas such as *The Practice, Ally McBeal,* and *Law & Order.* In these dramas defense attorneys vigorously battle the prosecution, and the jury often finds that their clients are not guilty. These images are reinforced by news stories about defense attorneys such as Johnnie Cochran and Robert Shapiro, whose efforts helped acquit O. J. Simpson of murder charges in 1995. In 1997, the attorneys defending the Oklahoma City bombing suspects captured the attention of news reporters. While these images are drawn from reality, they do not give a true picture of the typical defense attorney, focusing as they do on the few highly publicized cases that result in jury trials. By contrast, most cases are processed through plea bargaining, discretionary dismissals, and other decisions by actors in the justice system. In these cases the defense attorney may seem less like the prosecutor's adversary and more like a partner in the effort to dispose of cases as quickly and efficiently as possible through negotiation.

The Role of the Defense Attorney

To be effective, defense attorneys must have knowledge of law and procedure, skill in investigation, experience in advocacy, and, in many cases, relationships with prosecutors and judges that will help a defendant obtain the best possible outcome. In the American legal system the defense attorney performs the key function of making sure that the prosecution proves its case in court or has substantial evidence of guilt before a guilty plea leads to conviction and punishment.

As shown in Figure 8.7, the defense attorney advises the defendant and protects his or her constitutional rights at each stage of the criminal justice process. The defense attorney advises the defendant during questioning by the police, represents him or her at each arraignment and hearing, and serves as advocate for the defendant during the appeal process if there is a conviction. Without a defense attorney, prosecutors and judges might not respect the rights of the accused. Defendants have little ability to represent themselves in court effectively without knowing the technical details of law and court procedures. Dr. Jack Kevorkian, the doctor famous for assisting the suicides of terminally ill people, was acquitted of criminal charges in three trials in which he was represented by an attorney. When he attempted to represent himself in a later case, his ineffective presentation of evidence and ignorance of court procedures may have contributed to his conviction and imprisonment (Belluck, 1999).

While filling their roles in the criminal justice system, the defense attorneys also give psychological support to the defendant and his or her family. Relatives are often bewildered, frightened, and confused. The defense attorney is the only legal actor available to answer the question, "What will happen next?" In short, the attorney's relationship with the client is very important. An effective defense requires respect, openness, and trust between attorney and client. If the defendant refuses to follow the attorney's advice, the lawyer may feel obliged to withdraw from the case to protect his or her own professional reputation.

8.7 Typical actions of a defense attorney processing a felony case

Defense attorneys are advocates for the accused. They have an obligation to challenge points made by the prosecution and advise clients about constitutional rights.

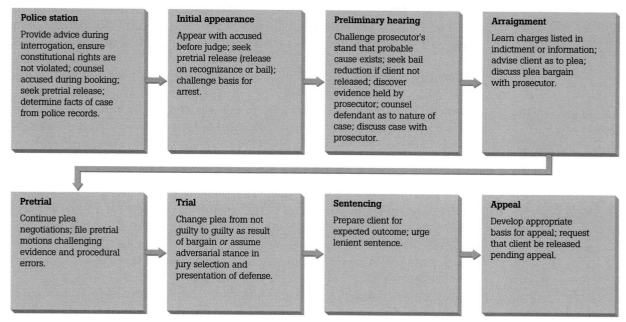

Police station

Provide advice during interrogation, ensure constitutional rights are not violated; counsel accused during booking; seek pretrial release; determine facts of case from police records.

Initial appearance

Appear with accused before judge; seek pretrial release (release on recognizance or bail); challenge basis for arrest.

Preliminary hearing

Challenge prosecutor's stand that probable cause exists; seek bail reduction if client not released; discover evidence held by prosecutor; counsel defendant as to nature of case; discuss case with prosecutor.

Arraignment

Learn charges listed in indictment or information; advise client as to plea; discuss plea bargain with prosecutor.

Pretrial

Continue plea negotiations; file pretrial motions challenging evidence and procedural errors.

Trial

Change plea from not guilty to guilty as result of bargain *or* assume adversarial stance in jury selection and presentation of defense.

Sentencing

Prepare client for expected outcome; urge lenient sentence.

Appeal

Develop appropriate basis for appeal; request that client be released pending appeal.

Realities of the Defense Attorney's Job

How well do defense attorneys represent their clients? The television image of defense attorneys is usually based on the due process model, in which attorneys are strong advocates for their clients. In reality, the enthusiasm and effectiveness of defense attorneys' efforts may vary. Several factors affect the performance of defense attorneys. Attorneys who are inexperienced, uncaring, or overburdened have trouble representing their clients effectively. The attorney may quickly agree to a plea bargain and then work to persuade the defendant to accept the agreement. The attorney's self-interest in disposing of cases quickly, receiving payment, and moving on to other cases may cause the attorney to, in effect, work with the prosecutor to pressure the defendant to plead guilty. Although skilled defense attorneys will also consider a plea bargain in the earliest stages of a case, their use of plea bargaining will be guided by their role as an advocate for the defendant. An effective defense attorney does not try to take every case all the way to trial. In many cases, a negotiated plea with a predictable sentence will serve the defendant better than a trial spent fending off more serious charges. Good defense attorneys seek to understand the facts of the case and to judge the nature of the evidence to reach the best possible outcome for their client. Even in the plea-bargaining process, this level of advocacy requires more time, effort, knowledge, and commitment than some attorneys are willing or able to provide.

The defense attorney's job is made all the more difficult because neither the public nor defendants fully understand the attorney's duties and goals. The public often views defense attorneys as protectors of criminals. The attorney's basic duty

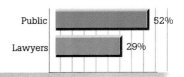
is not to save criminals from punishment but to protect constitutional rights, keep the prosecution honest in preparing and presenting cases, and prevent innocent people from being convicted. Surveys indicate that lawyers place much greater emphasis on the importance of the right to counsel than does the public. Look at the question presented in What Americans Think. Do you think that the public underestimates the necessity of representation by an attorney? Alternatively, might this data indicate that the public believes criminal defendants already have too many rights?

In performing tasks that ultimately benefit both the defendant and society, the defense attorney must evaluate and challenge the prosecution's evidence. However, defense attorneys can rarely arrange for guilty defendants to go free. Keep in mind that when prosecutors decide to pursue serious charges, they have already filtered out weaker cases. The defense attorney often negotiates the most appropriate punishment in light of the resources of the court, the strength of the evidence, and the defendant's prior criminal record.

Defendants who, like the public, have watched hours of *The Practice* on television, often expect their attorneys to fight vigorous battles against the prosecutor at every stage of the justice process. They do not realize that plea agreements negotiated in a friendly, cooperative way may be in their best interest. Public defenders in particular are often criticized because the defendants cannot choose their legal representatives. The defendants often assume that if the state provided an attorney for them, the attorney must be working for the state instead of on their behalf.

⑦ **How does the image of the defense attorney differ from the attorney's actual role?**

Private Counsel: An Endangered Species?

The United States has an estimated 800,000 practicing lawyers and very few studies have sought to determine how many lawyers specialize in each area of law. The most well-known study of attorneys discovered that fewer than twenty thousand accept criminal cases on a "more than occasional" basis and only about fourteen thousand work as public defenders. The study found that the number and quality of privately retained lawyers varied among cities, depending on legal, institutional, and political factors (Wice, 1978).

Given the small proportion of lawyers engaged in criminal practice, some questions arise: Who handles criminal cases? What are their qualifications? The average criminal lawyer practices alone, not as a member of a law firm, and comes from a middle-class, nonprofessional background and graduated from a lesser law school. Many entered private criminal practice after working as a government lawyer, often in prosecution. Paul Wice found that 38 percent of his sample of private criminal lawyers had been prosecutors and that 24 percent had been public defenders, had worked for legal services (doing civil law work), or had held civil service positions (1978:75).

Three groups of lawyers might be called specialists in criminal defense because they handle criminal cases on a regular basis. The first group is composed of nationally known attorneys who charge large fees in highly publicized cases.

Nationally known criminal defense specialist Johnnie Cochran is one of the small number of attorneys who have built their reputations on taking highly publicized cases for large fees.

O. J. Simpson's defense team included two attorneys who had built their reputations by defending famous clients: F. Lee Bailey, who defended heiress Patricia Hearst, and Alan Dershowitz, who handled the appeal for boxer Mike Tyson. Each large city has a small group of defense attorneys who are the lawyers of choice for defendants who can afford to pay high fees. O. J. Simpson's other attorneys, Johnnie Cochran and Robert Shapiro, were well known in Los Angeles for their success in big cases. These attorneys make handsome incomes by representing white-collar criminals, drug dealers, and affluent people charged with crimes. When business executives are charged with drunk driving, for example, they may be willing to pay top dollar to attorneys who can help them avoid conviction and the loss of their driver's license. Attorneys may join this select group by winning highly publicized cases, but usually not enough clients can pay high fees to permit many lawyers to make large amounts of money.

The largest group of attorneys in full-time criminal practice are courthouse regulars who accept many cases for small fees and who participate daily in the criminal justice system as either retained or assigned counsel. These attorneys handle a large volume of cases quickly. They negotiate guilty pleas and try to convince their clients that these agreements are good deals. They depend on the cooperation of prosecutors, judges, and other courtroom actors, with whom they form exchange relationships to reach plea bargains quickly.

In addition to these defense specialists, many private attorneys sometimes take criminal cases. These attorneys often have little trial experience and lack well-developed relationships with other actors in the criminal justice system. Their clients might be better served by a courthouse regular who has little interest in each case but whose relationships with prosecutors and judges will produce more favorable plea bargains.

The Environment of Criminal Practice

Defense attorneys have a difficult job. Much of their work involves preparing clients and their relatives for the likelihood of conviction and punishment. Although they may know that their clients are guilty, they may become emotionally involved because they are the only judicial actors who know the defendants as human beings and see them in the context of their family and social environment.

Most defense lawyers constantly interact with lower-class clients whose lives and problems are depressing. They may also visit the local jail at all hours of the day and night. Thus, their work setting is far removed from the fancy offices and expensive restaurants of the world of corporate attorneys. As described by one defense attorney, "The days are long and stressful. I spend a good deal of time in jail, which reeks of stale food and body odor. My clients often think that because I'm court-appointed, I must be incompetent" (Lave, 1998).

Defense lawyers must also struggle with the fact that criminal practice does not pay well. Public defenders have fairly low salaries, and attorneys appointed to represent poor defendants are paid small sums. If private attorneys do not demand payment from their clients at the start of the case, they may find that they must persuade the defendants' relatives to pay—because many convicted offenders have no incentive to pay for legal services while sitting in a prison cell. To perform their jobs well and gain satisfaction from their careers, defense attorneys must focus on goals other than money, such as their key role in protecting people's constitutional rights. However, because they are usually on the losing side, it can be hard for them to feel like professionals—with high self-esteem and satisfying work.

Defense attorneys face other pressures as well. If they mount a strong defense and gain an acquittal for their client, the public may blame them for using "technicalities" to keep a criminal on the streets. If they embarrass the prosecution in court, they may harm their prospects for reaching good plea agreements for future clients. Thus, criminal practice can bring major financial, social, and psychological burdens to attorneys. As a result, many attorneys are "burned out" after a few years; and few stay in the field past the age of 50.

CHECK POINT

⑧ **How is the private defense bar organized?**

⑨ **What special pressures do defense attorneys face?**

Counsel for Indigents

Since the 1960s, the Supreme Court has interpreted the "right to counsel" in the Sixth Amendment to the Constitution as requiring that the government provide attorneys for indigent defendants who face the possibility of going to prison or jail. Indigent defendants are those who are too poor to afford their own lawyers. The Court has also required that attorneys be provided early in the criminal justice process to protect suspects' rights during questioning and pretrial proceedings. A summary of key rulings on the right to counsel is set forth in Table 8.1.

Research on convicted offenders indicates that 76 percent of those serving time in state prisons and half of those in federal prisons said that they had received publicly provided legal counsel. An additional 83 percent of those in county jails said that they were provided with counsel by the state (Smith and

DeFrances, 1996). The portion of defendants who are provided with counsel because they are indigent has increased greatly in the past three decades.

There is debate about the quality of counsel given to indigent defendants (Worden, 1991). Ideally, experienced lawyers would be appointed soon after arrest to represent the defendant in each stage of the criminal justice process. Ideal conditions do not always exist, however. Inexperienced and uncaring attorneys may be appointed to represent indigent defendants. Sometimes this is done during court proceedings, so that the attorney has no time to prepare the case. Even conscientious attorneys may be unable to provide top-quality counsel if they have heavy caseloads or are not paid money to enable them to spend the time required to handle the case well.

If they lack the time and desire to interview the client and prepare the case, the appointed counsel may persuade defendants to plead guilty right in the courtroom during their first and only brief conversation. When the lawyers assigned to provide counsel to poor defendants cooperate with the prosecutor easily, without even asking the defendant about his or her version of events, convicted offenders not surprisingly often believe that their interests were not represented in the courtroom. This point was made clearly by an inmate who, when asked whether he had a lawyer when he went to court, said, "No, I had a public defender" (Casper, 1971). Not all publicly financed lawyers who represent poor defendants ignore their clients' interests. However, the quality of counsel received by the poor may vary from courthouse to courthouse, depending on the quality of the attorneys, conditions of defense practice, and administrative pressure to reduce the caseload.

TABLE 8.1   The right to counsel: major Supreme Court rulings

CASE	YEAR	RULING
Powell v. Alabama	1932	Indigents facing the death penalty who are not capable of representing themselves must be given attorneys
Johnson v. Zerbst	1938	Indigent defendants must be provided with attorneys when facing serious charges in federal court
Gideon v. Wainwright	1963	Indigent defendants must be provided with attorneys when facing serious charges in state court
Douglas v. California	1963	Indigent defendants must be provided with attorneys for their first appeal
Miranda v. Arizona	1966	Criminal suspects must be informed about their right to counsel before being questioned in custody
United States v. Wade	1967	Defendants are entitled to counsel at "critical stages" in the process including post-indictment lineups
Argersinger v. Hamlin	1972	Indigent defendants must be provided with attorneys when facing misdemeanor and petty charges that may result in incarceration
Ross v. Moffitt	1974	Indigent defendants are not entitled to attorneys for discretionary appeals after their first appeal is unsuccessful
Strickland v. Washington	1984	To show ineffective assistance of counsel violated the right to counsel, defendants must prove that the attorney committed specific errors that affected the outcome of the case
Murray v. Giarratano	1989	Death row inmates do not have a right to counsel for habeas corpus proceedings asserting rights violations in their cases

Methods of Providing Indigents with Counsel

In the United States there are three main ways of providing counsel to indigent defendants: (1) the **assigned counsel** system, in which a court appoints a private attorney to represent the accused; (2) the **contract counsel** system, in which an attorney, a nonprofit organization, or a private law firm contracts with a local government to provide legal services to indigent defendants for a specified dollar amount; and (3) **public defender** programs, which are public or private nonprofit organizations with full-time or part-time salaried staff (Spangenberg and Beeman, 1995). The system in use in the majority of counties in each of the fifty states is presented in Figure 8.8. Note, however, that many counties use a combination of methods to provide representation. In particular, 23 percent of counties use both

assigned counsel
An attorney in private practice assigned by a court to represent an indigent. The attorney's fee is paid by the government with jurisdiction over the case.

contract counsel
An attorney in private practice who contracts with the government to represent all indigent defendants in a county during a set period of time and for a specified dollar amount.

public defender
An attorney employed on a full-time, salaried basis by the government to represent indigents.

public defenders and assigned counsel (Smith and DeFrances, 1996). In counties that have sufficient resources, cases may be sent to assigned counsel when public defenders' caseloads become too large. Table 8.2 highlights the different methods used in nine jurisdictions.

ASSIGNED COUNSEL   In the assigned counsel system, the court appoints a lawyer in private practice to represent an indigent defendant. This system is widely used in small cities and in rural areas, but even some city public defender systems assign counsel in some cases, such as in a case with multiple defendants, where a conflict of interest might result if one of them were represented by a public lawyer. But in other cities, such as Detroit, the private bar has been able to insist that its members receive a large share of the cases (see Table 8.2).

Assigned counsel systems are organized on either an ad hoc system or a coordinated basis. In ad hoc assignment systems, private attorneys tell the judge that they are willing to take the cases of indigent defendants. When an indigent requires counsel, the judge either assigns lawyers in rotation from a prepared list or chooses one of the attorneys who are known and present in the courtroom. In coordinated assignment systems, a court administrator oversees the appointment of counsel.

Use of the ad hoc system may raise questions about the loyalties of the assigned counsel. Are they trying to vigorously defend their clients or are they trying to please the judges to ensure future appointments? For example, Texas has been criticized for giving judges free rein to assign lawyers to cases without any supervising authority to ensure that the attorneys do a good job (Novak, 1999).

FIGURE 8.8   **Indigent defense system used by the majority of counties in each state**

Note that some states use a mixture of methods to provide counsel for indigents.

Public defender
Contract
Assigned counsel

SOURCE: U.S. Department of Justice, Bureau of Justice Statistics, *Bulletin* (September 1988).

TABLE 8.2 — Percentage of felony cases handled by different types of defense attorneys in nine jurisdictions

Jurisdictions vary in the percentage of cases handled by each form of counsel. Note how these courts are similar and how they differ. To what extent do local traditions, politics, and judicial leadership affect the type of system used?

TYPES OF DEFENSE ATTORNEYS	DETROIT, MI.	SEATTLE, WASH.	DENVER, CO.	NORFOLK, VIRGINIA	MONTEREY, CA.	GLOBE, AZ.	OXFORD, ME.	ISLAND, WASH.	SAN JUAN, WASH.
Public defender	18.3%	0.0%	74.6%	0.0%	72.6%	0.0%	0.0%	0.0%	61.3%
Assigned counsel	64.6	1.2	5.4	71.1	19.3	0.0	52.7	0.0	0.0
Contract attorneys	0.0	86.8	0.0	0.0	0.0	81.9	0.0	65.6	0.0
Private counsel	17.0	12.0	20.0	28.9	8.1	17.5	47.3	34.4	38.7
	99.9%	100.0%	100.0%	100.0%	100.0%	99.4%	100.0%	100.0%	100.0%
Total number of cases	458	606	370	463	409	170	224	125	31
Percentage indigent	82.9%	88.0%	80.0%	71.1%	91.9%	81.9%	52.7%	65.6%	61.3%

SOURCE: Roger Hanson and Joy Chapper, *Indigent Defense Systems, Report to the State Justice Institute.* Copyright © 1991 by National Center for State Courts. (Williamsburg, Va.: National Center for State Courts, 1991).

Additional concerns were raised in Texas and other states where judges run for election because lawyers often donate money to judges' political campaigns. Judges might return the favor by supplying their contributors with criminal defense assignments. As you read the lawyers' conversation in the Question of Ethics (p. 306), consider what you would do if you were a new lawyer seeking to gain experience in criminal defense work.

The fees paid to assigned defenders are often low compared with what a lawyer might otherwise charge (see Table 8.3). While a private practice attorney might charge clients at rates that exceed $150 per hour, hourly rates for appointed counsel in Illinois are merely $30 per hour for out-of-court tasks and $40 per hour for in-court work. These rates have remained unchanged since 1975. In many Texas counties, judges determine rates for themselves and some pay as little as $25 per hour to attorneys who represent indigent defendants (Novak, 1999). In 1999, the average hourly overhead cost for attorneys—the amount they must make just to pay their secretaries, office rent, and telephone bills—was $58 (National Legal Aid and Defender Association, 1999). If their hourly fees do not exceed their overhead costs, then attorneys are making no money at all for spending their time on these cases.

Low fees discourage skilled attorneys from taking criminal cases. Low fees may also induce a defender to persuade the client to plead guilty to a lesser charge. Many assigned defenders find that they can make more money by collecting a preparation fee of about $50, payable when an indigent client pleads guilty, than by going to trial. Trials are very time-consuming, and appointed attorneys often do not feel that the fees paid by the state are high enough to cover the amount of time required to prepare for trial, especially when the fee is a flat rate per case or trial instead of an hourly rate. Handling many quick plea bargains usually is more profitable than spending weeks preparing for a trial for which the fee may be only a few hundred dollars.

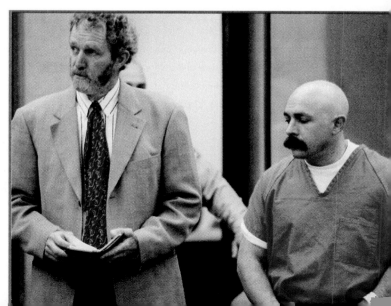

Public defenders are often thought to lack experience; yet research shows that they do the job well. In San Luis Obispo, California, Rex Allen Krebs appears with public defender James B. Maquire III at his arraignment. Krebs was charged with kidnapping, sodomy, rape, and murder of colleges students Rachel Newhouse and Aundria Crawford.

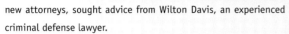

At a county bar association luncheon to honor recent law school graduates, Sarah Schweitzer, one of the new attorneys, sought advice from Wilton Davis, an experienced criminal defense lawyer.

"Mr. Davis, how can I build my reputation so that I attract clients?"

"The most obvious way is to start seeking assignments to represent indigent defendants. Go down to the courthouse and introduce yourself to Judge Garvey. Tell her that I sent you. If she likes you, she'll start giving you some misdemeanors and, if you do okay, you might start getting some felonies which pay a little bit better—although still not very much."

"Are cases assigned in rotation to lawyers on a list?"

Davis chuckled. "Not exactly. Judge Garvey has her own list and she decides on the order. Some people say that the attorneys who get the most assignments have two things in common. They are contributors to Judge Garvey's campaigns and their clients plead guilty quickly instead of going to trial. Working on those assigned cases will help you build a reputation, but they'll also make you appreciate the paying clients you get later. Paying clients really give you a chance to use your skills."

Schweitzer looked troubled. "Are you telling me I must donate money to Judge Garvey's campaigns and encourage my clients to plead guilty if I want to gain experience?"

Davis shook his head. "Look. I'm not telling you what to do with your clients. I'm just telling you how the system works around here."

■ What would you do if you were in Schweitzer's position as a new attorney seeking to gain experience in criminal law? If the system in this county poses ethical problems, who is at fault? The judge who runs the assignment process? The attorneys who cooperate to get more cases? The state and county governments that created this system for providing defense attorneys? How would you change this system to make it better?

Many organizations of judges and lawyers lobby Congress, state legislatures, and county councils to increase the amounts paid to assigned counsel. For example, the American Bar Association, the Federal Judges Association, and the National Legal Aid and Defender Association joined forces in 1999 to urge Congress to raise the pay for assigned counsel in federal criminal cases above the rate of $45 for out-of-court work and $65 for in-court work (National Legal Aid and Defender Association, 1999). Many members of Congress, however, do not wish to spend more money for the benefit of criminal defendants.

CONTRACT SYSTEM The contract system is used in a few counties, mainly in western states. Most states using this method do not have large populations. The government contracts with an attorney, a nonprofit association, or a private law firm to handle all indigent cases (Worden, 1994). Some jurisdictions use public defenders for most cases but contract for services in multiple-defendant cases that might present conflicts of interest, in extraordinarily complex cases, or in cases that require more time than the government's salaried lawyers can provide.

There are several kinds of contracts (Spears, 1991). The most common contract provides for a fixed yearly sum to be paid to the law firm that handles all cases. Some people fear that this method encourages attorneys to cut corners to preserve their profits, especially if more cases than expected come up during the year. Other contracts are based on a fixed price per case or per hour of work. Still other jurisdictions use a cost-plus contract, in which a new contract is negotiated when the estimated cost of counsel is surpassed. According to Robert Spangenberg and Marea Beeman (1995:49), "There are serious potential dangers with the contract model, such as expecting contract defenders to handle an unlimited caseload or awarding contracts on a low-bid basis only, with no regard to qualifications of contracting attorneys."

The contract system poses additional risks if the decision makers who choose the attorneys, whether the local judges or the county commission, seek to discourage attorneys from working too enthusiastically on behalf of criminal defendants. In one study, local judges seemed to decide not to renew one set of contract attorneys because those attorneys insisted on having preliminary hearings in each case and would not quickly plea bargain or waive their clients' rights to help speed cases through the courts. The next set of attorneys selected to handle cases by contract was primarily composed of former assistant prosecutors who were much more willing to cooperate with the prosecutor and judges in keeping cases moving steadily through the court (Eisenstein, Flemming, and Nardulli, 1988: 146).

CHAPTER EIGHT

TABLE
8.3 **Fees paid to assigned counsel in Colorado**

Colorado's statewide fee schedule applies to attorneys appointed to represent defendants when public defenders cannot accept a case. This arises, for example, when it would be a conflict of interest for a public defender's office to represent two or more co-defendants in the same case. Note that the hourly rates differ by seriousness of the charge and that there are maximum amounts for each type of case. Attorneys may seek court permission to exceed the hourly amounts when necessary.

STANDARD FEES	PER HOUR	
Death penalty cases	$65.00	
Type A felonies (e.g., violence)	$51.00	
Type B felonies (e.g., drugs)	$47.00	
Other (juvenile/traffic/misdemeanor)	$45.00	
MAXIMUM FEE PAYMENTS	WITH TRIAL	WITHOUT TRIAL
Class 1 felonies (death penalty, life, 51+ years)	$15,000	$7,500
Class 2 felonies (41- to 50-year sentences possible)	$ 7,500	$3,750
Class 3, 4, and 5 felonies (1- to 40-year sentences possible)	$ 5,000	$2,500
Misdemeanor	$ 1,000	$ 500
Juvenile	$ 1,500	$1,000

SOURCE: Colorado Office of the Alternate Defense Counsel, 1999.

PUBLIC DEFENDER   The public defender is a response to the legal needs of indigent defendants. The concept started in Los Angeles County in 1914, when attorneys were first hired by government to work full time in criminal defense. The most recent national survey found that public defender systems exist in 1,144 counties, covering more than 70 percent of the U.S. population (BJS, 1988). The public defender system, which is growing fast, is used in forty-three of the fifty most populous counties and in most large cities. There are about twenty statewide, state-funded systems; in other states they are organized and paid for by counties. Only two states, Maine and North Dakota, do not have public defenders.

The public defender system is often viewed as better than the assigned counsel system because public defenders are specialists in criminal law. Because they are full-time government employees, public defenders, unlike appointed counsel and contract attorneys, do not sacrifice their clients' cases to protect their own financial interests. Public defenders do face certain special problems, however.

Public defenders may have trouble gaining the trust and cooperation of their clients. Criminal defendants may assume that attorneys on the state payroll, even with the title "public defender," have no reason to protect the defendants' rights and interests. Lack of cooperation from the defendant may make it harder for the attorney to prepare the best possible arguments for use during hearings, plea bargaining, and trials.

Public defenders may also face heavy caseloads. In New York City's public defender program, for example, Legal Aid lawyers may handle as many as one hundred felony cases at any time. A public defender in Atlanta may be assigned as many as forty-five new cases *at a single arraignment* (Bright, 1994). Although the National Legal Aid and Defender Association recommends that defense attorneys

CLOSE

Counsel for the Indigent in Four Locales

seven years. Public defenders are paid less than their counterparts in the district attorney's office.

DENVER, COLORADO

With a population of 505,000, the city and county of Denver is the largest urban area in the Rocky Mountain region. The population tends to be divided between a relatively affluent majority and an impoverished class (15 percent of the population live below the poverty line) made up primarily of the 17 percent of the population that is African American or Hispanic.

Colorado has a statewide public defender system, which is responsible for all indigent cases except for those where there is a conflict (codefendants). The federal guidelines for determining indigency are used, but the information provided by defendants is not checked for accuracy. A $10 fee, waived for those in custody, is charged to those who apply for a public defender. An estimated 85 percent of felony defendants qualify for a public defender.

Twenty-six attorneys staff the Denver public defender's office. They are assisted by ten investigators and clerical staff. New defenders tend to be recent law school graduates who stay six to

DETROIT, MICHIGAN

Wayne County has a population of 2,164,300. Half of the citizens live in the city of Detroit, making it the sixth largest city in the United States. Almost 40 percent of the population is nonwhite and about 15 percent live below the poverty level. Wayne County has a relatively high crime rate.

Detroit provides attorneys to the indigent via assigned counsel and a nonprofit organization similar to a public defender agency. The assignments are distributed between two groups. Approximately 75 percent of the cases are assigned by judges to individual private attorneys; the remainder are allocated to the Legal Aid and Defenders Association (LADA), a nonprofit group. Attorneys are paid a fixed fee for their services based on the statutory punishment for the offense.

To be eligible for appointment as assigned counsel, attorneys must complete an application form listing professional experience, education, and criminal trial experience. Each applicant must be favorably reviewed by a committee of five judges. Once initially certified, an attorney can be assigned only those cases in which

handle no more than four hundred cases per year, public defenders in Connecticut averaged 1,045 cases per year in 1994 and, despite efforts to reduce caseload pressures, still averaged 618 cases in 1999 (Casey, 1999). Such heavy caseloads do not allow time for attorneys to become familiar with each case. Public defender programs are most effective when they have enough money to keep caseloads manageable. However, these programs do not control their own budgets and usually are not seen as high priorities by state and local governments. Thus they have difficulty obtaining the funds they need to give adequate attention to each defendant's case.

Some public defenders' offices try to make better use of limited resources by organizing assignments more efficiently. In some systems, every poor defendant has several public defenders, each handling a different stage or "zone" in the justice process. One attorney may handle all arraignments, another all preliminary hearings, and still another any trial work. No one attorney manages the entire case of any client. A study of Chicago felony cases found that 47 percent of defendants the penalty is twenty years or less imprisonment. With additional experience, assignment can be granted for the full range of cases.

Six hundred fifty attorneys are currently on the assigned counsel list. The pool is composed of about two hundred "hard-core" regulars who depend upon assignments for a substantial portion of their caseload and income. The remainder are "irregulars" who look to assignments to supplement their private civil and criminal practice.

The perception that the defense bar was too cozy with the judiciary and that African Americans were not receiving vigorous defense led to creation of LADA in the late 1960s. LADA is composed of twenty attorneys who by a Michigan Supreme Court order must receive 25 percent of felony case assignments.

At any one time each LADA attorney carries between thirty and thirty-five cases. In many ways LADA may be best understood as providing services as would a public defender organization with staff attorneys.

OXFORD, MAINE

With a population of only 50,200, Oxford County is located in the southwestern mountainous region of Maine. The per capita income averages $9,000 and about 13 percent of the population live below the federal poverty level. The crime rate is low by national standards. Less than one-half of 1 percent of the population are minorities.

Oxford County depends wholly on assigned counsel for indigent defense. By merely informing the court clerk, an attorney can receive assignments, which are given informally by the one visiting superior court judge who holds session for two or three weeks each month. At present only ten of the thirty-six attorneys practicing in the county receive indigent cases. Most of these attorneys also do private criminal and civil work.

Assigned counsel are paid by a voucher system and are allowed to charge $40 per hour for both in- and out-court work. Indigent defense is funded completely by the state.

GILA COUNTY, ARIZONA

Gila County is a large geographic area half the size of the state of Rhode Island. Globe, the county seat, is located about ninety miles east of Phoenix in the state's copper-mining country. The population is about 40,000 with 16 percent being Hispanic and Native American, and 13 percent living below the poverty level. The violent crime rate is 2,500 per 100,000 population.

Gila County contracts with four local attorneys for the provision of defense services to the indigent. Compensation for each attorney averages $45,000 per year. The county provides additional support for investigators. All of the contract attorneys also maintain a private criminal and civil practice.

SOURCE: Roger Hanson and Joy Chapper, *Indigent Defense Systems, Report to the State Justice Institute.* Copyright © 1991 by National Center for State Courts. (Williamsburg, Va.: National Center for State Courts, 1991).

received such sequential representation (Gilboy and Schmidt, 1979). Although the zone system may increase efficiency, there is a risk that cases will be processed in a routine way, without taking into account special factors. With limited responsibility for a given case, the attorney is less able to advise the defendant about the case as a whole and is unlikely to develop the level of trust needed to gain the defendant's cooperation.

With or without zone systems, overburdened public defenders find it difficult to avoid making routine decisions. One case may come to be viewed as very much like the next, and the process can become routine and repetitive. No one looks closely at cases to see if any special circumstances would justify a stronger defense.

The Close-Up above gives four views of how counsel is provided to indigents in different parts of the United States. Because state and local governments can decide how to provide defense attorneys for indigent defendants, the amount budgeted for criminal defense can vary from county to county. So, too, can the quality of counsel provided to poor defendants. Because state and local governments have limited funds, scholars have noted a "tendency to provide representation on the cheap," which raises concerns about the quality of representation (Spangenberg and Beeman, 1995:48).

The most recent comprehensive study of criminal defense systems was conducted in 1986. In 1999, a new national study began under the sponsorship of the U.S. Department of Justice's Bureau of Justice Statistics. Many observers believe that an increasing number of counties use public defenders and contract counsel. The new study will examine whether such a trend exists (Mickenberg and Wallace, 1998). The new study will also explore whether recommendations made in 1996 by the National Advisory Committee on Indigent Defense Services have been implemented. The National Advisory Committee identified several critical needs, including regularly scheduled training and performance standards for attorneys who represent indigent defendants (Hartman, Wallace, and Lyons, 1997).

⑩ **What are the three main methods of providing attorneys for indigent defendants?**

Private versus Public Defense

Publicly funded defense attorneys now handle up to 85 percent of the cases in many places, and private defense attorneys have become more and more unusual in many courts. Retained counsel may serve only upper-income defendants charged with white-collar crimes or drug dealers and organized crime figures who can pay the fees. This trend has made the issue of the quality of representation increasingly important.

Do defendants who can afford their own counsel get better legal services than those who cannot? Many convicted offenders say, "You get what you pay for," meaning that they would have received better counsel if they had been able to pay for their own attorneys. At one time, researchers thought public defenders entered more guilty pleas than did lawyers who had been either privately retained or assigned to cases. However, studies show little variation in case outcomes by various types of defense. For example, in a study of plea bargains in nine medium-sized counties in Illinois, Michigan, and Pennsylvania, the type of attorney representing the client appeared to make no difference in the nature of plea agreements (Nardulli, 1986). Other studies have also found few differences among assigned counsel, contract counsel, public defenders, and privately retained counsel with respect to case outcomes and length of sentence (Hanson and Chapper, 1991). Table 8.4 lists data on the relationship between type of counsel and case results in four cities.

⑪ **Are public defenders more effective than private defense attorneys?**

TABLE 8.4 **Case disposition and types of defense attorneys**

Few variations exist in case disposition among the defense systems used in each jurisdiction. Why do the cities differ in case outcomes?

| TYPE OF DISPOSITION | DETROIT, MICHIGAN | | | DENVER, COLORADO | | NORFOLK, VIRGINIA | | MONTEREY, CALIFORNIA | | |
	PUBLIC DEFENDER	ASSIGNED COUNSEL	PRIVATE COUNSEL	PUBLIC DEFENDER	PRIVATE COUNSEL	ASSIGNED COUNSEL	PRIVATE COUNSEL	PUBLIC DEFENDER	ASSIGNED COUNSEL	PRIVATE COUNSEL
Dismissals	11.9%	14.5%	12.8%	21.0%	24.3%	6.4%	10.4%	13.5%	8.9%	3.0%
Trial acquittals	9.5	5.7	10.3	1.8	0.0	3.3	5.2	1.7	1.3	0.0
Trial convictions	22.6	14.5	24.4	5.1	9.5	5.2	2.2	7.1	11.4	18.2
Guilty pleas	54.8	64.9	52.6	72.1	66.2	85.1	81.3	76.8	78.5	78.8
Diversion	1.2	0.3	0.0	0.0	0.0	0.0	0.7	1.0	0.0	0.0
	100.0%	99.9%	100.1%	100.0%	100.0%	100.0%	99.8%	101.1%	101.1%	100.0%
Total number of cases	84	296	78	276	74	329	134	294	79	33

SOURCE: Roger Hanson and Joy Chapper, *Indigent Defense Systems, Report to the State Justice Institute*. Copyright © 1991 by National Center for State Courts. (Williamsburg, Va.: National Center for State Courts, 1991).

Defense Counsel in the System

Most of the criminal lawyers in urban courts work in a difficult environment. They work very hard for small fees in unpleasant surroundings and often are not accorded respect by other lawyers or the public. Because plea bargaining is the main method of deciding cases, defense attorneys believe they must maintain close personal ties with the police, prosecutor, judges, and other court officials. Critics point out that the defenders' independence is undermined by daily inter-action with the same prosecutors and judges. When the supposed adversaries become close friends as a result of daily contact, the defense attorneys may no longer fight vigorously on behalf of their clients. Also, at every step of the justice process, from the first contact with the accused until final disposition of the case, defense attorneys depend on decisions made by other actors in the system. Even seemingly minor activities such as visiting the defendant in jail, learning about the case from the prosecutor, and setting bail can be difficult unless defense attorneys have the cooperation of others in the system. Thus defense attorneys may limit their activities to preserve their relationships with other courthouse actors.

For the criminal lawyer who depends on a large volume of petty cases from poor clients and assumes that they are probably guilty, the incentives to bargain are strong. If the attorney is to be assigned other cases, he or she must help make sure that cases flow smoothly through the courthouse. This requires a cooperative relationship with judges, prosecutors, and others in the justice system.

Despite their dependence on cooperation from other justice system officials to make their work go more smoothly, defense attorneys can sometimes use stub-bornness as a tactic. They can, for example, threaten to take a case all the way through trial to test whether the prosecutor is adamant about not reaching a favor-able plea agreement. Some paying clients may expect their counsel to play the role of combatant in the belief that they are not getting their money's worth unless there are verbal fireworks in the courtroom. Yet even when those fireworks do occur, one cannot be sure that the adversaries are engaged in a real contest. Studies have shown that attorneys whose clients expect a vigorous defense may

Defense attorneys in urban courts work in a difficult environment. Visiting the defendant in jail, learning about the case from the prosecutor, and setting bail can be difficult unless others in the system are cooperative.

engage in a courtroom drama commonly known as the "slow plea of guilty," in which the outcome of the case has already been determined but the attorneys go through the motions of putting up a vigorous fight. Defendants often have difficulty understanding the benefits of plea bargaining and friendly relationships between defense attorneys and prosecutors. Most cases that are pursued beyond the initial stages are not likely to result in acquittal, no matter how vigorously the attorney presents the defendant's case. In many cases the evidence of the defendant's guilt simply cannot be overcome by skilled lawyering. Thus good relationships can benefit the defendant by gaining a less-than-maximum sentence. At the same time, however, these relationships pose the risk that if the defense attorney and prosecutor are too friendly, the defendant's case will not be presented in the best possible way in plea bargaining or trial.

Some scholars have called defense attorneys "agent-mediators" because they often work to prepare the defendant for the likely outcome of the case—usually conviction (Blumberg, 1967). While such efforts may help the defendant gain a good plea bargain and become mentally prepared to accept the sentence, the attorney's efforts are geared to advance the needs of the attorney and the legal system. By mediating between the defendant and the system—for example, by encouraging a guilty plea—the attorney helps save time for the prosecutor and judge in gaining a conviction and completing the case. In addition, appointed counsel and contract attorneys may have a financial interest in getting the defendant to plead guilty quickly so that they can receive payment and move on to the next case.

A more sympathetic view of defense attorneys labels them "beleaguered dealers" who cut deals for defendants in a tough environment (Uphoff, 1992). While many of their actions help push cases through the courts, defense attorneys are under tremendous pressure to manage large caseloads in a difficult court environment. From this perspective, their actions in encouraging clients to plead guilty result from the difficult aspects of their jobs rather than from self-interest. Yet, as

CLOSE up

The **Public Defender:** Lawyer, **Social** Worker, **Parent**

Eddie, a nervous-looking heroin abuser with a three-page police record, isn't happy with his lawyer's news about his latest shoplifting arrest.

"The prosector feels you should be locked up for a long time," public defender William Paetzold tells Eddie in a closet-sized interview room in Superior Court. Barely big enough for a desk and two chairs, the room is known as "the pit."

Eddie, 34 and wide-eyed with a blond crew cut, twists a rolled-up newspaper in his hands. And as Paetzold goes over the evidence against him for the theft of $90.67 worth of meat from a supermarket, the paper gets tighter and tighter.

"So, you basically walked right through the doors with the shopping carriage?" Paetzold asks, scanning the police report.

"Well, there was another person involved and we really never got out of the store," Eddie replies quickly, now jingling a pocket-ful of change.

Eddie wants to take his case to trial. Paetzold doesn't like his chances with a jury.

"If you're going to base your whole case on that statement about not leaving the store, you're going to lose," he says. "If you lose, you're going to get five years."

Paetzold advises Eddie to consider pleading guilty in exchange for a lesser sentence.

Eddie rolls his eyes and grumbles. He thinks he deserves a break because he has been doing well in a methadone clinic designed to wean him from heroin.

"I'm not copping to no time," he says, shifting in his seat. "I'm not arguing the fact that I've been a drug addict my whole life, but I haven't been arrested since I've been in that program. I'm finally doing good and they want to bury me."

Paetzold says he will talk to the prosecutor and see what can be done.

"I'll be waiting upstairs," Eddie says, grabbing his newspaper and walking out past a small crowd of other clients waiting to see Paetzold or public defender Phillip N. Armentano.

Every client wants individual attention. Many expect Paetzold or Armentano to resolve their case with little or no punishment. And they don't care that the lawyers may have 25 other clients to see that morning demanding the same.

"A lot of what we do is almost like social work," says Armentano. "We have the homeless, the mentally ill, the drug addicts, and the alcoholics. Our job just isn't to try to find people not guilty, but to find appropriate punishment, whether that be counselling, community service or jail time."

"It's like being a parent," says Paetzold. "These clients are our responsibility and they all have problems and they want those problems solved now."

And like many parents, the lawyers often feel overwhelmed. Too many cases, not enough time or a big enough staff. Those obstacles contribute to another—the stigma that overworked public defenders are pushovers for prosecutors and judges.

"There's a perception that public defenders don't stand up for their clients," Armentano says. "We hear it all the time, 'Are you a public defender or a real lawyer?' There's a mistrust right from the beginning because they view us as part of the system that got them arrested."

With a caseload of more than a thousand clients a year, Paetzold and Armentano acknowledge that they cannot devote as much time to each client as a private lawyer can. But they insist that their clients get vigorous representation.

"Lawyers are competitors, whether you're a public defender or not," Paetzold says. "I think that under the conditions, we do a very good job for our clients."

SOURCE: Steve Jensen, "The Public Defender: He's One Part Lawyer, One Part Social Worker and One Part Parent," *Hartford Courant*, September 4, 1994, p. H1.

described in the Close-Up (see p. 313), some public defenders are able to maintain a personal interest in their clients.

CHECK POINT

⑫ **What special pressures face defense attorneys and how do these affect their work?**

Attorney Competence

The right to counsel is of little value when the counsel is not competent and effective. The adequacy of counsel provided to both private and public clients is a matter of concern to defense groups, bar associations, and the courts (Goodpaster, 1986). There are many examples of incompetent counsel (Gershman, 1993). Even in death penalty cases, attorneys have shown up for court so drunk that they could not stand up straight (Bright, 1994). In other cases, attorneys with almost no knowledge of criminal law have made blunders that have needlessly sent their clients to death row (Smith, 1997). For example, lawyers have fallen asleep during their clients' death penalty trials, yet one Texas judge found no problem with such behavior. He wrote that everyone has a constitutional right to have a lawyer, but "the Constitution does not say that the lawyer has to be awake" (Shapiro, 1997: 27). In other cases, it is less clear what should be viewed as inadequate counsel. What if a public defender's caseload is so large that he or she cannot spend more than a few minutes reviewing the files for most cases? What if, as a deliberate strategy to appear cooperative and thus stay in the judge's good graces, the defense attorney decides not to object to questionable statements and evidence presented by the prosecution? Because attorneys have discretion concerning how to prepare and present their cases, it is hard to clearly define what constitutes a level of performance that is so inadequate that it violates the defendant's constitutional right to counsel.

The U.S. Supreme Court has examined the question of what requirements must be met if defendants are to receive effective counsel. In two 1984 cases, *United States v. Cronic* and *Strickland v. Washington,* the Court set standards for effective assistance of counsel. Cronic had been charged with a complex mail fraud scheme, which the government had investigated for four and a half years. Just before trial, Cronic's retained lawyer withdrew and a young attorney—who had no trial experience and whose practice was mainly in real estate law—was appointed. The trial court gave the new attorney only twenty-five days to prepare for the trial, in which Cronic was convicted. The Supreme Court upheld Cronic's conviction on the ground that, although the new trial counsel had made errors, there was no evidence that the trial had not been a "meaningful" test of the prosecution's case or that the conviction had not been justified.

In *Strickland v. Washington,* the Supreme Court rejected the defendant's claim that his attorney did not adequately prepare for the sentencing hearing in a death penalty case and that the attorney sought neither character statements nor a psychiatric examination to present on the defendant's behalf. As it has done in later cases, the Court indicated its reluctance to second-guess defense attorney's actions. By focusing on whether errors by an attorney were bad enough to make the trial result unreliable and to deny a fair trial, the Court has made it hard for defendants to prove that they were denied effective counsel, even when defense attorneys perform very poorly. As a result, innocent people who were poorly represented have been convicted, even of the most serious crimes (Radelet, Bedeau, and Putnam, 1992).

When imprisoned people are proved innocent and released—sometimes after losing their freedom for many years—it serves as a reminder that the American justice system is imperfect. In 1996 four men, including two who had been on death row, were released from prison in Illinois after serving eighteen years for murders they did not commit (Terry, 1996). Such reminders highlight the importance of having quality legal counsel for criminal defendants. However, because state and local governments have limited funds, concerns will continue to be raised about the quality of defense attorneys' work.

⑬ **How has the U.S. Supreme Court addressed the issue of attorney competence?**

Summary

- American prosecutors, both state and federal, have significant discretion to determine how to handle criminal cases.
- There is no higher authority over most prosecutors that can overrule a decision to decline to prosecute (*nolle prosequi*) or to pursue multiple counts against a defendant.
- The prosecutor can play various roles, including trial counsel for the police, house counsel for the police, representative of the court, and elected official.
- Prosecutors' decisions and actions are affected by their exchange relationships with many other important actors and groups, including police, judges, victims and witnesses, and the public.
- Three primary models of prosecutors' decision-making policies are legal sufficiency, system efficiency, and trial sufficiency.
- The image of defense attorneys as courtroom advocates is often vastly different from the reality of pressured, busy negotiators constantly involved in bargaining with the prosecutor over guilty plea agreements.
- Relatively few private defense attorneys make significant incomes from criminal work, but larger numbers of private attorneys accept court appointments to handle indigent defendants' cases quickly for relatively low fees.
- Three primary methods for providing attorneys to represent indigent defendants are appointed counsel, contract counsel, and public defenders.
- Defense attorneys must often wrestle with difficult working conditions and uncooperative clients as they seek to provide representation, usually in the plea negotiation process.
- The quality of representation provided to criminal defendants is a matter of significant concern, but U.S. Supreme Court rulings have made it difficult for convicted offenders to prove that their attorneys did not provide a competent defense.

Questions for Review

1 What are the formal powers of the prosecuting attorney?

2 How are prosecutors affected by politics?

3 What considerations influence the prosecutor's decision about whether to bring charges and what to charge?

4 Why is the prosecuting attorney often cited as the most powerful office in the criminal justice system?

5 What are some of the problems faced by attorneys who engage in private defense practice?

6 What are the methods by which defense services are provided to indigents?

7 In what way is the defense attorney an agent-mediator?

8 Why might it be argued that publicly financed counsel serves defendants better than privately retained counsel?

Key Terms

accusatory process (p. 295)
assigned counsel (p. 303)
attorney general (p. 280)
contract counsel (p. 303)
count (p. 285)

defense attorney (p. 298)
discovery (p. 286)
legal sufficiency model (p. 293)
nolle prosequi (p. 286)
prosecuting attorney (p. 280)

public defender (p. 303)
system efficiency model (p. 294)
trial sufficiency model (p. 295)
United States attorney (p. 279)

For Further Reading

Buffa, Dudley W. *The Defense.* New York: Henry Holt, 1997; *The Prosecution: A Legal Thriller.* New York: Henry Holt, 1999. Novels focusing on court processes, judges, prosecutors, and defense attorneys written by a former criminal attorney.

Heilbroner, David. *Rough Justice: Days and Nights of a Young D.A.* New York: Pantheon Books, 1990. The experience of an assistant district attorney learning the ropes in New York's criminal courts.

Humes, Edward. *Mean Justice: A Town's Terror, a Prosecutor's Power, a Betrayal of Innocence.* New York: Simon & Schuster, 1999. An investigative reporter's examination of prosecutions in one California county in which apparently innocent people were sent to prison for crimes they did not commit.

Lewis, Anthony. *Gideon's Trumpet.* New York: Vintage, 1964. The classic case study of the case of Gideon v. Wainwright.

McIntyre, Lisa J. *The Public Defender: The Practice of Law in the Shadows of Repute.* Chicago: University of Chicago Press, 1987. A case study of the public defender's office in Cook County, Illinois.

Rowland, Judith, *The Ultimate Violation.* New York: Doubleday, 1985. A former San Diego district attorney describes her pioneering legal strategy to prosecute rapists.

Toobin, Jeffrey, *The Run of His Life: The People v. O. J. Simpson.* New York: Random House, 1996. A view of the trial from the perspectives of the prosecution and defense.

Tucker, John C. *May God Have Mercy.* New York: W. W. Norton, 1997. A former defense attorney turned writer reinvestigates and reconstructs a murder case in which the defendant, who was ultimately executed for the crime, was represented by inexperienced defense attorneys.

Turow, Scott. *Presumed Innocent.* New York: Farrar, Straus, and Giroux, 1987. Fictional account of the indictment and trial of an urban prosecutor for the murder of a colleague. Excellent description of an urban court system.

Going Online

❶ Go to the web site of the National District Attorneys Association at ww.ndaa.org. What purposes does the organization fulfill for prosecutors across the country? Pay particular attention to the description of the American Prosecution Research Institute. What are the Institute's goals? How might the Institute attempt to influence the development of law and policy?

❷ Go to the web site of the National Legal Aid and Defenders Association at www.nlada.org. What purposes does the organization fulfill for defense attorneys? How does the organization attempt to influence law and policy?

❸ Using InfoTrac College Edition: (1) Search for an article on "prosecutorial immunity." Are there any circumstances in which prosecutors can be sued for misconduct? If prosecutors can rarely be sued, how can the public hold prosecutors accountable for their actions? (2) Search for an article by or about a public defender. Could you imagine yourself working as a criminal defense attorney? Why or why not?

CHECK POINT ANSWERS

❶ United States attorney, state attorney general, prosecuting attorney (the prosecuting attorney is also called district attorney, county prosecutor, state's attorney, county attorney).

❷ Decides which charges to file, what bail amounts to recommend, whether to pursue a plea bargain, and what sentence to recommend to the judge.

❸ Trial counsel for the police, house counsel for the police, representative of the court, elected official.

❹ The prosecutor can determine the type and number of charges, reduce the charges in exchange for a guilty plea, or enter a *nolle prosequi* (thereby dropping some or all of the charges).

❺ Police, victims and witnesses, defense attorneys, judges.

❻ Legal sufficiency: is there sufficient evidence to pursue a prosecution? System efficiency: what will be the impact of this case on the system

with respect to caseload pressures and speedy disposition? Trial sufficiency: does sufficient evidence exist to ensure successful prosecution of this case through a trial?

❼ The public often views defense attorneys as protectors of criminals. Defendants believe that defense attorneys will fight vigorous battles at every stage of the process. The defense attorney's role is to protect the defendant's rights and to make the prosecution prove its case.

❽ A status hierarchy of private defense attorneys places a few nationally known specialists at the top; each city has a small group of attorneys for clients who can afford to pay high fees; at the bottom are courthouse regulars who accept small fees from many clients, including indigents whose cases are assigned by the court.

❾ Securing cases, collecting fees, persuading clients to accept pleas, accepting that they will lose most cases.

❿ Assigned counsel, contract system, public defender.

⓫ There seems to be little difference in outcomes.

⓬ They work very hard for small fees from multiple clients in unpleasant surroundings and are viewed negatively by the public.

⓭ The Supreme Court has addressed the issue of "ineffective assistance of counsel" in two 1984 cases: *United States v. Cronic* and *Strickland v. Washington.* The Court requires defendants to fulfill the difficult burden of showing that attorneys made specific errors that affected the outcome of the case and created an unfair proceeding.

Pretrial Processes

On September 16, 1999, Patrick Naughton was arrested at the Santa Monica Pier in California by FBI agents. He was charged with the federal crime of interstate travel with the intent to have sex with a minor. Many people are arrested each year and charged with offenses related to child pornography and sexual abuse, but Naughton's case grabbed the attention of the national news media. Although he was not yet 40 years old, Naughton was well known in the business community for his success in developing computer software and Internet enterprises. He had helped to invent the Java computer language, and he was in charge of Disney's online entertainment enterprises (Ith, 1999).

Naughton was arrested because he had allegedly arranged to meet a 13-year-old girl with whom he conversed online in an Internet chat room. According to the messages reportedly sent by Naughton to the girl, he wanted to meet her to "kiss, make out and play and stuff" (Ith, 1999). When Naughton traveled from Seattle to California to meet the girl, he was surprised to discover that his Internet conversations had been with an FBI agent posing as a teenage girl. Thus the FBI was waiting for Naughton when he arrived for his planned date with the young girl.

As in other criminal cases, the federal court faced the prospect of determining if Naughton should be released on bail and what the bail amount should be. The bail amount is usually based on the perceived dangerousness of the suspect, the seriousness of the charge, and the likelihood that the suspect might flee before the scheduled court dates. Because Naughton's net worth was estimated to exceed $13 million, he possessed the resources to flee (Ith, 1999). If you were the judge, what bail amount would you set to feel confident that Naughton would return to court voluntarily instead of fleeing and forfeiting the bail money? Bail for Naughton was set at $100,000. Was this too much or too little in light of Naughton's wealth and the nature of his crime?

One week later on the other side of the country in Lanexa, Virginia, 19-year-old Elizabeth Renee Otte was arrested for allegedly killing her 1-month-old baby by placing him in a microwave oven on September 23, 1999. Her family claimed that she became so severely disoriented after suffering an epileptic seizure that she put the baby into the microwave when she was intending to heat up the baby's bottle. District Judge Bruce Long set bail at $20,000, released Otte to the custody of her parents, and ordered her to undergo a psychiatric evaluation to determine if she is competent to stand trial (Timberg, 1999).

Important and difficult decisions are made during pretrial processes. With respect to bail, the judge must assess the risk of flight and potential threat—if any—to the community from releasing the suspect. The judge must also protect the presumption of innocence that is supposed to keep the criminal justice system from punishing defendants before they are proven guilty of a crime. Think about the bail amounts set for Naughton and Otte. Which one is accused of the most serious crime? Is that the same one who might be most likely to flee? Which one might pose the greatest danger to the community while released on bail? These are not easy questions to answer. Judges must use their best judgment, but no scientific formula can permit accurate predictions about criminal suspects' behavior.

Pretrial decisions can affect the ultimate outcome of a case. If Naughton was not released on bail, he might have trouble assisting his lawyers in preparing arguments and evidence for his defense. In Otte's case, an additional pretrial decision had to be made about her mental competence. If she were found to lack the necessary mental competence to stand trial, she could not be convicted of a crime for the death of her baby. Instead she might still spend years confined to a mental hospital. A pretrial competency evaluation is one key decision point that can affect the suspect's ultimate fate. As it turned out, in March 2000, Judge Thomas B. Hoover found that Otte was competent to stand trial, but he ordered a neurological evaluation to determine whether her epilepsy could have made her legally insane at the time of the tragic event (White, 2000).

There are other pretrial processes in which important decisions are also made. These processes include formal events, such as preliminary hearings to determine if enough evidence exists to pursue criminal charges, as well as informal interactions, such as plea bargaining discussions that might resolve the case prior to trial.

Up to 90 percent of people charged with serious crimes enter guilty pleas. Very few defendants have their cases decided by a jury or judge after a complete trial. Although Naughton's lawyer, Bruce Margolin, told news reporters that his client's intentions were not what the government claimed and Otte's family provided an explanation for the tragic event that might excuse the woman's actions, both defendants could eventually plead guilty (Ith, 1999). The incentive to plead guilty is very strong. By pleading guilty the defendant sometimes reduces the punishment, thus relieving anxiety about an uncertain outcome. The prosecutor gains a quick, certain conviction without the risk that a jury might return a verdict of not guilty. In Naughton's case, he entered a guilty plea in March 2000 to charges of crossing state lines with the intent to have sex with a minor (*Wall Street Journal*, 2000).

Plea bargaining can begin at any time after an arrested person has a lawyer. Negotiations may go on for weeks, as both the prosecutor and defense attorney try to figure out how strong the opposition's case would be if presented at trial. The fates of defendants are most often determined during pretrial processes through the discretionary decisions of prosecutors and the interactions of judges, defense attorneys, and prosecutors. The vast majority of cases are handled in ways that do not resemble the adversarial process described by the due process model.

In this chapter we focus on the pretrial period, when most major decisions about the fate of arrested persons are made. The links among the police, prosecution, defense, and court are most clearly revealed during this period. Of particular importance are the practices of bail and plea bargaining.

QUESTIONS
for Inquiry

- What are the methods for releasing the accused before trial?
- How does the bail system work, and how is bail set?
- Why might an accused person be detained before trial?
- What is plea bargaining and how does it affect the criminal justice system?
- What are the constitutional implications of plea bargaining?

From Arrest to Trial or Plea

At each stage of the pretrial process, key decisions are made that move some defendants to the next stage of the process and filter others out of the system. An innocent person could be arrested based on mistaken identification or misinterpreted evidence (Kridler, 1999). However, it is hoped that pretrial processes will force prosecutors and judges to review the available evidence and dismiss unnecessary charges against people who should not face trial and punishment.

After arrest, the accused is booked at the police station. This process includes taking photographs and fingerprints, which form the basis of the case record. Within forty-eight hours of an arrest without a warrant, the defendant must be taken to court for the initial appearance to hear which charges are being pursued, be advised of his or her rights, and be given the opportunity to post bail. The judge also has a chance to make sure that **probable cause** exists to believe that a crime has been committed and that the accused should be prosecuted for the crime.

If the police used an arrest warrant to take the suspect into custody, evidence has already been presented to a judge who believed that it was strong enough to support a finding of probable cause to proceed against the defendant.

Often, the first formal meeting between the prosecutor and the defendant's attorney is the **arraignment:** the formal court appearance in which the charges

probable cause
The criterion for deciding whether evidence is strong enough to uphold an arrest or to support issuing an arrest or search warrant. Also, the facts upholding the belief that a crime has been committed and that the accused committed the offense.

arraignment
The court appearance of an accused person in which the charges are read and the accused person, advised by a lawyer, pleads guilty or not guilty.

"Night stalker" Richard Ramirez, flanked by his attorneys, is arraigned in a Santa Ana, California, court on rape and murder charges. When defendants are thought to pose a threat, they may have their "day in court" from within a wired cage.

against the defendant are read and the defendant, advised by his or her lawyer, enters a plea of "guilty" or "not guilty." Most defendants will enter a plea of not guilty, even if they are likely to plead guilty at a later point. This is because, thus far, the prosecutor and defense attorney usually have had little chance to discuss a potential plea bargain. The more serious the charges, the more likely the prosecutor and defense attorney are to need time to assess the strength of the other side's case. Only then can plea bargaining begin.

At the time of arraignment, prosecutors begin to judge the evidence. This screening process has a major impact on the lives of accused persons, whose fate is largely at the mercy of the prosecutor's discretion (Barnes and Kingsnorth, 1996). If the prosecutor believes the case against the defendant is weak, the charges may simply be dropped. Prosecutors do not wish to waste their limited time and resources on cases that will not stand up in court. A prosecutor may also drop charges if the alleged crime is minor, if the defendant is a first offender, or if the prosecutor believes that the few days spent in jail before arraignment are enough punishment for the alleged offense. The decision to drop charges may also be influenced by jail overcrowding or the need to work on more serious cases. At times, prosecutors in making these decisions may discriminate against accused persons, based on race, wealth, or some other factor (Crew, 1991).

As discussed in Chapter 8, the prosecutor's key role in the criminal justice process causes the prosecutor to be viewed by many as the most powerful actor in the system. As a result of the discretionary power of prosecutors, two defendants who have committed the same offense may be treated in very different ways. For example, imagine two teenage high school dropouts caught shoplifting athletic shoes. One prosecutor may divert one defendant to an education program and drop the charges when the defendant begins to work seriously toward his or her high school diploma. Another prosecutor may pursue larceny charges against the other defendant that result in a short jail sentence. As cases move through the system, prosecutors' decisions to reduce charges for some defendants greatly affect the punishment eventually applied (Miller and Sloan, 1994). Thus, individual prosecutors play a major role in deciding which defendants will receive criminal punishment.

As Figure 9.1 shows, prosecutors use their decision-making power to filter many cases out of the system. The one hundred cases illustrated are typical felony cases. The percentages of cases will vary from city to city, depending on such factors as the effectiveness of police investigations and prosecutors' policies about which cases to pursue. For example, nearly half of those arrested did not ultimately face felony prosecutions. A small number of defendants were steered toward diversion programs. A larger number had their cases dismissed for various reasons—including lack of evidence, the minor nature of the charges, or first-time-offender status. Other cases were dismissed by the courts because the police and prosecutors did not present enough evidence to a grand jury or a preliminary hearing to justify moving forward.

In some cities, many cases are dropped before charges are filed. Prosecutors evaluate the facts and evidence and decide which cases are strong enough to carry

9.1 Typical outcomes of one hundred urban felony cases

Crucial decisions are made by prosecutors and judges during the period before trial or plea. Once cases are bound over for disposition, guilty pleas are many, trials are few, and acquittals are rare.

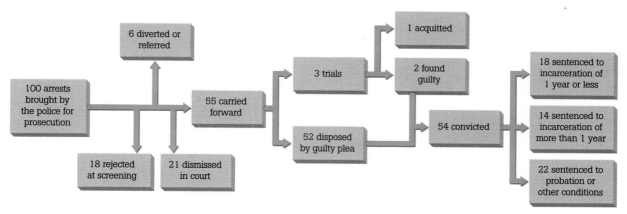

SOURCE: Barbara Boland, Paul Mahanna, and Ronald Stones, *The Prosecution of Felony Arrests, 1988* (Washington, D.C.: U.S. Department of Justice, Bureau of Justice Statistics, 1992), 2.

9.2 Disposition of felony arrests in three American cities

Note the differences in how cases are disposed of in these cities. How might prosecution policy models account for these differences?

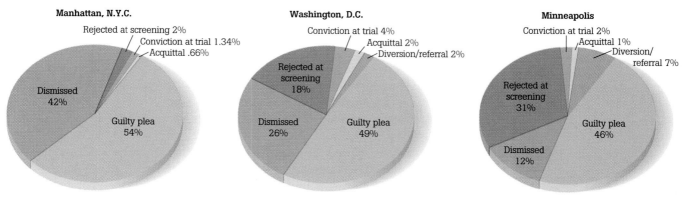

SOURCE: Barbara Boland, Paul Mahanna, and Ronald Stones, *The Prosecution of Felony Arrests, 1988* (Washington, D.C.: U.S. Department of Justice, Bureau of Justice Statistics, 1992), 6.

forward. The others are quickly dismissed. In other cities, formal charges are filed almost automatically on the basis of police reports, but many cases are dismissed when the prosecutor takes the time to closely examine each defendant's situation. In Figure 9.2, for example, Minneapolis prosecutors vigorously screen cases before filing any charges, while Manhattan prosecutors delay their evaluations of cases—and decisions to dismiss—until after formal charges are filed.

During the pretrial process defendants are exposed to the informal, "assembly-line" atmosphere of the lower criminal courts. Often, decisions are quickly made about bail, arraignment, pleas, and the disposition of cases. Moving cases as quickly as possible seems to be the major goal of many judges and attorneys during the pretrial process. Courts throughout the nation are under pressure to limit the number of cases going to trial. These pressures may affect the decisions of both judges and prosecutors, as well as the defense attorneys who seek to maintain good relationships with them. American courts often have too little money, too few staff members, and not enough time to give detailed attention to each case, let alone a trial.

In American courts, the defense uses the pretrial period to its own advantage. Preliminary hearings are an opportunity for defense attorneys to challenge the prosecution's evidence and make **motions** to the court requesting that an order be issued to bring about a specified action. Through pretrial motions, the defense may try to suppress evidence or learn about the prosecutor's case. A court hearing is held on the motion, and the attorney making the motion must be able to support the claim being made about procedures used in the arrest, the sufficiency of the evidence, or the exclusion of evidence. Typical pretrial motions by the defense include the following:

motion

An application to a court requesting that an order be issued to bring about a specified action.

1. Motion to quash a search warrant.
2. Motion to exclude evidence, such as a confession.
3. Motion for severance (separate trials in cases with more than one defendant).
4. Motion to dismiss because of delay in bringing the case to trial.
5. Motion to suppress evidence that was obtained by illegal means.
6. Motion for pretrial discovery of the evidence held by the prosecutor.
7. Motion for a change of venue because a fair trial cannot be held in the original jurisdiction.

Aggressive use of pretrial motions can be an effective strategy. They can become part of the jockeying for position between the prosecution and defense. Paul Wice (1978:148) cites the following reasons that defense attorneys file multiple motions:

What Americans Think

Question "Do you favor allowing the government to detain suspected criminals for more than 48 hours without being charged for a specific crime?"

1. It forces a partial disclosure of the prosecutor's evidence at an early date.
2. It pressures the prosecutor to consider plea bargaining early in the proceedings.
3. It forces exposure of primary state witnesses at an inopportune time for the prosecution.
4. It raises matters the defense may want called to the trial judge's attention early in the proceedings.
5. It forces the prosecutor to make decisions before final preparation of the case.
6. It allows the defendant to see the defense counsel in action, which has a salutary effect on the client-attorney relationship.

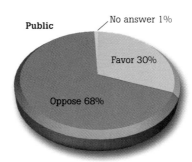

Public

No answer 1%
Favor 30%
Oppose 68%

The use and purposes of pretrial motions may contribute to a belief that the criminal justice system is not functioning properly. The use of motions gives defense attorneys a way to distract and disrupt the prosecutor's plans. Other factors may also contribute to a negative image of the justice system. As shown in Figure 9.1, as many as half of arrestees have their cases dismissed. Does this mean that the system has failed? Probably not.

Pretrial motions, which are filed in only a small percentage of cases, are a way for defense attorneys to seek further information about their client's case or call a judge's attention to a question about their client's rights. Because of the American system's emphasis on individual rights, court procedures are not designed just to make it easier for prosecutors to gain convictions.

Lawyers

No answer 1%
Favor 12%
Oppose 87%

SOURCE: Schmuel Lock, *Crime, Public Opinion, and Civil Liberties* (Westport, Conn.: Praeger, 1999), 193, 217.

As you consider the large numbers of dismissals, keep in mind that many of those people may be innocent or that the prosecutor may not have enough evidence to obtain a conviction. That so many cases are dismissed need not be viewed as a sign of weakness in the system. Instead, one strength of the system can be seen in the power of prosecutors and judges to dismiss charges when a conviction would be either unfair or unlikely. A close look at Figure 9.1 shows that the offenses that a prosecutor decides to pursue have a high conviction rate. Out of fifty-five typical cases carried forward, fifty-two will end with a guilty plea and two of the three defendants who had full trials will be convicted. These examples make it clear that the criminal justice system is effective in producing convictions when a prosecutor, with sufficient evidence, pursues a felony prosecution.

CHECK POINT

① What are the purposes of preliminary hearings, arraignments, and defense motions?

② Why and how are cases filtered out of the system?

(Answers are at the end of the chapter.)

Bail: Pretrial Release

It is often stated that defendants are presumed innocent until proved guilty or until they enter a guilty plea. However, people who are arrested are taken to jail. They are deprived of their freedom and, in many cases, subjected to miserable living conditions while they await the processing of their cases. The idea that people who are presumed innocent can lose their freedom—sometimes for many months—as their cases work their way toward trial clashes with the ideal of individual freedom. How strongly Americans are committed to preserving the ideal of freedom for people who have not yet been convicted of crimes is not clear. As indicated by one public opinion study (see What Americans Think), members of the public may be less concerned than lawyers about the ideal of freedom when it applies to suspected criminals.

A conflict is bound to occur because society must be protected by detaining people who are violent or may try to escape prosecution. However, every person who is charged with a criminal offense need not be detained. Thus, bail and other methods to release defendants are used on the condition that they will appear in court as required.

Bail is a sum of money or property specified by the judge that will be presented to the court by the defendant as a condition of pretrial release. The bail will be forfeited if the defendant does not appear in court as scheduled. The concept was developed in England so that sheriffs would not have to fill their jail cells with people awaiting trial. There is no constitutional right to release on bail, nor even a right to have the court set an amount as the condition of release. The Eighth Amendment to the U.S. Constitution forbids excessive bail, and state bail laws are usually designed to prevent discrimination in setting bail. They do not guarantee, however, that all defendants will have a realistic chance of being released before trial (Nagel, 1990).

bail

An amount of money specified by a judge to be paid as a condition of pretrial release to ensure that the accused will appear in court as required.

A Question of
Ethics

Jim Rourke stood in front of Desk Sergeant Jack Sweeney at the Redwood City Police Station. Rourke was handcuffed and waiting to be booked. He had been caught by Officers Rick Davis and Frank Timulty outside a building in a wealthy neighborhood, soon after the police had received a 911 call from a resident reporting that someone had entered her apartment. Rourke was seen loitering in the alley with a flashlight in his back pocket. He was known to the police because of his prior arrests for entering houses at night. As Timulty held Rourke, Davis went around behind the desk and spoke to Sergeant Sweeney in a soft voice.

"I know we don't have much on this guy, but he's a bad egg and I bet he was the one who was in that apartment. The least we can do is set the bail high enough so that he'll know we are on to him."

"Davis, you know I can't do that. You've got nothing on him," said Sweeney.

"But how's it going to look in the press if we just let him go? You know the type of people who live in Littleton Manor. There will be hell to pay if it gets out that this guy just walks."

"Well, he did have the flashlight. . . . I suppose that's enough to make him a suspect. Let's make the bail $1,000. I know he can't make that."

■ What is the purpose of bail? Was the bail amount appropriate in this instance? Should Rourke be held merely because of the suspicion that he might have entered the apartment? Do you think the case would have been handled in the same way if the call had come from a poorer part of town?

As early as 1835, the Supreme Court ruled that the purpose of bail was to ensure the presence of the accused in court to answer the indictment and submit to trial. This is consistent with the belief that accused persons are innocent until proved guilty and that they should not suffer hardship while awaiting trial. Because the accused has not been found guilty, bail should not be used as punishment. The amount of bail should therefore be high enough to ensure that the defendant appears in court for trial—but no higher.

But this is not the only purpose of bail. The community must be protected from further crimes that some defendants may commit while out on bail. Congress and some states have passed laws that permit preventive detention of defendants who are believed by the judge to pose a threat to any other person or to the community while awaiting trial.

The Reality of the Bail System

The reality of the bail system is far from the ideal. The question of bail may arise at the police station, at the initial court appearance in a misdemeanor case, or at the arraignment in most felony cases. As shown in Table 9.1, cities have their own systems for determining who will set bail for various kinds of crimes. For minor offenses, police officers may have a standard list of bail amounts. For serious offenses, bail will be set in court by a judge. In both cases, those setting bail may have discretion to set differing bail amounts for different suspects, depending on the circumstances of each case. As A Question of Ethics illustrates, this discretion creates the risk that officials will deprive some defendants of their freedom unfairly or for improper reasons.

In almost all courts, the amount of bail is based mainly on the judge's view of the seriousness of the crime and of the defendant's record. In part, this emphasis results from a lack of information about the accused. Because bail is typically determined within twenty-four to forty-eight hours after an arrest, there is little time to conduct a more thorough assessment. As a result, judges in many communities have developed standard rates: so many dollars for such-and-such an offense. In some cases, a judge may set a high bail if the police or prosecutor want a certain person to be kept off the streets.

Critics of the bail system argue that it discriminates against poor people. Imagine that you have been arrested and have no money. Should you be denied a chance for freedom before trial just because you are poor? What if you have a little money, but if you use it to post bail you will not have any left to hire your own attorney? Professional criminals and the affluent have no trouble making bail; many drug dealers, for instance, can readily make bail and go on dealing while awaiting trial. In contrast, a poor person arrested for a minor violation may spend the pretrial period in jail. Should dangerous, wealthy offenders be allowed out on bail while nonviolent, poor suspects are locked up?

According to a study of felony defendants in the nation's most populous counties, 62 percent were released before disposition of their cases, but the rates of release depended on the seriousness of the charges. Only 21 percent of murder defendants gained release while two-thirds of those charged with assault or drug offenses were released on bail. Among those who were released, half left jail within one day after their arrest and most of the others were in jail less than one week prior to release. Defendants who were unable to make bail faced the prospect of spending several months in jail because the median time period from arrest to adjudication ranges from seventy-three days for burglary defendants to more than three hundred days for murder defendants. The median time period for processing all felony cases was eighty-nine days (Reaves and Hart, 1999).

Among those who gained release, most had bail set at less than $5,000. Figure 9.3 shows the amounts of bail set for various types of felony offenses. Those who cannot make bail must remain in jail awaiting trial, unless they can obtain enough money to pay a bail bondsman's fee. Given the length of time between arraignment and trial in most courts and the hardships of pretrial detention, bondsmen are important to defendants in many cities.

Alex Kelly leaves Stamford Superior Court with his girlfriend after being released on $1-million bail until sentencing. Kelly was convicted of raping a Darien High School student. Three days before he was to come to trial he jumped bail and lived in Europe for eight years before his return to Connecticut to face the charges.

TABLE 9.1

The bail process in eleven major cities

Note that various actors make bail decisions. In most places, the initial level of bail for misdemeanors is set by a police officer who consults a schedule of amounts provided by the court.

CITY	WHO SETS BAIL		WHERE IT IS DONE		HOW IT IS DONE	
	MISDEMEANOR	FELONY	MISDEMEANOR	FELONY	MISDEMEANOR	FELONY
Washington	Desk sergeant	Judge	Station house	Court of general sessions	Schedule	Discretion
San Francisco	Clerk of criminal court	Judge	Hall of justice	Hall of justice	Schedule	Discretion
Los Angeles	Police captain	Judge	Station house	Regional	Schedule	Discretion
Oakland	Police captain	Judge	Station house	Courthouse		
Detroit	Desk sergeant Arresting magistrate	Arresting magistrate	Police station	Hall of justice	Schedule	Discretion
Chicago	Desk sergeant	Judge of bond court	Police station	Bond court or electronically	Schedule	Discretion
St. Louis	Desk sergeant	County circuit court judge	Police station	Police station or courthouse	Schedule	Flexible schedule
Baltimore	Desk sergeant	Judge	Police station	Police court	Schedule	Schedule
Indianapolis	Turnkey	Turnkey	City jail	City jail	Schedule	Schedule
Atlanta	Police	Police	Police headquarters	Police headquarters	Discretion/schedule	Discretion/schedule
Philadelphia	Desk sergeant	Magistrate and district attorney	Station house	Police headquarters	Schedule	Discretion

SOURCE: Paul B. Wice, *Freedom for Sale* (Lexington, Mass.: D.C. Heath, 1974), 26.

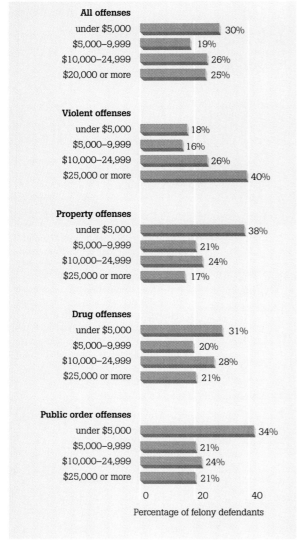

9.3

Bail amounts for felony defendants by type of offense

The amount of bail varies by offense.

All offenses
under $5,000	30%
$5,000–9,999	19%
$10,000–24,999	26%
$20,000 or more	25%

Violent offenses
under $5,000	18%
$5,000–9,999	16%
$10,000–24,999	26%
$25,000 or more	40%

Property offenses
under $5,000	38%
$5,000–9,999	21%
$10,000–24,999	24%
$25,000 or more	17%

Drug offenses
under $5,000	31%
$5,000–9,999	20%
$10,000–24,999	28%
$25,000 or more	21%

Public order offenses
under $5,000	34%
$5,000–9,999	21%
$10,000–24,999	24%
$25,000 or more	21%

Percentage of felony defendants

SOURCE: Brian Reaves and Timothy C. Hart, *Felony Defendants in Large Urban Counties, 1996: State Court Processing Statistics* (Washington, D.C.: U.S. Department of Justice, Bureau of Justice Statistics, 1999), 21.

Bail Bondsmen

The bail bondsman is a key figure in the bail process. Bail bondsmen (or women) are private businesspeople who are paid fees by defendants who lack the money to make bail. They are licensed by the state and are able to choose their own clients. In exchange for a fee, which may be 5 to 10 percent of the bail amount, the bondsman will put up the money (or property) to gain the defendant's release. Bondsmen are not obliged to provide bail money for every defendant who seeks to use their services. Instead, they decide which defendants are likely to return for court appearances. If the defendant skips town, the bondsman's money is forfeited.

Bondsmen may build relationships with police officers and jailers to obtain referrals. Many defendants may not know whom to call for help in making bail, and officers can steer them to a particular bondsman. This can lead to corruption if a bondsman pays a jailer or police officer to make such referrals. Moreover, these relationships may lead to improper cooperation, such as a bondsman refusing to help a particular defendant if the police would like to see that defendant remain in jail.

The role of the bondsman poses questions beyond the issue of corrupt relationships. Is it proper for a private, profit-seeking businessperson to decide who will gain pretrial release and to profit from a person who is "presumed innocent" but is threatened with the loss of his or her freedom? If charges are dropped or a defendant is acquitted, the bondsman still keeps the fee that was paid to make bail. This can be costly to a defendant, especially one who is poor. Although judges set the bail amount, the bondsmen often decide whether certain defendants will gain pretrial release.

Despite the problems posed by the bondsmen's role, they may provide benefits for the criminal justice system. Although bondsmen act in their own interest, they contribute to the smooth processing of cases (Dill, 1975). A major reason that defendants fail to show up for scheduled court appearances is forgetfulness and confusion about when and where they must appear. Courthouses in large cities are huge bureaucracies in which changes in the times and locations of hearings may not always be communicated to defendants. Bondsmen can help by reminding defendants about court dates, calling defendants' relatives to make sure that the defendant will arrive on time, and warning defendants about the penalties for failing to appear. In an informal way, they may act much like defense attorneys in explaining legal procedures to defendants and advising them that the case might best be resolved through a guilty plea. Bondsmen may also benefit the court system by locating defendants who have fled and put the bondsmen's money at risk. In the Hollywood films *Jackie Brown* and *Midnight Run*, bondsmen are shown as tough businesspeople who try to keep track of difficult and dangerous clients.

Although bounty hunters hired by bondsmen find a large percentage of defendants who have skipped out on bail, these independent operators have caused many problems. In highly publicized cases, bounty hunters have broken into the wrong homes, kidnapped innocent people mistaken for wanted criminals, and even shot and killed innocent bystanders (Drimmer, 1997). Bounty hunters' disregard for people's rights and public safety has led to calls for new laws to regulate the activities of bail bondsmen and the people they hire to hunt for fugitives.

The justice system may benefit in some ways from the activities of bondsmen. However, court and law enforcement officials could handle the same functions as well or better if they had the resources, time, and interest to make sure that released defendants return to court. If all courts had pretrial services offices such as those in the federal courts, defendants could be monitored and reminded to return to court without the risks of discrimination and corruption associated with the use of bail bondsmen (Marsh, 1994; Peoples, 1995; Carr, 1993).

Setting Bail

When the police set bail at the station house for minor offenses, there is usually a standard amount for a particular charge. By contrast, when a judge sets bail, the amount of bail and conditions of release are a product of interactions among the judge, prosecutor, and defense attorney. These actors discuss the defendant's personal qualities and prior record. The prosecutor may stress the seriousness of the crime, the defendant's record, and negative personal characteristics. The defense attorney may stress the defendant's good job, family responsibilities, and place in the community. Like other aspects of bail, these factors may favor affluent defendants over the poor, the unemployed, or people with unstable families. Yet many of these factors provide no clear information about how dangerous a defendant is or whether he or she is likely to appear in court.

Research studies highlight the disadvantages of the poor in the bail process. A study of Hispanic American arrestees in southwestern United States found that those who could afford to hire their own attorneys were seven times more likely to gain pretrial release than those who were represented at public expense (Holmes, Hosch, Daudistel, Perez, and Graves, 1996). This result may reflect the fact that affluent defendants are better able to come up with bail money, as well as the possibility that private attorneys fight harder for their clients in the early stages of the criminal process.

The amount of bail may also reflect racial or ethnic discrimination by criminal justice officials, or the social class of the defendant. A 1991 study by the State Bail Commission of cases in Connecticut showed that at each step in the process African American and Hispanic American males with clean records were given bail amounts that were double those given whites (see Figure 9.4). One reason for the difference might be that poor defendants often do not have jobs and a permanent residence, factors that have a strong influence in setting bail. The study also recognized that the higher bail might result from the fact that African Americans and Hispanics were more likely to be charged with a felony than whites. Yet the largest disparities in bail were in felony drug cases. In these cases the average bail for African Americans and Hispanic Americans was four times higher than for whites at the same courthouse (Houston and Ewing, 1991).

Mary Ellen's City Bail Bond in Denver, Colorado, promises "We'll put your feet back on the street." Providing bail bonds is a big business. Still, bondsmen retain discretion as to whether to provide bail to an individual defendant.

In some cases the police may request a high bail amount, especially if they have put a great deal of effort into catching the suspect or have had contact with the victim. Detectives sometimes visit judges' chambers before an arraignment to tell them about aspects of the case that the police do not want raised in open court.

In a classic study of bail setting in New York, Frederic Suffet recorded the interactions of the prosecutor, defense attorney, and judge. These interactions produced shared understandings about what range of bail would be set according to the seriousness of offense, the defendant's prior record, and the defendant's ties to the community. The prosecutor tended to have more influence than the defense attorney in the bail-setting process. When disagreements arose about bail, judges sided more often with prosecutors, in part because they tended to share similar views of the appropriate amount of bail. The defense attorney could try to negotiate with the prosecutor and persuade the judge to set a lower amount, but the "rules of the game" established the boundaries within which bail would be set for a particular person (Suffet, 1966). Certain bail patterns become established over time and accepted by the lawyers and judges in a courthouse. An experienced defense attorney will know better than to risk conflict with the prosecutor and judge by seeking low bail for an offender charged with a very serious crime or one with a significant prior record.

Because it is based on interactions and not a decision by the judge, the bail-setting process spreads out the responsibility for the bail decision. By including the prosecutor and the defense counsel in the process, the judge can create a buffer between the court and the public if the accused is released and commits a crime before appearing in court. In the federal courts, responsibility is further dispersed because bail is often set by U.S. magistrate judges, a judicial official who assists the regular U.S. district judges. For example, when a man accused of running an

FIGURE 9.4　The price of freedom in Connecticut

Bail can be set by several actors in the justice system. A study of 150,000 cases showed that the bail amount for African Americans and Hispanic Americans was double that for whites. Is this a result of discrimination? What other factors might be at work here?

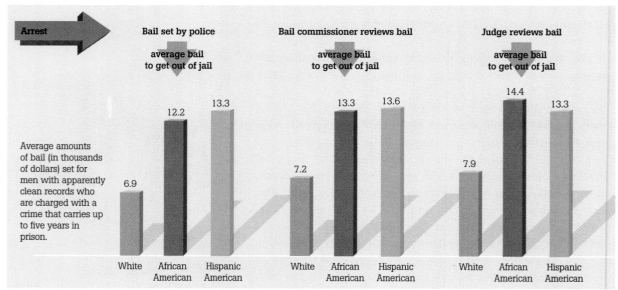

SOURCE: *Hartford Courant*, June 16, 1991, p. A1.

illegal gambling empire disappeared after paying his $600,000 bail, the local newspapers condemned the U.S. magistrate judge for disregarding the prosecutor's argument that the defendant should be held in jail without bail being set (Smith, 1990). The image and legitimacy of the judge and court may be protected by sharing responsibility and the risk of blame with other decision makers.

The local legal and political culture also plays a role in setting bail. In a study of bail systems in Detroit and Baltimore, Roy Flemming (1982) found clear contrasts in the treatment of felony defendants before trial. In the Detroit Recorder's Court, nearly 48 percent of felony defendants arraigned were freed on their own recognizance, the median bail for the rest was $2,000, and 32 percent were detained until the case was disposed of. In the Baltimore District Court, only 12 percent of the accused were freed on their own recognizance, the median bail was $4,650, and 41 percent awaited disposition of their case in jail.

Several factors contributed to these differences. The political climate in Detroit was described as "prodefendant" as a result of reforms instituted after the 1967 riots, in which thousands of black citizens were detained by extremely high bail. These reforms including the placing of a formal limit on the number of people who could be held in the Wayne County Jail and ensuring that bail-setting judges held secure positions. In Baltimore, by contrast, bail was set by "low-status court officials or commissioners with insecure tenure who were more highly vulnerable" to criticism by the police and other public officials. Because of their insecure position, they tended to take a cautious approach, setting higher bails and holding more people in jail. This was made possible by available jail space.

It has been argued that bail setting should be guided by six principles:

❶ The accused is entitled to release on his or her own recognizance.
❷ Nonfinancial alternatives to bail will be used when possible.
❸ The accused will receive a full and fair hearing.
❹ Reasons will be stated for the decision.
❺ Clear and convincing evidence will be offered to support a decision.
❻ There will be a prompt and automatic review of all bail determinations.

Many people argue that using these principles to set bail would hamper the ability of the justice system to deal with offenders and protect society. Others counter that personal freedom is so precious that failure to allow a person every opportunity to gain release is an even greater injustice.

③ **What factors affect whether bail is set and how much money or property a defendant must provide to gain pretrial release?**

④ **What positive and negative effects does the bail bondsman have on the bail system?**

Reforming the Bail System

Studies of pretrial detention in such cities as Philadelphia and New York raised questions about the need to hold defendants in jail. Criticisms of the bail system have focused on judges' discretion in setting bail amounts, the fact that the poor are deprived of their freedom while the affluent can afford bail, the negative

TABLE 9.2 **Pretrial release methods**

Financial Bond	Alternative Release Options
Fully secured bail. The defendant posts the full amount of bail with the court.	*Release on recognizance (ROR).* The court releases the defendant on his or her promise to appear in court as required.
Privately secured bail. A bondsman signs a promissory note to the court for the bail amount and charges the defendant a fee for the service (usually 10 percent of the bail amount). If the defendant fails to appear, the bondsman must pay the court the full amount. The bondsman frequently requires the defendant to post collateral in addition to the fee.	*Conditional release.* The court releases the defendant subject to his or her following specific conditions set by the court, such as attendance at drug treatment therapy or staying away from the complaining witness.
Percentage bail. The courts allow the defendant to deposit a percentage (usually 10 percent) of the full bail with the court. The full amount of the bail is required if the defendant fails to appear. The percentage bail is returned after disposition of the case, although the court often retains 1 percent for administrative costs.	*Third-party custody.* The defendant is released into the custody of an individual or agency that promises to ensure his or her appearance in court. No monetary transactions are involved in this type of release.
Unsecured bail. The defendant pays no money to the court but is liable for the full amount of bail should she or he fail to appear.	

SOURCE: U.S. Department of Justice, Bureau of Justice Statistics, *Report to the Nation on Crime and Justice*, 2d ed. (Washington, D.C.: Government Printing Office, 1988), 76.

---

citation

A written order or summons issued by a law enforcement officer directing an alleged offender to appear in court at a specified time to answer a criminal charge.

release on recognizance (ROR)

Pretrial release granted on the defendant's promise to appear in court because the judge believes that the defendant's ties in the community guarantee that he or she will appear.

---

aspects of bail bondsmen, and jail conditions for those detained while awaiting trial. Reform of the bail system has been attempted in response to these criticisms.

The effort to reform bail has led to changes in the number of defendants held in jail. Over time, the number of defendants released pending completion of their cases has increased. One classic study of twenty cities showed that the release rate in 1962 was 48 percent (Thomas, 1976:37–38). A recent survey of the seventy-five most populous counties found that nearly two-thirds of felony defendants were released before disposition of their cases. Only 7 percent of defendants were denied bail. Thus most defendants who stayed in jail were unable to come up with the bail amount required to gain pretrial release (Reaves, 1998). The increase in defendants released on bail—from 48 percent in 1962 to 62 percent in the late 1990s—occurred, in part, because of the use of certain pretrial release methods. These are listed in Table 9.2.

Citation

A **citation,** or summons, to appear in court—a "ticket"—is often issued to a person accused of committing a traffic offense or some other minor violation. By issuing the citation, the officer avoids taking the accused person to the station house for booking and to court for arraignment and setting of bail. Citations are now being used for more serious offenses, in part because the police want to reduce the amount of time they spend booking minor offenders and waiting in arraignment court for their cases to come up. In most jurisdictions, less than 5 percent of people who are given citations fail to appear. In some cities bail bondsmen have opposed this threat to their livelihood.

Release on Recognizance

Pioneered in the 1960s by the Vera Institute of Justice in New York City, the **release on recognizance (ROR)** approach is based on the assumption that judges will grant releases if the defendant is reliable and has roots in the community. Soon after the arrest, court personnel talk to defendants about their job, family, prior record, and associations. They then decide whether to recommend release. In the first three years of the New York project, more than ten thousand defendants were interviewed and about thirty-five hundred were released. Only 1.5 percent failed to appear in court at the scheduled time, a rate almost three times better than the rate for those released on bail (Goldfarb, 1965). Programs in other cities have had similar results, although Sheila Royo Maxwell's recent research raises questions about whether women and property crime defendants on ROR are less likely than other defendants to appear in court (Maxwell, 1999). Studies have also shown that the percentage of those released on their own recognizance does not greatly increase when a formal pretrial release program has been set up (Feeley, 1983).

Today ROR programs exist in almost every major jurisdiction (Eskridge, 1986). Often a pretrial release agency is part of the court. In some places it is tied to the probation department, and in some jurisdictions those who work to obtain the release of accused persons on their own recognizance are supported by private foundations.

Ten Percent Cash Bail

Although ROR is a useful alternative to money bail, judges are unwilling to release some defendants on their own recognizance. Some states (Illinois, Kentucky, Nebraska, Oregon, and Pennsylvania) have started bail programs in which the defendants deposit with the court an amount of cash equal to 10 percent of their bail. When they appear in court as required, 90 percent of this amount is returned to them. Begun in Illinois in 1964, this plan is designed to release as many defendants as possible without using bail bondsmen.

Bail Guidelines

To deal with the problem of unequal treatment, reformers have written guidelines for setting bail. The guidelines specify the standards judges should use in setting bail and also list appropriate amounts. Judges are expected to follow the guidelines but may deviate from them in special situations. The guidelines take into account the seriousness of the offense and the defendant's prior record to protect the community and ensure that released persons can be trusted to return for court appearances. When guidelines were tested in the Philadelphia Municipal Court, judges showed more consistency in setting bail for similar cases (Goldkamp and Gottfredson, 1985). However, a later effort to introduce guidelines into Miami's courts was less successful, in part, because judges and other court decision makers were less committed to the use of guidelines (Jones and Goldkamp, 1991).

Preventive Detention

Reforms have been suggested not only by those concerned with unfairness in the bail system but also by those concerned with stopping crime (Goldkamp, 1985). Critics of the bail system point to a link between release on bail and the commission of crimes, arguing that the accused may commit other crimes while awaiting trial. A study of the nation's most populous counties found that 14 percent of felony defendants released on bail were rearrested for another crime. Although only 9 percent of defendants with one prior conviction were rearrested during pretrial release, 29 percent of defendants with five or more prior convictions were rearrested (Reaves and Perez, 1994:1). To address this problem, legislatures have passed laws permitting detention of defendants without bail. As shown in Table 9.3, three-fourths of the states now have one or more provisions designed to ensure community safety in pretrial release.

For federal criminal cases, Congress enacted the Bail Reform Act of 1984, which authorizes **preventive detention** (Scott, 1985). Under the act, if prosecutors recommend that defendants be kept in jail, a federal judge holds a hearing to determine (1) if there is a serious risk that the person will flee; (2) if the person will obstruct justice or threaten, injure, or intimidate a prospective witness or juror; or (3) if the offense is one of violence or one punishable by life imprisonment or death. Upon finding that one or more of these factors makes it impossible to set

preventive detention
Holding a defendant for trial based on a judge's finding that, if the defendant were released on bail, he or she would endanger the safety of any other person and the community or would flee.

9.3

States with one or more provisions to ensure community safety in pretrial release

Concern that some persons on bail will commit other crimes while awaiting trial has caused some states to pass laws that limit pretrial release under certain conditions.

TYPE OF PROVISION	STATES THAT HAVE ENACTED THE PROVISIONS
Exclusion of certain crimes from automatic bail eligibility	Colorado, District of Columbia, Florida, Georgia, Michigan, Nebraska, Wisconsin
Definition of the purpose of bail to ensure appearance and safety	Alaska, Arizona, California, Delaware, District of Columbia, Florida, Hawaii, Minnesota, South Carolina, South Dakota, Vermont, Virginia, Wisconsin
Inclusion of crime control factors in the release decision	Alabama, California, Florida, Georgia, Minnesota, South Dakota, Wisconsin
Inclusion of release conditions related to crime control	Alaska, Arkansas, Colorado, Delaware, District of Columbia, Florida, Hawaii, Illinois, Iowa, Minnesota, New Mexico, North Carolina, South Carolina, South Dakota, Vermont, Virginia, Washington, Wisconsin
Limitations on the right to bail for those previously convicted	Colorado, District of Columbia, Florida, Georgia, Hawaii, Indiana, Michigan, New Mexico, Texas, Utah, Wisconsin
Revocation of pretrial release when there is evidence that the accused committed a new crime	Arizona, Arkansas, Colorado, District of Columbia, Georgia, Hawaii, Illinois, Maryland, Massachusetts, Michigan, Nevada, New Mexico, New York, Rhode Island, Texas, Utah, Vermont, Wisconsin
Limitations on the right to bail for crimes alleged to have been committed while on release	Arizona, Arkansas, California, Colorado, District of Columbia, Florida, Georgia, Hawaii, Illinois, Indiana, Maryland, Massachusetts, Michigan, Nebraska, Nevada, New Mexico, New York, Rhode Island, South Dakota, Texas, Utah, Vermont, Virginia, Washington, Wisconsin
Provisions for pretrial detention to ensure safety	Arizona, Arkansas, California, Colorado, District of Columbia, Florida, Georgia, Hawaii, Illinois, Indiana, Maryland, Massachusetts, Michigan, Nebraska, Nevada, New Mexico, New York, Rhode Island, South Dakota, Texas, Utah, Vermont, Virginia, Washington, Wisconsin

SOURCE: U.S. Department of Justice, Bureau of Justice Statistics, *Report to the Nation on Crime and Justice*, 2d ed. (Washington, D.C.: Government Printing Office, 1988), 77.

Schall v. Martin (1984)

Pretrial detention of a juvenile is constitutional to protect the welfare of the minor and the community.

United States v. Salerno and Cafero (1987)

Preventive detention provisions of the Bail Reform Act of 1984 are upheld as a legitimate use of governmental power designed to prevent people from committing crimes while on bail.

bail without endangering the community, the judge can order the defendant held in jail until the case is completed (Smith, 1990).

Critics of preventive detention argue that it violates the Constitution's due process clause because the accused is held in custody until a verdict is rendered. However, the Supreme Court has ruled that it is constitutional. In **Schall v. Martin** (1984), the Court said that the detention of a juvenile was useful to protect both the welfare of the minor and the community as a whole. The preventive detention provisions of the Bail Reform Act of 1984 were upheld in **United States v. Salerno and Cafero** (1987). The justices said that preventive detention was a legitimate use of governmental power because it was not designed to punish the accused. Instead, it deals with the problem of people who commit crimes while on bail. The ruling said that Congress has the power to try to prevent further damage to the community from these crimes. By upholding the federal law, the Court also upheld state laws dealing with preventive detention (Miller and Guggenheim, 1990).

Supporters of preventive detention claim that it ensures that drug dealers, who often treat bail as a business expense, cannot flee before trial. Martin Sorin (1984) argues that "pretrial criminals may account for as much as one-fifth of our nation's total crime problem." Researchers believe a small, easily identified group of defendants are not deterred by strict conditions for release and the prospect of bail being revoked. They commit crimes even with other charges pending against them and have no fears about being returned to jail. The Close-Up, "Preventive Detention: Two Sides of an Issue," presents a case in support of this argument (see p. 336). Research has shown that the nature and seriousness of the charge, a history of prior arrests, and drug use all have a strong bearing on the likelihood that a defendant will commit a crime while on bail. Some scholars contend, however, that the standards used to set bail are related to the likelihood that a defendant will not appear in court as scheduled or will commit another crime while awaiting trial (Goldkamp, 1985).

What is the likely impact of preventive detention? One study suggested that, while preventive detention had influenced federal pretrial release practices, the percentage of defendants released before trial remained fairly stable (Kennedy and Carlson, 1988). The researchers believe this stems from the fact that before the passage of the Bail Reform Act, although federal judges did not have clear authority to hold people without bail, they set high bail amounts for defendants they did not want to release. The Bail Reform Act allowed judges to be more honest and open about their bail decisions. Using their preventive detention authority, judges deny bail mainly in cases involving violence, drugs, or immigration—in which there is either danger to the public or a risk that the accused person will flee.

Those who are unable to post bail and are not released on their own recognizance are held in pretrial detention in the local jail until their court appearance. This has a major impact on these defendants.

CHECK POINT

⑤ What methods are used to facilitate pretrial release for certain defendants?

⑥ How did the U.S. Supreme Court rule in cases involving preventive detention? Why?

Pretrial Detention

People who are not released before trial must remain in jail. Often called the ultimate ghetto, American jails hold almost 500,000 people on any one day. Most are poor, half are in pretrial detention, and the rest are serving sentences (normally of less than one year) or are waiting to be moved to state prison or to another jurisdiction (Clear and Cole, 1997:144).

Urban jails also contain troubled people, many with mental health and drug abuse problems, who have been swept off the streets by police. Michael Welch

CLOSE up

Preventive Detention: Two Sides of an Issue

For Ricardo Armstrong, there is the despair of trying to reunite his family after spending four months in a Cincinnati jail for bank robbery before being acquitted of the crime.

For friends and family of Linda Goldstone, there is the anguish of knowing that she would still be alive if there had been a way to keep Hernando Williams in jail while he was facing rape and assault charges in Chicago.

Ricardo Armstrong was one of the first defendants held under the Bail Reform Act of 1984. The 28-year-old janitor, who had a prior burglary conviction, was denied bail after being charged with robbing two Ohio banks.

From the start, Mr. Armstrong had insisted that bank robbery charges against him were part of some nightmarish mix-up.

A Cincinnati jury agreed. After viewing bank photographs of the robber, the jury acquitted Mr. Armstrong in what was apparently a case of mistaken identity.

Justice, it seemed, had been served—but not before Mr. Armstrong had spent four months in jail—and his wife left their home and moved with their children a thousand miles away.

"Who's going to get me back those four months?" he now asks bitterly. "Who's going to get me back my kids?" The Bail Reform Act makes no provision for compensating defendants who are jailed and later acquitted.

Proponents of the Bail Reform Act concede that some injustices inevitably occur. But they note that other cases, involving dangerous defendants set free on bond, ring just as tragically for victims of crimes that could have been prevented.

Prosecutors point to the release of Hernando Williams as the classic example of the need for preventive detention. Even as Mr. Williams, free on $25,000 bond, drove to court to face charges [of raping and beating a woman he abducted at a shopping mall], another woman lay trapped inside his car trunk. This victim, Linda Goldstone, a 29-year-old birthing instructor, was abducted by Mr. Williams as she walked to Northwestern Hospital and was forced at gunpoint to crawl into his trunk.

Over a four-day period, Mrs. Goldstone was removed from the trunk periodically to be raped and beaten until she was shot to death. Mr. Williams has been sentenced to death.

"Linda Goldstone might well be alive today if we'd had this law then," said Richard M. Daley, the Cook County state's attorney.

SOURCE: Adapted from Dirk Johnston, "Preventive Detention: Two Sides of an Issue," *New York Times,* July 13, 1987, p. A13. Copyright (c) 1987 by The New York Times Company. Reprinted by permission.

calls this process, in which the police remove socially offensive people from certain areas, "social sanitation" (Welch, 1994:262).

Conditions in jails are often much harsher than those in prisons. People awaiting trial are often held in barracks-like cells with sentenced offenders. Thus, a "presumed innocent" pretrial detainee might spend weeks in the same confined space with troubled people or sentenced felons (Perkins, Stephan, and Beck, 1995). The problems of pretrial detention may be even worse in other countries where suspects have no opportunity for bail or a court system that is disorganized and lacks resources. As you read the Comparative Perspective concerning pretrial detention in Russia (see p. 338), ask yourself whether individual American jails could have similar conditions.

Although evidence of brutality surfaces periodically at some American jails, many aspects of the justice system in the United States help to prevent the problems experienced by pretrial detainees in Russia (Halbfinger, 1999). Jail conditions are frequently monitored by American judges. In addition, criminal defendants in the United States have a right to a speedy trial and other constitutional protections.

In many American cases, the period just after arrest is the most frightening and difficult time for suspects. Imagine freely walking the streets one minute and being locked in a small space with a large number of troubled and potentially dangerous cellmates the next. Suddenly you have no privacy and must share an open toilet with hostile strangers. You have been fingerprinted, photographed, and questioned—treated like the "criminal" that the police and the criminal justice system consider you to be. You are alone with people whose behavior you cannot predict. You are left to worry and wonder about what might happen. If you are female, you may be placed in a cell by yourself (Steury and Frank, 1990). Given the stressful nature of arrest and jailing, it is little wonder that most jail suicides and psychotic episodes occur during the first hours of detention.

The shock of arrest and detention can be made even worse by other factors. Many people are arrested for offenses they committed while under the influence of alcohol or some other substance. They may be less able to cope and adapt to their new situation. Young arrestees who face the risk of being victimized by older, stronger cellmates may sink into depression. Detainees also worry about losing their jobs while in jail, given that they do not know if or when they will be released.

Suspects not able to make bail are held awaiting trial. What is the impact on the jury of an accused who rises from the audience when his case is called, compared to an accused who is escorted by the jailer to the defense table?

Pretrial detention can last a long time. While most detainees have their cases adjudicated within three months, 12 percent must wait in jail for more than six months and 4 percent for more than a year (Reaves and Perez, 1994:13). Thus, the psychological and economic hardships faced by pretrial detainees and their families can be major and prolonged.

Pretrial detention not only imposes stresses and hardships that may reach crisis levels, but it also can affect the outcomes of cases. People who are held in jail can give little help to their defense attorneys. They cannot help find witnesses and perform other useful tasks on their own behalf. In addition, they may feel pressured to plead guilty to end their indefinite stay in jail. Even if they believe that they should not be convicted of the crime charged, they may prefer to start serving a prison or jail sentence with a definite end point. Some may even gain quicker release on probation or in a community corrections program by pleading guilty, while—ironically—they might stay in jail for a longer period of time by insisting on their innocence and awaiting a trial.

Defendants who post bail can return for their trial or sentencing hearing looking well groomed and neatly dressed, escorted into the courtroom by family members who thereby subtly indicate to the jury or judge that this "nice" person is not a criminal. Although detainees are supposed to be able to wear civilian clothing during their trials, they may be brought before the judge for preliminary hearings

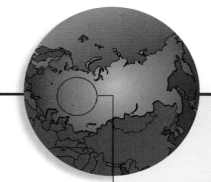

COMPARATIVE
perspective

Pretrial Detention in Russia

Prisoners almost always swear they are not guilty. In Russian pretrial detention centers, many inmates insist that they no longer care about proving their innocence. Pretrial detainees spend long periods in unhealthy conditions while investigations of their alleged offense are conducted.

"At first, all I wanted was a fair trial," Pyotr Kuznetsov, 51, said in a dank and stinking cell of Mastrosskaya Tishina, one of Moscow's largest and most infamous detention centers.

He said he had been arrested and brutally beaten for stealing less than $5 and had already spent 10 months behind bars awaiting trial. His lice-ridden 18th-century cell, built for 30, currently warehouses more than 100 men. The inmates share beds, sleeping in three shifts.

"All I want now is to get out of here, even to a labor camp," Mr. Kuznetsov said. "I've been in prison before, and it is not as bad as this."

Perhaps the most terrifying aspect of the Russian penal system is pretrial detention. Close to 300,000 people awaiting trial are now in jail. There, a death sentence stalks people who have not yet been convicted of a crime.

Unprotected from the TB [tuberculosis] epidemic (as many as 50 percent of Russian prisoners are believed to be infected) and other infectious diseases, many detainees end up spending two, three, and even four years awaiting their day in court in cells as packed as a rush-hour subway car.

The Russian legal system is so tortuous that people can find themselves detained for months or years even on minor charges. Prosecutors are legally required to complete a criminal investigation within two years, but there is no time limit for judges, who can keep a suspect waiting for trial indefinitely. The average stay in detention is 10 months.

In Soviet times, bail was dismissed as a capitalist folly. Today, bail is legal, but it remains a novelty, granted to less than two percent of the country's accused—usually to mobsters who have ready cash and connections to a compliant judge.

"Under our system, it is much harder to acquit than find a person guilty," Sergei Pasin, a judge in a Moscow appeals court explained. "Less than 1 percent of all cases end in an acquittal, and that is because before a judge can acquit, he must do a huge amount of work that is not done by

looking bedraggled and unshaven, wearing handcuffs and an orange jumpsuit. Such images may affect the judge's view of the defendant. Some believe that those unable to post bail are more likely to be convicted and receive harsher sentences than those who were released before trial. A study found a greater likelihood of imprisonment after trial for those who were detained before trial (Goldkamp, 1979). It is hard to know for certain if and how pretrial detention affects the outcomes of cases. Clearly, though, money bail systems often keep poor people in jail

In Russia, pretrial detention averages 10 months. Fewer than 2 percent of arrestees are given bail. In the Matrosskaya Tishina Detention Center in Moscow, 5,000 prisoners await trail in a Dickensian world of squalor, disease, and lice.

the police: requesting information, soliciting expert testimony, etc.

"The fact that time served before trial is subtracted from convicted prisoners' sentences can hardly be viewed as justice," Judge Pasin said. "The predetention centers are a far worse punishment than prison," he said. Prisons and labor camps in Russia are grim, but they are not nearly as overcrowded.

In a report on torture in Russia, Amnesty International said that "torture and ill-treatment occur at all stages of detention and imprisonment," but noted that it was most often reported in pretrial detention.

"Its main purpose appears to be to intimidate detainees and obtain confessions," the report said. Confessions, more than evidence, are a major part of criminal investigations in Russia.

■ How is the American criminal justice system different from Russia's? How do those differences affect the conditions of pretrial detention?

SOURCE: Alessandra Stanley, "Russians Lament the Crime of Punishment," *New York Times,* January 1, 1998, p. A1.

and let wealthier people out. Therefore, whatever adverse consequences flow from failing to make bail, poor people suffer the most.

___ CHECK POINT ___

⑦ **People are detained in jail for a number of reasons. What categories of people are found in jails?**

⑧ **What are the sources of stress for people in jail awaiting trial?**

Plea Bargaining

For the vast majority of cases, **plea bargaining**—also known as negotiating a settlement, copping a plea, or copping out—is the most important step in the criminal justice process. Very few cases go to trial; instead, a negotiated guilty plea arrived at through the interactions of prosecutors, defense lawyers, and judges determines what will happen to most defendants. Table 9.4 shows the percentages of guilty pleas in robbery and burglary cases in five jurisdictions. Note that the percentage varies little regardless of the number of trials, judges, and prosecutors. Table 9.5 shows the types of plea bargains made in these cases. The study reported in these tables is consistent with others, which have found that up to 90 percent of felony defendants in the United States plead guilty.

Thirty-five years ago, plea bargaining was not acknowledged or discussed publicly; it was the criminal justice system's "little secret." Doubts existed about whether it was constitutional, and it clashed with the image of the courtroom as a place where prosecutors and defense attorneys engage in legal battles as the jury watches "truth" emerge from the courtroom "combat." Yet quick resolution of cases through negotiated guilty pleas has been common. Scholars have found that guilty pleas have been a major means of disposing of criminal cases since at least the 1800s (Vogel, 1999). Scholars began to shed light on plea bargaining in the 1960s, and the U.S. Supreme Court endorsed the process in the 1970s. In 1971, for example, in *Santobello v. New York*, Chief Justice Warren Burger described plea bargaining in favorable terms in ruling that prosecutors were obliged to fulfill promises made during plea negotiations. According to Burger, " 'Plea bargaining' is an essential component of the administration of justice. Properly administered, it is to be encouraged." Burger also listed a number of reasons that plea bargaining was a "highly desirable" part of the criminal justice process:

TABLE 9.4 — Plea bargaining in five jurisdictions: robbery and burglary

The percentage of guilty pleas is about the same in all five cities regardless of the number of judges, the number of felony trials, and the number of indictments or informations.

	NEW ORLEANS	SEATTLE (KING COUNTY)	NORFOLK	TUCSON	DELAWARE COUNTY, PENN.
Population	562,000	1,157,000	285,500	500,000	600,000
Estimated annual indictments or informations filed	5,063	4,500	2,800	2,309	3,000
Number of felony judges	10	8	3	7	4
Number of prosecutors	63	69	15	30	30
Percentage of robbery and burglary defendants pleading guilty	81%	86%	78%	87%	80%
Number of felony trials per year	1,069	4,567	648	270	491
Type of defense counsel and estimated percentage of defendants covered	Public 65% Assigned 10% Retained 25%	Public 64% Assigned 16% Retained 20%	Assigned 75% Retained 25%	Public 70% Assigned 3% Retained 27%	Public 65% Retained 35%
Prosecutorial restrictions on plea bargaining	Limited charge bargaining	For high-impact cases	Minimal	For career criminals	Minimal

SOURCE: William F. McDonald, *Plea Bargaining: Critical Issues and Common Practices* (Washington, D.C.: National Institute of Justice, 1985), 7.

TABLE **9.5** **Types of plea concessions in robbery and burglary cases in five jurisdictions**

Although the percentage of cases ending in a guilty plea is similar in all of the cities (see Table 9.4), the type of plea bargain arrived at differs.

TYPE OF CONCESSION	NEW ORLEANS	SEATTLE (KING COUNTY)	NORFOLK	TUCSON	DELAWARE COUNTY, PENN.
Sentence recommendation only	56%	46%	32%	7%	2%
Sentence recommendation plus charge reduction and/or dismissal	4	42	37	3	31
Charge reduction and/or dismissal only	40	12	31	90	67

SOURCE: William F. McDonald, *Plea Bargaining: Critical Issues and Common Practices* (Washington, D.C.: National Institute of Justice, 1985), 7.

- If every case went to trial, federal and state governments would need many times more courts and judges than they now have.
- Plea bargaining leads to the prompt and largely final disposition of most criminal cases.
- Plea bargaining reduces the time that pretrial detainees must spend in jail. If they plead guilty to serious charges, they can be moved to prisons with recreational and educational programs instead of enduring the enforced idleness of jails.
- By disposing of cases more quickly than trials would, plea bargaining reduces the amount of time that released suspects spend free on bail. Therefore, the public is better protected from crimes that such suspects may commit while on pretrial release.
- Offenders who plead guilty to serious charges can move more quickly into prison counseling, training, and education programs designed to rehabilitate offenders.

In 1976, Justice Potter Stewart revealed the heart and soul of plea bargaining when he wrote in *Blackledge v. Allison* that plea bargaining "can benefit all concerned" in a criminal case. There are advantages for defendants, prosecutors, defense attorneys, and judges. Defendants can have their cases completed more quickly and know what the punishment will be, instead of facing the uncertainty of a judge's sentencing decision. Moreover, the defendant is likely to receive less than the maximum punishment that might have been imposed after a trial. Prosecutors are not being "soft on crime" when they plea bargain. Instead, they gain an easy conviction, even in cases in which enough evidence may not have been gathered to convince a jury to convict the defendant. They also save time and resources by disposing of cases without having to prepare for a trial. Private defense attorneys also save the

Scott Weiland, lead singer for the Stone Temple Pilots, plead guilty to a New York misdemeanor drug charge in exchange for probation, completion of a rehabilitation program, and staying out of trouble for a year. Unfortunately, Weiland lasted less than six months and was jailed in California for illegal drug use.

CLOSE up

Banning Plea Bargaining in Tennessee

In January 1997, William Gibbons, the district attorney [D.A.] for Shelby County, Tennessee, which includes the city of Memphis, introduced a policy of refusing to reduce charges of first- and second-degree murder and charges of robbery or rape that involved the use of a deadly weapon. These are generally considered the most violent and harmful of crimes. Under the policy, anyone indicted for these crimes must either plead guilty to the charge specified or go to trial. The operation of the policy raises interesting questions about the impact of bans on plea bargaining.

The District Attorney's Office hoped that the "no deal" policy and the resulting tough sentences for people convicted of these crimes would deter other potential offenders from committing violent crimes. Thus the ban on plea bargaining was accompanied by a public relations campaign to spread the word about the new policy. The marketing campaign, which would have cost

$1 million, was produced through contributions of free advertising, private fundraising led by a former Memphis mayor, and $200,000 in money confiscated from drug dealers by the county sheriff. "No Deal" signs, decals, and bumper stickers were distributed to businesses and neighborhood watch groups.

The District Attorney's Office claims that the ban on plea bargaining "had a positive impact in reducing violent felonies." The Office pointed to a 12 percent reduction in criminal homicides and a 12 percent reduction in robberies in 1997 as compared with 1996. In light of the fact that violent crime nationwide dropped steadily beginning in 1992 with, for example, declines of 11.4 percent for robberies and 7.4 percent for murders in 1998, can the district attorney accurately conclude that the reduction in Memphis is a result of the plea bargaining policy and not a general social trend?

The District Attorney's Office says that the effectiveness of the new policy stems from cooperation between the prosecutor and local law enforcement agencies:

time needed to prepare for a trial. They earn their fee quickly and can move on to the next case. Likewise, plea bargaining helps public defenders cope with large caseloads. Judges, too, avoid time-consuming trials and are spared the prospect of having to decide what sentence to impose on the defendant. Instead, they often adopt the sentence recommended by the prosecutor in consultation with the defense attorney, provided that it is within the range of sentences that they deem appropriate for a given crime and offender.

Because plea bargaining benefits all involved, it is little wonder that it existed long before it was publicly acknowledged by the legal community and that it still exists, even when prosecutors, legislators, or judges claim that they wish to abolish it. In California, for example, voters decided to ban plea bargaining for serious felony cases. Research showed, however, that when plea bargaining was barred in the felony trial courts, it did not disappear. It simply occurred earlier in the justice process, at the suspect's first appearance in the lower-level municipal court (McCoy, 1993). Efforts to abolish plea bargaining may also result in bargaining over the charges instead of over the sentence that will be recommended in exchange for a guilty plea. And if a prosecutor forbids his or her staff to plea bargain, judges may become more involved in negotiating and facilitating guilty pleas that result in predictable punishments for offenders.

The new policy is in large part possible because of a process by which representatives of the [District Attorney's] Office meet with representatives of the Memphis Police Department and the Shelby County Sheriff's Office to screen cases involving the violent crimes covered by the policy. This early review process helps to ensure that the D.A.'s Office has a good case with strong evidence before someone is charged and a proposed indictment is presented to the grand jury.

By filtering out cases for which the most serious charges are not justified and provable, does this review and screening process perhaps fulfill the function served by plea bargaining in other cities? Elsewhere, the plea negotiation process involves discussions between defense attorneys and prosecutors about the provable facts of a case so that both sides can reach agreement about the "going rate" of punishment for that particular offender and crime. In effect, then, might the Memphis screening process produce the same results in "no deal" cases that would have been produced anyway through plea negotiations in other cities?

In reality, the Memphis ban on plea bargaining is not absolute, even for the specified crimes to which it applies. There can be "exceptions based on legal, factual, or ethical grounds [that] must be approved by a supervisor [in the District Attorney's Office] and documented in writing." Although only 4 percent of cases have

produced reduced charges as approved exceptions, does the possibility of exceptions create incentives for defense attorneys to seek special deals for their clients? Does it create opportunities for prosecutors to use discretion to reduce charges against particular defendants or the clients of particular attorneys?

A critic might claim that the screening process and the opportunity to treat cases as exceptions to the "no deal" rule mean that the district attorney's policy has probably had little impact on the outcomes of criminal cases. Arguably, many of these cases might have produced the same results in a system that relied on plea negotiations. Moreover, it is difficult to prove that any reductions in crime rates are caused by the policy when similar drops in crime rates are simultaneously occurring throughout the country in cities that still rely on plea bargaining. Does that mean that the "no deal" policy and the accompanying advertising campaign are primarily a public relations effort to gain support and credit for the District Attorney's Office? Is it possible that the district attorney honestly believes that the "no deal" policy has positive benefits even if it may have produced little change? What do you think?

SOURCE: Thomas D. Henderson, "No Deals Policy" (1999), Office of the District Attorney General, Thirtieth Judicial District of Tennessee web page at www.personal.bellsouth.net/mem/d/a/dag30; and Michael J. Sniffen, "Crime Down for Seventh Straight Year," Associated Press report, October 17, 1999.

As you read the Close-Up concerning the ban on plea bargaining for several serious violent crimes in Memphis, Tennessee, consider the impact of the ban. The prosecutor claims that the ban has led to a drop in violent crime because potential criminals know that they will be severely punished under the "no deal" policy. Is this true? What other consequences might be produced by the ban on plea bargaining?

Exchange Relationships in Plea Bargaining

Plea bargaining is a set of exchange relationships in which the prosecutor, the defense attorney, the defendant, and sometimes the judge participate. All have specific goals, all try to use the situation to their own advantage, and all are likely to see the exchange as a success.

Plea bargaining does not always occur in a single meeting between prosecutor and defense attorney. One study showed that plea bargaining is a process in which prosecutors and defense attorneys interact again and again as they move farther along in the judicial process. As time passes, the prosecutor's hand may be strengthened by the discovery of more evidence or new information about the defendant's background (Emmelman, 1996). Often it is the prosecution rather than the defense that is in the best position to obtain new evidence (Cooney, 1994). However, the defense attorney's position may gain strength if the prosecutor does not wish to spend time going farther down the path toward a trial.

Tactics of Prosecutor and Defense

Plea bargaining between defense counsel and prosecutor is a serious game in which friendliness and joking may mask efforts to advance each side's cause. The pattern is a familiar one: initial humor, the statement of each side's case, resolution of conflict, and a final period of cementing the relationship. Throughout, each side tries to impress the other with its confidence in its own case while pointing out weaknesses in the other side's case. An unspoken rule of openness and candor is designed to keep the relationship on good terms. Little effort is made to conceal information that may later be useful to the other side in the courtroom.

Some attorneys do not follow these unwritten rules. One prosecutor said, "There are some attorneys with whom we never bargain, because we can't. We don't like to penalize a defendant because he has an ass for an attorney, but when an attorney cannot be trusted, we have no alternative." Studies show that the outcomes of plea bargaining may depend on the relationships between prosecutors and individual attorneys, as well as the defense counsel's willingness to fight for the client (Champion, 1989). Defense attorneys often feel that prosecutors do not see defendants as individuals because they have so little contact with the defendants and their families. Because defense lawyers get to know the defendants, their problems, and their families, they may become emotionally attached to them. As one defense lawyer said, "We have to impress the chief deputy prosecutor with the fact that he is dealing with humans, not with just a case. If the guy is guilty he should be imprisoned, but he should get only what is coming to him, no more."

A tactic that many prosecutors bring to plea-bargaining sessions is the multiple-offense indictment. One defense attorney commented, "Prosecutors throw everything into an indictment they can think of, down to and including spitting on the sidewalk. They then permit the defendant to plead guilty to one or two offenses, and he is supposed to think it's a victory" (Alschuler, 1968:54). Multiple-offense charges are especially important to prosecuting attorneys in difficult cases—in which, for instance, the victim is reluctant to provide information, the value of the stolen item is in question, and the evidence may not be reliable. The police often file charges of selling a drug when they know they can convict only for possession. Because the accused persons know that the penalty for selling is much greater, they are tempted to plead guilty to the lesser charge.

Defense attorneys may threaten to ask for a jury trial if concessions are not made. Their hand is further strengthened if they have filed pretrial motions that require a formal response by the prosecutor. Another tactic is to seek to reschedule pretrial activities in the hope that with delay witnesses will become unavailable, media attention will die down, and memories of the crime will be weakened by the time of the trial. Rather than resort to such legal tactics, some attorneys prefer to bargain on the basis of friendship. A defense attorney once said, "I never use the Constitution. I bargain a case on the theory that it's a 'cheap burglary' or a 'cheap purse snatching' or a 'cheap whatever.' Sure, I could suddenly start to negotiate by saying, 'Ha, ha! You goofed. You should have given the defendant a warning.' And I'd do just fine in that case, but my other clients would pay for this isolated success. The next time the district attorney had his foot on my throat, he'd push too" (Alschuler, 1968:79).

Often the bargain is arrived at in ways that might not be noticed by a casual observer. For example, vague references are often made to disposition of the case. Statements such as "I think I can sell this to the boss" or "I'll see what can be done" signal the end of a bargaining session and are viewed by the actors as an agreement on the terms of the exchange. On other cases the bargaining is more specific, with a direct promise that certain charges will be altered in exchange for a guilty plea.

Because bargaining is carried out mainly between the prosecutor and the defense attorney, the interests of the public and even of the defendant may take a back seat. If a case went all the way to trial, only evidence gathered in a legal manner could be used. Under plea bargaining, however, unconstitutional actions by police officers and other actors can be hidden from public view.

Neither the prosecutor nor the defense attorney is a free agent. Each must have the cooperation of both defendants and judges. Attorneys often cite the difficulty of convincing defendants that they should uphold their end of the bargain. Judges must cooperate by sentencing the accused according to the prosecutor's recommendation. Although their role requires that they uphold the public interest, judges may be reluctant to interfere with a plea agreement. Thus both the prosecutor and the defense attorney often confer with the judge about the sentence to be imposed before agreeing on a plea.

At the same time, however, the judicial role requires that the judge reject the agreement if it does not meet certain legal standards. Prosecutors and defense attorneys will evaluate each decision as an indication of the judge's future behavior. If a judge is unpredictable in supporting plea agreements, defense attorneys may be reluctant to reach agreements in later cases.

Pleas without Bargaining

Studies have shown that in many courts give-and-take plea bargaining does not occur for certain types of cases, yet there are as many guilty pleas as in other courts (Eisenstein, Flemming and Nardulli, 1988). The term *bargaining* may be misleading in that it implies haggling. Many scholars argue that guilty pleas emerge after an agreement to "settle the facts" is reached by the prosecutor, the defense attorney, and sometimes the judge (Utz, 1978). In this view the parties first study the facts of a case. What were the circumstances of the event? Was it really an assault or was it more of a shoving match? Did the victim antagonize the accused? Each side may hope to persuade the other that its view of the defendant's actions is backed up by provable facts. The prosecution wants the defense to believe that strong evidence proves its version of the event. The defense attorney wants to convince the prosecution that the evidence is not solid and that there is a risk of acquittal if the case is heard by a jury.

In some cases, the evidence is strong and the defense attorney has little hope of persuading the prosecutor otherwise. Through their discussions, the prosecutor and defense attorney seek to reach a shared view of the provable facts in the case. Once they agree on the facts, they will both know the appropriate charge, and they can agree on the sentence according to the locally defined "going rate" (the usual sentence for such an offense). At that point a guilty plea can be entered without any formal bargaining because both sides agree on what the case is worth in terms of the seriousness of the charge and the usual punishment. This process may be thought of as *implicit plea bargaining* because shared understandings create the expectation that a guilty plea will lead to a less-than-maximum sentence, even without any exchange or bargaining.

The going rates for sentences for particular crimes and offenders depend on local values and sentencing patterns. Often both the prosecutor and the defense attorney are members of a particular local legal culture and thus share an understanding about how cases should be handled. On the basis of their experiences in interacting with other attorneys and judges, they become keenly aware of local practices in the treatment of cases and offenders (Worden, 1995). Thus they may both know right away what the sentence will be for a first-time burglar or second-time robber. The sentence may differ in another courthouse because the local legal culture and going rates can vary.

These shared understandings are important for several reasons. First, they help make plea bargaining more effective because both sides understand which sentences apply to which cases. Instead of debating about whether a burglary case should be punished by a short prison term, both sides already know whether such a term is part of the going rate for burglary. Thus they can focus on the facts of the case and the characteristics of the defendant—especially his or her prior record—in deciding whether burglary is an appropriate charge in view of the provable facts. If the going rate does not apply to these facts or to a defendant with this record, both sides ought to be able to agree on a guilty plea to a lesser or related offense. Second, shared understandings help create a cooperative climate for plea bargaining, even if there are bad feelings between the prosecutor and the defense attorney. The local legal culture dictates how attorneys are expected to treat each other and thereby reach agreements. And third, the shared understandings help maintain the relationship between the attorneys.

Many cases are settled when one party makes an offer and the other simply agrees to it. Because courthouse actors know the definitions of criminal acts and the going rate for each, there is little bargaining. In one study, Douglas Maynard found that few cases were resolved through extensive bargaining. He believes that this is because the participants are able to "read" situations in a similar way and infer what resolution will be mutually acceptable. As he notes,

> such a process in plea bargaining is surely aided by the participants' knowledge of the courtroom subculture. The establishment by legal practitioners of "going rates" for run-of-the-mill, "normal" crimes . . . in local jurisdictions and the administration of these rates as a matter of course . . . is a well-documented practice. (Maynard, 1984:81)

Implicit plea bargaining through settling the facts is less likely to occur if there is turnover among prosecutors, defense attorneys, and judges. Bargaining is more likely over the most serious cases, such as murder and manslaughter, in which the sentence will probably be severe and may vary from case to case.

Just as the local legal culture and going rates may vary from courthouse to courthouse, so, too, can the routine procedures that affect plea bargaining. In some courts a "slow plea" process is dominant: defendants plead not guilty at first but change their pleas as the trial progresses. In 1996, Dallas Cowboys football star Michael Irvin was arrested when caught in a hotel room with two topless dancers and a quantity of cocaine and marijuana. In public, Irvin and his attorneys indicated that they would fight the case through trial. After the trial began, however, Irvin pleaded "no contest" to second-degree felony charges for cocaine possession. In exchange, the prosecutor dropped the marijuana charges and agreed to a sentence of probation and a fine (Justice, 1996). Apparently, Irvin's attorneys had been discussing plea possibilities with the prosecutor and both sides reached agreement after the trial had already begun.

In other courts, prosecutors may filter out part of the caseload by dropping cases or diverting offenders. These routines, norms, and expectations may vary greatly, and observers of any one courthouse may see patterns that do not match any textbook description.

CHECK POINT

⑨ **Why does plea bargaining occur?**

⑩ **What is implicit plea bargaining?**

Legal Issues in Plea Bargaining

Over the last few decades the United States Supreme Court has confronted questions about the voluntariness of the plea and the parties' obligation to uphold the plea bargain agreement. In ruling on these questions the Court has upheld the constitutionality of plea bargaining and sought to ensure that due process rights are upheld in plea agreements.

Whether the defendant enters a guilty plea voluntarily is a central concern. In *Boykin v. Alabama* (1969) the Court ruled that defendants must state that the plea was made voluntarily before a judge may accept the plea. Judges have created standard forms with questions for the defendant to affirm in open court before the plea is accepted. Trial judges also must learn whether the defendant understands the consequences of pleading guilty and ensure that the plea is not obtained through pressure or coercion.

Can a trial court accept a guilty plea if the defendant claims to be innocent? In *North Carolina v. Alford* (1970) the Court allowed a defendant to enter a guilty plea for the purpose of gaining a lesser sentence, even though he maintained that he was innocent. Henry C. Alford was charged with first-degree murder, a capital offense. Although he claimed to be innocent, Alford pleaded guilty to second-degree murder, a charge for which the death penalty was not allowed. After receiving a thirty-year sentence, he complained to the Supreme Court that the plea had been coerced by the threat of the death penalty. He argued that he had never admitted guilt. The Court disagreed, stating that "an individual accused of crime may voluntarily, knowingly, and understandingly consent to the imposition of a prison sentence even if he is unwilling or unable to admit his participation in the acts constituting the crime." One result of this ruling is that many courts now accept pleas based on the "Alford Doctrine," in which defendants plead guilty but say they are not guilty. However, the Supreme Court has stated that trial judges should not accept such a plea unless a factual basis exists for believing that the defendant is in fact guilty (Whitebread and Slobogin, 1993:647).

A second issue is whether the plea agreement is fulfilled. If the prosecutor has promised a lenient sentence, the promise must be kept. In *Santobello v. New York* (1971), the Supreme Court ruled that "when a [guilty] plea rests in any significant degree on a promise or agreement of the prosecutor, so that it can be said to be part of the inducement or consideration, such promise must be fulfilled." The Court also decided that defendants must also keep their side of the bargain. In the case of *Ricketts v. Adamson* (1987), John Harvey Adamson had agreed to plead guilty and testify against a codefendant in exchange for a reduction of the charges from first- to second-degree murder. He carried out the bargain but refused to testify again when the codefendant's conviction was reversed on

Boykin v. Alabama (1969)
Defendants must state that they are voluntarily making a plea of guilty.

North Carolina v. Alford (1970)
A plea of guilty may be accepted for the purpose of a lesser sentence by a defendant who maintains his or her innocence.

Santobello v. New York (1971)
When a guilty plea rests on a promise of a prosecutor, it must be fulfilled.

Ricketts v. Adamson (1987)
Defendants must uphold the plea agreement or suffer the consequences.

A Question of Ethics

Lisa Davidson stood silently in the courtroom of Judge Helen Iverson. Defense attorney Bill Dixon whispered in Davidson's ear as they waited for Judge Iverson to finish reading Davidson's file. "Are we ready to proceed?" asked the Judge.

"Yes, your honor," came the simultaneous replies from both Dixon and the prosecutor standing nearby.

Judge Iverson stared at Davidson momentarily with a serious expression. "Ms. Davidson, you are charged with larceny. Because it is your third offense, I can send to you prison. Do you understand that?"

"Yes, your honor," replied Davidson, her voice quivering.

"Are you pleading guilty to this crime because you are guilty?" asked the judge.

"Yes, your honor."

The judge continued. "Are pleading guilty of your own free will?"

"Yes, your honor."

"Did anyone threaten you to make you plead guilty?"

"No, your honor."

"Did anyone make any promises to you to induce you plead guilty?"

Davidson nodded her head. "Yes. Mr. Dixon said that if I plead guilty to this charge then the prosecutor promised that my sentence would be only. . . ."

"EXCUSE ME, JUDGE IVERSON." Dixon interrupted in a loud voice. "Could I please have a moment to speak with my client?" Judge Iverson nodded. Taking Davidson by the arm, Dixon moved her three feet farther away from the judge's bench. Dixon whispered into Davidson's ear as his hands punched the air with emphatic gestures. A few moments later, they returned to their positions, standing in front of the judge. "We are ready to continue, your honor," said Dixon.

Judge Iverson looked at Davidson once again. "Did anyone promise you anything to induce you to plead guilty?"

Davidson glanced sideways at Dixon before replying "No, your honor."

"You understand that you are waiving your constitutional right to a trial and you are freely waiving that right?"

"Yes, your honor."

"Then I find you guilty as charged and I will set sentencing for one month from today at 10 A.M."

■ Should Judge Iverson have accepted the guilty plea? What role did the defense attorney play in staging the guilty plea ceremony? Were there any ethical problems? What would you have done if you were the judge?

appeal. The prosecutor then withdrew the offer to reduce the charge. The Supreme Court upheld the prosecutor's action and said that Adamson had to suffer the consequences of his choice not to testify at the codefendant's second trial.

May prosecutors threaten to penalize defendants who insist upon their right to a jury trial? In a Kentucky case, Paul Hayes was indicted for forging an $88.50 check. The prosecutor offered to recommend a sentence of five years in prison if Hayes pleaded guilty but said that, if Hayes pleaded not guilty, he would be indicted under the state's habitual criminal act. If Hayes was then found guilty, he would receive a mandatory life sentence because he had two prior convictions. Hayes rejected the guilty plea, went to trial, and was sentenced to life imprisonment. On appeal, the Supreme Court ruled in *Bordenkircher v. Hayes* (1978) that in the "give and take" of plea bargaining, the prosecutor's conduct did not violate the constitution. Milwaukee judge Ralph Fine (1986) has charged that prosecutors around the country are now using this ruling as a tool to coerce defendants into pleading guilty.

Plea bargaining, then, is no longer a secret. The Supreme Court has ruled that it is constitutional and has emphasized the need to protect defendants' rights. The judge asks a series of questions to ensure that the method by which the bargain was reached meets the standards of a knowing and voluntary plea. At one time, this "copping-out ceremony" was a regular feature of the courtroom day. But judges are discussing plea bargaining more openly and indicating that they are aware of plea negotiations. In many cases, judges have entered into plea discussions with respect to sentences in cases before them. Examine the scene in A Question of Ethics. Are all of the courtroom actors behaving in an honest, ethical manner? Does this scene raise questions about how plea bargains operate?

Justifications for Plea Bargaining

As early as the 1920s the legal profession was opposed to plea bargaining. There were concerns about the risk of political influence over criminal cases. Today, the pressures created by crime in an urban society and the usefulness and actual practice of bargaining have increased professional groups' interest in procedures that will allow for the review of guilty pleas and for other safeguards. Plea bargaining is now justified on the grounds that it individualizes justice and that it is necessary from an administrative standpoint when there are not enough courts, prosecutors, and judges to handle an ever larger number of trials.

Individualized Justice

Judges individualize justice by fashioning sentences to the severity of the offense and the characteristics of the offender. Some argue, however, that the discretion of the judge has been reduced while the prosecutor has gained more control over the justice process. The federal courts and many states now use sentencing guidelines that limit the ability of judges to tailor sentences to each case and defendant. This approach suggests that if the criminal law is to be fair, the prosecutor's office must be able to determine the proper charge and punishment on the basis of the facts of the case, the defendant's willingness to show remorse, and other factors.

Legislatures, responding to public pressure, have promoted use of the guilty plea by passing laws requiring severe punishments. Criminal justice personnel individualize these punishments and make them less severe through plea bargaining. In this way, they develop shared understandings of what punishment is appropriate for each crime. They believe that defendants who do not cooperate or who insist on a trial and are then found guilty should receive harsher sentences than defendants who "go along."

Administrative Necessity

A second justification for plea bargaining is administrative necessity. Many defendants must be processed quickly for the courts to keep up with the arrests made by the police, especially in large cities. The demands on the judicial process—crowded court calendars, large prison populations, strains on judicial personnel—are overwhelming. A Manhattan prosecutor has said, "Our office keeps eight courtrooms extremely busy trying 5 percent of the cases. If even 10 percent of the cases ended in a trial, the system would break down. We can't afford to think very much about anything else" (Fine, 1986:55). Yet some courts in large cities use guilty pleas much less often (Eisenstein and Jacob, 1977).

Studies have also cast doubt on the assumption that plea bargaining is a contemporary practice that arose in response to increased caseloads. One study found that plea bargaining was practiced in both high- and low-volume courts as early as 1880 and that since then less than 10 percent of indictments have led to trials (Heumann, 1978). Others have shown that plea bargaining has been a feature of American criminal justice since the Civil War (Friedman, 1993:252).

Malcolm Feeley argues that the use of plea bargaining has increased in direct proportion to the adversarial nature of the system. The modern criminal justice system has increased due process requirements, devoted more resources to both prosecution and defense, developed a substantive criminal law, and made defense counsel more widely available. If one looks at conditions in the nineteenth century, often called the "golden era of trials," one finds

> a process that is difficult for the contemporary observer to recognize; those accused of criminal offense—misdemeanor or felony alike—were typically rushed through crowded and noisy courts either subject to a quick, one-sided trial lasting an hour or two or pressured to plead guilty by overbearing prosecutors whose practices were condoned by judges. All this took place without benefit of counsel. (Feeley, 1982)

Today, Feeley believes, the balance between the state and the accused is more even. This has intensified the adversary nature of the system, and thus the opportunity for negotiation.

Bordenkircher v. Hayes (1978)
A defendant's rights were not violated by a prosecutor who warned that declining to accept a guilty plea would result in a harsher sentence.

Criticisms of Plea Bargaining

Although plea bargaining is widely used, it has been deplored by a number of scholars and by groups such as the American Bar Association. The criticisms are of two main types. The first stresses due process and argues that plea bargaining is not fair because defendants give up some of their constitutional rights, especially the right to trial by jury. The second criticism stresses sentencing policy and points out that society's interest in appropriate punishments for crimes is reduced by plea bargaining. In urban areas with high caseloads, harried prosecutors and judges are said to make concessions based on administrative needs, resulting in lighter sentences than those required by the penal code.

Plea bargaining also comes under fire because it is hidden from judicial scrutiny. Because the agreement is most often made at an early stage, the judge has little information about the crime or the defendant and cannot evaluate the case. Nor can the judge review the terms of the bargain—that is, check on the amount of pressure put on the defendant to plead guilty. The result of "bargain justice" is that the judge, the public, and sometimes even the defendant cannot know for sure who got what from whom in exchange for what.

Other critics believe that overuse of plea bargaining breeds disrespect and even contempt for the law. They say criminals look at the judicial process as a game or a sham, much like other "deals" made in life.

Critics also contend that it is unjust to penalize persons who assert their right to a trial by giving them stiffer sentences than they would have received if they had pleaded guilty. The evidence here is unclear, although it is widely believed that an extra penalty is imposed on defendants who take up the court's time by asserting their right to a trial (Spohn, 1992). Critics note that federal sentencing guidelines also encourage avoidance of trial because they include a two-point deduction from an offender's base score—thus lowering the sentence—for "acceptance of responsibility" (McCoy, 1995).

In their analysis of robbery and burglary data from three California counties, David Brereton and Jonathan Casper (1981–1982) found that a greater proportion of defendants who went to trial received prison sentences, compared with those who pleaded guilty. Mark Cuniff's study (1987) of twenty-eight large jurisdictions also revealed that defendants who pleaded guilty were less likely to be sent to prison than those who were found guilty after a jury trial. Of interest is that cases decided by the judge alone in a bench trial resulted in about the same proportion of offenders going to prison as for cases in which the defendant pleaded guilty.

Figure 9.5 presents the results of a Bureau of Justice Statistics study that supports the view that offenders who go to trial receive harsher punishments. These results should be viewed with caution, because it is difficult to know the strength of the evidence against a defendant and the reason a plea bargain was not used to dispose of a case. When defendants view the stakes as high, however, they are more likely to take a chance on a jury trial.

Finally, another concern about plea bargaining is that innocent people will plead guilty to acts that they did not commit. Although it is hard to know how often this happens, some defendants have entered guilty pleas when they have not committed the offense. For example, the Colorado courts overturned a sentence on the ground that the defendant had been coerced by the judge's statement that he would "put him away forever if he did not accept the bargain"

9.5 Conviction by guilty plea, bench trial, or trial by jury: a comparison of prison sentences

Although it appears to be in the offender's interest to plead guilty for most crimes, there is not enough information in this graph to support such a conclusion. What else would you need to know?

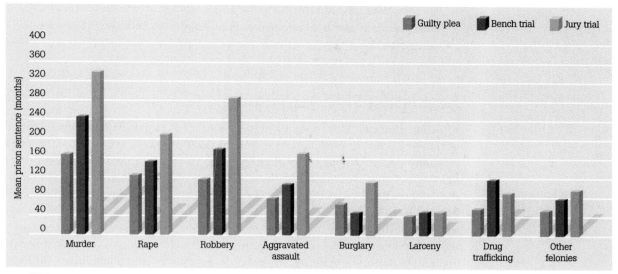

SOURCE: U.S. Department of Justice, Bureau of Justice Statistics, *Bulletin* (February 1990).

(*People v. Clark,* 1973). It may be hard for middle-class people to understand how anyone could possibly plead guilty when they are innocent. However, people with little education and low social status may lack the confidence to say "no" to an attorney who pressures them to plead guilty. Poor people may feel helpless in the stressful climate of the courthouse and jail. If they lack faith in the system's ability to protect their rights and find them not guilty, they may accept a lighter punishment rather than risk being convicted for a serious offense.

Reforming Plea Bargaining

Some believe that plea bargaining should be abolished. Others argue that it should be retained as long as it is done openly and counsel for the defense is present.

In some jurisdictions (Honolulu, New Orleans, El Paso, and the Bronx), efforts have been made to ban plea bargaining. In Alaska, the state attorney general told district attorneys to stop the practice. Judges feared that as a result the courts would be flooded with cases and the justice process would be bogged down. Neither fear was realized. While direct bargaining ceased, "implicit" bargaining remained. Prosecutors also screened more cases so that only the strongest ones went to trial. There was some increase in the punishment given in minor cases but little impact on the sentences received for serious cases (Rubenstein and White, 1979:367; Carns and Kruse, 1991).

In 1982 California voters passed Proposition 8, a victims' bill of rights. Included in this new law was a ban on plea bargaining in cases that involved serious crimes. However, the ban did not extend to cases decided in the municipal court. Candace McCoy (1993) has shown how Proposition 8 shifted plea bargaining to the lower courts, with only the most serious and disputed felonies being bound over to the superior court. Brian Forst concludes:

> It is clear that little good would be served by attempting to force all cases through the court [in trials]; many, perhaps most, pleas involve cases in which an offender has no defense and simply wishes to expedite the process, often in exchange for minor concessions by the prosecutor. (1995:336)

Evaluating Plea Bargaining

Pleading guilty, either to obtain a lighter sentence or as part of a bargain, is typical of the American criminal justice system. The guilty plea occurs in up to 90 percent of felony cases. Although it is often explained as a way to reduce the burden of heavy caseloads for criminal justice officials and defense attorneys, plea bargaining can benefit all the participants. The prosecutor gains a guilty plea and does not have to go to trial; the defense attorney can make more efficient use of his or her time; the judge moves cases through the process; and the defendant receives a lighter sentence. In view of the Supreme Court's decisions and increased public awareness of plea bargaining, the practice can be expected to continue and to be seen as legitimate.

CHECK POINT

⑪ **What issues concerning plea bargaining has the Supreme Court examined?**

⑫ **What are the justifications for plea bargaining?**

⑬ **What are the criticisms of plea bargaining?**

Summary

- Pretrial processes determine the fates of nearly all defendants through case dismissals, decisions defining the charges, and plea bargains that affect more than 90 percent of cases.
- Defense attorneys use motions to their advantage to gain information and delay proceedings to benefit their clients.
- The bail process provides opportunities for many defendants to gain pretrial release, but poor defendants may be disadvantaged by their inability to come up with the money or property needed to secure release. New preventive detention statutes may permit judges to hold defendants considered dangerous or likely to flee.
- Bail bondsmen are private businesspeople who provide money for defendants' pretrial release for a fee. Their activities create risks of corruption and discrimination in the bail process, but they may help the system by reminding defendants about court dates and tracking down defendants who disappear.

■ Although judges bear primary responsibility for setting bail, prosecutors are especially influential in recommending amounts and conditions for pretrial release.

■ Initiatives to reform the bail process include release on own recognizance (ROR), police-issued citations, and bail guidelines.

■ Pretrial detainees, despite the presumption of innocence, are held in difficult conditions in jails containing mixed populations of convicted offenders, detainees, and troubled people. The shock of being jailed creates risks of suicide and depression.

■ Most convictions are obtained through plea bargains, a process that exists because it fulfills the self-interest of prosecutors, judges, defense attorneys, and defendants.

■ Plea bargaining is facilitated by exchange relations between prosecutors and defense attorneys. In many courthouses, there is little actual bargaining, as outcomes are determined through the implicit bargaining process of settling the facts and assessing the "going rate" punishment according to the values of the local legal culture.

■ The U.S. Supreme Court has endorsed plea bargaining and addressed legal issues concerning the knowing and voluntary nature of pleas, guilty pleas by defendants who still claim to be innocent, and the obligations of prosecutors and defense attorneys to uphold the plea bargain agreement.

■ Plea bargaining has been justified for its ability to individualize justice and ease administrative burdens on courts. It has been criticized for pressuring defendants to surrender their rights and for reducing the sentences imposed on offenders.

Questions for Review

❶ What is the method of securing pretrial release for the accused?

❷ What are the criteria used to set bail?

❸ Is plea bargaining necessary? Why does it exist?

❹ What has the U.S. Supreme Court ruled about the constitutionality of plea bargaining? What safeguards has it imposed?

Key Terms and Cases

arraignment (p. 321)
bail (p. 325)
citation (p. 332)
motion (p. 324)
plea bargaining (p. 340)
preventive detention (p. 333)

probable cause (p. 321)
release on recognizance (ROR) (p. 332)
Bordenkircher v. Hayes (1978) (p. 349)
Boykin v. Alabama (1969) (p. 347)
North Carolina v. Alford (1970) (p. 347)
Ricketts v. Adamson (1987) (p. 347)

Santobello v. New York (1971) (p. 347)
Schall v. Martin (1984) (p. 334)
United States v. Salerno and Cafero (1987) (p. 334)

For Further Reading

Goldkamp, John. *Personal Liberty and Community Safety: Pretrial Release in Criminal Court.* New York: Plenum Publishing, 1995. An examination of issues surrounding bail and pretrial release.

Heumann, Milton. *Plea Bargaining.* Chicago: University of Chicago Press, 1978. How prosecutors, judges, and defense attorneys adapt to plea bargaining.

Maynard, Douglas W. *Inside Plea Bargaining.* New York: Plenum, 1984. Examination of the discourse surrounding plea bargaining as settlements are made by prosecutors and defense attorneys.

McCoy, Candace. *Politics and Plea Bargaining.* Philadelphia: University of Pennsylvania Press, 1993. A study of the 1982 California victim's rights legislation and its impact on plea bargaining.

Nasheri, Hedieh. *Betrayal of Due Process: A Comparative Assessment of Plea Bargaining in the United States and Canada.* Lanham, Md.: University Press of America, 1998. A critical study of differences and similarities in plea bargaining in two countries.

Taubman, Bryna. *Preppy Murder Trial.* New York: St. Martins, 1988. A description of the events leading to the plea bargain of Robert Chambers in the death of Jennifer Levin.

Uviller, H. Richard. *Virtual Justice: The Flawed Prosecution of Crime in America.* New Haven, Conn.: Yale University Press, 1996. A critical analysis of the stages of the criminal justice process, including an evaluation of plea bargaining.

Wice, Paul. *Freedom for Sale.* Lexington, Mass.: Lexington Books, 1974. A classic survey of bail and its operation.

Going Online

❶ Go to www.state.sd.us/state/executive/attorney/opinions/94.94-06.htm. Read the South Dakota attorney general's opinion on the authority of out-of-state bail bondsmen and bounty hunters to take fugitives into custody. What problems do states face in trying to regulate and control the pursuit of fugitives who arrive from out-of-state?

❷ Go to www.ajc.state.ak.us/Reports/pleafram.htm. Read the report on banning plea bargaining in Alaska. What has been the impact of banning plea bargaining?

❸ **Using InfoTrak College Edition,** type in your password. Search for the phrase *plea bargain* and find an article on Alan Eagleson, the former director of the National Hockey League Players'

Association. What kind of deal did Eagleson receive in pleading guilty to fraud charges in both the United States and Canada? Do you believe that Eagleson received adequate punishment for his crimes?

CHECK POINT ANSWERS

❶ Preliminary hearings inform defendants of their rights and determine if there is probable cause. Arraignments involve the formal reading of charges and the entry of a plea. Motions seek information and the vindication of defendants' rights.

❷ Cases are filtered out through the discretionary decisions of prosecutors and judges when they believe that there is inadequate evidence to proceed, or when prosecutors believe that their scarce resources are best directed at other cases.

❸ Bail decisions are based primarily on the judge's evaluation of the seriousness of the offense charged and the defendant's prior record. The decisions are influenced by the prosecutor's recommendations and the defense attorney's counterarguments about the defendant's personal qualities and ties to the community.

❹ Bondsmen may help the system by reminding defendants about their court dates and finding them if they fail to appear. However, bondsmen also may contribute to corruption and discrimination.

❺ Bail reform alternatives include police citations, release on own recognizance, and 10 percent cash bail.

❻ The U.S. Supreme Court ruled that preventive detention did not violate the Constitution's ban on excessive bail because such detentions are not punishment and are merely a way to protect the public.

❼ The jail population includes pretrial detainees for whom bail was not set or those who are too poor to pay the bail amount required. People convicted of misdemeanors are also in jail, serving short sentences, along

with people convicted of felonies awaiting transfer to prison and people with psychological or substance abuse problems who have been swept off the streets.

8 Pretrial detainees face the stress of living with difficult and potentially dangerous cellmates. They also face uncertainty about what will happen to their case, their families, their jobs, and their ability to contribute to preparing a defense.

9 Plea bargaining occurs because it serves the self-interest of all relevant actors: defendants gain a certain, less-than-maximum sentence; prosecutors gain swift, sure convictions; defense attorneys get prompt resolu-

tion of cases; judges do not have to preside over as many time-consuming trials.

10 Implicit plea bargaining occurs when prosecutors and defense attorneys use shared expectations and interactions to settle the facts of the case and reach a resolution based on the going rate for sentences in the local legal culture.

11 The U.S. Supreme Court has examined whether the defendant pleads guilty in a knowing and voluntary way, guilty pleas from defendants who still claim to be innocent, and prosecutors' and defendants' obligations to fulfill their plea agreements.

12 The justifications for plea bargaining

are (1) the opportunity to individualize justice during an era when legislatures mandate harsh punishments and limit judges' sentencing discretion, and (2) administrative necessity because of overcrowded courts.

13 The criticisms of plea bargaining include concerns about pressures on defendants to surrender their rights and concerns that society's mandated criminal punishments are improperly reduced.

CHAPTER TEN

Trial and Post-Trial Processes

Om January 3, 1999, Kendra Webdale, 32-year-old record company receptionist and aspiring screen writer, waited on a subway platform in New York City. As a subway train roared into the station, she was suddenly grabbed from behind and thrown on to the tracks in the path of the oncoming train. Webdale was killed instantly under the wheels of the train. Meanwhile, her attacker, 29-year-old Andrew Goldstein, a complete stranger who had never met Webdale, silently sat down as other people on the platform prevented him from leaving (Rohde, 1999).

Goldstein, a mental patient suffering from schizophrenia, who had stopped taking his medication, confessed to the police (Anderson, 1999). In his taped confession, Goldstein said, "And then the train is almost there and I said, 'Oh no, it happened.' You know, I, I, I got into the fit again, like I've done in the past, and I pushed the woman, not meaning to push her on the tracks" (Winerip, 1999b).

Although Goldstein's confession and the witnesses present on the subway platform made perfectly clear who caused Kendra Webdale's death, Goldstein had the right to a trial. He had a right to be defended by an attorney as he forced the prosecution to prove its case before twelve jurors drawn from among the citizens of New York City. At issue in Goldstein's trial was not whether he pushed Webdale, but whether he could be punished for committing a crime. Because of Goldstein's mental illness, his lawyer, Harvey Fishbein, argued that he should be found not guilty by reason of insanity. Fishbein did not argue that Goldstein should be freed. Instead, the lawyer sought to persuade the jury that Goldstein should be judged legally insane so that he could be sent to a secure mental hospital instead of being sentenced to twenty-five years to life in prison (Rohde, 1999).

The prosecutor, William Greenbaum, portrayed Goldstein as someone who knew what he was doing when he killed Webdale. As the attack was described by Greenbaum, Goldstein carefully timed his shove to send the victim directly in front of the oncoming train and took care to maintain his own balance on the platform in the process. The prosecution's psychiatrist, Dr. Angela Hegarty, testified that the attack stemmed from Goldstein's hatred for women, not from his mental illness (Italiano, 1999a). In response, defense attorneys blamed the government for the shortage of beds in mental hospitals that kept Goldstein walking the streets even when he repeatedly requested to be hospitalized (Rohde, 1999). The defense psychiatrist, Dr. Spencer Eth, blamed the attack on uncontrollable thoughts and feelings caused by Goldstein's mental illness (Italiano, 1999a).

After the month-long presentation of evidence at trial, the twelve jurors, four women and eight men, in November 1999 spent six days locked together in a room deliberating Goldstein's fate. Occasionally they asked for testimony to be read to them again as they continued to discuss and debate. On the sixth day, they told the judge that they were hopelessly deadlocked with ten jurors favoring conviction and two jurors believing that Goldstein was insane. The judge declared a mistrial and thereby forced the prosecution to plan to try Goldstein again in front of an entirely new jury in 2000. In March, Goldstein was convicted of murder after a second trial and sentenced in May to 25 years to life in prison, the maximum possible.

The American system regards the trial as the best method for determining a defendant's guilt. Yet a trial is not a scientific process. Instead of calm, consistent evaluations of evidence, trials involve unpredictable human perceptions and reactions. One of the holdout jurors in Goldstein's first trial was a man awaiting sentencing after being convicted of punching a police officer (Italiano, 1999c). His presence on the jury raised questions about whether the prosecution had adequately investigated the jurors' backgrounds when participating in jury selection. The other holdout juror was a former social worker who worked with mentally ill people (Italiano, 1999b). If someone with professional experience believed that the insanity defense was justified, does that raise questions about whether the other jurors were qualified and capable of making accurate judgments about Goldstein's mental state at the time of the crime? As demonstrated by Goldstein's case, the American system permits jurors drawn from the community to make some of the most important and difficult decisions in the justice process.

The Goldstein case occupies the top layer of Samuel Walker's criminal justice wedding cake—as one of those celebrated cases that go to trial and command great public attention. The horrific nature of the crime attracted significant public attention. The seriousness of the charge and potential punishment created little incentive for Goldstein to enter a guilty plea. And Goldstein's father, a physician, could afford to pay for defense attorneys and expert witnesses during a long, expensive trial (Italiano, 1999b). By contrast, judges hear guilty pleas from and hand out hundreds of sentences to less publicized defendants whose crimes are equally horrible. As discussed in Chapter 9, most defendants plead guilty or are judged in a bench trial without jury. The number of full jury trials is small compared with the total number of cases processed by the judicial system.

Although trials are relatively unusual, they are important. Not only do they provide the method for deciding highly disputed cases, but they communicate to the public the values and rules by which society lives. Issues of proper evidence, defendant's rights, and citizens' participation in judicial decision making through jury service are illustrated in trial processes and reinforced in post-trial processes.

QUESTIONS for Inquiry

- What are the stages of a criminal trial?
- How are juries chosen?
- What is the basis for an appeal of a conviction?

Trial: The Exceptional Case WWW

Most Americans are familiar with the image of the criminal trial. As portrayed in so many movies and television shows, the prosecutor and defense attorney face off in a tense courtroom conflict. Each attorney attempts to use evidence, persuasion, and emotion to convince a **jury** of citizens to favor its arguments about the defendant's guilt or innocence. Because trials are conducted in public, they are a kind of stylized drama. As Steven Phillips (1977:109) has said, the trial

> is also politics, in both the noblest and the basest senses of the word. A criminal trial is an almost primordial confrontation between the individual and society. At stake are values no less important than individual liberty on the one hand, and the need for social order on the other. It is also pragmatic, grass-roots clubhouse politics in its rawest form. Trial by jury is publicity, the news media, and the making and unmaking of reputations. Many a political career has begun or ended in a criminal courtroom.

The trial process is based on the assumption that an open battle between opposing lawyers is the best way to discover the truth. The authors of the Constitution apparently shared this assumption: the Sixth Amendment says the accused shall enjoy a speedy and public trial by an impartial jury "in all criminal prosecutions" (Langbein, 1992). In theory, each side will present the best evidence and arguments it can muster for its side, and the jury will make a decision based on thorough consideration of the available information about the case.

However, trials are human processes, and the truth is not guaranteed to emerge in the final verdict. Many factors may keep a trial from achieving its goal of revealing the truth. The rules of evidence may prevent one side from presenting the most useful evidence. One side may have impressive expert witnesses that the other side cannot afford to counter with its own experts. One side's attorney may be more persuasive and likeable, and thus may sway the jury in spite of the

jury
A panel of citizens selected according to law and sworn to determine matters of fact in a criminal case and to deliver a verdict of guilty or not guilty.

Only 4 percent of felony cases go to jury trial, yet these, such as that of Louise Woodward, convicted of second-degree murder for causing the death of 9-month old Matthew Eappen, often attract great attention. They can be likened to morality plays, as skilled attorneys for the prosecution and defense battle in front of the jury.

bench trial
Trial conducted by a judge who acts as fact finder and determines issues of law. No jury participates.

evidence. The jurors or judge may bring into the courtroom their own prejudices, which cause them to favor some defendants or automatically assume the worst about others. Fundamentally, great faith is placed in the trial process as the best means society has for giving complete consideration of a defendant's potential guilt, yet the process will not always work as it should.

Trials determine the fates of very few defendants. Although the right to trial by jury is ingrained in American ideology—it is mentioned in the Declaration of Independence, three amendments to the Constitution, and countless opinions of the Supreme Court—only 9 percent of felony cases go to trial. Of these, 4 percent are jury trials, and 5 percent are **bench trials** presided over by a judge without a jury (BJS, 1999k:432). Defendants may choose a bench trial if they believe a judge will be more capable of making an objective decision, especially if the charges or evidence are likely to arouse emotional reactions in jurors.

Even though relatively few cases go to trial, trials have a powerful influence on plea bargaining. Attorneys plea bargain while considering the question, "What will a jury do if we go to trial?" For example, in a highly publicized Pennsylvania murder case in which a drifter shot two graduate students who were hiking the Appalachian Trail, both sides agreed to a guilty plea because of their predictions and fears about what a jury might do. In particular, the defendant's fears about receiving the death penalty for a first-degree murder conviction outweighed his hope that jurors might convict him only of manslaughter if they accepted his claim that the students had provoked the attack (Pohlman, 1999).

A defense attorney's certainty that a jury would convict his or her client may create an incentive to compromise and seek a plea bargain. Similarly, for a prosecutor with doubts about the strength of the evidence, a plea bargain for a lesser sentence may be less risky than the possibility that a jury might acquit the defendant at trial. Trials can even influence police officers' decision to arrest if they anticipate that jurors will strongly disapprove of their tactics in questioning or searching a suspect.

Trials take considerable time and resources. Attorneys frequently spend weeks or months preparing—gathering evidence, responding to their opponents' motions, planning trial strategy, and setting aside from one day to several weeks to present the case in court. From the perspective of judges, prosecutors, and defense attorneys, plea bargaining is an attractive alternative for purposes of completing cases quickly.

Deciding to Go to Trial

Some cases simply cannot be resolved through plea bargaining. Think back to the wedding cake model of criminal justice described in Chapter 1. Prominent or wealthy defendants can pay their attorneys to fight a case to the very end and therefore can demand trials even if they do not face especially serious charges. And defendants who face harsh penalties—such as life in prison or death—may have little incentive to plead guilty. At least with a trial, the jury could find that the prosecutor did not present enough evidence to prove guilt "beyond a reasonable doubt." When the prosecutor and defense attorney cannot agree about the provable facts in a case during the plea bargaining process, either party may seek a trial instead of compromising with the opposition. The fact-finding function of the jury trial serves to resolve such a dispute. The defendant's prior record may also influence the state's decision to go to trial. If the evidence against a repeat offender is weak, the prosecutor may prefer to risk having a jury find the accused not guilty instead of striking a bargain that would yield only a minimal punishment. The state may lose the trial but still convey to the defendant the message, "We are after you."

The seriousness of the charge is probably the most important factor influencing the decision to go to trial. A trial is rarely demanded by defendants charged with property crimes. Murder, felonious assault, or rape—all charges that bring long prison terms—are more likely to require judge and jury. In a study of the nation's seventy-five largest counties, 32 percent of murder cases went to trial, the largest percentage for any crime. Eleven percent of assault cases and 10 percent of rape cases went to trial. For all other crimes, trials occurred in 7 percent of cases or less (Reaves, 1998). When the penalty is harsh, many defendants seem willing to risk the possibility of conviction at trial. But note in Table 10.1 the differences in the percentages of defendants going to trial for several offenses in various cities. What might be the reasons for differences from one city to another and for one offense or another? Think about how prosecutors' policies or sentencing practices in different cities may increase or decrease the incentives for a defendant to plead guilty. Some scholars believe that more defendants choose jury trials in the United States than in Canada, in part, because so many American trial judges are former prosecutors who want to look tough on crime to gain reelection. Thus the defendants would rather have a jury than a judge decide their fate. By contrast, Canadian judges are appointed to office and fewer are former prosecutors (Friedland and Roach, 1997).

TABLE 10.1

Percentage of indicted cases that went to trial, by offense

The percentages of cases that went to trial differ both by offense and by jurisdiction. It seems that the stiffer the possible penalty, the greater the likelihood of a trial.

JURISDICTION	HOMICIDE	SEXUAL ASSAULT	ROBBERY	LARCENY	DRUG OFFENSES
Indianapolis, Ind.	38%	18%	21%	12%	9%
Los Angeles, Calif.	29	20	12	5	7
Louisville, Ky.	57	27	18	10	11
New Orleans, La.	22	18	16	7	7
St. Louis, Mo.	36	23	15	6	6
San Diego, Calif.	37	2	12	5	3
Washington, D.C.	43	32	22	12	10

SOURCE: Adapted from U.S. Department of Justice, Bureau of Justice Statistics, *Report to the Nation on Crime and Justice*, 2d ed. (Washington, D.C.: Government Printing Office, 1988), 84.

What Americans Think

1. In October 1995, a jury acquitted Hall of Fame football star O. J. Simpson of murder charges in the stabbing deaths of his ex-wife and a man. A national poll in February 1999 asked, "Do you personally believe that the charges that O. J. Simpson murdered [the two people. . .] are definitely true, probably true, probably not true, or definitely not true?"

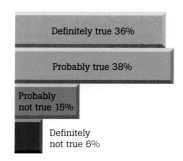

Definitely true 36%

Probably true 38%

Probably not true 15%

Definitely not true 6%

2. In 1997, Terry Nichols was convicted of conspiracy and manslaughter for working with Timothy McVeigh to bomb the federal building in Oklahoma City in 1995, a bombing that killed more than one hundred people. McVeigh was convicted of first-degree murder and received a death sentence. Nichols was sentenced to prison. A national poll in 1998 asked, "Overall, do you agree or disagree with the jury's verdict in this trial [finding him guilty of manslaughter instead of first-degree murder]?"

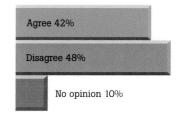

Agree 42%

Disagree 48%

No opinion 10%

continued on next page

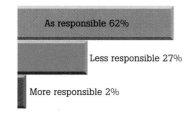
Because the adversary process is designed to get to the truth, the rules of criminal law, procedure, and evidence govern the conduct of the trial. Trials are based on the idea that the prosecution and defense will compete before a judge and jury so that the truth will emerge. Above the battle, the judge sees to it that the rules are followed and that the jury impartially evaluates the evidence and reflects the community's interest. In a jury trial, the jury is the sole evaluator of the facts in a case.

The adversary process and inclusion of citizen-jurors in decision making often make trial outcomes difficult to predict. The verdict hinges not only on the nature of the evidence, but also on the effectiveness of the prosecution and defense and attitudes of the jurors. In the aftermath of highly publicized trials, public opinion often clashes with the decisions made by judges and juries. As you examine the public opinion data on popular disagreement with trial decisions, consider whether these disagreements indicate that Americans find the trial process unsatisfactory. Do these results indicate that jurors are manipulated by attorneys in adversary process? Alternatively, are jurors better positioned than the public to recognize the facts that are relevant to each case?

Eighty percent of all jury trials worldwide take place in the United States (Hans and Vidmar, 1986:109). Among the legal systems of the world, it is only in common law countries such as Australia, Canada, Great Britain, and the United States that a group of citizens drawn from the community determines the guilt of criminal defendants. In civil law countries, this function is usually performed by a judge or judges, often assisted by two or three nonlawyers serving as "assessors."

Juries perform six vital functions in the criminal justice system:

❶ Prevent government oppression by safeguarding citizens against arbitrary law enforcement.

❷ Determine whether the accused is guilty on the basis of the evidence presented.

❸ Represent diverse community interests so that no one set of values or biases dominates decision making.

❹ Serve as a buffer between the accused and the accuser.

❺ Educate citizens selected for jury duty about the criminal justice system.

❻ Symbolize the rule of law and the community foundation that supports the criminal justice system.

As a symbol of law, juries demonstrate to the public—and to defendants—that decisions about depriving individuals of their liberty will be made carefully by a group of citizens who represent the community's values. In addition, juries provide the primary element of direct democracy in the judicial branch of government. Through participation on juries, citizens use their votes to determine the outcomes of cases (Smith, 1994). This branch of government, which is dominated by judges and lawyers, offers few other opportunities for citizens to shape judicial decisions directly.

In the United States, a jury in a criminal trial traditionally comprises twelve citizens, but some states now allow as few as six citizens to make up a jury. This reform was recommended to modernize court procedures and reduce expenses. It costs less for the court to contact, process, and pay a smaller number of jurors. The use of small juries was upheld by the Supreme Court in ***Williams v. Florida*** (1970). In *Burch v. Louisiana* (1979), the Supreme Court ruled that six-member juries in criminal trials must vote unanimously to convict a defendant, but unanimity is not required for larger juries. Some states permit juries to convict defendants by

***Williams v. Florida* (1970)**
Juries of fewer than twelve members are constitutional.

10.1   **Jury size for felony and misdemeanor trials**

All states require twelve-member juries in capital cases; six states permit juries of fewer than twelve members in felony cases. Does the smaller number of people on a jury have advantages or disadvantages? Would you rather have your case decided by a twelve- or six-person jury?

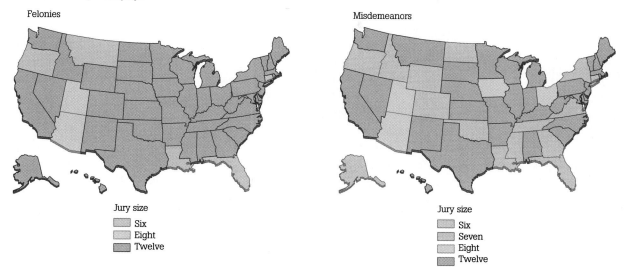

Felonies   Misdemeanors

Jury size
- Six
- Eight
- Twelve

Jury size
- Six
- Seven
- Eight
- Twelve

SOURCE: U.S. Department of Justice, Bureau of Justice Statistics, *Report to the Nation on Crime and Justice*, 2d ed. (Washington, D.C.: Government Printing Office, 1988), 86.

votes of 10 to 2 or 9 to 3 (see Figure 10.1 for jury size requirements in each state). The change to six-person juries has its critics, who charge that the smaller group is less representative of the conflicting views in the community and too quick to bring in a verdict (Amar, 1997).

CHECK POINT

① What are three of the functions that juries serve for the criminal justice system?

② What has the Supreme Court decided concerning the size and unanimity requirements of juries?

③ Approximately what percentage of criminal cases reach their conclusion through a trial?

(Answers are at the end of the chapter.)

The Trial Process

The trial process generally follows eight steps: (1) selection of the jury, (2) opening statements by prosecution and defense, (3) presentation of the prosecution's evidence and witnesses, (4) presentation of the defense's evidence and witnesses, (5) presentation of rebuttal witnesses, (6) closing arguments by each side, (7) instruction of the jury by the judge, and (8) decision by the jury. The details of each step may vary according to each state's rules. Although the proportion of trials may be small, it is important to understand each step in the process and to consider the broader impact of this institution.

During jury selection, attorneys for each side may question prospective jurors to determine whether they are biased in ways that would make them incapable of rendering a fair verdict.

Jury Selection

The selection of the jury, which is outlined in Figure 10.2, is a crucial first step in the trial process. Because people always apply their experiences, values, and biases in their decision making, prosecutors and defense attorneys actively seek to identify potential jurors who may be automatically sympathetic or hostile to their side. When they believe they have identified such potential jurors, they try to find ways to exclude the jurors who may sympathize with the other side while striving to keep the jurors who may favor their side. Lawyers do not necessarily achieve these goals, because the selection of jurors involves the decisions and interactions of prosecutors, defense attorneys, and judges, each of whom has different objectives in the selection process.

Jurors are selected from among the citizens whose names have been placed in the jury pool. The composition of the jury pool has a tremendous impact on the ultimate composition of the trial jury. In most states, the jury pool is drawn from lists of registered voters, but research has shown that nonwhites, the poor, and young people register to vote at much lower rates than the rest of the population. As a result, members of these groups are underrepresented on juries (Fukurai, 1996). In many cases, the presence or absence of these groups may make no difference in the ultimate verdict. In some situations, however, members of these groups may interpret evidence differently than do their older, white, middle-class counterparts who dominate the composition of juries (Ugwuegbu, 1999). For example, the poor, nonwhites, and young people may be more likely to have had unpleasant experiences with police officers and therefore be less willing to believe automatically that police officers always tell the truth. While a middle-class juror may believe

FIGURE 10.2 **Jury selection process for a twelve-member jury**

Potential jurors are drawn at random from a source list. From this pool, a panel is selected and presented for duty. The voir dire examination may remove some, while others will be seated. The fourteen jurors selected include two alternates.

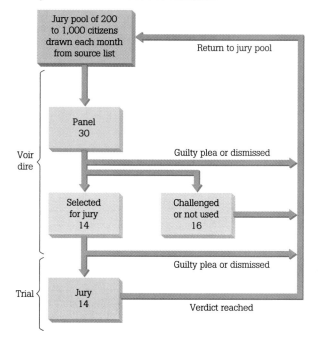

someone began the day intending to commit a crime if he or she left home carrying a pocketknife, a poor juror may disagree and simply view the carrying of a pocketknife as normal, expected behavior among people in rough neighborhoods who are concerned about protecting themselves (Cowan, Thompson, and Ellsworth, 1984:60). Some jurisdictions have addressed the problem of unrepresentative jury pools by seeking to broaden the sources from which the jurors' names are drawn (Kairys, Kadane, and Lehoczky, 1977). They have supplemented the lists of registered voters with other lists, such as those for driver's licenses, hunting licenses, and utility bills (Newman, 1996).

People in some occupations, such as doctors, lawyers, and police officers, are often not called for jury duty. Other potential jurors may be excused from duty if service would cause an economic or physical hardship. As illustrated in A Question of Ethics, some people attempt to avoid jury duty because it is inconvenient for them. This evasion also affects jury composition. Only about 15 percent of adult Americans have ever been called for jury duty. Because of the exclusions from service, retired people and homemakers with grown children tend to be overrepresented on juries because they are less inconvenienced by serving. To make jury duty less onerous, many states have moved to a system called "one-day-one-trial," in which jurors serve for either one day or for the duration of one trial.

The courtroom process of **voir dire** (which means "to speak the truth") is used to question prospective jurors to screen out those who might be biased or incapable of making a fair decision. Attorneys for each side, as well as the judge, may question jurors about their background, knowledge of the case, and acquaintance with any participants in the case. Jurors will also be asked whether they or their immediate family members have been crime victims or otherwise involved in a criminal case in a manner that may prevent them from making open-minded decisions about the evidence and the defendant. If a juror's responses indicate that he or she will not be able to make fair decisions, the juror may be **challenged for cause.** The judge must rule on the challenge, but if the judge agrees with the attorney, then the juror is excused from that specific case. There is usually no limit on the number of jurors that the attorneys may challenge for cause. It is not easy, however, for attorneys to identify all of a juror's biases through brief questioning (Dillehay and Sandys, 1996).

Although challenges for cause are ultimately under the judge's control, the prosecution and defense can exert their own control over the jury's composition through the use of **peremptory challenges.** Using these challenges, the prosecution and defense can exclude prospective jurors without giving specific reasons. Attorneys use peremptory challenges to exclude jurors whom they think will be unsympathetic to their arguments (Hoffman, 1999). Attorneys usually use hunches about which jurors to challenge; there is little evidence that they can accurately identify which jurors will be sympathetic or unsympathetic to their side (White, 1995). Normally, the defense is allowed eight to ten peremptory challenges, and the prosecution six to eight.

A Question of Ethics

The return address on the official-looking envelope read "Jury Commissioner, District Court, Plainville, Massachusetts." Having a good idea of the contents, Donald Rotman tore open the envelope and pulled out a computer-generated form that read: "Donald A. Rotman, You are hereby summoned to be available for duty as a trial juror and are directed to report to the District Court of the Commonwealth of Massachusetts, 61 South Street, Plainville, at 9:00 A.M. on July 10. Failure to appear as instructed by law may subject you to a penalty as provided by law. Your juror number is 89367. The term of your jury duty will be one day or one trial."

"Hell! I can't do that, I want to go to Cape Cod that week. There must be some way out of this." Rotman looked at the bottom of the form and read, "You may apply to be excused from this duty if you are: an attorney; caring for a child under three; student or teacher during the school year," and about five other categories, none of which applied to him.

"This is no big deal. Everyone does it. I'll just tell them I'm going to summer school. They won't check."

■ Is getting out of jury duty no big deal? What are the implications of Donald's action? If Donald is required to serve on a jury, how might justice be affected by the fact that he had planned to spend that week on vacation? What exemptions to service should exist?

voir dire
A questioning of prospective jurors to screen out persons the attorneys think might be biased or incapable of delivering a fair verdict.

challenge for cause
Removal of a prospective juror by showing that he or she has some bias or some other legal disability. The number of such challenges permitted to attorneys is unlimited.

peremptory challenge
Removal of a prospective juror without giving any reason. Attorneys are allowed a limited number of such challenges.

In applying peremptory challenges, attorneys are not necessarily seeking to have a jury made up of the most open-minded people. Instead, they would prefer to have people who lean toward their own position. Wealthy defendants may hire jury consultants—psychologists who advise them on what kinds of people are likely to be on their side (Barber, 1994). For example, a jury consultant might advise a defense attorney to avoid having the parents of teenage daughters on the jury in rape cases. The consultants may have survey research showing that such parents' views are affected by fears that their own daughters might become victims some day. Although jury consultants claim credit when their clients are acquitted, research has questioned whether consultants can accurately predict how different people are likely to decide a particular case (Diamond, 1990).

The use of peremptory challenges has raised concerns that attorneys can use them to exclude, for example, African American jurors when an African American is on trial (Kennedy, 1997). In a series of decisions in the late 1980s and early 1990s, the Supreme Court prohibited using peremptory challenges to systematically exclude potential jurors because of their race or gender (e.g., *Batson v. Kentucky*, 1986). This does not mean that prosecutors and defense attorneys cannot use a peremptory challenge to exclude a nonwhite or female juror. However, if the prosecution or defense is accused by the opposition of excluding prospective jurors based on race or gender, then the attorney must give the judge a reason for the exclusion that has nothing to do with race or gender. In practice, however, the enforcement of this prohibition on race and gender discrimination is up to the trial judge (Smith and Ochoa, 1996). If a trial judge is willing to accept flimsy excuses for race-based and gender-based exclusions, then the attorneys can ignore the ban on discrimination (Bray, 1992). As you read the Close-Up opposite, ask yourself whether peremptory challenges have a positive or negative effect on jury selection. Do you think peremptory challenges should be abolished?

The jury selection process sets the stage for the trial by putting into place the decision makers who will decide the defendant's fate. Although voir dire takes place before the trial begins, jury selection can be viewed as the first step in trial. Some lawyers say that trials are won or lost in jury selection. If a lawyer succeeds in seating a favorable jury, he or she may have a receptive audience that will readily support one side's arguments and evidence.

CHECK POINT

④ **What is voir dire?**

⑤ **What is the difference between a peremptory challenge and a challenge for cause?**

Opening Statements

After the jury has been selected, the trial begins. The clerk reads the complaint (indictment or information) detailing the charges, and the prosecutor and the defense attorney may, if they desire, make opening statements to the jury to summarize the position that each side intends to take. The statements are not evidence. The jury is not supposed to regard the attorneys' statements as proving or disproving anything about the case. Judges normally keep tight control so that the attorneys will not make prejudicial or inflammatory remarks that may improperly sway the jury. Lawyers use this phase of the trial to establish themselves with the jurors and emphasize points they intend to make later. Lawyers view the opening

CLOSE up

The **Peremptory** Challenge **Controversy**

In 1987, Jimmy Elem faced trial on robbery charges in a Missouri state court. During jury selection, the prosecutor used peremptory challenges to exclude two African American men from the jury. Elem's attorney objected and claimed that the prosecutor appeared to be improperly excluding potential jurors because of their race. Under the U.S. Supreme Court's decision in *Batson v. Kentucky* (1986), the trial judge was obligated to ask the prosecutor to provide a nonracial reason for removing the jurors when an appearance exists of race-based exclusion in a prosecutor's use of peremptory challenges. In response to the judge's question, the prosecutor replied,

> I struck [juror] number twenty-two because of his long hair. He had long curly hair. He had the longest hair of anybody on the panel by far. He appeared to me to not be a good juror for that fact, the fact that he had long hair hanging down shoulder length, curly unkempt hair. Also he had a mustache and a goatee type beard. And juror number twenty-four also has a mustache and goatee type beard. Those are the only two people on the jury . . . with the facial hair. . . . And I don't like the way they looked, with the way the hair is cut, both of them. And the mustaches and the beards look suspicious to me.

The trial judge accepted the prosecutor's explanation and the trial moved forward. Elem subsequently filed a habeas corpus action in the federal courts claiming that the prosecutor had used a flimsy, nonsensical excuse to cover the fact that the exclusions were based on race. The U.S. Court of Appeals agreed with Elem and declared that peremptory challenges that appear to be based on race are valid only if based on reasons related to the individuals' qualifications to be a good juror. The Court of Appeals did not believe that having curly or long hair affected one's ability to be a good juror.

Missouri carried the case forward to the U.S. Supreme Court. In a 7-to-2 decision, the Supreme Court reversed and said that prosecutors can put forward silly, superstitious, and implausible reasons as long as the trial judge accepts the exclusion as being based on something other than race or gender. Thus it is possible to violate the Constitution by using peremptory challenges in a racially discriminatory or sexist manner if the prosecutor or defense attorney can provide some alternative excuse that is accepted by the judge.

Many attorneys like the peremptory challenge because they believe that they can identify people who are biased and thereby remove them from the jury. Often these attorneys perceive potential jurors to be biased based on the jurors' facial expressions or body language. Social science research does not support lawyers' claims that they can use such hunches to tell if a potential juror will be biased.

Although the U.S. Constitution does not say anything about peremptory challenges, Supreme Court Justice Antonin Scalia claims that peremptory challenges should be retained because they are part of such a long tradition in the jury selection process. Others argue that peremptory challenges enhance the legitimacy of the trial process by letting defendants feel as if they had some influence over the composition of the jury. By contrast, Supreme Court Justice Thurgood Marshall indicated that peremptory challenges should be abolished because they were frequently used to discriminate or add bias to the jury. To Marshall, if there is not enough evidence of bias to justify a challenge for cause, then the person should be allowed to serve on the jury. He or she should not be denied the opportunity to participate in this important aspect of judicial decision making just because one lawyer does not like the expression on his or her face or the color of his or her skin.

■ If you were a state legislator and someone proposed a bill to abolish peremptory challenges in jury selection, how would you vote? Do you think peremptory challenges are helpful or harmful in the trial process?

statement as an opportunity to show the jury that they are trustworthy, friendly, and believable. Their fundamental goal is that the jurors will believe what they say throughout the trial.

Presentation of the Prosecution's Evidence

One of the basic protections of the American criminal justice system is the presumption that the defendant is innocent until proved guilty. The prosecution has the burden of proving beyond a reasonable doubt, within the demands of the court procedures and rules of evidence, that the individual named in the indictment committed the crime. That does not mean absolute certainty is required, only that the evidence is such that there is no reasonable doubt.

By presenting evidence to the jury, the prosecution must establish a case showing that the defendant is guilty. Evidence is classified as real evidence, demonstrative evidence, testimony, direct evidence, and circumstantial evidence. **Real evidence** might include such objects as a weapon, business records, fingerprints, or stolen property. These are real objects involved in the crime. **Demonstrative evidence** is presented for jurors to see and understand without testimony. Real evidence is one form of demonstrative evidence, but other forms of demonstrative evidence are used to make points to jurors without being items involved in the crime. These other forms of demonstrative evidence include maps, X-rays, photographs, models, and diagrams. Most evidence in a criminal trial, however, consists of the **testimony** of witnesses. Witnesses at a trial must be legally competent. Thus the judge may be required to determine whether the witness whose testimony is challenged has the intelligence to tell the truth and the ability to recall what was seen. Witnesses with inadequate intelligence or mental problems may not be regarded as qualified to present testimony. **Direct evidence** refers to eyewitness accounts—for example, "I saw John Smith fire the gun." **Circumstantial evidence** requires that the jury infer a fact from what the witness observed: "I saw John Smith walk behind his house with a gun. A few minutes later I heard a gun go off, and then Mr. Smith walked toward me holding a gun." The witness's observation that Smith had a gun and that the witness then heard a gun go off does not provide the direct evidence that Smith fired his gun; yet the jury may link the described facts and infer that Smith fired his gun. After a witness has given testimony, he or she may be cross-examined by counsel for the other side.

The rules of evidence govern the facts that may be admitted into court for the judge and jury to consider. Real evidence that has been illegally seized, for example, may be excluded under the Fourth Amendment's protection against unreasonable searches and seizure. Statements by the defendant may also be excluded if they were made without proper warnings to the defendant about the Fifth Amendment right to remain silent. Testimony that is hearsay or opinion cannot become a formal part of the trial record, except under specific circumstances. Hearsay testimony would be, for example, a witness saying, "I heard this other witness say that she heard the defendant admit guilt." Courts do not regard third-hand comments as reliable as evidence concerning the defendant that is directly seen or heard by a witness. Likewise, witnesses cannot say "I believe" or "I think" something happened. Usually only expert witnesses can express opinions. Other witnesses must describe what they saw or heard.

The judge decides, with reference to these rules, what evidence may be heard. In making such decisions, the judge must weigh the importance of the evidence and balance it against the need for a fair trial. The attorney for each side

---

real evidence

Physical evidence such as a weapon, records, fingerprints, stolen property—objects involved in the crime.

---

demonstrative evidence

Evidence that is not based on witness testimony but that demonstrates information relevant to the crime, such as maps, X-rays, and photographs; includes real evidence involved in the crime.

---

testimony

Oral evidence provided by a legally competent witness.

---

direct evidence

Eyewitness accounts.

---

circumstantial evidence

Evidence provided by a witness from which a jury must infer a fact.

challenges the other side's presentation of evidence. If evidence is presented that violates the rules, reflects untrustworthy hearsay or opinion statements, or is not relevant to the issues in the case, an attorney will object to the presentation. In effect, the attorney is asking the judge to rule that the opponent's questionable evidence cannot be considered by the jury.

After the prosecution has presented all of the state's evidence against the defendant, the court is informed that the people's case rests. It is common for the defense then to ask the court to direct the jury to bring forth a verdict of not guilty. Such a motion is based on the defense argument that the state has not presented enough evidence to prove its case; it has not established all the elements of the crime charged. The judge rules on this motion, sustaining or overruling it. If the motion is sustained (it rarely is), the trial ends; if it is overruled, the defense presents its evidence.

Presentation of the Defense's Evidence

The defense is not required to answer the case presented by the prosecution. As it is the state's responsibility to prove the case beyond a reasonable doubt, it is theoretically possible—and in fact sometimes happens—that the defense rests its case immediately. Usually the accused's attorney employs one strategy or a combination of three strategies: (1) contrary evidence is introduced to rebut or cast doubt on the state's case, (2) an alibi is offered, or (3) an affirmative defense is presented. The Andrew Goldstein defense team relied on the final approach in presenting an insanity defense in the subway murder case. An affirmative defense is a legal excuse that permits the jury to find the defendant not responsible for the crime. As discussed in Chapter 3, defenses include self-defense, insanity, duress, and necessity.

A key issue for the defense is whether the accused will take the stand. The Fifth Amendment protection against self-incrimination means that the defendant does not have to testify. The Supreme Court has ruled that the prosecutor may not comment on, nor can the jury draw inferences from, the defendant's decision not to appear in his or her own defense. The decision is not made lightly, because if the defendant does testify, the prosecution may cross-examine. Cross-examination,

Barry Sheck, attorney for Louise Woodward, presents evidence that an earlier skull fracture, and not a shaking of 8-month-old Matthew Eappens by his client, had caused the death.

which is questioning by the opposing attorney, is broader than direct examination. The prosecutor may question the defendant not only about the crime but also about his or her past. If the defendant testifies and thereby submits to cross-examination, the prosecutor often is able to introduce testimony about prior convictions.

Another consideration for many criminal lawyers is that juries may expect to hear both sides of what happened. Lawyers recognize that if jurors do not hear the defendant testify, they may begin to favor a guilty verdict. Jurors may wonder what is being hidden by the defendant who chooses not to testify. Although jurors are not supposed to make assumptions about the defendant's guilt, there is always a risk that some of them will do so.

Presentation of Rebuttal Witnesses

When the defense's case is complete, the prosecution may present witnesses whose testimony is designed to discredit or counteract testimony presented on behalf of the defendant. Evidence previously introduced by the prosecution may not be rehashed, but new evidence may be presented. If the prosecution brings rebuttal witnesses, the defense has the opportunity to question them and to present new witnesses in rebuttal.

Closing Arguments by Each Side

When each side has completed its presentation of the evidence, prosecution and defense make closing arguments to the jury. The attorneys review the evidence of the case for the jury, presenting interpretations of the evidence that are favorable to their own side. The prosecutor may use the summation to show that the individual pieces of evidence are connected together to form a basis for concluding that the defendant is guilty. The defense may set forth the applicable law and try to show that (1) the prosecution has not proved its case beyond a reasonable doubt and (2) the testimony raised questions but did not provide answers. Each side may remind the jury of its duty not to be swayed by emotion and to evaluate the evidence impartially. Yet, some attorneys may hope that the jurors react emotionally, especially if they think that those emotions will benefit their side.

Veteran attorneys feel that the closing argument is a major chance to appeal directly to the members of the jury. Some lawyers use the emotional and spellbinding techniques of experienced actors in their summations to sway the jury. But for many the summation is also an opportunity to show the defendant, other possible clients, or their supervisors that they are skilled courtroom performers who have put their full effort into the trial.

Judge's Instructions to the Jury

The jury decides the facts of the case, but the judge determines the law. Before the jurors depart for the jury room to decide the defendant's fate, the judge instructs them on how the law should guide their decision. The judge may discuss basic legal principles such as proof beyond a reasonable doubt, the legal requirements necessary to show that all the elements have been proved by the prosecution, or the rights of the defendant. More specific aspects of the law bearing on the decision—such as complicated court rulings on the nature of the insanity defense or the ways certain types of evidence have been gathered—may be included in the judge's instructions. In complicated trials, the judge may spend an entire day instructing the jury.

The concept of **reasonable doubt** is at the heart of the jury system. The prosecution is not required to prove the guilt of the defendant beyond all doubt. Instead, if a juror is

> satisfied to a moral certainty that this defendant . . . is guilty of any one of the crimes charged here, you may safely say that you have been convinced beyond a reasonable doubt. If your mind is wavering, or if you are uncertain . . . you have not been convinced beyond a reasonable doubt and must render a verdict of not guilty. (Phillips, 1977:214)

A vote for acquittal should not be based on sympathy or the reluctance of a jury to perform a disagreeable task.

The experience of listening to the judge may become an ordeal for the jurors, who must hear and understand perhaps two or three hours of instruction on the law and the evidence (Bradley, 1992). It is assumed that somehow jurors will fully absorb these details upon first hearing them, so that they will thoroughly understand how they are supposed to decide the case in the jury room (Kramer and Koenig, 1990). Finally, the judge explains the charges and the possible verdicts. Trials usually involve multiple charges, and the judge must instruct the jurors in such a way that their decisions will be consistent with the law and the evidence.

Decision by the Jury

After they have heard the case and have been instructed by the judge, the jurors retire to a room where they have complete privacy. They elect a foreperson to run the meeting, and deliberations begin. Until now, the jurors have been passive observers of the trial, unable to question witnesses or to discuss the case among themselves; now they can discuss the facts that have been presented. Throughout their deliberations the jurors may be sequestered—kept together day and night, away from the influences of newspapers and conversations with family and friends. If jurors are allowed to spend nights at home, they are ordered not to discuss the case with anyone. The jury may request that the judge reread to them portions of the instructions, ask for additional instructions, or hear portions of the transcript detailing what was said by specific witnesses.

In almost every state and in the federal courts, the verdict must be unanimous in criminal cases. Only Louisiana, Montana, Oregon, Oklahoma, and Texas permit majority decisions in a criminal case whose jury is composed of twelve people. As illustrated by Andrew Goldstein's case at the start of the chapter, if the jury becomes deadlocked and cannot reach a verdict, the trial ends with a hung jury and the prosecutor must decide whether to try the case all over again in front of a new jury. When a verdict is reached, the judge, prosecution, and defense reassemble in the courtroom to hear it. The prosecution or the defense may request that the jury be polled: each member individually tells his or her vote in open court. This procedure presumably ensures that no juror has felt pressured to agree with the other jurors. If the verdict is guilty, the judge may continue bail or may incarcerate the convicted person to await a presentence report. If the verdict is not guilty, the defendant is freed. Because the Fifth Amendment guarantees that a person shall not be "twice put in jeopardy of life or limb," prosecutors may not appeal a jury's finding or prosecute the same charges against the defendant again.

American jury trials place great faith in the ability of citizens to understand legal rules and evaluate evidence without being unduly affected by biases and preconceived beliefs. These trials also rely on the opposing attorneys to present a complete and accurate picture of the evidence even though the adversarial process

reasonable doubt
The standard used by a juror to decide if the prosecution has provided enough evidence for conviction. Jurors should vote for acquittal if they think there is a reasonable doubt.

encourages attorneys to present, mischaracterize, and withhold evidence in ways that help their side in the case. The American trial process also relies heavily on trial judges to make proper rulings on the admissibility of evidence and to provide appropriate jury instructions. Because these judges are elected in many states, fears sometimes arise that they will be inclined to facilitate convictions to appear "tough on crime" in the voters' eyes. Does this adversarial, politically connected, and citizen-involved trial process provide the best mechanism for finding the truth and doing justice in the most serious criminal cases? As you read the Comparative Perspective (p. 374), consider the French courts' concerns about the American process and examine whether the French trial process presents any advantages. Could the American trial process be improved by borrowing any elements from France?

CHECK POINT

6. **What are the stages in the trial process?**
7. **What are the kinds of evidence presented during a trial?**

Evaluating the Jury System

The question of which factors in a trial lead to the jury's verdict is always intriguing. The 1957 film *Twelve Angry Men* depicts jury deliberations and the emotions that often rule decision making. The character portrayed by actor Henry Fonda, initially the lone holdout against conviction, gradually persuades other members as doubts are raised about the evidence presented by the prosecution. After hours of deliberation in a hot, cramped room, a vote for acquittal is finally reached.

Social scientists have been hampered in studying the process of juror decision making because of the secrecy of the jury room (Levine, 1996). Instead researchers must study simulated juries—groups of people who pretend to be a jury when they hear and decide a case presented to them as part of a research study. Early

Jury foreman Joe Collins, right, talks with the media after the jury gave John William King a death sentence in the Jasper, Texas, dragging death of James Byrd, Jr. Social scientists are still uncertain as to the factors influencing juries.

research at the University of Chicago Law School found that, consistent with theories of group behavior, participation and influence in the process are related to social status. Men were found to be more active participants than women, whites more active than minority members, and the better educated more active than those less educated. Much of the discussion in the jury room was not directly concerned with the testimony but rather with trial procedures, opinions about the witnesses, and personal reminiscences (Strodtbeck, James, and Hawkins, 1957). In 30 percent of the cases, a vote taken soon after entering the jury room was the only one necessary to reach a verdict; in the rest of the cases, the majority on the first ballot eventually prevailed in 90 percent of the cases (Broeder, 1959). Because of group pressure, only rarely did a single juror produce a hung jury. Although some individual jurors may view the case differently, they may doubt their own views or go along with the others if everyone else disagrees. More recent findings have upheld the importance of group pressure on decision making (Hastie, Penrod, and Pennington, 1983). Do you think changes have occurred in group behavior since the original research?

In evaluating the jury system, researchers have tried to discover whether juries and judges view cases differently. Harry Kalven and Hans Zeisel (1966) attempted to answer this question by examining more than thirty-five hundred criminal trials in which juries played a part. They found that the judge and jury agreed on the outcome in 75.4 percent of the trials, but that a jury was more lenient than a judge. The total conviction rate by juries was 64.5 percent; by judges, 83.3 percent. The very high rate of conviction supports the idea that the filtering process removes many doubtful cases before trial. A study by Robert Roper and Victor Flango (1983) challenged the earlier Kalven and Zeisel findings. In examining data from all fifty states, Roper and Flango found that juries convicted felons at a higher rate than did judges and that judges tended to convict more people charged with misdemeanors.

A recent examination of trials in the seventy-five largest counties found that 84 percent of jury trials ended in convictions but only 72 percent of bench trials ended in convictions (Reaves and Hart, 1999). These numbers alone do not reveal whether judges and juries decide cases differently. The different conviction percentage may also stem from a tendency of defendants facing more ironclad evidence to pin their hopes on the ability of the defense attorney to persuade jurors to acquit. By contrast, they may view judges as less susceptible to persuasion.

Kalven and Zeisel's analysis of the factors that caused disagreement between judge and jury revealed that 54 percent of disagreements were attributable to "issues of evidence," about 29 percent to "sentiments on the law," about 11 percent to "sentiments on the defendant," and about 6 percent to other factors. Juries clearly do more than merely deal with questions of fact. Much of the disagreement between judge and jury was favorable to the defendant, an indication that citizens recognize certain values that fall outside the official rules. In weighing the evidence, the jury was strongly impressed by a defendant who had no criminal record and took the stand, especially when the charge was serious. Juries tend to take a more liberal view of such issues as self-defense than judges and are likely to minimize the seriousness of an offense if they dislike some characteristic of the victim (Adler, 1994:200–207). For example, if the victim of an assault is a prostitute, the jury may minimize the assault. Judges have more experience with the justice process. Thus, they appear more likely to label as guilty defendants whose cases were sent forward by police and prosecutors who believed that there was strong evidence of guilt.

Comparing
Trial Processes:
France and the United States

In 1977, Helen "Holly" Maddux, a 30-year-old woman from a wealthy Texas family, disappeared. She had been living in Philadelphia with her boyfriend, Ira Einhorn, a former hippie leader who had developed a network of friends among prominent people as he ran for mayor and organized artistic events and self-discovery courses. He even spent one semester as a visiting fellow at Harvard University's John F. Kennedy School of Government. Eighteen months after Einhorn claimed that Maddux went out and never returned from a trip to the store, her decomposed remains were found in a trunk in his closet. Einhorn proclaimed his innocence and gained release on bail with the assistance of his attorney, former Philadelphia district attorney and later U.S. senator Arlen Specter, and the support of prominent Philadelphians who thought this leading advocate of peace and love could never commit a murder.

When Einhorn's trial date approached, he disappeared. Investigators later learned that he had fled the country. Sightings of Einhorn were reported in Ireland and Sweden, but authorities could not find him. When Philadelphia's district attorney became concerned that witnesses' memories might fade over time, Einhorn was tried *in absentia* in 1993. A trial "*in absentia*" means that the trial was conducted even though the defendant was absent. Einhorn was convicted of murder.

Assistant District Attorney Richard DiBenedetto continued to investigate Einhorn's whereabouts, just as he had done for years. In 1997, DiBenedetto directed French police to a house where Einhorn's former Swedish girlfriend resided under an assumed name. The police found a man who said his name was "Mallon," but his fingerprints matched those of Ira Einhorn.

Einhorn hired an attorney to fight against his extradition—the process of returning a fugitive to face charges in another jurisdiction. His attorneys argued that the United States has an unfair criminal trial process because it permitted defendants to be tried *in absentia*, it used the death penalty, and it did not obey the European Convention on Human Rights. According to an American writer who followed Einhorn's case closely, his attorneys were fundamentally raising questions about the fairness of American trials and the justice process (Levy, 1997):

> *However, the underlying argument, it would appear, was to urge the French judges to send a message to the "barbarians" in the United States. . . . [They wanted France to] send a message on human rights to the new masters of the world order across the ocean.*

The French judges agreed with the attorneys' arguments. The judges refused to send Einhorn back to the United States to stand trial and he was released from custody. Government officials in the United States protested the decision and its implication that American trial processes are unfair. In an effort to satisfy French criticisms of the trial *in absentia,* the Pennsylvania legislature passed a special law to give Einhorn a new trial if he were ever returned to the United States. After two additional years of appeals, a French court ordered Einhorn returned to the United States in 1999. He was not transported from France immediately because he was entitled to further appeals in the French courts.

If French judges are so critical of American trial processes that they would permit a suspected murderer to live freely in their country, what does that say about their view of the United States? Moreover, in what ways might French judges view their own trial processes as superior?

Judges in France are deeply involved in all aspects of criminal trials in France, from investigation of defendants through jury deliberations after a trial. French judges are not elected officials and efforts are made to separate the French judiciary from electoral politics. To become a judge in France, law students must take a competitive examination to gain entry into the graduate school for future judges. Based on their performance in graduate school and their achievement on additional tests, they may gain positions at the lower levels of the judiciary, which is a branch of the national civil service. French judges have the protected tenure of civil servants and, unlike so many American state judges, never need to worry about running for reelection to retain their seats on the bench.

Criminal investigations and trials in France differ fundamentally from those in the United States because French judges are so deeply involved in each step of the process. A judge called an "examining magistrate," rather than a police official or prosecutor, is in charge of investigating criminal cases. There are fears that some examining magistrates might become overly familiar with police and prosecutors and thereby

lose their neutral perspective. However, the examining magistrate is positioned to be an independent investigator unlike American police and elected prosecutors who are under political pressure to gain convictions in an adversarial system.

After the investigation is completed, the trial serves as a mechanism to check the quality of the investigation. Trials for serious criminal cases take place in the Courts of Assize. A chief trial judge assumes responsibility for the case. The chief trial judge asks the questions during the trial when the witnesses and defendant testify. Instead of having adversarial prosecutors and defense attorneys attempting to persuade the jury with carefully phrased and often deceptive questions, the French chief trial judge is responsible for all questioning and no cross-examination of witnesses is permitted. The chief trial judge typically asks many questions about the defendant's background and character because the trial does not need to focus solely on the evidence about the crime. Because judges control the pretrial investigation and the presentation of evidence in the courtroom, it may be less likely that defendants are treated differently because of their wealth. Unlike in the United States, where the quality of defense representation may vary depending on whether the defendant can afford to hire his or her own attorney, French judges are positioned to make sure that sufficient and proper evidence is presented on behalf of all defendants.

Throughout the trial, the chief judge is joined by two associate judges and nine jurors from the community. Both the prosecution and defense can use peremptory challenges to eliminate a few of the jurors, but they do not engage in the extensive

questioning of jurors that can occur in American trials concerning serious crimes.

At the end of the trial, the three judges and nine jurors deliberate in secret. By having judges participate in the jury's verdict, legal professionals can influence the outcome of the case. Participation by professionals may help to keep the jurors focused on the relevant facts and law. However, the participation of judges may also lead jurors to defer to the legal professionals and thereby fail to express viewpoints that reflect public sentiments about the case. Judges do not automatically control the verdict but the jurors and judges vote by secret ballot. Eight of the twelve must vote in favor of conviction for the defendant to be found guilty. Thus a defendant can be found guilty even when four jurors disagree. The sentence is determined by a majority vote of the jurors and judges. Thus citizen-jurors have greater direct input into sentencing in France. In the United States, jurors affect the eventual sentence by determining which offenses will be the basis for the conviction. If they want to see a lighter sentence, they can convict on fewer charges or a lesser offense. However, they do not control the sentence because that is usually determined by a judge. By contrast, French jurors can vote directly on the sentence and even out-vote the judges in determining the sentence. Thus criminal punishment in France may be shaped directly by community representatives instead of legal professionals.

Is the French trial process superior to the processes in the United States? Would it be beneficial for American courts to give judges greater control over criminal investigations, the presentation of evidence, and deliberations about guilt? Would it be

COMPARATIVE **perspective** continued

beneficial to give American jurors the direct authority to determine the sentence for each offender? The Einhorn extradition dispute between France and the United States did not rest solely on the nature of American jury trials. Instead, it seemed to reflect a broader sense that some French judges had doubts about the fairness of the American criminal justice process. The differences between the French and American systems as well as the French criticisms of the American process stem from differences in the respective countries' values and traditions.

SOURCE: Drawn from Henry J. Abraham, *The Judicial Process*, 6th ed. (New York: Oxford University Press, 1986); Steven Levy, "A Guru Goes Free," *Newsweek*, December 15, 1997; Robert Moran, "Pennsylvania Governor Signs Provision for Einhorn Retrial," *Philadelphia Inquirer*, January 29, 1998; Herbert Jacob, Erhard Blankenburg, Herbert M. Kritzer, Doris Marie Provine, and Joseph Sanders, *Courts, Law, and Politics in Comparative Perspective* (New Haven, Conn.: Yale University Press, 1996), 177–248; and Julie Stoiber, "Fugitive Ira Einhorn Loses a Round in Extradition Appeal," *Philadelphia Inquirer*, May 28, 1999.

Jury Duty

The *Juror's Manual* of the United States District Court says that jury service is "perhaps the most vital duty next to fighting in the defense of one's country." Every year nearly two million Americans respond to the call to perform this civic duty, even though doing so usually entails personal and financial hardship. They must miss time from work, arrange for childcare, drive through downtown traffic, and pay for parking. The court's daily pay rate for jurors is usually minimal. In addition, not all employers pay for time lost from the job.

Most jurors experience great frustration with the system as they wait endless hours in barren courthouse rooms. Often they are placed on a jury only to have their function preempted by a sudden change of plea to guilty during the trial. The result is wasted juror time and wasted money. Unfortunately, what could be a valuable civic education often leaves jurors with an unnecessarily negative impression of the entire criminal justice system.

To deal with some of the more negative aspects of jury duty, some courts have introduced the "one-day-one-trial" system. Traditionally, citizens are asked to be jurors for a thirty-day term, and although only a few may be needed for a particular day, the entire pool may be present in the courthouse for the full thirty-day period. In the new system, jurors serve for either one day or the duration of one trial. Prospective jurors who are challenged at voir dire or who are not called to a courtroom are dismissed at the end of their first day and have thus fulfilled their jury duty. Those who are accepted on a jury are required to serve for the duration of that trial, normally about three days. The consensus of jurors, judges, and court administrators is that the one-trial system is a great improvement.

CHECK POINT

⑧ What factors may affect a jury's decision differently than that of judges?

⑨ What reform has improved jurors' experience with the court system and reduced the frustrations of jury service?

Trial: The Impact of Delay   WWW.

One of the oldest concepts of the common law is that justice delayed is justice denied. Defendants who must wait for months with charges hanging over their heads are likely to suffer adverse consequences. These consequences include disrupted relationships with friends and family, the time and expense of preparing a defense, and perhaps even the loss of liberty and jobs if held in jail without bail. Such defendants may eventually be found "not guilty" and thus will have suffered these harms needlessly and unfairly. Thus the interests of fairness and justice demand that cases be handled as quickly as possible without unnecessary delays.

In the United States a speedy trial is guaranteed by the Sixth Amendment to the Constitution, and the Supreme Court has said that swift justice is an important safeguard to prevent undue incarceration before trial, to minimize anxiety accompanying public accusation, and to limit the possibilities that long delay will impair the abilities of accused persons to defend themselves.

Delay is usually described as occurring when something "goes wrong" with the system. Much of the research on delay has focused on problems in the courts: lack of coordination between police, prosecutors, and courts; poor organization and supervision of administrative personnel; too little money; too few prosecutors and judges; and too many complicated procedures. It has been suggested that the problems would go away if the numbers of judges and courtrooms were increased, if professional administrators were hired, and if sound management were instituted.

Studies by the National Center for State Courts question these assumptions. When researchers examined the size, caseload, and management procedures of urban trial courts, they found that it is not always true that criminal cases are disposed of quickly and effectively only where there is a small volume of neither serious nor complex cases (Church, Carlson, Lee, and Tan, 1978; Mahoney, Sipes, and Ito, 1985). As shown in Table 10.2, the researchers uncovered very little relationship between processing time and the number of felony filings per judge. The data show that the courts with the largest caseloads are not those with the slowest disposition times and that the comparatively underworked courts are not speedier.

The Pittsburgh court handles more cases per judge and is slower than the small-volume courts in Sacramento and Salinas; the Cleveland court is substantially slower than might be expected for its size; and the large Detroit court processes criminal cases at a faster pace than similar courts. The courts of Jersey City are not particularly distinguished by the numbers of their filings, or judges, yet they are the slowest of those examined.

TABLE 10.2   Court structure and case delay

The data show little relationship among the number of judges, the case filings per judge, and processing time. If these are not the variables that explain delay, what might be at work?

JURISDICTION	NUMBER OF FTE* JUDGES	FILINGS PER FTE JUDGE	MEDIAN PROCESSING TIME (DAYS)
Salinas, Calif.	3.40	383	62
Dayton, Ohio	4.00	555	56
St. Paul, Minn.	5.00	495	77
Jersey City, N.J.	6.63	360	198
Pittsburgh, Pa.	7.00	843	153
Sacramento, Calif.	11.00	331	165
Cleveland, Ohio	16.50	574	135
Detroit, Mich.	34.00	480	71

*FTE = Full-time equivalent.

SOURCE: John Goerdt, Chris Lomvardias, and Geoff Gallas, *Reexamining the Pace of Litigation in Thirty-Nine Urban Trial Courts* (Williamsburg, Va.: National Center for State Courts, 1991), Tables 2.2, 2.5.

Why do some courts process cases much more quickly than others? The answer appears to be found in the local legal culture and the social organization of the criminal justice system, not the formal structure of courts. The participants become adapted to a certain pace of litigation, and these expectations are translated into other expectations regarding how cases should proceed. What is viewed as the normal speed for the disposition of criminal cases in one system may be viewed as unduly fast in another. As this book has emphasized, decisions are made in the context of an organization in which participants exercise a great deal of discretion. Local norms, role relationships, and the incentives of the major actors determine how cases are processed. Unless the defendant is being held without bail while awaiting trial, there is little incentive for speed. The defense may even request a continuance—a postponement—to delay the making of key decisions, hoping that developments will favor the defendant as time passes. Not all judges are committed to making sure that cases keep moving steadily forward and thus attorneys may succeed in stalling if the judge does make sure that trials are scheduled in a timely manner.

Continuances: Accommodations in the System

continuance
An adjournment of a scheduled case until a later date.

The **continuance** is a prime example of the type of accommodation that causes delay. From a legal standpoint, the judge has the discretion to grant continuances—the postponement of a case—so that the defense will have an opportunity to prepare its case. The need for time to obtain counsel, to prepare pretrial motions, to obtain evidence, or to find a witness can be used as a reason for postponement. The prosecution can also request continuances. Although they are less likely to have a request granted than the defense, especially if the defendant is being held for trial, prosecutors do receive a significant number of continuances in most courts.

Continuances have the effect of decreasing the number of defendants convicted as the number of court appearances increases. Defendants are able to delay a trial to wear out witnesses, remain out on bail as long as possible, or wait for community interest to diminish. Even some defendants in pretrial detention may prefer a further stay in jail to a case decided quickly (Levin, 1975).

Rules for Speedy Trials

Congress and several states have tackled the problem of delay by enacting rules for speedy trials. These rules typically require that cases move from arrest to trial within certain strict time limits. The rules also provide for the dismissal of charges if the case is not brought to trial within the time specified. In 1974 Congress passed the Federal Speedy Trial Act, which sets the maximum period from arrest to indictment at thirty days and from indictment to trial at seventy days (Garner, 1987). Cases that do not meet these requirements may be dismissed either with or without the option of reinstatement of the charges, but it is expected that charges will not be reinstated without good reason. Defendants may waive their right to a speedy trial under the rules, and they frequently do so by requesting continuances so their attorneys can have more time to prepare. The prosecution can also get an extension of the limits, but only if the "ends of justice" will thus be served or if there is a "judicial emergency."

In assessing the results of the Speedy Trial Act, Malcolm Feeley (1983) found that most federal judges have not taken it seriously. However, the legislation has had some indirect effects. First, the federal courts' planning processes have led to improved procedures and better organization within the courts. Second, the administrative improvements have led to better decisions about allocating and using the courts' personnel, time, and money. Third, the backlog of civil cases has grown as the courts have worked to bring criminal cases to trial before the charges have to be dismissed. In many courts it appears that only the formal requirements of the act have been met and that the problem of delay remains because the "ends of justice" exception is used extensively.

Assessing Delay

Delay benefits not only defendants seeking lenient treatment but also defense attorneys, prosecutors, and judges. It helps attorneys maximize their fees, please their clients, and enhance their reputations for skill. Although a move to delay a case is usually initiated by the defense attorney, it cannot succeed without the cooperation of the judge and sometimes the prosecutor, too. Prosecutors presumably understand the need to reach accommodations that will result in a bargained plea. Judges also realize that postponement usually helps prevent a full-length trial that would tie up the courtroom for an extended period. But the prosecutor and judge recognize that by assisting the defense attorney, they ensure the attorney's cooperation in the plea negotiation process.

Although changes have been proposed to reduce delay in the criminal courts, such changes will not be successful unless it is recognized that courtroom actors have individual and multiple goals. The personal needs of the defense attorney, prosecutor, and judge—especially their need to cooperate for smooth plea bargaining—have been shown to be stronger than the broader goal of processing offenders quickly. Thus the goals of fixing the system cannot be expected to dominate the criminal court until the participants see incentives that are more rewarding than fulfillment of their current needs.

CHECK POINT

⑩ **Why do defense attorneys seek continuances?**

⑪ **Why is it difficult to solve the problems of delay in the courts?**

Appeals

Imposition of a sentence does not mean that it must be served immediately; the defendant has the right to appeal the verdict to a higher court. An **appeal** is based on a claim that one or more errors of law or procedure were made during the investigation, arrest, or trial process (Smith, 1999b). Such claims usually assert that the trial judge made errors in courtroom rulings or in improperly admitting evidence that was gathered by the police in violation of some constitutional right. A defendant might base an appeal, for example, on the claim that the judge did not instruct the jury correctly or that a guilty plea was not made voluntarily.

appeal
A request to a higher court that it review actions taken in a completed trial.

Appeals are typically based on questions of procedure, not on issues of the defendant's guilt or innocence. The appellate court will not normally second-guess a jury. Instead it will check to make sure that the trial followed proper procedures. If there were significant errors in the trial, then the conviction is set aside. The defendant may be tried again if the prosecutor decides to pursue the case again. Most criminal defendants must file an appeal shortly after trial to have an appellate court review the case. By contrast, many states provide for an automatic appeal in death penalty cases. The quality of defense representation is important because the appeal must usually meet short deadlines and carefully identify appropriate issues (Wasserman, 1990).

Most judges hate to have their decisions overturned by a higher court. Correcting errors through the appeals process encourages trial judges to be careful in making decisions. Appellate courts also encourage consistent application of the law throughout a state, region, or, in U.S. Supreme Court cases, the entire nation. If judges in different parts of a state are interpreting a provision of the criminal code differently, the appellate court can issue a decision to clarify the issue and ensure consistent application of the law.

Basis for Appeals

Unlike most other Western countries, the United States does not allow the terms of the sentence to be appealed in most circumstances. An appeal may be filed when it is contended that the judge selected penalties that did not accord with the law or that there were violations of either due process or equal protection. But if the law gave the judge the discretion to impose a sentence of, for example, ten years in a particular case, and the defendant thought that the offense warranted only eight, it would be unusual for the sentence to be overturned on appeal unless an improper sentencing procedure was followed. It would be necessary to show that the decision was illegal, unreasonable, or unconstitutional.

A case originating in a state court is usually appealed through that state's judicial system. When a state case involves a federal constitutional question, however, it may be appealed to the U.S. Supreme Court. Almost four-fifths of all appeals are decided by state courts.

The number of appeals in both the state and federal courts has increased during the past decade. What is the nature of these cases? A five-state study by Joy Chapper and Roger Hanson (1989) showed that (1) although a majority of appeals occur after trial convictions, about a quarter result from nontrial proceedings such as guilty pleas and probation revocations; (2) homicides and other serious crimes against persons account for more than 50 percent of appeals; (3) most appeals arise from cases in which the sentence is five years or less; and (4) the issues raised at appeal tend to concern the introduction of evidence, the sufficiency of evidence, and jury instructions.

Most appeals are unsuccessful. In almost 80 percent of the cases Chapper and Hanson examined, the decision of the trial courts was affirmed. Most of the other decisions produced new trials or resentencing; relatively

TABLE 10.3

Percentage distribution of alternative outcomes in five state appellate courts

Although the public thinks defendants exercising their right of appeal will be released, this study shows that 20 percent have their convictions reversed, but only a few are acquitted by the appellate court.

APPEAL OUTCOME	PERCENTAGE OF APPEALS	PERCENTAGE OF APPEALS REVERSED
Conviction affirmed	79.4	—
Conviction reversed	20.6	100.0
Acquittal	1.9	9.4
New trial	6.6	31.9
Resentencing	7.3	35.3
Other	4.8	23.4

SOURCE: Joy Chapper and Roger Hanson, *Understanding Reversible Error in Criminal Appeals* (Williamsburg, Va.: National Center for State Court, 1989).

few decisions (1.9 percent) produced acquittals on appeal. Table 10.3 shows the percentage distribution of the outcomes from the appellate process. The appellate process rarely provides a ticket to freedom for someone convicted of a crime.

Habeas Corpus

After people use their avenues of appeal, they may pursue a writ of habeas corpus if they claim that their federal constitutional rights were violated during the lower-court processes. Known as "the great writ" from its traditional role in English law and its enshrinement in the U.S. Constitution, **habeas corpus** is a judicial order requesting that a state or federal judge examine whether an individual is being properly detained in a jail, prison, or mental hospital. If there is no legal basis for the person to be held, then the judge may grant the writ and order the person to be released. In the context of criminal justice, convicted offenders claim that their imprisonment is improper because one of their constitutional rights was violated during the investigation or adjudication of their case. Statutes permit offenders convicted in both state and federal courts to pursue habeas corpus actions in the federal courts. After first seeking favorable decisions by state appellate courts, convicted offenders can start their constitutional claims anew in the federal trial-level district courts and subsequently pursue their habeas cases in the federal circuit courts of appeal and the U.S. Supreme Court.

Only about 1 percent of habeas petitions are successful (Flango, 1994b). One reason may be that an individual has no right to be represented by counsel when pursuing a habeas corpus petition. Few offenders have sufficient knowledge of law and legal procedures to identify and present constitutional claims effectively in the federal courts (Hanson and Daley, 1995).

In the late 1980s and early 1990s, the U.S. Supreme Court issued many decisions that made it more difficult for convicted offenders to file habeas corpus petitions (Alexander, 1993; Smith, 1995a). The Court created tougher procedural rules that are more difficult for convicted offenders to follow. The rules also unintentionally created some new problems for state attorneys general and federal trial courts that must examine the procedural rule affecting cases rather than simply address the constitutional violations that the offender claims occurred (Smith, 1995c). In 1996, Congress enacted and President Bill Clinton signed the Antiterrorism and Effective Death Penalty Act, which placed additional restrictions on habeas corpus petitions. In *Felker v. Turpin* (1996) the U.S. Supreme Court upheld the statute. These reforms were based, in part, on a belief that prisoners' cases are clogging the federal courts (Smith, 1995b). Yet common perceptions about prisoners' cases frequently do not reflect an accurate understanding of convicted offenders' cases and the burden they pose for the federal courts (Thomas, 1989; Thomas, Keeler, and Harris, 1986). It remains to be seen how these judicial and legislative reforms will affect convicted offenders' opportunities to gain post-conviction reviews of alleged constitutional rights violations during criminal investigations and trials.

Evaluating the Appellate Process

The public seems to believe that many offenders are being "let off" through the appellate process. In addition, frustrated by the problems of crime, some conservatives have argued that opportunities for appeal should be limited. They claim

habeas corpus
A writ or judicial order requesting the release of a person being detained in a jail, prison, or mental hospital. If a judge finds the person is being held improperly, the writ may be granted and the person released.

that too many offenders delay imposition of their sentences and that others completely evade punishment by filing appeals endlessly. This practice not only increases the workload of the courts but also jeopardizes the concept of the finality of the justice process. However, given that 90 percent of accused persons plead guilty, the number of cases that might be appealed is greatly diminished.

Consider what follows a defendant's successful appeal, which is by no means a total and final victory. An appeal that results in reversal of the conviction normally means that the case is remanded to the lower court for a new trial. At this point the state must consider whether the procedural errors in the original trial can be overcome and whether it is worth additional expenditure to bring the defendant into court again. Frequently, the prosecutor pursues the case again and gains a new, proper conviction of the defendant. And the appeal process sometimes generates new plea negotiations that produce a second conviction with a lesser sentence that reflects the reduced strength of the prosecutor's case.

The appeals process performs the important function of righting wrongs. Beyond that, its presence is a constant influence on the daily operations of the criminal justice system as prosecutors and trial judges must consider how their decisions and actions will later be evaluated by a higher court.

CHECK POINT

12 **How does the appellate court's job differ from that of the trial court?**

13 **What is a habeas corpus petition?**

Summary

- Through the dramatic courtroom battle of prosecutors and defense attorneys, trials are presumed to provide the best way to discover the truth about a criminal case.
- Less than 10 percent of cases go to trial, and most of those are bench trials in front of a judge, not jury trials.
- Cases go to trial because they involve defendants who are wealthy enough to pay attorneys to fight to the very end, they involve charges that are too serious to create incentives for plea bargaining, or they involve serious disagreements between the prosecutor and defense attorney about the provable facts and appropriate punishment.
- The U.S. Supreme Court has ruled that juries need not be made up of twelve members, and twelve-member juries can, if permitted by state law, convict defendants by a majority vote instead of a unanimous vote.
- Juries serve vital functions for society by preventing arbitrary action by prosecutors and judges, educating citizens about the justice system, symbolizing the rule of law, and involving citizens from diverse segments of the community in judicial decision making.

■ The jury selection process, especially in the formation of the jury pool and the exercise of peremptory challenges, often creates juries that do not fully represent all segments of a community.

■ The trial process consists of a series of steps: jury selection; opening statements, presentation of prosecution's evidence, presentation of defense evidence, presentation of rebuttal witnesses, closing arguments, judge's jury instructions, and the jury's decision.

■ Rules of evidence dictate what kinds of information may be presented in court for consideration by the jury. Types of evidence are real evidence, demonstrative evidence, testimony, direct evidence, and circumstantial evidence.

■ Delays are common in criminal cases because of the use of continuances and because delay often is in the interests of participants in the system. Delay is not necessarily caused by large caseloads in a court as courts with small caseloads often process cases more slowly, depending on the practices and expectations of decision makers within those courts.

■ Speedy trials are guaranteed by the Sixth Amendment and by the laws of many states and federal governments, yet these rules are frequently not fully implemented.

■ Convicted offenders have the opportunity to appeal, although defendants who plead guilty—unlike those convicted through a trial—often have few grounds for an appeal.

■ Appeals focus on claimed errors of law or procedure in the investigation by police and prosecutors or the decisions by trial judges. Relatively few offenders win their appeals, and most of those simply gain an opportunity for a new trial, not release from jail or prison.

■ After convicted offenders have used all of their appeals, they may file a habeas corpus petition to seek federal judicial review of claimed constitutional rights violations in their cases. Very few petitions are successful.

Questions for Review

❶ Because there are so few jury trials, what types of cases would you expect to find adjudicated in this manner? Why?

❷ If so few cases ever reach a jury, why are juries such an important part of the criminal justice system?

❸ What is the impact of appeals on the criminal justice system?

❹ What is a habeas corpus petition?

Key Terms and Cases

appeal (p. 379)
bench trial (p. 360)
challenge for cause (p. 365)
circumstantial evidence (p. 368)
continuance (p. 378)

demonstrative evidence (p. 368)
direct evidence (p. 368)
habeas corpus (p. 381)
jury (p. 359)
peremptory challenge (p. 365)

real evidence (p. 368)
reasonable doubt (p. 371)
testimony (p. 368)
voir dire (p. 365)
Williams v. Florida (1970) (p. 363)

For Further Reading

Adler, Stephen. *The Jury: Disorder in the Court.* New York: Doubleday, 1994. A newspaper reporter analyzes the jury system by interviewing jurors after publicized verdicts and reconstructing how they made their decisions.

Geis, Gilbert, and Leigh B. Bienen. *Crimes of the Century: From Leopold and Loeb to O. J. Simpson.* Boston: Northeastern University Press, 1998. An examination of several of the most famous criminal trials in American history.

Hastie, Reid, Steven Penrod, and Nancy Pennington. *Inside the Jury.* Cambridge: Harvard University Press, 1983. A study of the jury process and the elements of decision making.

Levine, James P. *Juries and Politics.* Pacific Grove, Calif.: Brooks/Cole, 1992. An overview of the jury system in the United States with a special perspective on the influence of politics.

Pohlman, H. L. *The Whole Truth? A Case of Murder on the Appalachian Trail.* Amherst, Mass.: University of Massachusetts Press, 1999. An analysis of a high publicized murder case, including the defendant's and attorneys' considerations about whether to seek a jury trial.

Wishman, Seymour. *Anatomy of a Jury.* New York: Times Books, 1986. Inside the jury room.

Going Online

❶ Go to www.firstline.com/jury.html to compare the right to a jury in criminal trials in Canada with the right in the United States. In the United States, the defendant decides whether to have a jury trial or a bench trial. Who decides in Canada?

❷ Go to www.fija.org/kriho/. Bearing in mind that this web site was set up by a political interest group that is seeking to advance its views, read the articles about Laura Kriho, a juror who faced criminal charges for her statements during jury deliberations. Should jurors be able to say anything they want to say during deliberations? Do you think Kriho should have faced criminal prosecution for what she did?

❸ **Using InfoTrac College Edition,** after searching for the subject word *jury*, read two articles about jury nullification. What is jury nullification? Should jurors be permitted to exercise this power?

CHECK POINT ANSWERS

❶ The six functions of juries are to safeguard citizens against arbitrary law enforcement, determine the guilt of the accused, represent diverse community interests and values, serve as buffer between accused and accuser, educate citizens about the justice system, and symbolize the law.

❷ The Supreme Court has said that juries can have as few as six jurors, except in death penalty cases, in which twelve are required, and convictions can occur through less-than-unanimous verdicts.

❸ Only 9 percent of cases go to trial; 4 percent are jury trials and 5 percent are bench trials.

❹ Voir dire is the jury selection process in which lawyers and judges ask questions of prospective jurors and make decisions about using peremptory challenges and challenges for cause to shape the jury's composition.

❺ A challenge for cause is based on an indication that a prospective juror cannot make a fair decision. Such challenges must be approved by the judge. A peremptory challenge can be made by the attorney without giving a reason, unless an allegation arises that the attorney is using such challenges systematically to exclude people because of their race or gender.

❻ The stages in the trial process are jury selection, attorneys' opening statements, presentation of prosecution's evidence, presentation of defense's evidence, presentation of rebuttal witnesses, closing arguments by each side, judge's instructions to the jury, and the jury's decision.

❼ The kinds of evidence are real evidence, demonstrative evidence, witness testimony, direct evidence, and circumstantial evidence.

❽ Jurors may be impressed with defendants who take the stand or those that have no criminal record, and jurors may discount cases in which they dislike the victims.

9 The one-day-one-trial reform has improved the jury system in the minds of jurors, judges, and court administrators.

10 Defense attorneys seek continuances because delay is often advantageous—not only to allow more time to prepare, but also to make it harder for the prosecution to have witnesses appear in court and to remember the details of their intended testimony against the defendant.

11 The problems of delay are difficult to solve because they are not caused simply by the size of a court's case-load, and they often stem from the self-interest, agreement, and cooperation of judges, defense attorneys, and prosecutors.

12 Unlike trial courts, which have juries, hear evidence, and decide if the defendant is guilty or not guilty, appellate courts focus only on claimed errors of law or procedure in trial court proceedings. Victory for a defendant in a trial court means an acquittal and instant freedom. Victory in an appellate court may mean only a chance at a new trial—which often leads to a new conviction.

13 The habeas corpus process may be started after all appeals have been filed and lost. Convicted offenders ask a federal court to review whether any constitutional rights were violated during the course of a case investigation and trial. If rights were violated, the person's continued detention in prison or jail may be improper.

CHAPTER ELEVEN

Punishment and Sentencing

"All rise!" Everyone stood as Oakland County, Michigan, Circuit Court Judge Jessica Cooper entered the room. On this day in April 1999, the courtroom was packed with attorneys, reporters, and onlookers. Judge Cooper was about to sentence Dr. Jack Kevorkian for second-degree murder in the death of Thomas Youk, a 52-year-old from suburban Detroit who suffered from Lou Gehrig's disease.

Kevorkian, a retired pathologist, claimed to have helped more than 130 people commit suicide in his campaign to legalize assisted suicide. This was the fifth time that Michigan prosecutors had charged Kevorkian with the deaths of seriously ill people. Three trials had ended in acquittal and the fourth in a mistrial. In those trials he had not been charged with murder, but with violating laws against assisted suicide. In many of these cases family members of the deceased defended his actions.

In this trial Kevorkian, charged with first-degree murder, insisted on being his own defense counsel. Undoubtedly a key point in the trial was when prosecutors showed a videotape of the doctor injecting Youk with the lethal chemicals. The videotape was shown nationally on the CBS News program *60 Minutes* along with an interview in which Kevorkian dared prosecutors to bring charges against him. After deliberating for thirteen hours, the jury returned a guilty verdict of second-degree murder, which does not require the showing of premeditation.

Before pronouncing the sentence Judge Cooper asked Kevorkian if he had anything to say. His response was simply, "I have no comment, your honor." Melody Youk, widow of Thomas Youk, gave a statement in which she criticized the prosecution and said that Kevorkian was merely carrying out her husband's wishes. Terrance Youk, a brother of the deceased, urged the judge to show leniency and said that prosecutors had been "disingenuous" by casting his late brother as Kevorkian's victim. But Prosecutor John Skrznski said that Kevorkian had used Youk as part of his efforts to rally support for euthanasia.

Rather than simply announcing the terms of the punishment, Judge Cooper took pains to review the case and to explain the reasons for the sentence. Speaking to the defendant she said,

> This is a court of law and you said you invited yourself here to take a final stand. But this trial was not an opportunity for a referendum. The law prohibiting euthanasia was specifically reviewed and clarified by the Michigan Supreme Court several years ago in a decision involving your very own cases, sir. We are a nation of laws. We have a civilized and nonviolent way of resolving conflict. You can criticize the law. You can gripe. You can lecture. You can petition the voters. But you may not take the law into your own hands. When you purposely inject another human being with what you know is a lethal dose, that, sir, is murder.

Reviewing Michigan's sentencing guidelines Judge Cooper then announced that Kevorkian was to be incarcerated from ten to twenty-five years. She denied bail pending an appeal on the grounds that she could not be certain that Kevorkian could be trusted to stop assisting suicides.

Outside the courtroom opponents of Kevorkian, many in wheelchairs, burst into applause after the sentencing. The offender smiled as he was led out of the courtroom by bailiffs.

Sentencing is a crucial point in the criminal justice system. After guilt is established, a decision must be made about what to do with the defendant. The interest of the public—even in a highly publicized case—seems to drop at this point. Usually the convicted criminal is out of sight and the case is out of the public's mind. But for the offender, sentencing is the beginning of corrections.

The criminal justice system aims to solve three basic questions: What conduct is criminal? What determines guilt? What should be done with the guilty? Earlier chapters emphasized the first two problems. The answers given by the legal system to the first question are the basic rules of society: do not murder, rob, sell drugs, commit treason. The process for determining guilt or innocence is spelled out in the law, but it is greatly influenced by administrative and interpersonal considerations of the actors in the criminal justice system. In this chapter we will begin to examine the third problem, sanction and punishment. We will consider the four goals of punishment: retribution, deterrence, incapacitation, and rehabilitation. We will then explore the forms punishment takes to achieve its goals. These are incarceration, intermediate sanctions, probation, and death.

QUESTIONS
for Inquiry

- What are the goals of punishment?
- What really happens in sentencing?
- What types of sentences may judges impose?
- Does the system treat wrongdoers equally?

The Goals of Punishment

Criminal sanctions in the United States have four main goals: retribution (deserved punishment), deterrence, incapacitation, and rehabilitation. Throughout the history of Western civilization the design of criminal punishments has been shaped by the dominant philosophical and moral orientations of the time. Ultimately, all criminal punishment is aimed at maintaining the social order. However, each goal represents a different approach to advancing society's interests.

Punishments reflect the dominant values of a particular moment in history. By the end of the 1960s, for example, the number of Americans who were sentenced to imprisonment decreased because of a widespread commitment to rehabilitating offenders through counseling, education, and other forms of assistance. By contrast, since the mid-1970s record numbers of offenders have been sentenced to prison because of an emphasis on imposing strong punishments for the purposes of retribution, deterrence, and incapacitation (see What Americans Think). At the beginning of the twenty-first century, voices are calling for the addition of restorative justice as a fifth goal of the criminal sanction.

Retribution—Deserved Punishment

Retribution is punishment inflicted on a person who has violated a criminal law and so deserves to be penalized. The biblical expression "An eye for an eye, a tooth for a tooth" illustrates the philosophy underlying retribution. Retribution means that those who commit a particular crime should be punished alike, in proportion to the gravity of the offense or to the extent to which others have been made to suffer. Retribution is deserved punishment; offenders must "pay their debts."

Some scholars claim that the desire for retribution is a basic human emotion. They maintain that if the state does not provide retributive sanctions to reflect community revulsion at offensive acts, citizens will take the law into their own hands to punish offenders. Under this view, the failure of government to satisfy the people's desire for retribution could produce social chaos.

This argument may not be valid for all crimes, however. If a rapist is inadequately punished, then the victim's friends, family, and other members of the community may be tempted to exact their own retribution. But what about a young adult smoking marijuana? If the government failed to impose retribution for this offense, would the community care? The same apathy may hold true for offenders who commit other nonviolent crimes that have a modest impact on society. Yet in these seemingly trivial situations, retribution may be useful and necessary to remind the public of the general rules of law and the important values it protects.

What Americans Think

Question "Which of these four purposes do you think should be the most important in sentencing adults?"

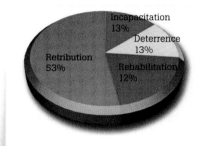

SOURCE: Jurg Gerber and Simone Engelhardt-Greer, "Just and Painful: Attitudes toward Sentencing Criminals," *Americans View Crime and Justice,* eds. Timothy J. Flanagan and Dennis R. Longmire (Thousand Oaks, Calif.: Sage Publications, 1996), 69.

retribution

Punishment inflicted on a person who has violated a criminal law and so deserves to be penalized. The severity of the sanction should fit the seriousness of the crime.

Since the late 1970s retribution as a justification for the criminal sanction has aroused new interest, largely because of dissatisfaction with the philosophical basis and practical results of rehabilitation. Using the concept of "just deserts or deserved punishment" to define retribution, some theorists argue that one who infringes on the rights of others deserves to be punished. This approach is based on the philosophical view that punishment is a moral response to harm inflicted on society. In effect, these theorists believe that basic morality demands that wrongdoers be punished (von Hirsch, 1976:49). According to this view, punishment should be applied only for the wrong inflicted and not primarily to achieve other goals such as deterrence, incapacitation, or rehabilitation.

Deterrence

Many people see criminal punishment as a basis for affecting the future choices and behavior of individuals. Politicians frequently talk about being tough on crime so as to send a message to would-be criminals. This deterrence approach has its roots in eighteenth-century England among the followers of the social philosopher Jeremy Bentham.

Bentham was struck by what seemed to be the pointlessness of retribution. His fellow reformers adopted Bentham's theory of utilitarianism, which holds that human behavior is governed by the individual's calculation of the benefits versus the costs of one's acts. Before stealing money or property, for example, potential offenders would consider the punishment that others have received for similar acts and would thereby be deterred.

There are two types of deterrence (Stafford and Warr, 1993). **General deterrence** presumes that members of the general public will be deterred by observing the punishments of others and conclude that the costs of crime outweigh the benefits. For

general deterrence

Punishment of criminals that is intended to be an example to the general public and to discourage the commission of offenses by others.

Former nurse Orville Lynn Majors, convicted of giving lethal injections to six hospital patients in Brazil, Indiana, waits with his attorney to hear his fate. The judge sentenced him to 360 years in prison. What should be the goal of his punishment?

general deterrence to be effective, the public must be constantly reminded about the likelihood and severity of punishment for various acts. They must believe that they will be caught, prosecuted, and given a specific punishment if they commit a particular crime. Moreover, the punishment must be severe enough that they will be impressed by the consequences of committing crimes. For example, public hanging was once considered to be an effective general deterrent.

By contrast, **special deterrence,** also called *specific* or *individual deterrence,* targets the decisions and behavior of offenders who have already been convicted. Under this approach, the amount and kind of punishment are calculated to discourage the criminal from repeating the offense. The punishment must be sufficiently severe to cause the criminal to say, "The consequences of my crime were too painful. I will not commit another crime because I do not want to risk being punished again."

There are obvious difficulties with the concept of deterrence (Stafford

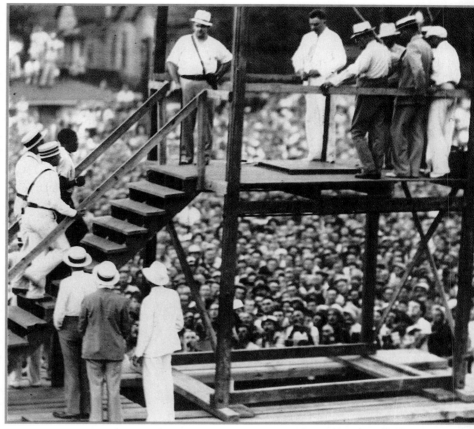

Public executions are thought to strengthen general deterrence. The hanging of Rainey Bethea in Owensboro, Kentucky, in 1936 was the last such execution in the United States. Why have we moved executions out of public view?

and Warr, 1993). Deterrence assumes that all people act rationally and think before they act. Deterrence does not account for the many people who commit crimes while under the influence of drugs or alcohol, or those whose harmful behavior stems from psychological problems or mental illness. Deterrence also does not account for people who act impulsively in stealing or damaging property. In other cases, the low probability of being caught defeats both general and special deterrence. To be generally deterrent, punishment must be perceived as relatively fast, certain, and severe. But that is not always the case.

Knowledge of the effectiveness of deterrence is limited (Nagin, 1998). For example, social science is unable to measure the effects of general deterrence; only those who are not deterred come to the attention of researchers. A study of the deterrent effects of punishment would have to examine the impact of different forms of the criminal sanction on various potential lawbreakers. How can it ever be determined how many people—or even if *any* people—stopped themselves from committing a crime because they were deterred by the prospect of prosecution and punishment? Therefore, while legislators often cite deterrence as a rationale for certain sanctions, no one knows the extent to which sentencing policies based on deterrence achieve their objectives. Because contemporary American society has shown little ability to reduce crime by imposing increasingly severe sanctions, the effectiveness of deterrence for many crimes and criminals should be questioned.

special deterrence
Punishment that is inflicted on criminals to discourage them from committing any future crimes.

Incapacitation

Incapacitation assumes that society can remove an offender's capacity to commit further crimes by detention in prison or by execution. Many people express such sentiments, urging "lock-'em up and throw away the key!" In primitive societies, banishment from the community was the usual method of incapacitation. In early America, offenders often agreed to move away or to join the army as an alternative to some other form of punishment. In contemporary America, imprisonment is the usual method of incapacitation. Offenders can be confined within secure institutions and effectively prevented from committing additional harm against society for the duration of their sentence. Capital punishment is the ultimate method of incapacitation.

Any sentence that physically restricts an offender can have the effect of incapacitating the person, even when the underlying purpose of the sentence is retribution, deterrence, or rehabilitation. Sentences based on incapacitation are future-oriented. Whereas retribution requires focusing on the harmful act of the offender, incapacitation looks at the offender's potential future actions. If the offender is likely to commit future crimes, then a severe sentence may be imposed—even for a relatively minor crime.

For example, under the incapacitation theory, a woman who kills her abusive husband as an emotional reaction to his verbal insults and physical assaults could receive a light sentence. As a one-time impulse killer who felt driven to kill by unique circumstances, she is not likely to commit additional crimes. By contrast, someone who shoplifts merchandise from a store and has been convicted of the offense on ten previous occasions may receive a severe sentence. The criminal record and type of crime indicate that he or she will commit additional crimes if released. Thus incapacitation focuses on characteristics of the offenders instead of characteristics of their offenses.

Does it offend the American sense of justice that a person could receive a more severe sentence for shoplifting than for manslaughter? This is one of the criticisms of incapacitation. Questions also arise about how to determine the length of sentence. Presumably, offenders will not be released until the state is reasonably sure that they will no longer commit crimes. However, can any person's behavior be accurately predicted? Moreover, on what grounds can people be punished for anticipated future behavior that cannot be accurately predicted?

In recent years greater attention has been paid to the concept of **selective incapacitation,** whereby offenders who repeat certain kinds of crimes are sentenced to long prison terms. Research has suggested that a relatively small number of offenders are responsible for a large number of violent and property crimes (Clear, 1994:103). Burglars, for example, tend to commit many offenses before they are caught. Thus, these "career criminals" should be locked up for long periods (Auerhahn, 1999). Such policies could be costly, however. Not only would correctional facilities have to be expanded, but the number of expensive, time-consuming trials also might increase if more severe sentences caused more repeat offenders to plead not guilty. Another difficulty with this policy is that no accurate predictions can be made of which offenders will commit more crimes upon release.

Luis Felipe, founder of the New York chapter of the Almighty Latin Kings and Queens Nation, was sentenced to life in solitary confinement by Federal Judge John S. Martin, Jr. Felipe had ordered murders from prison by writing to his followers outside. The judge forbade him to write or to be visited by anyone except his lawyer and close relatives.

incapacitation

Depriving an offender of the ability to commit crimes against society, usually by detaining the offender in prison.

selective incapacitation

Making the best use of expensive and limited prison space by targeting for incarceration those individuals whose incapacity will do the most to reduce crime in society.

Rehabilitation

Rehabilitation refers to the goal of restoring a convicted offender to a constructive place in society through some form of vocational or educational training or therapy. Many people find rehabilitation the most appealing modern justification for use of the criminal sanction. Americans want to believe that offenders can be treated and resocialized so that they will lead a crime-free, productive life. Over the last hundred years, rehabilitation advocates argued that techniques are available to identify and treat the causes of criminal behavior. If the offender's criminal behavior is assumed to result from some social, psychological, or biological imperfection, the treatment of the disorder becomes the primary goal of corrections.

Rehabilitation is focused on the offender. Its objective does not imply any consistent relationship between the severity of the punishment and the gravity of the crime. People who commit lesser offenses can receive long prison sentences if experts believe that a long period of time will be required to successfully rehabilitate them. By contrast, a murderer might win early release by showing signs that the psychological or emotional problems that led to the killing have been corrected.

According to the concept of rehabilitation, offenders are treated, not punished, and they will return to society when they are "cured." Consequently, judges should not set fixed sentences but ones with maximum and minimum terms so that parole boards may release inmates when they have been rehabilitated. Such sentences are known as indeterminate sentences because no fixed release date is set by the judge. The indeterminate sentence is justified by the belief that if prisoners know when they are going to be released, they will not make an effort to engage in the treatment programs prescribed for their rehabilitation. If, however, they know that they will be held until they are cured, they will cooperate with counselors, psychologists, and other professionals seeking to treat their problems.

From the 1940s until the 1970s, the goal of rehabilitation was so widely accepted that treatment and reform of the offender were generally regarded as the only issues worth serious attention. Crime was assumed to be caused by problems affecting individuals, and modern social sciences had the tools to address those problems. During the past twenty-five years, however, the assumptions of the rehabilitation model have been questioned. Studies of the results of rehabilitation programs have challenged the idea that criminal offenders can be cured (Martinson, 1974). Moreover, it is no longer taken for granted that crime is caused by identifiable, curable problems such as poverty, lack of job skills, low self-esteem, and hostility toward authority. Instead, some scholars argue that the cause of criminal behavior for individual offenders cannot always be identified.

Clearly, many legislatures, prosecutors, and judges have abandoned the rehabilitation goal in favor of retribution, deterrence, or incapacitation. Yet on the basis of opinion polls researchers have found public support for rehabilitative programs (McCorkle, 1993:240; Applegate, Cullen, and Fisher, 1997:237–258). Prison wardens have also supported such programs (Cullen, Latessa, Burton, and Lombardo, 1993:69).

rehabilitation
The goal of restoring a convicted offender to a constructive place in society through some form of vocational or educational training or therapy.

New Approaches to Punishment

During the past decade many people have called for shifts away from punishment goals that focus either on the offender (rehabilitation, specific deterrence) or the crime (retribution, general deterrence, incapacitation). In keeping with the focus

restoration

Punishment designed to repair the damage done to the victim and community by an offender's criminal act.

on community justice—police, courts, corrections—advocates are calling for **restoration** (through restorative justice) to be added to the goals of the criminal sanction (Basemore and Umbreit,1994).

The restorative justice perspective views crime as more than a violation of penal law. The criminal act also practically and symbolically denies community. It breaks trust among citizens and requires community members to determine how "to contradict the moral message of the crime that the offender is above the law and the victim beneath its reach" (Clear and Karp, 1999). Crime victims suffer losses involving damage to property and self that result from the act. Crime also challenges the very essence of community, to the extent that community life depends on a shared sense of trust, fairness, and interdependence. Shifting the focus to restorative justice requires a three-way approach that involves the offender, the victim, and the community. Mediation can be used involving the three actors in devising ways that all agree are fair and just for the offender to repair the harm done to victim and community.

This new approach to community justice means that losses suffered by the crime victim are restored, the threat to local safety is removed, and the offender again becomes a fully participating member of the community. The Vermont Reparative Sentencing Boards, described in the Close-Up opposite, are one way of implementing the goal of restoration.

Although the four goals of the criminal sanction are often discussed as if they are distinct, they overlap a great deal. A sentence of imprisonment can be philosophically justified in terms of its primary goal of incapacitation, but the secondary functions of retribution and deterrence are also present. Deterrence is such a broad concept that it mixes well with all the other purposes.

To see how these goals might be enacted in real life, consider again the sentencing of Dr. Jack Kervorkian for killing Thomas Youk. Table 11.1 show various hypothetical sentencing statements that the judge might have given, depending on prevailing correctional goals.

TABLE 11.1

The goals of punishment

At sentencing the judge usually gives reasons for the punishments imposed. Here are statements that Judge Jessica Cooper might have given to Dr. Jack Kevorkian, each promoting a different goal for the sanction.

GOAL	JUDGE'S POSSIBLE STATEMENT
Retribution	I am imposing this sentence because you deserve to be punished for killing Thomas Youk. Your criminal behavior is the basis of the punishment. Justice requires that I impose a sanction at a level that illustrates the importance that the community places on the sanctity of life.
Deterrence	I am imposing this sentence so that your punishment for killing Thomas Youk will serve as an example and deter others who may contemplate similar actions. In addition, I hope that this sentence will deter you from ever again committing an illegal act.
Incapacitation	I am imposing this sentence so that you will be incapacitated and hence unable to kill a person in the free community during the length of this term.
Rehabilitation	The trial testimony and information contained in the presentence report makes me believe that there are aspects of your personality that led you to kill Thomas Youk. I am therefore imposing this sentence so that you can receive treatment that will rectify your behavior so you will not commit another crime.

CLOSE

Restorative Justice
in Vermont

One night in Morrisville, Vermont, Newton Wells went looking for a good time and wound up in an experiment.

The 22-year-old college student was charged with assault after nearly driving into two police officers who were breaking up a party. Facing a felony conviction, Wells took a different way out. He pleaded guilty to a lower charge and volunteered to be sentenced by a county "reparative" board. Instead of a judge, a businessman, a counselor, a retired chemistry teacher and a civil servant issued his punishment.

Flinty Vermonters have a long history with community sanctions. In Colonial days, thieves were nailed by their ear lobes to the village hitching post, the better to contemplate their wrongs. Today, offenders are more likely to be sentenced to make public apologies, restitution or chop wood for the elderly—to "repair" the community. . . .

Restorative justice programs are designed to compensate victims, rehabilitate offenders and involve the community, in a new and a direct way, in the justice process. . . .

Vermont's sentencing boards, which have been meting punishments statewide since late 1995, are not without controversy. Defense lawyers say sanctions can vary widely, raising the issue of fairness. Others question the constitutionality of private citizens acting as judges.

And then there is what might be called the "Crucible" factor: the unease even some Vermonters feel about letting fellow citizens sit in judgment upon them. . . .

The boards, typically four to six volunteers, handle misdemeanors and low-grade felonies such as drunken driving and writing bad checks. And while such crimes normally would not merit jail time, removing the cases from the traditional criminal justice system has the side benefit of freeing corrections department resources.

People accused of non-violent crimes agree to be sent to the community sentencing program as part of a plea bargain that is approved by a judge.

Board members meet with offenders in hour-long sessions, hear explanations and apologies, and tailor the penalties.

The idea is to make the punishment related to the crime, often in a novel way.

In Morrisville, college student Wells was ordered to work 30 hours with troubled youths, and to meet with the police he menaced so that they could vent their anger about his driving.

In Rutland, a man who drove 105 mph down a residential street was sentenced to work with brain-injured adults, some of them survivors of high-speed crashes.

In Hyde Park, a teen-ager who vandalized a home got 55 hours on a work crew. His job was repairing plaster on an aging opera house. . . .

Panel members get involved in ways they never could if they were serving as jurors. In Rutland, Jack Aicher tells shoplifters they've committed crimes against the "community." Everyone pays higher prices, he says, to cover the store's loss.

Victims are encouraged to sit in on hearings but to date few have. Board members say some may fear facing their antagonists, while others don't wish to be inconvenienced. Flor Tutiakoff of Barre says board members try to act as surrogates for the "victims and the entire community."

Proponents say board sanctions are typically tougher than conventional probation. But offenders opt for the citizen panels to get their sentences concluded quickly. In Vermont, probation can last more than a year and can include special sanctions such as drug tests and rehabilitation programs. Reparative board punishments are concluded within 90 days.

In the corrections department's view, the boards have worked out well. Citizens handled about 650 cases [in 1996] or one-third of Vermont's ordinary probation caseload. They will soon handle 100% if corrections officials get their way.

Meanwhile, the percentage of non-violent offenders in the state's eight prisons has dropped from about 50% to 28%. The decline is ascribed, in part, to the effect of the boards. By handling low-level offenders, the community panels have freed state probation officers to deal with more serious cases. Those probation officers are then able to monitor criminals serving their sentences in work camps or on furlough rather than in jail as a way of relieving overcrowding.

SOURCE: *USA Today*, February 12, 1997, at www.usatoday.com.

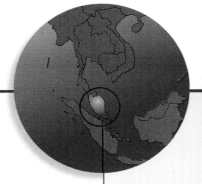

COMPARATIVE
perspective

Corporal Punishment
in Singapore

A Singapore court's decision to sentence Michael Fay, an American teenager, to receive a flogging for vandalizing cars with spray paint produced a predictable nod of approval from many Singaporeans, long accustomed to their government's firm hand. For many Americans the punishment seemed unduly harsh; yet others expressed the view that this might be the answer to the U.S. crime problem.

Michael Fay was sentenced to six strokes of the cane; four months in prison; and a $2,230 fine after pleading guilty to two counts of vandalism, two counts of mischief, and one count of possessing stolen property. Canings, the term for floggings, in Singapore are carried out by a jailer trained in martial arts who uses a moistened, four-foot rattan cane. The offender is stripped, bound by the hands and feet to a wooden trestle. Pads covering his kidneys and groin are the only protection from the cane. Should he pass out, a doctor will revive him before the caning continues. The wounds generally take two weeks to heal; scarring is permanent.

After Singapore gained independence from Britain, the government imposed increasingly harsh penalties for a range of crimes, culminating in laws against such offenses as armed robbery and drug trafficking carrying a mandatory death penalty. Singapore has dropped some traditional safeguards, such as jury trials, on grounds that guilty criminals were manipulating the system to walk free.

As the ways that the goals are applied through the various forms of punishment are considered, keep in mind the underlying goal—or mix of punishment goals—that justifies each form of sanction.

CHECK POINT

① **What are the four primary goals of the criminal sanction?**
② **What are the difficulties in showing that a punishment acts as a deterrent?**
(Answers are at the end of the chapter.)

Forms of the Criminal Sanction

Incarceration, intermediate sanctions, probation, and death are the basic ways that the criminal sanction, or punishment, is applied in the United States. Most people think of incarceration as the usual punishment. As a consequence, much of the public thinks that using alternatives to incarceration, such as probation, means that offenders are "getting off." However, community-based punishments such as

Statistics comparing the small city-state of Singapore with Los Angeles, with its roughly equal population of about 3.5 million, provide a dramatic contrast. In 1993, 58 murders, 80 rapes, 1,008 robberies, and 3,162 car thefts were reported in Singapore. Los Angeles Police Department statistics for the same period show 1,100 homicides, 1,855 rapes, 39,227 robberies, and 65,541 car thefts. There are fewer than 3,800 full-time police officers in Singapore; all guns are outlawed, except those belonging to the police and armed forces. Gun possession carries a stiff prison term, and those who fire one during a crime face a mandatory death sentence.

Another difference with Los Angeles is the makeup of the society itself. In Singapore 77 percent of the residents are ethnic Chinese and 14 percent conservative Muslim Malays living in relative isolation on a small island. There is virtually no poverty—80 percent of the people own their homes—and the family remains the backbone of society. There are few divorces, and children live at home until marriage. As in many Asian societies, public shame, for the criminal and for his family, is a potent deterrent.

According to Singapore officials, sentences are intended not just as punishment but as a deterrent. For example, when an 18-year-old man who was called "educationally subnormal" repeatedly kissed a woman in an elevator, he was charged with molestation. A court sentenced him to six months in prison. When the man's lawyer appealed, Chief Judge Yong Pung How, saying "sentences have been too light; they are not having a deterrent effect," increased the punishment to include three whacks of the rattan cane.

SOURCE: Adapted from Charles P. Wallace, "Singapore's Justice System: Harsh, Temptingly Effective," *Hartford Courant,* April 4, 1994, p. 1.

probation and intermediate sanctions are imposed almost three times as often as prison sentences. Although these are the sanctions used in the United States, the form and severity of punishment vary across cultures, as seen in the Comparative Perspective above on the use of corporal punishment in Singapore. Consider the reaction in the United States to the flogging of Michael Fay. Why have corporal punishments (inflicting pain on the body of the offender) disappeared in Western countries? Should flogging be reinstituted?

Many judges and researchers believe that sentencing structures in the United States are both too severe and too lenient. That is, many offenders who do not warrant incarceration are sent to prison, and many who should be given more restrictive punishments receive minimal probation supervision. Advocates of more effective sentencing practices increasingly support a range of punishment options, with graduated levels of supervision and harshness. As Figure 11.1 shows, simple probation lies at one end of this range and traditional incarceration lies at the other. It is argued that by using this type of sentencing scheme, authorities can maintain expensive prison cells for violent offenders. At the same time, less restrictive community-based programs can be used to punish nonviolent offenders.

As the various forms of criminal sanctions are examined, bear in mind that applying these legally authorized punishments is complex. Judges are given wide discretion in determining the appropriate sentence within the parameters of the penal code.

FIGURE 11.1 Escalating punishments to fit the crime

This list includes generalized descriptions of many sentencing options used in jurisdictions across the country.

PROBATION
Offender reports to probation officer periodically, depending on the offense, sometimes as frequently as several times a month or as infrequently as once a year.

INTENSIVE SUPERVISION PROBATION
Offender sees probation officer three to five times a week. Probation officer also makes unscheduled visits to offender's home or workplace.

RESTITUTION AND FINES
Used alone or in conjunction with probation or intensive supervision and requires regular payments to crime victims or to the courts.

COMMUNITY SERVICE
Used alone or in conjuntion with probation or intensive supervision and requires completion of set number of hours of work in and for the community.

SUBSTANCE ABUSE TREATIMENT
Evaluation and referral services provided by private outside agencies and used alone or in conjumction with either simple probation or intensive supervision.

SOURCE: *Seeking Justice: Crime and Punishment in America* (New York: Edna McConnell Clark Foundation, 1997), 32–33.

Incarceration

Imprisonment is the most visible penalty imposed by U.S. courts. Although less than 30 percent of persons under correctional supervision are in prisons and jails, incarceration remains the standard for punishing those who commit serious crimes. Imprisonment is thought to have a significant effect in deterring potential offenders. However, incarceration is expensive. It also creates the problem of reintegrating offenders into society upon release.

In penal codes, legislatures stipulate the type of sentences and the amount of prison time that may be imposed for each crime. Three basic sentencing structures are used: (1) indeterminate sentences (thirty-six states), (2) determinate sentences (fourteen states), and (3) mandatory sentences (all states). Each type of sentence makes certain assumptions about the goals of the criminal sanction, and each provides judges with varying degrees of discretion (Bureau of Justice Assistance, 1998:4).

Indeterminate Sentences

When the goal of rehabilitation dominated corrections, legislatures enacted indeterminate (often termed indefinite) sentences. In keeping with the goal of treatment, **indeterminate sentences** give correctional officials and parole boards significant control over the amount of time a prisoner serves. Penal codes with indeterminate sentences specify a minimum and a maximum amount of time to be served in prison (for example, one to five years, three to ten years, or one year to life). At the time of sentencing, the judge informs the offender of the range of the

---

indeterminate sentence

An indefinite period set by a judge that specifies a minimum and a maximum time served in prison. Sometime after the minimum, the offender may be eligible for parole. Because it is based on the idea that the time necessary for treatment cannot be set, the indeterminate sentence is closely associated with rehabilitation.

DAY REPORTING

Clients report to a central location every day where they file a daily schedule with their supervision officer showing how each hour will be spent: at work, in class, at support group meetings, etc.

HOUSE ARREST AND ELECTRONIC MONITORING

Used in conjunction with intensive supervision and restricts offender to home except when at work, school, or treatment.

HALFWAY HOUSE

Residential settings for selected inmates as a supplement to probation for those completing prison programs and for some probation or parole violators. Usually coupled with community service work and/or substance abuse treatment.

BOOT CAMP

Rigorous military-style regimen for younger offenders designed to accelerate punishment while instilling discipline, often with an educational component.

PRISONS AND JAILS

More serious offenders serve their terms at state or federal prisons, while county jails are usually designed to hold inmates for shorter periods.

---

determinate sentence
A sentence that fixes the term of imprisonment at a specific period of time.

presumptive sentence
A sentence for which the legislature or a commission sets a minimum and maximum range of months or years. Judges are to fix the length of the sentence within that range, allowing for special circumstances.

sentence. The offender also learns that he or she will probably be eligible for parole at some point after the minimum term has been served. "Good time" may be subtracted from either the minimum or maximum; good time is earned by good behavior in prison or participation in a rehabilitation program. The actual release date is decided by the parole board.

Determinate Sentences

Dissatisfaction with the rehabilitation goal and support for the concept of deserved punishment led many legislatures in the 1970s to shift to **determinate sentences.** With a determinate sentence, a convicted offender is imprisoned for a specific period of time (for example, two years, five years, or ten years). At the end of the term, minus credited good time, the prisoner is automatically freed. The time of release is not tied to participation in treatment programs or to the offender's likelihood of returning to criminal activities, as judged by the parole board.

Some determinate sentencing states have adopted penal codes that stipulate a specific term for each crime category; others allow the judge to choose a range of time to be served. Some states emphasize a determinate **presumptive sentence:**

Incarceration is the greatest restriction on freedom. Since 1980 the number of people in prison has more than doubled.

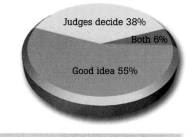
mandatory sentence

A sentence determined by statutes and requiring that a certain penalty be imposed and carried out for convicted offenders who meet certain criteria.

Gloria L. Van Winkle, with her children, was sentenced to life under the Kansas "three strikes" law for possession of $40 worth of cocaine. The cost of the long-term incarceration of nonviolent drug offenders is raising questions about the effectiveness of mandatory sentences.

the legislature or often a commission specifies a term based on a time range (for example, fourteen to twenty months) into which most cases should fall. Only in special circumstances should judges deviate from the presumptive sentence. Whichever variation is used, however, the offender theoretically knows at sentencing the amount of time to be served. One result of determinate sentencing is that by reducing the judge's discretion, legislatures have tended to limit sentencing disparities and to ensure the terms will correspond to those the elected body thinks are appropriate (Griset, 1993).

Mandatory Sentences

Politicians and the public have continued to complain that offenders are released before serving long enough terms, and legislatures have responded (see What Americans Think). All states and the federal government now have some form of **mandatory sentences** (often called mandatory minimum sentences), stipulating some minimum period of incarceration that people convicted of selected crimes must serve. The judge may not consider the circumstances of the offense or the background of the offender, and they may not impose nonincarcerative sentences. Mandatory prison terms are most often specified for violent crimes, drug violations, habitual offenders, or crimes in which a firearm was used.

The "three strikes and you're out" laws adopted by twenty-four states and the federal government are an example of mandatory sentencing (Turner, Sundt, Applegate, and Cullen, 1995). These laws require that judges sentence offenders with three felony convictions (in some states two or four convictions) to long prison terms, sometimes to life without parole (Vitiello, 1997). In California and Georgia, the two states making the greatest use of them, the laws have had the unintended consequences of clogging the courts, lowering rates of plea bargaining, and causing desperate offenders to violently resist arrest (Butterfield, 1996b). One study has shown that the law has had little impact on the reduction of rates for serious crime or petty theft (Stolzenberg and D'Alessio, 1997).

Although legislators may assume that mandatory sentences will be imposed and criminal behavior reduced, this intent may be thwarted by the decisions of judges and prosecutors. California prosecutors vary greatly as to whether they

charge under the law; those in Alameda and San Francisco have minimized its use. Regional voter support for the law may account for the disparity (*Sacramento Bee,* March 31, 1996:A1ff). The impact of the California "three strikes" law shows that:

- The law does incapacitate habitual offenders for a long time, but no hard evidence proves that it has had a deterrence effect on crime commission.
- The law targets repeat felons but captures mostly nonviolent offenders.
- Wide discretion and racial disparity in applying the law raise questions of legality and fairness.
- Prison problems are exacerbated by demand for space, high costs of building and staffing, and escalation of geriatric inmate health care costs (*Sacramento Bee,* March 31, 1996)

The experience of other mandatory sentencing laws suggests the types of impact that "three strikes" states should expect. For example, when New York imposed tough, mandatory sentences for drug dealers in 1973, these sentences merely raised the stakes so high for the defendant that the prosecutors had to reduce charges to get guilty pleas. Critics say that the impact has been to "pack the prisons, force plea deals and hit small-timers the hardest" (Wren, 1998). In a study of laws requiring mandatory sentences for crimes in which firearms are used, Thomas Marvell and Carlisle Moody found that such sentences had little influence on either reducing crime or increasing prison populations (Marvell and Moody, 1995).

The Sentence versus Actual Time Served

Regardless of the discretion judges have to fine-tune the sentences they give, the prison sentences that are imposed may bear little resemblance to the amount of time actually served. In reality, parole boards in indeterminate sentencing states have broad discretion in release decisions once the offender has served a minimum portion of the sentence. In addition, offenders can have their prison sentence reduced by earning good time for good behavior, at the discretion of the prison administrator.

All but four states have good-time policies (BJA, 1998). Days are subtracted from prisoners' minimum or maximum term for good behavior or for participating in various types of vocational, educational, or treatment programs. Corrections officials consider these policies necessary for maintaining institutional order and reducing crowding. The possibility of receiving good-time credit is an incentive for prisoners to follow institutional rules. Good time is also taken into consideration by prosecutors and defense attorneys during plea bargaining. In other words, they think about the actual amount of time a particular offender is likely to serve.

The amount of good time that one can earn varies among the states, usually from five to ten days a month. In some states, once ninety days of good time are earned they are vested; that is, the credits cannot be taken away as a punishment for misbehavior. Prisoners who then violate the rules risk losing only days not vested.

Judges in the United States often prescribe long periods of incarceration for serious crimes, but good time and parole reduce the amount of time spent in prison. Figure 11.2 shows the estimated time actually served by offenders sent to state prisons versus the mean (or the average) sentence imposed. Note that the

FIGURE **11.2** **Estimated time served in state prison compared with
mean length of sentence**

Most offenders serve a third or less of
their mean sentences. Why is there such
a difference between the sentence and
actual time served?

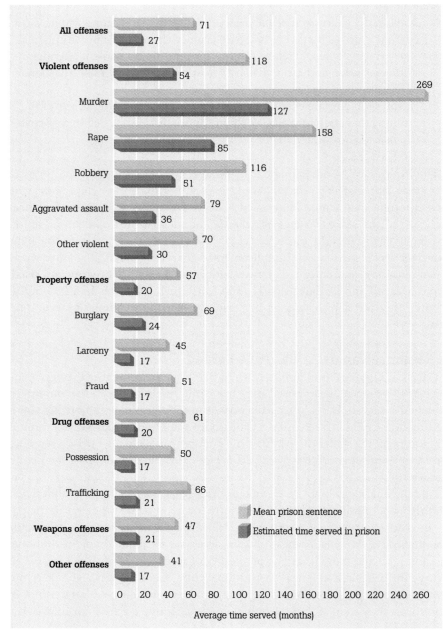

SOURCE: U.S. Department of Justice, Bureau of Justice Statistics, *State Court Sentencing of Convicted Felons, 1994*
(Washington, D.C.: Government Printing Office, 1998).

national average for time served is twenty-seven months, or 38 percent of the
mean sentence of seventy-nine months.

In viewing these statistics, note that the data are based on persons released
from prison. As a result, this understates the amount of time served for those
incarcerated for serious offenses given very long terms, some of whom may
never be released. Also, national data often hide the impact of variations in sentencing and releasing laws in individual states. In many states, because of prison

crowding and release policies, offenders are serving less than 20 percent of their sentences. In other states, where "three strikes" and "truth-in-sentencing" laws are employed, the average time served will be longer than the national average.

Truth in Sentencing

Calls for truth-in-sentencing have arisen when the public has learned that the actual time served is much less than expected. Truth-in-sentencing refers to the requirement that offenders serve a substantial proportion (usually 85 percent for violent crimes) of their prison sentence before being released on parole (BJS, 1999i). This has become such a "hot," politically attractive idea that the federal government has allocated most of the $10 billion for prison construction, authorized under the 1994 federal crime bill, only to those states adopting truth-in-sentencing (Donziger, 1996:24). Critics maintain that truth-in-sentencing will increase prison populations at a tremendous cost. M. A. Jones and James Austin (1995) have estimated that, with the 85 percent rule, the national prison population would rise to 1.6 million by the end of the year 2000 at a cost of $32.5 billion to $37 billion dollars in construction and operating costs.

Studies in Texas and Illinois project major increases in the prison population, new construction, and operating funds. If Texas should impose the 85 percent rule for only *aggravated* violent offenses, it would need to add 30,600 beds, costing $980 million to construct and $510 million to operate. A statute has been proposed in Illinois to impose the 85 percent rule on *all* inmates. Should it pass the prison population would double at an additional cost of $4.6 billion in operating and $1.5 billion in construction costs (Austin, 1997). Todd Clear argues that although inmates may currently be serving a smaller proportion of their time, they are actually serving sentences about as severe as, and in some cases more severe than, a decade ago (Clear, 1996).

Intermediate Sanctions

Prison crowding and the low levels of probation supervision have spurred interest in the development of **intermediate sanctions,** punishments that are less severe and costly than prison, but more restrictive than traditional probation (Morris and Tonry, 1990). Intermediate sanctions provide a variety of restrictions on freedom, such as fines, home confinement, intensive probation supervision, restitution to victims, community service, boot camp, and forfeiture of possessions or stolen property. According to estimates, if murderers and rapists, those previously incarcerated, and those with a prior sentence for violence were excluded from consideration for intermediate punishments, 29 percent of those who are now headed for prison could be sanctioned in the community (Petersilia and Turner, 1989).

In advocating intermediate punishments, Norval Morris and Michael Tonry (1990:37) stipulate that these sanctions should not be used in isolation, but rather in combination to reflect the severity of the offense, the characteristics of the offender, and the needs of the community. In addition, intermediate punishments must be supported and enforced by mechanisms that take seriously any breach of the

intermediate sanctions
A variety of punishments that are more restrictive than traditional probation but less severe and less costly than incarceration.

Community service, such as assisting in a homeless shelter, is one form of intermediate punishment. Advocates of these sanctions stress that offenders need to recognize responsibility for their acts.

conditions of the sentence. Too often criminal justice agencies have devoted few resources to enforcing sentences that do not involve incarceration. If the law does not fulfill its promises, offenders may feel that they have "beaten" the system, which makes the punishment meaningless. Citizens viewing the ineffectiveness of the system may develop the attitude that nothing but stiffer sentences will work.

Probation

probation
A sentence that the offender is allowed to serve in the community under supervision.

The most frequently applied criminal sanction is **probation,** a sentence that an offender serves in the community under supervision. Nearly 60 percent of adults under correctional supervision are on probation. Probation is designed to maintain supervision of offenders while they attempt to straighten out their lives. Probation is a judicial act, granted by the grace of the state, not extended as a right. Conditions are imposed specifying how an offender will behave through the length of the sentence. Probationers may be ordered to undergo regular drug tests, abide by curfews, enroll in educational programs or remain employed, stay away from certain parts of town or certain people, and meet regularly with probation officers. If the conditions of probation are not met, the supervising officer recommends to the court that the probation be revoked and that the remainder of the sentence be served in prison. Probation may also be revoked for commission of a new crime.

Although probationers serve their sentences in the community, the sanction is often tied to incarceration. In some jurisdictions, the court is authorized to modify an offender's prison sentence after a portion is served by changing it to probation. This is often referred to as **shock probation** (or *split probation*): an offender is released after a period of incarceration (the "shock") and resentenced to probation. An offender on probation may be required to spend intermittent periods, such as weekends or nights, in jail. Whatever the specific terms of the probationary sentence, it emphasizes guidance and supervision in the community.

shock probation
A sentence in which the offender is released after a short incarceration and resentenced to probation.

Probation is generally advocated as a way of rehabilitating offenders whose crimes are less serious or whose past records are clean. It is viewed as less expensive than imprisonment, and more effective. Imprisonment may embitter youthful or first-time offenders and mix them with hardened criminals so that they learn more sophisticated criminal techniques.

Death

Although other Western democracies abolished the death penalty years ago, the United States continues to use it. Capital punishment was carried out regularly prior to the late 1960s. Amid debates about the constitutionality of the death penalty and with public opinion polls showing opposition to it, the U.S. Supreme Court suspended its use from 1968 to 1976. Eventually, the Court decided that capital punishment does not violate the Eighth Amendment's prohibition on cruel and unusual punishments. Executions resumed in 1977 as a majority of states began, once again, to sentence murderers to death.

The numbers of persons facing the death penalty has increased dramatically, as Figure 11.3 reveals. As of the end of 1999, more than 3,625 persons were awaiting execution in thirty-seven of the thirty-eight death penalty states. Two-thirds of those on death row are in the South, with the greatest number found in Texas, Georgia, Alabama, and Florida (see Figure 11.4). Although about 250 people are sent to death row each year, since 1977 the annual number of executions has never exceeded 98 (in 1999). From 1930 through 1967, in contrast, more than 3,800 men and women were executed in the United States, 199 of them in 1935, the deadliest year. Use of the penalty has spread in recent years from its southern base to states around the country.

The Death Penalty and the Constitution

Death obviously differs from other punishments in that it is final and irreversible. The Supreme Court has therefore examined the decision-making process in capital cases to ensure that the Constitution's requirements regarding due process, equal protection, and cruel and unusual punishment are fulfilled. Because life is in the balance, capital cases must be conducted according to higher standards of fairness and more careful procedures than other kinds of cases. Several important Supreme Court cases illustrate this concern.

Mumia Abu-Jamal, sentenced to death in Philadelphia for the killing of a police officer, charges that the criminal justice system is racist as evidenced by his prosecution, trial, and sentence.

FIGURE 11.3 Persons under sentence of death and persons executed, 1953–1999

Since 1976 approximately 250 new offenders have been added to death row each year, yet the number of executions has never been greater than 98. What explains this situation?

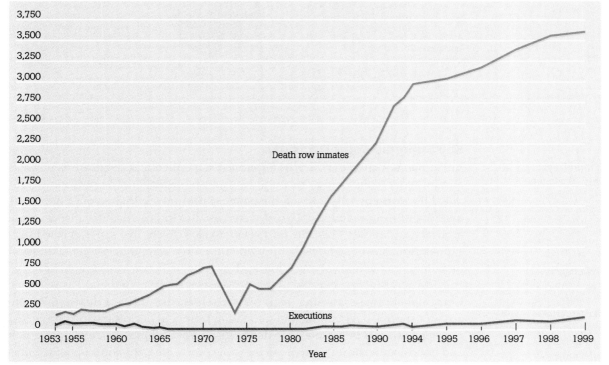

SOURCE: NAACP Legal Defense and Education Fund, *Death Row, USA* (Fall 1999); and Death Penalty Information Center at www.essential org/dpic/.

FIGURE

11.4 **Death row census, 1999**

Many of the inmates on death row are concentrated in certain states. African Americans make up about 13 percent of the U.S. population, yet make up 43 percent of the death row population. How might you explain this higher percentage of death sentences in proportion to the population?

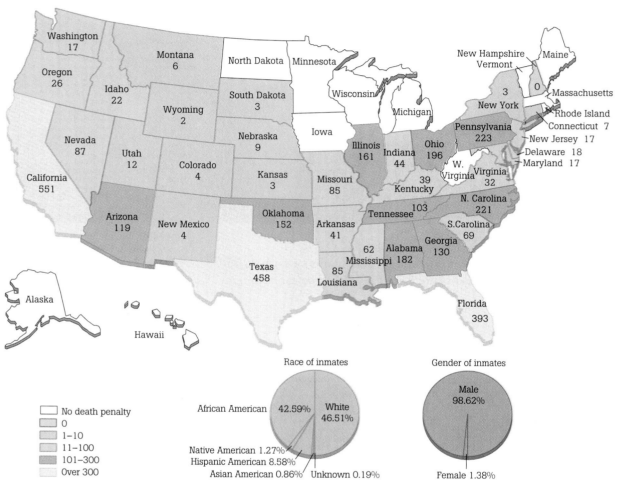

Legend:
- No death penalty
- 0
- 1–10
- 11–100
- 101–300
- Over 300

SOURCE: NAACP Legal Defense and Education Fund, *Death Row, USA* (Fall 1999).

Key Supreme Court Decisions

Furman v. Georgia (1972)

The death penalty, as administered, constituted cruel and unusual treatment.

In *Furman v. Georgia* (1972), the Supreme Court ruled that the death penalty, as administered, constituted cruel and unusual punishment. The decision invalidated the death penalty laws of thirty-nine states and the District of Columbia. A majority of justices found the procedures used to impose death sentences were arbitrary and unfair. Over the next several years, thirty-five states enacted new capital punishment statutes that provided for more careful decision making and more modern methods of execution, such as lethal injection (see Figure 11.5)

Gregg v. Georgia (1976)

Death penalty laws are constitutional if they require judge and jury to consider certain mitigating and aggravating circumstances in deciding which convicted murderers should be sentenced to death.

The new laws were tested in the 1976 case of *Gregg v. Georgia.* The Supreme Court upheld those laws that required the sentencing judge or jury to take into account specific aggravating and mitigating factors in deciding which convicted murderers should be sentenced to death. Instead of deciding the defendant's guilt and imposing the death sentence in the same proceeding, the court upheld "bifurcated" proceedings. This two-part process has a trial that determines guilt or

CHAPTER ELEVEN

FIGURE
11.5 Methods of execution authorized by the states

The number of states authorizing the use of lethal injection is increasing. What reasons might be given for the acceptance of this method?

Legend:
- No death penalty
- Lethal injection
- Electrocution
- Lethal gas
- Lethal injection/electrocution
- Lethal injection/lethal gas
- Lethal injection/hanging
- Lethal injection/firing squad

SOURCE: U.S. Department of Justice, Bureau of Justice Statistics, *Bulletin* (December 1997), 5.

innocence and then a separate hearing that focuses exclusively on the issues of punishment. It ensures a thorough deliberation before someone is given the ultimate punishment.

Under the *Gregg* decision, the prosecution may use the punishment-phase hearing to focus attention on the existence of "aggravating factors," such as excessive cruelty or a defendant's prior record of violent crimes. The defense may focus on "mitigating factors," such as the offender's youthfulness, mental retardation, or lack of a criminal record. These aggravating and mitigating factors must be weighed before the judge or jury can decide to impose a death sentence.

The U.S. Supreme Court may have dealt a fatal blow to the hopes of death penalty opponents in 1987. In the case of **McCleskey v. Kemp,** the Court rejected a challenge to Georgia's death penalty law on the grounds of racial discrimination. Warren McCleskey, an African American, was sentenced to death for the killing of a white police officer. Before the U.S. Supreme Court, McCleskey's attorney cited research that showed a disparity in the imposition of the death penalty in Georgia based on the race of the victim and, to a lesser extent, the race of the defendant. Researchers had examined more than two thousand Georgia murder cases and found that defendants charged with killing whites had received the death penalty eleven times more often than had those convicted of killing African Americans. Although 60 percent of homicide victims in Georgia are African Americans, all seven people put to death in that state since 1976 had been convicted of killing white people, and six of the seven murderers were African Americans (Baldus, Woodworth, and Pulaski, 1994).

McCleskey v. Kemp (1987)
Rejected a challenge of Georgia's death penalty on grounds of racial discrimination.

By a 5-4 vote the justices rejected McCleskey's assertion that Georgia's capital sentencing practices violated the equal protection clause of the Constitution by producing racial discrimination. A slim majority of justices declared that McCleskey would have to prove that the decision makers acted with a discriminatory purpose in deciding his case. The Court also concluded that statistical evidence showing discrimination throughout the Georgia courts did not provide adequate proof. McCleskey was executed in 1991.

Continuing Legal Issues

In recent years a shift has occurred in the challenges to capital punishment. The case law since *Furman* indicates that capital punishment is legal so long as it is imposed fairly. However, opponents now argue that certain classes of death row inmates should not be executed because they are insane, were underage at the time they committed the crime, are mentally retarded, or did not have effective counsel. A fifth issue, the length of appeals, has been a major concern of Chief Justice William H. Rehnquist.

EXECUTION OF THE INSANE Insanity is a recognized defense for commission of a crime. But should people who become mentally disabled while on death row be executed? The Supreme Court responded to this question in 1986 in *Ford v. Wainwright*. In 1974 Alvin Ford was convicted of murder and sentenced to death. Only after he was incarcerated did he begin to exhibit delusional behavior.

With evidence of these delusions, Ford's counsel invoked the procedures of the Florida law governing the determination of competency of a condemned inmate. Three psychiatrists examined Ford for thirty minutes in the presence of witnesses, including counsel and correctional officials. Each psychiatrist filed a separate and conflicting report with the governor, who subsequently signed a death warrant. Ford then appealed to the Supreme Court.

Justice Thurgood Marshall, writing for the majority, concluded that the Eighth Amendment prohibited the state from executing the insane—the accused must comprehend both the fact that he had been sentenced to death and the reason for it. Marshall cited the common law precedent that questioned the retributive and deterrent value of executing a mentally disabled person. In addition, he argued, the idea is offensive to humanity. The justices also found the Florida procedures defective because they did not provide for a full and fair hearing on the competence of the offender.

Although the Supreme Court has ruled that the insane should not be executed, the issue of how competence should be determined remains unresolved. A second issue concerns the morality of treating an offender's mental illness so that he or she *can* be executed, a policy opposed by the American Medical Association. The Supreme Court has not directly addressed this issue with regard to death row inmates.

EXECUTION OF JUVENILES The laws of eight states do not specify a minimum age for offenders receiving capital punishment. In some states the minimum age is the same as the age at which a juvenile may be tried as an adult (BJS, 1997a). Since 1642, when the Plymouth Colony in Massachusetts hanged a teenage boy for bestiality, about three hundred juveniles have been executed in the United States (Rosenbaum, R., 1989; NAACP Legal Defense and Educational Fund, 1999). Death penalty opponents have argued that adolescents do not have the same capacity as adults to understand the consequences of their actions. The United States is one of only five nations in the world—the others are Iran, Nigeria, Pakistan, and Saudi Arabia—that permits the execution of individuals for crimes committed when they were minors.

The Supreme Court has been divided on the issue of the death penalty for juveniles. In *Thompson v. Oklahoma* (1988) the Court narrowly decided that William Wayne Thompson, who was 15 when he committed murder, should not be executed. A plurality of four justices held that executing juveniles was not in accord with the "evolving standards of decency that mark the progress of a maturing society." The dissenters said that Thompson had been correctly sentenced under Oklahoma law. Within a year the Court again considered the issue in *Stanford v. Kentucky* (1989) and *Wilkins v. Missouri* (1989). This time the justices upheld the death sentences imposed on offenders who were 16 and 17 years old at the time of their crime. All of the justices agreed that interpretation of the cruel and unusual punishment clause rests on the "evolving standards of decency that mark the progress of a maturing society." However, the justices disagreed as to the factors that should be used to make that determination.

The Supreme Court has sanctioned executions of juveniles under some circumstances. On January 25, 2000, Texas put to death Glen Alan McGinnis, who was 17 years old when he fatally shot a laundromat clerk. The Vatican, the European Union, and the American Bar Association were among the organizations that pleaded for his life. McGinnis became the eighth juvenile offender executed in Texas since 1976 (*New York Times*, January 26, 2000:A12.). Currently seventy males are on death row who were under the age of 18 at the time their offenses occurred (Death Penalty Information Center, 2000). The 1998–1999 schoolyard killings in Jonesboro, Arkanas, and seven other communities raised calls to lower the age at which young people may be executed.

EXECUTION OF THE RETARDED   An estimated 250 offenders on the nation's death rows are classified as retarded and they account for 13 percent of executions (Streib, 1998:212). It is argued that retarded people have difficulty defending themselves in court because they have problems remembering details, locating witnesses, and testifying credibly in their own behalf. It is also asserted that executing the retarded serves neither retributive nor deterrent purposes, because the general public may believe that their disability caused the offenders to commit crimes (Fetzer, 1989).

In 1989 the Supreme Court decided that the Eighth Amendment does not prohibit execution of the mentally retarded. The case involved Johnny Paul Penry, a convicted killer with an intelligence quotient (IQ) of about 70 and the mental capacity of a 7-year-old. The court noted that only Georgia and Maryland prohibited execution of the mentally retarded. Now, years after the Supreme Court decision, Penry is still on death row in Texas, in part because of the lengthy appeals process.

In contrast, Alabama electrocuted Horace Dunkins Jr., who had an IQ of 69, in 1989. Adding to the injustice was the botched execution. Because the first bolt of electricity left Dunkins still alive, a second flick of the switch was needed to kill him (*New York Times*, July 15, 1989:6).

EFFECTIVE COUNSEL   In *Strickland v. Washington* (1984) the Supreme Court ruled that defendants in capital cases had the right to representation that meets an "objective standard of reasonableness." As noted by Justice Sandra Day O'Connor, the appellant must show "that there is a reasonable probability that, but for the counsel's unprofessional errors, the result of the proceeding would be different."

David Washington was charged with three counts of capital murder, robbery, kidnapping, and other felonies, and an experienced criminal lawyer was appointed as counsel. Against his attorney's advice Washington confessed to two murders, waived a jury trial, pleaded guilty to all charges, and chose to be sentenced by the trial judge. Believing the situation was hopeless, his counsel did not adequately prepare for the sentencing hearing. On being sentenced to death, Washington appealed. The Supreme Court rejected Washington's claim that his attorney was ineffective because he did not call witnesses, seek a presentence investigation report, or cross-examine medical experts on the defendant's behalf.

In 1999, the *Chicago Tribune* conducted an extensive investigation of capital punishment in Illinois. Reporters found that thirty-three defendants sentenced to death since 1977 were represented by an attorney who had been, or was later, disbarred or suspended for conduct that was "incompetent, unethical or even criminal." These attorneys included David Landau, who was disbarred one year after representing a Will County defendant sentenced to death, and Robert McDonnell, a convicted felon and the only lawyer in Illinois to be disbarred twice. McDonnell represented four men who landed on death row (Armstrong and Mills, 1999). In March 2000, a federal judge in Texas ordered the release of Calvin Jerold Burdine after sixteen years on death row. At his 1984 trial, Burdine's counsel slept through long portions of the proceedings. As the judge said, "Sleeping counsel is equivalent to no counsel at all." (*New York Times,* March 2, 2000:A19)

APPEALS   The long appeals process for death penalty cases is a source of ongoing controversy. Congress, state legislatures, and the Supreme Court have made efforts to shorten the time between sentencing and execution. In 1998 the average length of time on death row prior to execution was ten years and ten months (BJS, 1999h). During this time sentences are reviewed by the state courts and through the writ of habeas corpus by the federal courts.

Chief Justice Rehnquist has actively sought to reduce the opportunities for capital punishment defendants to have their appeals heard by multiple courts. In 1996 President Bill Clinton signed a new law that requires death row inmates to file habeas petitions within one year and requires federal judges to issue their decisions within strict time limits. In January 2000 the Florida legislature passed legislation designed to limit the number of appeals to a five-year period (*New York Times,* January 9, 2000:rwk5).

Appellate review is a time-consuming and expensive process, but it also has an impact. From 1977—the year the Supreme Court upheld the constitutionality of revised state capital punishment laws—to 1998, a total of 5,416 people entered prison under sentence of death. During those twenty-one years, 432 people were executed, and 2,029 were removed from death row as a result of appellate court decisions and reviews, commutations, or death while awaiting execution (BJS, 1998d:9).

Michael L. Radelet, William S. Lofquist, and Hugo Adam Bedau (1996:907) have examined the cases of sixty-eight death row inmates later released because of doubts about their guilt. These cases account for one of every five inmates executed during the period 1970–1996. Correction of the miscarriage of justice for about one-third of the defendants took four or less years, but it took nine years or longer for another third of the defendants. Had the expedited appeals process and limitations on habeas corpus been in effect, would these death sentences have been overturned?

A group photo of twenty-eight of the seventy-five former death row inmates released because later evidence proved their innocence. The group assembled at a conference on Wrongful Convictions and the Death Penalty held at Northwestern University.

The Death Penalty: A Continuing Controversy

As we enter the new century, the death penalty remains controversial. In January 2000, Governor George Ryan of Illinois called for a moratorium on executions in his state. He noted that since 1976 Illinois had executed twelve people yet freed thirteen from death row as innocent. He was followed by a similar call from Kansas Governor Bill Graves, the Louisiana State Bar Association, and the Philadelphia City Council. At the federal level, Vermont Senator Patrick Leahy has introduced the *Innocent Protection Act of 2000* that would make it easier for inmates to have DNA evidence tested and the results used to challenge their convictions.

Although public opinion polls show high support for the death penalty and about three hundred new death sentences are imposed each year, the number of executions remains low. Mark Costanzo (1997:123) points to surveys that show the public is about evenly split when respondents are asked to choose between life imprisonment without parole and death. Does this mean that Americans are ambivalent about carrying out the punishment? What might it say about capital punishment in the next decade? Debate on this important public policy issue has gone on for more than two hundred years, yet there is still no consensus.

Opponents of the death penalty argue that poor people and members of minority groups receive a disproportionate number of death sentences. Yet some researchers have challenged this view (Rothman and Powers, 1994)

Opponents further note that the cost to try, convict, and execute a murderer is much higher than trying that individual as a noncapital case and keeping him or her in prison for twenty years. A study of death penalty cases in North Carolina showed that the extra cost to the public of prosecuting a capital case is $216,000. And if the case ultimately results in an execution, the extra cost is more than $2.16 million (Cook and Slawson, 1993). Data from other parts of the country support this view (*Sacramento Bee*, March 28, 1988:1; *New York Newsday*, June 14, 1989:60.).

Proponents of the death penalty claim that it deters criminals from committing violent acts and that justice demands that retribution, regardless of cost, be accorded murderers. They further argue that, given the high level of violent crimes in the United States, the severest penalties must be retained. To give someone a life sentence of incarceration for murder diminishes the worth of the victim,

What Americans Think

Question "Are you in favor of the death penalty for a person convicted of murder?"

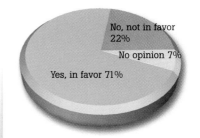

No, not in favor 22%

No opinion 7%

Yes, in favor 71%

SOURCE: U.S. Department of Justice, Bureau of Justice Statistics, *Sourcebook of Criminal Justice Statistics, 1998* (Washington, D.C.: Government Printing Office, 1999), Table 2.58.

is costly to society, and does not lessen the possibility that the offender will do further harm either while incarcerated or on release on parole. In answer to the charge that the death penalty is administered in an arbitrary and capricious manner, scholars such as Walter Berns and Joseph Bessette say that "the system now in place serves as a filter, reserving the death penalty for the worst offenders (Berns and Bessette, 1998:A16).

The criminal sanction takes many forms, and offenders are punished in various ways to serve various purposes. Table 11.2 summarizes how these sanctions operate and how they reflect the underlying philosophies of punishment.

CHECK POINT

③ **What are the three types of sentences used in the United States?**

④ **What are thought to be the advantages of intermediate sanctions?**

⑤ **What requirements specified in *Gregg v. Georgia* must exist before a death sentence may be imposed?**

TABLE 11.2   **The punishment of offenders**

The goals of the criminal sanction are carried out in a variety of ways, depending upon the provisions of the law, the characteristics of the offender, and the discretion of the judge. Judges may impose sentences that combine several forms to achieve punishment objectives.

FORM OF SANCTION	DESCRIPTION	PURPOSES
Incarceration	Imprisonment.	
Indeterminate sentence	Specifies a maximum and minimum length of time to be served.	Incapacitation, deterrence, rehabilitation.
Determinate sentence	Specifies a certain length of time to be served.	Retribution, deterrence, incapacitation.
Mandatory sentence	Specifies a minimum amount of time for given crimes that must be served.	Incapacitation, deterrence.
Good time	Subtracts days from an inmate's sentence because of good behavior or participation in prison programs.	Rewards behavior, relieves prison crowding, helps maintain prison discipline.
Intermediate sanctions	Punishment for those requiring sanctions more restrictive than probation but less restrictive than prison.	Retribution, deterrence.
Administered by the judiciary		
Fine	Money paid to state by offender.	Retribution, deterrence.
Restitution	Money paid to victim by offender.	Retribution, deterrence.
Forfeiture	Seizure by the state of property illegally obtained or acquired with resources illegally obtained.	Retribution, deterrence.
Administered in the community		
Community service	Requires offender to perform work for the community.	Retribution, deterrence.
Home confinement	Requires offender to stay in home during certain times.	Retribution, deterrence, incapacitation.
Intensive probation supervision	Requires strict and frequent reporting to probation officer.	Retribution, deterrence, incapacitation.
Administered institutionally		
Boot camp/shock incarceration	Short–term institutional sentence emphasizing physical development and discipline, followed by probation.	Retribution, deterrence, rehabilitation
Probation	Allows offender to serve a sentence in the community under supervision.	Retribution, incapacitation, rehabilitation
Death	Execution.	Incapacitation, deterrence, retribution.

The Sentencing Process

Regardless of how and where the decision has been made—misdemeanor court or felony court, plea bargain or adversarial context, bench or jury trial—judges have the responsibility for imposing sentences.

Sentencing is often difficult and is often not just a matter of applying clear-cut principles to individual cases. In one case, a judge may decide to sentence a forger to prison as an example to others, although he is no threat to community safety and he probably does not need rehabilitative treatment. In another case, the judge may impose a light sentence on a youthful offender who, although he has committed a serious crime, may be a good risk for rehabilitation if he can be moved quickly back into society. As Judge Robert Satter notes in the Close-Up (see p. 413), sentencing requires balancing the scales of justice between society, violated by a crime, and the defendant, fallible, but nonetheless human.

Legislatures establish the penal codes that set forth the sentences judges may impose. These laws generally give judges wide powers of discretion in sentencing. They may combine various forms of punishment to tailor the sanction to the offender. The judge may specify, for example, that the prison terms for two charges are to run either concurrently (at the same time) or consecutively (one after the other), or that all or part of the period of imprisonment may be suspended. In other situations, the offender may be given a combination of a suspended prison term, probation, and a fine. Judges may also suspend a sentence as long as the offender stays out of trouble, makes restitution, or seeks medical treatment. The judge may also delay imposing any sentence but retain the power to set penalties at a later date if the offender misbehaves.

Within the discretion allowed by the code, various elements in the sentencing process influence the decisions of judges. Social scientists believe several factors influence the sentencing process: (1) the administrative context of the courts, (2) the attitudes and values of judges, (3) the presentence report, and (4) sentencing guidelines.

The Administrative Context of the Courts

Judges are significantly influenced by the administrative context within which they impose sentences. As a result, differences are found, for example, between the assembly-line style of justice in the misdemeanor courts and the more formal proceedings found in felony courts.

Misdemeanor Courts: Assembly-Line Justice

Misdemeanor or lower courts have limited jurisdiction because they normally can impose prison sentences of only less than one year. These courts hear about 90 percent of criminal cases. Whereas felony cases are processed in lower courts only for arraignments and preliminary hearings, misdemeanor cases are processed completely in the lower courts. Only a minority of cases adjudicated in lower courts end in jail sentences; most cases result in fines, probation, community service, restitution, or a combination of these punishments.

Wichita, Kansas, Judge Richard Shull sentences a drug offender. With a range of intermediate sanctions, judges are able to tailor the sentence to the particular needs of the offender and the community.

CLOSE

A **Trial Judge** at Work:
Judge Robert **Satter**

I am never more conscious of striving to balance the scales of justice than when I am sentencing the convicted. On one scale is society, violated by a crime, on the other is the defendant, fallible, but nonetheless human.

As a trial judge I am faced with the insistent task of sentencing a particular defendant who never fails to assert his own individuality. . . .

George Edwards was tried before me for sexual assault, first degree. The victim, Barbara Babson, was a personable woman in her late twenties and a junior executive in an insurance company. She described on the stand what had happened to her:

I was returning to my Hartford apartment with two armloads of groceries. As I entered the elevator, a man followed me. He seemed vaguely familiar but I couldn't quite place him. When I reached my floor and started to open my door, I noticed him behind me. He offered to hold my bags. God, I knew right then I was making a mistake. He pushed me into the apartment and slammed the door. He said, "Don't you know me? I work at Travelers with you." Then I remembered him in the cafeteria and I remembered him once staring at me. Now I could feel his eyes roving over my body, and I heard him say, "I want to screw you." He said it so calmly at first, I didn't believe him. I tried to talk him out of it. When he grabbed my neck, I began to cry and then to scream. His grip tightened, and that really scared me. He forced me into the bedroom, made me take off my clothes.

"Then," she sobbed, "he pushed my legs apart and entered me."

"What happened next?" the state's attorney asked.

"He told me he was going to wait in the next room, and if I tried to leave he would kill me. I found some cardboards, wrote HELP! on them, and put them in my window. But nobody came.

Eventually I got up the courage to open the door, and he had left. I immediately called the police."

Edwards's lawyer cross-examined her vigorously, dragging her through the intimate details of her sex life. Then he tried to get her to admit that she had willingly participated in sex with the defendant. Through it all, she maintained her poise. She left the stand with her version of the crime intact.

Edwards took the stand in his own defense. A tall man with bushy hair, he was wearing baggy trousers and a rumpled shirt. In a low voice he testified that the woman had always smiled at him at work. He had learned her name and address and gone to her apartment house that day. When he offered to help her with her bundles, she invited him into her apartment. She was very nice and very willing to have sex. He denied using force.

I did not believe him. I could not conceive that Miss Babson would have called the police, pressed the charges, and relived the horrors of the experience on the stand if the crime had not been committed as she testified. The jury did not believe him either. They readily returned a verdict of guilty.

First-degree sexual assault is a class B felony punishable by a maximum of twenty years in the state prison. If I had sentenced Edwards then, I would have sent him to prison for many years. But sentencing could take place only after a presentence report had been prepared by a probation officer.

The report was dropped off in my chambers a few days before the sentencing date. Unlike the trial, which had portrayed Edwards in the context of the crime, the presentence report portrayed the crime in the context of Edwards's life.

It revealed that Edwards was thirty-one years old, born of a black father and white mother. He had graduated from high school and had an associate's degree from a community college. . . . Edwards had worked successfully as a coordinator of youth programs in the inner city of Hartford. Simultaneously he had taken computer courses. At the time of the crime, he was a computer programmer at Travelers Insurance Company. Edwards was separated from his wife and child, and fellow employees had recently noticed a personality change in him; he seemed withdrawn, depressed, and sometimes confused. His only criminal offense was a disorderly conduct charge three months before the crime, which had not been prosecuted.

I gazed out the window of my chambers and reflected. What should be my sentence?

Before the rescheduled date, I had weighed the factors, made up my mind, and lived with my decision for several days. In serious criminal cases I do not like to make snap judgments from the bench. I may sometimes allow myself to be persuaded by the lawyers' arguments to reduce a preconceived sentence, but never to raise it.

I nod to the state's attorney to begin. He asks to have Miss Babson speak first. She comes forward to the counsel table. "That man," she says, pointing to Edwards, "did a horrible thing. He should be severely punished not only for what he did to me, but for what he could do to other women. I am furious at him. As far as I am concerned, Judge, I hope you lock him up and throw away the key."

She abruptly stops and sits down. The state's attorney deliberately pauses to let her words sink in before he stands up. Speaking with less emotion but equal determination, he says,

This was a vicious crime. There are not many more serious than rape. The defendant cynically tried to put the blame on the victim. But it didn't wash. She has been damaged in the most fundamental way. And the defendant doesn't show the slightest remorse. I urge the maximum punishment of twenty years in prison.

Edwards's lawyer starts off by mentioning his client's lack of a criminal record. Then he goes on, "George and his wife have begun living together again with their child, and they are trying to pick up the pieces of their lives. More important," the lawyer continues, "George started seeing a psychiatrist six weeks ago."

The lawyer concludes, "If you will give George a suspended sentence, Your Honor, and make a condition of probation that he

stay in treatment, he won't be before this court again. George Edwards is a good risk."

I look at Edwards. "Do you have anything you want to say, Mr. Edwards?"

The question takes him by surprise. Gathering his thoughts, he says with emotion, "I'm sorry for what I did, Judge. I'm sorry for Barbara, and I understand how she feels. I'm sorry for my wife. I'm . . ." His voice trails off.

I gaze out the courtroom window struggling for the words to express my sentence. I am always conscious that the same sentence can be given in a way that arouses grudging acceptance or deep hostility.

Mr. Edwards, you have committed a serious crime. I am not going to punish you to set an example for others, because you should not be held responsible for the incidence of crime in our society. I am going to punish you because, as a mature person, you must pay a price for your offense. The state's attorney asks for twenty years because of the gravity of the crime. Your attorney asks for a suspended sentence because you are attempting to deal with whatever within you caused you to commit the crime. Both make valid arguments. I am partially adopting both recommendations. I herewith sentence you to state prison for six years.

Edwards wilts. His wife gasps. I continue.

However, I am suspending execution after four years. I am placing you on probation for the two-year balance of your term on the condition that you continue in psychiatric treatment until discharged by your doctor. The state is entitled to punish you for the crime that you have committed and the harm you have done. You are entitled to leniency for what I discern to be the sincere effort you are making to help yourself.

Edwards turns to his wife, who rushes up to embrace him. Miss Babson nods to me, not angrily, I think. She walks out of the courtroom and back into her life. As I rise at the bench, a sheriff is leading Edwards down the stairwell to the lockup.

SOURCE: Robert Satter, *Doing Justice: A Trial Judge at Work* (New York: Simon & Schuster, 1990), 170–181. Copyright (c) 1990 by Robert Satter. Reprinted by permission of the author.

Most lower courts are overloaded and allot minimal time to each case. Judicial decisions are mass produced because actors in the system share three assumptions. First, any person appearing before the court is guilty, because doubtful cases have presumably been filtered out by the police and prosecution. Second, the vast majority of defendants will plead guilty. Third, those charged with minor offenses will be processed in volume, with dozens of cases being decided in rapid succession within a single hour. The citation will be read by the clerk, a guilty plea entered, and the sentence pronounced by the judge for one defendant after another.

Defendants whose cases are processed through the lower court assembly line may appear to receive little or no punishment. However, people who get caught in the criminal justice system experience other punishments, whether or not they are ultimately convicted. A person who is arrested but then released at some point in the process still incurs various tangible and intangible costs. Time spent in jail awaiting trial, the cost of a bail bond, and days of work lost have an immediate and concrete impact. Poor people may lose their jobs or be evicted from their homes if they fail to work and pay their bills for even a few days. For most people, simply being arrested is a devastating experience. It is impossible to measure the psychic and social price of being stigmatized, separated from family, and deprived of freedom (Feeley, 1979).

Felony Courts

Felony cases are processed and offenders are sentenced in courts of general jurisdiction. Because of the seriousness of the crimes, the atmosphere is more formal and generally lacks the chaotic, assembly-line environment of misdemeanor courts. Caseload burdens can affect how much time is devoted to individual cases. Exchange relationships among courtroom actors can facilitate plea bargains and shape the content of prosecutors' sentencing recommendations. Sentencing decisions are ultimately shaped, in part, by the relationships, negotiations, and agreements among the prosecutor, defense attorney, and judge. Table 11.3 shows the types of felony sentences imposed for different conviction offenses.

Attitudes and Values of Judges

All lawyers recognize that judges differ from one another in their sentencing decisions. The differences can be explained in part by the conflicting goals of criminal justice, administrative pressures, and the influence of community values. Sentencing decisions also depend on judges' attitudes toward the law, toward a particular crime, or toward a type of offender.

Judges are products of different backgrounds and have different social values. Martin Levin's now classic study of the criminal courts of Pittsburgh and Minneapolis showed the influence of judges' values on sentencing behavior. He found that Pittsburgh judges, all of whom came from humble backgrounds, exhibited a greater empathy toward defendants than did judges in

TABLE 11.3   Types of felony sentences imposed by state courts

Although a felony conviction is often equated with a sentence to prison, almost a third of felony offenders are given probation.

MOST SERIOUS CONVICTION OFFENSE	PERCENTAGE OF FELONS SENTENCED TO		
	PRISON	JAIL	PROBATION
All offenses	38%	31%	31%
Violent offenses	57	22	21
Murder	92	3	5
Sexual assault	63	16	21
Robbery	73	14	13
Aggravated assault	42	30	28
Other violent	38	34	27
Property offenses	34	28	38
Burglary	45	26	29
Larceny	31	32	37
Fraud	26	24	50
Drug offenses	35	37	28
Possession	29	41	30
Trafficking	39	33	27
Weapons offenses	40	27	33
Other offenses	31	32	37

NOTE: For persons receiving a combination of sanctions, the sentence designation came from the most severe penalty imposed—prison being the most severe, followed by jail and then probation.

SOURCE: U.S. Department of Justice, Bureau of Justice Statistics, *Felony Sentences in State Courts, 1996* (Washington, D.C.: Government Printing Office, 1999), 2.

Minneapolis, who tended to come from upper-class backgrounds. While the Pittsburgh judges tried to make decisions that they believed would help straighten out the troubled defendants' lives, the Minneapolis judges were more inclined to follow the law precisely and to emphasize society's need for protection from crime (Levin, 1998).

It is widely assumed that judges are predisposed to treat female offenders less severely than men. Research on sentencing in Pennsylvania suggests that judges are concerned not only with an offender's prior record and level of involvement in the crime, but also such practical considerations as the responsibility for children, pregnancy, and availability of prison space (Steffensmeier, Kramer, and Strifel, 1993). Kathleen Daly and Rebecca Bordt (1995) found that gender effects are more likely to be found for felony offenses, for those prosecuted in urban courts, and in the decision to incarcerate, than in the length of sentence.

Presentence Report

Even though sentencing is the judge's responsibility, the **presentence report** has become an important ingredient in the judicial mix. Usually a probation officer investigates the convicted person's background, criminal record, job status, and mental condition to suggest a sentence that is in the interests of both the offender and society. Although the primary purpose of the presentence report is to help the judge select the sentence, it also assists in the classification of probationers, prisoners, and parolees for treatment planning and risk assessment. In the report, the probation officer makes judgments about what information to include and what conclusions to draw from that information. In some states, however, probation officers present only factual material to the judge and make no sentencing recommendation. The probation officer is not required to follow evidentiary rules and may include hearsay statements as well as first-hand information. The Close-Up gives an example of a presentence report (see p. 418).

Although presentence reports are represented as diagnostic evaluations, critics point out that they are not scientific and often reflect stereotypes. John Rosencrance has argued that in practice the presentence report primarily serves to maintain the myth of individualized justice. He found that the present offense and the prior criminal record determine the probation officer's final sentencing recommendation (Rosencrance, 1988:235). He learned that officers begin by reviewing the case and typing the defendant as one who should fit into a particular sentencing category. Their investigations are then conducted mainly to gather further information to buttress their early decision.

The presentence report is one means by which judges ease the strain of decision making. The report lets judges shift partial responsibility to the probation department. Because a substantial number of sentencing alternatives are open to judges, they often rely on the report for guidance. A Question of Ethics (p. 419) illustrates some of the difficulties faced by a judge who must impose a sentence with little more than the presentence report to go on.

Sentencing Guidelines

Since the 1980s **sentencing guidelines** have been established in the federal courts and in seventeen states, and they are being developed in three other states (BJA, 1998). Guidelines are designed to indicate to judges the expected sanction for particular types of offenses. They are intended to limit the sentencing discretion of

presentence report
Report prepared by probation officer, who investigates a convicted offender's background to help the judge select an appropriate sentence.

sentencing guidelines
A mechanism to indicate to judges the expected sanction for certain offenses, to reduce disparities in sentencing.

CLOSE

up

SAMPLE PRESENTENCE
REPORT

STATE OF NEW MEXICO

Corrections Department
Field Service Division
Santa Fe, New Mexico 87501

Date: January 4, 2000

To: The Honorable Manuel Baca

From: Presentence Unit, Officer Brian Gaines

Re: Richard Knight

EVALUATION

Appearing before Your Honor for sentencing is 20-year-old Richard Knight, who on November 10, 1999, pursuant to a Plea and Disposition Agreement, entered a plea of guilty to Aggravated Assault Upon a Peace Officer (Deadly Weapon) (Firearm Enhancement), as charged in Information Number 95-5736900. The terms of the agreement stipulate that the maximum period of incarceration be limited to one year, that restitution be made on all counts and charges whether dismissed or not, and that all remaining charges in the Indictment and DA files 39780 be dismissed.

The defendant is an only child, born and raised in Albuquerque. He attended West Mesa High School until the eleventh grade, at which time he dropped out. Richard declared that he felt school was "too difficult" and that he decided that it would be more beneficial for him to obtain steady employment rather than to complete his education. The defendant further stated that he felt it was "too late for vocational training" because of the impending one-year prison sentence he faces, because of the Firearm Enhancement penalty for his offense.

The longest period of time the defendant has held a job has been for six months with Frank's Concrete Company. He has been employed with the Madrid Construction Company since August 1998 (verified). Richard lives with his parents who provide most of his financial support. Conflicts between his mother and himself, the defendant claimed, precipitated his recent lawless actions by causing him to "not care about anything." He stressed the fact that he is now once again "getting along" with his mother. Although the defendant contends that he doesn't abuse drugs, he later contradicted himself by declaring that he "gets drunk every weekend." He noted that he was inebriated when he committed the present offense.

In regard to the present offense, the defendant recalled that other individuals at the party attempted to stab his friend and that he and his companion left and returned with a gun to settle the score. Richard claimed remorse for his offense and stated that his past family problems led him to spend most of his time on the streets, where he became more prone to violent conduct. The defendant admitted being a member of the 18th Street Gang.

RECOMMENDATION

It is respectfully recommended that the defendant be sentenced to three years incarceration and that the sentence be suspended. It is further recommended that the defendant be incarcerated for one year as to the mandatory Firearm Enhancement and then placed on three years probation under the following special conditions:

① That restitution be made to Juan Lopez in the amount of $622.40.

② That the defendant either maintain full-time employment or obtain his GED [general equivalency diploma], and

③ That the defendant discontinue fraternizing with the 18th Street Gang members and terminate his own membership in the gang.

judges and to reduce disparity among sentences given for similar offenses. Although statutes provide a variety of sentencing options for particular crimes, guidelines attempt to direct the judge to more specific actions that *should* be taken. The range of sentencing options provided for most offenses is based on the seriousness of the crime and on the criminal history of an offender.

Legislatures—and in some states and the federal government, commissions—construct sentencing guidelines as a grid of two scores (Tonry, 1993:140). As shown in Table 11.4, one dimension relates to the seriousness of the offense, and the other to the likelihood of offender recidivism. The offender score is obtained by totaling the points allocated to such factors as the number of juvenile, adult misdemeanor, and adult felony convictions; the number of times incarcerated; the status of the accused at the time of the last offense, whether on probation or parole or escaped from confinement; and employment status or educational achievement. Judges look at the grid to see what sentence should be imposed on a particular offender who has committed a specific offense. Judges may go outside of the guidelines if aggravating or mitigating circumstances exist; however, they must provide a written explanation of their reasons for doing so (Kramer and Ulmer, 1996).

Sentencing guidelines are to be reviewed and modified periodically so that recent decisions will be included. Given that guidelines are constructed on the basis of past sentences, some critics argue that because the guidelines reflect only what has happened, they do not reform sentencing. Others question the choice of characteristics included in the offender scale and charge that some are used to mask racial criteria (Petersilia and Turner, 1987). However, Lisa Stolzenberg and Stewart J. D'Alessio (1994) studied the Minnesota guidelines and found, compared with preguideline decisions, an 18 percent reduction in disparity for the prison/no prison outcome and a 60 percent reduction in disparity of length of prison sentences.

Although guidelines have been found to make sentences more uniform, many judges object to having their discretion limited in this manner (Weinstein, 1992). In particular, many scholars and judges view the U.S. Sentencing Commission Guidelines as impossibly complex, politically motivated, and unduly harsh (Rothman, 1994; *Washington Post*, October 6, 1996).

A Question of Ethics

Seated in her chambers, Judge Ruth Carroll read the presentence investigation report of the two young men she would sentence when court resumed. She had not heard these cases. As often happens in this overworked courthouse, the cases had been given to her only for sentencing. Judge Harold Krisch had handled the arraignment, plea, and trial.

The codefendants had held up a convenience store in the early morning hours, terrorizing the young manager and taking $47.50 from the till.

As she read the reports, Judge Carroll noticed that they looked similar. Each offender had dropped out of high school, had held a series of low-wage jobs, and had one prior conviction for which probation was imposed. Each had been convicted of Burglary 1, robbery at night with a gun.

Then she noticed the difference. David Bukowski had pleaded guilty to the charge in exchange for a promise of leniency. Richard Leach had been convicted on the same charge after a one-week trial. Judge Carroll pondered the decisions that she would soon have to make. Should Leach receive a stiffer sentence because he had taken the court's time and resources? Did she have an obligation to impose the light sentence recommended for Bukowski by the prosecutor and the defender?

There was a knock on the door. The bailiff stuck his head in. "Everything's ready, your honor."

"Okay, Ben, let's go."

■ How would you decide? What factors would weigh in your decision? How would you explain your decision?

CHECK POINT

⑥ **What are the four factors thought to influence the sentencing behavior of judges?**

TABLE 11.4 Minnesota sentencing guidelines grid (presumptive sentence length in months)

The italicized numbers in the grid are the range within which a judge may sentence without the sentence being considered a departure. The criminal history score is computed by adding one point for each prior felony conviction, one-half point for each prior gross misdemeanor conviction, and one-quarter point for each prior misdemeanor conviction.

	LESS SERIOUS ← CRIMINAL HISTORY SCORE → MORE SERIOUS						
SEVERITY OF OFFENSE (ILLUSTRATIVE OFFENSES)	0	1	2	3	4	5	6 OR MORE
Sale of simulated controlled substance	12	12	12	13	15	17	19 *18–20*
Theft-related crimes ($2,500 or less) Check Forgery ($200–$2,500)	12	12	13	15	17	19	21 *20–22*
Theft crimes ($2,500 or less)	12	13	15	17	19 *18–20*	22 *21–23*	25 *24–26*
Nonresidential burglary theft crimes (more than $2,500)	12	15	18	21	25 *24–26*	32 *30–34*	41 *37–45*
Residential burglary simple robbery	18	25	27	30 *29–31*	38 *36–40*	46 *43–49*	54 *50–58*
Criminal sexual conduct, second degree	21	26	30	34 *33–35*	44 *42–46*	54 *50–58*	65 *60–70*
Aggravated robbery	48 *44–52*	58 *54–62*	68 *64–72*	78 *74–82*	88 *84–92*	98 *94–102*	108 *104–112*
Criminal sexual conduct, first degree Assault, first degree	86 *81–91*	98 *93–103*	110 *105–115*	122 *117–127*	134 *129–139*	146 *141–151*	158 *153–163*
Murder, third degree Murder, second degree (felony murder)	150 *144–156*	165 *159–171*	180 *174–186*	195 *189–201*	210 *204–216*	225 *219–231*	240 *234–246*
Murder, second degree (with intent)	306 *299–313*	326 *319–333*	346 *339–353*	366 *359–373*	386 *379–393*	406 *399–413*	426 *419–433*

■ At the discretion of the judge, up to a year in jail and/or other nonjail sanctions can be imposed instead of prison sentences as conditions of probation for most of these offenses. If prison is imposed, the presumptive sentence is the number of months shown.
□ Presumptive commitment to state prison for all offenses.

NOTE: First-degree murder is excluded from the guidelines by law and is punished by life imprisonment.

SOURCE: *Seeking Justice: Crime and Punishment in America* (New York: Edna McConnell Clark Foundation, 1997).

Who Gets the Harshest Punishment?

The prison population in most states contains a higher proportion of African American and Hispanic American men than is found in the general population. Women are less represented in jails and prisons (Daly and Tonry, 1997). Poor people are more likely to be convicted of crimes than those with higher incomes. Are these disparities the result of the prejudicial attitudes of judges, police officers, and prosecutors? Are poor people more likely to commit crimes that elicit a strong response from society? Are enforcement resources distributed so that certain groups are subject to closer scrutiny than other groups?

Charges of racial discrimination have been leveled at all stages of the criminal justice process, however much of the harshest criticism has focused on judges' sentencing decisions. Some argue that African Americans and Hispanics receive much harsher sentences than do whites who commit the same crimes. These critics say that American judges are mainly white men and use their sentencing discretion inappropriately (Mann, 1993). Other scholars contend that sentencing decisions are not racially motivated (Wilbanks, 1987).

Another serious dilemma for the criminal justice system concerns those who are falsely convicted and sentenced. Whereas much public concern is expressed over those who "beat the system" and go free, comparatively little attention is paid to those who are innocent, yet convicted. The development of DNA (deoxyribonucleic acid) technology has increased the number of people convicted by juries and later exonerated by science. Since 1989, DNA testing has excluded the primary suspect in 25 percent of sexual assault cases referred to the FBI (Connors, Lundregan, Miller, and McEwen, 1996).

Each year several cases of the conviction of innocent persons come to national attention. Two examples, announced within days of each other, come from Illinois:

> Since 1977 Illinois executed eleven people and eleven others were freed after it was decided their conviction was wrongly decided. Four of these men, who had spent nearly twenty years in prison for a double murder, were released after a Northwestern University journalism class uncovered police and prosecution bungling. Cook County paid $36 million to settle a lawsuit brought by the four (*San Francisco Chronicle,* March 6, 1999:A3).

> In 1999 seven DuPage (Illinois) County prosecutors and deputy sheriffs went on trial accused of knowingly using false evidence or withholding evidence so as to convict a man of the 1983 rape and murder of a 10 year old girl. Rolando Cruz spent 10 years on death row and was exonerated only when one of the sheriff's officers recanted his testimony (*New York Times,* March 3, 1999:A1).

How prevalent are such miscarriages of justice? Objective evidence is unclear. Eyewitness error, unethical conduct by police and prosecutors, community pressure, false accusations, inadequacy of counsel, and plea bargaining pressures are usually cited as contributing to wrongful convictions. Beyond the fact that the real criminal is presumably still free in such cases, the standards of society are damaged when an innocent person has been wrongfully convicted.

Summary

- Four goals of the criminal sanction are acknowledged in the United States—retribution, deterrence, incapacitation, and rehabilitation.
- Restoration is a new approach to punishment.
- These goals are carried out through incarceration, intermediate sanctions, probation, and death.
- Penal codes vary as to whether the permitted sentences are indeterminate, determinate, or mandatory. Each type of sentence makes certain assumptions about the goals of the criminal sanction.
- Good time allows correctional administrators to reduce the sentence of prisoners who live according to the rules and participate in various vocational, educational, and treatment programs.

■ Capital punishment is allowed by the U.S. Supreme Court if the judge and jury are allowed to take into account mitigating and aggravating circumstances.

■ Judges have considerable discretion in fashioning sentences to take into account factors such as the seriousness of the crime, the offender's prior record, and mitigating and aggravating circumstances.

■ The sentencing process is influenced by the administrative context of the courts, the attitudes and values of the judges, and the presentence report.

■ Sentencing guidelines have been formulated in many states as a way of reducing disparity among the sentences given offenders in similar situations.

Questions for Review

❶ What are the major differences among retribution, deterrence, incapacitation, and rehabilitation?

❷ What is the major purpose of restoration?

❸ What are the forms of the criminal sanction?

❹ What purposes do intermediate sanctions serve?

❺ What has been the Supreme Court's position on the constitutionality of the death penalty?

❻ Is there a link between sentences and social class and race?

Key Terms and Cases

determinate sentence (p. 399)
general deterrence (p. 390)
incapacitation (p. 392)
indeterminate sentence (p. 398)
intermediate sanctions (p. 403)
mandatory sentence (p. 400)
presentence report (p. 417)

presumptive sentence (p. 399)
probation (p. 404)
rehabilitation (p. 393)
restoration (p. 394)
retribution (p. 389)
selective incapacitation (p. 392)
sentencing guidelines (p. 417)

shock probation (p. 404)
special deterrence (p. 391)
Furman v. Georgia (1972) (p. 406)
Gregg v. Georgia (1976) (p. 406)
McCleskey v. Kemp (1987) (p. 407)

For Further Reading

Costanzo, Mark. *Just Revenge.* New York: St. Martin's Press, 1997. Analyzes the costs and consequences of the death penalty. Finds that when given an option there is higher support for life without parole than for death.

Gaylin, Willard. *The Killing of Bonnie Garland,* 2d ed. New York: Simon & Schuster, 1995. True story of the murder of a Yale student by her boyfriend and the reaction of the criminal justice system to the crime. Raises important questions about the

goals of the criminal sanction and the role of the victim in the process.

Johnson, Robert. *Death Work,* 2d ed. Belmont, Calif.: Wadsworth, 1998. A look at those on death row—prisoners and correctional officers—and the impact of capital punishment on their lives.

Prejean, Helen. *Dead Man Walking.* New York: Random House, 1993. An account by a Roman Catholic nun of her association with Patrick Sonnier,

a condemned prisoner in Louisiana, as he faces execution.

Satter, Robert. *Doing Justice: A Trial Judge at Work.* New York: Simon & Schuster, 1990. One judge's view of his daily caseload and the factors influencing his decisions.

Scheck, Barry, Peter Neufeld, and Jim Dwyer. *Actual Innocence.* New York: Doubleday, 2000. Describes the harrowing stories of ten men wrongly convicted and the efforts of the Innonence Project to free them.

Tonry, Michael. *Sentencing Matters.* New York: Oxford University Press, 1996. Examination of sentencing reforms over the past quarter century; critiques of the just deserts model, sentencing guidelines, and mandatory penalties.

Zimring, Franklin E., and Gordon Hawkins. *Incapacitation.* New York: Oxford University Press, 1995. Examines the theoretical issues surrounding incapacitation and its use to justify imprisonment today.

Going Online

1 Go to the web site of Families Against Mandatory Minimums (FAMM) at www.famm.org. Click to "All About Mandatory Minimums." What is the principle characteristic of this type of sentence? What has been its impact according to FAMM?

2 The web site of the Death Penalty Information Center at www. essential.org/dpic/ contains a wealth of information. Under "Information Topics" examine the data concerning the race of the victim and the race of the offender. Compare intraracial versus interacial punishments.

3 Using InfoTrac College Edition, search for the subject "capital punishment." Find an article on the relationship between the news media and capital punishment. What impact does the news media have on public perceptions of the death penalty?

CHECK POINT ANSWERS

1 Retribution, deterrence, incapacitation, rehabilitation.

2 It is impossible to show who has been deterred from committing crimes; punishment is not always certain; people act impulsively rather than rationally; people commit crimes while on drugs.

3 Determinate, indeterminate, and mandatory sentences.

4 Intermediate sanctions give judges a greater range of sentencing alternatives, reduce prison populations, cost less than prison, and increase community security.

5 Judge and jury must be able to consider mitigating and aggravating circumstances, proceedings must be divided into a trial phase and a punishment phase, and there must be opportunities for appeal.

6 The administrative context of the courts, the attitudes and values of judges, the presentence report, and sentencing guidelines.

Should Mandatory Minimum Sentences for Drug Offenders Be Abolished?

I nside the maximum security unit of the Kansas State Prison for Women, Gloria Van Winkle is in the seventh year of a life term for possession of $40 worth of cocaine. A mother of two and a drug addict with two prior convictions, she was arrested after a convicted thief told undercover agents she was smoking crack and they set up a sting. In Kentucky, Louie Cordell, a 55-year-old father of nine with no prior convictions, is finishing a mandatory five-year federal sentence for growing 141 marijuana plants. Anthony Papa, who ran a small auto repair shop in New York City, agreed to deliver a little more than four ounces of cocaine to earn $500. Recipients of the cocaine turned out to be two undercover agents. Papa is in Sing Sing serving fifteen years to life.

All of the prisoners described above are nonviolent drug offenders sentenced under mandatory minimum laws, among the most politically popular crime-fighting measures in recent years. Such laws require the judge to impose a sentence of at least a specific amount of time if certain criteria are met. For example, a person convicted by a federal court of possessing half a kilogram or more of cocaine powder must be sentenced to at least five years in prison. The judge has no discretion to weigh the characteristics of the offender and the circumstances of the offense. In the federal system and in many states, early release on parole or through "good-time" reductions do not apply to these sentences.

Although some types of mandatory sentences have existed for many years, their use greatly expanded during the 1980s as a weapon in the "war on drugs." The mandatory aspect of these laws reflects a belief that judges cannot be relied upon to dispense sentences that are "tough." Since 1984, each Congress has enacted new laws extending mandatory sentences for various drug and firearms offenses, violent crimes, drug crimes involving firearms, and involvement in a drug crime conspiracy. All states and the federal government now have mandatory minimum sentencing laws targeted to certain types of offenses.

Proponents of mandatory minimums argue that their certainty and severity help ensure that incarceration's goals will be achieved. Those goals included punishing the convicted, ensuring that they will not commit additional crimes while in prison, and deterring others from committing similar offenses. Critics of the laws say that by taking away the discretionary power of judges, sentences are mechanically imposed without consideration for mitigating factors. In many jurisdictions judges may impose a lesser sentence only if the prosecutor agrees that the defendant has provided "substantial assistance" in bringing others to justice. Critics believe that mandatory minimums result in too many draconian sentences that are unjust.

The most obvious impact of mandatory minimums is the great increase of drug offenders in America's prisons and jails. Since 1978, the number of violent offenders entering prison doubled, the number of nonviolent offenders tripled, and the number of nonviolent drug offenders increased eightfold. In Massachusetts nearly 50 percent of drug offenders have no record of violent crime. In New York, seventy thousand inmates and 47 percent of new offenders entering prison have committed only nonviolent drug crimes. Analysts have calculated that nationally the $24 billion to incarcerate nonviolent offenders is almost 50 percent larger than the entire federal welfare budget and is six times what the government spends on child care.

But do mandatory minimums reduce the use of drugs? A RAND study found that they are not a cost-effective method for reducing drug use. Enforcement usually targets low-level street dealers, mules, and addicts rather than the "kingpins" who import and distribute drugs to the market. Sentencing street dealers to long terms results in high incarceration costs without reducing sales because the offender is easily replaced in the marketplace. Some argue that shifting to discretionary sentences of reasonable length and spending the money saved on drug treatment and prevention would be more efficient.

Since 1993 several states have repealed or reformed their drug sentencing laws. In Michigan, which required a mandatory life sentence with no parole for possession of more than 650 grams of cocaine or heroin, the law now specifies twenty years to life with the possibility of parole after fifteen years. Arizona now offers treatment instead of prison to nonviolent drug offenders. Similar reform efforts are under way in Iowa, Massachusetts, New York, Oregon, Pennsylvania, and South Carolina. In 1994 Congress adopted a "safety valve" provision that applies to federal drug cases. Under this law, judges are permitted to sentence offenders below the mandatory minimum (but not less than two years in prison) if the offender has a minimal prior record, if no violence was used in the offense, and if the offender provides "substantial assistance" to the prosecution. Twenty percent of federal drug cases are now sentenced in this manner. However, Congress has not taken the step to make the "safety valve" applicable to cases sentenced prior to 1994.

For Mandatory Minimum Sentences for Drug Offenders

Supporters of mandatory minimum sentences argue that drugs are a major problem that has a devastating impact on American society. Sentencing offenders to long prison terms removes them from the community so that they cannot commit new crimes. Long sentences also send a message of deterrence to others who might be tempted to enter the drug culture. Long sentences are cost-effective because drug offenders cost society much more in the community than in prison by victimizing others through their criminal acts.

To summarize the arguments for mandatory minimum sentences:

- Long prison terms are an effective way of dealing with drug offenders because, while incarcerated, they are unable to sell or use drugs.
- Long prison terms serve as a deterrent to others.
- Mandatory sentences are necessary to ensure that judges follow the legislature's intent of imposing harsh sentences.
- Mandatory sentences aid prosecutors in securing the assistance of defendants who will implicate others in exchange for charges that bring a lesser term.

Against Mandatory Minimum Sentences for Drug Offenders

Critics of mandatory minimum sentences for drug offenders point to the length and the mechanistic, inflexible characteristics of these sentences. They argue that the judge should be able to tailor the sentence to the offender and the crime. Sentencing discretion has been shifted from the judge to the prosecutor whose charging decision has the de facto impact of setting the sentence. Too many people, they say, are serving long terms way out of proportion to the circumstances of their offense. Mandatory minimums have filled prisons with low-level drug offenders serving long sentences at enormous and growing cost to taxpayers. The impact of these sentences has devastated low-income and minority communities.

To summarize the arguments against mandatory minimum sentences for drug offenders:

- Judges should have the ability to tailor sentences to the individual circumstances of the offense and the offender.
- Mandatory minimum sentences are too long and out of proportion to the severity of the offenses.

- Mandatory minimum sentences without provisions for good time or parole provide no incentive for offenders to enter treatment or educational programs.
- Mandatory minimums have resulted in the incarceration of great numbers of first-time, nonviolent drug offenders at tremendous cost to society.

What Should U.S. Policy Be?

As fear of crime and drugs became a hot issue in the 1980s, political leaders sought to toughen policies to severely punish offenders. Long, mandatory minimum sentences were imposed by Congress and most states to target those who were convicted of violent crimes and those who imported, distributed, and sold drugs, especially crack cocaine. One result was to greatly increase the number of drug offenders sent to prison. Researchers have pointed out that incarceration is very costly and that large numbers of those given long mandatory minimum sentences were low-level nonviolent drug offenders.

Calls are now being heard to reform the mandatory minimum strategy so that it will be used for only the most serious offenders. Yet legislators may be hesitant to make these changes because they fear the consequence of appearing to be "soft on crime." Should mandatory minimum sentences be changed? Should good time and parole be made available to nonviolent drug offenders? Should treatment, not imprisonment, become the policy objective? What are the costs to the community and to offenders and their families if the present policies are maintained?

Corrections

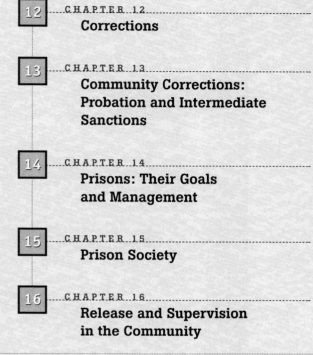

Throughout history the debate has continued about the most appropriate and effective ways to punish lawbreakers. Over time the corrections system has risen to peaks of excited reform, only to drop to valleys of despairing failure. In Part Four, how the American system of criminal justice now deals with offenders is examined. The process of corrections is intended to penalize the individual found guilty, to impress upon others that violators of the law will be punished, to protect the community, and to rehabilitate and reintegrate the offender into law-abiding society.

Chapters 12 through 16 will discuss how various influences have structured the U.S. correctional system and how offenders are punished. As these chapters unfold, recall the processes that have occurred before the sentence was imposed and how they are linked to the ways offenders are punished in the correctional portion of the criminal justice system.

Corrections

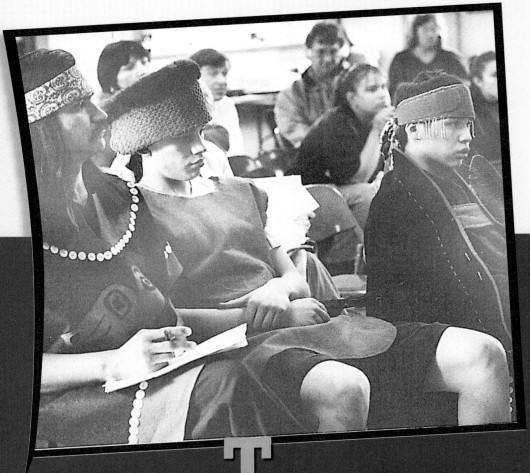

Two teenage Native Americans, convicted of robbing and beating a pizza delivery driver in Everett, Washington, were sentenced by the Tlingit Tribal Court to spend twelve to eighteen months on separate uninhabited islands off the Alaskan coast. Such a banishment was not an option according to the Washington state penal code, which required that the Superior Court of Snohomish County sentence first-time robbery offenders to three to five years in prison. With the court's approval, however, the alternative punishment was arranged by Rudy James, a Tlingit tribal elder. The Tlingit offenders, Adrian Guthrie and Simon Roberts, were given only sleeping bags, forks for digging clams, axes, and enough food to carry them through the first five days. They were expected to live alone without modern conveniences (*New York Times,* September 1, 1994:1).

Banishment is an ancient punishment that has not been formally imposed by a U.S. court since the beginning of the republic. The punishment of these two young offenders shows that prison is not the only form of corrections. Students of criminal justice are not surprised to learn that less than one-third of offenders under supervision are in prisons and jails. Most offenders are punished in the community through probation, intermediate sanctions, and parole. But because of the folklore, films, and songs about prison life in the culture, most Americans understandably think of incarceration when they think of corrections.

corrections

The variety of programs, services, facilities, and organizations responsible for the management of people who have been accused or convicted of criminal offenses.

Corrections refers to the great number of programs, services, facilities, and organizations responsible for the management of people accused or convicted of criminal offenses. In addition to prisons and jails, corrections includes probation, halfway houses, education and work release, parole supervision, counseling, and community service. Correctional programs operate in Salvation Army hostels, forest camps, medical clinics, and urban storefronts.

Since the early 1970s, corrections has experienced unprecedented growth. This growth means that more Americans than ever have direct experience with the corrections system. Now more than 5.7 million adults and juveniles receive correctional supervision from more than 500,000 administrators, psychologists, officers, counselors, social workers, and other professionals. An astounding 2.9 percent of U.S. adults (1 of every 20 men and 1 of every 100 women) are incarcerated or on probation or parole.

The expansion of corrections is particularly alarming considering that 1 of every 6 African American adult males and 1 of 3 African American males in their 20s are under some form of correctional supervision. In some cities, such as Baltimore, Detroit, and Philadelphia, as much as half of this group is being supervised.

Corrections is authorized by all levels of government, is administered by both public and private organizations, and costs almost $35 billion a year (BJS, 1999k:3). This chapter will examine (1) the history of corrections, (2) the organization of corrections, and (3) the directions incarceration is headed.

QUESTIONS
for Inquiry

How has the American system of corrections developed?

What roles are played by federal, state, and local governments in corrections?

Why has the prison population more than doubled in the last ten years?

Development of Corrections

How did corrections get where it is today? Why are offenders now placed on probation or incarcerated instead of whipped or burned as in colonial times? Over the past two hundred years, ideas about punishment have moved like a pendulum from one direction to far in another direction (see Figure 12.1 and Table 12.1). As the development of present-day policies is reviewed, think about how future changes in society may lead to new forms of corrections.

FIGURE 12.1 **Development of corrections in the United States**

Correctional policies have evolved over time. Elements from each era can be found in corrections procedures today.

1700s

CORPORAL PUNISHMENT
During the colonial and early post–Revolutionary years, Americans used physical punishment, a legacy from Europe.

1800s

PENITENTIARY MOVEMENT
A major idea of the Enlightenment, which shook Europe and the United States in the early 1800s, was that criminals should be placed in institutions where they would have opportunities for work and penitence.

1950s

REHABILITATION MODEL
The rise of psychology shifted the emphasis of corrections to reform of offenders through treatment programs.

1970s

COMMUNITY MODEL
Criticisms of correctional institutions led to the belief that most offenders should be supervised in the community so that they could be reintegrated into society.

1980s—Present

INCARCERATION MODEL
Contemporary crime control policies place greater emphasis on the incarceration of offenders.

TABLE 12.1 **History of corrections in America**

Note the extent to which correctional policies have shifted from one era to the next and are influenced by societal factors.

	CORRECTIONAL MODEL					
Colonial (1600s—1790s)	Penitentiary (1790s—1860s)	Reformatory (1870s—1890s)	Progressive (1890s—1930s)	Medical (1930s—1960s)	Community (1960s—1970s)	Crime Control (1970s—2000s)
Features						
Anglican Code	Separate confinement	Indeterminate sentences	Individual case approach	Rehabilitation as primary focus of incarceration	Reintegration into community	Determinate sentences
Capital and corporal punishment, fines	Reform of individual	Parole	Administrative discretion	Psychological testing and classification	Avoidance of incarceration	Mandatory sentences
	Power of isolation and labor	Classification by degree of individual reform	Broader probation and parole	Various types of treatment programs and institutions	Vocational and educational programs	Sentencing guidelines
	Penance	Rehabilitative programs	Juvenile courts			Risk management
	Disciplined routine	Separate treatment for juveniles				
	Punishment according to severity of crime					
Philosophical basis						
Religious law	Enlightenment	National Prison Association Declaration of Principles	The Age of Reform	Biomedical science	Civil rights movement	Crime control
Doctrine of predestination	Declaration of Independence		Positivist school	Psychiatry and psychology	Critique of prisons	Rising crime rates
	Human perfectability and powers of reason	Crime as moral disease	Punishment according to needs of offender	Social work practice	Small is better	Political shift to the right
	Religious penitence	Criminals as "victims of social disorder"	Focus on the offender	Crime as signal of personal "distress" or "failure"		New punitive agenda
	Power of reformation		Crime as an urban, immigrant ghetto problem			
	Focus on the act					
	Healing power of suffering					

Invention of the Penitentiary

Enlightenment

A movement during the eighteenth century in England and France, in which concepts of liberalism, rationalism, equality, and individualism dominated social and political thinking.

The late eighteenth century stands out as a remarkable period. At that time scholars and social reformers in Europe and America were rethinking the nature of society and the place of the individual in it. During the **Enlightenment,** as this period was called, philosophers and reformers challenged tradition with new ideas about the individual, about limitations on government, and about rationalism. Such thinking was the major intellectual force behind the American Revolution, and it also affected the new nation's views on law and criminal justice. Reformers began to raise questions about the nature of criminal behavior and the methods of punishment. At a time of overcrowded and unmanaged jails, brutal corporal punishment, and rising crime, the first great period of correctional reform was launched.

Prior to 1800, Americans copied the Europeans in using physical punishment as the main criminal sanction. Flogging, branding, and maiming were the methods of controlling deviance and maintaining public safety. For more serious crimes, offenders were hanged on the gallows. For example, in the state of New York about 20 percent of all crimes on the books were capital offenses. Criminals were regularly sentenced to death for picking pockets, burglary, robbery, and horse stealing (Rothman, 1971:49). Jails existed throughout the country, but they were only for holding people awaiting trial or punishment or people unable to pay their debts. As in England, houses of correction existed in the American colonies where offenders were sentenced to terms of "hard labor" as a means of turning them from crime (Hirsch, 1992).

The French scholar Michel Foucault has written about the spread of Enlightenment ideas during the late eighteenth century (Foucault, 1977). Before the French Revolution of 1789, European governments tried to control crime by making punishments such as torture and hanging into public spectacles. Criminals were often branded to display their offense. The dismembered bodies of capital offenders were put on display. In the early nineteenth century, such practices gradually were replaced by "modern" penal systems that emphasized fitting the punishment to

Until the early 1800s Americans followed the European practice of relying upon punishment that was physically brutal, such as death, flogging, and branding. This whipping post and pillory in New Castle, Delaware, continued to be used well into the 19th century.

the individual offender. The new goal was not to inflict pain on the offender's body but to change the individual and set him or her on the right path.

Clearly, this constituted a major shift in policy. The change from physical (corporal) punishment to correction of the offender reflected new ideas about the causes of crime and the possibility of reforming behavior.

Many people promoted the reform of corrections, but John Howard (1726–1790), sheriff of Bedfordshire, England, was especially influential. His book *The State of Prisons in England and Wales,* published in 1777, described his observations of the prisons he visited (Howard, 1929). Among generally horrible conditions, he was particularly concerned about the lack of discipline.

Public response to the book resulted in Parliament's passing the Penitentiary Act of 1779, which called for the creation of a house of hard labor where offenders would be imprisoned for up to two years. The institution would be based on four principles:

1. A secure and sanitary building.
2. Inspection to ensure that offenders followed the rules.
3. Abolition of the fees charged offenders for their food.
4. A reformatory regime.

At night prisoners were to be confined to individual cells. During the day they were to work silently in common rooms. Prison life was to be strict and ordered. Influenced by his Quaker friends, Howard believed that the new institution should be a place of industry. But more important, it was to be a place where criminals could have an opportunity for penitence (sorrow and shame for their wrongs) and repentance (willingness to change their ways). In short, the purposes of this **penitentiary** were to punish and to reform.

The penitentiary legislation was enacted during Howard's lifetime but not implemented in England until 1842, fifty years after his death. Although his own

penitentiary
An institution intended to punish criminals by isolating them from society and from one another so they can reflect on their past misdeeds, repent, and reform.

country was slow to act, Howard's idea of the penitentiary traveled across the Atlantic to the United States where it took root.

CHECK POINT

① **What was the Enlightenment and how did it influence corrections?**

② **What were the main goals of the penitentiary?**

(Answers are at the end of the chapter.)

Reform in the United States

From 1776 to around 1830, a new revolution occurred in the American idea of criminal punishment. Although based on the work of English reformers, the new correctional philosophy reflected many ideas expressed in the Declaration of Independence, including an optimistic view of human nature and of individual perfectibility. Emphasis shifted from the assumption that deviance was part of human nature to a belief that crime was a result of environmental forces. The new nation's humane and optimistic ideas were to be focused on reforming the criminal.

In the first decades of the nineteenth century, the creation of penitentiaries in Pennsylvania and New York attracted the attention of legislators in other states and investigators from Europe. Even travelers from abroad with no special interest in corrections made it a point to include a penitentiary on their itinerary, much as they planned visits to a southern plantation, a textile mill, or a frontier town. By the mid-1800s, the U.S. penitentiary had become world famous.

The Pennsylvania System

A number of groups in the United States dedicated themselves to reforming the institutions and practices of criminal punishment. One of these groups was the Philadelphia Society for Alleviating the Miseries of Public Prisons, formed in 1787 under the leadership of Dr. Benjamin Rush, one of the signers of the Declaration of Independence. This group, which included many Quakers, was inspired by Howard's ideas. They argued that criminals could best be reformed if they were placed in penitentiaries—isolated from one another and from society to consider their crimes, repent, and reform.

Eastern State Penitentiary located outside Philadelphia became the model for the Pennsylvania system of "separate" confinement. The building was designed to ensure that each offender was separated from all human contact so that he could reflect upon his misdeeds.

In 1790 the Pennsylvania legislature authorized construction of two penitentiaries for the solitary confinement of "hardened and atrocious offenders." The first, created out of an existing three-story stone structure in Philadelphia, was the Walnut Street Jail. This building, forty by twenty-five feet, had eight dark cells, each measuring six by eight by nine feet, on each floor. A yard was attached to the building. Only one inmate occupied each cell, and no communications of any kind were allowed. From a small, grated window high on the outside wall prisoners "could perceive neither heaven nor earth."

From this limited beginning the Pennsylvania system of **separate confinement** evolved. It was based on five principles:

❶ Prisoners would not be treated vengefully but should be convinced that through hard and selective forms of suffering they could change their lives.

❷ Solitary confinement would prevent further corruption inside prison.

❸ In isolation, offenders would reflect on their transgressions and repent.

❹ Solitary confinement would be punishment because humans are by nature social animals.

❺ Solitary confinement would be economical because prisoners would not need long periods of time to repent, fewer keepers would be needed, and the costs of clothing would be lower. (Sellin, 1970)

> **separate confinement**
> *A penitentiary system, developed in Pennsylvania, in which each inmate was held in isolation from other inmates. All activities, including craft work, took place in the cells.*

The opening of the Eastern Penitentiary near Philadelphia in 1829 culminated forty-two years of reform activity by the Philadelphia Society. On October 25, 1829, the first prisoner, Charles Williams, arrived. He was an 18-year-old African American and had been sentenced to two years for larceny. He was assigned to a cell twelve by eight by ten feet with an individual exercise yard eighteen feet long. In the cell was a fold-up steel bed, a simple toilet, a wooden stool, a workbench, and eating utensils. Light came from an eight-inch window in the ceiling. Solitary labor, Bible reading, and reflection were the keys to the moral rehabilitation that was supposed to occur within the penitentiary. Although the cell was larger than most in use today, it was the only world the prisoner would see throughout the entire sentence. The only other human voice heard would be that of a clergyman who would visit on Sundays. Nothing was to distract the penitent prisoner from the path toward reform.

Unfortunately, the system did not work. The Walnut Street Jail became overcrowded as more and more offenders were held for longer periods. It became a "warehouse of humanity." Politicians influenced operation of the jail. A second Pennsylvania penitentiary near Pittsburgh was soon declared outmoded because isolation was not complete and the cells were too small for solitary labor. As in the other institutions, overcrowding became a problem, and the Pittsburgh institution was demolished in 1833.

The New York System

In 1819 New York opened a penitentiary in Auburn that evolved as a rival to Pennsylvania's concept of separate confinement. Under New York's **congregate system,** prisoners were held in isolation at night but worked with fellow prisoners in shops during the day. They worked under a rule of silence and were even forbidden to exchange glances while on the job or at meals. The men were to have the benefits of labor as well as meditation. They lived under tight control, on a simple diet, and worked to pay for a portion of their keep.

> **congregate system**
> *A penitentiary system, developed in Auburn, New York, in which each inmate was held in isolation during the night but worked and ate with fellow prisoners during the day under a rule of silence.*

American reformers, seeing the New York approach as a great advance, copied it throughout the Northeast. Because the inmates produced goods for sale, advocates said operating costs would be covered. At an 1826 meeting of prison reformers in Boston, the New York system was described in glowing terms:

> At Auburn, we have a more beautiful example still, of what may be done by proper discipline, in a prison well constructed. . . . The unremitted industry, the entire subordination, and subdued feeling among the convicts [have] probably no parallel among any equal number of convicts. In their solitary cells, they spend the night with no other book than the Bible, and at sunrise they proceed in military order, under the eye of the turnkey in solid columns, with the lock march to the workshops. (Goldfarb and Singer, 1973:30)

During this period, advocates of the Pennsylvania and New York plans debated on public platforms and in the nation's periodicals. Advocates of both systems agreed that the prisoner must be isolated from society and placed on a disciplined routine. They believed that criminality was a result of corruption pervading the community that the family and the church did not sufficiently counterbalance. Only when offenders were removed from the temptations and influences of society and kept in a silent, disciplined environment could they reflect on their sins and offenses and become useful citizens. The convicts were not inherently depraved; rather, they were victims of a society that had not protected them from vice. While offenders were being punished, they would become penitent and motivated to place themselves on the right path.

Reformatory Movement

By the middle of the nineteenth century, reformers had become disillusioned with the penitentiary. Neither the Pennsylvania nor the New York systems nor any of their imitators had achieved rehabilitation or deterrence. This failure was seen as the result of poor administration rather than as a sign of weakness of the basic concept. Within forty years of being built, penitentiaries had become overcrowded, understaffed, and minimally financed. Discipline was lax, brutality was common, and administrators were viewed as corrupt. At Sing Sing Penitentiary in Ossining, New York, for example, investigators in 1870 discovered "that dealers were publicly supplying prisoners with almost anything they could pay for" and that convicts were "playing all sorts of games, reading, scheming, trafficking" (Rothman, 1980:18).

The Cincinnati Declaration of Principles

In 1870 the newly formed National Prison Association (predecessor of today's American Correctional Association) met in Cincinnati. The association issued a Declaration of Principles, which signaled a new round of penal reform. Progressive reformers advocated a new design for **penology.** The goal of punishment should be the moral regeneration of criminals, but the means to achieve this goal should be changed. Like the Quakers, these reformers also believed that rehabilitation should be done behind walls. However, the Cincinnati Declaration stated that prisons should reward offenders who reformed with release. Fixed sentences should be replaced by sentences of indeterminate length, and proof of reformation should replace the "mere lapse of time" in decisions about when to release a prisoner. This program of reformation required a progressive classification of prisoners based on improvements in their character.

penology

A branch of criminology dealing with the management of prisons and the treatment of offenders.

Elmira Reformatory

The first **reformatory** took shape in 1876 at Elmira, New York, when Zebulon Brockway was appointed superintendent. Brockway believed that diagnosis and treatment were the keys to reform and rehabilitation. He questioned each new inmate to explore the social, biological, psychological, and "root cause" of the offender's deviance. An individualized work and education treatment program was then prescribed. Inmates followed a rigid schedule of work during the day, followed by courses in academic, vocational, and moral subjects during the evening.

Designed for first-time felons aged 16–30, the approach at Elmira incorporated a "mark" system of classification, indeterminate sentences, and parole. Each offender entered the institution at grade 2, and if he earned nine marks a month for six months by working hard, completing school assignments, and causing no problems, he could be moved up to grade 1, which was necessary for release. If he failed to cooperate and violated the rules, he would be demoted to grade 3 and could not return to the path toward eventual release until he had completed three months of satisfactory behavior. This system placed "the prisoner's fate, as far as possible, in his own hands" (Pisciotta, 1994:20).

By 1900 the reformatory movement had spread throughout the nation, yet by the outbreak of World War I in 1914, it was already in decline. In most institutions the architecture, the attitudes of the guards, and the emphasis on discipline differed little from past orientations. Too often, the educational and rehabilitative efforts took a back seat to the traditional emphasis on punishment. Even Brockway admitted that it was difficult to distinguish between inmates whose attitudes had changed and those who merely lived by prison rules. Being a good prisoner became the way to win parole, but this did not guarantee that the prisoner had truly changed.

reformatory
An institution for young offenders emphasizing training, a mark system of classification, indeterminate sentences, and parole.

CHECK POINT

③ **How did the Pennsylvania and New York systems differ?**

④ **What was the significance of the Cincinnati Declaration of Principles?**

Improving Prison Conditions for Women

Until the beginning of the nineteenth century, female offenders in Europe and North America were treated no differently than males and were not separated from them when they were incarcerated. Only with John Howard's 1777 exposé of prison conditions in England and the development of the penitentiary in Philadelphia did attention begin to focus on the plight of the female offender. Among the English reformers, Elizabeth Gurney Fry, a middle-class Quaker, was the first person to press for changes. When she and fellow Quakers visited London's Newgate Prison in 1813, they were shocked by the conditions in which the female prisoners and their children were living (Zedner, 1995:333).

News of Fry's efforts spread to the United States, and the Women's Prison Association was formed in New York in 1844 with the goal of improving the treatment of female prisoners and separating them from males. Elizabeth Farnham, head matron of the women's wing at Sing Sing from 1844 to 1848, sought to implement Fry's ideas but was thwarted by the male overseers and legislators and was forced to resign.

Until 1870 most women inmates were housed in the same prisons as men and treated essentially the same. The first separate, female-run prison was established in Indianapolis in 1873.

Although the National Prison Association's Cincinnati meeting was a turning point in American corrections, the Declaration of Principles did not address the problems of female offenders. It only endorsed the creation of separate treatment-oriented prisons for women. Although the House of Shelter, a reformatory for women, was created in Detroit following the Civil War, not until 1873 was the first independent female-run prison opened in Indiana. Within fifty years thirteen other states had followed this lead.

Three principles guided female prison reform during this period: (1) the separation of women prisoners from men, (2) the provision of care in keeping with the needs of women, and (3) the management of women's prisons by female staff. "Operated by and for women, female reformatories were decidedly 'feminine' institutions' " (Rafter, 1983:147). As time passed, the original ideas of the reformers faltered. In 1927 the first federal prison for women was opened in Alderson, West Virginia, with Mary Belle Harris as warden. Yet, by 1935 the women's reformatory movement had "run its course, having largely achieved its objective (establishment of separate prisons run by women)" (Rafter, 1983:165).

Reforms of the Progressives

In the first two decades of the twentieth century, reformers known as the Progressives attacked the excesses of big business and urban society and advocated government actions against the problems of slums, vice, and crime. The Progressives believed that science could help solve social problems. They urged that knowledge from the social and behavioral sciences should replace religious and traditional moral wisdom as the guiding ideas of criminal rehabilitation. The two main goals of the Progressives were to improve social conditions thought to be the breeding grounds of crime and to improve ways of rehabilitating individual deviants. Both objectives had their roots in the positivist school of criminology, which focused on the behavior of the offender, as discussed in Chapter 2.

By the 1920s, probation, indeterminate sentences, the presentence report, parole, and treatment programs were being promoted as a more scientific approach to criminality. All of these components remain in corrections today, although they are not necessarily used strictly in accordance with the Progressives' goals and methods.

 CHECK POINT

⑤ **What were the principles guiding reform of corrections for women in the nineteenth century?**

rehabilitation model
A model of corrections that emphasizes the need to restore a convicted offender to a constructive place in society through some form of vocational or educational training or therapy.

Rehabilitation Model

Although the Progressives were instrumental in advancing the new penal ideas, not until the 1930s were attempts made to implement fully what became known as the **rehabilitation model** of corrections. Taking advantage of the new prestige of the social sciences, penologists helped shift the emphasis of corrections. The new approach took the social, intellectual, or biological deficiencies of criminals to be the causes of their crimes. The essential elements of parole, probation, and the indeterminate sentence were already in place in most states, so incorporating the rehabilitation model meant adding classification systems to diagnose offenders and treatment programs to rehabilitate them.

Because penologists likened the new correctional methods to those used by physicians in hospitals, this approach was often referred to as the **medical model.** Correctional institutions were to be staffed with persons who could diagnose the causes of an individual's criminal behavior, prescribe a treatment program, and determine when the offender was cured and could be safely released to the community.

Following World War II, rehabilitation won new followers. Group therapy, behavior modification, counseling, and several other approaches became part of the "new penology." Yet even during the 1950s, when the medical model was at its height, only a small proportion of state correctional budgets was allocated for rehabilitation. What frustrated many persons committed to treatment was that, even while states adopted the rhetoric of the rehabilitation model, the institutions were still run with custody as the overriding goal.

The rehabilitation model failed to achieve its goals and became discredited in the 1970s. The problem was that it presumed that corrections officials and psychologists could make consistent, accurate judgments about when particular prisoners had been rehabilitated. Studies of treatment programs showed that some prisoners successfully reentered society, while others returned to their criminal ways. Corrections officials apparently did not know precisely which techniques would be effective or whether every prisoner had the potential to be rehabilitated. As a result of dissatisfaction with the rehabilitation model, new reforms emerged.

medical model

A model of corrections based on the assumption that criminal behavior is caused by biological or psychological conditions that require treatment.

Community Model

Correctional goals and methods have been influenced by the social and political values of particular periods. During the 1960s and early 1970s, U.S. society experienced the civil rights movement, the War on Poverty, and resistance to the war in Vietnam. It was a time that challenged the conventional ways of government. In 1967 the President's Commission on Law Enforcement and the Administration of Justice reported that

> crime and delinquency are symptoms of failures and disorganization of the community. . . .
> The task of corrections, therefore, includes building or rebuilding social ties, obtaining
> employment and education, securing in the larger sense a place for the offender in the rou-
> tine functioning of society. (President's Commission on Law Enforcement and Administration
> of Justice, 1967:7).

This model of **community corrections** was based on the assumption that the goal of corrections should be to reintegrate the offender into the community. Proponents viewed prisons as artificial institutions that hindered offenders from finding a crime-free lifestyle. The emphasis should be on increasing opportunities for offenders to be successful citizens instead of on providing psychological treatment. Programs were supposed to help offenders find jobs and remain connected to their families and the community. Imprisonment was to be avoided, if possible, in favor of probation, so that offenders could seek education and vocational training that would help their adjustment. The small proportion of offenders who had

community corrections

A model of corrections based on the goal of reintegrating the offender into the community.

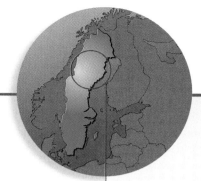

Corrections
in Sweden

The Kriminalvardsstyrelsen—literally the "criminal care administration"—is the agency that runs the Swedish corrections system. Inmates make fun of this name. As one said, "We are not prisoners, or inmates, or convicts. We are consumers of criminal care!" Rehabilitation and reintegration of offenders are the overriding goals of the Swedish correctional system. Why are correctional policies in the United States so different from those in Sweden? Are there social, economic, and political factors that help explain these differences?

On a given day, the Kriminalvardsstyrelsen is responsible for about four thousand inmates serving sentences and about seven hundred awaiting trial. In most countries, a half dozen institutions would be considered more than enough to hold the small number of inmates. But in Sweden the treatment focus emphasizes small institutions, hence

there are nineteen national prisons, designed for people sentenced to more than one year; fifty-six local institutions, used primarily to house people with terms of less than one year, and twenty-four remand prisons holding people awaiting trial. The maximum capacity of these institutions ranges from ten to three hundred, most hold between twenty to forty, more akin to halfway houses in the United States. The prisons have a total capacity for seventeen hundred inmates housed in "open" institutions—without walls or fences—and twenty-four hundred in closed facilities.

Over the course of a year approximately seventeen thousand people are sentenced to prison. The five offenses that most often lead to incarceration are: property crimes, drug offenses, drunk driving, grand larceny, and offenses against other legislation.

The time served in Sweden by serious offenders is shorter than in the United States. The penal code authorizes incarceration at either a fixed term of fourteen days to ten years, or a life sentence. The latter is rare and is usually commuted to a determinate sentence of between fifteen and twenty years.

to be incarcerated would spend a minimal amount of time in prison before release on parole. To promote reintegration, correctional workers were to serve as advocates for offenders in dealing with governmental agencies providing employment counseling, medical treatment, and financial assistance.

Community corrections has been the goal of corrections in Sweden for more than thirty years. In that country sentences are short by American standards, prisons are small, and offenders work industries. As you read the Comparative Perspective (see p. 440), ask yourself why this orientation has not been successful in the United States.

The community model was dominant until the late 1970s. It gave way to a new punitiveness in criminal justice in conjunction with the rebirth of the determinate sentence. Advocates of reintegration claim, as did advocates of previous

Sixty-five percent of Swedish prisoners serve sentences of three months or less; 13 percent, three to six months; 9.5 percent, six to twelve months; 8 percent, twelve to twenty-four months; and only 4 percent, more than two years. Included are drunk drivers (30 percent of all offenders sent to prison) and 75 percent of those convicted of a traffic offense who receive the maximum sentence of one month. In Sweden, no distinction is made between felons and misdemeanants: all enter the same correctional system.

The "Act on Correctional Treatment in Institutions" passed in 1974 puts great emphasis upon the reintegration of prisoners into the community. It states that the "natural" form of correctional care is noninstitutional and that every effort should be made to keep offenders out of prison and to maximize contacts with the outside world for those who are incarcerated. To accomplish this goal judges are instructed to make greater use of probation; inmates in local institutions are given the right to leave the facility during the day to work, study, and participate in recreation; furloughs for short or long terms are authorized; and long-term

prisoners not viewed as security risks are given short-term periods of release to study, secure treatment, or for other reasons that would facilitate the prisoner's adjustment to society.

The factory program at the national prison Tillberga is an example of the reintegrative thrust of Swedish penology. There are about eighty inmates at this facility, and of these, about forty are employed in the construction of prefabricated houses, which are sold on the open market. All inmate-workers are members of the national construction union and are paid free-market wages negotiated by that union. The union agreed to this idea on three conditions: that the inmates would be paid the same wages as other building-trade members; that the houses would be sold at the same price as private companies; and that the housing market remained strong.

However, because the inmates do not pay national income taxes (normally 30 percent of a wage), their pay envelop contains 70 percent of that received by their outside counterparts. Many prisoners are not attracted to the Tillberga scheme because they are given only 25 percent

of their wages to spend. The remainder is placed in a savings account that the inmate receives upon release. Success of the program at Tillberga has led to development of a similar industry based on clothing manufacture at another national prison.

Sweden has a reputation of taking social welfare policies further than any developed nation. The Swedish political ideology emphasizes the similarities among citizens instead of the differences and encourages a sense of collective responsibility, which seeks to protect the rights and needs of its weakest members. Governmental policies have been developed to assist these citizens, even those who have broken the law. As a Swedish official noted in a United Nations report, "A society without slums cannot let its prisoners live under slum conditions; a society which has accepted collective responsibility for the physical and economic welfare of its citizens cannot abuse the rights even of those who transgress its laws."

SOURCE: Adapted from Michael S. Serrill, "Profile/Sweden," *Corrections Magazine* 3 (June 1977):11; and Richard J. Terrill, *World Criminal Justice Systems*, 2d ed. (Cincinnati, Ohio: Anderson Publishing Company, 1992), 196–205.

---

reforms, that the idea was never adequately tested. Nevertheless, community corrections remains one of the significant ideas and practices in the recent history of corrections.

Crime Control Model

As the political climate changed in the 1970s and 1980s, legislators, judges, and officials responded with a renewed emphasis on a **crime control model of corrections.** This more punitive approach to criminality makes greater use of incarceration (especially for violent offenders and career criminals), longer sentences, mandatory sentences, and strict supervision of probationers and parolees.

crime control model of corrections

A model of corrections based on the assumption that criminal behavior can be controlled by more use of incarceration and other forms of strict supervision.

Some states have added "supermax" prisons such as Pelican Bay, California, for violent offenders or those with chronic behavior problems. In such institutions inmates spend up to twenty-three hours a day in their cells. They are shackled whenever they are out of their cells, during recreation, showers, and telephone calls. All of these measures are designed to send a message to other inmates.

By 2000, the success of these "get-tough" policies was demonstrated by the record number of persons incarcerated, the greater amount of time being served, and the huge size of the probation population. In some states the political fervor to be tough on criminals resulted in the reinstitution of chain gangs and the removal of television sets, body-building equipment, and college courses from prisons. Some advocates point to the crime control policies as the reason for the fall of the crime rate. Others ask whether the crime control policies have made a difference, considering the smaller number of males in the crime-prone age group, and other changes in American society.

The history of corrections in America has been a series of swings from one model to another. As the twenty-first century begins, the time may be ripe for another look at correctional policy. The language now used in criminal justice journals differs markedly from that found in their pages thirty years ago. The optimism that once suffused corrections has waned. The financial and human costs of the retributive crime control policies of the 1990s are now being scrutinized. Are the costs of incarceration and surveillance justified? Have corrections policies reduced crime and made society safer? Many researchers think not. Looking to the future, will there be a new direction for corrections? If so, what will be its focus?

CHECK **POINT**

⑥ **What are the underlying assumptions of the rehabilitation, community, and crime control models of corrections?**

Organization of Corrections in the United States

The organization of corrections in the United States is fragmented: each level of government has some responsibility for corrections. The federal government, the fifty states, the District of Columbia, the 3,047 counties, and most cities all have at least one correctional facility and many correctional programs. Public and private organizations administer corrections at an average annual cost of more than $30 billion (Smeltz, 1995). State and local governments pay about 95 percent of the cost of all correctional activities in the nation (BJS, 1999k:3).

The scope of federal criminal laws is less broad than that of state laws; as a result, only about 200,000 adults are under federal correctional supervision. In most areas, maintaining prisons and parole is the responsibility of the state, while counties have some jails for misdemeanor offenders but no authority over the short-term jails operated by towns and cities. Jails are operated mainly by local governments (usually sheriff's departments), but in six states they are integrated with the state prison system. Most correctional activities are part of the executive branch of

TABLE **12.2**   **Distribution of correctional responsibilities in Philadelphia County, Pennsylvania**

Note the various correctional functions performed by different government agencies.

	CORRECTIONAL FUNCTION	LEVEL AND BRANCH OF GOVERNMENT	RESPONSIBLE AGENCY
Adult corrections	Pretrial detention	Municipal/executive	Department of Human Services
	Probation supervision	County/courts	Court of Common Pleas
	Halfway houses	Municipal/executive	Department of Human Services
	Houses of corrections	Municipal/executive	Department of Human Services
	County prisons	Municipal/executive	Department of Human Services
	State prisons	State/executive	Department of Corrections
	County parole	County/executive	Court of Common Pleas
	State parole	State/executive	Board of Probation and Parole
Juvenile corrections	Detention	Municipal/executive	Department of Public Welfare
	Probation supervision	County/courts	Court of Common Pleas
	Dependent/neglect	State/executive	Department of Human Services
	Training schools	State/executive	Department of Public Welfare
	Private placements	Private	Many
	Juvenile aftercare	State/executive	Department of Public Welfare
Federal corrections	Probation/parole	Federal/courts	U.S. courts
	Incarceration	Federal/courts	Federal Bureau of Prisons

SOURCE: Taken from the annual reports of the responsible agencies.

government, but most probation offices are attached to the judiciary and are paid for by county government. Facilities and programs for juveniles are separate.

The fragmentation of corrections is illustrated in Table 12.2, which shows how correctional responsibilities are distributed in the Philadelphia metropolitan area. Note that all levels of government—federal, state, county, and municipal—operate correctional programs. Various departments within these levels are responsible for implementing programs.

Federal Corrections System

The correctional responsibilities of the federal government are divided between the Department of Justice, which operates prisons through the Federal Bureau of Prisons, and the Administrative Office of the United States Courts, which is responsible for probation and parole supervision.

Federal Bureau of Prisons

The Federal Bureau of Prisons, which was created by Congress in 1930, now operates a system of prisons located throughout the nation and housing more than 100,000 inmates, supervised by a staff of more than thirty thousand (Federal Bureau of Prisons, 1998:51). Facilities and inmates are classified by security level, ranging from Level 1 (the least secure, camp-type settings such as the Federal Prison Camp in Tyndall, Florida) through Level 5 (the most secure such as the "supermax" penitentiary in Florence, Colorado). Between these extremes are

Levels 2 through 4 federal correctional institutions—other U.S. penitentiaries, administrative institutions, medical facilities, and specialized institutions for women and juveniles. The Bureau enters into contractual agreements with states, cities, and private agencies to provide community services such as halfway houses, prerelease programs, and electronic monitoring.

Because of the nature of federal criminal law, prisoners in most federal facilities are different from those in state institutions. Federal prisoners are often a more sophisticated type of criminal, from a higher socioeconomic status, who have committed crimes of extortion, mail fraud, bank robbery, and arson. However, since the beginning of the "war on drugs" in the 1980s, the proportion of drug offenders has increased and now makes up about 60 percent of the incarcerated population. Fewer offenders (less than 7 percent of the federal prison population) have committed crimes of violence than are found in most state institutions. About 25 percent of federal prisoners are citizens of other countries (Federal Bureau of Prisons, 1998:46).

Federal Probation and Parole Supervision

Probation and parole supervision for federal offenders are provided by the Federal Probation and Pretrial Services System, a branch of the Administrative Office of the U.S. Courts. Probation officers are appointed by the federal judiciary and serve the court. The first full-time federal probation officer was appointed in 1927; today 3,842 are assigned to the judicial districts across the country. They assist with presentence investigations but are primarily involved in supervising those on probation and offenders released either on parole or mandatory release. Their average caseload is seventy people (BJS, 1999k:477).

The Pretrial Services Act of 1982 required pretrial services to be established in each federal judicial district. These services are performed either by probation officers or independently in a separate office of pretrial services. The responsibilities of pretrial services officers are to "collect, verify, and report to the judicial officer information pertaining to the pretrial release of each person charged with an offense" (Administrative Office of the U.S. Courts, 1993).

State Corrections Systems

Although states vary considerably in how they organize corrections, in all states the administration of prisons is part of the executive branch of state government. This point is important because probation is often part of the judiciary, parole may be separate from corrections, and in most states jails are run by county government. The differences can be seen in the proportion of correctional employees who work for the state. In Connecticut, Rhode Island, and Vermont, for example, 100 percent are state employees, compared with 47 percent in California. The remaining 53 percent in California work for county or municipal governments.

Community Corrections

Probation, intermediate sanctions, and parole are the three major ways that offenders are punished in the community. States vary in how they carry out these punishments. In many states probation and intermediate sanctions are administered by the judiciary, often by county and municipal governments. By contrast, parole is a function of state government. The decision to release an offender from prison is made by the state parole board in those states with discretionary release. Parole boards are a part of either the department of corrections or an independent agency. In states with mandatory systems, release is made by the department of corrections. Supervision of parolees in the community is also by an agency of state government.

Central to the community corrections approach is a belief in the "least restrictive alternative," the idea that the criminal sanction should be applied only to the minimum extent necessary to meet the community's need for protection, the seriousness of the offense, and society's need for offenders to get their deserved punishment. To this end probation and parole services are geared to assist and reintegrate the offender into the community.

State Prison Systems

A wide range of state correctional institutions, facilities, and programs exists for adult felons, including prisons, reformatories, prison farms, forestry camps, and halfway houses. This variety does not exist for women because of the smaller female prisoner population.

States vary considerably in the number, size, type, and location of correctional facilities. Michigan's prison at Jackson, for example, has a capacity of thirty-five hundred, whereas specialized institutions house fewer than one hundred inmates. Some states (such as New Hampshire) have centralized incarceration in a few institutions, and other states

In many states prisons are so crowded that offenders are backed up in county jails awaiting transfer. These inmates in the Franklin County, North Carolina, jail have little to do but wait for prison space to open up.

(such as California, New York, and Texas) have a wide mix of sizes and styles— secure institutions, diagnostic units, work camps, forestry centers, and prerelease centers. For example, Alabama has thirteen correctional institutions (prisons), a disciplinary rehabilitation unit, an honor farm, a boot camp, a state cattle ranch, a prison for women, and youth center for male felons under age 25, in addition to eleven community-based facilities (American Correctional Association, 1996:4).

State correctional institutions are classified by their level of security, and their type of population shifts according to the special needs of the offenders. The security level is indicated by the physical characteristics of the buildings.

The maximum security prison (where 35 percent of state inmates are confined) is built like a fortress, usually surrounded by stone walls with guard towers and designed to prevent escape. New facilities are surrounded by double rows of chain-link fences with rolls of razor wire in between and along the top of the fences. Inmates live in cells that include plumbing and sanitary facilities. The barred doors may be operated electronically so that an officer can confine all prisoners to their cells with the flick of a switch. The purpose of the maximum security facility is custody and discipline; there is a military-style approach to order. Prisoners follow a strict routine. Some of the most famous prisons, such as Stateville, Attica, Yuma, and Sing Sing, are maximum security facilities.

The medium security prison (holding 47 percent of state inmates) resembles the maximum security prison in appearance. Because it is organized on a somewhat different basis, its atmosphere is less rigid and tense. Prisoners have more privileges and contact with the outside world through visitors, mail, and access to radio and television. The medium security prison emphasizes rehabilitative programs because inmates are not perceived to be hardened criminals, although in most states they have probably committed serious crimes.

The minimum security prison (with 18 percent of state inmates) houses the least violent offenders, long-term felons who have clean disciplinary records, and inmates who have nearly completed their term. The minimum security prison does not have the guard towers and stone walls associated with correctional institutions. Often chain-link fencing surrounds the buildings. Prisoners usually live in dormitories or even in small private rooms instead of in barred cells. There is more personal freedom: inmates may have television sets, choose their own clothes, and move about casually within the buildings. The system relies on rehabilitation programs and offers opportunities for education and work release. Although outsiders may think that little punishment goes on inside the minimum security facility, it is still a prison; restrictions are placed on inmates, and they remain segregated from society.

State Institutions for Women

Because only 6.4 percent of the incarcerated population are women, there are relatively few women's facilities. Although the ratio of arrests is approximately 6 men to 1 woman, the ratio of admissions to state correctional institutions is 18 men to 1 woman. A higher proportion of women defendants is sentenced to probation and intermediate punishments, partly as a result of male offenders' tendency to commit most of the violent crimes. However, the growth rate in number of incarcerated women has exceeded that for men since 1981. From 1985 to 1998 the male population in state and federal prisons increased 211 percent, whereas that of women increased by 311 percent. During the past ten years the number of women in state prisons for drug offenses has increased almost 450 percent (BJS, 1998c).

Female offenders are incarcerated in 141 institutions for women and 161 coed facilities (BJS, 1997b:54). In some states with no separate facilities for women, offenders are assigned to a separate section of the state prison; other women offenders are housed in neighboring states by intergovernmental contract.

Conditions in correctional facilities for women are more pleasant than those of similar institutions for men. Usually the buildings have no gun towers and barbed wire. Because of the small population, however, most states have only one facility, which is often located in a rural setting far removed from urban centers. Thus women prisoners may be more isolated than men from their families and communities. Pressure from women's organizations and the apparent rise in the incidence of crime committed by women may bring about a greater equality in corrections for men and women.

CHECK **POINT**

⑦ **What agencies of the U.S. government are responsible for prisons and probation?**

⑧ **What agencies of state government are responsible for incarceration, probation, intermediate sanctions, and parole?**

Private Prisons

Corrections is a multibillion-dollar government-funded enterprise that purchases supplies and services from the private sector. Many jurisdictions have long contracted with private vendors to provide specific institutional services and to operate aftercare facilities and programs. Businesses furnish food and medical services, educational and vocational training, maintenance, security, and industrial programs. All of this has been referred to as "the corrections-commercial complex" (Lilly, 1993: 150).

One response to prison and jail crowding and staff costs rising has come from private entrepreneurs who argue that they can build and run prisons at least as effectively, safely, and humanely as any level of government can, at a profit and at a lower cost to taxpayers. The management of entire institutions for adult felons under private contract is a recent approach, launched in the 1980s (Shichor, 1995).

The first privately operated correctional institution was the Intensive Treatment Unit, a twenty-bed, high-security, dormitory-style training school for delinquents, which was opened in 1975 by the RCA Corporation in Weaversville, Pennsylvania. In January 1986, Kentucky's Marion Adjustment Center became the first privately owned and operated (by the U.S. Corrections Corporation) facility for the incarceration of adult felons sentenced at least to a level of minimum security. By the end of 1999 there were 158 private prisons for adults in operation, with a total capacity of 117,867 inmates in thirty states plus the District of Columbia and Puerto Rico. The $1 billion-a-year private prison business is dominated by Corrections Corporation of America and Wackenhut Corrections Corporation, which together hold more than three-quarters of the market share of the private prison business (Thomas and Bolinger, 1999).

The major advantages claimed by advocates of privately operated prisons are that they provide the same level of care as the states but more cheaply and flexibly. Charles Logan's study (1992) of private prisons points to the difficulties of measuring the costs and quality of these institutions. One issue is that many of the "true costs" (fringe benefits, contracting supervision, federal grants) are not taken into consideration. The quoted rates of existing private facilities vary widely. In Texas, the state pays the private companies about $30 a day on average for each prisoner compared with $39.50 per day in state-run facilities. However, the $39.50 figure includes expensive maximum-security prisons, which the private companies do not run. The private prison rate in Texas is equivalent to $10,950 per year, much less than the costs per inmate held in most states (*New York Times,* June 24, 1997:A19). A report by the U.S. General Accounting Office found that in a study of similar prisons in Tennessee—one private and two government—the per diem rates were almost the same (*New York Times,* July 13, 1997:D5).

Provision of correctional services by private companies may result in lower costs, but public agencies must constantly monitor contracts to ensure compliance. The profit incentive may result in poor services, as evidenced by a 1995 detainee uprising at an Elizabeth, New Jersey, jail run by Esmore Correctional Services Corporation for the Immigration and Naturalization Service. Undercutting a bid by Wackenhut Corporation by $20 million, Esmore violated the contract by understaffing, abuse of detainees, inadequate physical conditions, and health hazards (*New York Times,* July 23, 1995:1). In the Northeast Ohio Correctional Center, owned by the Correctional Corporation of America, twenty inmates were stabbed, two of the fatally, during the first ten months of operations (*New York Times,* April 15, 1999:1).

Political, fiscal, ethical, and administrative issues must be examined before corrections can become too heavily committed to the private ownership and operation of prisons. The political issues, including ethical questions of the propriety of delegating social-control functions to persons other than the state, may be the most difficult to overcome. Some people believe that the administration of justice is a basic function of government that should not be delegated. They fear that correctional policy would be skewed because contractors would use their political influence to continue programs not in the public interest—for instance, they would press to maintain high occupancy levels, and they would be interested only in skimming off the best inmates, leaving the most troublesome to the public correctional system. The fiscal value of private corrections cannot yet be demonstrated. However, labor unions have opposed these incursions into the public sector, pointing out that the salaries, benefits, and pensions of workers in other spheres such as private security are lower than those of their public counterparts. Finally, questions have risen about quality of services, accountability of service providers to corrections officials, and problems related to contract supervision. Opponents cite the many instances in which privately contracted services in group homes, day-care centers, hospitals, and schools have been terminated because of reports of corruption, brutality, or substandard services.

A movement is growing for greater government regulation of private prisons. In Ohio, Texas, Tennessee, and several other states, legislatures have enacted or are considering new laws to ensure that the private prison industry lives up to its contractual obligations. A number of members of Congress have introduced bills to prohibit federal inmates from serving their time in private prisons (*New York Times*, April 15, 1999:1).

The idea of privately run correctional facilities has stimulated much interest among the general public and within the criminal justice community. There may be further privatization of criminal justice services, or privatization may become only a limited venture initiated at a time of prison crowding, fiscal constraints on governments, and a revival of the free-enterprise ideology. The controversy about privatization has, however, forced corrections to rethink some strongly held beliefs. In this regard the possibility of competition from the private sector may have a positive impact.

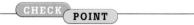
CHECK POINT

⑨ **What are the arguments in favor of and opposed to privately run prisons?**

Jails: Local Correctional Facilities

The U.S. jail has been called the "poorhouse of the twentieth century" (Goldfarb, 1975:29). Most Americans do not distinguish between jails and prisons, but there is an important distinction. The jail is a strange correctional hybrid: part detention center for people awaiting trial, part penal institution for sentenced misdemeanants, and part holding facility for social misfits of one kind or another. Prisons usually hold only offenders sentenced to terms longer than one year. Locating correctional facilities and programs in the community to serve those who do not require long-term incarceration has been thought to be important, but local jails and short-term institutions in the United States are generally considered to be poorly managed custodial institutions (McConville, 1995:297).

There are approximately thirty-three hundred jails in the United States with the authority to detain individuals for more than forty-eight hours. The twenty-five largest hold 27 percent of the nation's jailed inmates. The Los Angeles County Men's Central Jail holds more than six thousand people. Most jails, however, are much smaller: 67 percent hold fewer than fifty persons (BJS, 1998a:8). Small jails are becoming less numerous because of new construction and new regional, multicounty facilities.

CHAPTER TWELVE

FIGURE

12.2 Characteristics of adult inmates in U.S. jails

Compared with the American population as a whole, jails are disproportionately inhabited by males, minorities, the poorly educated, and those with low incomes.

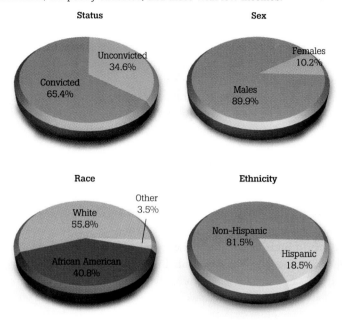

Status

Unconvicted 34.6%

Convicted 65.4%

Sex

Females 10.2%

Males 89.9%

Race

White 55.8%

Other 3.5%

African American 40.8%

Ethnicity

Non-Hispanic 81.5%

Hispanic 18.5%

SOURCE: U.S. Department of Justice, Bureau of Justice Statistics, *Special Report* (April 1998).

The most recent one-day census of the jail population found 567,079 inmates (212 per 100,000 adult residents), a 100 percent increase in ten years (BJS, 1998a:6). The characteristics of these inmates are shown in Figure 12.2. But the number of persons held at any one time in jail does not tell the complete story. Many people are held for less than twenty-four hours; others may reside in jail as sentenced inmates for up to one year; a few may await their trial for more than a year. The turnover rate is so great that more than 13 million Americans are jailed in one year. More citizens see the inside of jails than see the inside of prisons, mental hospitals, and halfway houses combined (BJS, 1995a:13)

Jails are usually locally administered by elected officials (sheriffs or county administrators). Only in Alaska, Connecticut, Delaware, Hawaii, Rhode Island, and Vermont are they run by the state government. Jails have traditionally been run by law enforcement agencies. It seems reasonable that the agency that arrests, detains, and transports defendants to court should also administer the facility that holds them, but generally neither sheriffs nor their deputies have much interest in corrections. They think of themselves as police officers and of the jail as merely an extension of law enforcement activities. However, more than half the jail inmates are sentenced offenders under correctional authority.

The primary function of jails is to hold persons awaiting trial and persons who have been sentenced for misdemeanors to terms of no more than one year. But this description is deceptive, because on a national basis about 35 percent of jail inmates are pretrial detainees. In some states, convicted felons may serve more than one year in jail instead of in prison. For 87 percent of the sentenced population, stays in jail are less than one month. Others held in jail are persons awaiting transportation to prison and persons convicted of parole or probation violations. This backup of inmates has caused difficulties in some states for judges and jail administrators who must often put misdemeanants on probation because no jail space is available.

Jails and police lockups shoulder responsibility for housing not only criminal defendants and offenders but also those persons viewed as problems by society. The criminal justice system is thus linked to other agencies of government. People with mental problems have become a new part of the jail population. They are often reported to the police when they act in a deviant manner that, although not illegal, is upsetting to the citizenry (urinating in public, appearing disoriented, shouting obscenities, and so on). The police must handle such situations, and temporary confinement in the lockup or jail may be necessary if no appropriate social service facilities are available. This situation has been likened to a revolving door that shifts these "street people" from the police station to the jail. After an appearance in court, they are often released to the streets to start their cycle through the system all over again.

Because of constant inmate turnover and because local control provides an incentive to keep costs down, correctional services are usually lacking. Recreational facilities and treatment programs are not found in most jails. Medical services are generally minimal. Such conditions add to the idleness and tensions of time spent in jail. Suicides and high levels of violence are hallmarks of many jails. In any one year almost half the people who die while in jail have committed suicide.

The mixture of offenders of widely diverse ages and criminal histories is another often-cited problem in U.S. jails. Because most inmates are viewed as temporary residents, little attempt is made to classify them for either security or treatment purposes. Horror stories of the mistreatment of young offenders by older, stronger, and more violent inmates occasionally come to public attention. The physical condition of most jails aggravates this situation, because most are old, overcrowded, and lacking basic facilities. Many sentenced felons prefer to move on to state prison where the conditions are likely to be better.

As criminal justice policy has become more punitive, jails, like prisons, have become crowded. Surveys have documented increases averaging 6 percent during each of the past five years. Even with new construction and with alternatives such as release on recognizance programs, diversion, intensive probation supervision, and house arrest with electronic monitoring, the jail population continues to rise. With the cost of building new facilities as high as $100,000 per cell and the cost of incarcerating an inmate about $20,000 per year, the $4.5 billion annual cost of operating jails is a great financial burden for local governments.

CHECK POINT

⑩ **What are the functions of jails?**

⑪ **List three of the problems affecting jails.**

Issues in Corrections

From 1940 until 1973 the number of persons incarcerated in the United States remained fairly stable and the characteristics of those individuals changed little. During the 1940s and 1950s, the incarceration rate was maintained at about 110 per 100,000 population. For a brief period in the late 1960s, when the trend was to stress rehabilitation and community corrections, the incarceration rate decreased. Paradoxically, although crime in the United States has been declining for the past eight years, the number of people in prison continues to climb. As criminologist Alfred Blumstein asks, "With so dramatic an increase in the incarceration rate, why have we not seen a significant decline in the crime rates?" (1998:129).

As noted by Allen Beck of the Bureau of Justice Statistics, this growth has brought about dramatic changes in the demographic and offense composition of the prison population. African Americans and Hispanics make up a much larger percentage of inmates than ever. Prisoners are more likely to be middle-aged, and more women are being incarcerated. Since 1980 the percentage of inmates serving time for violent offenses has declined, and the number incarcerated for drug offenses has increased (Beck, 1997:1–14).

Incarceration Trends

Every June and December a census of the U.S. prison population is taken for the Bureau of Justice Statistics. As shown in Figure 12.3, from a low of 98 per 100,000 population in 1972, the incarceration rate has steadily risen, and by January 1999 (the last census published) it was 461 per 100,000. This corresponds to the 1,217,592 men and 84,427 women in state and federal prisons. An additional 592,462 were inmates in local jails (BJS, 1999c:2, 3). Incarceration rates are second

FIGURE 12.3 **Incarceration in federal and state prisons per 100,000 population, 1940–1998**

Between 1940 and 1970 the incarceration rate was steady. Only since 1975 has there been a continuing increase. The rate today is more than double what it was in 1985.

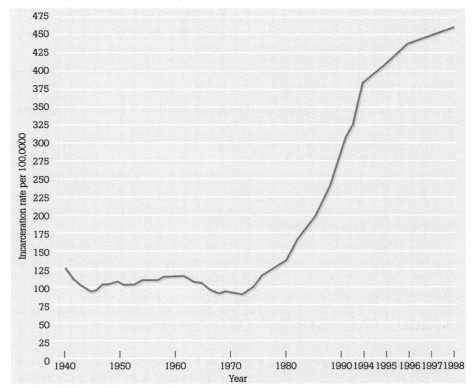

SOURCE: U.S. Department of Justice, Bureau of Justice Statistics, *Bulletin* (August 1999).

Behind Bars
in North America
and Europe

Most Western countries have put more people behind bars in recent years but in none has the incarceration rate risen higher than in the U.S. The cause of the extraordinary American figure is not higher levels of crime, for the crime rate in the U.S. is about the same as in western Europe (except for the rate of homicide, which is two to eight times greater, mostly because of the ready availability of guns).

The high U.S. rate—which rivals those of former Soviet nations—can be traced primarily to a shift in public attitudes toward crime that began about 30 years ago as apprehension about violence and drugs escalated. Politicians were soon exploiting the new attitudes with promises to get criminals off the streets. Presidents Ronald Reagan and George Bush promoted tough-on-crime measures, including the "War on Drugs." Bill Clinton, breaking with previous Democratic candidates, endorsed the death penalty and as president signed an anticrime bill that called for more prisons and increases in mandatory sentencing. Governors in about half the states signed "three strikes and you're out" legislation. Local officials who make most of the day-to-day decisions that affect incarceration, including police, prosecutors, judges and probation officers, were strongly influenced by the law-and-order rhetoric of governors and presidents. Increasingly, they opted for incarceration of law-breakers in local jails or in state prisons.

As a result, the length of sentences, already severe by western European standards, became even more punitive. Consequently, the number of those locked up rose more than fivefold between 1972 and 1998 to more than 1.8 million. Most of those sentenced in recent years are

only to Russia in North America and Europe as shown in the Comparative Perspective above.

The skyrocketing prison population has created a correctional crisis of overcrowding. In many states the new inmates have been put into already bulging institutions; some offenders are held in county jails and temporary quarters while others make do in corridors and basements. Faced with such conditions, courts in some states have demanded that changes be made, because they believe the overcrowding violates the Constitution.

But it is important to emphasize that the size and growth of the prison population is not evenly distributed across the country. As Figure 12.4 shows, seven of the ten states with the highest incarceration rates are in the South. In 1998 the South incarcerated 520 people for each 100,000 inhabitants, a ratio much higher than the national average of 461 (BJS, 1999c). Because Arizona, California, and Nevada are included in the top ten, the South is not alone with high incarceration rates.

Why this increase? Little relationship exists between the crime rate and the incarceration rate. If this is the case, what factors explain the growth? Five reasons are often cited for the increase: (1) increased arrests and more likely incarceration, (2) tougher sentencing, (3) prison construction, (4) the "war on drugs," and (5)

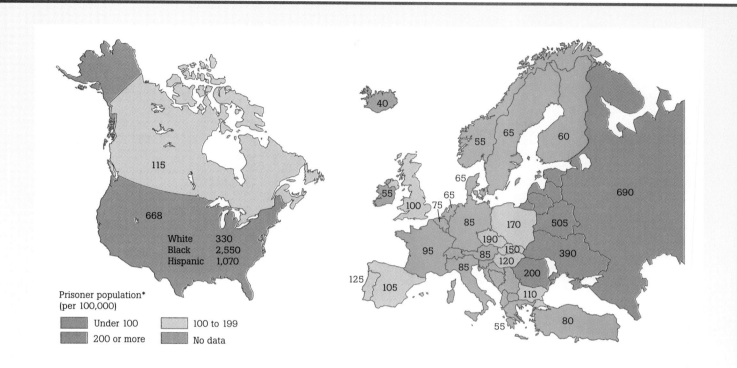

Prisoner population*
(per 100,000)

- Under 100
- 100 to 199
- 200 or more
- No data

White   330
Black   2,550
Hispanic 1,070

SOURCE: Roger Doyle, "By the Numbers," *Scientific American* (August 1999), 25.

*U.S. rate includes jail and prison populations.

perpetrators of nonviolent crimes, such as drug possession, that would not ordinarily be punished by long prison terms in other western countries. The rise in the population behind bars happened while the rate of property crime victimization was falling steeply and while the rate of violent crime victimization was generally trending downward.

state politics. None of these reasons should be viewed as a single explanation, with some having a greater impact than others.

Increased Arrests and More Likely Incarceration

Some analysts have argued that the billions of dollars spent on the crime problem may be paying off. When the crime rate began to rise in the mid-1960s, the incarceration rate was proportionally low. Crime rates for serious offenses have now declined, but arrest rates have gone up. Between 1980 and 1990 the adult arrest rate increased 45 percent, yet for some offenses the growth was much greater. For example drug violations were up 114 percent, aggravated assaults were up 74 percent, and sexual assaults other than rape were up 60 percent. In recent years arrest rates for most serious crimes have dropped (Beck, 1997:9).

Compounding this increase in arrest rates has been an increase in the probability of being sent to prison on conviction. Reacting to public opinion and legislative actions, judges have been more willing to sentence serious offenders to prison.

Not only has the number of arrests increased, but so has the likelihood of going to prison upon conviction.

FIGURE 12.4 Sentenced prisoners in state institutions per 100,000 population, December 31, 1998

What can be said about the differences in incarceration rates among the states? There are not only regional differences but also differences between adjacent states that seem to have similar socioeconomic and crime characteristics

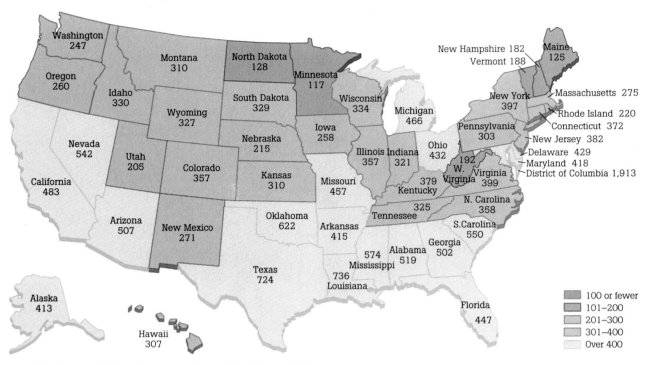

SOURCE: U.S. Department of Justice, Bureau of Justice Statistics, *Bulletin* (August 1999).

Between 1980 and 1994 (the latest available data) the likelihood of incarceration upon arrest increased fivefold for drug violations, fourfold for weapons offenses, and twofold for larceny-theft, motor vehicle theft, and sexual assault other than rape. For only one crime—murder/nonnegligent manslaughter—did the likelihood of incarceration for a serious offense decrease (Beck, 1997:11).

Not only is the probability of a prison sentence greater today than in the past, but also increased numbers of offenders are being sent to prison for probation and parole violations. In 1980, 82.4 percent of those entering prison did so directly as a result of a court sentence. This percentage dropped to 64.5 percent in 1994, reflecting an increase in the number sent to prison for violating conditions of community supervision. Allen Beck's analysis (1997:10) shows that 42 percent of the growth in total admissions to state prisons from 1980 to 1994 can be attributed to this factor.

Tougher Sentencing Practices

Some observers think that a hardening of public attitudes toward criminals is reflected in longer sentences, in a smaller proportion of those convicted getting probation, and in fewer being released at the time of the first parole hearing.

As discussed in Chapter 11, in the past few decades the states and the federal government have passed laws that increase sentences for most crimes. In addition, new mandatory sentencing laws greatly limit the discretion of judges in determining the length of sentences for certain offenders. The shift to determinate sentences, the new "truth-in-sentencing" laws, and a drop in the percentage of

CLOSE up

Connecticut: Trying to Build Its Way Out

In the early 1980s Connecticut's prison system became over-crowded, driven by the public demand that the criminal justice system "get tough" on crime. A state long wedded to the concepts of rehabilitation and community corrections, Connecticut's incarceration rate in 1981 was 95 per 100,000 population, well below the national rate of 153. As political pressures increased, however, the legislature toughened sentencing laws, eliminated supervised home release, and mandated that an increasing portion of sentences be served. Immediately the incarceration rate began to rise.

In 1987 Connecticut launched a $1 billion construction effort to double capacity by adding thirteen new prisons and expanding nine others. Connecticut's prison-building program was rivaled in scope only by California's. The expansion was inaugurated at a time when the state's economy was booming and there was a budget surplus. However, by the time the new facilities came on line in the early 1990s, a recession had set in and the state had a major budget deficit. Opening the new prisons became a problem as operating costs skyrocketed. Several stood vacant awaiting legislative appropriations to hire additional staff, yet the flow of newly sentenced offenders continued to increase.

From 1985 to 1997 the number of Connecticut inmates increased from 5,790 to 14,100, the correctional budget rose from $92.5 million to $417 million, and the incarceration rate swelled from 127 to 387 per 100,000 inhabitants (the highest in the Northeast). All of this has occurred in a state in which the amount of reported crime has not changed appreciably, although the number of arrests, especially for drug offenses, increased dramatically. In 1994 Connecticut led all states by recording a one-year prisoner growth rate of 20 percent. By 1995 the new prisons were operational and filled.

prisoners released on their first appearance before the parole board have increased the amount of time served for most offenses.

The tougher sentences do not seem to be the major factor for keeping offenders in prison for longer periods. Rather, it is the increased amount of time served (BJS, 1999b). Now a smaller percentage of state inmates are being released on their first appearance before the parole board. The number of releases dropped from 37 per 100 state prisoners in 1990 to 31 per 100 in 1996. The average time served by violent offenders rose to forty-nine months in 1997 from forty-three months in 1993. Keeping people in prison longer seems to account for much of the growth of the incarcerated population (Butterfield, 1999a:A10).

Prison Construction

The increased rate of incarceration may be related to the creation of additional space in the nation's prisons. Public attitudes in favor of more punitive sentencing policies influence legislators to approve building more prisons. However, the impact of new prisons may present a variation of the "Field of Dreams" scenario—build them and they will come. As Joseph Davey has noted, "the presence of empty state-of-the-art prison facilities can encourage a criminal court judge to incarcerate a defendant who may otherwise get probation" (Davey, 1998:84).

Prison construction during the 1990s was a growth industry with 213 state and federal prisons built in the first five years of the decade at an estimated

$30 billion (*New York Times,* August 8, 1997:A16). For health and security reasons, crowded conditions in existing facilities cannot be tolerated. Many states attempted to build their way out of this dilemma, because the public seemed to favor more punitive sentencing policies, which would require more prison space (see the Close-Up on p. 455).

Building costs are perhaps one of the greatest deterrents to prison expansion. The average cost of a new cell is $75,000, but because states borrow the construction money, the interest on this debt means that a new cell actually costs well over $100,000. For a hypothetical five hundred-bed medium-security facility, the base construction cost would be around $31 million. However, the true cost of constructing and operating a comparable prison begins with this base cost, plus costs for architects' fees, furnishings, and site preparation, raising the total to $41 million for the facility. To this must be added operating costs, which, estimated conservatively at $19,000 per inmate per year, totals $9.5 million per year. The thirty-year bill to taxpayers for construction and operations thus totals about $250 million, not the $31 million mentioned in legislative debates (Edna McConnell Clark Foundation, 1997:9).

The "War on Drugs"

Crusades against the use of drugs have been a recurring theme of American politics since the late 1800s. The latest manifestation began in 1982 when President Ronald Reagan declared another "war on drugs" and asked Congress to set aside more money for drug enforcement personnel and for prison space. This came at a time when the country was scared by the advent of crack cocaine, which ravaged many communities and resulted in increasing the murder rate. In 1987 Congress imposed stiff mandatory minimum sentences for federal drug law violations. These sentencing laws were copied by many states. The war continued into the Bush and Clinton administrations, as both presidents urged Congress to appropriate billions more for an all-out law enforcement campaign against drugs.

The "war on drugs" succeeded on one front by packing the nation's prisons with drug law offenders, but many scholars believe that is about all it has achieved. With additional resources and pressures for enforcement, the number of persons sentenced to prison for drug offenses has increased steadily. In 1980 only 19 per 1,000 new court commitments to state prisons were for drug offenses; by 1994 this had risen to 80 per 1,000. The number of women incarcerated for drug offenses rose by 888 percent from 1986 to 1996, in contrast to a rise of 129 percent for all nondrug offenses (Mauer, Potler, and Wolf, 1999). Today, 21 percent of state prisoners are incarcerated for drug offenses and the percentage in federal prisons is even higher, at almost 60 percent of inmates (BJS, 1999c).

But is imprisonment a cost-effective way of dealing with the problem of drugs? The harsh laws have not reduced drug use and the "ceaseless march of new drug offenders and the mounting costs of prisons" are moving some people to question the assumptions behind the "war" (Egan, 1999b). In particular it is asked if sentencing people to long terms for low-level, nonviolent drug offenses is cost-effective (DiIulio, 1999). John J. DiIulio Jr. argues that the incarceration of large numbers of drug-only offenders is not an efficient use of valuable prison space. Some of the cells could be better reserved for high-rate property and violent offenders (DiIulio, Piehl, and Useem, 1998).

State Politics

Incarceration rates vary among the regions and states, but why do states with similar characteristics differ in their use of prisons? Can it be that local political factors influence correctional policies?

One might think that there is an association among the states between variation in crime rates and variation in incarceration rates—the more crime, the more prisoners. Yet as shown by Davey, some states with high crime rates do not have corresponding high incarceration rates. Even when states have similar socioeconomic and demographic characteristics—poverty, unemployment, racial composition, drug arrests—it was not possible to explain variations in incarceration rates. For example, North Dakota and South Dakota have similar social characteristics and crime rates, yet the incarceration rate in South Dakota rose 300 percent from 1972 to 1992 and today remains three times as high as that found in North Dakota (Davey, 1998:27). One can even find similar and contiguous states such as Connecticut and Massachusetts, Arizona and New Mexico, or Minnesota and Wisconsin, where the state with the higher crime rate has the lower incarceration rate.

Since the 1970s most politicians have felt that the public demanded that they be "tough on crime." Governors and legislators have pushed for tougher sentences and greater use of incarceration as a way of reducing crime. Davey found that in seven states that elected "law-and-order" governors, there was a "rapid increase in the rate of imprisonment without regard to changes in the crime rate." In contiguous states where governors advocated less punitive policies, imprisonment rates did not increase (Davey, 1998:111).

Correctional Policy Trends

It is difficult to point to one factor as the major cause of the doubling of the incarceration rate during the past decade. A number of plausible hypotheses exist. Given current public attitudes toward crime and punishment, fear of crime, and the expansion of prison space, incarceration rates will likely remain high (see What Americans Think). Perhaps only when the costs of this form of punishment have a greater impact on the pockets of taxpayers will attitudes and policies shift, with a greater emphasis being placed on alternatives to incarceration.

CHECK POINT

⑫ **List four explanations for the great increase in the incarcerated population.**

⑬ **Why might additional construction only aggravate the problem?**

What Americans Think

Question "Would you favor or oppose each of the following measures that have been suggested as ways to reduce prison overcrowding?"

Percentage Responding That They Favor

Shortening sentences
8%

Allowing prisoners early release for good behavior and participation in educational and work programs
64%

Developing local programs to keep more nonviolent and first-time offenders active and working in the community
90%

Giving the parole board more authority to release offenders early
21%

Increasing taxes to build more prisons
33%

SOURCE Timothy J. Flanaghan, "Reform or Punish: Americans' Views of the Correctional System," *Americans View Crime and Justice*, Timothy J. Flanagan and Dennis R. Longmire, eds. (Thousands Oaks, CA: Sage Publications, 1996), pp. 88, 192.

Summary

■ From colonial days to the present, the methods of criminal sanctions that are considered appropriate have varied.

■ The development of the penitentiary brought a shift away from corporal punishment.

- The Pennsylvania and New York systems were competing approaches to implementing the ideas of the penitentiary.
- The Declaration of Principles of 1870 contained the key elements for the reformatory and rehabilitation models of corrections.
- The administration of corrections in the United States is fragmented in that various levels of government are involved.
- Jails, which are administered by local government, hold persons awaiting trial as well as sentenced offenders.
- Prison populations have more than doubled during the past decade; there has also been a great increase in facilities and staff to administer them.

Questions for Review

❶ What were the major differences between the Pennsylvania and New York systems in the nineteenth century?

❷ What are some of the pressures on administrators of local jails?

❸ What are the types of correctional programs that exist in your state? What agencies of government run them?

❹ Why are private prisons a corrections option that is attractive to some state legislators?

❺ What explanations might be given for the increased use of incarceration during the past two decades?

Key Terms

community corrections (p. 439)
congregate system (p. 435)
corrections (p. 430)
crime control model
 of corrections (p. 441)

Enlightenment (p. 432)
medical model (p. 439)
penitentiary (p. 433)
penology (p. 436)
reformatory (p. 437)

rehabilitation model (p. 438)
separate confinement (p. 435)

For Further Reading

Clear, Todd R., and George F. Cole. *American Corrections.* 5th ed. Belmont, Calif.: Wadsworth, 2000. An overview of American corrections.

Davey, Joseph Dillion. *The Politics of Prison Expansion: Winning Elections by Waging War on Crime.* Westport, Calif.: Praeger, 1998. Examines increases in the crime rate and increases in the incarceration rate at the state level. Finds that political factors influenced prison expansion in the period since 1972.

DiIulio, John, Jr. *No Escape: The Future of American Corrections.* New York: Basic Books, 1991. Essays on the governing of prisons and other issues related to the future of corrections.

Foucault, Michel. *Discipline and Punish.* Translated by Alan Sheridan. New York: Pantheon, 1977. Describes the transition of the focus of correctional punishment from the body of the offender to the reform of the individual.

Irwin, John, and James Austin. *It's About Time: America's Imprisonment Binge,* 2d ed. Belmont, Calif.: Wadsworth, 1997. Argues that the "grand imprisonment experiment" that has dominated recent American crime reduction policy has failed miserably and should be abandoned.

Rothman, David J. *Conscience and Convenience.* Boston: Little, Brown, 1980. Argues that conscience

activated the Progressives to reform corrections, yet the new structures for rehabilitation operated for the convenience of administrators.

Rothman, David J. *The Discovery of the Asylum: Social Order and Disorder in the New Republic.* Boston: Little, Brown, 1971. Rothman notes that before the nineteenth century deviants were cared for in the community. Urbanization and industrialization brought this function to government institutions.

Shichor, David. *Punishment for Profit: Private Prisons/Public Opinion.* Thousand Oaks, Calif.: Sage, 1995. Surveys the history and current debate over private prisons.

Going Online

❶ Write a short paper describing the organization, staffing, and facilities of the department of corrections in your state. You can access this information by linking to the web page of your state doc through "The Blue Leprecon's Correctional Directory" at www.tiac.net/users/leprecon/blue.htm.

❷ Go to the web site of the Bureau of Justice Statistics at www.ojp.usdoj.gov/bjs/. Click on publications and then access the bulletin "Prisoners in 1998." How many prisoners were held in your state on December 31, 1998? What was the incarceration rate? Compare the numbers and rates of two adjacent states. Can you explain differences among the three states?

❸ **Using InfoTrac College Edition,** search for the subject "prison reformers" and read an article about Elizabeth Fry. What were conditions like in British prisons? What did Fry try to accomplish?

CHECK POINT ANSWERS

❶ A period in the late eighteenth century when philosophers rethought the nature of society and the place of the individual in the world. New ideas about society and government arose from the Enlightenment.

❷ Four principles: secure and sanitary building, systematic inspection, abolition of fees, and a reformatory regime.

❸ The Pennsylvania system of separate confinement held inmates in isolation from one another. The New York congregate system kept inmates in their cells at night, but they worked in shops during the day.

❹ The Declaration of Principles advocated indeterminate sentences, rehabilitation programs, classifications based on improvements in character, and release on parole.

❺ Separation of women prisoners from men, care in keeping with women's needs, women's prisons staffed by women.

❻ Rehabilitation model: criminal behavior is the result of a biological, psychological, or social deficiency; clinicians should diagnose the problem and prescribe treatment; when cured, the offender may be released. Community model: the goal of corrections is to reintegrate the offender into the community, so rehabilitation should be carried out in the community rather than in prison if possible; correction workers should serve as advocates for offenders in their dealings with government agencies. Crime control model: criminal behavior can be controlled by greater use of incarceration and other forms of strict supervision.

❼ The Federal Bureau of Prisons of the Department of Justice and the Administrative Office of the U.S. Courts, which handles probation.

❽ Prisons: department of corrections. Probation: judiciary or executive branch department. Intermediate sanctions: judiciary, probation department, department of corrections. Parole: executive agency.

❾ In favor: costs are lower yet conditions are the same or better than prisons run by the government. Opposed: incarceration should be a function of government, not an enterprise for private profit. Private interests can skew public policy.

❿ Holding of offenders before trial and incarceration of offenders sentenced to short terms.

⓫ High population turnover, lack of services, scarce resources.

⓬ Increased arrests and more likely incarceration, tougher sentencing, prison construction, the "war on drugs."

⓭ New prison beds will quickly become filled because judges will be less hesitant to sentence people to prison and because the corrections bureaucracy needs the space to be used.

CHAPTER THIRTEEN

Community Corrections

Probation and Intermediate Sanctions

Todd Harrison raked his way across the littered lot as he and his coworkers moved about in the Bayside, Florida, recreation area. He wore the "uniform" provided by the probation department—an orange-colored hard hat and vest. He wore his own sunglasses and a T-shirt emblazoned "B.U.M." Harrison was one of ten probationers working under the watchful eye of Rich Clark, a community service supervisor employed by the nonprofit organization Upward Now, Inc. Two years before, Harrison had been sentenced to three years on probation and one hundred hours of community service for a larceny conviction. Because Todd was 19 at the time and had no prior record, the judge had given him a community sentence instead of sending him to prison—the usual sentence for more experienced criminals convicted of the same offense. Harrison lives with his mother, works the late shift at a convenience store, reports to his probation officer monthly, and spends five hours every

Although most people think of corrections as prisons and jails, almost three-quarters of offenders are supervised within the community.

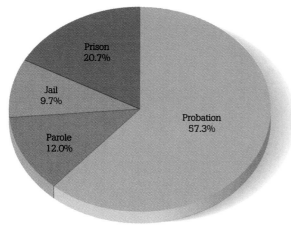

Prison 20.7%
Jail 9.7%
Parole 12.0%
Probation 57.3%

SOURCE: U.S. Department of Justice, Bureau of Justice Statistics, *Sourcebook of Criminal Justice Statistics, 1998* (Washington, D.C.: Government Printing Office, 1999), Table 6.1

Saturday under the supervision of Clark to complete his community service. Things are looking up for Todd Harrison as he moves toward completion of his punishment.

Since the early nineteenth century, supervision in the community has been recognized as an appropriate punishment for some offenders. Although probation had been developed in the 1840s and was widely used by the 1920s, incarceration remained the usual sentence for serious crimes until the 1960s. At that time, with a new emphasis on community corrections, judges sentenced increased numbers of offenders to sanctions carried out in the community. Community corrections in the 1960s and 1970s continued the rehabilitative emphasis of earlier periods—to reform bad guys into good guys (Peterson and Palumbo, 1997: 83). As a result, incarceration rates fell as probation was viewed as the "punishment of choice" for most first-time offenders. However, as Americans wearied of crime in the 1980s, legislatures passed tough sentencing laws and specified incarceration as the new priority punishment. The "war on drugs" further increased the number of offenders incarcerated, as well as adding to the numbers under probation supervision. By the late 1980s, criminal justice scholars recognized that many imprisoned offenders, if properly supervised, could be punished more cheaply and effectively in the community. Yet probation was clearly inappropriate for offenders whose crimes were serious and who could not be effectively supervised by officers with large caseloads. What was needed was a set of intermediate sanctions, less restrictive of freedom than prison, but more restrictive than probation. Unlike community corrections of the 1970s, intermediate sanctions were to be "a less costly way of handling criminals while still protecting public safety" (Peterson and Palumbo. 1997:83). These sanctions came to include intensive probation supervision, home confinement, monetary sanctions, and boot camps (Morris and Tonry, 1990:3).

In years to come, community corrections can be expected to play a much greater role in the criminal justice system. As shown in Figure 13.1, already two-thirds of offenders are under correctional supervision in the community. This portion is likely to increase as states try to deal with the high costs of incarceration. Probation and intermediate sanctions appear to many criminal justice experts to be less expensive and just as effective as imprisonment (Petersilia, 1996).

QUESTIONS for Inquiry

- What are the philosophical assumptions underlying community corrections?
- How did probation evolve, and in what ways are probation sentences implemented today?
- What are the types of intermediate sanctions, and how are they administered?
- What are the key issues facing community corrections as the twenty-first century begins?

Community Corrections: Assumptions

Community corrections seeks to keep offenders in the community by building ties to family, employment, and other normal sources of stability and success. This model of corrections assumes that the offender must change, but it recognizes that factors within the community that might encourage criminal behavior (unemployment, for example) must also change.

Four factors are usually cited in support of community corrections. First, many offenders' criminal records and current offenses are not serious enough to warrant incarceration. Second, community supervision is cheaper than incarceration. Third, rates of **recidivism,** or returning to crime, for those under community supervision are no higher than for those who go to prison. Some studies show that just being in prison raises the offender's potential for recidivism, perhaps by hardening attitudes toward society or transmitting criminal skills and behaviors. Fourth, when compared with alternative sentences and their consequences, incarceration is more destructive to both the offender and society. In addition to the pains of imprisonment and the harmful effects of prison life, incarceration adds to the suffering of family members, particularly children.

Community corrections is based on the goal of finding the "least restrictive alternative"—punishing the offender only as severely as needed to protect the community and to satisfy the public. Advocates call for programs to assist offenders in the community so they will have opportunities to succeed in law-abiding activities and to reduce their contact with the criminal world.

recidivism
A return to criminal behavior.

CHECK POINT

① **What are the four main assumptions underlying community corrections?**

(Answers are at the end of the chapter.)

Probation: Correction without Incarceration

Probation is the conditional release of the offender into the community under the supervision of correctional officials. Probationers live at home and work at regular jobs, but they must report regularly to their probation officers. They must also abide by certain conditions, such as submitting to drug tests, obeying curfews, and staying away from certain people or parts of town. Although probation is mainly used for lesser offenses, states are increasingly using probation for more serious felonies, as shown in Figure 13.2.

Probation may be combined with other sanctions, such as fines, restitution, and community service. Fulfillment of these other sanctions may, in effect, become a condition for successful completion of probation. The sentencing court retains authority over the probationer, and if he or she violates the conditions or commits another crime, the judge may order the entire sentence to be served in prison.

Often the judge imposes a prison term but then suspends serving of that sentence and instead places the offender on probation. Increasingly, however, judges in some states are using the tactics of shock probation or split sentences, in which

probation
A sentence allowing the offender to serve the sanctions imposed by the court in the community under supervision.

FIGURE 13.2 Felony sentences to probation in state courts

Although most people on probation have been convicted of misdemeanors, states have increasingly used this sanction for serious offenders. Shown here are the percentages sentenced to probation listed by their most serious charge for which they were convicted.

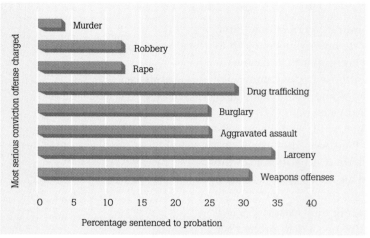

SOURCE: U.S. Department of Justice, Bureau of Justice Statistics, *Bulletin* (January 1997), 2.

a period in prison is followed by probation. This reflects a theory that a taste of imprisonment will jar some offenders sufficiently to change their lives, making them obey the conditions of their probation and "go straight."

The number of probationers now under supervision is at a record high and is still rising. Much has been written about overcrowded prisons, but the adult probation population has also been increasing—by about 3 percent a year, up 22 percent since 1990 (BJS, 1998f). Today, more than three million offenders are on probation, yet probation budgets in many states have been cut and caseloads increased as greater resources are diverted instead to prisons.

Although probation has many benefits that cause it to be chosen over incarceration, the public often sees it as merely a "slap on the wrist" for offenders. This view is so widespread that even a scholarly work on correctional policy has referred to probation as a kind of "standing joke" (Davis and Smith, 1994). With caseloads in some urban areas comprised of as many as three hundred probationers, officers are unable to provide the level of supervision necessary.

Origins and Evolution of Probation

The historical roots of probation lie in the procedures for reprieves and pardons of early English courts. Probation itself, however, developed in the United States. John Augustus, a Boston boot maker, was the world's first probation officer. He persuaded a judge in the Boston Police Court in 1841 to give him custody of a convicted offender for a brief period and then helped the man to appear rehabilitated by the time of sentencing.

Massachusetts developed the first statewide probation system in 1880, and by 1920 twenty-one other states had followed suit. The federal courts were authorized to hire probation officers in 1925. By the beginning of World War II, forty-four states had probation systems.

Probation began as a humanitarian effort to allow first-time and minor offenders a second chance. Probation officers guided clients toward law-abiding and productive lives. Early probationers were expected not only to obey the law, but also to behave in a morally acceptable fashion. Officers sought to provide moral leadership to help shape probationers' attitudes and behavior with respect to family, religion, employment, and free time.

By the 1920s, the development of psychology led probation officers to shift their emphasis from moral leadership to therapeutic counseling. This shift brought three important changes. First, the officer no longer primarily acted as a community supervisor charged with enforcing a particular morality. Second, the officer became more of a clinical social worker whose goal was to help the offender solve psychological and social problems. Third, the offender was expected to become actively involved in the treatment. The pursuit of rehabilitation as the primary goal of probation gave the officer extensive discretion in defining and treating the offender's problems. Officers used their judgment to evaluate each offender and develop a treatment approach to the personal problems that presumably had led to crime.

During the 1960s, a new shift occurred in probation techniques. Rather than counseling offenders, probation officers provided them with concrete social services, in the form of assistance with employment, housing, finances, and education. This emphasis on reintegrating offenders and remedying the social problems they faced was consistent with federal efforts to wage a "war on poverty." Instead of being a counselor or therapist, the probation officer was an advocate, dealing with private and public institutions on the offender's behalf.

In the late 1970s, the orientation of probation changed yet again as the goals of rehabilitation and reintegration gave way to "risk control." This approach, still dominant today, attempts to minimize the probability that an offender will commit a new offense. Risk control reflects two basic goals. First, based on the deserved punishment ideal, the punishment should fit the offense, and correctional intervention should neither raise nor lower the level of punishment. Second, according to the community protection criterion, the amount and type of supervision are determined according to the risk that the probationer will return to crime.

CHECK POINT

② **Who was John Augustus and what did he do?**

③ **What is the major goal of probation today?**

Organization of Probation

Although probation is viewed as a form of corrections, in many states it is administered locally by the judiciary. As shown in Figure 13.3, there are seven different jurisdictional arrangements for adult and juvenile probation. In about 25 percent of the states, probation is a responsibility of county and local government. The state sets the standards and provides financial support and training courses, but about two-thirds of all persons under probation supervision are handled by locally administered programs. In many jurisdictions, although the state is formally responsible for all probation services, the locally elected county judges are in charge.

This seemingly odd arrangement produces benefits as well as problems. On the positive side, having probationers under the supervision of the court permits judges to keep closer tabs on them and to order incarceration if the conditions of probation are violated. On the negative side, some judges know little about the goals and methods of corrections, and the probation responsibility adds to the administrative duties of already overworked courts.

One strong reason for judicial control is that probation works best when the judge and the supervising officer have a close relationship. Proponents of this system say that judges need to work with probation officers whom they can trust, whose presentence reports they can accurately evaluate, and whom they can rely to report on the success or failure of individual cases.

For the sake of their clients and the goals of the system, probation officers need direct access to corrections and other human services agencies. However, these agencies are located within the executive branch of government. A number of states have combined probation and parole services in the same agency to

FIGURE 13.3 **The seven jurisdictional arrangements for probation, by state**

The organization of probation varies, depending on the traditions and politics of state and local governments.

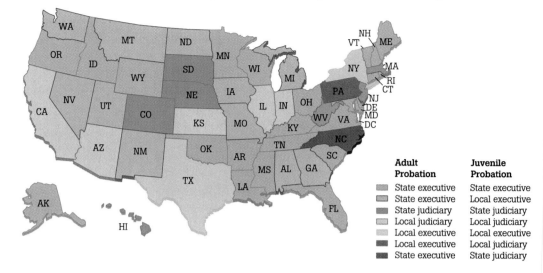

Adult Probation	Juvenile Probation
State executive	State executive
State executive	Local executive
State judiciary	State judiciary
Local judiciary	Local judiciary
Local executive	Local executive
Local executive	Local judiciary
State executive	State judiciary

SOURCE: American Correctional Association, *ACA Directory, 1995* (College Park, Md.: American Correctional Association, 1995).

better coordinate resources and services. Others point out, however, that probationers are different from parolees. Parolees already have served prison terms, frequently have been involved in more serious crimes, and often have been disconnected from mainstream society. By contrast, most probationers have not developed criminal lifestyles to the same degree and do not have the same problems of reintegration into the community.

Probation Services

Probation officers play roles similar to both police personnel and social workers. In addition to assisting the judiciary with presentence investigations, probation officers supervise clients to keep them out of trouble and enforce the conditions of the sentence. This law enforcement role involves discretionary decisions about whether to report violations of probation conditions. Probation officers are also expected to play a social worker role by helping clients obtain the housing, employment, and treatment services they need. Not surprisingly, individual officers may emphasize one role over the other, and the potential conflict between the roles is great. But studies have shown that most probation officers have backgrounds in social services and lean toward that role.

A continuing issue for probation officers is the size of their caseloads. How many clients can an officer effectively handle? In the 1930s, the National Probation Association recommended a 50-unit caseload, and in 1967 the President's Commission on Law Enforcement and Administration of Justice reduced it to 35. However, the national average is currently about 117, and some caseloads exceed 300 (Petersilia, 1996, 1998). The oversized caseload is usually identified as one of the major obstacles to successful operation of probation. Recent evidence indicates, however, that the size of the caseload is less significant than the nature of the supervision experience, the classification of offenders, the professionalism of the officer, and the services available from the agencies of correction. In other words, the number of offenders handled by each probation officer is less

Providing direct supervision of drug offenders has become a dangerous task for probation officers. Here, the probation officer has police assistance in bringing a client to court for revocation.

important than the quality of the services and the supervision the probationers get (Petersilia and Turner, 1993).

During the past decade, probation officials have developed methods of classifying clients according to their service needs, the element of risk they pose to the community, and the chance that they will commit another offense. Through this process probationers may be supervised less as they continue to live within the conditions of their sentence. Risk classification schemes fit the deserved-punishment model of the criminal sanction in that the most serious cases receive the greatest restrictions and supervision.

Whether serious cases receive more supervision is influenced by a number of factors. Consider the "war on drugs." It has significantly increased probation levels in urban areas because large numbers of drug dealers and people convicted of drug possession are placed on probation. Many of these offenders have committed violent acts and live in inner-city areas marked by drug dealing and turf battles to control drug markets. Under these conditions, direct supervision can be a dangerous task for the probation officer. In some urban areas, probationers are merely required to telephone or mail reports of their current residence and employment. In such cases, it is hard to see how any goal of the sanctions—deserved punishment, rehabilitation, deterrence, or incapacitation—is being realized. If none of these objectives is met, the offender is getting off.

④ What are the major tasks of probation officers?

Revocation of Probation

Does probation work? By "work," most mean: do probationers remain crime-free? Did they recidivate? Current data make it difficult to accurately answer this question. Patrick Langan and Mark Cunniff (1992) found that within three years

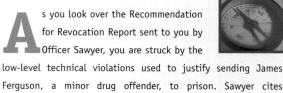

A s you look over the Recommendation for Revocation Report sent to you by Officer Sawyer, you are struck by the low-level technical violations used to justify sending James Ferguson, a minor drug offender, to prison. Sawyer cites Ferguson's failure to attend all the drug treatment sessions, to complete his community service, and to pay a $500 fine. You call Sawyer in to discuss the report.

"Bill, I've looked over your report on Ferguson and I'm wondering what's going on here. Why isn't he fulfilling the conditions of his probation?"

"I'm really not sure, but it seems he just doesn't want to meet the conditions. I think he's got a bad attitude, and I don't like the guys he hangs around with. He's always mouthing off about the 'system' and says I'm on his case for no reason."

"Well, let's look at your report. You say that he works for Capital Services cleaning offices downtown from midnight till 8 A.M. yet has to go to the drug programs three mornings a week and put in ten hours a week at the Salvation Army Thrift Store. Is it that he isn't trying or does he have an impossible situation?"

"I think he could do it if he tried, but also, I think he's selling cocaine again. Perhaps he needs to get a taste of prison."

"That may be true, but do you really want to revoke his probation?"

■ What's going on here? Is Sawyer recommending revocation because of Ferguson's attitude and the suspicion that he is selling drugs again? Do the technical violations warrant prison?

___Mempa v. Rhay (1967)___
*Probationers have the right
to counsel at a revocation
and sentencing hearing.*

___Gagnon v. Scarpelli (1973)___
*Before probation can be revoked,
a two-stage hearing must be held
and the offender provided with
specific elements of due process.*

43 percent of felons given probation were rearrested. Looking at all probationers Michael Geerken and Hennessey Hayes (1993:549) found that between one-fifth and one-third violated the provisions of their sentences. Because probation is usually granted in conjunction with a suspended jail or prison sentence, incarceration may follow revocation. Revocation of probation can occur for either a technical violation or a new arrest.

Technical violations occur when a probationer fails to meet the conditions of a sentence by, for instance, violating curfew, failing a drug test, or using alcohol. Officers have discretion as to whether or not they bring this fact to the attention of the judge. Peter Burke (1997:12) found nationwide motions to revoke probation were for failing a drug urinalysis test, 27 percent; failing to participate in treatment, 20 percent; absconding, 18.5 percent; committing a new felony, 12 percent; failing to report, 10 percent; committing a new misdemeanor, 4 percent; and committing other technical violations, 8.5 percent.

Probation officers and judges have widely varying notions of what constitutes grounds for revoking probation as seen by Officer Sawyer's attitude in A Question of Ethics (p. 000). Once the officer has decided to call a violation to the attention of the court, the probationer may be arrested or summoned for a revocation hearing. Given that the contemporary emphasis is on avoiding incarceration except for flagrant and continual violation of the conditions of probation, most revocations today occur because of a new arrest or conviction. Yet one study in California found that many of these "failures" stayed on probation after their convictions, even though the new offense was often serious. This study suggests that once a person is on probation, serious misbehavior will not necessarily result in removal from the community (Petersilia, Turner, Kahan, and Peterson, 1985:39).

In 1967 the U.S. Supreme Court gave its first opinion concerning the due process rights of probationers at a revocation hearing. In *Mempa v. Rhay* (1967) the justices determined that a state probationer had a right to counsel at a revocation and sentencing hearing, but the Court did not refer to any requirement for a hearing. This issue was addressed in *Gagnon v. Scarpelli* (1973), in which the justices ruled that before probation or parole can be revoked, the offender is entitled to a preliminary and a final hearing and to specific elements of due process. When a probationer is taken into custody for violating the conditions of probation, a preliminary hearing must be held to determine whether probable cause exists to believe that the incident occurred. If there is a finding of probable cause, a final hearing, where the revocation decision is made, is mandatory. At these hearings the probationer has the right to cross-examine witnesses and to be given notice of the alleged violations and a written report of the proceedings. The Court ruled, though, that the probationer does not have an automatic right to counsel—this decision is to be made on a case-by-case basis. At the final hearing, the judge decides whether to continue probation or to impose tougher restrictions, such as incarceration.

The case of *Griffin v. Wisconsin* (1987) is a good example of the clash between the Bill of Rights and community corrections. Learning that Joseph Griffin might have a gun, probation officers searched his apartment without a warrant. The Supreme Court noted the practical problems of obtaining a search warrant while the probationer was under supervision. The Court said the probation agency must be able to act before the offender damaged himself or society. In Griffin's case the Court felt that the agency had satisfied the Fourth Amendment's reasonableness requirement.

CHECK POINT

⑤ **What are the grounds for probation revocation?**

⑥ **What rights does a probationer have while revocation is being considered?**

Assessing Probation

Probation is at a crossroads. Some critics see probation as nothing more than a slap on the wrist, an absence of punishment. Yet the importance of probation for public safety has never been greater: in one sample of large urban counties it was estimated that 17 percent of people arrested for a felony were on probation (Reaves and Smith, 1995).

Because of their probation officers' huge caseloads, probationers often receive very little guidance, supervision, or assistance. Joan Petersilia observes that because of low funding and large caseloads, probation supervision in many urban jurisdictions "amounts to simply monitoring for rearrest." Sixty percent of all Los Angeles probationers are tracked solely by computer and have no contact with officers (Petersilia, 1996). Nationally three out of five felony probationers see a probation officer no more than once a month at best. While the credibility of probation is low in the eyes of the public, its workload is growing dramatically and, in view of the crowding in prisons and jails, will probably continue to do so.

How effective can probation be? From one-fifth to one-third of probationers fail to fulfill the conditions of their sentence. Although this recidivism rate is lower than for those who have been incarcerated, researchers question whether this is a direct result of supervision or an indirect result of the maturing of the probationers. Most offenders placed on probation do not become career criminals, their criminal activity is short-lived, and they become stable citizens as they obtain jobs and get married. Most of those who are arrested a second time do not repeat their mistake again.

What rallies support for probation is its relatively low cost: keeping an offender on probation instead of behind bars costs roughly $1,000 a year, a savings of more than $20,000 a year (Abadinsky, 1997). However, these savings may not satisfy community members who hear of a sex offender on probation who repeats his crime.

In recent years as prisons have become overcrowded, increasing numbers of felony offenders have been placed on probation. Almost half (46 percent) of all convicted felons are given probation (Petersilia, 1996:21). More than 75 percent of probationers are addicted to drugs or alcohol. These factors present new challenges for probation, because officers can no longer assume that their clients pose little threat to society and that they have the skills to live productive lives in the community.

To offer a viable alternative to incarceration, probation services need the resources to appropriately supervise and assist their clients. The new demands on probation have brought calls for increased electronic monitoring and for risk management systems that provide different levels of supervision for different kinds of offenders.

Intermediate Sanctions in the Community

Dissatisfaction with the traditional means of probation supervision, coupled with the crowding and high cost of prisons, has resulted in a call for a new kind of intermediate sanctions in the community. The call is for sanctions that restrict the offender more than simple probation does and that constitute punishment for more serious offenders.

The case for intermediate sanctions can be made on several grounds, but Norval Morris and Michael Tonry said it this way: "Prison is used excessively; probation is used even more excessively; between the two is a near vacuum of purposive and enforced punishments" (1990:3). This view is based on the fact that 46 percent of convicted felons are given prison, the most severe sentence, while probation, the least severe, is given to 47 percent. Hence more than 90 percent of all convicted felons receive either the most or least severe of possible penalties (Langan, 1994:791). Morris and Tonry have urged that punishments be created that are more restrictive than probation yet match the severity of the offense and the characteristics of the offender, and that can be carried out while still protecting the community.

Advocates of intermediate sanctions also point to the lower cost of community punishments than prison or jail. As states struggle with the soaring costs of corrections, the idea that these could be lessened by punishing more offenders in the community sounds promising. Table 13.1 shows the costs of the range of punishments in four states. But are lower costs the only factor to increase public support for intermediate sanctions?

Intermediate sanctions may be viewed as a continuum—a range of punishments that vary in levels of intrusiveness and control, as shown in Figure 13.4. Probation plus a fine or community service may be appropriate for minor offenses, while six weeks of boot camp followed by intensive probation supervision might be right for serious crimes. But some question whether offenders will be able to fulfill the conditions added to probation? Moreover, if prisons are overcrowded, is incarceration a believable threat if offenders fail to comply (Blomberg and Lucken, 1993:470)?

Across the country, many different types of intermediate sanctions are being used. They can be divided into (1) those administered primarily by the judiciary (fines, restitution, and forfeiture), (2) those primarily administered in the community with a supervision component (home confinement, community service, day reporting centers, and intensive probation supervision), and (3) those that are administered inside institutions and followed by community supervision (boot camp). Furthermore, sanctions may be imposed in combination—for example, a fine and probation, or boot camp with community service and probation.

TABLE 13.1

Costs of incarceration and community sanctions in four states

In a study of Colorado, North Carolina, Ohio, and Virginia, probation and intermediate sanctions proved far less expensive than incarceration.

CORRECTIONAL METHOD	COST PER YEAR PER OFFENDER
Prison	$17,794
Jail	12,494
Probation	869
Intensive supervision	2,292
Community service	2,759
Day reporting	2,781
House arrest	402
Electronic monitoring	2,011
Halfway house	12,494
Boot camp	23,707

SOURCE: *Seeking Justice: Crime and Punishment in America* (New York: Edna McConnell Clark Foundation, 1997), 34.

CHAPTER THIRTEEN

FIGURE 13.4 Continuum of intermediate sanctions

Judges may use a range of intermediate sanctions, from those in which the offender requires a low level of control to those in which the offender requires a high level of control.

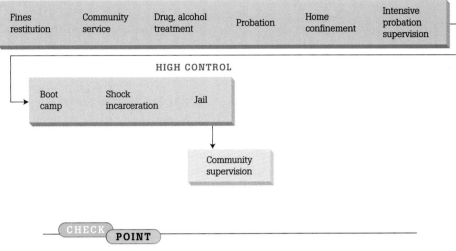

LOW CONTROL

| Fines restitution | Community service | Drug, alcohol treatment | Probation | Home confinement | Intensive probation supervision |

HIGH CONTROL

| Boot camp | Shock incarceration | Jail |

Community supervision

CHECK POINT

⑦ **What is the main argument for intermediate sanctions?**

⑧ **What is meant by a continuum of sanctions?**

Intermediate Sanctions Administered Primarily by the Judiciary

A number of intermediate sanctions are administered primarily by the judiciary. Three—fines, restitution, and forfeiture—are discussed here. Because all three involve the transfer of money or property from the offender to the government or crime victim, the judiciary is considered the proper branch not only to impose the sanction but also to collect what is due.

Fines

Fines are routinely imposed today for offenses ranging from traffic violations to felonies. Studies have shown that the fine is used widely as a criminal sanction and that well over $1 billion in fines are collected annually by courts across the country (Hillsman, Sichel, and Mahoney, 1983). Yet, judges in the United States make little use of fines as the sole punishment for crimes more serious than motor vehicle violations. Instead, fines typically are used in conjunction with other sanctions, such as probation and incarceration; for example, two years of probation and a $500 fine.

The American resistance to using fines as the sole punishment for serious offenders stands in marked contrast to European countries. The criminal code of the Netherlands explicitly states that the fine is the preferred penalty for all offenses and judges must provide a statement justifying their use of other sanctions. In Germany, 81 percent of all sentenced offenders must pay a fine, including 73 percent of those convicted for crimes of violence. In Sweden fines are used in 91 percent of cases; in England 47 percent of indictable offenses (roughly equivalent to an American felony) (Tonry, 1998a:698).

fine
A sum of money to be paid to the state by a convicted person as punishment for an offense.

Day Fines in Germany:
Could the Concept Work in the United States?

Monetary sanctions are used extensively in Europe in part because of the existence of the day-fine system. Under this system the amount of the fine is related not only to the seriousness of the crime but also to the offender's income. Could a day-fine system work in the United States?

Modern implementation of fines related to the income of the offender began with creation of the day-fine system in Finland in 1921, followed by its development in Sweden (1931) and Denmark (1939). The Federal Republic of Germany instituted day fines in 1975. Since then, there has been a major change in the punishments of offenders so that now more than 80 percent of those convicted receive a fine-alone sentence.

Judges determine the amount of the day fine through a two-stage process. First, judges relate the crime to offense guidelines, which have established the minimum and maximum number of day-fine units for each offense. For example, according to the guidelines, theft may be punished by a day fine within the range of ten to fifty units. Judges choose the number of units by considering the culpability of the offender and by examining the offender's motivation and the circumstances surrounding the crime. Second, the value of these units is determined. The German day fine is calculated as the cost of a day of freedom: the amount of income an offender would have forfeited if incarcerated for a day. One day-fine unit is equal to the offender's average net daily

Many judges cite the difficulty of collecting fines as the reason that they do not impose this punishment more often. For most other punishments, the judges rely on another agency of government—such as the sheriff, probation, or corrections—to carry out the sentence. But monetary penalties are typically imposed by a judge and collected by the court's staff. However, enforcing fines often takes a back seat to the demanding flow of criminal prosecutions, sentencing decisions, and probation revocations. Perhaps the judiciary sees little incentive to expend its own resources in administering the collection of fines given that the proceeds are not earmarked for the courts.

In addition, judges point out that because so many offenders are poor, it is difficult for them to pay fines, and they might even commit additional illegal acts to get the money. Furthermore, reliance on fines as an alternative to incarceration might enable affluent offenders to "buy" their way out of jail with little discomfort, while the poor would have to serve time. Finally, in cases in which a poor offender can pay, payment might be most burdensome to his or her family, who would suffer the loss of bare necessities.

Fines are used extensively in Europe and are strongly enforced (Tonry and Hamilton, 1995:16). They are normally the only punishment for a wide range of crimes, with amounts geared to the severity of the offense and the resources of the offender. To deal with the concern that fines exact a heavier toll on the poor than on the wealthy, Sweden and Germany have developed the day fine, which is income (considering salary, pensions, welfare benefits, interests, and so on), without deductions for family maintenance, so long as the offender and the offender's dependents have a minimal standard of living. Finally, the law calls for publication of the number of units and their value for each day fine set by the court so that the sentencing judgment is publicly known.

For example, say a judge is faced with two defendants who have separately been convicted of theft. One defendant is a truck driver who earns an average of DM [deutsche mark] 100 per day and the other is a business manager whose earnings average DM 300 per day. The judge uses the guidelines and decides that the circumstances of the theft and the criminal record of each offender are the same. The judge decides that forty day-fine units should be assessed to each. By multiplying these units by the average daily income for each, the truck driver's fine is DM 4,000 and the manager's fine is DM 12,000.

Since the day-fine system was introduced in Germany, there has been an increase in the use of fines and a decrease in short-term incarceration. The size of fines has also increased, reflecting the fact that affluent offenders are now being punished at levels corresponding to their financial worth. Likewise, fines for poor offenders have remained relatively low. These results have been accomplished without an increase in the default rate.

■ Some Americans believe that day fines would be more equitable than the current system of low fines for all, regardless of wealth. Others believe that to levy higher fines against rich people than poor people is unjust because the wealthy person is being penalized for working hard for a high income. What do you think?

described in the Comparative Perspective above. They achieve fairness by imposing different levels of fines on offenders who have committed the same offense, but who have different levels of income.

The day-fine concept has been adapted to the U.S. system and tested in several jurisdictions. Evaluations in Staten Island, New York, and Milwaukee, Wisconsin, found day-fine systems worked well in regular courts. In Staten Island, 70 percent of those assessed a day fine paid in full. However, in Milwaukee only 37 percent paid in full. Not surprisingly offenders with the lowest incomes were less likely to pay (McDonald, Greene, and Worzella, 1992). Evaluations of other day-fines projects in the United States are disappointing (Turner and Petersilia, 1996).

Restitution

In its simplest form, **restitution** is repayment by an offender to a victim who has suffered some form of financial loss from the crime. It is *reparative* in that it seeks to repair the harm done. In the Middle Ages restitution was a common way to settle a criminal case (Karmen, 1996:297). The offender was ordered to pay the victim or do the victim's work. The growth of the modern state saw the decline of such punishments based on "private" arrangements between offender and victim. Instead, the state prosecuted offenders, and punishments focused on the wrong the offender had done to society. Victim restitution has remained a part of the U.S. criminal justice system, though it is largely unpublicized. In many instances,

restitution
Repayment—in the form of money or service—by an offender to a victim who has suffered some financial loss from the offense.

restitution derives from informal agreements between law enforcement officials and offenders at the police station, during plea bargaining, or in the prosecutor's sentence recommendations. Only since the late 1970s, however, has restitution been institutionalized in many jurisdictions, usually as one of the conditions of probation. Judge Lois Forer of the Philadelphia Court of Common Pleas was a pioneer in the use of restitution and made extensive use of it for incarcerated offenders as well as those on probation. A study showed that most offenders ordered to pay restitution completed their probation successfully (Weitekamp, 1995:68).

As with fines, convicted offenders have differing abilities to pay restitution, and the conditions inevitably fall more harshly on less affluent offenders who cannot easily pay. Someone who has the "good fortune" to be victimized by an affluent criminal may receive full compensation, while someone victimized by a poor offender may never receive a penny.

Restitution is more easily imposed when the "damage" inflicted can be easily measured—value of property destroyed or stolen, or medical costs, for instance. But what should be the restitution for the terror of an attempted rape?

Forfeiture

With passage of two laws in 1970—the Racketeer Influenced and Corrupt Organizations Act (RICO) and the Continuing Criminal Enterprise Act (CCE), Congress resurrected forfeiture, a criminal sanction that had not been used in the United States since the American Revolution. By amending these laws in 1984 and 1986, Congress improved procedures for implementing forfeiture. Similar laws are now found in most states, particularly to deal with controlled substances and organized crime.

forfeiture
Seizure by the government of property and other assets derived from or used in criminal activity.

Forfeiture is seizure by the government of property and other assets derived from or used in criminal activity. Forfeiture proceedings take civil or criminal forms. Under civil forfeiture, property used in criminal activity (contraband, equipment to manufacture illegal drugs, automobiles) can be seized without a finding of guilt (see Chapter 3). Criminal forfeiture is a punishment imposed as a result of conviction that requires the offender to give up assets related to the crime.

Assets seized by federal and state agencies through forfeiture can be considerable. For example, the Drug Enforcement Administration alone annually seizes assets (including cash, real estate, vehicles, vessels, and airplanes) valued at more than a half billion dollars (BJS, 1999k:378).

Forfeiture is controversial. Critics argue that civil forfeiture confiscates property without a court hearing and is a violation of rights. Concern has also been raised about the excessive use of this sanction, because forfeited assets often go into the budget of the law enforcement agency taking the action (Blumenson and Nilsen, 1998).

In a 1993 opinion, the Supreme Court ruled that the Eighth Amendment's ban on excessive fines requires that the seriousness of the offense be related to the property that is taken (*Austin v. United States*). The ruling places limits on the government's ability to seize property and invites the judiciary to monitor the government's forfeiture activities when they are challenged by convicted offenders.

Critics argue that many times ownership of the seized property is unclear. For example, in Hartford, Connecticut, a woman's home was seized because her grandson, unbeknownst to her, was using it as a base for selling drugs. The U.S. Supreme Court upheld the forfeiture by Michigan of an automobile jointly owned by a married couple in which the husband engaged in sexual activity with a prostitute. The court said that even though the wife had no knowledge of her husband's activity she had no claim on half the value of the car (*Bennis v. Michigan*, 1996).

In April 2000, Congress enacted a law to provide greater protection for innocent property owners against seizure by federal law enforcement agencies. Under the new law, innocent owners' property cannot be seized if they can demonstrate their innocence by a preponderance of evidence (*Lansing State Journal,* 2000).

CHECK POINT

⑨ **Distinguish between fines, restitution, and forfeiture.**

⑩ **What are some of the problems of implementing these sanctions?**

Intermediate Sanctions Administered in the Community

One basic argument for intermediate sanctions is that probation, as traditionally practiced, is inadequate for the large numbers of offenders who probation officers must supervise today. Probation leaders have responded to this criticism by developing new intermediate sanction programs and expanding old ones. New programs often rely on increases in surveillance and control. Old programs have been revamped to become more efficient and redesigned to fit more probationers. Four are examined here: home confinement, community service, day reporting centers, and intensive supervision probation.

Home Confinement

With technological innovations that provide for electronic monitoring, **home confinement,** in which convicted offenders must remain at home during specific periods, has gained attention. Offenders under home confinement (often called house arrest) may face other restrictions, for example, the usual probation rules against alcohol and drugs as well as strictly monitored curfews and check-in times.

Some offenders are allowed to go to a place of employment, education, or treatment during the day but must return to their residence by a specific hour. Those supervising home confinement may telephone offenders' homes at various times of the day or night to speak personally with offenders to make sure they are complying.

Home confinement has the advantage of flexibility, because it can be used as a sole sanction or in combination with other penalties. It can be imposed at almost any point in the criminal justice process: during the pretrial period, after a short term in jail or prison, or as a condition of probation or parole (Renzema, 1992:41). In addition, home confinement relieves the government of responsibility for providing food, clothing, and housing for the offender, as it must do in prisons. Home confinement programs have grown and proliferated.

The development of electronic monitoring equipment has made home confinement an enforceable sentencing option. Reliable estimates of the number of offenders currently being monitored are difficult to obtain because manufacturers of the equipment consider this confidential information. However, the best

home confinement

A sentence requiring the offender to remain inside his or her home during specified periods.

Larry Ingles, given a one-year sentence of home confinement for driving while intoxicated (DWI), answers his electronic monitoring call. Failure to answer the telephone within three minutes may result in revocation of probation.

estimates are that about ninety thousand people are being monitored at any given time.

There are two basic types of electronic systems. The first, an "active" system, is a continuously signaling device that is attached to the probationer, along with a receiver-dialer attached to the probationer's home telephone. When the signal stops, the dialer notifies a central monitoring station that the offender is not in the house. The second, a "passive" system, is a computer programmed to telephone the probationer randomly or at specific times. The offender has a certain number of minutes to answer the phone and to verify that he or she is the person under supervision.

Home confinement, enforced by electronic monitoring, is much less expensive than imprisonment (especially because the offender is often required to pay to use the system) and tougher than probation. However, some critics are concerned that home confinement has merely widened the net of social control—that persons who formerly would have been placed on "regular" probation will now be given home confinement with its greater restrictions. Other observers have pointed out, however, that with prisons full and increased numbers of high-risk offenders on probation, home confinement is a necessary shift in correctional policy.

Despite favorable publicity, certain legal, technical, and correctional issues must be addressed before home confinement with electronic monitoring can become a standard punishment. First, some criminal justice scholars question its constitutionality: monitoring may violate the Fourth Amendment's protection against unreasonable searches and seizures. The issue is a clash between the constitutional protection for reasonable expectations of privacy and the invasion of one's home by surveillance devices. As Ronald Corbett and Gary Marx have said, "We appear to be moving toward, not away from, a 'maximum-security society' " (1991). Second, technical problems with the monitoring devices are still extensive, often giving erroneous reports that the offender is home (Clear and Braga, 1995:434). Third, offender failure rates may prove to be high. Being one's own warden is difficult, and visits by former criminal associates and other enticements may become problematic for many offenders (Renzema, 1992:41). The offenders' tolerance levels for home confinement have not yet been researched, but some observers believe that four months of full-time monitoring is about the limit before a violation will occur (Clear and Braga, 1995:435). Furthermore, some crimes can be committed while the offender is at home such as child abuse, drug sales, and assaults.

Community Service

community service
A sentence requiring the offender to perform a certain amount of unpaid labor in the community.

A **community service** sentence requires the offender to perform a certain amount of unpaid labor in the community. Community service may take a variety of forms, including assisting in social service agencies, cleaning parks and roadsides, or assisting the poor. The sentence specifies the number of hours to be worked and usually requires supervision by a probation officer. Community service can be tailored to the skills and abilities of offenders. For example, less educated offenders might pick up litter along the highway, while those with schooling may teach reading in evening literacy classes. Many judges order community service when an offender cannot pay a fine. A symbolic value also is served in the offender's effort to make reparation to the community offended by the crime.

Although community service has many supporters, some labor unions and workers criticize it for possibly taking jobs away from law-abiding citizens. In addition, some believe that if community service is the only sanction, it may be too mild a punishment, especially for upper-class and white-collar criminals.

Day Reporting Centers

Another intermediate sanction option is **day reporting centers**—community correctional centers to which the offender must report each day to carry out elements of the sentence. Designed to ensure that probationers' employment and treatment stipulations attached to their sentences are followed, these centers also increase the likelihood that probation supervision will be considered credible by offenders and the general public. Originally developed in Great Britain, the day reporting center concept has been applied extensively in the United States since 1990.

Most day reporting centers incorporate multiple correctional methods. For example, in some centers offenders are required to be in the facility for eight hours or to report for drug urine checks before going to work. Centers that have a rehabilitation component carry out drug and alcohol treatment, literacy programs, and job searches. Others "provide contact levels equal to or greater than intensive supervision programs, in effect, creating a community equivalent to confinement" (Diggs and Peiper, 1994:9–13).

Most of these programs have not yet been formally evaluated. One study of New York City's program found that its stiff eligibility requirements resulted in few cases entering the center. In Connecticut, however, more than six thousand offenders report daily to such centers (Parent, 1990). A study of six day reporting centers in Massachusetts found that about 80 percent of offenders successfully completed the program (McDivitt and Miliano, 1992:160). In determining success with regard to recidivism, it is important to examine who is being treated. If such centers are used only for selected offenders with a low risk of returning to crime, then it will be difficult to know whether the centers themselves are effective.

day reporting center
A community correctional center where an offender reports each day to comply with elements of a sentence.

CHECK POINT

⑪ **How effective is home confinement? What are some of the problems of this form of sanction?**

⑫ **What goes on at a day reporting center?**

Intensive Supervision Probation

Intensive supervision probation (ISP) has been presented as a means of dealing in the community with offenders who need greater restrictions than traditional programs can provide. Jurisdictions in every state have programs to intensively supervise such offenders. Intensive supervision probation uses probation as an intermediate form of punishment by imposing conditions of strict reporting to a probation officer who has a limited caseload. ISP programs are of two general types: probation diversion and institutional diversion. Probation diversion puts offenders thought to be too risky for routine supervision under intensive surveillance. Institutional diversion selects low-risk offenders sentenced to prison and provides supervision for them in the community (Clear and Braga, 1995:429). Daily contact between the probationer and the probation officer may cut rearrest rates and provide treatment services in the community. Offenders have incentives to obey rules, knowing that they must meet with their probation officers daily and in some cases must speak with them even more frequently. Additional restrictions often are imposed on offenders, as shown in Table 13.2.

ISP programs have been called "old-style" probation because each officer has only twenty clients and frequent face-to-face contacts are required. But questions

intensive supervision probation (ISP)
Probation granted under conditions of strict reporting to a probation officer with a limited caseload.

TABLE 13.2   **Key features of selected ISP programs**

Intensive supervision probation (ISP) entails more than daily contacts with a probation officer; twenty-three other restrictions are often imposed. Given a choice, would you prefer ISP or a short prison term?

PROGRAM FEATURE	NUMBER OF STATES USING FEATURE	PERCENTAGE OF ISP PROGRAMS WITH FEATURE
Curfew/house arrest	25	80.6%
Electronic monitoring	6	19.3
Mandatory (high needs) referrals/special conditions	22	70.9
Team supervision	18	58.1
Drug monitoring	27	87.1
Alcohol monitoring	27	87.1
Community service	21	67.7
Probation fees	13	41.9
Split sentence/shock incarceration	22	70.9
Community sponsors	4	12.9
Restitution	21	67.7
Objective risk assessment	30	96.7
Objective needs assessment	29	93.5

SOURCE: James M. Byrne, Arthur I. Lurigio, and Christopher Baird, "The Effectiveness of the New Intensive Supervision Programs," *Research in Corrections* 2 (September 1989):16. Reprinted by permission.

have been raised about how much of a difference constant surveillance can make to probationers with numerous problems. Such offenders frequently need help to get a job, counseling to deal with emotional and family situations, and a variety of supports to avoid drug or alcohol problems that may have contributed to their criminality. Yet ISP may be a way of getting the large number of felons who are drug addicted into treatment (Gendreau, Cullen, and Bonta, 1994).

ISP has become popular among politicians, probation administrators, judges, and prosecutors because it presents a "tough" image of community supervision and addresses the problem of prison crowding. Most require a specific number of monthly contacts with officers; performance of community service; curfews; drug and alcohol abuse testing; and referral to appropriate job training, education, or treatment programs.

Observers have warned that ISP is not a "cure" for the rising costs and other problems facing corrections systems. Ironically, ISP can also increase the number of probationers sent to prison. All evaluations of ISP find that, probably because of the closer contact with clients, probation officers uncover more violations of rules than they do in regular probation. Therefore, ISP programs often have higher failure rates than regular probation, even though their clients produce fewer arrests (Tonry and Lynch, 1996:116).

This was precisely what researchers found in a series of important experiments testing ISP effectiveness. Offenders in California counties were randomly assigned to either ISP or regular probation. Results indicted no differences in overall arrest rates but substantial differences in probation failure rates. ISP clients did much worse under the stricter rules—possibly because ISP makes detecting rules violations easier (Petersilia and Turner, 1990)

Another surprising finding is that when given the option of serving prison terms or participating in ISP, many offenders have chosen prison. In New Jersey, 15 percent of offenders withdrew their applications for ISP once they learned the conditions and requirements. Similarly, when offenders in Marion County, Oregon, were asked if they would participate in ISP, one-third chose prison instead (Petersilia, 1990:24). Apparently some offenders would rather spend a short time in prison, where conditions differ little from their accustomed life, than a longer period under demanding conditions in the community. To these offenders, ISP does not represent freedom because it is so intrusive and the risk of revocation is perceived as high.

Despite problems and continuing questions about its effectiveness, ISP has rejuvenated probation. Some of the most effective offender supervision is being carried out by these programs (Clear and Hardyman, 1990:42). As with regular probation, the size of a probation officer's caseload, within reasonable limits, is often less important for preventing recidivism than the quality of supervision and assistance provided to probationers. If ISP is properly implemented, it may improve the quality of supervision and services that foster success for more kinds of offenders.

CHECK POINT

⑬ **How does intensive supervision probation differ from traditional probation?**

Intermediate Sanctions Administered in Institutions and the Community

Among the most publicized intermediate sanctions are the **boot camps** now operated by thirty-six states and the Federal Bureau of Prisons (Bourque, Han, and Hill, 1996). Often referred to as **shock incarceration,** these programs vary, but all are based on the belief that young offenders can be "shocked" out of their criminal ways. Boot camps put offenders through a thirty- to ninety-day physical regimen designed to develop discipline and respect for authority. Like the Marine Corps, most programs emphasize a spit-and-polish environment and keep the offenders in a disciplined and demanding routine that seeks ultimately to build self-esteem. Most camps also include education, job training programs, and other rehabilitation services. On successful completion of the program, offenders are released to the community. At this point probation officers take over, and the conditions of the sentence are imposed.

A New Jersey boot camp includes a "stabilization and reintegration program" that follows graduation. This entails intensive supervision for up to eighteen months and some help getting back into school and finding a job. Yet even with this support, eleven of the fifty-one cadets who graduated from three classes are back in jail. Another two are missing (*New York Times*, September 3, 1996:B1). The Close-Up describes the problems faced by Nelson Colon upon returning to his Camden neighborhood after four months at a New Jersey boot camp (see p. 480).

boot camp/shock incarceration
A short-term institutional sentence, usually followed by probation, that puts the offender through a physical regimen designed to develop discipline and respect for authority.

Boot camps for young offenders have received much publicity since they were introduced in the 1980s. Advocates believe that they build self-esteem and discipline. Skeptics point to contrary evidence and wonder if this is another false correctional panacea.

CLOSE up

After **Boot Camp,** A Harder **Discipline**

Nelson Colon misses waking up to the blast of reveille. He sometimes yearns for those sixteen-hour days filled with military drills and nine-mile runs. He even thinks fondly of the surly drill instructors who shouted in his face.

During his four months at New Jersey's boot camp, Colon adapted to the rigors of military life with little difficulty. He says it was much easier than what he faces now. He is back in his old neighborhood, trying to stay away from old friends and old ways.

So far, Mr. Colon, 18, has managed to stay out of trouble since he graduated with the camp's first class of twenty cadets in June. Yet each day, he said, he fears he will be pulled back onto the corner, only two blocks away, where he was first arrested for selling drugs at age 15.

A 10 P.M. curfew helps keep Colon off the streets. His parole officer checks in with him almost daily, sometimes stopping by at 11 o'clock to make sure he is inside. Colon is enrolling in night classes to help him earn his high school equivalency certificate, and he plans on attending Narcotics Anonymous meetings.

His biggest problems are the same ones that tens of thousands of Camden residents confront daily. Camden's unemployment rate exceeds 20 percent. This troubled city has few jobs, particularly for young men who have dropped out of high school. Colon has found work as a stock clerk in a sneaker store, but it is miles away at a shopping center on a busy highway, and he has no transportation there.

Selling drugs paid considerably more than stacking shoe boxes and did not require commuting. Colon says he pushes those thoughts of easy money out of his head and tries to remember what the boot camp's drill instructors told him over and over again.

"They used to tell us, 'It's up to you.' You have to have self-accountability. You have to be reliable for your own actions, not because some person wanted you to do it. They taught us not to follow, to lead. That was one of the most important things."

Colon said his immediate goal was to find a job that he could get to more easily and then save enough to get as far away from Camden as possible. "I want to get out of here," he said.

"The people's mentality here is real petty. Life isn't nothing to them. The other night, they killed one of the guys I grew up with. They shot him a couple of times. My old friends came around and knocked on my door at 1 o'clock in the morning to tell me." He said it was his eighth childhood friend to die.

SOURCE: Adapted from *New York Times,* September 3, 1995, p. B1.

Evaluations of boot camp programs have faded the initial optimism about such approaches (Tonry, 1996:108–114). Critics suggest that the emphasis on physical training ignores young offenders' real problems. Some point out that, like the military, boot camp builds esprit de corps and solidarity, characteristics that have the potential for improving the leadership qualities of the young offender and therefore enhancing a criminal career. In fact, follow-up studies of book camp graduates show they do no better than other offenders after release from the program (MacKenzie, 1995). It has also been found that, like intensive supervision probation, boot camps do not automatically reduce prison crowding (MacKenzie and Piquero, 1994).

Some correctional practitioners now recognize that boot camps have not achieved their goals. The director of the Arizona Department of Corrections asked the legislature to eliminate the program, arguing that with an 85 percent failure rate it was neither cost-effective nor successful in reducing recidivism (Petersen and Palumbo, 1997:85). Colorado and South Dakota have closed their camps. Georgia, one of the initial book camp states, is phasing out its program, while California and Florida are scaling back theirs.

Defenders of boot camps argue that the camps are accomplishing their goals, but that education and employment opportunities are lacking back in the participants' inner-city communities. A national study found that few boot camp graduates received any after-care assistance upon returning to their community (Bourque, Han, and Hill, 1996). Because boot camps have been popular with the public, which imagines that strict discipline and harsh conditions will instill positive attitudes in young offenders, such camps are likely to continue operating whether or not they are more effective than probation or prison. Some criminal justice experts believe the entire boot camp experiment has been a cynical political maneuver. As Franklin Zimring has said, "Boot camps are rapidly becoming yesterday's enthusiasm" (*Newsweek,* February 21, 1994:26).

⑭ **What are some typical activities at a boot camp?**

Implementing Intermediate Sanctions

Although the use of intermediate sanctions has spread rapidly, three major questions have emerged about their implementation: (1) Which agencies should implement the sanctions? (2) Which offenders should be admitted to these programs? (3) Will the "community corrections net" widen as a result of these policies so that more people will come under correctional supervision?

Administrative politics is an ongoing factor in corrections, as in any public service organization. In many states, agencies compete for the additional funding needed to run the programs. The traditional agencies of community corrections, such as probation offices, could receive the funding, or the new programs could be contracted out to nonprofit organizations. Probation organizations argue that they know the field, have the experienced staff, and—given the additional resources—could do an excellent job. They correctly point out that a great many offenders sentenced to intermediate sanctions are also on probation. Critics of giving this role to probation services argue that the established agencies are not receptive to innovation. They say that probation agencies place a high priority on the traditional supervision function and would not actively help clients solve their problems.

The different types of offenders that are given an intermediate sanction prompt a second issue in the implementation debate. One school of thought focuses on the seriousness of the offense and the other on the problems of the offender. If offenders are categorized by the seriousness of their offense, they may be given such close supervision that they will not be able to abide by the sentence. Sanctions for serious offenders may accumulate to include, for example, probation, drug testing, addiction treatment, and home confinement (Blomberg and Lucken, 1993). As the number of sentencing conditions is increased, even the most willing probationer finds it hard to fulfill every one of them.

Some agencies want to accept into their intermediate sanctions program only those offenders who will succeed. These agencies are concerned about their success ratio, especially because of threats to future funding if the program does not reduce recidivism. Critics point out that this strategy leads to "creaming," taking the most promising offenders and leaving those with worse problems to traditional sanctions.

The third issue concerns **net widening,** a process in which the new sanction increases instead of reduces the control over offender's lives. This can occur when a judge imposes a more intrusive sentence than usual. For example, rather than merely giving an offender probation, the judge might also require that the offender perform community service. Critics of intermediate sanctions argue that they have created

net widening
Process in which the new sentencing options increase instead of reduce control over the offenders' lives.

- Wider nets. Reforms increase the proportion of individuals in society whose behavior is regulated or controlled by the state.
- Stronger nets. Reforms augment the state's capacity to control individuals by intensifying the state's intervention powers.
- Different nets. Reforms transfer or create jurisdictional authority from one agency or control system to another.

The creation of intermediate sanctions has been a major development in corrections. These sanctions have been advocated as a less costly alternative to incarceration and a more effective alternative to probation. But how have they been working? Michael Tonry and Mary Lynch have written the discouraging news that "Few such programs have diverted large numbers of offenders from prison, saved public monies or prison beds, or reduced recidivism rates" (1996:99). With incarceration rates still at record highs and probation caseloads increasing, intermediate sanctions will probably play a major role in corrections during the first decade of the new century. However, correctional reform has always had its limitations, and intermediate sanctions may not achieve the goals of their advocates (Cullen, Wright, and Applegate, 1996:69).

CHECK POINT

⑮ **What are three problems in the implementation of intermediate sanctions?**

The Future of Community Corrections

In 1980 there were 1.4 million Americans under community supervision; by 1999 this figure had grown to 3.9 million, an increase of more than 250 percent (BJS, 1998f). Yet, despite this tremendous growth, community corrections often lacks public support. Intermediate sanctions and other forms of community corrections suffer from the image of being "soft on crime." As a result, some localities provide adequate resources for prisons and jails but not for community corrections.

Community corrections also faces the reality that offenders today require closer supervision (Petersilia and Turner, 1990). The crimes, criminal records, and drug problems of these offenders are often worse than those of lawbreakers of earlier eras. In New York, for example, 77 percent of probationers are convicted felons, and about a third of those have been found guilty of violent crimes. Yet, these people are supervised by probation officers whose caseloads number in the hundreds (Petersilia, 1993:61). Such officers cannot provide effective supervision and services to all their probationers.

Despite research findings that suggest probation and intermediate sanctions "do not reduce recidivism, corrections costs, and prison crowding while simultaneously enhancing public safety," Tonry believes that these forms of social control have a future (1998a:700). Achieving it, however, will be a formidable task.

Community corrections is burdened by even greater caseload pressures than in the past. With responsibility for about three-fourths of all offenders under correctional supervision, community corrections needs an infusion of additional resources.

To succeed, public support for community corrections is essential but it will be forthcoming only if citizens believe that offenders are being given appropriate punishments. Citizens must realize that policies designed to punish offenders in the community yield not mere "slaps on the wrists" but meaningful sanctions, even while these policies allow offenders to retain and reforge their ties to their families and society. Joan Petersilia has argued that too many crime control policies are focused solely on the short term. She believes that long-term investments in community corrections will pay off for both the offender and the community (Petersilia, 1996). But before new policies can be put in place, there must be a shift of public opinion in support of community corrections.

Summary

- Community supervision through probation and intermediate sanctions is a growing part of the criminal justice system.
- Probation is imposed on about two-thirds of offenders. Persons with this sentence live in the community according to conditions set by the judge and under the supervision of a probation officer.
- Intermediate sanctions are designed as punishments that are more restrictive than probation and less restrictive than prison.
- The range of intermediate sanctions allows judges to design sentences that incorporate one or more of the punishments.
- Some intermediate sanctions are implemented by courts (fines, restitution, forfeiture), others in the community (home confinement, community service, day reporting centers, intensive supervision probation) and in institutions and the community (boot camps).
- Increasingly, electronic monitoring is being used with many community sanctions.
- The use of community corrections is expected to grow in the twenty-first century, in spite of the problems of implementing them.

Questions for Review

1. What is the aim of community corrections?
2. What is the nature of probation and how is it organized?
3. What is the purpose of intermediate sanctions?
4. What are the primary forms of intermediate sanctions?
5. Why is net widening a concern?

Key Terms and Cases

boot camp/shock incarceration (p. 479)
community service (p. 476)
day reporting center (p. 477)
fine (p. 471)
forfeiture (p. 474)

home confinement (p. 475)
intensive supervision
  probation (ISP) (p. 477)
net widening (p. 482)
probation (p. 463)

recidivism (p. 463)
restitution (p. 473)
Gagnon v. Scarpelli (1973) (p. 468)
Mempa v. Rhay (1967) (p. 468)

For Further Reading

Anderson, David. *Sensible Justice: Alternatives to Prison.* New York: The New Press, 1998. A comprehensive review of the arguments for alternatives to incarceration. Develops a politically feasible case for expanded use of alternatives.

Byrne, James M., Arthur J. Lurigio, and Joan Petersilia. *Smart Sentencing: The Emergence of Intermediate Sanctions.* Newbury Park, Calif.: Sage, 1992. A collection of papers exploring various issues in the design and implementation of intermediate sanctions programs.

Clear, Todd R., and Vincent O'Leary. *Controlling the Offender in the Community.* Lexington, Mass.: Lexington Books, 1983. Examination of risk assessment, classification, and supervision in the context of community corrections.

McCarthy, Belinda, and Bernard McCarthy. *Community-Based Corrections.* 3d ed. Belmont, Calif.: Wadsworth, 1997. A thorough overview of community corrections and its role in the criminal justice system.

Morris, Norval, and Michael Tonry. *Between Prison and Probation: Intermediate Punishments in a Rational Sentencing System.* New York: Oxford University Press, 1990. Urges development of a range of intermediate punishments that can be used to sanction offenders more severely than probation but less severely than incarceration.

Tonry, Michael, and Kate Hamilton, eds. *Intermediate Sanctions in Overcrowded Times.* Boston: Northeastern University Press, 1995. Summaries of research on intermediate sanctions in the United States and England.

Going Online

1. Using the Internet, go to the web page of the New York State Probation Officers Association: www.nyspoa. com. Click on "professional information" and then click on "1999 probation salaries." Are you surprised by the salaries for probation officers? Do these officers receive adequate pay for the kind of work they do?

2. Using the Internet, go to the Community Corrections web page at www.corrections.com/link/ community.html. Click on "Carolina Correctional Services." Read the Carolina Correctional Services' ideals and goals for community corrections. Do you believe that offenders are adequately punished if these ideals are followed?

3. **Using InfoTrac College Edition,** search for the subject "community corrections." Read about a community corrections program in New York. Does this program offer advantages when compared with incarceration of offenders?

CHECK POINT ANSWERS

❶ Many offenders' crimes and records do not warrant incarceration; community supervision is cheaper; recidivism rates for those supervised in the community are no higher than for those who serve prison time; incarceration is more destructive to the offender and society.

❷ A Boston boot maker who became the first probation officer by taking responsibility for a convicted offender before sentencing; called the "father of probation."

❸ Risk control.

❹ To assist judges by preparing presentence reports, and to provide assistance and supervision to offenders in the community.

❺ An arrest for a new offense, and a technical violation of the conditions of probation that were set by the judge.

❻ Right to a preliminary and final hearing, right to cross-examine witnesses, right to notice of the alleged violations, and right to a written report of the proceedings. Right to counsel is determined on a case-by-case basis.

❼ Judges need a range of sentencing options that are less restrictive than prison and more restrictive than simple probation.

❽ A range of punishments reflecting different degrees of intrusiveness and control over the offender.

❾ A fine is a sum of money paid to the government by the offender. Restitution is a sum of money paid to the victim by the offender. Forfeiture is the taking by the government of assets derived from or used in criminal activity.

❿ Most offenders are poor and cannot pay, offenders may commit additional crimes to pay monetary sanctions, and resources are not allocated by the courts for collection and enforcement.

⓫ Home confinement may violate the Fourth Amendment's protections against unreasonable searches, monitoring devices have technical problems, and failure rates are high because offenders cannot tolerate home confinement for very long.

⓬ Drug and alcohol treatment, job searches, educational programs, and sometimes just offenders reporting in.

⓭ In ISP the offender is required to make more strict and frequent reporting to an officer with a much smaller caseload.

⓮ Boot camps maintain a spit-and-polish environment and strict discipline, involve offenders in physical activity, and provide educational, vocational, and rehabilitative services.

⓯ Which agencies should implement the sanctions? Which offenders should be admitted to these programs? Will the "community corrections net" be widened?

Prisons
Their Goals and Management

On Easter Sunday in 1993 a fight broke out in the recreation yard at the Southern Ohio

Correction Facility in Lucasville, a "supermax" prison reserved for the most violent and

incorrigible offenders. Within minutes, the fight grew into a full-scale riot. Eight correc-

tional officers were taken hostage by the 450 prisoners who barricaded themselves inside

Cellblock L. The prisoners held their ground—and their hostages—for more than a week.

During the uprising, prisoners murdered others whom they regarded as "snitches," and six

inmate bodies were dumped into the recreation yard.

When the prisoners threatened to kill one of the hostages, a spokesperson for the state

said it was a "standard threat they've been issuing." Shortly thereafter, correctional officer

Robert Vallandingham was murdered. Another hostage told the media that the officer was

killed because the prisoners were angry that their threats were not being taken seriously.

According to George Skatzes, an inmate who negotiated with authorities on behalf of his fellow prisoners, "We are going to remain no matter what they put on us. . . . If we die, we die" (*Newsweek*, April 26, 1993:52–53). Eventually, the prisoners negotiated their surrender, the remaining hostages were released, and the state began prosecuting some prisoners on criminal charges stemming from the riot and murders.

These periodic eruptions of prisoners bring public attention to the life behind bars. Maximum security prisons such as Lucasville are not the only correctional institutions that simmer with trouble. Many others—even most—experience the racial conflict, gangs, allegations of brutality, and inmate violence that can bring tensions inside to the boiling point. Violence is relatively infrequent only because most institutions manage to keep the lid on the cauldron.

Incarceration—what does it mean to the inmates, the officers, and the public? What goes on inside U.S. prisons? In this chapter the goals of the more than twelve hundred American prisons in operation are examined, as well as how prisons are managed and the crucial role of the correctional officer.

QUESTIONS
for Inquiry

- How is a prison organized?
- How do contemporary institutions differ from the old-style "big-house" prisons?
- What are the assumptions of each model of incarceration?
- How is a prison governed?
- What is the role of correctional officers?
- What constitutional rights do prisoners have?

The Modern Prison: Legacy of the Past

American correctional institutions have always been more varied than movies or novels portray them. Fictional depictions of prison life are typically set in a fortress, the "big house"—the maximum security prisons where the inmates are tough and the guards are just as tough or tougher. Although big houses predominated in much of the country during the first half of the twentieth century, many prisons were built on another model. In the South, for instance, prisoners worked outside at farm labor, and the massive walled structures were not so common.

The typical big house of the 1940s and 1950s was a walled prison with large, tiered cell blocks, a yard, shops, and industrial workshops. The prisoners, in an average population of about twenty-five hundred per institution, came from both urban and rural areas, were usually poor, and, outside the South, were predominantly white. The prison society was essentially isolated; access to visitors, mail, and other communication was restricted. Prisoners' days were strictly structured, with rules enforced by the guards. There was a basic division between inmates and staff; rank was observed and discipline maintained. In the big house, few treatment programs existed; custody was the primary goal.

During the 1960s and early 1970s, when the rehabilitation model was dominant, many states built new prisons and converted others into "correctional institutions." Treatment programs administered by counselors and teachers became a major part of prison life, although the institutions continued to give priority to the custody goals of security, discipline, and order.

During the past thirty years, as the population of the United States has changed, so has the prison population. There has been a major increase in the number of African American and Hispanic American inmates. More inmates come from urban areas, and more have been convicted of drug-related and violent offenses. Former street gangs, often organized along racial lines, today regroup inside prisons, and in many institutions they have raised the level of violence. Another major change has been the rise of public employee unions, which correctional officers have joined. They have used collective bargaining to improve working conditions, safety procedures, and training.

As discussed in Chapter 12, the last two decades have doubled the number of persons held in prisons. This increase has led to greater tensions inside overcrowded institutions. Although today's correctional administrators seek to provide humane incarceration, they must struggle with limited resources and shortages of cell space. Thus, the modern prison faces many of the difficult problems that confront other parts of the criminal justice system: racial conflicts, legal issues, limited resources, and growing populations. Despite these challenges, can prisons still achieve their objectives? The answer to this question depends, in part, on how the goals of incarceration are defined.

① **How does today's prison differ from the "big house" of the past?**

(Answers are at the end of the chapter.)

custodial model

A model of incarceration that emphasizes security, discipline, and order.

Goals of Incarceration

Security is what most people consider the dominant purpose of a prison, given the nature of the inmates and the need to protect the staff and the community. High walls, barbed-wire fences, searches, checkpoints, and regular counts of inmates serve the security function: few inmates escape. More importantly, these features set the tone for the daily operations. Prisons are expected to be impersonal, quasi-military places where strict discipline, minimal levels of amenities, and restrictions on freedom carry out the punishment of criminals.

Three models of incarceration have been prominent since the early 1940s: custodial, rehabilitation, and reintegration. Each is associated with one style of institutional organization.

❶ The **custodial model** is based on the assumption that prisoners have been incarcerated for the purpose of incapacitation, deterrence, or retribution. It emphasizes security, discipline, and order and subordinates the prisoner to the authority of the warden. Discipline is

Some legislators have argued that weight lifting, basketball, and other prison physical exercise activities are frills that should be restricted. Wardens, however, believe that these activities are important means of keeping prisoners busy and reducing tensions.

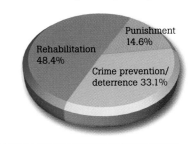

What Americans Think

Question "Once people who commit crimes *are in prison,* which of the following do you think should be *the most important goal of prison?"*

Punishment
14.6%

Rehabilitation
48.4%

Crime prevention/
deterrence 33.1%

SOURCE: U.S. Department of Justice, Bureau of Justice Statistics, *Sourcebook of Criminal Justice Statistics, 1998* (Washington, D.C.: Government Printing Office, 1999), Table 2.51.

---

rehabilitation model

A model of corrections that emphasizes the provision of treatment programs designed to reform the offender.

---

reintegration model

A model of a correctional institution that emphasizes maintaining the offender's ties to family and community as a method of reform, recognizing that the offender will be returning to society.

---

strict, and most aspects of behavior are regulated. This model was prevalent in corrections before World War II, and it dominates most maximum security institutions today.

❷ The **rehabilitation model,** developed during the 1950s, emphasizes treatment programs designed to reform the offender. According to this model, security and housekeeping activities are viewed primarily as preconditions for rehabilitative efforts. As all aspects of the organization should be directed toward rehabilitation, professional treatment specialists have a higher status than other employees. Since the rethinking of the rehabilitation goal in the 1970s, treatment programs still exist in most institutions, but very few prisons conform to this model today.

❸ The **reintegration model** is linked to the structures and goals of community corrections. This model emphasizes maintaining the offenders' ties to family and community as a method of reform, recognizing that they will be returning to society. Prisons that have adopted the reintegration model gradually give inmates greater freedom and responsibility during their confinement, moving them to halfway houses or work release programs before giving them community supervision.

Correctional institutions that conform to each of these models can be found, but most prisons are mainly custodial. Nevertheless, treatment programs do exist, and because almost all inmates return to society at some point, even the most custodial institutions must prepare them for their reintegration. Public opinion on the goals of prisons are found in What Americans Think.

Much is asked of prisons. As Charles Logan notes, "We ask them to correct the incorrigible, rehabilitate the wretched, deter the determined, restrain the dangerous, and punish the wicked" (1993:19). Prisons are expected to pursue many different and often incompatible goals, so as institutions they are almost doomed to fail. Logan believes the mission of prisons is confinement. He argues that the basic purpose of imprisonment is to punish offenders fairly and justly through lengths of confinement proportionate to the seriousness of their crimes. If the goal of incarceration is to do justice through confinement, then he summarizes the prison's function is "to keep prisoners—to keep them in, keep them safe, keep them in line, keep them healthy, and keep them busy—and to do it with fairness, without undue suffering, and as efficiently as possible" (Logan, 1993). If the purpose of prisons is punishment through confinement under fair and just conditions, what are the implications for correctional managers?

 **CHECK POINT**

② **What three models of prison have been predominant since the 1940s?**

 # Prison Organization

The prison differs from almost every other institution or organization in modern society. Its physical facilities are different, and it is distinct because it is a place where a group of employees manage a group of captives. Prisoners are required to live according to the rules of their keepers, and their movements are sharply restricted. Unlike managers of other governmental agencies, prison managers:

- cannot select their clients,
- have little or no control over the release of their clients,
- must deal with clients who are there against their will,
- must rely on clients to do most of the work in the daily operation of the institution—work they are forced to do and for which they are not paid, and
- must depend on the maintenance of satisfactory relationships between clients and staff.

With these unique characteristics, how should a prison be run? What rules should guide administrators? As the description above indicates, wardens and other key personnel are asked to perform a difficult job, one that requires skilled and dedicated managers.

Three Lines of Command

Most prisons are expected to fulfill goals related to keeping (custody), using (working), and serving (treating) inmates. Because individual staff members are not equipped to perform all functions, there are separate organizational lines of command for the groups of employees that carry out these different tasks. One group is charged with maintaining custody over the prisoners, another group supervises them in their work activities, and a third group attempts to treat them.

The custodial employees are the most numerous. They are normally organized along military lines, from warden to captain to officer, with accompanying pay differentials down the chain of command. The professional personnel associated with the using and serving functions, such as industry supervisors, clinicians, and teachers, are not part of the custodial structure and have little in common with its staff. All employees are responsible to the warden, but the treatment personnel and the civilian supervisors of the workshops have their own salary scales and titles. The formal organization of staff responsibilities in a typical prison is shown in Figure 14.1.

The multiple goals and separate employee lines of command often mean the administration of prisons is marked by ambiguity and conflict. There is ambiguity in the often contradictory goals imposed on prisons, as noted by Logan. Conflict between different segments of staff (custodial versus treatment, for instance), as well as between staff and inmates, presents significant challenges for administrators.

FIGURE 14.1 Formal organization of a prison for adult felons

Prison staff are divided into various sections consistent with the goals of the organization. Custodial employees are the most numerous.

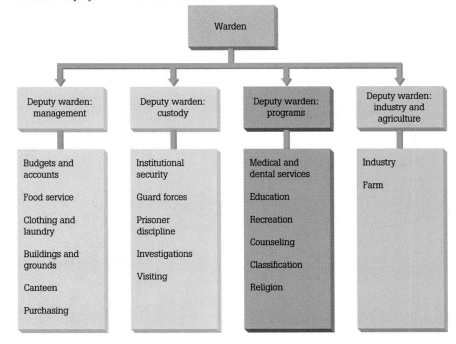

So how do prisons function? The U.S. prison may not conform to the ideal goals of corrections, and the formal organization of staff and inmates may bear little resemblance to the ongoing reality of the informal relations, but somehow order is kept and a routine is followed.

The Importance of Management

One of the amazing facts about prisons is that most of the time they work. Order is maintained and activities are carried out, despite the wide variation in administrative policies and practices at different prisons.

Although most prisons have similar organizational structures, management styles vary. John DiIulio (1987) studied the management of selected prisons in California, Michigan, and Texas. He found differences in leadership philosophy, political environment, and administrative style of individual wardens. He believes that prisons can be governed, violence can be minimized, and services can be provided to inmates if correctional managers provide proper leadership.

DiIulio suggests that prison systems perform well if managers work competently with the political and other pressures that make for administrative uncertainty and instability. In particular, he points to the success of wardens whose management style can be characterized as "management by walking around." This means that wardens must be "hands-on" and proactive, paying close attention to details, instead of waiting for problems to arise. They must know what is going on inside, yet also recognize the need for outside support. This means they are not strangers either in the cell blocks or in the aisles of the state legislatures (DiIulio, 1987:242; DiIulio, 1993b:438). From this perspective, making prisons work is a function of leadership and the application of management principles.

CHECK POINT

③ How are prisons different from other organizations in society?

④ What are the multiple goals pursued in today's prisons?

⑤ Which management style does John DiIulio believe is most effective?

"Management by Walking Around" is a style that successful wardens have adopted. This means that they must be "hands-on" and proactive, paying close attention to details, rather than waiting for problems to arise.

Who Is in Prison?

The age, education, and criminal history of the inmate population help determine how correctional institutions function. What are the characteristics of inmates in the nation's prisons? Do most offenders have long records of serious offenses, or are significant numbers of inmates first-time offenders who have committed minor crimes? Do all prisoners "need" incarceration? These questions are crucial to an understanding of the work of wardens and correctional officers.

Data on the characteristics of prisoners are limited. However, in a national survey of state prisons, the Bureau of Justice Statistics found that most prisoners are males in their late 20s to early 30s, have less than a high school education, and are disproportionately members of minority groups (see Figure 14.2).

The most recent studies indicate that inmates who are recidivists and who are convicted of violent crimes make up an overwhelming portion of the prison population. More than 60 percent of inmates have been either incarcerated or on probation at least twice; 45 percent of them, three or more times; and nearly 20 percent, six or more times. Two-thirds of the inmates were serving a sentence for a violent crime or had previously been convicted of a violent crime. These are major

FIGURE 14.2 Sociodemographic and offense characteristics of state prison inmates

These data show the types of people found in state prisons. What do they indicate about the belief that many offenders do not "need" to be incarcerated?

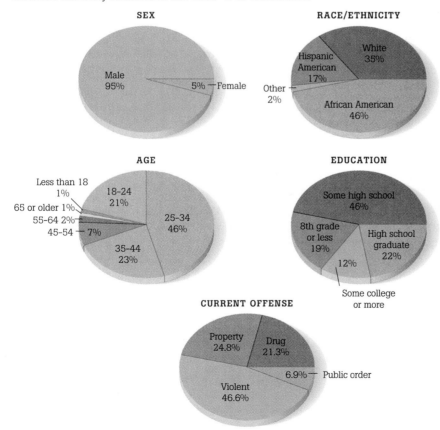

SOURCE: U.S. Department of Justice, Bureau of Justice Statistics, *Survey of State Prison Inmates* (Washington, D.C.: Government Printing Office, 1993), 3.

shifts from the prison populations of earlier decades, when only about 40 percent of all inmates had committed such offenses (BJS, 1993b:3).

Besides these shifts in the prison population, four additional factors affect correctional operations: the increased number of elderly prisoners, the many prisoners with acquired immune deficiency syndrome (AIDS) or the human immunodeficiency virus (HIV) that causes AIDS, the thousands of prisoners who are mentally ill, and the increase in the number of prisoners sentenced to long terms of incarceration.

Elderly Prisoners

Correctional officials have recently become aware of the increasing number of inmates over age 55. That number is now more than thirty thousand, with about one thousand over 75 years old (BJS, 1998c:10; *New York Times,* November 1, 1995:A1). About half of these inmates are serving long sentences; the other half committed crimes late in life. Although older prisoners still make up a small proportion of the total inmate population, their numbers are doubling every four years. If "three strikes" and "truth-in-sentencing" laws are fully implemented, the number of elderly prisoners will become a major problem for corrections within the next decade.

Elderly prisoners have security and medical needs that differ from those of the average inmate. In a number of states, special sections of the institution have been designated for this older population so they will not have to mix with the younger, tougher inmates. Elderly prisoners are more likely to develop chronic illnesses such as heart disease, stroke, and cancer (Zimbardo, 1994). In California the average yearly maintenance and medical costs for inmates over age 55 is $46,800, double that of the norm (*Hartford Courant,* February 18, 1997:A6). A paradox of the incarceration of the elderly is that while in prison the offender's life will be prolonged and his medical care will be much better than if he is discharged (Morris and Rothman, 1995:253).

Prisoners with HIV/AIDS

In the coming years, AIDS is expected to be the leading cause of death among males aged 35 and younger. With 68 percent of the adult inmate population under age 35, correctional officials must cope with the problem of HIV as well as AIDS and related health issues. In 1998 there were more than forty thousand HIV-positive inmates (2.3 percent of the prison population) and almost nine thousand verified offenders (0.5 percent of the prison population) with AIDS. The rate of confirmed AIDS cases in state and federal prisons is five times higher than in the total U.S. population. More than nine hundred inmates died of AIDS while incarcerated in 1996, the second largest single cause of inmate death (BJS, 1999d:95). Because many inmates who are HIV infected are undiagnosed, these numbers underestimate the scope of the problem.

The high incidence of HIV/AIDS among prisoners can be traced to increased incarceration of drug offenses. Many of these inmates have engaged in intravenous drug use, shared needles, or traded sex for drugs or money. Male homosexual activity, forbidden in prison, is also a major way that HIV is transmitted. Some argue that government has a compelling interest to educate prisoners about the risk of unprotected sex or drug use in prison and even beyond the walls (Merianos, Marquart, and Damphousse, 1997:84–87).

To deal with offenders who have AIDS symptoms or who test positive for the virus, prison officials can develop policies on methods to prevent transmission of the disease, housing of those infected, and medical care for inmates with the full range of symptoms. Administrators are confronting a host of legal, political, medical, budgetary, and attitudinal factors as they decide what actions the institution should take.

Mentally Ill Prisoners

Mass closings of public hospitals for the mentally ill began in the 1960s. At the time new antipsychotic drugs made treating patients in the community seem a more humane and less expensive alternative to long-term hospitalization. But it soon became apparent that community treatment works only if the drugs are taken, and that clinics and halfway houses exist to assist the mentally ill.

Homelessness has become the most public sign of the lack of programs for the mentally ill. But with the expansion of prisons and the greater emphasis on public order offenses, arrest and incarceration have become the price many people pay for their illness.

Currently far more mentally ill are in the nation's jails and prisons (almost 300,000) than in state hospitals (62,000) (BJS, 1999j). The incarceration rate of the mentally ill is four times that of the general population. In some correctional institutions, such as New York City's Riker's Island with three thousand mentally ill inmates, the prison has become the state's largest psychiatric facility (Winerip, 1999a:42). Over the last ten years the mentally ill portion of Connecticut's prison population has gone from 24 percent to 40 percent (Watson, 1999:A8). In Los Angeles 50 percent of those entering the county jail are identified as mentally ill (Butterfield, 1998c:A26).

Although some inmates benefit from the regular medication they receive in jail or prison, others suffer as the stress of confinement deepens their depressions, intensifies delusions, or often leads to mental breakdown. Many commit suicide.

Correctional workers are usually unprepared to deal with the mentally ill. Cell-block officers may not know how to respond to disturbed inmates. Although most correctional systems have mental health units that segregate the ill, many inmates with psychiatric disorders live among other prisoners in the general population where they are teased and otherwise exploited.

Few prisons have well-developed mental health treatment programs. An exception is Ohio where mental health units have been created in each facility and one prison has been set aside to house only the mentally ill. However, most prisons rely on the generous dispensing of medication to keep the mentally ill stable and functioning.

Long-Term Prisoners

More prisoners serve long sentences in the United States than in any other Western nation. While the average first-time offender serves about twenty-two months, an estimated 11 to 15 percent of all prisoners—well over 100,000—will serve more than seven years in prison. About 9 percent of these are serving life sentences, and another 24 percent are serving sentences of more than twenty-five years. These long-term prisoners are often the same people who will become elderly inmates, with all of the attendant problems (Flanagan, 1995:10).

Studies show substantial differences in the way the long-termer responds to incarceration. Some, but not others, experience severe stress, depression, and other health problems (Bonta and Gendreau, 1995). When severe emotional stress occurs, it tends to take place earlier, rather than later, in the sentence.

Long-term prisoners are generally not seen as control problems. They are charged with disciplinary infractions about half as often as short-term inmates. However, they do represent a management problem for administrators, who must find ways of making prison life livable for those who are going to be there a long time. According to Timothy Flanagan (1991), an authority on long-term inmates, administrators need to adhere to three main principles: (1) maximize opportunities for the inmate to exercise choice in living circumstances, (2) create opportunities for meaningful living, and (3) help the inmate maintain contact with the outside world. Most long-term inmates will eventually be released after spending their prime years incarcerated. Will offenders be able to support themselves when they return to the community at age 50, 60, or 70?

In the context of overcrowded facilities, the contemporary inmate population presents several challenges to correctional workers. Resources may not be available to provide rehabilitative programs for most inmates. Even if the resources exist, the goal of maintaining a safe and healthy environment may tax the staff's abilities. These difficulties are multiplied still further by the presence of AIDS and the increasing numbers of elderly and long-term prisoners. The contemporary corrections system is having to deal with a different type of inmate, one who is more prone to violence, and with a prison society where racial tensions are great. How well this correctional challenge is met will have an important impact on American society.

CHECK POINT

⑥ **What are the major characteristics of today's prisoners?**

Governing a Society of Captives

Much of the public believes that prisons are operated in an authoritarian manner. In such a society, correctional officers give orders and inmates follow orders. Strictly enforced rules specify what the captives may and may not do. Staff members have the right to grant rewards and to inflict punishment. In theory, any inmate who does not follow the rules could be placed in solitary confinement. Because the officers have a monopoly on the legal means of enforcing rules and can be backed up by the state police and the National Guard if necessary, many people believe that no question should arise as to how the prison is run.

But what quality of life should be maintained in prison? According to John DiIulio, a good prison is one that "provides as much order, amenity, and service as possible given the human and financial resources" (1987:12). Order is the absence of individual or group misconduct, such as assault and rape, that threatens the security of others. Amenities are those things that enhance the comfort of the inmates—good food, clean cells, and recreational opportunities. Service includes programs to improve the lives of inmates: vocational training, remedial education, and work opportunities.

If the premise is accepted that well-run prisons are important for the inmates, staff, and society, what are the problems that must be faced and solved by correctional administrators? Four factors distinguish the governing of prisons from the administration of other public institutions: (1) the defects of total power, (2) the limited rewards and punishments that can be used by officials, (3) the exchange relations between correctional officers and inmates, and (4) the strength of inmate leadership. In reviewing each of these, also consider what administrative and leadership styles can best be used by corrections managers to achieve the goal of a prison that is safe, humane, and able to serve the needs of the inmates.

The Defects of Total Power

Imagine a prison society that comprises hostile and uncooperative captives ruled by force, a society in which prisoners can be legally isolated from one another, physically abused until they cooperate, and put under continuous surveillance. Theoretically, such a society is possible. In reality, however, the power of officers is limited, because many prisoners have little to lose by misbehaving, and unarmed officers have only limited ability to force compliance with rules. Perhaps more important is that forcing people to carry out complex tasks is basically inefficient. Prison efficiency is further diminished by the realities of the usual ratio of 1 officer to 40 inmates and the potential danger of the situation (Hepburn, 1985).

Rewards and Punishments

Correctional officers often rely on rewards and punishments to gain cooperation. To maintain security and order among a large population in a confined space, they impose extensive rules of conduct. Instead of using force to ensure obedience, however, they reward compliance and punish rule violators by granting and denying privileges.

Several policies may be followed to promote control. One is to offer cooperative prisoners rewards such as choice job assignments, residence in the honor unit, and favorable parole reports. "Good time" is given to inmates who do not break rules. Informers may also be rewarded, and administrators may ignore conflict among inmates on the assumption that it keeps prisoners from uniting against authorities.

The system of rewards and punishments has some deficiencies. One is that the punishments for rule breaking do not represent a great departure from the prisoners' usual circumstances. Because inmates are already deprived of many freedoms and valued goods—heterosexual relations, money, choice of clothing, and so on—not being allowed to attend, say, a recreational period does not carry much weight. Finally, authorized privileges are given to the inmate at the start of the sentence and are taken away only if rules are broken. However, as an inmate approaches release, opportunities for furloughs, work release, or transfer to a halfway house can serve as incentives to obey rules.

Gaining Cooperation: Exchange Relationships

One way that correctional officers obtain inmate cooperation is by tolerating minor rule infractions in exchange for compliance with major aspects of the custodial regime. The correctional officer is the key official in these exchanges given

PART FOUR

A Question of Ethics

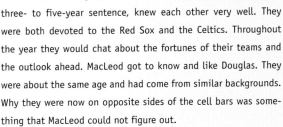

After three years of daily contact, correctional officer Bill MacLeod and Jack Douglas, who was serving a three- to five-year sentence, knew each other very well. They were both devoted to the Red Sox and the Celtics. Throughout the year they would chat about the fortunes of their teams and the outlook ahead. MacLeod got to know and like Douglas. They were about the same age and had come from similar backgrounds. Why they were now on opposite sides of the cell bars was something that MacLeod could not figure out.

One day Douglas called to MacLeod and said that he needed money because he had lost a bet gambling on the Red Sox. Douglas said that his wife would send him the money but that it couldn't come through the prison mail to him in cash. And a check or money order would show on his commissary account.

"The guy wants cash. If he doesn't get it, I'm dead." Douglas took a breath and then rushed on with his request. "Could you bring it in for me? She'll mail the money to you at home. You could just drop the envelope on my bed."

"You know the rules. No gambling and no money," said MacLeod.

"But I'm scared shitless. It will be no big deal for you and it will make all the difference for me. Come on, we've gotten along well all these years. I think of you as being different from those other officers."

■ What should MacLeod do? Is this kind of request likely to be a one-time occurrence with Douglas? What if MacLeod's sergeant finds out? What if other inmates learn about it?

that they work closely with the prisoners throughout the day in the cell block, workshop, or recreation area. They count prisoners, sign passes, check groups of inmates as they come and go, and search for contraband. These are the minor details of an officer's eight-hour shift.

Although the formal rules require a social distance between officers and inmates, physical closeness makes them aware that each is dependent on the other. The officers need the cooperation of the prisoners so that they will look good to their superiors, and the inmates depend on the guards to relax the rules or occasionally look the other way. For example, officers in a Midwestern prison told Stan Stojkovic that flexibility in rule enforcement was especially important as it related to the ability of prisoners to cope with their environment. As one officer said, "Phone calls are really important to guys in this place. . . . You cut off their calls and they get pissed. So what I do is give them a little extra and they are good to me." Yet the officers also told Stojkovic that they would be crazy to intervene to stop illicit sex or drug use (Stojkovic, 1990).

Correctional officers must be careful not to pay too high a price for the cooperation of their charges. Officers who establish sub-rosa, or secret, relationships can be manipulated by prisoners into smuggling contraband or committing other illegal acts. Officers are under pressure to work effectively with prisoners and may be blackmailed into doing illegitimate favors in return for cooperation. A dilemma that correctional officers frequently face is posed in A Question of Ethics.

Inmate Leadership

Some officials also try to use inmate leaders to control other convicts. Inmate leaders have been "tested" over time so that they are neither pushed around by other inmates nor distrusted as stool pigeons. Because the staff can also rely on them, they serve as the essential communications link between staff and inmates. Their ability to acquire inside information and gain access to higher officials brings inmate leaders the respect of other prisoners and special privileges from officials. In turn, they distribute these benefits to other prisoners, thus bolstering their own influence within the society.

In the traditional prison of the big-house era, officials were more successful at using inmate leaders to maintain order than are today's administrators. In most of today's institutions, prisoners are divided by race, ethnicity, age, and gang affiliation, so that no single leadership structure exists.

The Challenge of Governing Prisons

The factors of total power, rewards and punishments, exchange relationships, and inmate leadership exist in every prison and must be managed. How they are managed greatly influences the quality of prison life. DiIulio's research (1987) challenges the common assumption of many correctional administrators that "the cons run the joint." Instead, successful wardens have made their prisons "work" by applying management principles within the context of their own style of leadership. Prisons can be governed, violence can be minimized, and services can be provided to the inmates if correctional executives and wardens exhibit leadership. Governing prisons is an extraordinary challenge, but it can be and has been effectively accomplished. The Close-Up describes the unique management practices of Warden Dennis Luther (see p. 500).

⑦ **What four factors make the governing of prisons different from administering other public institutions?**

Correctional Officers: The Linchpin of Management

A prison is supposed to simultaneously keep, use, and serve its inmates. The achievement of these goals depends heavily on the performance of its correctional officers. Their job is not easy. Not only do they work long and difficult hours with a hostile client population, but their superiors also expect them to do so with few resources or punishments at their disposal. Most of what they are expected to do must be accomplished by gaining and keeping the cooperation of the prisoners.

The Officer's Role

In the contemporary prison the officer is the crucial professional because he or she has the closest contact with the prisoners and is expected to perform a variety of

Correctional officers are the linchpins of management because they are in constant contact with inmates. They must enforce the rules and yet gain the cooperation of the prisoners. A difficult job!

CLOSE up

A Model Prison

Set in the woods outside of Bradford, Pennsylvania, is the Federal Correctional Institution, McKean. Opened in 1989 as a medium-security facility, it houses more than one thousand male inmates. Until he retired in July 1995, Dennis Luther was McKean's warden, an administrator who, during his sixteen years in prison work, gained a reputation for unorthodox policies.

At a time when politicians were railing against "country club" prisons and the need to "make 'em bust rocks," Warden Luther ran an institution that earned a 99.3 accreditation rating from the American Correctional Association, the highest in the Bureau of Prisons. Badly overcrowded and with an increasing number of violent offenders, McKean cost taxpayers $15,370 a year for each inmate, well below the federal average of $21,350. Amazingly in six years there were: no escapes, no murders, no suicides, and only three serious assaults against staff and six recorded against inmates.

How did Warden Luther do it? According to Luther each prison has its own culture, which is often violent and abusive, based on gangs. The staff in such institutions feel they are unable to change it. At McKean, Warden Luther set out to build a different type of culture, one based on the unconditional respect for the inmates as people. As he says, "If you want people to behave responsibly, and treat you with respect then you treat other people that way."

This credo has been translated into twenty-eight beliefs, the product of Luther's years of experience. These "Beliefs about the Treatment of Inmates" are posted all over the institution to remind both staff and inmates alike of their responsibilities. They include:

1. Inmates are sent to prison as punishment and not for punishment.
2. Correctional workers have a responsibility to ensure that inmates are returned to the community no more angry or hostile than when they were committed.
3. Inmates are entitled to a safe and humane environment while in prison.
4. You must believe in man's capacity to change his behavior.
10. Be responsive to inmate requests for action or information. Respond in a timely manner and respond the first time an inmate makes a request.
12. It is important for staff to model the kind of behavior they expect to see duplicated by inmates.
14. There is an inherent value in self-improvement programs such as education, whether or not these programs are related to recidivism.
18. Staff cannot, because of their own insecurities, lack of self-esteem or concerns about their masculinity, condescend or degrade inmates.
26. Inmate discipline must be consistent and fair.

tasks. Correctional officers are no longer responsible merely for "guarding." Instead, they are expected to counsel, supervise, protect, and process the inmates under their care. But the officer also works as a member of a complex bureaucratic organization and is expected to deal with clients impersonally and to follow formal procedures. Fulfilling these contradictory role expectations is difficult in itself, and the difficulty is exacerbated by the physical closeness of the officer and inmate over long periods. Yet John Hepburn and Paul Knepper found that officers who played a human services role rather than a purely custody role had greater job satisfaction (1993:315).

Merely posting the "Beliefs" in prominent places will not create a superior prison culture. The credo must be put into practice. Here are some examples:

❶ *Front Line Staff.* If you want to get front-line staffers to treat inmates with respect, top managers must treat staffers with respect. As Luther has said, "Line-level people have good ideas, not only about how to do their job, but about how to do your job better." With this in mind he created the Line Staff Advisory Board, a rotating group of front-line workers who meet with him to talk through complaints, suggestions, and rumors.

❷ *"Management by Walking Around."* Through contact with staff and inmates in the dining hall, in the yard, and in the cell blocks, a warden becomes a visible presence who can hear suggestions and complaints. Often he or she is able to nip problems before they fester and explode. This presence sets an example of the extent to which the warden is concerned about the problems of inmates and staff.

❸ *Inmate Involvement.* Regular "town hall" meetings with inmates provide opportunities for two-way communications. Proposed changes in regulations or procedures are first brought to the inmates for comment. For example, items to be offered in the commissary.

❹ *Inmate Benefit Fund.* The Inmate Benefit Fund (IBF) was created to generate money inmates could use to purchase items for which taxpayer dollars were not available. Using their own funds, inmates could order items from Bradford stores and restaurants that would ease their stay in McKean. Orders were placed with the IBF and delivered to the institution for a modest handling charge. With two thousand inmates, substantial sums were generated by these surcharges. The inmates could use these funds to purchase additional educational and recreational programs for the population. Besides helping inmates gain access to these programs, the IBF spending contributed to the local economy.

❺ *Education.* McKean has a higher percentage of inmates enrolled in classes than almost any other federal prison. Luther believes that prison time should be spent preparing offenders for their return to the community. Courses are taught by staff members of the prison's education department, professors from neighboring colleges, and inmates. The latter teach Adult Continuing Education course and act as mentors and tutors.

Luther expects inmates to be responsible and he holds them to a higher standard than found in most prisons. After a few minor incidents the warden ordered "closed movement" during evening hours. This restricted inmate activity and was meant to be permanent. A group of inmates asked if he would restore "open movement" if the prison was incident-free for ninety days. Luther agreed and the prison has remained "open."

Inmates who meet the standards are rewarded. Weekly inspections are held in each cell block and inmates who score high are given additional privileges. Those whose disciplinary record is clean and excel in the programs can earn their way to the "honor unit." And those who show consistently good behavior are allowed to attend supervised picnics on Family Day.

Dennis Luther is convinced that his methods will work in any prison, even those plagued by violence, overcrowding, and gangs. Many staff members feel the same way. They believe that McKean is a shining example of the difference good management can make.

SOURCE: Drawn from Robert Worth, "A Model Prison," *Atlantic Monthly* (November 1995), 38–44; and Tom Peters, *Liberation Management* (New York: Alfred A. Knopf, 1992), 247–255.

Just as there is an inmate culture that emphasizes certain values and norms, there is a code of behavior that encourages solidarity among officers (see Table 14.1). Many correctional officers are nostalgic for the days of the big house when their purpose was clear, their authority was unchallenged, and they were respected by inmates.

Recruitment of Officers

Employment as a correctional officer is not a glamorous, sought-after occupation. The work is thought to be boring, the pay is low, and career advancement is

TABLE 14.1   The officer code reinforces camaraderie among correctional officers

1   Always go to the aid of an officer in distress.

2   Don't "lug" drugs.
    Bringing drugs or alcohol into the prison places
    fellow officers in danger.

3   Don't rat.
    Never rat on an officer to an inmate.
    Never testify against a fellow officer.

4   Never make a fellow officer look bad in front of inmates.

5   Always support an officer in a dispute with an inmate.

6   Always support officer sanctions against inmates.

7   Don't be a white hat ["bleeding heart"].
    Don't be too lenient or sympathetic to inmates.

8   Maintain officer solidarity versus all outside groups.
    Don't talk about the institution to outsiders.

9   Show positive concern for fellow officers.
    Never leave another officer a problem.
    Help your fellow officer with problems outside the institution.

SOURCE: Adapted from Kelsey Kauffman, *Prison Officers and Their World* (Cambridge, Mass.: Harvard University Press, 1988), 86–114. Reprinted by permission.

almost nonexistent. Studies have shown that one of the primary incentives for becoming involved in correctional work is the security that civil service status provides. In addition, because most correctional facilities are located in rural areas, prison work often is better than other available employment. Because correctional officers are recruited locally, most of them are rural and white, in contrast to the majority of prisoners who come from urban areas and are often either African American or Hispanic American. Yet there are also correctional officers who see their work as a way of helping people, often the people most in need in the society.

Today, because they need more well-qualified correctional officers, most states have given priority to recruiting quality personnel. Salaries have been raised so that the yearly average entry-level pay runs between $16,000 in some southern and rural states to more than $30,000 in states such as Massachusetts and New Jersey (BJS, 1995b:98). In addition to their salaries, most officers can earn overtime pay, supplementing base pay by up to 30 percent.

Special efforts have been made to recruit women and minorities. Today approximately 32 percent of correctional officers are members of minority groups and 19 percent are women (BJS, 1999k:81). Women officers are no longer restricted to working with female offenders. For example, women make up 23 percent of Alabama's correctional officers, and 97 percent work in male institutions (BJS, 1999k:81).

How do these increases in the number of minority and female officers shape the work environment among correctional officers? Dana Britton found in her study that black male and female officers are less satisfied with their jobs than their white male counterparts. She also found that black and Hispanic male officers felt they were more effective working with the inmates than did their white counterparts. And female correctional officers were also found to be more contented with their work than male officers (Britton, 1997). Contrary to the assumption of some male officers that females cannot handle the job, Denise Jenne and Robert Kersting (1996) found that women officers tended to respond to violent situations as aggressively as their male coworkers.

For most correctional workers, a position as a custody officer is a dead-end job. Although officers who perform well may be promoted to higher ranks within the custodial staff, very few ever move into administrative positions. Yet in some states and in the Federal Bureau of Prisons, there are career paths for persons with college degrees to advance to management positions.

Use of Force

As with the police, the use of force by correctional officers is a controversial issue. Although corporal punishment and the excessive use of force are not permitted, correctional officers may use force in many situations. They often find themselves in confrontations with inmates who challenge their authority or are attacking fellow inmates. Officers are unarmed and outnumbered, yet are expected to maintain order and uphold institutional rules. Under these conditions corrections officers feel that they are justified in using force.

When and how much force may be used? All correctional agencies now have formal policies and procedures with regard to the legitimate use of force. In general these policies emphasize that only levels of force necessary to achieve legitimate goals are acceptable. Officers violating these policies may be subject to an inmate lawsuit and dismissal. There are five situations in which the use of force is legally acceptable.

❶ Self-defense: If officers are threatened with physical attack, they may use a level of force that is reasonable to protect themselves from harm.

❷ Defense of Third Persons: Like self-defense an officer may use force to protect an inmate or another officer. Again, only reasonably necessary force may be used.

❸ Upholding Prison Rules: If prisoners refuse to obey prison rules, it may be necessary for officers to use force to maintain safety and security. For example, if an inmate refuses to return to his or her cell it may be necessary to use handcuffs and forcefully transfer the prisoner.

❹ Prevention of a Crime: Force may be used to stop a crime from being committed; for example, theft or destruction of property.

❺ Prevention of Escapes: Officers may use force to prevent escapes because they threaten the well-being of society and order within correctional institutions. Although escape from a prison is a felony, officials may not shoot the fleeing inmate at will as in the past. Today, agencies differ as to their policies toward escapees, some limit the use of deadly force to prisoners thought to be dangerous, others require warning shots. However, officers in Nebraska and Texas may face disciplinary action if they fail to use deadly force. Although the U.S. Supreme Court has limited the ability of police officers to shoot fleeing felons, the rule has not been applied to correctional officers.

Correctional officers face difficult pressures that challenge their ability to maintain self-control and professional decision making. Inmates often challenge officers in subtle ways such as moving slowly, but they may also use verbal abuse to provoke officers. Correctional officers are expected to run a "tight ship" and maintain order, often in threatening situations where they are outnumbered and dealing with troubled people who are difficult to control. In confrontation situations they must coolly exercise discretion so as to defuse hostility, yet uphold the rules—a difficult task at best.

Collective Bargaining

Correctional officers have been unionized only since the 1970s. When many states passed laws permitting collective bargaining by public employees, unions were allowed to seek members among correctional officers. Now, correctional employees are unionized in more than half of the states. Like other labor organizations, unions representing prison employees seek better wages and working conditions for their members. Because the members are public employees, most are prevented by law from engaging in strikes, but work stoppages and "sickouts" have occurred in a number of prisons.

The great expansion of the incarcerated population over the past decade has increased the number of correctional employees from 223,078 in 1989 to more than 350,000 in 1999 (BJS, 1999k:81) In some states this has strengthened the power of officers' unions. In California, where the number of officers has increased 500 percent since 1980, their union has become a potent political force that lobbies not only for better wages and working conditions but also for expansion of prison facilities. This union has become a major contributor to political campaigns. It worked for passage of the state's "three strikes" law, lobbied against private prisons, supported the victims' rights movement, and pushed for the hiring of more correctional officers (*New York Times,* November 7, 1995:1).

As a result of unionization, relationships between employees and administration are now more formalized. With the rights and obligations of each side specified in contracts, old-style wardens cannot dictate working conditions. Unionization has brought officers not only better pay and job security but also more control over their work.

Correctional officers are responsible for the smooth day-to-day functioning of prisons. As they deal with inmates, officers must recognize that the rights of prisoners must be respected.

CHECK POINT

⑧ **Why are correctional officers called the "linchpin of management"?**

⑨ **What role do officer unions play in today's corrections?**

Prisoners' Rights

hands-off policy

Judges should not interfere with the administration of correctional institutions.

Ruffin v. Commonwealth (1871)

By committing a crime, the prisoner has become a slave of the state and has forfeited all personal rights.

Cooper v. Pate (1964)

Prisoners are entitled to the protection of the Civil Rights Act of 1871 and may challenge the conditions of their confinement in federal courts.

Prior to the 1960s, most courts maintained a **hands-off policy** with respect to prisons. Only a few state courts had recognized rights for prisoners (Wallace, 1994). In general, judges felt that prisoners did not have protected rights and that courts should defer to the expertise of correctional administrators in deciding how to run prisons. Most judges followed the belief of the Virginia judge in *Ruffin v. Commonwealth* (1871) that prisoners did not have rights.

But since the 1960s prisoners have gained access to the courts to contest decisions made by officers and aspects of their incarceration that they believe violate basic rights. Judicial decisions have defined and recognized the constitutional rights of incarcerated offenders and the need for correctional policies and procedures that respect these rights (Smith, C. E., 1993).

The greatest departure from the hands-off policy was in 1964 when the Supreme Court ruled in *Cooper v. Pate* that state prisoners are entitled to the protections of the Civil Rights Act of 1871 and may challenge conditions of their confinement in the federal courts. This legislation (designated as Volume 42 *United States Code,* Section 1983, or 42 U.S.C. 1983) imposes civil liability on any state official who deprives another of constitutional rights.

Because of the decision in *Cooper v. Pate,* the federal courts now recognize that prisoners, under the Section 1983 provisions, may sue state officials over such things as brutality by guards, inadequate nutrition and medical care, theft of personal property, and the denial of basic rights.

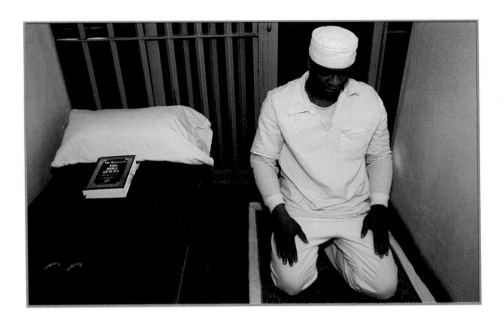

The first amendment to the Constitution provides for the free exercise of religion. The Black Muslims have been a major factor in forcing correctional administrators to recognize that right for prisoners.

The first successful prisoners' rights cases involved the most excessive of prison abuses: brutality and inhuman physical conditions. Gradually, however, prison litigation has focused more directly on the daily activities of the institution, especially on the administrative rules that regulate inmates' conduct. The result has been a series of court decisions concerning the First, Fourth, Eighth, and Fourteenth Amendments to the Constitution. (The full text of these amendments is in Appendix A.)

—— CHECK POINT ——————————————————————————

⑩ **What is meant by the hands-off policy?**

⑪ **Why is the case of *Cooper v. Pate* important to the expansion of prisoners' rights?**

First Amendment

The First Amendment guarantees freedom of speech, press, assembly, petition, and religion. Many of the restrictions of prison life—access to reading materials, censorship of mail, and rules affecting some religious practices—have been successfully challenged by prisoners in the courts.

Since 1970 the federal and state courts have extended the rights of freedom of speech and expression to prisoners. They have required correctional administrators to show why restrictions on these rights must be imposed (see Table 14.2). For example, in 1974 the Supreme Court said that censorship of mail could be allowed only when officials could demonstrate a substantial governmental interest in maintaining security (*Procunier v. Martinez*). The result: markedly increased communication between inmates and the outside world. However, in *Turner v. Safley* (1987) the Court upheld a Missouri ban on correspondence between inmates, saying that such a regulation was reasonably related to legitimate penological interests.

TABLE 14.2 Prisoners' rights under the First Amendment: selected interpretations

The Supreme Court has made several decisions affecting prisoners' rights to freedom of speech and expression and freedom of religion.

CASE	DECISION
Freedom-of-speech cases	
Procunier v. Martinez (1974)	Censorship of mail is permitted only to the extent necessary to maintain prison security.
Turner v. Safley (1987)	Inmates do not have a right to receive mail from one another, and this mail can be banned if "reasonably related to legitimate penological interests."
Thornburgh v. Abbott (1989)	Rules permitting wardens to reject incoming publications deemed detrimental to security, good order, and discipline are constitutional.
Freedom-of-religion cases	
Fulwood v. Clemmer (1962)	The Muslim faith must be recognized as a religion, and officials my not restrict members from holding services.
Gittlemacker v. Prasses (1970)	The state must give inmates the opportunity to practice their religion but is not required to provide a member of the clergy.
Cruz v. Beto (1972)	Prisoners who hold other unconventional beliefs may not be denied the opportunity to practice their religion.
Kahane v. Carlson (1975)	Orthodox Jewish inmates have the right to a diet consistent with their religious beliefs unless the government can show cause why it cannot be provided.
Theriault v. Carlson (1977)	The first Amendment does not protect so-called religions that are obvious shams, that tend to mock established institutions, and whose members lack religious sincerity.
O'Lone v. Estate of Shabazz (1987)	The rights of Muslim prisoners are not violated when work assignments make it impossible for them to attend religious services if no alternative exists.

Fulwood v. Clemmer (1962)
Black Muslims have the same right to worship and practice their religion that inmates of other faiths have.

Cruz v. Beto (1972)
Inmates whose faiths are not the conventional ones practiced in the United States should have reasonable opportunities to practice their faith.

The First Amendment also prevents Congress from making laws respecting the establishment of religion or prohibiting its free exercise. Although freedom of belief has not been challenged, cases concerning the free exercise of religion have caused the judiciary some problems, especially when the religious practice may interfere with prison routine.

The growth of the Black Muslim religion in prisons set the stage for suits demanding that this group be granted the same privileges as other faiths (special diets, access to clergy and religious publications, opportunities for group worship). In the 1970s many prison administrators believed that the Black Muslims were primarily a radical political group posing as a religion, and they did not grant them the benefits accorded to persons who practiced conventional religions.

In *Fulwood v. Clemmer* (1962), the U.S. District Court of the District of Columbia ruled that Black Muslims have the same right to practice their religion and hold worship services as do inmates of other faiths. In another case (*Cruz v. Beto,* 1972), the Supreme Court declared that a Buddhist prisoner must be given reasonable opportunities to practice his faith, like those given fellow prisoners belonging to religions more commonly practiced in the United States.

However, in *O'Lone v. Estate of Shabazz* (1987), the court ruled that a Muslim's rights were not violated when prison officials would not alter his work schedule so that he could attend Friday afternoon Jumu'ah services. Ahmad Uthman Shabazz's work assignment took him outside of the prison, and officials claimed that returning him for services would create a security risk. The justices ruled that the policy was related to a legitimate penological interest.

Muslim, Orthodox Jewish, Native American, and other prisoners have gained some of the rights considered necessary for the practice of their religions. Court decisions have upheld prisoners' rights to be served meals consistent with religious dietary laws, to correspond with religious leaders and possess religious literature, to wear a beard if one's religious belief requires it, and to assemble for religious services. In sum, members of these religious minorities have broken new legal ground in First Amendment issues.

Fourth Amendment

The Fourth Amendment prohibits "unreasonable" searches and seizures, but courts have not been active in extending these protections to prisoners. Thus regulations viewed as reasonable to maintain security and order in an institution may be justified. For example, the decision in ***Hudson v. Palmer*** (1984) upheld the right of officials to search cells and confiscate any materials found.

Table 14.3 outlines some of the U.S. Supreme Court's Fourth Amendment opinions. They reveal the fine balance between the right to privacy and institutional need. Body searches have been harder for administrators to justify than cell searches, for example. But body searches have been upheld when they are part of a policy clearly related to an identifiable and legitimate institutional need and not conducted with the intent to humiliate or degrade (*Smith v. Fairman,* 1982). Some courts have ruled that staff members of one sex may not supervise inmates of the opposite sex during bathing, use of the toilet, or strip searches (*Lee v. Downs,* 1981). Yet the authority of female guards to "pat down" male prisoners, excluding the genital area, has been upheld (*Smith v. Fairman,* 1982). These cases illustrate the lack of clear-cut constitutional principles in such matters.

Eighth Amendment

The Constitution's prohibition of cruel and unusual punishments has been tied to prisoners' need for decent treatment and minimum health standards. Three principal tests have been applied by courts under the Eighth Amendment to determine whether conditions are unconstitutional: (1) whether the punishment shocks the conscience of a civilized society, (2) whether the punishment is unnecessarily cruel, and (3) whether the punishment goes beyond legitimate penal aims.

Federal courts have ruled that, although some aspects of prison life may be acceptable, the combination of various factors—the totality of conditions—may be such that life in the institution may constitute cruel and unusual punishment. When courts have found brutality, unsanitary facilities, overcrowding, and inadequate food, judges have used the Eighth Amendment to order sweeping changes and, in some cases, even to take over administration of entire prisons or corrections systems. In these cases judges have ordered wardens to follow specific internal procedures and to spend money on certain improvements (see Table 14.4).

In several dramatic cases, prison conditions were shown to be so bad that judges have demanded change (Chilton, 1991). In ***Ruiz v. Estelle*** (1980), the court ordered the Texas prison system to

TABLE **14.3**

Prisoners' rights under the Fourth Amendment: selected interpretations

The Supreme Court has often considered the issue of unreasonable searches and seizures.

CASE	DECISION
Bell v. Wolfish (1979)	Strip searches, including searches of body cavities after contact visits, may be carried out when the need for such searches outweighs the personal rights invaded.
Lee v. Downs (1981)	Staff members of one sex may not supervise inmates of the opposite sex in toilet and shower areas even if providing a staff member of the same sex is inconvenient to the administration.
U.S. v. Hitchcock (1972)	A warrantless search of a cell is not unreasonable, and documentary evidence found there is not subject to suppression in court. It is not reasonable to expect a prison cell to be accorded the same level of privacy as a home or automobile.
Hudson v. Palmer (1984)	Officials may search cells without a warrant and seize materials found there.

TABLE 14.4

Prisoners' rights under the Eighth Amendment: selected interpretations

In several key cases, the Supreme Court has ruled on whether correctional actions constitute cruel and unusual punishments.

CASE	DECISION
Estelle v. Gamble (1976)	Deliberate indifference to serious medical needs of prisoners constitutes the unnecessary and wanton infliction of pain, and thus violates the Eighth Amendment.
Ruiz v. Estelle (1980)	Conditions of confinement in the Texas prison system are unconstitutional.
Rhodes v. Chapman (1981)	Double-celling and crowding do not necessarily constitute cruel and unusual punishment. It must be shown that the conditions involve "wanton and unnecessary infliction of pain" and are "grossly disproportionate" to the severity of the crime warranting imprisonment.
Whitley v. Albers (1986)	A prisoner shot in the leg during a riot does not suffer cruel and unusual punishment if the action was taken in good faith to maintain discipline instead of for the mere purpose of causing harm.
Wilson v. Seiter (1991)	Prisoners must not only prove that prison conditions are objectively cruel and unusual but also show that they exist because of the deliberate indifference of officials.

Hudson v. Palmer (1984)
Prison officials have a right to search cells and confiscate from inmates any materials found.

Ruiz v. Estelle (1980)
Conditions of confinement in the Texas prison system were unconstitutional.

address a series of unconstitutional conditions (Crouch and Marquart, 1989; Martin and Ekland-Olson, 1987). Judicial supervision of the system continued for a decade, finally ending in 1990.

Many conditions that violate the rights of prisoners may be corrected by administrative action, training programs, or a minimal expenditure of funds, but remedying an overcrowded population requires expanding facilities or reducing the intake rate. Prison officials have no control over the capacities of their institutions or over the number of offenders sent to them by the courts. New facilities are expensive, and they require appropriations by legislatures and, often, approval of bond issues by voters.

CHECK POINT

⑫ **Which amendment to the Bill of Rights has been most influential in expanding prisoners' rights?**

Fourteenth Amendment

One word and two clauses of the Fourteenth Amendment are relevant to the question of prisoners' rights. The relevant word is *state*, which is found in several clauses of the Fourteenth Amendment. It was not until the 1960s that the Supreme Court ruled that, through the Fourteenth Amendment, most of the Bill of Rights restricts state government actions affecting criminal justice.

The first important clause concerns procedural due process. In the 1970s the Supreme Court began to insist on procedural fairness in the disciplining of prisoners. Two of the most sensitive of institutional decisions are the process that sends inmates to solitary confinement and the method by which inmates may lose good-time credit because of misconduct.

Wolff v. McDonnell (1974)
Basic elements of procedural due process must be present when decisions are made about the disciplining of an inmate.

The equal protection clause is the second important clause with respect to prisoners. Claims that prisoners have been denied equal protection of the law are based on claims of racial, gender, or religious discrimination.

Due Process in Prison Discipline

In the case of *Wolff v. McDonnell* (1974), the Court ruled that basic elements of procedural due process must be present when decisions are made about the disciplining of inmates. Specifically, prisoners have a right to receive notice of the complaint, to have a fair hearing, to confront witnesses, to get help in preparing for the hearing, and to be given a written statement of the decision. Yet the Court has also said that there is no right to counsel at a disciplinary hearing (*Baxter v. Palmigiano*, 1976).

As a result of the Supreme Court decisions, some of which are outlined in Table 14.5, most prisons have established rules that provide elements of due process in disciplinary proceedings. In many institutions, a disciplinary committee receives the

TABLE 14.5 Prisoners' rights under the Fourteenth Amendment: selected interpretations

The Supreme Court has ruled in several key cases concerning procedural due process and equal protection.

CASE	DECISION
Wolff v. McDonnell (1974)	The basic elements of procedural due process must be present when decisions are made concerning the disciplining of an inmate.
Baxter v. Palmigiano (1976)	Although due process must be accorded, an inmate has no right to counsel in a disciplinary hearing.
Vitek v. Jones (1980)	The involuntary transfer of a prisoner to a mental hospital requires a hearing and other minimal elements of due process such as notice and the availability of counsel.
Sandin v. Conner (1995)	Transfer to disciplinary segregation is not the type of atypical, significant deprivation of liberty that requires due process protections as outlined in Wolff.

Since the 1960s state prisoners have been able to sue officials for violations of their civil rights in the federal courts. To facilitate these actions the Supreme Court ordered that prisoners have access to law libraries.

charges, conducts hearings, and decides guilt and punishment. Such committees are usually made up of administrative personnel, but sometimes inmates or outside citizens are included. Even with these protections, the fact remains that prisoners are powerless and may fear further punishment if they too strongly challenge the disciplinary decisions of the warden.

Equal Protection

In 1968 the Supreme Court firmly established that racial discrimination may not be official policy within prison walls (*Lee v. Washington*). Segregation is justified only temporarily during periods when violence between the races is imminent. Equal protection claims have also been upheld in relation to religious freedoms and access to reading materials. For example, the cases brought by members of the Black Muslim religion concerned both the First Amendment right to religious freedom and the Fourteenth Amendment right to equal protection.

The most recent cases concerning equal protection deal with issues concerning female offenders. In *Pargo v. Elliott* (1995), Iowa female inmates argued that their equal protection rights were violated because programs and services were not at the same level as those provided male inmates. The court ruled that because of differences and needs, identical treatment is not required for men and women. It concluded that there was no evidence of "invidious discrimination."

CHECK POINT

⑬ **Which two clauses of the Fourteenth Amendment have been interpreted by the Supreme Court to apply to prisoners' rights?**

Redress of Grievances

Decisions of the U.S. Supreme Court make headlines, but the public never hears about many prisoners' rights suits. In 1997, state prisoners filed almost forty-two thousand suits in the federal courts under the Civil Rights Act of 1871 (42 U.S.C.

1983) contesting conditions of their confinement. In these Section 1983 civil rights suits prisoners were seeking improvements in prison conditions, medical care, return of property, or compensation for abuse by officers.

Few of these suits are successful. Roger A. Hanson and Henry W. K. Daley (1995) found that 74 percent of Section 1983 cases were dismissed because the plaintiff had not followed the court's rules or because there was no evidence of a constitutional rights violation. Most prisoner petitions are written without the assistance of counsel and are often filed in error because of misinterpretations of the law. Ultimately only 2 percent of the cases went to trial and only half were decided in favor of the prisoner.

Although successful Section 1983 cases are few, individual inmates have won redress, or remedy, of their grievances. Some have received monetary compensation for neglect; others have been given the medical attention they desired; still other cases have brought judicial orders that have ended certain correctional practices.

Courts may respond to prisoners' requests in specific cases, but judges cannot possibly oversee the daily activities within institutional walls. As a result of the increase in conditions-of-confinement cases, correctional authorities have acted to ensure that fair procedures are followed and that unconstitutional practices are stopped. Publication of institutional rules, obligations, and procedures is one of the first and most important steps required to meet these goals. In most states, grievance procedures have been developed so that prisoner complaints may be addressed before they result in a lawsuit.

CHECK POINT

⑭ **What has been the function of 42 U.S.C. 1983 in relation to prisoners' rights?**

⑮ **What procedures are required in prisoner disciplinary proceedings?**

A Change in Judicial Direction?

During the last twenty years the Supreme Court has been less supportive of expanding prisoners' rights, and a few decisions reflect a retreat. In particular, the Court ruled in 1986 that prisoners could sue for damages in federal court only if officials had inflicted injury intentionally or deliberately (*Daniels v. Williams*). The chief justice wrote that due process was meant to prevent only an "abuse of power" by public officials and that lack of due care or carelessness was not included. This reasoning was extended in **Wilson v. Seiter** (1991) where the Court ruled that a prisoner's conditions of confinement are not unconstitutional unless it can be shown that prison administrators had acted with "deliberate indifference" to basic human needs (Call, 1995; Smith, 1995a). Even with regard to First Amendment rights (inmate-to-inmate correspondence and attendance at Black Muslim religious services) the Court upheld prison policies (*Turner v. Safley*, 1987; *O'Lone v. Estate of Shabazz*, 1987).

In 1996, Congress passed the Prison Reform Litigation Act, limiting the authority of federal judges to interfere in the operations of correctional institutions. To stem the number of Section 1983 cases, this act made it difficult for

Wilson v. Seiter (1991)
The standard of review of official conduct is whether state policies or actions by correctional officers constitute "deliberate indifference" to constitutional rights.

prisoners to file cases without paying court fees, a problem for most inmates (Cripe, 1997). Since the act was passed there has been a drop in Section 1983 filings (Cheesman, Hanson, and Ostrom, 1998). In addition, the Supreme Court's 1996 decision in *Lewis v. Casey* makes it more difficult for federal judges to ensure that prisoners have enough access to prison law libraries and legal assistance to permit them to prepare their cases.

Impact of the Prisoners' Rights Movement

The prisoners' rights movement can be credited with some general changes in American corrections since the late 1970s (Feeley and Hanson, 1990). The most obvious are concrete improvements in institutional living conditions and administrative practices. Law libraries and legal assistance are now generally available; communication with the outside is easier; religious practices are protected; inmate complaint procedures have been developed; and due process requirements are emphasized. Prisoners in solitary confinement undoubtedly suffer less neglect than they did before. Although overcrowding is still a major problem in most institutions, many conditions are much improved and the more brutalizing elements of prison life have been diminished (Jacobs, 1995:63).

Until *Ruiz v. Estelle*, the staff in many Texas prisons relied on a select group of inmates know as "building tenders" (BTs) to handle the rank-and-file. These BTs had extensive power over their fellow inmates.

Individual cases may have made only a dent in correctional bureaucracies, but over time real changes have occurred. The prisoners' rights movement has clearly influenced correctional officials. The threat of lawsuits and public exposure has placed many in the correctional bureaucracy on guard. On the one hand, it can be argued that this wariness has merely further bureaucratized corrections, requiring staff to prepare extensive and time-consuming documentation of their actions to protect themselves from lawsuits. On the other hand, judicial intervention has forced corrections to rethink existing procedures and organizational structures. As part of the wider changes in the "new corrections," new administrators, increased funding, reformulated policies, and improved management procedures have been, at least in part, influenced by the prisoners' rights movement.

Extending constitutional rights to prisoners has by no means been a speedy process, and the courts have addressed only limited areas of the law. The impact of these decisions on the behavior of correctional officials has not yet been measured, but evidence suggests that court decisions have had a broad effect. Wardens and their subordinates may now be refraining from traditional disciplinary actions that might result in judicial intervention. In sum, after two hundred years of judicial neglect of the conditions under which prisoners are held, courts now look more closely at the situation of the incarcerated.

Lewis v. Casey (1996)
Limits the power of federal judges to ensure that prisoners have adequate access to prison law libraries and other legal resources.

Summary

- Three models of incarceration have been prominent since the 1940s. The custodial model emphasizes the maintenance of security. The rehabilitation model views security and housekeeping activities as mainly a framework for treatment efforts. The reintegration model recognizes that prisoners must be prepared for their return to society.
- The public's belief that the warden and officers have total power over the inmates is outdated.
- Good management through effective leadership can maintain the quality of prison life as measured by levels of order, amenities, and service.
- Correctional officers, because they are constantly in close contact with the prisoners, are the real linchpins in the prison system. The effectiveness of the institution lies heavily on their shoulders.
- The prisoners' rights movement, through lawsuits in the federal courts, has brought many changes to the administration and conditions of American prisons.

Questions for Review

1. How do modern prisons differ from those in the past?
2. What are the characteristics of prisons that make them different from other institutions?
3. What must a prison administrator do to ensure successful management?
4. What are some of the management problems associated with special offender populations, such as those who are elderly, those serving long sentences, or those who have contracted AIDS?
5. What Supreme Court decisions are most significant to corrections today? What effect has each had on correctional institutions?

Key Terms and Cases

custodial model (p. 489)
hands-off policy (p. 504)
rehabilitation model (p. 490)
reintegration model (p. 490)
Cooper v. Pate (1964) (p. 504)

Cruz v. Beto (1972) (p. 506)
Fulwood v. Clemmer (1962) (p. 506)
Hudson v. Palmer (1984) (p. 508)
Lewis v. Casey (1996) (p. 511)
Ruffin v. Commonwealth (1871) (p. 504)

Ruiz v. Estelle (1980) (p. 508)
Wilson v. Seiter (1991) (p. 510)
Wolff v. McDonnell (1974) (p. 508)

For Further Reading

DiIulio, John J., Jr. *Governing Prisons.* New York: Free Press, 1987. A critique of the sociological perspective on inmate society. DiIulio argues that governance by correctional officers is the key to the maintenance of good prisons and jails.

Goodstein, Lynne, and Doris Layton MacKenzie, eds. *The American Prison: Issues in Research and Policy.* New York: Plenum Press, 1989. An excellent collection of essays on various prison issues.

Jacobs, James B. *Stateville.* Chicago: University of Chicago Press, 1977. A classic study of the management of a large state prison over half a century.

Johnson, Robert. *Hard Time: Understanding and Reforming the Prison.* 2d ed. Belmont, Calif.: Wadsworth, 1996. A significant contribution to understanding prison society.

Kauffman, Kelsey. *Prison Officers and Their World*. Cambridge, Mass.: Harvard University Press, 1988. Looks at the work of correctional officers, their roles, and their place within the prison environment.

Martin, Steve J., and Sheldon Ekland-Olson. *Texas Prisons: The Walls Came Tumbling Down*. Austin: Texas Monthly Press, 1987. Impact of the federal courts on the Texas prison system.

Zimmer, Lynn. *Women Guarding Men*. Chicago: University of Chicago Press, 1986. Exploration of the innovation of women as correctional officers in prisons for men.

Going Online

❶ Using the Internet, go to the web page of the National Commission on Correctional Health Care: www.corrections.com/ncchc/index.html. What is the National Commission? What must a health care provider do to become certified by the Commission?

❷ Look up www.geocities.com/capitolhill/4815/onduty.htm. Read the six scenarios of problems that confront correctional officers. For each scenario answer the question "What would you do?" Explain your reasons.

❸ **Using InfoTrac College Edition,** search for the subject "prisoners' rights." Click on "religion." Find and read an article that will help you understand the impact of the U.S. Supreme Court's decision in *O'Lone v. Estate of Shabazz*. Did the Court make a good decision?

CHECK POINT ANSWERS

❶ The characteristics of the inmate population have changed. More inmates are from urban areas and have been convicted for drug-related or violent offenses, the inmate population is fragmented along racial and ethnic lines, prisoners are less isolated from the outside world, and correctional officers have used collective bargaining to improve their working conditions.

❷ The custodial, rehabilitation, and reintegration models.

❸ It is a place where a group of workers manages a group of captives.

❹ Keeping (custody), using (working), serving (treatment).

❺ Management by walking around.

❻ Today's prisoners are largely males in their late 20s to early 30s with less than a high school education. They are disproportionately members of minority groups.

❼ The defects of total power, a limited system of rewards and punishments, exchange relations between correctional officers and inmates, and the strength of inmate leadership.

❽ They are in daily contact with the inmates.

❾ The unions represent members in negotiations with management over salaries and working conditions; they also lobby for expansion of prisons and the hiring of more officers, among other issues.

❿ Judges' belief that prisoners do not have protected rights and that the courts should not become involved in the administration of prisons.

⓫ *Cooper v. Pate* allowed state prisoners to challenge the conditions of their confinement in the federal courts.

⓬ The First Amendment rights concerning free speech and free exercise of religion.

⓭ The due process and equal protection clauses.

⓮ 42 U.S.C. 1983 is the provision of the *United States Code* that allows state prisoners to challenge conditions of their confinement in the federal courts.

⓯ The prisoner should receive notice of the complaint, a fair hearing, assistance in preparing for the hearing, and written notice of the decision. The prisoner should also be able to confront witnesses.

Prison Society

We're crowded into the back of the police van, fifteen convicts en route to the state prison. I'm handcuffed to two other men, the chains gleaming dully at wrists and ankles. The man on my right lifts his hand to smoke, the red eye of his cigarette burning through the darkness of the van. When he exhales, the man at my left coughs, the sound in his lungs suggesting that he's old, maybe sick. I want to ask what he's in for. But I don't speak, restrained by my fear, a feeling that rises cold up the back of my spine. For a long time no one else speaks either, each man locked in his own thoughts. It's someone up front, a kid, his voice brittle with fear, who speaks first. "What's it like down there—in the joint? Is it as bad as they say?"

"Worse," someone answers. "Cell blocks are dirty. Overcrowded. Lousy chow. Harassment. Stabbings."

"How do you live there?"

"You don't exactly live. You go through the motions. Eat, sleep, mind your own business. Do drugs when you can get them. Forget the world you came from."

This description of the "way in" was written by an inmate who was incarcerated in the Arizona penal system for seven years. It conveys much of the anxiety not only of the new "fish" but also of the old con. What is it like to be incarcerated? What does it mean to the inmates, the guards, and the administrators? Are the officers in charge or do the prisoners "rule the joint"?

In many ways the interior of the American maximum security prison is a foreign land. Observers of the criminal justice system need to gain an awareness of the social dimensions of prison life: its traditions, the roles played there, and the patterns of interpersonal relations. Although the walls and guns may give the impression that everything goes by strict rules and with predictable, machinelike precision, the human dimension might be overlooked if only the formal organization and rules are studied. The lives of the incarcerated are the subjects of this chapter.

QUESTIONS for Inquiry

- What is it like to be in prison, and how do prisoners adapt to life in the joint?
- How are social relationships among female prisoners different from those among male prisoners?
- What is the nature of violence in prisons?
- What can be done about prison violence?

The Convict World

Because a prison population is made up of felons and many of them are prone to violence, prisons might be expected to be scenes of frequent revolt, if prison officials did not maintain strict discipline. However, definite limits have been placed on correctional administrators' ability to keep order in a society of prisoners that has its own order within that imposed by the institution. Examining the convict world will foster an understanding of the day-to-day operation of a prison, the prison subculture, and the means by which prisoners adapt to their social and physical environments.

Inmates in today's prisons do not serve their terms in isolation. Rather, prisoners form a society with traditions, norms, and a leadership structure (Sykes, 1958). Some members of this society may choose to associate with only a few close friends; others form cliques along racial or "professional" lines (Carroll, 1974). Still others may be the politicians of the convict society: they attempt to represent convict interests and distribute valued goods in return for support. Just as there is a social culture in the free world, there is a prisoner subculture on the "inside." Membership in a group provides mutual protection from theft and physical assault, the basis of wheeling and dealing activities, and a source of cultural identity (Irwin, 1980).

As in any society, the convict world has certain norms and values. Often described as the **inmate code,** the values and norms develop within the prison social system and help to define the inmate's image of the model prisoner.

inmate code

The values and norms of the prison social system that define the inmates' idea of the model prisoner.

As Robert Johnson notes, "The public culture of the prison has norms that dictate behavior 'on the yard' and in other public areas of the prison such as mess halls, gyms, and the larger program and work sites" (1996:113). He suggests that the culture emphasizes the use of hostility and manipulation in one's relations with fellow inmates and staff. It makes caring and friendly behavior, especially with respect to the staff, look servile and silly.

Chuck Terry, with twelve years of personal experience on the "inside" says that male prisoners must project an image of "fearlessness in the way they walk, talk and socially interact" (1997:26). Thus inmates must suppress expressions of one's true feelings, because showing emotion is seen as a weakness.

The code also emphasizes the solidarity of all inmates against the staff. For example, inmates should never inform on one another, pry into one another's affairs, run off at the mouth, or put another inmate on the spot. They must be tough and not trust the officers or the principles for which the guards stand. Further, guards are "hacks" or "screws"; the officials are wrong and the prisoners are right.

Some sociologists believe that the code emerges within the institution as a way to lessen the pain of imprisonment (Sykes, 1958); others believe that it is part of the criminal subculture that prisoners bring with them (Irwin and Cressey, 1962). The inmate who follows the code can be expected to enjoy a certain amount of admiration from other inmates as a "right guy" or a "real man." Those who break the code are labeled "rat" or "punk" and will probably spend their prison life at the bottom of the convict social structure, alienated from the rest of the population and targeted for abuse (Sykes, 1958:84).

A single, overriding inmate code may not exist in today's prison. Instead, convict society has divided itself along racial lines (Carroll, 1974; Irwin, 1980). Apparently reflecting tensions in American society, many prisons now are marked by racially motivated violence, organizations based on race, and voluntary segregation by inmates by race whenever possible—for example, in recreation areas and dining halls.

Interviews with ex-convicts in California painted a picture of prison society in a greater degree of turmoil than in the past. This turmoil was created by the presence of gangs, changes in the type of person incarcerated, and changes in prison policy. As the researchers found, "All these elements coalesced to create an increasingly unpredictable world in which prior loyalties, allegiances, and friendships were disrupted" (Hunt, Riegel, Morales, and Waldrof, 1993:398–409).

In a society without a single code of behavior that is accepted by all, the task of administrators becomes much more difficult. They must be aware of the different groups, recognize the norms and rules that members follow, and deal with the leaders of many cliques rather than with a few inmates who have risen to top positions in the inmate society.

CHECK **POINT**

① **What are the key elements of the inmate code?**

② **Why is it unlikely that a single, overriding inmate code exists in today's prisons?**

(Answers are at the end of the chapter.)

Adaptive Roles

On entering prison, a newcomer ("fish") is confronted by the question, "How am I going to do my time?" Some may decide to withdraw into their own world and isolate themselves from their fellow prisoners. Others may decide to become full participants in the convict social system. Their choice, which is influenced by prisoners' values and experiences, will, in turn, help to determine the strategies for survival and success that they will use while in prison.

Four terms describe the basic role orientations most male inmates use to adapt to prison: *doing time, gleaning, jailing,* and functioning as a *disorganized criminal* (Irwin, 1970:67).

Those who are *doing time* view their prison term as a brief, inevitable break in their criminal careers, as merely a cost of doing business. They try to serve their terms with the least amount of suffering and the greatest amount of comfort. They avoid trouble by living by the inmate code, finding activities to fill their days, forming friendships with a few other convicts, and generally doing what they think is necessary to survive and to get out as soon as possible.

Inmates who are *gleaning* try to take advantage of prison programs to better themselves and improve their prospects for success after release. They use the resources at hand: libraries, correspondence courses, vocational training, schools. Some make a radical conversion away from a life of crime.

Jailing is the choice of those who cut themselves off from the outside and try to construct a life within the prison. These are often "state-raised" youths who have spent much of their lives in institutional settings and who identify little with the values of free society. These are the inmates who seek power and influence in the prison society, often becoming key figures in the politics and economy of the joint.

A fourth role orientation—the *disorganized criminal*—describes inmates who are unable to develop any of the other three orientations. They may be of low intelligence or afflicted with psychological or physical disabilities. They have difficulty functioning in prison society. They are "human putty" to be manipulated by others. These are also the inmates who cannot adjust to prison life and who develop emotional disorders, attempt suicide, and violate prison rules (Adams, 1992).

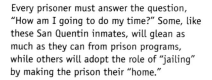

Every prisoner must answer the question, "How am I going to do my time?" Some, like these San Quentin inmates, will glean as much as they can from prison programs, while others will adopt the role of "jailing" by making the prison their "home."

As the number of roles suggests, prisoners are not part of an undifferentiated mass. Individual convicts choose to play specific roles in the prison society. The roles they choose reflect the physical and social environment they have experienced and also influence the relationships and interactions they will develop in prison. How do most prisoners serve their time? Although the media generally portray prisons as violent, chaotic places, research shows that most inmates want to get through their sentence without trouble. As journalist Pete Earley (1992:44) found in his study of Leavenworth Prison in Kansas, about 80 percent of inmates try to avoid trouble and do their time as easily as possible.

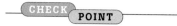

③ **What are the four role orientations found in prisons for adult males?**

The Prison Economy

In prison, as outside, individuals desire goods and services. Although the state feeds, clothes, and houses all prisoners, amenities are sparse. Prisoners are deprived of everything but bare necessities. Their diet and routine are monotonous and their recreational opportunities are few. They experience a loss of individual identity (because of uniformity of treatment) and a lack of responsibility. In short, the prison is relatively unique in having been deliberately designed as "an island of poverty in the midst of a society of relative abundance" (Williams and Fish, 1974:40).

In recent years the number of items that a prisoner may purchase or receive through legitimate channels has increased. In some state institutions, for example, inmates may own television sets, civilian clothing, and hot plates. However, these few luxuries are not enjoyed by all prisoners, nor do they satisfy lingering desires for a variety of other goods. Some state legislatures have decreed that amenities will be prohibited and that prisoners should live in a Spartan environment.

Recognizing that prisoners do have some needs that are not met, prisons have a commissary or "store" from which inmates may, on a scheduled basis, purchase a limited number of items—toilet articles, tobacco, snacks, and other food products—in exchange for credits drawn on their "bank accounts." The size of a bank account depends on the amount of money deposited on the inmate's entrance, gifts sent by relatives, and amounts earned in the low-paying prison industries.

But the peanut butter, soap, and cigarettes of the typical prison store in no way satisfy the consumer needs and desires of most prisoners. Consequently, an informal, underground economy is a major element in prison society. Many items taken for granted on the outside are inordinately valued on the inside. For example, talcum powder and deodorant become more important because of the limited bathing facilities. Goods and services that a prisoner would not have consumed at all outside prison can have exaggerated importance inside prison. Unable to enjoy their accustomed alcoholic beverages, some offenders will seek the same effect by sniffing glue. Or to distinguish themselves from others, offenders may pay laundry workers to iron a shirt in a particular way.

Mark Fleisher's research at the United States Penitentiary at Lompoc, California (1989:151), and David Kalinich's study of the State Prison of Southern Michigan in Jackson (1980) have documented the existence of prison economies. They learned that a market economy provides the goods and services not available or not allowed by prison authorities. As a principal feature of the prison culture, this informal economy reinforces the norms and roles of the social system and influences the nature of interpersonal relationships. The extent of the underground economy and its ability to produce desired goods and services—food, drugs, alcohol, sex, preferred living conditions—vary according to the extent of official surveillance, the demands of the consumers, and the opportunities for entrepreneurship. Inmates' success as "hustlers" will determine the luxuries and power they can enjoy.

The standard currency in the prison economy is cigarettes. Because having real money is prohibited and a barter system is somewhat restrictive, "cigarette money" is a useful substitute. Cigarettes are not contraband, are easily transferable, have a stable and well-known standard of value, and come in "denominations" of singles, packs, and cartons. And they are in demand by smokers. Even those who do not smoke keep cigarettes for prison currency.

Certain positions in the prison society enhance opportunities for entrepreneurs. For example, inmates assigned to work in the kitchen, warehouse, and administrative office steal food, clothing, building materials, and even information to sell or trade to other prisoners. The goods may then become part of other market transactions. Thus, the exchange of a dozen eggs for two packs of cigarettes may result in the reselling of the eggs in the form of egg sandwiches made on a hot plate for five cigarettes each. Meanwhile, the kitchen worker who stole the eggs may use the income to get a laundry worker to starch his shirts, to get drugs from a hospital orderly, or to pay a "punk" for sexual favors.

But economic transactions may lead to violence when goods are stolen, debts are not paid, or agreements are broken. Disruptions of the economy may occur when officials conduct periodic "lockdowns" and inspections. Confiscation of contraband may result in temporary shortages and price readjustments, but gradually business returns. The prison economy, like that of the outside world, allocates goods and services, rewards and sanctions, and it is closely linked to the society it serves.

CHECK POINT

④ Why does an underground economy exist in prison?

⑤ Why are prison administrators wary of the prison economy?

 # Women in Prison

Most studies of prisons have been based on institutions for males. How do prisons for women differ from prisons for men, and what are the special problems of female inmates?

Women constitute only 6.4 percent (about eighty-three thousand) of the entire U.S. prison population. However, the growth rate in the number of incarcerated women has exceeded that of men since 1981. This growth is particularly acute in the federal system, which, because of the "war on drugs," has had to absorb an additional six thousand female inmates during the past ten years (Fleisher, Rison, and Helman, 1997). In state prisons the number of women incarcerated for drug

Compared with the convict society in prisons for males, many female prisoners, such as these in Alabama's Julia Tutwiler Prison, form pseudofamilies, developing strong bonds with family members.

offenses increased almost 450 percent in the 1990s (*New York Times Magazine,* June 2, 1996:35). Barbara Owen and Barbara Bloom (1995:166) argue that the increased number of women in prison has significantly affected the delivery of programs, housing conditions, medical care, staffing, and security.

Men's and women's prisons differ in a number of ways. Women's prisons are smaller and less security-conscious, and the relationships between inmates and staff are less structured. Women inmates are less committed to the inmate code, and physical aggression and violence seem to be less common in women's institutions. The hidden economy is not as well developed. And because women serve shorter sentences, there is perhaps more fluidity in the prison society as new members join and others leave.

Although institutional facilities for women are generally smaller, better staffed, and less fortress-like than those for men, these advantages may pale when the problems of remoteness and heterogeneity are considered. Because few states operate more than one prison for women and some operate none, inmates are generally far removed from their families, friends, and attorneys. In addition, because the number of inmates is small, there is less pressure to design programs to meet an individual offender's security and treatment needs. Rehabilitation programs are few, and in many cases dangerous inmates are not segregated from those who have committed minor offenses.

Incarcerated women are young (their average age is 29) and poorly educated (less than half have finished high school). They were employed before conviction at unskilled jobs, and about 60 percent are African Americans or Hispanic Americans. Nearly half were caring for dependents when they were admitted, most without a male companion. Few had alcohol problems, but about half were drug abusers (Pollock-Byrne, 1990:57). Figure 15.1 presents some of the characteristics of female prisoners.

CHECK POINT

⑥ **What reasons are given for the neglect of facilities and programs in women's prisons?**

Like their male counterparts, female prisoners typically are young, have low education levels, are members of minority groups, and are incarcerated for a serious offense.

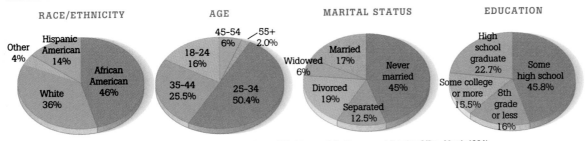

SOURCE: U.S. Department of Justice, Bureau of Justice Statistics, *Special Report* (Washington, D.C.: Government Printing Office, March 1994).

Social Relationships

In a classic study, Esther Heffernan (1972:41–42) discovered that three terms in prison slang—*square, cool,* and *in the life*—correspond to the real-world identities of noncriminal, professional, and habitual offenders in women's correctional institutions. *Square* has the same meaning it has in outside world: the word describes a person who holds to conventional norms and values. For example, a woman who killed her husband in a moment of rage is likely to be square. She attempts to maintain a conventional life while incarcerated, strives to gain the respect of officers and fellow inmates, and seeks to be a "good Christian woman." *Cool* refers to professional criminals who "keep busy, play around, stay out of trouble, and get out." They attempt to manipulate others and get through their incarceration on "easy time," seeking to gain as many amenities as they can without risking a longer stay.

By contrast, *in the life* is to be antisocial in prison, just as one was on the outside. Those who are in the life are habitual offenders who have been involved in prostitution and drugs. Because they have frequently served previous prison terms, they interact with others with similar experiences and find community within the prison. It is important to them to stand firm against authority (Heffernan, 1972:41–42).

In one of the few recent studies of prison culture, Barbara Owen found that the inmates at the Central California Women's Facility developed various styles of doing time. She found that the vast majority wanted to avoid "the mix"—"behavior that can bring trouble and conflict with staff and other prisoners" (Owen, 1998:179). A primary feature of the mix is anything for which one can lose "good time" or can result in being sent to administrative segregation. Being in the mix was related to " 'homo-secting,' involvement in drugs, fights, and 'being messy,' that is being involved in conflict and trouble." Owen found most women wanted to do their time and go home, but some "are more at home in prison and do not seem to care if they 'lost time.' " The culture of being in the mix is not imported from the outside but is internal to the prison, as some inmates prefer the pursuit of drugs, girl friends, and fighting (Owen, 1998:179).

What types of social relationships do women prisoners maintain? As in all types of penal institutions, homosexual relationships are found. Among women prisoners, these relationships are more likely to be voluntary than coerced. More importantly, female inmates tend to form pseudofamilies in which they adopt various roles—father, mother, daughter, sister—and interact as a unit (Propper, 1982;

CLOSE

up

Surviving in **Prison**

I was scared when I went to Bedford Hills. But I knew a few things by then. Like if you act quiet and hostile, people will consider you dangerous and won't bother you. So when I got out of isolation and women came up and talked to me, I said, "I left my feelings outside the gate, and I'll pick 'em up on my way out." I meant I wasn't going to take no junk from anyone. I made a promise if anybody hit me, I was gonna send 'em to the hospital.

When you go in, if you have certain characteristics, you're classified in a certain way. First of all, if you are aggressive, if you're not a dependent kind of woman, you're placed in a position where people think you have homosexual tendencies. If you're in that society long, you play the game if it makes it easier to survive.

And it makes it easier if people think you're a stud broad. I played the game to make it easier so they would leave me alone. I didn't have money to use makeup and I couldn't see going through any changes. You're in there and the women are looking for new faces. Since I was quiet and not too feminine-looking, I was placed in a certain box in other people's minds. I let them think that's what box I was in—'cause it was a good way to survive. My good friends knew better. But I had three good friends and they were considered "my women"—so they in turn were safe, too. You have to find ways to survive. You cultivate ways to survive. It's an alien world and it has nothing to do with functioning in society better. What I learned there was to survive there.

SOURCE: Kathryn Watterson Burkhart, *Women in Prison* (New York: Doubleday, 1976), 89–90.

Girshick, 1999). Heffernan views these "play" families as a "direct, conscious substitution for the family relationships broken by imprisonment, or . . . the development of roles that perhaps were not fulfilled in the actual home environment" (Heffernan, 1972:41–42). Such links help relieve the tensions of prison life, assist the socialization of the new inmate, and allow individuals to act according to clearly defined roles and rules. (For a survival method that one woman chose, see the Close-Up above.)

Male and Female Subcultures Compared

The prison subculture of women has many parallels with that of men—and a number of major differences. Comparisons are complicated by the nature of the research, because most studies have been conducted in single-sex institutions, and theories and concepts first developed in male prisons have been then applied to female institutions. However, the following facts may explain the subcultures:

- Nearly half of male inmates, but only a third of female inmates, are serving time for violent offenses.
- There is less violence in prisons for women than in prisons for men.
- Women show greater responsiveness to prison programs.
- Men's prison populations are divided by security level; most women serve time in facilities where the entire population is mixed.
- Men tend to segregate themselves by race; this is less true with women.
- Men rarely become intimate with their keepers; many women share their lives with officers.

A principal difference between men's and women's prisons lies in interpersonal relations. Male prisoners seem to have a greater sense that they act as individuals and that their behavior is evaluated by the yardstick of the prison culture. As James Fox noted in his comparative study of four prisons for men and one for women, men believe they must demonstrate physical strength and consciously avoid any mannerisms that may imply homosexuality. Male prisoners have their gangs or cliques but not the network of "family" relationships that has been found among female prisoners. Fox found little sharing in men's institutions. Men are expected to do their own time. The norms stress autonomy, self-sufficiency, and the ability to cope with one's own problems (Fox, 1982).

According to Fox, women at the Bedford Hills Correctional Facility in New York were less likely to look toward achievement of status or recognition within the prisoner community or "to impose severe restrictions on the sexual (or emotional) conduct of other members" (Fox, 1982:100). In prisons for women, close ties seem to exist among small groups of inmates. These extended families, which may include homosexual couple relationships, provide emotional support and emphasize the sharing of resources.

The little data that exist indicate that women are less likely to engage in violent acts against fellow inmates than are men (Kruttschnitt and Krmopotich, 1990:371). Some researchers have attributed the distinctive female prison subculture to the nurturing, maternal qualities of women. Others have criticized this analysis as a stereotype of female behavior, imputing to women sex-specific personality characteristics.

CHECK POINT

⑦ **How do the social relationships among women prisoners differ from those of their male counterparts?**

Programs and the Female Role

The two major criticisms of programs in women's prisons are that they lack the variety of the vocational and educational programs available in male institutions, and that existing programs tend to conform to sexual stereotypes of "female" occupations—cosmetology, food service, housekeeping, sewing. Such training does not correspond to the wider employment opportunities available to women in today's world. This is especially true for many who must support their households as single parents.

Research conducted in the 1970s by Ruth Glick and Virginia Neto (1977) confirmed that fewer programs were offered in women's than in men's institutions and that the existing programs lacked variety. Merry Morash and her colleagues noted changes that had taken place during the 1980s, but they, too, found that gender stereotypes shaped the content of vocational programs (Morash, Haarr, and Rucker, 1994). The American Correctional Association reported in 1990 that prisons have few work assignments for incarcerated women, but those that do exist do teach marketable job skills (1990). However, the range of offerings in many prisons for women has since increased to add business education, computer training, auto repair, and carpentry to the more traditional offerings.

Better-paying jobs in contemporary America are open only to those persons with the education necessary to cope with the complexities of the workplace.

The educational level of most female offenders limits their access to these occupations. In some institutions less than half of the inmates have completed high school. These women are sometimes assigned to the classroom so that they can earn the general equivalency diploma (GED), while other inmates may do college work through correspondence study or courses offered in the institution.

Medical Services

Women's prisons also lack proper medical services. Yet women usually have more serious health problems because of their higher incidence of asthma, drug abuse, diabetes, and heart disorder; many women also have gynecological problems (Bershard, 1985; Yang, 1990). A national survey revealed that a higher percentage of female than male state inmates tested positive for HIV, that 15 percent of females had spent a night in a mental hospital before incarceration, and 62 percent had used drugs during the month before entering prison (BJS, 1999k: Tables 6.76, 6.59). A higher proportion of women than men report receiving medical services in prison, yet women's institutions are less likely than men's to have full-time medical staff or hospital facilities.

Saying that corrections must "defuse the time bomb," Leslie Acoca argues that failure to provide women inmates with basic preventive and medical treatments such as immunizations, breast cancer screenings, and management of chronic diseases "is resulting in the development of more serious health problems that are exponentially more expensive to treat." She says that poor medical care for the incarcerated merely shifts costs to overburdened community health care systems after release (Acoca, 1998).

Pregnancies raise numerous issues for correctional policy, including availability of special diets, the right to an abortion, access to a delivery room and medical personnel, and the length of time that newborns can remain with incarcerated mothers. Most pregnant inmates have characteristics (older than 35, history of drug abuse, prior multiple abortions, and sexually transmitted diseases) that indicate the potential for a high-risk pregnancy requiring special medical care. Many prison systems are attempting to address this problem by allowing nursing infants to stay with their mothers, creating in-prison nurseries, instituting counseling programs, and improving standards of medical care (Wooldredge and Masters, 1993).

Shirley Carone and David Smith with David Jr. during visiting hours at Central California Women's Facility. That David not only takes care of their son but married Shirley and visits her four times a week is most unusual in the world of women's prisons.

Mothers and Their Children

Incarcerated mothers worry a great deal about their children. The best available data indicate that almost 80 percent of women inmates are mothers and on average have two dependent children. On any given day, 167,000 American children—two-thirds of whom are under 10 years old—have mothers who are in jail or prison. One study found that approximately half of these children do not see their mothers at any time while they are in prison (*New York Times*, November 30,1992:A10).

Because about 76 percent of incarcerated mothers were single caretakers of minor children before they entered prison, they do not have

husbands or male partners able and willing to make a home for the children (Acoca, 1997). In a study of the effects of separation on 133 inmates and their children, Phyllis Jo Baunach found that the children were most often cared for by their maternal grandmothers. This arrangement gave the inmates some peace of mind (Baunach, 1985:75). When an inmate had no relative to care for the children, they were often put up for adoption or placed in state-funded foster care. This development can be a source of lingering emotional pain and distress for both the mother and child.

Mothers have difficulty maintaining contact with their children because of the distance of prisons from the children's homes, restrictions on visiting hours, intermittent telephone privileges, and conditions for meeting with offspring during visits. In some correctional institutions, child visitors must abide by the same rules governing visits by adults: no physical contact and strict time limits.

Programs to address the needs of imprisoned mothers and their children are being designed. In some states, children may meet with their mothers at almost any time, for extended periods, and in playrooms or nurseries where contact is possible. Some states arrange transportation for visits. In both Nebraska and South Dakota, for example, children may stay with their mothers for up to five days a month. A few prisons have family visiting programs that allow the inmate, her legal husband, and her children to be together, often in a mobile home or apartment, for periods up to seventy-two hours.

In most states a baby born in prison must be placed with a family member or social agency within three weeks. This policy interferes with the early mother-infant bonding thought to be crucial for human development. Some innovative programs now allow them to remain together longer. For example, at the Women's Correctional Institution at Bedford Hills, New York, mothers and their newborns move to a special nursery wing and can stay there for up to one year. Their primary responsibility is to care for their children and to learn parenting skills.

The future of women's correctional institutions is hard to predict. More women are being sent to prison now, and more have committed the violent crimes and drug offenses that used to be more typical of male offenders. Will these changes affect the adaptive roles and social relationships that differentiate women's prisons from men's? Will women's prisons need to become more security-conscious and to enforce rules through more formal relationships between inmates and staff? These are important issues that need study.

CHECK POINT

⑧ **List some of the problems encountered by women prisoners in maintaining contact with their children.**

⑨ **How are children cared for while their mothers are incarcerated?**

Prison Programs

Modern correctional institutions differ from those of the past in the number and variety of programs for inmates. Prison industries were a part of early penitentiaries; educational, vocational, and treatment programs were added when

As the saying goes, "Idle hands are the Devil's playground." Experienced administrators know that the more programs offered, the less likely inmates' boredom will translate into "mischief-making."

rehabilitation goals became prevalent. In the 1990s, as the public called for harsher punishment of criminals, legislators gutted prison educational and treatment programs as "frills" that only "coddled" inmates. In addition, the great increase in the number of prisoners has limited access to programs that are available.

Administrators argue that programs are important in dealing with the problem of time on the prisoners' hands. They know that the more programs prisons offer, the less likely inmate idleness is to turn into hostility—the less cell time, the fewer tensions. New evidence suggests that inmate education and jobs may positively affect the running of prisons, as well as reduce recidivism (Butterfield, 1995a).

Classification of Prisoners

Determining the appropriate program for an individual prisoner usually involves a **classification** process. A committee of department heads for security, treatment, education, and industry evaluates the inmate's security level, treatment needs, work assignment, and eventually readiness for release. Unfortunately, classification decisions are often based on administrative rather than inmate needs. Certain programs are limited, and the demand for them is great. Inmates may find that the few places in the electrician's course are filled and that there is a long waiting list. Or inmates may be excluded from programs because prison housekeeping work takes priority. Inmates from the city may be assigned to farm work because that is where they are needed. Prisoners are often angered and frustrated by the classification process and the limited availability of programs. Release on parole can depend on a good record of participation in these programs, yet entrance for some inmates is blocked.

classification
The process of assigning an inmate to a category specifying his or her needs for security, treatment, education, work assignment, and readiness for release.

CHECK POINT

⑩ Why are prison programs important from the standpoint of prison administrators?

⑪ What is the process for assigning inmates to programs?

Educational Programs

It has been estimated that more than 200,000 federal and state prisoners partici-pate in education programs, making education the most popular prison program (*Corrections Compendium,* March 1994:5–6). Educational programs give inmates a range of opportunities to take academic courses. In many systems, all prisoners who have not completed eighth grade are assigned full time to the prison school. Many programs provide remedial help with basic reading, English, and math skills. They also permit prisoners to earn high school equivalency diplomas. Some institutions offer courses in cooperation with a college or university, although funding for such programs has come under attack. The Comprehensive Crime Control Bill of 1994 bans federal funding to prisoners for post-secondary educa-tion (Kunen, 1995). Some state legislatures have passed similar laws under pres-sure from people who argue that tax dollars should not be spent on the college tuition of prisoners when law-abiding students must pay for their own education. Studies have shown that prisoners assigned to education programs are good risks to avoid committing crimes after release (Andrews and Bonta, 1994). Anne Piehl found that male inmates in the Wisconsin prison system who were enrolled in high school classes were 10 percent less likely to be rearrested four years after their release than those who did not participate (Butterfield, 1995a). However, it is unclear whether education helps to rehabilitate these offenders or whether the types of prisoners (gleaners) assigned to education programs tend to be those motivated to avoid further crimes.

Vocational Education

Vocational education programs are designed to teach skills such as plumbing, automobile mechanics, printing, and computer programming. Unfortunately, most such programs are unable to keep abreast of the technological advances and needs of the free market. Too many programs train inmates for trades that already have an adequate labor supply or in which new methods have made the skills taught obsolete. Some vocational programs are even designed to prepare inmates for outside careers that are closed to former felons. For example, many states pro-hibit former felons from working in restaurants where alcohol is sold, yet training in food preparation is taught in many prisons.

Prison Industries

Prison industries, which trace their roots to the early workshops of New York's Auburn Penitentiary, are intended to teach work habits and skills that will assist prisoners' reentry into the outside workforce. In practice, institutions rely on prison labor to provide basic food, maintenance, clerical, and other institutional services. In addition, many prisons contain manufacturing facilities that produce goods, such as office furniture and clothing, to be used in correctional and other state institutions.

The prison industries system has had a checkered career (Conley, 1980). During the nineteenth century, factories were established in many prisons, and inmates manufactured items that were sold on the open market. With the rise of the labor movement, however, state legislatures and Congress passed laws restricting the sale of prison-made goods so that they would not compete with those made by free workers (Hawkins, 1983). In 1979 Congress lifted restrictions on the interstate sale of prison-made products and urged correctional administrators to explore with the private sector possible improvements for prison industry programs. Industrial programs would relieve idleness, allow inmates to earn wages that they could save until release, and reduce the costs of incarceration. The Federal Bureau of Prisons and some states have developed industries, but generally their products are not sold on the free market and the percentage of prisoners employed varies greatly. For example, in Georgia and Minnesota more than 50 percent of prisoners are employed in industries, while in Kentucky and Maine only 5 percent work in prison industries (Waunder, 1994). A later survey by the American Correctional Association revealed that the number of inmates employed in prison industries ranged from 1 percent to a high of 30 percent, with the average at 9 percent (Butterfield, 1995a).

Although the idea of employing inmates sounds attractive, the economic value may be offset by the inefficiencies of prison work. Turnover is great because many inmates are transferred among several institutions or released over a two-year period. Many prisoners have low education levels and lack steady work habits, making it difficult for them to perform many of the tasks of modern production. An additional cost to efficiency is the need to periodically stop production to count heads and to check that tools and materials have not been stolen (Flanagan and Maguire, 1993).

Rehabilitative Programs

Rehabilitative programs seek to treat the personal defects thought to have brought about the inmate's criminality. Most people agree that rehabilitating offenders is a desirable goal, but the amount of emphasis that should be given to these programs is much debated.

Reports in the 1970s cast doubt on the ability of treatment programs to stem recidivism. They also questioned the ethics of requiring inmates to participate in rehabilitative programs in exchange for the promise of parole (Martinson, 1974). Supporters of treatment programs argue that certain programs, if properly run, work for certain offenders (Palmer, 1992; Andrews, Zinger, Hoge, Bonta, Gendreau, and Cullen, 1990).

In most correctional systems, a range of psychological, behavior, and social services programs is still available. How much they are used seems to vary according to the goals of the institution and the attitudes of the administrators. Nationally, very little money is spent for treatment services, and these programs reach only 5 percent of the inmate population. Rehabilitative programs remain a part of correctional institutions, but their emphasis has diminished. Incarceration's current goal of humane custody implies no effort to change inmates.

CHECK POINT

⑫ Why have legislatures and the general public been so critical of educational and rehabilitative programs in prisons?

⑬ What problems are encountered in vocational training programs?

⑭ Why have legislatures restricted prison industries?

Violence in Prison

Prisons provide a perfect recipe for violence. They confine in cramped quarters thousands of men, some with histories of violent behavior. While incarcerated, they are not allowed contact with women, and they live under highly restrictive conditions. Sometimes these conditions spark collective violence, as in the riots at Attica, New York (1971), Santa Fe, New Mexico (1980), Atlanta, Georgia (1987), and Lucasville, Ohio (1993) (Useem and Reisig, 1999).

Although such events are widely reported in the news media, few people are aware of the level of everyday interpersonal violence in U.S. prisons. For example, each year about 150 prisoners commit suicide, about 70 perish in deaths "caused by another," and 400 die of unspecified causes (BJS, 1999d:95). Annually there are about twenty-five thousand assaults by other inmates (*USA Today*, August 8, 1997:1). Great numbers of prisoners live in a state of constant uneasiness, always on the lookout for persons who might subject them to homosexual demands, steal their few possessions, or otherwise make their lives more painful. Yet some researchers point out that the level of violence varies by offender age, institutional security level, and administrative effectiveness (Maitland and Sluder, 1998:55).

Assaultive Behavior and Inmate Characteristics

For the person entering prison for the first time, the anxiety level and fear of violence are especially high. As one fish asked, "Will I end up fighting for my life?" (Schmid and Jones, 1991:415). Gary, an inmate at Leavenworth, told Pete Earley, "Every convict has three choices, but only three. He can fight (kill someone), he can hit the fence (escape), or he can fuck (submit)" (1992:55).

Racial and ethnic gangs dominate prison society in some institutions. As a correctional officer, how would you deal with these members of the white supremacist Aryan Brotherhood gang incarcerated in Ferguson Prison, Texas?

Assaults in correctional institutions raise serious questions for administrators, criminal justice specialists, and the general public. What are the causes of prison violence and what can be done about it? These questions are considered as the three main categories of prison violence are examined: prisoner-prisoner, prisoner-officer, and officer-prisoner.

To begin to understand that violence, however, we must first understand more about the inmates, because violent behavior in prisons is related to the types of people who are incarcerated and the characteristics they bring with them (Innes and Verdeyen, 1997:1). Three of these characteristics stand out: age, attitudes, and race.

Age

Young males between the ages of 16 and 24, both inside and outside prison, are more prone to violence than their elders (Simon, 1993:263). Not surprisingly, 96 percent of adult prisoners are men, with an average age at the time of admission of 27.

The young not only have greater physical strength, but they also lack the commitments to career and family that are thought to restrict antisocial behavior. In addition, many young men have difficulty defining their position in society, so many of their interactions with others are interpreted as challenges to their status.

"Machismo," the concept of male honor and the sacredness of one's reputation as a man, requires physical retaliation against those who insult one's honor. Observers have argued that many homosexual rapes are nonsexual; rather, they are political—attempts to impress on the victim the power of the aggressor and to define the target's role as passive or "feminine" (Rideau and Wikberg, 1992:79). Some inmates adopt a preventive strategy of trying to impress their colleagues with their bravado. The reaction of others to this behavior may be counterchallenge. The potential for violence among such prisoners is clear.

Attitudes

One sociological theory of crime suggests that a subculture of violence exists among certain socioeconomic, racial, and ethnic groups. This subculture, found in the lower class, has a value system in which violence is "tolerable, expected, or required" (Wolfgang and Ferracuti, 1967:263). Arguments are settled and decisions are made by the fist rather than by verbal persuasion. Many inmates bring these attitudes into prison with them.

Race

Race has become a major divisive factor in today's prisons, reflecting tensions in the larger society. Racist attitudes seem to be acceptable in most institutions and have become part of the convict code. The fact of forced association, having to live with persons with whom one would not be likely to associate with on the outside, exaggerates and amplifies racial conflict. Violence against members of another race may be how some inmates deal with the frustrations of their lives both inside and outside prison. In addition, the presence of gangs organized along racial lines contributes to violence in prison.

Prisoner-Prisoner Violence

Although prison folklore may attribute violence to brutal guards, most of the violence in prison is inmate to inmate. Data on inmate assaults are poorly reported, however Matthew Silberman (1995:9) found a rate at "Central" of 32.64 attacks per 1,000 inmates; and Ben Crouch and James Marquart (1989:201) found a similar rate in eight Texas prisons. These levels of violence are not necessarily related to the size of the prisoner population in a particular facility. The sad fact is that uncounted inmates are injured by assaults. As Hans Toch has observed, the climate of violence in prisons has no free-world counterpart: "Inmates are terrorized by other inmates, and spend years in fear of harm. Some inmates request segregation, others lock themselves in, and some are hermits by choice" (1976:47–48). Yet it might also be argued that most prisoners come from violent neighborhoods. But are they safer in prison than on the outside?

Racial or ethnic gangs are now linked to acts of violence in many prison systems. These gangs make certain prisons more dangerous than any American neighborhoods, as they continue gang wars inside prison (Trout, 1992:62). Gangs are organized primarily to control an institution's drug, gambling, loan sharking, prostitution, extortion, and debt-collection rackets. In addition, gangs protect their members from other gangs and instill a sense of macho camaraderie (Hunt, Riegel, Morales, and Waldorf, 1993:398).

Contributing to prison violence is the usual "blood-in, blood-out" basis for gang membership: a would-be member must stab a gang's enemy to be admitted, and once in cannot drop out without endangering his own life. Given the racial and ethnic foundation of the gangs, violence between them can easily spill into the general prison population. Many administrators attempt to separate rival gangs by housing them in separate units of the prison or break up gangs by moving some of their members to other facilities.

Prison gangs exist in the institutions of forty states and also in the federal system, according to a national survey by the American Correctional Association (see Figure 15.2). The survey identified thirty-nine major individual gangs nationwide; overall membership totaled about 6 percent of the U.S. prison population (American Correctional Association, 1993).

Although the gangs are small, they are tightly organized enough that they have arranged the killing of opposition gang leaders housed in other institutions. Administrators say that prison gangs, like organized crime groups, tend to pursue their "business" interests, yet they are also a major source of inmate-inmate violence as they discipline members, enforce orders, and retaliate against other gangs (Buentello, 1992:58).

The racial composition of prison gangs has been documented in a number of states. In California, for example, a Chicano gang—the Mexican Mafia—took over the rackets in San Quentin in the 1960s. In reaction other gangs formed including La Nuesra Familia; CRIPS (Common Revolution in Progress); the Texas Syndicate; the Black Guerrilla Family; and the Aryan Brotherhood (American Correctional Association, 1993). Recent immigration patterns are reflected in new Chinese, Southeast Asian, and Central American gangs entering U.S. prisons (Huff and Meyer, 1997:11).

For many victims of prisoner-prisoner violence, the only way to escape physical abuse, homosexual threats, or the fear of assault is to enter the protective custody unit found in most prisons. Life is not pleasant for these inmates. Usually, they are let out of their cells only briefly to exercise and shower (McGee, Warner, and Harlow, 1998). Inmates who ask to "lock up" have little chance of returning to the general prison population without being viewed as a weakling—a snitch or a punk—to be preyed on.

FIGURE

15.2 **States with prison gangs**

Racial and ethnic gangs are major causes of prison violence. What factors may account for the role of gangs in American prisons?

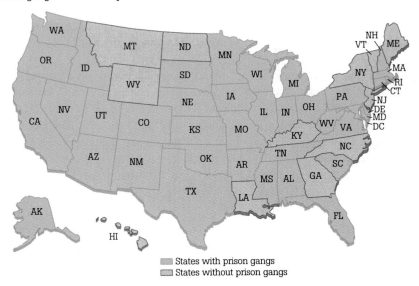

States with prison gangs
States without prison gangs

SOURCE: American Correctional Association, *Gangs in Correctional Institutions: A National Assessment* (Laurel, Md: American Correctional Association, 1993).

CHECK POINT

(15) **Which inmate characteristics are thought to be factors in prison violence?**

(16) **Why are gangs such a threat to prison order?**

Prisoner–Officer Violence

The mass media have focused on riots in which guards are taken hostage, injured, and killed. However, violence against officers typically occurs in specific situations and against certain individuals. The number of such incidents is surprising: in 1995, more than fourteen thousand prison staff members were injured by inmate assaults (*USA Today*, August 8, 1997:1). Correctional officers do not carry weapons within the institution because a prisoner may seize them. However, prisoners do manage to obtain lethal weapons and can use the element of surprise to injure an officer. In the course of a workday an officer may encounter situations that require the use of physical force against an inmate—for instance, breaking up a fight or moving a prisoner to segregation. Officers know that such situations are especially dangerous and may enlist others to help them minimize the risk of violence. The officer's greatest fear is unexpected attacks. These may take the form of a missile thrown from an upper tier, verbal threats and taunts, or an officer's "accidental" fall down a flight of stairs. The fact that officers must be constantly watchful against personal attacks adds to the level of stress and keeps many officers at a distance from contact with the inmates.

Officer-Prisoner Violence

A fact of life in many institutions is unauthorized physical violence by officers against inmates. Stories abound of guards giving individual prisoners "the treatment" when supervisors are not looking. Many guards view physical force as an everyday, legitimate procedure. In some institutions, authorized "goon squads" comprising physically powerful officers use their muscle to maintain order and the status quo.

How can it be determined when prison officers are using force legitimately, and when they are using physical violence to punish individual prisoners? Correctional officers are expected to follow departmental rules in their dealings with prisoners, yet supervisors are generally unable to directly observe staff-prisoner confrontations. Further, prisoner complaints about officer brutality are often not believed until an individual officer involved gains a reputation for harshness. Still, wardens may feel they must uphold the actions of their officers to retain their support.

Decreasing Prison Violence

Five factors contribute to prison violence: (1) inadequate supervision by staff members, (2) architectural design that promotes rather than inhibits victimization, (3) the easy availability of deadly weapons, (4) the housing of violence-prone prisoners near relatively defenseless persons, and (5) a general high level of tension produced by close quarters (Bowker, 1982:64). The physical size and condition of the prison and the relations between inmates and staff also have a bearing on violence.

The Effect of Architecture and Size

The fortress-like prison certainly does not create an atmosphere for normal interpersonal relationships, and the size of the larger institutions can create management problems. The massive scale of the megaprison, which may hold up to three thousand inmates, provides opportunities for aggressive inmates to hide weapons, dispense private "justice," and engage more or less freely in other illicit activities. The size of the population in a large prison may also result in some inmates "falling through the cracks," being misclassified and forced to live among more violent offenders.

The Role of Management

The degree to which inmate leaders are allowed to take matters into their own hands can affect the level of violence among inmates. When administrators run a tight ship, security measures prevent sexual attacks in dark corners, the making of "shivs" and "shanks" (knives) in the metal shop, and open conflict among inmate groups. A prison must give each inmate defensible space, and an administrative goal should be the assurance that every inmate is secure from physical attack.

Effective prison management may decrease the level of assaultive behavior by limiting opportunities for attacks. Wardens and correctional officers must therefore recognize the types of people with whom they are dealing, the role of prison gangs, and the structure of institutions. John DiIulio argues that no group of inmates is "unmanageable [and] no combination of political, social, budgetary, architectural, or other factors makes good management impossible" (1990a:12). He points to such varied institutions as the California Men's Colony, New York City's Tombs and Rikers Island, the Federal Bureau of Prisons, and the Texas Department of Corrections under the leadership of George Beto. At these institutions, good management practices resulted in prisons and jails where inmates can "do time" without fearing for their personal safety. Wardens who exert leadership and effectively manage their prisons maintain an environment of governance so that problems do not fester and erupt into violent confrontations.

In sum, prisons must be made safe places. Because the state puts offenders there, it has a responsibility to prevent violence and maintain order. If violence is to be excluded from prisons, limitations may have to be placed on prisoners' movement within the institution, contacts with the outside, and the right to choose their associates. Yet these measures may run counter to the goal of producing men and women who will be accountable when they return to society.

⑰ **List the five factors thought to contribute to prison violence.**

Summary

- Inmates do not serve their time in isolation but are members of a subculture with its own traditions, norms, and leadership structure.
- Inmates deal with the pain of incarceration by assuming an adaptive role and lifestyle.
- To meet the needs of prisoners for goods and services not provided by the state, an underground economy exists in the society of captives.
- Only a small portion of the inmate population is female. This is cited as the reason for the limited programs and services available to women prisoners.
- Social relationships among female inmates differ from those of their male counterparts. Women tend to form pseudofamilies in prison. Many women experience the added stress of being responsible for their children on the outside.
- Educational, vocational, industrial, and treatment programs are available in prisons. Administrators believe these programs are important for maintaining order.
- Prison violence is a major problem confronting administrators. The characteristics of the inmates and the rise of gangs contribute to this problem.

Questions for Review

1. What is meant by an adaptive role? Which roles are found in male prison society? In female prison society?
2. What is the currency used in the underground prison economy?
3. In what ways is the convict society in institutions for women different from that in institutions for men?
4. What are the major categories of prison violence?
5. What factors contribute to prison violence?

Key Terms

classification (p. 527)
inmate code (p. 516)

For Further Reading

Baunach, Phyllis Jo. *Mothers in Prison.* New Brunswick, N.J.: Transaction Books, 1985. A survey of incarcerated mothers and their relationships with their children.

Earley, Pete. *The Hot House: Life inside Leavenworth Prison.* New York: Bantam Books, 1992. An eyewitness account of daily life in the United States Penitentiary in Leavenworth, Kansas, written by the first journalist given unlimited access to a maximum security institution of the Federal Bureau of Prisons.

Rideau, Wilbert, and Ron Wilkburg. *Life Sentences: Rage and Survival behind Bars.* New York: Times Books, 1992. Describes life inside the Louisiana State Penitentiary. Written by two former editors of The Angolite, the prison newspaper.

Rierden, Andi. *The Farm: Life inside a Women's Prison.* Amherst, Mass.: University of Massachusetts Press, 1997. A case study of changes in the inmate population and administration during the late 1980s to early 1990s at Connecticut's Niantic Correctional Institution.

Sheehan, Susan. *A Prison and a Prisoner.* Boston: Houghton Mifflin, 1978. A fascinating description of life in Green Haven Prison and the way one prisoner "makes it" through "swagging," "hustling," and "doing time."

It contains an excellent discussion of the inmate economy.

Timilty, Joseph. *Prison Journal.* Boston: Northeastern University Press, 1997. The experiences of a Boston politician, sentenced to federal prison following his trial on a white-collar conspiracy charge.

Useem, Bert, and Peter Kimball. *States of Siege: U.S. Prison Riots, 1971–1986.* New York: Oxford University Press, 1989. A survey of prison riots with case studies of the upheavals at Attica, Joliet, Santa Fe, Jackson, and Moundsville. Summary chapters consider the nature and causes of prison riots.

Going Online

1. Using the Internet, go to the web page of the Correctional Industries Association: www.corrections.com/ industries/. Find and read the Association's Legislative Position Statement. Does the Association invite or discourage state regulation of prison industries? Why?
2. Using the Internet, go to the web page for the Massachusetts Department of Corrections roster of prison gangs: www.magnet.state.ma.us/ doc/gang/othgang.htm#white. Read about the gangs represented in Massachusetts prisons. How should officials address the problem of multiple, diverse gangs within prisons?
3. **Using InfoTrac College Edition,** search for the subject "prisoners." Click on "woman prisoners." Find an article about the daily life of four women in prison in Maryland. How has prison affected the lives of these women and their outlook on the future?

1 The values and norms of prison society that emphasize inmate solidarity.

2 The prison society is fragmented by racial and ethnic divisions.

3 Doing time, gleaning, jailing, and functioning as a disorganized criminal.

4 To provide goods and services not available through regular channels.

5 The prison economy is responsible for the exploitation of other prisoners and has the potential for violence.

6 The small number of female inmates compared with the number of males.

7 Men are more individualistic and their norms stress autonomy, self-sufficiency, and the ability to cope with one's own problems. Women are more sharing with one another.

8 The distance of prisons from homes, intermittent telephone privileges, and unnatural visiting environment.

9 Children are either with relatives or in foster care.

10 Programs keep prisoners busy and reduce security problems.

11 Classification by a committee according to the needs of the inmate or of the institution.

12 They are thought to "coddle" prisoners and give them resources not available to free residents.

13 Too many programs train inmates for trades for which there is already an adequate labor supply or in which the skills are outdated. They are inefficient because of the low education level and poor work habits of the

prisoners. Production has to be stopped for periodic head counts and checks on tools and materials.

14 Pressures from labor unions whose members make competing products at higher wages.

15 Age, gender, machismo.

16 Competition between rival gangs, violence as condition for membership in gangs, and enforcement of gang orders.

17 Inadequate supervision, architectural design, availability of weapons, housing of violence-prone inmates with the defenseless, and the high level of tension of people living in close quarters.

CHAPTER SIXTEEN

Release and Supervision in the Community

After three years, three months, and four days in Stanhope Correctional Facility, Ben Brooks was ready to go before the Board of Parole. He woke with butterflies in his stomach, realizing that at nine o'clock he was to walk into the hearing room to confront a roomful of strangers. As he lay on his bunk he rehearsed the answers to the questions he thought the board members might ask: "How do you feel about the person you assaulted? What have you done with your time while incarcerated? Do you think you have learned anything here that will convince the board that you will follow a crime-free life in the community? What are your plans for employment and housing?" According to prison scuttlebutt, these were the types of questions asked and you had to be prepared to answer that you were sorry for your past mistakes, had taken advantage of the prison programs, had a job waiting for you, and planned to live with your family. You had to "ring bells" with the board.

At breakfast, friends dropped by Ben's table to reassure him that he had it made. As one said, "Ben, you've done everything they've said to do. What else can they expect?" That was the problem, *What did they expect?*

At eight-thirty Officer Kearney came by the cell. "Time to go, Ben." They walked out of the housing unit and down the long prison corridors to a group of chairs outside the hearing room. Other prisoners were already seated there. "Sit here, Ben. They'll call when they're ready. Good luck."

At ten minutes past nine the door opened and an officer called, "First case, Brooks." Ben got up, walked into the room. "Please take a seat, Mr. Brooks," said the African American seated in the center at the table. Ben knew he was Reverend Perry, a man known as being tough but fair. To his left was a white man, Mr. MacDonald, and to his right a Hispanic woman, Ms. Lopez. The white man led the questioning.

"Mr. Brooks. You were convicted of armed robbery and sentenced to a term of six to ten years. Please tell the board what you have learned during your incarceration."

Ben paused and then answered hesitantly, "Well, I learned that to commit such a stupid act was a mistake. I was under a lot of pressure when I pulled the robbery and now am sorry for what I did."

"You severely injured the woman you held up. What might you tell her if she were sitting in this room today?"

"I would just have to say, I'm sorry. It will never happen again."

"But this is not the first time you have been convicted. What makes you think it will never happen again?"

"Well this is the first time I was sent to prison. You see things a lot differently from here."

Ms. Lopez spoke up. "You have a good prison record—member of the Toastmaster's Club, gotten your high school equivalency diploma, kept your nose clean. Tell the board about your future plans should you be released."

"My brother says I can live with him until I get on my feet, and there is a letter in my file telling you that I have a job waiting at a meat-processing plant. I will be living in my hometown but I don't intend to see my old buddies again. You can be sure that I am now on the straight and narrow."

"But you committed a heinous crime. That woman suffered a lot. Why should the board believe that you won't do it again?"

"All I can say is that I'm different now."

"Thank you, Mr. Brooks," said Reverend Perry. "You will hear from us by this evening." Ben got up and walked out of the room. It had only taken eight minutes, yet it seemed like hours. Eight minutes during which his future was being decided. Would it be back to the cell or out on the street? It would be about ten hours before he would receive word from the board as to his fate.

Today, scenes similar to this one still occur, but fewer states maintain parole boards or allow boards the wide discretion they had in the past. This chapter will examine the mechanisms for prison release and the supervision of offenders in the community. Special attention will be paid to the problems confronting offenders as they reenter society. Try to imagine yourself as Ben Brooks. Three weeks after his appearance before the board, he left Stanhope, having been given transportation back to his hometown, a check for $100, a list of rules to follow, and a date to report to his parole officer. What do you think was his first reaction to family, friends, and a community he had not seen in years?

RELEASE AND SUPERVISION IN THE COMMUNITY

QUESTIONS
for Inquiry

- What is parole, and how does it operate today?
- What effects do mandatory and discretionary release have on the criminal justice system?
- What programs ease the transition of the offender back to society, and how are ex-offenders supervised in the community?
- What is the purpose of the pardon?
- What restrictions does society place on ex-offenders?

Parole: Reentry into Society

Parole is the *conditional* release of an offender from incarceration but not from the legal custody of the state. During most of the twentieth century the term *parole* referred to both a release mechanism and a method of community supervision. The term still has this general meaning, but because some states adopted determinate sentencing and parole guidelines, a distinction must now be made between a release mechanism and supervision. Although the releasing mechanisms have changed, most former prisoners are still required to serve a period of time under parole supervision.

Only felons are released on parole; adults convicted of misdemeanors are usually released immediately after they have finished serving their sentences. Every year almost 400,000 felons are conditionally released from prison and allowed to live under parole supervision in the community. Today 685,000 people are under parole supervision, a rate of 346 for every 100,000 adult Americans (BJS, 1998c).

parole
The conditional release of an inmate from incarceration under supervision after part of the prison sentence has been served.

The Origins of Parole

Parole in the United States evolved during the nineteenth century from the English, Australian, and Irish practices of conditional pardon, apprenticeship by indenture, transportation of criminals from one country to another, and the issuance of "tickets of leave." These were all methods of moving criminals out of prison. Such practices generally did not develop as part of any coherent theory of punishment or to promote any particular goal of the criminal sanction. Instead, they were responses to problems of overcrowding, unemployment, and the cost of incarceration.

The practice of punishing offenders by keeping them under the authority of the government, yet not confined to an institution, developed as Britain was establishing colonies. As early as 1587, England had passed the Act of Banishment, by which criminals and "rogues" could be sent to the colonies as laborers for the king in exchange for a pardon. The pardons initially were unconditional, but they eventually became conditional after the offender had completed a period of service. During the eighteenth century, English convicts were released and indentured to private persons to work in the colonies until the end of a set term.

After the American colonies gained independence, Australia became the major colonial destination for offenders banished from England. The governor of Australia was given the power to pardon felons. Initially, unconditional pardons were given to offenders with good work records and good behavior. As problems arose with the behavior of some pardoned offenders, the pardons became conditional. The essential condition was a requirement that prisoners support themselves and remain within a specific district. This method of parole, known as ticket of leave, was similar to the modern concept of parole, except that the released prisoner was not under government supervision.

A key figure in developing the concept of parole in the nineteenth century was Captain Alexander Maconochie, an administrator of British penal colonies in Tasmania and elsewhere in the South Pacific. Later he served as a prison governor in England. A critic of definite prison terms, Maconochie devised a system of rewards for good conduct, labor, and study. He developed a classification procedure by which prisoners could pass through stages of increasing responsibility and freedom: (1) strict imprisonment, (2) labor on government chain gangs, (3) freedom within a limited area, (4) a ticket of leave or parole resulting in a conditional pardon, and (5) full restoration of liberty. Like modern correctional practices, this procedure assumed that prisoners should be prepared gradually for release. In the transition from imprisonment to conditional release to full freedom, the roots of the American system of parole can be seen.

Maconochie's idea of requiring prisoners to earn their early release caught on first in Ireland. There, Sir Walter Crofton built on Maconochie's idea that an offender's progress in prison and a ticket of leave were linked. Prisoners who graduated through Crofton's three successive levels of treatment were released on parole with a series of conditions. Most significant was the requirement that parolees submit monthly reports to the police. In Dublin, a special civilian inspector helped releasees find jobs, visited them periodically, and supervised their activities.

CHECK POINT

① **In what countries did the concept of parole first develop?**

② **What were the contributions of Alexander Maconochie and Sir Walter Crofton?**
   (Answers are at the end of the chapter.)

The Development of Parole in the United States

In the United States, parole developed during the prison reform movement of the latter half of the nineteenth century. Relying on the ideas of Maconochie and Crofton, American reformers such as Zebulon Brockway of the Elmira State Reformatory in New York began to experiment with the concept of parole. After New York adopted indeterminate sentences in 1876, Brockway started to release prisoners on parole. Under the new sentencing law, prisoners could be released when their prison conduct showed they were ready to return to society.

As originally implemented, the parole system in New York did not require supervision by the police. Instead, volunteers from citizens' reform groups assisted with the parolee's reintegration into society. As parole became more common and applied to larger numbers of offenders, states replaced the volunteer supervisors with correctional employees.

Many individuals and groups in the United States opposed the release of convicts before they had completed the entire sentence that they had earned by their crimes. However, the use of parole continued to spread. By 1900, twenty states had parole systems; and by 1932, forty-four states and the federal government had them (Friedman, 1993:304). Today every state has some procedure for the release of offenders before the end of their sentences.

Although it has been used in the United States for more than a century, parole remains controversial. To many people, parole allows convicted offenders to avoid serving the full sentence they deserve. Public anger has been fueled by periodic news stories about parolees committing other crimes; for example, the kidnapping and murder of 12-year-old Polly Klaas by California parolee Richard Davis, or the rape and murder of 7-year-old Megan Kanka by a paroled New Jersey sex offender. Public pressure to be tougher on criminals has led half the states and the federal government to restructure their sentencing laws and release mechanisms (Petersilia, 1999).

Release Mechanisms

Except for the small number who die in prison, all inmates will eventually be released to live in the community. Until the mid-1970s all states and the federal government had systems that allowed parole boards to determine the exact date for an inmate to leave prison. With the critique of rehabilitation, the move to determinate sentencing, and the public's view that the system was "soft" on criminals, parole boards were abolished or their powers reduced in many states. Reflecting the climate of the times parole boards across the country have become more hesitant to grant it. In Texas, for example, 57 percent of all cases considered for parole release in 1988 were approved; by 1998 that figure had dropped to 20 percent (Fabelo, 1999).

There are three basic mechanisms for persons to be released from prison: (1) discretionary release, (2) mandatory release, and (3) unconditional release. Figure 16.1 shows the percentage of felons released by the various mechanisms.

Discretionary Release

States retaining indeterminate sentences allow **discretionary release** by the parole board within the boundaries set by the sentence and the penal law. This is a conditional release to parole supervision. This approach (illustrated by the case of Ben Brooks) lets the parole board assess the prisoner's readiness for release within the minimum and maximum terms of the sentence. As it reviews the prisoner's file and asks questions about the prisoner, the parole board focuses on the nature of the offense, the inmate's behavior, and participation in rehabilitative programs. This process places great faith in the ability of board members to accurately predict the future behavior of offenders.

discretionary release
The release of an inmate from prison to conditional supervision at the discretion of the parole board within the boundaries set by the sentence and the penal law.

FIGURE 16.1 Methods of release from state prison

Felons are released from prison to the community, usually under parole supervision, through means that vary depending on the law.

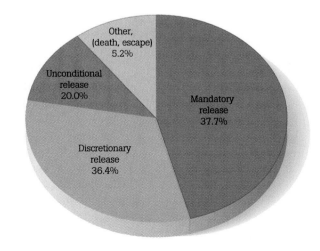

SOURCE: U.S. Department of Justice, Bureau of Justice Statistics, *National Corrections Reporting Program, 1996* (Washington, D.C.: Government Printing Office, 1998), 36.

Mandatory Release

Mandatory release is so named because it occurs after an inmate has served time equal to the total sentence minus "good time," if any, or to a certain percentage of the total sentence as specified by law. Mandatory release is found in federal jurisdictions and states with determinate sentences and parole guidelines (see Chapter 11). Without a parole board to make discretionary decisions, mandatory release is a matter of bookkeeping to check the correct amount of good time and other credits and make sure the sentence has been accurately interpreted. The prisoner is released to the supervision of a parole officer for the remainder of the sentence minus good time. Yet, because of the growth of prison populations, many states have devised ways to get around the rigidity of mandatory release by placing inmates in the community through furloughs, home supervision, halfway houses, emergency release, and other programs (Griset, 1995:307).

Unconditional Release

An increasing percentage of prisoners are given **unconditional release.** These are inmates who are released from any further correctional supervision and cannot be returned to prison for any remaining portion of the sentence for a current offense. Such offenders have been incarcerated until the end of their sentence, had their sentence commuted, or been pardoned.

The Organization of Releasing Authorities

Parole boards tend to be organized either as a part of a department of corrections or as an independent agency of government. Some commentators have argued that a parole board must be independent so that its members can be insulated from the activities and influence of corrections staff. According to this viewpoint, an independent parole board is less likely to be influenced by staff considerations such as the need to reduce the prison population and the desire to punish inmates who do not conform to institutional rules.

Whether a parole board is independent or a part of the corrections department, it cannot exist in a vacuum. Board members cannot ignore the public's attitudes and fears about crime. If a parolee commits a crime and public indignation is aroused, the board members inevitably will make decisions more cautiously to avoid public condemnation and embarrassment. Members of one parole board said they had to be very cautious in releasing prisoners; if parolees committed additional crimes, the news media always blamed the board for improperly releasing unworthy offenders.

Parole boards also are susceptible to influence from departments of corrections and must maintain good working relations with them. For example, if even an autonomous board develops a conflict with the department, the department may not cooperate in providing the board with information it needs. Information about particular offenders may become "unavailable," or the state may provide biased information about particular offenders that officials wish to see punished. By contrast, a board that is closely tied to corrections officials may have access to information and receive complete cooperation. However, such a board runs the risk of being viewed by prisoners and the general public as merely the rubber stamp of the department.

Most people assume that parole boards are made up of experts on human behavior who can accurately evaluate whether an offender is ready for release. In some states this view is reasonably accurate. However, no one can predict human behavior with complete accuracy, especially when dealing with offenders, many of whom have histories of substance abuse or violent behavior or are unable to function well in society because of illiteracy and other problems.

In other states, parole board members are chosen with political considerations in mind. Governors seek to appoint citizens who fit specific racial, geographic, occupational, and other demographic criteria. In the recent past, for example, the Mississippi board consisted of a contractor, a businessman, a farmer, and a clerk; the Florida board included a journalist, an attorney, and a member with experience in both business and probation; the state of Washington board had persons with training and experience in sociology, government, law, the ministry, and juvenile rehabilitation. Parole boards act much like a jury: they can apply the community's values in determining whether particular offenders deserve to be released.

CHECK POINT

③ Distinguish among mandatory release, discretionary release, and unconditional release.

④ What are the two ways that parole boards are organized?

The Decision to Release

An inmate's eligibility for release to community supervision on parole depends on requirements set by law and on the sentence imposed by the court. In the states with determinate sentences or parole guidelines, release is mandatory once the offender has served the required amount of time. In nearly half the states, however, the release decision is discretionary, and the parole board has the authority to establish a release date. The board bases the date on the sufficiency of rehabilitation and the individual's characteristics as an inmate.

Based on the assumptions of indeterminate sentences and rehabilitative programs, discretionary release is designed to allow the parole board to release inmates to conditional supervision in the community when they are judged "ready" to live as law-abiding citizens (Talarico, 1988).

Eligibility for a release hearing in discretionary states varies greatly. Appearance before the parole board is a function of the individual sentence, statutory criteria, and the inmate's conduct before incarceration. Often the inmate is eligible for release at the end of the minimum term of the sentence minus good time. In other states eligibility is at the discretion of the parole board or is calculated at one-third or one-half of the maximum sentence.

As an example of the computation of parole eligibility, consider the case of Ben Brooks (see Figure 16.2). At the time of sentencing Brooks had been held in jail for six months awaiting trial and disposition of his case. He was given a sentence of a minimum of five years and a maximum of ten years for robbery with violence. Brooks did well at Stanhope, the maximum security prison to which he was sent. He did not get into trouble and was thus able to save up good-time credit at the rate of one day for every four that he spent on good behavior. In addition, he was

FIGURE

16.2 **Computing parole eligibility for Ben Brooks**

Various "good-time" reductions to the minimum sentence are allowed in most correctional systems to determine eligibility for parole. Note how a five- to ten-year sentence can be reduced to a stay of three years, four months.

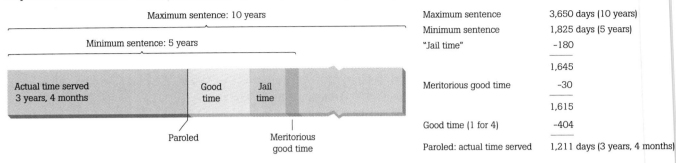

Maximum sentence	3,650 days (10 years)
Minimum sentence	1,825 days (5 years)
"Jail time"	–180
	1,645
Meritorious good time	–30
	1,615
Good time (1 for 4)	–404
Paroled: actual time served	1,211 days (3 years, 4 months)

given meritorious credit of thirty days when he completed his high school equivalency test after attending the prison school for two years. After serving three years, three months, and four days of his sentence, he appeared before the board of parole and was granted release into the community.

What criteria guide the parole board as it makes a decision? A formal statement of standards may list elements such as inmates' attitudes toward their families, their insights into the causes of their past conduct, and the adequacy of their parole plan. Additional considerations might include whether offenders have accepted responsibility for their actions and whether they have a plan for steady employment after release. Written statements from the victim, defense attorney, prosecutor, and offender's family may also be presented to the board (McLeod, 1989).

Although the published criteria may help familiarize inmates with the board's expectations, the actual decision is discretionary and is typically based on other kinds of information. A survey of parole boards found that nine items were ranked as "important" in the release decision. In order of importance these were: (1) offender's current offense, (2) history of prior violence, (3) prior felony convictions, (4) possession of a firearm, (5) previous incarceration, (6) prior parole adjustment, (7) prison disciplinary record, (8) psychological reports, and (9) victim input (Runda, Rhine, and Wetter, 1994). It is frequently said that parole boards release only good risks, but as one parole board member stated, "There are no good-risk men in prison. Parole is really a decision of when to release bad-risk persons."

Other considerations weigh heavily on the board members. If parole is not regularly awarded to most prisoners who gain eligibility, morale among all inmates may suffer as they fear that they will not gain release at the anticipated time. The seeming arbitrariness of parole boards was one of the major causes of prison riots during the 1970s. The prospect of gaining parole is a major incentive for many prisoners to follow rules and cooperate with corrections officials.

Parole board members are also concerned about being criticized by the public for making controversial decisions. Notorious offenders such as Sirhan Sirhan, the man convicted of assassinating presidential candidate Robert F. Kennedy in 1968, and multiple murderer Charles Manson are unlikely ever to gain parole release even if they behave well in prison.

The Prisoners' Perspective: How to Win Parole

"If you want to get paroled, you've got to be in a program." This statement reflects one of the most controversial aspects of discretionary release: its link to treatment. Although corrections authorities emphasize the voluntary nature of most treatment services and clinicians argue that therapy cannot be successful in a coercive atmosphere, the fact remains that inmates believe they must "play the game."Most parole boards cite an inmate's progress in self-improvement programs as one of the criteria for release. A Connecticut inmate noted, "The last time I went before the board they wanted to know why I hadn't take advantage of the programs. Now I go to A.A. and group therapy. I hope they will be satisfied."

Although prisoners' participation in programs is technically voluntary, the link between participation and release poses many legal and ethical problems, as illustrated by the case of Jim Allen in A Question of Ethics.

In some states, inmates convicted of drug or sex offenses may be expected to participate in treatment programs. However, the correctional system may not have enough places in these programs to serve all of them. Offenders may wait long periods before gaining admission, or they may be in an institution that does not have the treatment they need. Because they cannot force the prison system to transfer them to the appropriate institution, inmates may become frustrated hearing about other people gaining parole while they are not given an opportunity to prove themselves to the board. Moreover, some kinds of treatment programs, especially for sex offenders, may involve intrusive counseling therapies or medications that have lingering physical effects and a limited likelihood of success. Yet, faced with the threat of denial of parole if they refuse to participate, prisoners may not feel able to decline such treatments.

Structuring Parole Decisions

In response to criticism that the release decisions of parole boards are arbitrary, many states have adopted parole guidelines to assist board members. As with sentencing guidelines, a "severity scale" ranks crimes according to their seriousness and a "salient factor" score measures the offender's criminal history (drug arrests, prior record, age at first conviction, and so on) and risk factors considered relevant to successful completion of parole (see Tables 16.1 and 16.2). By placing the offender's salient factor score next to his or her particular offense on the severity scale, the board and correctional officials may calculate the **presumptive parole date** soon after the offender enters prison. This is the date by which the inmate can expect to be released if there are no disciplinary or other problems during incarceration. The presumptive parole date may be modified on a scheduled basis. The date of release may be advanced

The five members of the parole board questioned Jim Allen, an offender with a long history of sex offenses involving teenage boys. Now approaching 45 and having met the eligibility requirement for a hearing, Allen respectfully answered the board members.

Toward the end of the hearing, Richard Edwards, a dentist who had recently been appointed to the board, spoke up: "Your institutional record is good, you have a parole plan, a job has been promised, and your sister says she will help you. All of that looks good, but I just can't vote for your parole. You haven't attended the behavior modification program for sex offenders. I think you're going to repeat your crime. I have a 13-year-old son, and I don't want him or other boys to run the risk of meeting your kind."

Allen looked shocked. The other members had seemed ready to grant his release.

"But I'm ready for parole. I won't do that stuff again. I didn't go to that program because electroshock to my private area is not going to help me. I've been here five years of the seven-year max and have stayed out of trouble. The judge didn't say I was to be further punished in prison by therapy."

After Jim Allen left the room, the board discussed his case. "You know, Rich, he has a point. He has been a model prisoner and has served a good portion of his sentence," said Brian Lynch, a long-term board member. "Besides we don't know if Dr. Hankin's program works."

"I know, but can we really let someone like that out on the streets?"

▉ Are the results of the behavior-modification program for sex offenders relevant to the parole board's decision? Is the purpose of the sentence to punish Allen for what he did or for what he might do in the future? Would you vote for his release on parole? Would your vote be the same if his case had received media attention?

prison. This is the date by which the inmate can expect to be released if there are no disciplinary or other problems during incarceration. The presumptive parole date may be modified on a scheduled basis. The date of release may be advanced

presumptive parole date
The presumed release date stipulated by parole guidelines if the offender serves time without disciplinary or other incidents.

TABLE 16.1 Criminal history/risk assessment under the Oregon Guidelines for Adult Offenders

The amount of time to be served is related to the severity of the offense and to the criminal history/risk assessment of the inmate. The criminal history score is determined by adding the points assigned each factor in this table.

	CRIMINAL HISTORY/RISK FACTOR	POINTS	SCORE
A	No prior felony convictions as an adult or juvenile:	3	
	One prior felony conviction:	2	
	Two or three prior felony convictions:	1	
	Four or more prior felony convictions:	0	_____
B	No prior felony or misdemeanor incarcerations (that is, executed sentences of ninety days or more) as an adult or juvenile:	2	
	One or two prior incarcerations:	1	
	Three or more prior incarcerations:	0	_____
C	Verified period of three years conviction-free in the community prior to the present commitment:	1	
	Otherwise:	0	_____
D	Age at commencement of behavior leading to this incarceration was _____ :		
	Date of birth was _____ / _____ / _____ .		
	Twenty-six or older and at least one point received in A, B, or C:	2	
	Twenty-six or older and no points received in A, B, or C:	1	
	Twenty-one to under 26 and at least one point received in A, B, or C:	0	
	Twenty-one to under 26 and no points received in A, B, or C:	0	
	Under 21:	0	_____
E	Present commitment does not include parole, probation, failure to appear, release agreement, escape, or custody violation:	2	
	Present commitment involves probation, release agreement, or failure to appear violation:	1	
	Present commitment involves parole, escape, or custody violation:	0	
F	Has no admitted or documented substance abuse problem within a three-year period in the community immediately preceding the commission of the crime conviction:	1	
	Otherwise:	0	
	Total history/risk assessment score:		_____

SOURCE: Adapted from State of Oregon, Board of Parole, ORS Chapter 144, Rule 255–35–015.

because of good conduct and superior achievement, or it may be postponed if there are disciplinary infractions or a suitable community supervision plan is not developed.

CHECK POINT

⑤ What are the major factors considered by parole boards in exercising discretionary release?

⑥ What do prisoners believe improves their chances for release?

TABLE 16.2 **Number of months to be served before release under the Oregon guidelines**

The presumptive release date is determined by finding the intersection of the criminal history score (Table 16.1) and the category of the offense. An offender with an assessment score between 6 and 8, convicted of a category 3 offense, could expect to serve between ten and fourteen months.

	CRIMINAL HISTORY/RISK ASSESSMENT SCORE			
OFFENSE SEVERITY	11–9 EXCELLENT	8–6 GOOD	5–3 FAIR	2–0 POOR
Category 1: Bigamy, criminal mischief I, dogfighting, incest, possession of stolen vehicle	6	6	6–10	12–18
Category 2: Abandonment of a child, bribing a witness, criminal homicide, perjury, possession of controlled substance	6	6–10	10–14	16–24
Category 3: Assault III, forgery I, sexual abuse, trafficking in stolen vehicles	6–10	10–14	14–20	22–32
Category 4: Aggravated theft, assault II, coercion, criminally negligent homicide, robbery II	10–16	16–22	22–30	32–44
Category 5: Burglary I, escape I, manslaughter II, racketeering, rape I	16–24	24–36	40–52	56–72
Category 6: Arson I, kidnapping I, rape II, sodomy I	30–40	44–56	60–80	90–130
Category 7: Aggravated murder, treason	96–120	120–156	156–192	192–240
Category 8: Aggravated murder (stranger–stranger, cruelty to victim, prior murder conviction)	20–168	168–228	228–288	288–life

SOURCE: Adapted from State of Oregon, Board of Parole, ORS Chapter 144, Rule 255–75–026 and Rule 255–75–035.

The Impact of Release Mechanisms

Parole release mechanisms do more than simply determine the date at which a particular prisoner will be sent back into the community. Parole release also has an enormous impact on other parts of the system, including sentencing, plea bargaining, and the size of prison populations (Walker, 1993:141).

One important effect of discretionary release is that an administrative body—the parole board—can shorten a sentence imposed by a judge. Even in states that have mandatory release, various potential reductions built into the sentence mean that the full sentence is rarely served. Good time, for example, can reduce punishment even if there is no parole eligibility.

To understand the impact of release mechanisms on criminal punishment, the amount of time actually served in prison must be compared with the sentence specified by the judge. In some jurisdictions, up to 80 percent of felons sentenced to prison are released to the community after their first appearance before a parole board. Eligibility for discretionary release is ordinarily determined by the minimum term of the sentence minus good time and jail time. As noted, good time allows the minimum sentence to be reduced for good behavior during incarceration or for exceptional performance of assigned tasks or personal achievement. Jail time—credit given for time spent in jail while an offender awaits trial and sentencing—also shortens the period that must be served before an inmate's first appearance before the parole board.

Although states vary considerably, on a national basis felony inmates serve an estimated average of a little over two years before release. Offenders who receive long sentences serve a smaller proportion of such sentences than do offenders given shorter sentences. For example, a robbery offender may be given a term of 12 to 60 months and serve 69 percent of the term before being released after

23 months. By contrast, an offender sentenced to a term of 181 to 240 months will serve 38 percent of the term, 83 months. Figure 16.3 shows the average time served for selected offenses.

The probability of release well before the end of the formal sentence encourages plea bargaining by both prosecutors and defendants. Prosecutors can reap the benefits of quick, cooperative plea bargains that look tough in the eyes of the public. Meanwhile, the defendant agrees to plead guilty and accept the sentence because of the high likelihood of early release through parole.

Besides the benefits of parole to prosecutors, supporters of discretion for the paroling authority argue that parole offers invaluable benefits for the overall system. Discretionary release makes the penal code less harsh. If the legislature must establish exceptionally strict punishments as a means of conveying a "tough-on-crime" image to frustrated and angry voters, parole can permit sentence adjustments that make the punishment fit the crime. Everyone convicted of larceny may not have caused the same amount of harm, yet some legislatively mandated sentencing schemes may impose equally strict sentences on everyone convicted of larceny. Early release on parole can be granted to an offender who is less deserving of strict punishment, such as someone who voluntarily makes restitution, cooperates with the police, or shows genuine regret.

A major criticism of the effect of parole is that it has shifted responsibility for many of the primary criminal justice decisions from a judge, who holds legal procedures uppermost, to an administrative board, where discretion rules. Having

FIGURE 16.3 **Estimated time to be served (in months) by state prisoners for selected offenses**

The data indicate that the average felony offender going to prison for the first time spends about two years in prison. How would you expect the public to react to that fact?

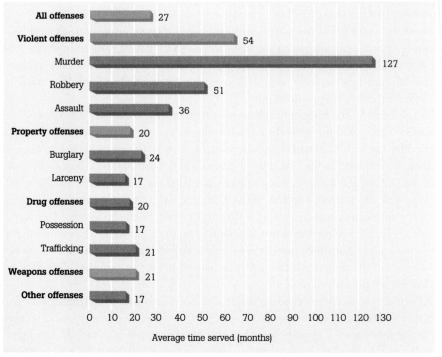

SOURCE: U.S. Department of Justice, Bureau of Justice Statistics, *Bulletin* (January 1997), 4.

legal education, judges are knowledgeable about constitutional rights and basic legal protections. In contrast, parole board members may not have such knowledge. In most states with discretionary release, parole decision hearings are secret, with only board members, the inmate, and correctional officers present. Often no published criteria guide decisions, and prisoners are given no reason for denial or granting of parole. Should society place such power in the hands of parole boards? Because there is so little oversight over their decision making and so few constraints on their decisions, some parole board members will make arbitrary or discriminatory decisions that are inconsistent with the values underlying the constitutional system and civil rights. Generally, the U.S. legal system seeks to avoid determining people's fate through such methods.

⑦ **What are the influences of parole release on the rest of the criminal justice system?**

Supervision in the Community

Parolees are released from prison on condition that they abide by laws and follow rules, known as **conditions of release** designed both to aid their readjustment to society and control their movement. The parolee may be required to abstain from alcohol, keep away from undesirable associates, maintain good work habits, and not leave the state without permission. If they violate these conditions, they may be returned to prison to serve out the rest of their sentence behind bars. Except Maine and Virginia, all states have some requirement for post-prison or parole supervision, and nearly 80 percent of all released prisoners are subject to some form of conditional community or supervision release (Petersilia, 1999).

 The restrictions are justified on the ground that people who have been incarcerated must readjust to the community so they will not simply fall back into preconviction habits and associations. Some people hold that trying to impose on parolees standards of conduct not imposed on others is both wrong and likely to fail. Moreover, new parolees find themselves in such daunting circumstances that they may have great difficulty living according to the rules.

 The day they come out of prison, parolees face a staggering array of problems. In most states, they are given only clothes, a token amount of money, a list of rules governing their conditional release, and the name and address of the parole officer to whom they must report within twenty-four hours. Although a promised job is often a condition for release, an actual job may be another matter. Most former convicts are unskilled or semiskilled, and the conditions of release may prevent them from moving to areas where they could find work. If the parolee is African American, male, and under 30, they join the largest group of unemployed in the country.

 Parolees have the added handicap of former convict status. In most states, laws prevent former prisoners from working in certain types of establishments—where alcohol is sold, for example—thus ruling out many jobs. In many trades, union affiliation is a requirement for employment, and there are restrictions on the

conditions of release
Restrictions on parolees' conduct that must be obeyed as a legally binding requirement of being released.

admission of new members. Finally, many parolees, as well as other ex-convicts, face a significant dilemma. If they are truthful about their backgrounds, many employers will not hire them. If they are not truthful, however, they can be fired for lying if the employer ever learns about their conviction. Some problems that parolees encounter when they reenter the community are illustrated in the Close-Up, opposite. As you read about Jerome Washington's experience, ask yourself what problems you might encounter after a long term in "max."

Other reentry problems may plague parolees. For many, the transition from the highly structured life in prison to the open society is too difficult to manage. Many just do not have the social, psychological, and material resources to cope with the temptations and complications of modern life. For these parolees, freedom may be short-lived as they fall back into forbidden activities such as drinking, using drugs, and stealing.

Finally, offenders must adjust not only to the challenges and temptations of living in a free society but also to changes that have taken place while they were in prison. This transitional period is believed to be the critical time that will determine whether the offender can avoid returning to crime.

Community Programs Following Release

To assist parolees reentering society, various programs have been developed. Some help prepare offenders for release while they are still in prison; others provide employment and housing assistance after release. Together, the programs are intended to help the offender progress steadily toward reintegration into the community.

Programs of partial confinement prior to parole are used to test the offender's readiness for full release. While the prisoner is still confined, correctional staff must evaluate a variety of issues. Community-based corrections assumes that the goal is to choose, from the several alternatives to incarceration, the least restrictive alternative that will lead to eventual reintegration. Thus, staff members must first

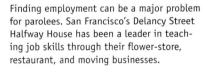

Finding employment can be a major problem for parolees. San Francisco's Delancy Street Halfway House has been a leader in teaching job skills through their flower-store, restaurant, and moving businesses.

CLOSE up

Returning to America

Returning to America after living in France, China, Swaziland, or the high Himalayas is one thing, but returning to America after serving sixteen years and three months in maximum security [mostly in Attica] is something altogether different.

In 1972 when I went to prison, [Richard M.] Nixon was president and politicians were still thought to be ethical; Patti Hearst was involved in a self-kidnapping conspiracy with the SLA [Symbionese Liberation Army], the Supreme Court was reasonably balanced; the Vietnam War was winding down, but the weekly body count was still news. The HIV virus was unknown and free sex had more fans than the Super Bowl game. Although everybody was not living the American Dream, and some people felt that life was hopeless, most were optimistic about their future and many had a strong commitment to social activism. People cared, and even the most disadvantaged could still dream without fear of having nightmares.

Soon after I got out I was with my brother Freddy. We were standing at Columbus Circle, a major hub, a New York City crossroads. Freddy was my guide. He asked where I'd like to go; what I'd like to do; what I'd like to see. Did I want to meet new people, or just hang out, drift from place to place? Suddenly, life was a smorgasbord, a cornucopia of enticements and alluring temptations. I didn't know where to start, what to do first. Prison was my immediate reference point and, there, decisions related to physical movement were made by the guards, not by me. "We can't stand here all day," my brother said, over and over.

"Go slow," I told myself as I recalled a number of prisoners who shortly after being released returned to prison with new convictions, and new sentences. They tried to make everything happen at once, all at the same time. Like children, they wanted instant gratification. Played all their cards at the same time, swung before the ball got to the plate, struck out and found themselves back in a cell where their only landscape was the sun setting against the prison wall.

After my release from prison, the world presented me with a lot of maybes and possibilities. It takes time to sort things out, put them into workable categories. Sometimes while walking on the streets, I feel as though a spaceship left me on the wrong planet. At other times everything seems natural and falls into place. Still, a bit of uncertainty lurks behind everything, everywhere.

I decided to do life the same way I did prison. Nothing fancy. One step at a time, one day at a time, and most of all, don't forget to breathe.

"Let's just hang out," I told my brother, "go with the flow, move with the groove."

Freddy was supportive and sensitive. He understood that I needed to relearn the rhythm of the streets, tune in on the city, explore my new freedom and tune out on prison. I had no preference which direction we'd walk, or which street we'd take. Freddy didn't seem to have any preference either. He just started off, leaving me to stay where I was or to catch up. I learned a quick but important lesson. It was this kind of small, ordinary decision—often taken for granted and overlooked—that I missed most in prison. Now, by just walking off and letting me decide what to do, Freddy was tuning me in again to this level of free choice.

The morning after my release from prison found me in Harlem. I was staying with Bert, a long-time family friend. I awoke at dawn. There was no excitement. No stage fright or butterflies to signal the first day of the rest of my life. Looking up from sleep I could have dreamed my release from prison the day before. The sky was as gray as a prison sky—the same sky I had seen for the past sixteen years and three months.

Not long after I went to prison, I woke in the middle of the night and sat up on the side of the bed. The cell was so quiet I could hear cockroaches foraging in my garbage.

"When I get out of prison," I said to myself, "sex can wait." Thinking of what I would most like to do, I said, "I'm going to eat strawberries! Big! Fresh! Red strawberries!" And that became my mantra for the rest of the time I was in prison.

On the day I was released, Kathrin, a friend, a sister, my confidante, came to pick me up. She was there with her camera, taking photos of me as I walked through the last gate to freedom. She drove me to the house where she lived with her husband and son, and fed me steamed shrimp, French champagne, and strawberries!

Jerome Washington, a writer, is now discharged from parole supervision and is living in California.
SOURCE: Jerome Washington, *Iron House: Stories from the Yard* (New York: Vintage, 1994), 155–163.

consider whether a particular offender should be moved to a halfway house within the community. The staff must also consider whether the offender has the necessary skills to obtain employment and become self-sufficient.

Among the many programs developed to assist offenders, three are especially important: work and educational release, furloughs, and residential programs. Although similar in many ways, each offers a specific approach to helping formerly incarcerated individuals reenter the community.

Work and Educational Release

work and educational release

The daytime release of inmates from correctional institutions so they can work or attend school.

Programs of **work and educational release,** in which inmates are released from correctional institutions during the day so that they may work or attend school, were first established in Vermont in 1906. However, the Huber Act, passed by the Wisconsin legislature in 1913, is usually cited as the model on which such programs are based. By 1972, most states and the federal government had instituted these programs.

Although most work and educational release programs are justifiable as rehabilitation, many correctional administrators and legislators also like them because they cost relatively little. In some states, a portion of the inmate's earnings from work outside may be deducted for room and board. One of the problems of administering the programs is that the person on release is often viewed by other inmates as privileged, and such perceptions can lead to resentment and conflict within the prison. Another problem is that in some states, organized labor complains that jobs are being taken from free citizens. Furthermore, the releasee's contact with the community increases the chances that contraband may be brought into the institution. To deal with such bootlegging and to assist in the reintegration process, some states and counties have built special work and educational release units in urban areas where offenders live away from the prison.

Furloughs

furlough

The temporary release of an inmate from a correctional institution for a brief period, usually one to three days, for a visit home. Such programs help maintain family ties and prepare inmates for release on parole.

Isolation from loved ones is one of the pains of imprisonment. Although conjugal visits have been a part of correctional programs in many countries, they have been used in only a few U.S. correctional systems. Many penologists view the **furlough** —the temporary release of an inmate from a correctional institution for a visit home—as a meaningful alternative. Consistent with the focus on community corrections, brief home furloughs are being used more frequently in the United States. In some states, an effort is made to ensure that all eligible inmates are able to use the furlough privilege on Thanksgiving and Christmas. In other states, however, the program has been much more restrictive, and often only those about to be released are given furloughs.

Furloughs are thought to offer an excellent means of testing an inmate's ability to cope with the larger society. Through home visits, the inmate can renew family ties and relieve the tensions of confinement. Most administrators also feel that furloughs are good for prisoners' morale. The general public, however, does not always support the concept. Public outrage is inevitable if an offender on furlough commits another crime or fails to return. Correctional authorities are often nervous about using furloughs because they fear being blamed for a violent incident.

Residential Programs

community correctional center

An institution, usually in an urban area, that houses inmates soon to be released. Such centers are designed to help inmates establish community ties and thus promote their reintegration with society.

The **community correctional center** is an institution that houses soon-to-be-released inmates and connects them to community services, resources, and support. It may take a number of forms and serve a variety of offender clients. Throughout the country, halfway houses, prerelease centers, and correctional service centers can be found. Most programs require offenders to reside at the facility while they work in the community or visit with their families. Other facilities are designed primarily to provide services and programs for parolees. Often these facilities are established in former private homes or small hotels, creating a homey, less institutional environment. Individual rooms, group dining rooms, and other homelike features are maintained whenever possible.

The term **halfway house** has been applied to a variety of community correctional facilities and programs in which felons work in the community but reside in the halfway house during nonworking hours. Halfway houses range from secure institutions in the community with programs designed to assist inmates who are preparing for release on parole to group homes where parolees, probationers, or persons diverted from the system are able to live with minimal supervision and direction. Some halfway houses are organized to deliver special treatment services, such as programs designed to deal with alcohol, drug, or mental problems.

The number of halfway houses in the United States and the number of clients housed in them are not known. Most halfway houses are operated under contract by private, nonprofit organizations. Their capacity is about twenty-five residents, who generally stay eight to sixteen weeks. There are three models of release or transfer to halfway houses. In one model, halfway houses serve as a preparation station for offenders who will soon be released on parole. In this setting, they can prepare for the challenges of returning to life in free society. In the second model, offenders are paroled from prison directly to a halfway house, where officials can monitor their adjustment and help them reintegrate. The third model involves paroling offenders directly into the community and making the halfway house available as a resource for parolees who need support or assistance (Latessa and Travis, 1992).

Residential programs have problems. Few neighborhoods want to host halfway houses or treatment centers for convicts. Community resistance has been a significant impediment to the development of community-based corrections facilities and even has forced some successful facilities to close. Community corrections programs have become a major political issue, as have programs for the mentally disabled and the retarded. Many communities, often wealthier ones, have blocked placement of halfway houses or treatment centers within their boundaries. One result of the NIMBY ("not in my backyard") attitude is that many centers are established in deteriorating neighborhoods inhabited by poor people, who lack the political power and resources to block unpopular programs.

The future of residential programs is unclear. Originally advocated for both rehabilitative and financial reasons, they do not seem to be saving as much money for the correctional system as officials had hoped. Medical care, education, vocational rehabilitation, and therapy are expensive. Thus, the costs of quality community programs are likely to be about the same as the costs of incarceration. Effective programs require the services of teachers, counselors, and other professional personnel. Moreover, to be truly effective, these officials must work with small numbers of offenders. The savings from having fewer custodial personnel in community programs may be offset by the costs of counseling and other professional services.

If recidivism rates of offenders who have been involved in community treatment were proven to be lower, the expenditures might more readily be justified.

halfway house
A correctional facility housing convicted felons who spend a portion of their day at work in the community but reside in the halfway house during nonworking hours.

However, the available data are discouraging. The excitement and optimism that greeted the community correctional movement may have been unwarranted.

CHECK **POINT**

⑧ **What are three programs designed to ease the reentry of offenders into the community?**

Parole Officer: Cop or Social Worker?

After release, a parolee's principal contact with the criminal justice system is through the parole officer who has the dual responsibility of providing surveillance and assistance. Thus, parole officers are asked to play two different, some might say incompatible, roles: cop and social worker. It has always been a question as to which role should dominate the officer's work.

Traditionally parole was designed to help offenders make the transition from prison to the community. Officers were expected to help offenders find housing and employment as well as to address personal problems. Increasingly however, parole supervision has shifted away from providing assistance and more toward surveillance, drug testing, monitoring curfews, and collecting restitution. Safety and security have become major issues in parole services (Lynch, 1998). As noted by Joan Petersilia, "parole supervision has been transformed ideologically from a social service to a law enforcement system" (Petersilia, 1999).

The Parole Officer as Cop

In their role as police officer, parole officers are given the power to restrict many aspects of the parolee's life, to enforce the conditions of release, and to initiate revocation proceedings if parole conditions are violated. Like other officials in the criminal justice system, parole officers have extensive discretion in low-visibility situations. In many states, parole officers have the authority to search the parolee's house without warning, to arrest him or her without the possibility of bail for suspected violations, and to suspend parole pending a hearing before the board. Firearms are now provided in most jurisdictions. This authoritarian component of the parole officer's role can give the ex-offender a sense of insecurity and hamper the development of mutual trust.

Parole Officer Corey Burke drops by unannounced to visit a paroled sex offender in the man's apartment. Burke sees his job as neither to exact retribution nor to offer compassion, but to keep parolees from committing another crime.

The parole officer is responsible for seeing that the parolee follows the conditions imposed by the parole board. The conditions imposed by Connecticut's Board of Parole are substantial and not atypical. Consider how difficult it must be for a parole officer to monitor the following twelve conditions, especially when the officer is responsible for many parolees at once.

❶ Upon release from the institution, you must follow the instructions of the institutional parole officer (or other designated authority of the Division of Parole) with regard to reporting to your supervising parole officer and/or fulfilling any other obligations.

❷ You must report to your parole officer when instructed to do so and must permit your parole officer or any parole officer to visit you at your home and place of employment at any time.

❸ You must work steadily, and you must secure the permission of your parole officer before changing your residence or your employment, and you must report any change of residence or employment to your parole officer within twenty-four hours of such change.

❹ You must submit written reports as instructed by your parole officer.

❺ You must not leave the state of Connecticut without first obtaining permission from your parole officer.

❻ You must not apply for a motor vehicle operator's license, or own, purchase, or operate any motor vehicle without first obtaining permission from your parole officer.

❼ You must not marry without first obtaining written permission from your parole officer.

❽ You must not own, possess, use, sell, or have under your control at any time any deadly weapons or firearms.

❾ You must not possess, use, or traffic in any narcotic, hallucinatory, or other harmful drugs in violation of the law.

❿ You must support your dependents, if any, and assume toward them all moral and legal obligations.

⓫ (a) You shall not consume alcoholic beverages to excess. (b) You shall totally abstain from the use of alcoholic beverages or liquors. (Strike out either a or b, leaving whichever clause is applicable.)

⓬ You must comply with all laws and conduct yourself as a good citizen. You must show by your attitude, cooperation, choice of associates, and places of amusement and recreation that you are a proper person to remain on parole.

The law enforcement powers are granted to parole officers to protect the community from offenders who are coming out of prison. However, because these powers diminish the possibility for the officer to develop a close relationship with the client, they may weaken the officer's other role of assisting the parolee's readjustment to the community (Clear and Latessa, 1993:441).

The Parole Officer as Social Worker

Parole officers must act as social workers by helping the parolee find a job and restore family ties. Officers must be prepared to channel parolees to social agencies, such as psychiatric, drug, and alcohol clinics, where they can obtain help. As caseworkers, officers work to develop a relationship that allows parolees to confide their frustrations and concerns.

Because parolees are not likely to do this if they are constantly aware of the parole officer's ability to send them back to prison, some researchers have suggested that parole officers' conflicting responsibilities of cop and social worker should be separated. Parole officers could maintain the supervisory aspects of the position, and other personnel—perhaps a separate parole counselor—could perform the casework functions. Another option would be for parole officers to be charged solely with social work duties, while local police check for violations. In Japan and a few other countries, citizen volunteers are involved in helping the newly released offender adjust to the community and become a law-abiding citizen (see Comparative Perspective on p. 558).

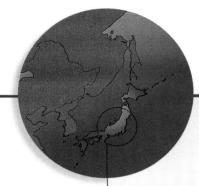

perspective

Parole Supervision in Japan

Parole supervision and aftercare services in Japan are characterized by the extensive participation of community volunteers. Would Americans be willing to volunteer to play such a role?

When Japan reorganized its correctional services after World War II, it was argued that probation and parole supervision should be organized to combine a professional staff and volunteer community corrections workers. A shortage of funds precluded an expanded professional service, and a historical record of volunteer services had contributed to the rehabilitation of offenders. Japan also had a tradition of voluntary social welfare systems firmly rooted in the community. The Offender's Rehabilitation Law called on all people to "render help, in accordance with their position and ability, in order to achieve the goals (of rehabilitation of offenders, etc.)." With passage of the Volunteer Probation Officer Law in 1950, people were nominated to serve in this capacity. They were charged with helping offenders to rehabilitate themselves in society and with fostering a constructive public attitude that would help to promote crime prevention.

Today, almost fifty thousand volunteers work on an individual basis with the one to ten cases assigned to them and are supervised by eight hundred professional officers. Appointed for two-year terms, volunteers are assigned according to their place of residence to one of 764 "rehabilitation areas." The volunteers in each area form an association of officers that is nationally linked to provide for volunteer solidarity, to coordinate training, and to gain resources.

Volunteer officers tend to be older (more than half are over 50) and are from a variety of backgrounds. The largest group (23 percent) comes from such primary

The Parole Bureaucracy

Huge caseloads make effective supervision practically impossible in most states. Parole caseloads range from fifty to seventy people. Although this is smaller than probation caseloads, offenders who have just been released from prison require more extensive services that those on probation. One reason is that parolees, by the very fact of their incarceration, have generally committed much more serious crimes than probationers. Another reason is that probationers continue their lives in the community while living under a set of restrictive conditions, whereas parolees are making a difficult transition from the highly structured prison environment to a society in which they have previously failed to live as law-abiding citizens. It is exceptionally difficult for a parole officer to monitor, control, and assist clients who may have little knowledge of or experience with living successfully within society's rules.

industries as agriculture, fishing, and forestry. The second largest category (18 percent) is comprised of individuals officially classified as unemployed but composed mainly of homemakers and the retired. Religious professionals comprise the next largest category. Only 5 percent of the officers are lawyers, doctors, and other professionals, somewhat in contrast to the community activities of this group in Western countries. Although there is a diversity of backgrounds, most volunteers are middle class.

The volunteer regularly meets a client at home and also visits the client's family. The volunteer continues to observe the offender in these contacts and tries to advise, assist, and support him or her. Assistance is also given to the offender's family, with due respect to the dignity and freedom of the individual. Sometimes the volunteer has to visit the client's place of employment. The greatest concern of the volunteer is how to maintain client contact while at the same time keeping the offender's criminal background from the knowledge of neighbors and employers. The frequency of contact with the client is generally twice a month, but in special cases it occurs almost every day. Volunteers feel they should be readily available to their clients and their families, even during weekends or late at night in case of emergency, particularly in remote areas where professional services are few.

The volunteer probation and parole service in Japan is believed to have unique merits lacked by the professional officer. The nonofficial nature of the relationship between volunteer and offender is thought to be positive. It is believed that through this relationship the offender can regain self-respect and identify with the law-abiding culture. Another merit is the "local" nature of the volunteers. As members of the community where their clients live, volunteers know the particular setting and local customs. Yet some of the professional officers believe that they could do a better job at the grass roots-level than the volunteers.

The nature of probation and parole in Japan draws heavily upon that country's unique sense of community. By sharing a common culture and social experience, the Japanese are closely bound to one another in a consensual society. For offenders, rehabilitation requires earning one's way back into community membership.

■ The Japanese approach to probation and parole is quite different from the United States. Perhaps it would be successful only in a country where there is not great cultural diversity and where community pressures are a major aspect of social control. Do you agree?

SOURCE: Drawn from Yasuyoshi Shiono, "Use of Volunteers in the Non-Institutional Treatment of Offenders in Japan," *International Review of Crime Policy* 27 (1969):25–31; Kenichi Nakayama, "Japan," in *Major Criminal Justice Systems,* 2d ed., ed. George F. Cole, Stanislaw Frankowski, and Marc G. Gertz (Newbury Park, Calif.: Sage, 1987), 168; L. Craig Parker Jr., *Parole and the Community-Based Treatment of Offenders in Japan and the United States* (New Haven, Conn.: University of New Haven Press, 1986); and Elmer H. Johnson, *Japanese Corrections* (Carbondale, Ill.: Southern Illinois University Press, 1996).

The parole officer works within a bureaucratic environment. Because the difficulties faced by many parolees are so complex, the officer's job is almost impossible. At the same time, like most other human services organizations, parole agencies are short on resources and expertise. As a result, they frequently must classify parolees and give priority to those most in need. To serve those with the greatest need, most parole officers spend more time with the newly released. As the officer gains confidence in the parolee, the level of supervision can be reduced. Depending on how the parolee has functioned in the community, he or she eventually may be required to check in with the officer only periodically rather than submit to regular home visits, searches, and other intrusive monitoring.

CHECK POINT

⑨ What are some of the rules most parolees must follow while they are supervised in the community?

⑩ What are the major tasks of parole officers?

Adjustment to Life outside Prison

With little preparation, the ex-offender moves from the highly structured, author-itarian life of the institution into a world that is filled with temptations and com-plicated problems. Suddenly, ex-convicts who are not accustomed to undertaking even simple tasks such as going to the store for groceries are expected to assume pressing, complex responsibilities. Finding a job and a place to live are not the only problems the newly released person faces. The parolee must also make sig-nificant social and psychological role adjustments. A male ex-convict, for example, is suddenly required to become not only a parolee but also an employee, a neigh-bor, a father, a husband, and a son. The expectations, norms, and social relations in the free world are different from those learned in prison. The relatively predictable inmate code is replaced by society's often unclear rules of behavior—rules that the offender had failed to cope with during his or her previous life in free society.

The "Dangerous" Parolee

The public's assumptions about ex-offenders are shaped by news reports of brutal crimes committed by parolees. The murder of 12-year-old Polly Klaas by a parolee and the rape and murder of 7-year-old Megan Kanka by a paroled sex offender stimulated legislators in more than thirty-five states to enact "sexual offender noti-fication" laws. These laws require that the public be notified of the whereabouts of "potentially dangerous" sex offenders. In some states paroled sex offenders must register with the police, while in others, the immediate neighbors must be informed (Lieb, Quinsey, and Berliner, 1998:43).

The impact of these laws have had a number of unintended consequences. Incidents have occurred in which parolees have been "hounded" from communi-ties, where the media have televised the parolee's homecoming, and where neigh-bors have assaulted parolees they erroneously thought were sex offenders. In a number of states the legislation is written so broadly that statutory rape, consen-sual sodomy, and third-degree assault that might constitute inappropriate touch-ing or sexual contact are included in the notification mandate. Real estate agents

Paroled child molester Richard Marter, alone in a motel, has been hounded out of Riverside and Beverly, New Jersey. Residents learned of his past through the Megan's Law requirement that neighbors be notified when a sex offender moves into an area.

have also found it difficult to sell property in neighborhoods where registered sex offenders live (*Hartford Courant,* April 7, 1999).

The fact of repeat violence fuels a public perception that parolees represent a continuing threat to the community. This preoccupation with potential parolee criminality makes it harder for parolees to make it on the outside. Although the new laws are directed primarily at people who have committed sex offenses against children, there is concern that the community will target all parolees. This will make it even more difficult for ex-offenders to successfully reenter society.

Parole and Recidivism

The reentry problems of parolees are reflected in their revocation rate. Unfortunately, the best available study of parolee recidivism rates is now more than fifteen years old (BJS, 1989). That national study showed that 63 percent of inmates were arrested for a felony or serious misdemeanor within three years of their release from prison. The Bureau of Justice Statistics does collect data on each state's parole population and the number successfully completing supervision. Forty-four percent of ex-inmates successfully completed parole in 1997 (BJS, 1998f). As seen in What Americans Think, much of the public believes that those who recidivate should not be released on parole.

It is not surprising that the recidivism rate is so high, considering that the average ex-inmate has been convicted of serious crimes (83 percent for violent or property offenses), has a criminal record of multiple arrests (8.4 prior arrests), and has been incarcerated before (67 percent) (BJS, 1998f). These are not the people who have run afoul of the law only once, when they made a bad decision or acted impulsively. Instead, most prisoners have committed serious crimes and have a long history of difficulties with the criminal justice system. The numbers indicate that a large percentage of today's inmates are criminals who will resort to their old habits upon release. In addition, the experience of spending time in prison is essentially designed to punish people for their harmful acts. By itself, the experience of incarceration is unlikely to teach anyone how to succeed in the community. The artificial environment of prisons moves people farther away from the atmosphere, attitudes, habits, and responsibilities that make for success in American society.

 **POINT**

⑪ **What are some of the major problems faced by parolees?**

⑫ **What are "offender notification laws"?**

⑬ **Why are recidivism rates high?**

Revocation of Parole

Always hanging over the ex-inmate's head is the potential revocation of parole and a return to prison for: (1) committing a new crime or (2) violating the conditions of release (a "technical violation"). The public tends to view the high number of revocations as a failure of parole. Corrections officials point to the great number of parolees who are required to remain drug-free, be employed, and pay restitution—conditions that are difficult for many to fulfill. One result is that the greater number of parolees being returned to prison has contributed to crowding and pressures to build more institutions.

What Americans Think

Question "Tell me whether you think the following proposal is a good idea or a bad idea."

Refuse parole to any prisoner who has been paroled before for a serious crime.

Good idea 75%

SOURCE: Timothy J. Flanagan, "Reform or Punish: Americans' View of the Correctional System," in *Americans View Crime and Justice,* ed. Timothy J. Flanagan and Dennis R. Longmire (Thousand Oaks, Calif.: Sage Publications, 1996), 84.

<u>*Morrissey v. Brewer* (1972)</u>

Due process rights require a prompt, informal inquiry before an impartial hearing officer before parole may be revoked. The parolee may present relevant information and confront witnesses.

If the parole officer alleges that a technical violation has occurred, the U.S. Supreme Court requires a two-step revocation proceeding (***Morrissey v. Brewer,*** 1972). In the first stage the parole authority determines whether there is probable cause to believe the conditions have been violated. The parolee has the right to be notified of the charges, to be informed of the evidence, to be heard, to present witnesses, and to confront the parole board's witnesses. In the second stage the parole authority decides if the violation is severe enough to warrant return to prison.

The number of parole revocations is difficult to determine because most published data do not distinguish between parolees returned to prison for technical violations and those sent back for new criminal offenses. One study found that 22 percent of state inmates were on parole at the time of their recommitment to prison. Eighty percent were returned following conviction on a new offense, while the remainder were in prison for a technical violation (BJS, 1995c:2).

Alfred Blumstein and Allen J. Beck (1999) studied parole violations by offenders sentenced for six serious crimes (murder, robbery, assault, burglary, drugs, and sex offenses). They found that these violators represent an increasing fraction of all admissions to prison. In 1980 serious offense parole violators comprised 18 percent of all admissions, by 1996 that had grown to 35 percent. The largest fraction of these offenders were initially sentenced for burglary and robbery. Drug offenders comprised the largest percentage of growth of violators during the period, reflecting the increased number of paroled drug offenders.

Great variations are found among the states as to the number of parolees returned to prison. In California nearly 80 percent of parolees fail to successfully complete supervision, and parole violators make up 65 percent of prison admissions (Austin and Lawson, 1998). However, in many states the failure rate is as low as 25 percent. Nationally about 41 percent of parolees are returned to prison (BJS, 1998f).

Because prisons are crowded, most revocations occur only when the parolee has been arrested on a serious charge. Given the size of the normal caseload, most parole officers are unable to monitor parolees closely and thus may be unaware of technical violations. Under the requirements for prompt and fair hearings, some parole boards discourage officers from issuing violation warrants following infractions of parole rules unless there is evidence of new crimes.

 **CHECK** **POINT**

⑭ **What two conditions may result in the revocation of parole?**

⑮ **What due process requirements must be followed in the parole revocation process?**

The Future of Parole

Parole has been under attack since the 1970s as a symbol of leniency where criminals are "let out" early (Petersilia, 1999). Public outrage is heightened when the media report the gruesome details of violent crimes committed by parolees. Calls by legislators for the abolition of parole have been politically popular. It is argued that without parole criminals would serve longer terms and there would be greater honesty in sentencing. As a result fourteen states and the federal government have abolished early release by a parole board for all offenders, and several other states have restricted its use. Where discretionary release has been retained many boards have limited the number of prisoners granted parole.

Correctional experts argue that parole plays an important role in the criminal justice system given that early release from prison must be earned. Without discretionary release parole boards are unable to individualize punishment or "correct" disparities in sentencing. Finally, parole release is a crucial mechanism used by officials to deal with crowded prisons.

Where the emphasis of community supervision in the 1970s was on assisting the parolee, today's emphasis is much more on monitoring and surveillance. The conditions of release have increased so that most parolees are now required to remain drug-free, employed, and attend a range of treatment programs. Parole officers must now spend much of their time checking to see that these conditions are fulfilled. This careful scrutiny can lead to an increase in technical revocations.

Advances in the use of electronic surveillance technology have made it possible to keep track of parolees. Although electronic monitoring of offenders sentenced to home confinement has taken place since the 1980s, some agencies are now experimenting with global positioning systems (GPS) to track parolees. These systems require the parolee to carry a transmitting device with them at all times. The device transmits a signal to the satellite system developed by the military for surveillance purposes, which routes the information back to central control (Renzema, 1998). Electronic surveillance has been criticized as not providing the human element of direct contract with a parole officer and as a threat to personal liberty (Clear and Cole, 2000:478).

As prison populations rise, demands that felons be allowed to serve part of their time in the community will undoubtedly mount. These demands will not come from the public, which typically believes that all offenders should serve their full sentences. Instead, they will come from the legislators and corrections officials who recognize that the money and facilities to incarcerate all offenders for the complete terms of their sentences are lacking. Although many offenders are not successfully integrated into the community, most offenders will end up back in free society whether or not they serve their full sentences. Parole and community programs represent an effort to address the inevitability of their return. Even if such programs do not prevent all offenders from leaving the life of crime, they do help some to turn their lives around.

Pardon WWW

References to **pardon** are found in ancient Hebrew law, and the church and the monarchies had the power of clemency in medieval Europe. Pardon later became known as the "royal prerogative of mercy" in England.

In the United States, the president or the state governor may grant clemency in individual cases. In each state the executive receives recommendations from the state's board of pardons (often combined with the board of parole) concerning individuals who are thought to be deserving of the act. Pardons serve three main purposes: (1) to remedy a miscarriage of justice, (2) to remove the stigma of a conviction, and (3) to mitigate a penalty. Although full pardons for miscarriages of justice are rare, from time to time society is alerted to the story of some individual

pardon
An action of the executive branch of state or federal government excusing an offense and absolving the offender from the consequences of the crime.

who has been released from prison after the discovery that he or she was incarcerated by mistake. The more typical activity of pardons boards is to erase the criminal records of first-time offenders—often young people—so they may enter those professions whose licensing procedures keep out former felons, may obtain certain types of employment, and in general will not have to bear the stigma of a single mistake.

Civil Disabilities of Ex-Felons

Once a person has been released from prison, paid a fine, or completed parole or probation, the debt to society—in theory—has been paid and the punishment has ended. For many offenders, however, a criminal conviction is a lifetime burden. In most states, certain civil rights are forfeited forever, some fields of employment are closed, and some insurance or pension benefits may be denied. It does not matter if an ex-convict successfully obtains steady employment, raises a family, and contributes time to community organizations.

The extent of civil disabilities varies greatly among the states. In some states, the activities of persons who have been convicted of certain crimes have specific restrictions. A conviction for forgery, for example, prevents employment in the banking or stock-trading fields. In other states, blanket restrictions are placed on all felons regardless of the circumstances of the crime. These restrictions are removed only upon completion of the sentence, after a period subsequent to completion of the sentence, or upon action of a board of pardons. One survey has shown that between 1986 and 1996 states increased their restrictions on released inmates (Olivares, Burton, and Cullen, 1996).

The civil rights to vote and hold public office are generally limited upon conviction. Thirty-two states disenfranchise parolees and fourteen states bar for life ex-offenders. The Sentencing Project (1998) estimates that 3.9 million Americans, including 1.4 million African American men (13 percent of black men), cannot vote because of their felony convictions. Thus in Alabama and Florida 31 percent of African American men are permanently disenfranchised, and in Iowa, Mississippi, New Mexico, Virginia, Washington, and Wyoming, the ratio is 1 to 4. Felons are denied other civil rights—such as eligibility to serve on juries, parental rights, and access to public employment—in many states (Love and Kuzma, 1996).

Although most former felons may not believe that restrictions on their civil rights will make it difficult for them to lead normal lives, barriers to certain fields of employment are a problem. Ironically, many prison vocational programs lead to occupations from which former inmates may be barred. In various states, restricted occupations include nurse, beautician, barber, real estate salesperson, dentist, chauffeur, employee in a place where alcoholic beverages are served, cashier, stenographer, and insurance agent (Love and Kuzma, 1996). Many observers assert that the restrictions push offenders toward menial jobs at low pay and may lead them back to crime.

Critics of civil disability laws point out that, upon fulfilling the penalty imposed for a crime, the former offender should be assisted to full reintegration into society. They argue that it is counterproductive for the government to promote rehabilitation with the goal of reintegration while at the same time preventing offenders from fully achieving that goal. Supporters of these laws respond that they are justified by the possibility of recidivism and the community's need for protection. Between these two extremes is the belief that not all persons convicted of felonies should be treated equally and that society can be protected adequately by the placement of restrictions on only certain individuals.

CHECK POINT

⑯ **What are the purposes served by the pardon?**

⑰ **What is a civil disability? List three examples.**

Summary

- Conditional release from prison on parole is the primary method by which inmates return to society. While on parole they remain under correctional supervision.

- There are three types of release: mandatory, discretionary, and unconditional.

- Parole boards exercise the discretion to consider various factors in making the release decision.

- Parolees are released from prison on the condition that they do not again violate the law and that they live according to rules designed both to help them adjust to society and to control their movements.

- Parole officers are assigned to assist ex-inmates to make the transition to society and to ensure that they follow the conditions of their release.

- Upon release, offenders face a number of problems: they must find housing and employment and renew relationships with family and friends.

- Community corrections assumes that reentry should be a gradual process through which parolees should be assisted. Halfway houses, work and educational release, furloughs, and community correctional centers are geared to ease the transition.

- Society places restrictions on many ex-felons. State and federal laws prevent offenders from entering certain professions and occupations. Voting rights and the right to hold public office are often denied to ex-felons.

- Some offenders are able to obtain pardons for their crimes and have their civil rights reinstated, usually after successfully completing their time on parole.

Questions for Review

1 What are the basic assumptions of parole?

2 How do mandatory release, discretionary release, and unconditional release differ?

3 What is the role of the parole officer?

4 What problems confront parolees upon their release?

Key Terms and Cases

community correctional center (p. 554)
conditions of release (p. 551)
discretionary release (p. 543)
furlough (p. 554)

halfway house (p. 555)
mandatory release (p. 544)
pardon (p. 563)
parole (p. 541)

presumptive parole date (p. 547)
unconditional release (p. 544)
work and educational release (p. 554)
Morrissey v. Brewer (1972) (p. 562)

For Further Reading

McCleary, Richard. *Dangerous Men: The Sociology of Parole,* 2d ed. Albany, N.Y.: Harrow and Heston, 1992. A study of the bureaucracy of parole supervision.

Rhine, Edward E., William R. Smith, and Ronald W. Jackson. *Paroling Authorities: Recent History and Current Practice.* Laurel, Md.: American Correctional Association, 1991. Results of a national survey con-

ducted by the American Correctional Association Task Force on Parole.

Simon, Jonathan. *Poor Discipline: Parole and the Social Control of the Underclass.* Chicago: University of Chicago Press, 1993. Explores the use of parole to control poor and disadvantaged members of society.

Stanley, David. *Prisoners among Us.* Washington, D.C.: Brookings Institution, 1975. Still the only major

published account of parole release decision making. The book emphasizes parole board discretion.

Von Hirsch, Andrew, and Kathleen J. Hanrahan. *The Question of Parole.* Cambridge, Mass.: Ballinger, 1979. Examines parole from the "just deserts" perspective and urges its reform.

Going Online

1 Access New Jersey's Megan Law informational web site at www.state.nj.us/1ps/megan.htm. Describe the requirements imposed on released sex offenders. What is the process of neighborhood notification? What are the likely benefits and drawbacks of this policy?

2 What is the impact of felony disenfranchisement laws in the United States? Find out on the Internet at www.sentencingproject.org. What reforms does The Sentencing Project hope will be enacted?

3 **Using InfoTrac College Edition,** type the keyword *parole.* Access the article by Donald Evans, "One Hundred Years of Conditional Release in Canada," *Corrections Today* (August 1999). Write a short essay describing the similarities and differences between parole in Canada and in your own state. What are the current goals of parole in Canada?

❶ England, Australia, Ireland.

❷ Maconochie developed a classification procedure through which prisoners could get increasing responsibility and freedom. Crofton built on Maconochie's idea of an offender's progress in prison and the ticket of leave to supervision in the community.

❸ Mandatory release is the required release of an inmate from incarceration to community supervision upon the expiration of a certain time period, as specified by a determinate sentencing law or parole guidelines. Discretionary release is the release of an inmate from incarceration to conditional supervision at the discretion of the parole board within the boundaries set by the sentence and the penal law. Unconditional release is the release of an inmate from incarceration without any further correctional supervision; the inmate cannot be returned to prison for any remaining portion of the sentence for the current offense.

❹ As part of the department of corrections or independent of the department.

❺ The severity of the offense, rehabilitation program participation by the inmate, readiness for parole, the attitude of the offender, and the attitude of the victim.

❻ Participation in prison educational and treatment programs.

❼ Parole release encourages plea bargaining, relieves prison crowding, makes the sentence less harsh, and encourages good behavior in prison.

❽ Work and educational release programs, furlough programs, residential programs.

❾ Make required reports to parole officer, do not leave the state without permission, do not use alcohol or drugs, maintain employment, attend required treatment programs.

❿ Surveillance and assistance.

⓫ Finding housing and employment, having a shortage of money, and reestablishing relationships with family and friends.

⓬ Laws requiring certain types of parolees (usually sex offenders) to notify the police or residents that they are living in the community.

⓭ Many parolees are career criminals, and the problems of reentry and close parole supervision are difficult adjustments.

⓮ Arrest for a new crime, or a technical violation of one or more of the conditions of parole.

⓯ In a two-step hearing process, the parolee has the right to be notified of the charges, to know the evidence against him or her, to be heard, to present witnesses, and to confront witnesses.

⓰ To remedy a miscarriage of justice, to remove the stigma of a conviction, to mitigate a penalty.

⓱ Ex-felons forfeit certain civil rights such as the right to vote, to serve on juries, to hold public office. Ex-felons are restricted from certain types of employment.

Is There a Prison-Commercial Complex?

Forty years ago President Dwight D. Eisenhower warned of the strong, unwarranted influence of the "military-industrial complex." He was concerned about the extent to which the armed forces of the United States and the manufacturers of military hardware shared an interest in the ever-expanding defense budget. Today critics are pointing to a similar "prison-commercial complex" made up of bureaucratic, political, and economic interests that encourage increased spending on imprisonment, regardless of need.

One of the anomalies of the past decade is that as crime rates have fallen, the prison population has continued to grow. Some point to the new effectiveness of policing, the "war on drugs," mandatory minimum sentences, and truth-in-sentencing laws as contributing to the rising incarceration rate. It is said that crime has fallen because of tough incarceration policies and that compared with other countries there is still too much violent crime. As economist Michael Block has said, "There are too many prisoners because there are too many criminals committing too many crimes."

Others believe that with corrections costing more than $35 billion per year, expansion has been encouraged by the profits to be made in prison supplies and construction; by the increased value of stock in private prison corporations; by the greater number of corrections jobs in impoverished rural areas; by the expanded fiefdoms of prison bureaucrats; by the growth of correctional officer labor unions; and by the votes for politicians who pass "tough on crime" legislation.

The existence of a prison-commercial complex is based on what political scientists call an "iron triangle." This refers to relationships built on the mutuality of interests of legislators who promote policies to endear themselves to voters and interest groups, government agencies that are able to expand their influence by carrying out these policies, and businesses that have an economic interest in these policies. These relationships are stable and endure because each of the three parties can deliver something the others need.

Why are so many people in the United States locked up? Are government agencies, legislators, and businesses merely responding to public demand that criminals should be isolated from society? Is there a "prison-commercial complex" that has influenced the upward spiral of the number of prisoners?

There Is a Prison-Commercial Complex

Supporters of the belief that there is a prison-commercial complex argue that high incarceration rates during a period of falling levels of crime are influenced by the "punishment industry." They say that in the American free-enterprise system the penal system is highly influenced by, and responsive to, market interests. Corporations doing business with corrections have a mutuality of interests with government agencies seeking to expand their domain and with legislators promoting tough crime policies.

People holding this view point to the 400 percent increase in corrections spending since 1979, the 600 percent increase in funds for prison construction, and the expectation that these allocations will continue to grow at an annual rate of 5 to 10 percent. They cite the spectacular growth of private prisons corporations and the billions of dollars spent to purchase goods and services. For example, some note that the annual meeting of the American Correctional Association (ACA) has become an enormous trade show. The ACA, whose advertising proclaims that "corrections is an industry," plays a central role in facilitating the buying and selling of goods and services found in today's prisons and jails.

Besides the growth of businesses serving corrections, labor unions have also benefited by the rise in the number of prison employees now set at more than 350,000. In many states correctional officers have become a potent political force and have lobbied for expansion of the system. In California, the correctional officers' union contributed $1 million to the reelection campaign of Governor Pete Wilson.

To summarize the arguments that there is a prison-commercial complex that has promoted incarceration:

- Spending for incarceration continues to rise and in most states exceeds appropriations for most government services.
- There is a mutuality of interests among correctional agencies, businesses, and legislators that supports high incarceration.
- Correctional workers and their unions support the addition of employees.
- Legislators believe that voters expect them to be "tough on crime."

There Is No Prison-Commercial Complex

Supporters of the use of incarceration for offenders who have committed serious felonies say that there is no prison–commercial complex. They believe that crime continues to be a major national problem and that criminals must be dealt with severely. Prison expansion is driven by the need to provide space for the increased number of offenders incarcerated for longer terms and not by business interests hoping to profit from the crime problem.

Defenders of contemporary sentencing policies also say that the growth of the prison population has helped to lower crime rates. Some argue that the drop in crime is more a function of the large numbers of offenders who are put away. They say that crime would have increased if so many people had not been locked up.

The philosophical perspective of supporters of current policies is that treating criminals severely is just and that incarcerated felons deserve to be punished because their crimes are serious. They argue that incarceration is expensive but to allow felons to live in society where they will continue their criminal ways is many times more costly. Contemporary punishment policies enjoy public support and are not the result of pressures of commercial interests.

To summarize the arguments against a prison-commercial complex:

- Increased incarceration rates are not being pushed by commercial interests but reflect current public policies.
- Incarceration is being used to punish individuals who have committed serious offenses. Justice demands that they be punished in this manner.
- Incarceration policies have been successful in lowering the crime rate.
- The public's support of incarceration policies is reflected by the actions of Congress and the state legislatures.

What Should U.S. Policy Be?

Incarceration is expensive. It costs a great deal of money to build and operate prisons, but there are also human costs to offenders and their families. In addition, one cannot measure the psychological, economic, and social costs that years of incarceration extract from families and friends. Some analysts believe that these governmental and human costs do not outweigh the costs of crime to crime victims and the community. They dispute the idea that a prison-commercial complex is promoting the expansion of corrections.

A number of questions about incarceration warrant serious attention in the years ahead. Does incarceration have an impact—one way or the other—on the crime rate? Is incarceration rising during a period of decreased criminality because it is being promoted by economic interests? Should imprisonment be used more sparingly, only for the most serious offenders?

PART FIVE

The Juvenile Justice System

Crimes committed by juveniles are a serious national problem. *The Uniform Crime Reports* show that just over one-third of the people arrested for an index crime are under 18 years of age. Children who are

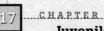

CHAPTER 17
Juvenile Justice

charged with crimes, who have been neglected by their parents, or whose behavior is judged to require official action enter the juvenile justice system, an independent process that is interrelated with the adult system.

Many of the procedures used in handling juvenile problems are similar to those used with adults, but the overriding philosophy of juvenile justice is somewhat different, and the state may intrude into the lives of children to a much greater extent. In recent years political and legal moves have been made to reduce the differences in the procedures of the two systems.

Juvenile Justice

Shortly after 11 A.M. on Tuesday, April 27, 1999, Denver police officer John Lietz received a phone call from Matthew Depew, the son of a fellow cop who lived in Littleton, Colorado. Depew told Officer Lietz that he and seventeen other Columbine High School students were trapped in a storage room off the school cafeteria, hiding from classmates with guns. Lietz could hear gunfire in the background and told Depew to barricade the door. Several times he heard the shooters trying to break down the door. Depew told Lietz that he was going to die. "Please tell my father I love him," he said (*Newsweek*, May 3, 1999:25).

For a long, tragic day, two armed teenagers—Dylan Klebold and Eric Harris—laid siege to Columbine High. When the terror ended, the killers, twelve students, and a teacher were dead; twenty-three students were wounded. The shootings in Littleton shocked the nation, not only because of the number of dead and wounded, but also because this was the ninth such incident in twenty-six months in which American teenagers had shot and killed their teachers and fellow students. The events in Alaska, Arkansas, California, Colorado, Kentucky, Mississippi, Oregon, Pennsylvania, and Tennessee were lead stories in the news for weeks.

The school shootings raised important issues concerning gun control, Internet violence, parental guidance, and education. In the wake of the shootings the country was divided over the reasons behind this outbreak of teen violence. Some people pointed to the availability of guns and the lack of parental control of their children. Others cited violence in films, television, video games, and the Internet. The horrific conduct, and the way it forced itself onto the public agenda, led to calls for fundamental reforms of juvenile justice. Predictable calls came for "getting tough" with serious offenders, as well as demands for actions to strengthen families and reduce youth alienation.

As the twenty-first century begins, crimes committed by juveniles are no longer limited to vandalism, petty theft, and drag racing. The *West Side Story* image of tough 1960s teenage hoodlums fighting each other with fists, and occasionally with knives, has been displaced by the more frightening image of contemporary juveniles who kill each other—and innocent bystanders—with guns. Moreover, well-armed juvenile offenders do not just target each other. They may commit precisely the same crimes as the worst adult offenders, including homicides, in the course of small-time robberies involving items such as team jackets and basketball shoes.

At the same time that society confronts the frightening recognition that young offenders can commit terrible acts, no consensus has been reached on how to solve this problem. Separate institutions and processes have been developed to handle crimes by juveniles, but this structure has been questioned. Should juveniles continue to be treated differently from adults when they commit crimes, assuming that juveniles can be taught to change their ways? Or should all criminals be treated alike by being tough on everyone who commits violent crimes?

Why is there a chapter on juvenile justice in this book, which has focused primarily on the justice system that deals with crimes committed by adults? The juvenile justice system is a separate but interrelated part of the broader criminal justice system. While the formal processes of juvenile justice differ from those in the adult system, the differences primarily concern emphasis. The activities and concerns of policing, courts, or corrections cannot be separated from the problems of youth. With juveniles committing a significant portion of criminal offenses, serious attention must be paid to this system.

QUESTIONS for Inquiry

- What is the extent of youth crime in the United States?
- How did the juvenile justice system develop, and what assumptions was it based on?
- What determines the jurisdiction of the juvenile justice system?
- How does the juvenile justice system operate?
- What are some of the problems facing the American system of juvenile justice?

Youth Crime in the United States

In Denver a child visiting the zoo was hit by a bullet intended by one teenager for another. A 17-year-old Salt Lake City boy was kicked and then shot to death by a group of his fellow high school students. A British tourist was killed while at a rest stop; a 13-year-old boy was one of the suspects. Such dramatic criminal acts make headlines, but are these only isolated incidents or is the United States facing a major increase in youth crime?

The juvenile crime incidents just described are rare. In a nation with thirty million people under 18, there are 2.84 million arrests of juveniles each year, with 123,400 (4 percent) for violent crime. After rising from 1988 to 1994, the juvenile violent crime rate has now returned to 1989 levels (OJJDP, 1999:115). Compare this with the thirteen million adults who are arrested for 367,000 violent crimes per year. Yet when Americans are asked to identify the two or three most serious problems facing children, they cite drugs and crime (see What Americans Think).

As shown in Figure 17.1, youths commit index crimes out of proportion to their numbers. But juveniles also commit such "youthful crimes" as curfew violations, loitering, and being a runaway. About 1 in 20 in the under-18 cohort is taken into police custody each year and nearly a million are processed by juvenile courts. Most juvenile crimes are committed by young males; only 26 percent of arrestees under 18 years of age are females (OJJDP, 1999:115). Some researchers have estimated that 1 boy in 3 will be arrested by the police at some point before his eighteenth birthday.

Explanations for the rise of youth violence have confounded many criminologists (Moore and Tonry, 1998:1–26). Between 1985 and 1994 the homicide rate among juveniles more than doubled. Juveniles aged 13–18 made up 20 percent of all arrests by police for violent crime (Cook and Laub, 1998:35). The rise in youth violence has not been limited to the United States. Since the mid-1980s an increase in youth violence also was evident in ten European countries, including England, Germany, Sweden, Italy, and France (Pfeiffer, 1998).

What Americans Think

Question "What do you think are the two or three most serious problems facing children in America today?"

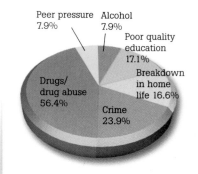

SOURCE: U.S. Department of Justice, Bureau of Justice Statistics, *Sourcebook of Criminal Justice Statistics, 1997* (Washington, D.C.: Government Printing Office, 1998), Table 2.5.

Violence committed by juveniles has fallen to 1989 levels, yet the public believes it is a major national problem. Legislators have argued for tougher policies to deal with juvenile delinquents.

FIGURE **17.1** **Percentage of arrests of persons under 21 years**

Although they make up fewer than 10 percent of the population, those aged 15 to 21 are arrested for index crimes out of proportion to their numbers. Property offenses are those most often committed by young people, although the number of violent crimes committed by this group is rising.

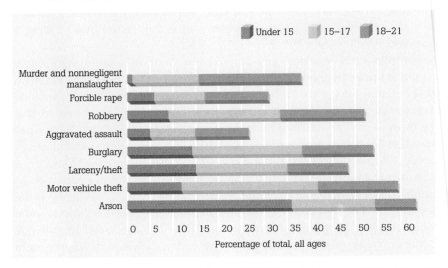

SOURCE: U.S. Department of Justice, *Crime in the United States—1998* (Washington, D.C.: Government Printing Office, 1999).

In America the "epidemic" of violent youth crime coincided with an increase in drug arrests, particularly in nonwhite urban areas. As Alfred Blumstein points out, this reflected in part the extent to which drug enforcement focused on street drug markets in inner-city areas, which more often involved young black drug dealers. He suggests that as more juveniles were recruited into the drug trade, they armed themselves with guns and used those firearms in battles over market turf. With the under-18 cohort expected to enlarge during the next decade it is expected that violent crime will rise (Blumstein, 1996).

Youth gangs have become another dangerous presence in most American cities. Gangs such as the Black P Stone Nation, CRIPS (Common Revolution in Progress), and Bloods first came to police attention in the 1970s. Since then there has been a proliferation of gangs across the country. The National Youth Gang Survey estimates that there are more than thirty-one thousand gangs with 846,000 members (OJJDP, 1999:77). During the past decade not only have their numbers increased but they also have moved into suburban and rural areas. Many of the gangs that are now in the adult correctional system have their younger counterparts on the streets. Today's gangs have become a major element in the drug trade and the crimes of violence it spawns.

As frightening as the problem of juvenile crime is today, some experts are concerned about the future. Looming on the horizon is what John DiIulio has called "a demographic crime bomb" (Traub, 1996:50). DiIulio and other criminologists point to a thirty-nine-million-strong youth cohort, the largest since the 1950s, whose members are now under 15 years old and who will enter their crime-prone years about 2005. Not only is this group large, but a greater portion of its members also may be exposed to social factors that contribute to youth crime—single-parent households, child abuse, drugs, poor inner-city schools, and poverty. At the same time, government has cut back on programs designed to help this population.

Juvenile delinquency, neglect, and dependency have been concerns since the beginning of the Republic, yet not until the early twentieth century did a separate system to deal with these problems evolve. The contemporary juvenile justice system has gone through a major shift of emphasis.

CHECK POINT

① **Why do criminologists believe there will be a great increase in youth crime by the year 2005?**

(Answers are at the end of the chapter.)

The Development of Juvenile Justice

The system and philosophy of juvenile justice that began in the United States during the social reform period of the late nineteenth century remained unchallenged until the Supreme Court's 1967 decision in *In re Gault* ushered in the juvenile rights period. The idea that children should be treated differently from adults originated in the common law and in the chancery courts of England.

The common law had long prescribed that children under 7 years of age were incapable of felonious intent and were therefore not criminally responsible. Children aged 7 to 14 could be held accountable only if it could be shown that they understood the consequences of their actions.

The English chancery courts, established during the Middle Ages, heard only civil cases—mainly concerning property. However, under the doctrine of ***parens patriae,*** which held the king to be the father of the realm, the chancery courts exercised protective jurisdiction over all children, particularly those involved in questions of dependency, neglect, and property. At this time juvenile offenders were dealt with by the criminal courts. But the concept of *parens patriae* was important for the development of juvenile justice, because it legitimized actions of the state on behalf of the child.

The English procedures were maintained in the American colonies and continued into the nineteenth century. The earliest attempt by a colony to deal with problem children was passage of the Massachusetts Stubborn Child Law in 1646. With this law, the Puritans of the Massachusetts Bay Colony imposed the view that the child was evil and emphasized the need of the family to discipline and raise youths. Those who would not obey their parents were dealt with by the law.

Table 17.1 outlines the shifts in how the United States has dealt with the problems of youth. Five periods of American juvenile justice history can be defined. Each period was characterized by changes in juvenile justice that reflected the social, intellectual, and political currents of the time. During the past two hundred years, population shifts from rural to urban areas, immigration, developments in the social sciences, political reform movements, and the continuing problem of youth crime have all influenced how Americans have treated juveniles.

parens patriae
The state as parent; the state as guardian and protector of all citizens (such as juveniles) who are unable to protect themselves.

CHECK POINT

2. Until what age were children exempt from criminal responsibility under common law?
3. What was the jurisdiction of the English chancery court?
4. What is meant by the doctrine of *parens patriae*?

The Refuge Period (1824–1899)

As the population of American cities began to grow in the half-century following independence, the problem of youth crime and neglect was a concern for reformers. Just as the Quakers of Philadelphia had been instrumental during the early 1800s in reforming correctional practices, other groups supported changes to educate and protect youths. These reformers focused their efforts primarily on the urban immigrant poor, seeking to have parents declared "unfit" if their children roamed the streets and were apparently "out of control." Not all such children were engaged in criminal acts, but the reformers believed that children whose parents did not discipline and train them to abide by the rules of society would end up in prison. The state's power was to be used to prevent delinquency. The solution was to create institutions where these children could learn good work and study habits, live in a disciplined and healthy environment, and develop "character."

TABLE 17.1 Juvenile justice developments in the United States

PERIOD	MAJOR DEVELOPMENTS	CAUSES AND INFLUENCES	JUVENILE JUSTICE SYSTEM
Puritan 1646–1824	Massachusetts Stubborn Child Law (1646)	A Puritan view of child as evil B Economically marginal agrarian society	Law provides: A Symbolic standard of maturity B Support for family as economic unit
Refuge 1824–1899	Institutionalization of deviants; House of Refuge in New York established (1825) for delinquent and dependent children	A Enlightenment B Immigration and industrialization	Child seen as helpless, in need of state intervention.
Juvenile court 1899–1960	Establishment of separate legal system for juveniles; Illinois Juvenile Court Act (1899)	A Reformism and rehabilitative ideology B Increased immigration, urbanization, large–scale industrialization	Juvenile court institutionalized legal irresponsibility of child.
Juvenile rights 1960–1980	Increased "legalization" of juvenile law; *Gault* decision (1967); Juvenile Justice and Delinquency Prevention Act (1974) calls for deinstitutionalization of status offenders	A Criticism of juvenile justice system on humane grounds B Civil rights movement by disadvantaged groups	Movement to define and protect rights as well as to provide services to children.
Crime control 1980–present	Concern for victims, punishment for serious offenders, transfer to adult court of serious offenders, protection of children from physical and sexual abuse	A More conservative public attitudes and policies B Focus on serious crimes by repeat offenders	System more formal, restrictive, punitive; increased percentage of police referrals to court; incarcerated youths stay longer periods.

SOURCE: Adapted from U.S. Department of Justice, *A Preliminary National Assessment of the Status Offender and the Juvenile Justice System* (Washington, D.C.: Government Printing Office, 1980), 29; and Barry Krisberg, Ira M. Schwartz, Paul Litsky, and James Austin, "The Watershed of Juvenile Justice Reform," *Crime and Delinquency* 32 (January 1986), 5–38.

The first of these institutions was the House of Refuge of New York, which opened in 1825. This half-prison and half-school housed destitute and orphaned children as well as those convicted of crimes (Friedman, 1993:164). Similar facilities followed in Boston, Philadelphia, and Baltimore. Children were placed in these homes by court order usually because of neglect or vagrancy. They often stayed until they were old enough to be legally regarded as adults. The houses were run according to a strict program of work, study, and discipline.

Recognizing the right of the state to place children in such institutions, the Pennsylvania Supreme Court in 1838 upheld the doctrine of *parens patriae*. A father brought a suit, objecting to the commitment of his daughter (by his wife without his knowledge) to the Philadelphia House of Refuge as an "incorrigible." The justices said that the courts as guardians of the community could supersede the desires of the natural parents who were not equal to the task of rearing a child. If parents fail to fulfill their responsibility of training their children to be productive, law-abiding adults, the state should assume it by training the children "to industry (and) by imbuing their minds with the principles of morality and religion."

Some states created "reform schools" to provide the discipline and education needed by wayward youth in a "homelike" atmosphere, usually in rural areas. The first, the Lyman School for Boys, opened in Westboro, Massachusetts, in 1848. A similar Massachusetts reform school for girls was opened in 1855 for "the instruction . . . and reformation, of exposed, helpless, evil disposed and vicious girls" (Friedman, 1993:164). Institutional programs began in New York in 1849, Ohio in 1850, and in Maine, Rhode Island, and Michigan in 1906.

In New York, the Children's Aid Society was created in 1853. The society emphasized the need to place neglected and delinquent children in private homes. Like the reform advocates of adult corrections, the children's aid societies emphasized placement in rural areas, away from the crime and bad influences of the city. Farmers had an economic incentive to take in these extra "hands," who arrived on "orphan trains" throughout the Midwest.

Despite these reforms, children could still be arrested, detained, tried, and imprisoned. Even in states that had institutions for juveniles, the criminal justice process for children was the same as for adults.

The Juvenile Court Period (1899–1960)

With most states providing services to neglected youth by the end of the nineteenth century, the problem of juvenile criminality became the focus of attention. Progressive reformers pushed for the state to provide individualized care and treatment to deviants of all kinds—adult criminals, the mentally ill, juvenile delinquents. They urged adoption of probation, treatment, indeterminate sentences, and parole for adult offenders and succeeded in establishing similar programs for juveniles.

Referred to as the "child savers," these upper-middle-class reformers sought to use the power of the state to "save" children from a life of crime (Platt, 1977). They were influenced by a concern about the role of environmental factors on behavior and a belief that benevolent state action could solve social problems. They also believed the claim of the new social sciences that they could treat the problems underlying deviance.

Reformers wanted a separate juvenile court system that could address the problems of individual youths using flexible procedures that, as one reformer

Three boys sit in the Denver court chambers of Judge Ben Lindsey, an early leader of the juvenile justice movement. Lindsey urged that the keynotes of the court be empathy, trust, and the working together of court officials, parents, and children.

said, "banish entirely all thought of crime and punishment" (Rothman, 1980:213). They put their idea into action with the creation of the juvenile court.

Passage of the Juvenile Court Act by Illinois in 1899 established the first comprehensive system of juvenile justice. The act placed under one jurisdiction cases of dependency, neglect, and delinquency ("incorrigibles and children threatened by immoral associations as well as criminal lawbreakers") for children under 16. The act had four major elements:

- A separate court for delinquent, dependent, and neglected children.
- Special legal procedures that were less adversarial than were found in the adult system.
- Separation of children from adults in all portions of the justice system.
- Programs of probation to assist the courts in deciding what is in the best interest of the state and the child.

Activists such as Jane Addams and Julia Lathrop, both of the settlement house movement, Henry Thurston, a social work educator, and the National Congress of Mothers successfully promoted the juvenile court concept, so that ten states by 1904 had implemented procedures similar to those of Illinois. By 1917 all but three states provided for a juvenile court.

The philosophy of the juvenile court derived from the idea that the state should deal with a child who broke the law much as a wise parent would deal with a wayward child. The doctrine of *parens patriae* again helped legitimize the system. Procedures would be informal and private, records would be confidential, children would be detained apart from adults, and probation and social worker staffs would be appointed. Even the vocabulary and physical setting of the juvenile system were changed to emphasize diagnosis and treatment rather than findings of guilt. The term *criminal behavior* was replaced by *delinquent behavior* when it referred to the acts of children. But the new term also emphasized that the juvenile court could deal with **status offenses,** behaviors that were not criminal if committed by adults. Status offenses might include smoking cigarettes, consensual sexual activity, truancy, or living a "wayward, idle, and dissolute life" (Feld, 1993:203). The terminology reflected the underlying belief that these children could be "cured" and returned to society as law-abiding citizens.

status offense

Any act committed by a juvenile that is considered unacceptable for a child, such as truancy or running away from home, but that would not be a crime if it were committed by an adult.

By separating juveniles from the adult criminal justice system and providing a rehabilitative alternative to punishment, the juvenile courts rejected not only the criminal law's scope but also its due process protections. Because procedures were not to be adversarial, lawyers were unnecessary; psychologists and social workers, who could determine the juvenile's underlying behavior problem, were the main professionals attached to the system. Judge Julian Mack, a pioneer of the juvenile justice movement, summarized the questions to be placed before a juvenile court: "The problem for determination by the judge is not, has this boy or girl committed a specific wrong, but what is he, how has he become what he is, and what had best be done in his interest and in the interest of the State to save him from a downward career" (Mack, 1909:119). But these reforms were instituted in a system where children lacked the due process rights held by adults.

The Juvenile Rights Period (1960–1980)

Until the early 1960s, few questioned the necessity for the sweeping powers of juvenile justice officials. Then, with the due process revolution expanding the rights of adult defendants, lawyers and scholars began to criticize the extensive discretion given to juvenile justice officials. In essence these critics believed that the juvenile justice system had failed to fulfill its promise.

More appeals of juvenile court decisions began to go to the U.S. Supreme Court. In *Kent v. United States* (1966) the Court extended due process rights to children. In this case a 16-year-old boy was sent from the juvenile to the adult court without his lawyer present. He was convicted of rape and robbery in the adult court and sentenced to a thirty- to ninety-year prison term. The Supreme Court found the procedure for transferring the case to the adult court to be inadequate and ruled that juveniles had the right to counsel at a hearing at which a juvenile judge may waive jurisdiction and pass the case to the adult court.

In re Gault (1967) extended due process rights to juveniles. Fifteen-year-old Gerald Gault had been sentenced to six years in a state training school for making a prank phone call. Had he been an adult, the maximum punishment for making such a call would have been a fine of $5 to $50 or imprisonment for two months at most. Gault was convicted and sentenced in an informal proceeding without being represented by counsel. The justices held that a child in a delinquency hearing must be given certain procedural rights, including notice of the charges, right to counsel, right to confront and cross-examine witnesses, and protection against self-incrimination. Writing for the majority, Justice Abe Fortas emphasized that due process rights and procedures have a place in juvenile justice: "Under our Constitution the condition of being a boy does not justify a kangaroo court."

The precedent-setting *Gault* decision was followed by a series of cases further defining the rights of juveniles. In the case of *In re Winship* (1970) the Supreme Court held that proof must be established "beyond a reasonable doubt" and not on "a preponderance of the evidence" before a juvenile may be classified as a delinquent for committing an act that would be a crime if it were committed by an adult. The Court was not willing to give juveniles every due process right: it held in *McKeiver v. Pennsylvania* (1971) that "trial by jury in the juvenile court's adjudicative stage is not a constitutional requirement." But in *Breed v. Jones* (1975) the Court extended the protection against double jeopardy to juveniles by requiring that, before a case is adjudicated in juvenile court, a hearing must be held to determine if it should be transferred to the adult court.

In re Gault (1967)
Juveniles have the right to counsel, to confront and examine accusers, and to have adequate notice of charges when there is the possibility of confinement as a punishment.

In re Winship (1970)
The standard of proof beyond a reasonable doubt applies to juvenile delinquency proceedings.

McKeiver v. Pennsylvania (1971)
Juveniles do not have a constitutional right to a jury trial.

Breed v. Jones (1975)
Juveniles cannot be found delinquent in juvenile court and then transferred to adult court without a hearing on the transfer; to do so violates the protection against double jeopardy.

Although the court decisions seem to have placed the rights of juveniles on a par with those of adults, critics have charged that the states have not fully implemented these rights. The law on the books is different from the law in action. Most notably, writes Barry Feld, "In many states half or less of all juveniles receive the assistance of counsel to which they are constitutionally entitled" (1993:239).

Another area of change concerned status offenders—juveniles who have committed acts that are not illegal if they are committed by an adult, such as skipping school or running away from home. In 1974 Congress passed the Juvenile Justice and Delinquency Prevention Act, which included provisions for taking status offenders out of corrections institutions. Since then efforts have been made to divert such children out of the system, to reduce the possibility of incarceration, and to rewrite status offense laws.

As juvenile crime rates continued to rise during the 1970s, the public called for tougher approaches in dealing with delinquents. In the 1980s, at the same time that stricter sanctions were imposed on adult offenders, juvenile justice policies shifted more directly to crime control.

The Crime Control Period (1980–Present)

Policies on juvenile crime have shifted since 1980 to an emphasis on crime control. With the public demanding a "crackdown on crime," legislators have responded by changing the system. Greater attention is now being focused on repeat offenders, with policy makers calling for harsher punishment for juveniles who commit crimes.

Schall v. Martin (1984)
Juveniles can be held in preventive detention if there is concern that they may commit additional crimes while awaiting court action.

In *Schall v. Martin* (1984), the Supreme Court significantly departed from the trend toward increased juvenile rights. Fourteen-year-old Gregory Martin was arrested in New York City and held in a secure detention facility awaiting a hearing on robbery and weapons charges. The Court upheld the constitutionality of New York's law allowing the preventive detention of juveniles. Noting that any attempt to structure such rights "must be qualified by the recognition that juveniles, unlike adults, are always in some form of custody," the Court confirmed that the general notion of *parens patriae* was a primary basis for the juvenile court, equal in importance to the Court's desire to protect the community from crime. Thus, juveniles may be held in preventive detention before trial if they are deemed a "risk" to the community.

The *Schall* decision reflects the ambivalence permeating the juvenile justice system. On one side are the liberal reformers, who call for increased procedural and substantive legal protections for juveniles accused of crime. On the other side are conservatives devoted to crime control policies and alarmed by the rise in juvenile crime.

The present crime control policy has brought many more juveniles to be tried in adult courts. As noted by Alex Kotlowitz, "the crackdown on children has gone well beyond those accused of violent crimes" (1994:40). Data from the National Juvenile Court Data Archive show delinquency cases adjudicated in the adult criminal courts to have increased from sixty-five hundred in 1987 to ten thousand in 1996 (OJJDP, 1999:170).

In spite of the increasingly tough policies directed at juvenile offenders, changes that occurred during the juvenile rights period continue to have a profound impact. Lawyers are now routinely present at court hearings and other stages of the process, adding a note of formality that was not present thirty years ago. Status offenders seldom end up in secure, punitive environments such as training schools. The juvenile justice system looks more like the adult justice system than it did, but it still is less formal. Its stated intention is also less harsh: to keep juveniles in the community whenever possible.

Public support for a get-tough stance toward older juveniles seems to be growing. The juvenile court, where the use of discretion and the desire to rehabilitate were uppermost, has become a system of rules and procedures similar to adult courts. With deserved punishment more prominent as a correctional goal, more severe sentences are being given to juveniles who are repeat offenders. Examine how Norway deals with youth crime by reading the Comparative Perspective (p. 583).

POINT

⑤ **What was the function of a House of Refuge?**

⑥ **What were the major elements of the Illinois Juvenile Court Act of 1899?**

⑦ **What was the main point of the decision in *In re Gault*?**

The Juvenile Justice System

Juvenile justice operates through a variety of procedures in different states; even different counties within the same states will vary. The offenses committed by juveniles are mostly violations of state laws, so there is little federal involvement in the juvenile justice system. Still, an overall national pattern can be discerned. In general, the system functions through many of the existing organizations of the state adult criminal justice system but often in specialized juvenile programs. For instance, although some large cities have juvenile sections in their police departments, the patrol officer usually has contact with delinquents when a disturbance or crime has been reported. In many states, special probation officers work with juveniles, but they function as part of the larger probation service. Some correctional systems maintain separate facilities for children but are still organized under a commissioner who is responsible for both adult and juvenile institutions.

Even though differences exist from state to state or county to county, the juvenile justice system is characterized by two key factors: (1) the age of clients and (2) the categories of cases under juvenile instead of adult court jurisdiction.

Age of Clients

Age normally determines whether a person is processed through the juvenile or adult justice system. The upper age limit for a juvenile varies from 16 to 18: in thirty-eight states and the District of Columbia it is the eighteenth birthday; in eight states, the seventeenth; and in the remainder, the sixteenth. As discussed in Chapter 3, common law assumes that children under the age of 7 are incapable of committing crimes. Between 7 and 14, they are thought to have the capacity for criminal behavior. Over the age of 14, they are held responsible for their actions.

In forty-nine states, judges have the discretion to transfer juveniles to adult courts through a waiver hearing. Figure 17.2 shows the age at which juveniles can be transferred to adult court by a judge's giving up jurisdiction over the case.

perspective

The Hidden Juvenile Justice System in Norway

Norway has a social worker-dominated juvenile justice system. Yet, as the writer points out, where care and protection are the goals of the system, power and secrecy prevail. Aspects of the American system, as it was before the Supreme Court insisted that juvenile justice be conducted with due process of law, are seen in Norway.

There is no punishment for crimes in Norway for a child who is under fifteen. No special courts have been established with jurisdiction to try criminal cases against juvenile offenders. Older teenagers may be tried in ordinary courts of law and sentenced to prison. Sentences for most crimes, however, consist of only a suspended sentence or probation or several months in an open prison.

In practice, the public prosecutor, who represents the police, will transfer the juvenile case directly to a division of the "social office," the *barnevern*—literally, child protection. Alternatively, the judge, after the trial, will refer the youth to the *barnevern*. Police evidence is turned over to the social workers, not for prosecution, but for "treatment."

The usual first step in treatment is that the *barnevern* takes emergency custody of the child and places the child in a juvenile institution, or *ungdomshjem* (youth home). If the parents or guardians do not give consent, there will be a meeting of the . . . child welfare committee. An attorney may represent the parents at this stage; there is no legal fee in serious cases. At the meeting [the social welfare committee] will hear the lawyer's and parents' arguments against the placement. The concern is not with evidence about the crimes but, rather, with appropriate treatment for the child. . . .

The *barnevern* is most often associated in the public mind with handling of cases of child abuse and neglect. In such a case, the board will turn over custody of the child to the *barnevern* social workers who will place the child in a foster home or youth home. Once the custody is removed from the parents, the burden of proof is on the parents to retain custody. Social workers in alcoholism treatment are well aware of numerous such cases of recovering alcoholics who, even after recovery, have been unable to retain custody of their children. . . .

In contrast to the American juvenile court, the Norwegian model is wholly social worker dominated. The function of the judge is to preside over the hearing and to maintain proper legal protocol, but it is the child welfare office that presents the evidence and recommendations and directs the course of the case. The five laypersons who constitute the [social welfare committee] are advised by the child welfare office well before the hearing of the "facts" of the case. Before the hearing, the youth will have been placed in a youth home or mental institution "on an emergency basis"; the parents' rights to custody will have already been terminated.

The process of the hearing itself is thus a mere formality after the fact. . . . [There] is an overwhelming unanimity among members of the board and between the board and social worker administrators. . . . [All] the arguments of the clients and of their lawyers [seem to] "fall on deaf ears." . . .

Proof of guilt brought before the committee will generally consist of a copy of the police report of the offenses admitted by the accused and a school report written by the principal after he or she has been informed of the lawbreaking. Reports by the *barnevern*-appointed psychologist and social worker are also included. The *barnevern*, in its statement, has summarized the reports from the point of view of its arguments (usually for placement). Otherwise, the reports are ignored.

The hearing itself is a far cry from standard courtroom procedure. The youth and his or her parents may address the board briefly. The attorney sums up the case for a return to the home. Expert witnesses may be called and questioned by the board concerning, for instance, their treatment recommendations.

Following the departure of the parties concerned, the *barnevern* office presents what amounts to "the case for the prosecution." There is no opportunity to rebut the testimony and no opportunity for cross-examination. . . .

Placement in an institution is typically for an indefinite period. No notice of the disposition of the matter is given to the press. This absence of public accountability may serve more to protect the social office than the child.

Children receive far harsher treatments than do adults for similar offenses. For instance, for a young adult first offender the typical penalty for thievery is a suspended sentence. A child, however, may languish in an institution for years for the same offense.

A *barnevern*'s first work ought to be to create the best possible childhood. However, the *barnevern* also has a control function in relation to both the parents and the child,

and the controller often feels a stronger duty to the community than to the parents and child. The fact of institutionalization of children with behavior problems clearly reflects this social control function. This process has been going on for some time. Approximately half of the 8,174 children under care of the child welfare committee were placed outside the home and the other half placed under protective watch. . . .

The Norwegian *barnevern* is a powerful body vested with the responsibility of child protection. When this department wishes to remove a child from the home, the child welfare committee is called into session. Then with a semblance of legal formality, the decision is put into effect. The child is placed outside the home "until further notice." . . .

The system of justice for children accused of crimes or behavioral problems is therefore often very harsh in Norway. This is in sharp contrast to the criminal justice system in general, which is strikingly lenient. Where punishment is called treatment, however, the right of the state can almost become absolute. The fact that the state is represented by social work administrators creates a sharp ethical conflict for those whose first duty is to the client.

What we see in Norway today is a process of juvenile justice that has not changed substantially since the 1950s. Due to flaws within the system, including the lack of external controls, the best intentions of social workers "have gone awry." Where care and protection were intended, power and secrecy have prevailed. Juvenile justice in Norway today is the justice of America yesterday.

SOURCE: Katherine Van Wormer, "The Hidden Juvenile Justice System in Norway: A Journey Back in Time," *Federal Probation* (March 1990), 57–61.

FIGURE 17.2   **The youngest age at which juveniles may be transferred to adult criminal court by waiver of juvenile jurisdiction**

The waiver provisions of states vary greatly, and no clear regional or other factor explains the differences.

Legend:
- No specific age
- 10 years
- 12 years
- 13 years
- 14 years
- 15 years
- 16 years
- No judicial waiver provision

SOURCE: U.S. Department of Justice, Office of Juvenile Justice and Delinquency Prevention, *Trying Juveniles as Adults in Criminal Court* (Washington, D.C.: Government Printing Office, 1998), 14–15.

Categories of Cases under Juvenile Court Jurisdiction

Four types of cases are under the jurisdiction of the juvenile justice system: delinquency, status offenses, neglect, and dependency. Mixing together young criminals and children who suffer from their parents' inadequacies is a practice that dates from the early history of juvenile justice.

Connecticut laws outlining the powers of the juvenile court illustrate the range of authority of the system. As the law provides,

> Juvenile matters include all proceedings concerning uncared-for, neglected, or dependent children and youth and delinquent children within this state, termination of parental rights of children committed to a state agency, matters concerning families with service needs and contested termination of parental rights transferred from the probate court, but do not include matters of guardianship and adoption or matters affecting property rights of any child or youth over which the probate court has jurisdiction (Connecticut, General Laws, Sec.47b–21).

Chicago police discovered nineteen children living in this squalid, rodent-infested apartment. The kitchen stove did not work, and the children were sharing food with dogs. Six adults were charged with contributing to the neglect of children.

Delinquent children have committed acts that if committed by an adult would be criminal—for example, auto theft, robbery, or assault. Juvenile courts handle about 1.8 million delinquency cases each year, 77 percent involving males and 30 percent involving African Americans. Among the criminal charges brought before the juvenile court, 22 percent are for crimes against the person, 50 percent for property offenses, 10 percent for drug law violations, and 19 percent for public order offenses (OJJDP, 1999:144). Table 17.2 shows the distribution of delinquency cases that are referred to juvenile court.

Recall that status offenses are acts that are illegal only if they are committed by juveniles. Status offenders have not violated a penal code; instead they are charged with being ungovernable or incorrigible: as runaways, truants, or persons in need of supervision (**PINS**). Status offenders make up about 10 percent of the juvenile court caseload. Although females are charged with only 15 percent of delinquency cases, they are involved in 42 percent of the status offense cases.

Some states do not distinguish between delinquent offenders and status offenders; they label both as juvenile delinquents. Those judged to be ungovernable and those judged to be robbers may be sent to the same correctional institution. Beginning in the early 1960s, many state legislatures attempted to distinguish status offenders and to exempt them from a criminal record. In states that have decriminalized status offenses, juveniles who participate in these activities may now be classified as dependent children and placed in the care of child-protective agencies.

Juvenile justice also deals with problems of neglect and dependency—situations in which children are viewed as being hurt through no fault of their own because their parents have failed to provide a proper environment for them. Such situations have been the concern of most juvenile justice systems since the beginning of the twentieth century. The state's proper role was seen as acting as a parent to a child whose own parents are unable or unwilling to provide proper care. Illinois, for example, defines a **neglected child** as one who is not receiving proper care because of some action or inaction of his or her parents. This may include not being sent to school, not receiving medical care, being abandoned, living in an injurious environment, or not receiving some other care necessary for the child's well-being. A **dependent child** either is without a parent or guardian or is not receiving proper care because of the physical or mental disability of that person. The law governing neglected and dependent children is broad and includes situations in which the child is viewed as a victim of adult behavior.

Nationally about 75 percent of the cases referred to the juvenile courts are delinquency cases, 20 percent of which are status offenses. About 20 percent are dependency and neglect cases, and about 5 percent involve special proceedings, such as adoption. The system, then, deals with both criminal and noncriminal

TABLE 17.2

Distribution of delinquency cases referred to juvenile court

About 75 percent of the juvenile court caseload involves criminal charges against youths.

PERCENTAGE OF TOTAL CASES REFERRED	
22% **Crimes against persons**	
Homicide	less than 1%
Forcible rape	less than 1
Robbery	2
Aggravated assault	5
Simple assault	12
Other personal offenses	1
Other violent sex offenses	1
50% **Property crimes**	
Burglary	8%
Larceny-theft	24
Motor vehicle theft	3
Arson	1
Vandalism	7
Trespassing	4
Stolen property offenses	2
Other property offenses	2
10% **Drug violations**	10%
19% **Public order offenses**	
Obstruction of justice	7%
Disorderly conduct	5
Weapons offenses	2
Liquor law violations	1
Nonviolent sex offenses	1
Other public order offenses	3

SOURCE: U.S. Department of Justice, Office of Juvenile Justice and Delinquency Prevention, *Juvenile Offenders and Victims: 1999 National Report* (Washington, D.C.: Government Printing Office, 1999), 144.

delinquent
A child who has committed an act that if committed by an adult would be criminal.

PINS
Acronym for "person in need of supervision," a term that designates juveniles who are either status offenders or thought to be on the verge of trouble.

neglected child
A child who is not receiving proper care because of some action or inaction of his or her parents.

dependent child
A child who has no parent or guardian or whose parents are unable to give proper care.

cases. Often juveniles who have done nothing wrong are categorized, either officially or in the public mind, as delinquents. In some states little effort is made in pre-judicial detention facilities or in social service agencies to separate the classes of juveniles.

CHECK POINT

⑧ **What are the jurisdictional criteria for the juvenile court?**

Juvenile Justice Process

Underlying the juvenile justice system is the philosophy that the police, judges, and correctional officials should be primarily concerned with the interests of the child. Prevention of delinquency is the system's justification for intervening in the lives of juveniles who are involved in either status or criminal offenses.

In theory at least, juvenile proceedings are to be conducted in a nonadversarial environment, and the juvenile court is a place where the judge, social workers, clinicians, and probation officers work together to diagnose the child's problem and select a treatment program to attack that problem.

Juvenile justice is a bureaucracy based on an ideology of social work and is staffed primarily by persons who think of themselves as members of the helping professions. Even the recent emphasis on crime control and punishment has not removed the treatment philosophy from most juvenile justice systems. However, implementation of this philosophy may be stymied by political pressures and limits on resources so that the focus is on punishing offenders instead of emphasizing the prevention of delinquency.

Like the adult criminal justice system, juvenile justice functions within a context of exchange relationships between officials of various government and private agencies that influence decisions. The juvenile court must deal not only with children and their parents, but also with patrol officers, probation officers, welfare officials, social workers, psychologists, and the heads of treatment institutions—all of whom have their own goals, perceptions of delinquency, and concepts of treatment.

How are juveniles processed by the juvenile justice system? Figure 17.3 outlines the sequence of steps that are taken from the point of police investigation through to correctional disposition. As you examine this figure, compare the procedures with those of the criminal justice system for adults. Note the various options available to decision makers and the extensive discretion that they may exercise.

Police Interface

Many police departments, especially in cities and larger towns, have special juvenile units. A survey of law enforcement agencies with more than one hundred sworn officers found that 93 percent had special units concerned with drug education in the schools, 89 percent had units working on juvenile crime, and 60 percent had units dealing with youth gangs (BJS, 1998b).

FIGURE

17.3 The Juvenile Justice System

Decision makers have many options for the disposition of juvenile offenders compared with the criminal justice system for adults.

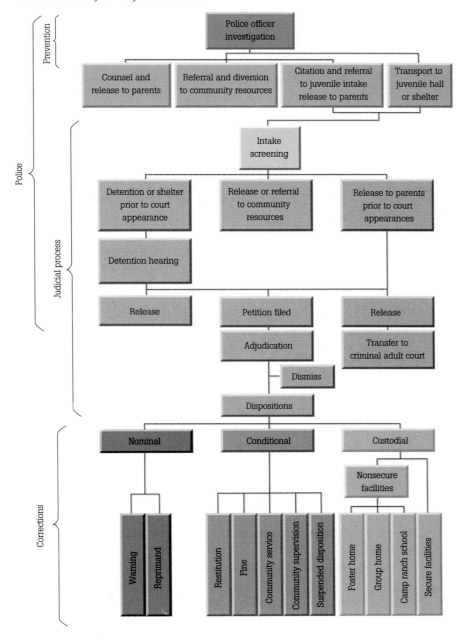

SOURCE: National Advisory Commission on Criminal Justice Standards and Goals, *Report of the Task Force on Juvenile Justice and Delinquency Prevention* (Washington, D.C.: Law Enforcement Assistance Administration, 1976).

The juvenile officer is often selected and trained to relate to youths, is knowledgeable about relevant legal issues, and is sensitive to the special needs of young offenders. This officer is also an important link between the police and other community institutions, such as schools and other organizations serving young people.

Most complaints against juveniles are brought by the police, although they may be initiated by an injured party, school officials, or even the parents. The

17.4 Disposition of juveniles taken into police custody

The police have discretion in the disposition of juvenile arrest cases. What factors may influence how a case is disposed?

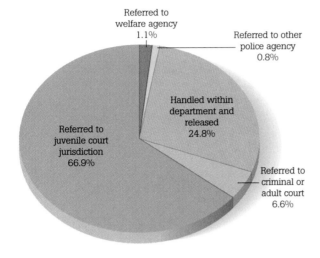

Referred to welfare agency
1.1%

Referred to other police agency
0.8%

Handled within department and released
24.8%

Referred to juvenile court jurisdiction
66.9%

Referred to criminal or adult court
6.6%

SOURCE: U.S. Department of Justice, Bureau of Justice Statistics, *Sourcebook of Criminal Justice Statistics, 1998* (Washington, D.C.: Government Printing Office, 1999), Table 4.25

police must make three major decisions with regard to the processing of juveniles:

❶ Whether to take the child into custody.
❷ Whether to request that the child be detained following apprehension.
❸ Whether to refer the child to court.

The police exercise enormous discretion in these decisions. They do extensive screening and make informal adjustments in the street and at the stationhouse. In communities and neighborhoods where the police have developed close relationships with the residents or where policy dictates, the police may deal with violations by giving warnings to the juveniles and notifying their parents. Figure 17.4 shows the disposition of juveniles taken into police custody.

Initial decisions about what to do with a suspected offender are influenced by such factors as the officer's attitude toward the juvenile, the juvenile's family, the offense, and the court; the predominant attitude of the community; and the officer's conception of his or her own role.

A classic study of the police in a metropolitan city of 450,000 revealed that the choice of disposition of juvenile cases at the stage of arrest depended mostly on the prior record of the child, but second in importance was the offender's demeanor (Piliavin and Briar, 1976:197). Juveniles who had committed minor offenses but were respectful and contrite were defined by the officers as worthy candidates for rehabilitation and were given an informal reprimand. Those who were argumentative or surly were defined as "punks" who needed to be taught a lesson through arrest. The researchers found that only 4 percent of the cooperative youths were arrested, in comparison with 67 percent of those who were uncooperative.

To summarize, several key factors influence how the police dispose of a case of juvenile delinquency:

❶ The seriousness of the offense.
❷ The willingness of the parents to cooperate and to discipline their child.
❸ The child's behavioral history as reflected in school and police records.
❹ The extent to which the child and the parents insist on a formal court hearing.
❺ The local political and social norms concerning dispositions in such cases.

In dealing with juveniles, police confront questions on whether or not the *Miranda* warnings and the *Mapp* unreasonable search and seizure rulings apply. Although the language of these decisions is not explicit, most jurisdictions now provide the *Miranda* protections. But questions remain as to the ability of juveniles to waive these rights. In 1979 the Supreme Court ruled in *Fare v. Michael C.* that a child may waive his or her rights to an attorney and to protections against self-incrimination. But the Court said that juvenile court judges must evaluate the totality of circumstances under which the minor made these decisions to ensure that they were voluntary.

On the issue of unreasonable searches and seizures as required by the Fourth Amendment, the Court has not been as forthcoming. State courts interpreted *Gault* to extend these provisions, but in 1985 the Supreme Court ruled in

Fare v. Michael C. (1979)

By examining the totality of the circumstances, trial court judges must evaluate the voluntariness of juveniles' waiving their rights to an attorney and to protections against self-incrimination.

New Jersey v. T.L.O. that school officials can search students and their lockers. The justices recognized that children do have Fourth Amendment rights, yet a search could be viewed as reasonable if it (1) is based on a suspicion of lawbreaking and (2) is required to maintain order, safety, and discipline in the school.

Although young people commit many serious crimes, the juvenile function of police work is concerned largely with order maintenance. In most incidents of this sort the law is ambiguous, and blame cannot easily be assigned. Many offenses committed by juveniles that involve physical or monetary damage are minor infractions: breaking windows, hanging around the business district, disturbing the peace, adolescent sexual behavior, and shoplifting. Here the function of the investigating officer is not so much to solve crimes as to handle the often legally uncertain complaints involving juveniles. The officer seeks both to satisfy the complainant and to keep the youth from future trouble. Given this emphasis on settling cases within the community—rather than on strictly enforcing the law—the police power to arrest is a weapon that can be used to deter juveniles from criminal activity and to encourage them to conform to the law.

Intake Screening at the Court

The juvenile court processing of delinquency cases begins with a referral in the form of a petition, not an arrest warrant as in the adult system. Eighty-five percent of the petitions are brought by law enforcement agencies, but parents, school officials, social service agencies, and victims also make referrals to the court.

When a petition is filed, an intake hearing is held, presided over by a hearing officer who is often an attorney, a probation officer, or social worker. During this stage, the hearing officer reviews the case to determine whether the alleged facts are sufficient for the juvenile court to take jurisdiction or whether some other action would be in the child's interest.

Nationally, 45 percent of all referrals are disposed of at this stage, without formal processing by a judge. **Diversion** is the process of screening children out of the system without a decision by the court. In 47 percent of these cases the charges are dismissed and about one-third are diverted to an informal probation, 6 percent are placed in a mental health facility or other treatment facility, while 21 percent are dealt with through some agreed-upon alternative sanction.

Pretrial Procedures

When a decision is made to refer the case to the court (55 percent of cases) an initial hearing is held. Here, the juveniles are informed of their rights and that if a plea is given it must be voluntary.

If the juvenile is to be detained pending trial, most states require a **detention hearing.** This hearing is held to determine if the youth is to be released to a parent or guardian, or to be held in a detention facility until adjudication. Many states do not provide the right to bail for children and the Supreme Court upheld preventive detention in *Schall v. Martin* (1984). Some children will be detained to keep them from committing other crimes while awaiting trial. Others are held to protect them from the possibility of harm from gang members or parents. Still others may not appear in court as required if released. Nationally, about 18 percent of all delinquency cases involve detention between referral to the juvenile court and disposition of the case (OJJDP, 1999:152).

___*New Jersey v. T.L.O.* (1985)___
School officials may search a student based on a reasonable suspicion that the search will produce evidence that a school or a criminal law has been violated.

___diversion___
The process of screening children out of the juvenile justice system without a decision by the court.

___detention hearing___
A hearing by the juvenile court to determine if a juvenile is to be detained or released prior to adjudication.

Nathaniel Abraham, who at age 11 fatally shot a stranger walking into a Pontiac, Michigan convenience store, became the youngest American ever convicted in an adult court of murder. The case highlighted a national trend toward putting children on trial as adults.

The conditions in many detention facilities are poor; abuse is often reported. Although much attention is focused on the adjudication processes of the juvenile court and the sanctions imposed by judges, many more children are punished through confinement in detention centers and jails before any court action has taken place than are punished with sentences of incarceration by the courts.

Transfer to Adult Court

One of the first decisions to be made is whether a case should be transferred to the criminal (adult) justice system. In forty-nine states juvenile court judges may **waive** their jurisdiction and the case is transferred. Consideration is given to the seriousness of the charge, the age of the juvenile, and the poor prospects of rehabilitation (OJJDP, 1998). In thirteen states prosecutors have the authority to file a case directly with the adult court. In twenty-six states certain violent crimes such as murder, rape, and armed robbery are excluded by law from the jurisdiction of the juvenile courts (NIJ: 1997).

As a "tougher" approach to juvenile crime took hold in the 1970s, the number of cases transferred have increased dramatically. However, waived cases still represent less than 2 percent of delinquency cases. The likelihood of waiver varies by offense, offender age, and offender race. Since 1985 there has been a slight increase in the percentage of African Americans subjected to the waiver (BJS, 1997e). Among juveniles transferred to the adult court for violent crimes, only 59 percent are convicted of that offense. This suggests that the waiver decision is not automatically the toughest option for a serious offender (BJS, 1998h). Many states now place on the youth the burden of proving that he or she is amenable to treatment in the juvenile instead of the adult court (Zimring, 1991). Attitudes about transferring juveniles to the adult court are shown in What Americans Think.

waive

Procedure by which the juvenile court waives its jurisdiction and transfers a juvenile case to the adult criminal court.

One result of the increased number of juveniles tried in adult court has been the doubling, between 1985 and 1997, of the number of under-18-year-olds sent to adult state prisons. A recent study by the Bureau of Justice Statistics found that 61 percent of young inmates were incarcerated for violent crimes, 22 percent for property crimes, 11 percent for drug offenses, and 5 percent for public order offenses (BJS: Press Release, February 27, 2000).

Adjudication

Adjudication is the trial stage of the juvenile justice process. If the child has not admitted to the charges and the case has not been transferred to the adult court, an adjudication hearing is held to determine the facts in the case and, if appropriate, label the juvenile "delinquent."

The Supreme Court's decision in *Gault* (1967) and other due process rulings mandated changes in criminal proceedings that have changed the philosophy and actions of the juvenile court. Contemporary juvenile proceedings are more formal than those of the past, although still more informal than adult courts. Copies of petitions with specific charges must be given to the parents and child; counsel may be present and free counsel may be appointed if the juvenile cannot pay; witnesses may be cross-examined; and a transcript of the proceedings must be kept.

As with other Supreme Court decisions, local practice may differ sharply from the procedures spelled out in the high court's rulings. Juveniles and their parents often waive their rights in response to suggestions from the judge or probation officer. The lower social status of the offender's parents, the intimidating atmosphere of the court, and judicial hints that the outcome will be more favorable if a lawyer is not present are reasons the procedures outlined in *Gault* may not be followed. The litany of "getting treatment," "doing what's right for the child," and "working out a just solution" may sound enticing, especially to people who are unfamiliar with the intricacies of formal legal procedures. In practice, then, juveniles still lack many of the protections given to adult offenders. Some of the differences between the juvenile and adult criminal justice systems are listed in Table 17.3.

The increased concern about crime has given prosecuting attorneys a more prominent part in the system. In keeping with the traditional child-saver philosophy, prosecuting attorneys rarely appeared in juvenile court prior to the *Gault* decision. Now that a defense attorney is present, the state often is represented by legal counsel as well. In many jurisdictions, prosecutors are assigned to deal specifically with juvenile cases. Their functions are to advise the intake officer, administer diversion programs, negotiate pleas, and act as an advocate during judicial proceedings (BJS, 1997e).

Juvenile proceedings and court records have traditionally been closed to the public to protect the child's privacy and potential for rehabilitation. However, judges in the adult courts may not have access to juvenile records. This means that persons who have already served time on juvenile probation or in institutions are erroneously perceived to be first offenders when they are processed for crimes as adults. Some people argue that adult courts should have access to juvenile records and that young criminals should be treated more severely to deter them from future illegal activity.

What Americans Think

Question "Tell me for each of the following statements whether you strongly agree, agree, neither agree or disagree, or strongly disagree:

1. a juvenile charged with a serious property crime should be tried as an adult.
2. a juvenile charged with selling illegal drugs should be tried as an adult.
3. a juvenile charged with a serious violent crime should be tried as an adult."

Percentage responding "Strongly agree" or "agree."

Serious property crime 62%

Selling illegal drugs 69%

Serious violent crime 87%

SOURCE: Ruth Triplett, "The Growing Threat: Gangs and Juvenile Offenders," *Americans View Crime and Justice*, eds. Timothy J. Flanagan and Dennis R. Longmire (Thousand Oaks, Calif.: Sage Publications, 1996), 142.

THE JUVENILE JUSTICE SYSTEM

TABLE 17.3 The adult and juvenile criminal justice systems

Compare the basic elements of the adult and juvenile systems. To what extent does a juvenile have the same rights as an adult? Are the different decision-making processes necessary because a juvenile is involved?

	ADULT SYSTEM	JUVENILE SYSTEM
Philosophical assumptions	Decisions made as result of adversarial system in context of due process rights	Decisions made as result of inquiry into needs of juvenile within context of some due process elements
Jurisdiction	Violations of criminal law	Violations of criminal law, status offenses, neglect, dependency
Primary sanctioning goals	Retribution, deterrence, rehabilitation	Retribution, rehabilitation
Official discretion	Widespread	Widespread
Entrance	Official action of arrest, summons, or citation	Official action, plus referral by school, parents, other sources
Role of prosecuting and defense attorneys	Required and formalized	Sometimes required; less structured; poor role definition
Adjudication	Procedural rules of evidence in public jury trial required	Less formal structure to rules of evidence and conduct of trial; no right to public jury in most states
Treatment programs	Run primarily by public agencies	Broad use of private and public agencies
Application of Bill of Rights amendments		
Fourth: Unreasonable searches and seizures	Applicable	Applicable
Fifth: Double jeopardy	Applicable	Applicable (re waiver to adult court)
Self–incrimination	Applicable (*Miranda* warnings)	Applicable
Sixth: Right to counsel	Applicable	Applicable
Public trial	Applicable	Applicable in less than half of states
Trial by jury	Applicable	Applicable in less than half of states
Fourteenth: Right to treatment	Not applicable	Applicable

Jonathan McDonald, 13, listens to Juvenile Court Shane Burleigh during his arraignment in Port Huron, Michigan. McDonald and three other teenagers face adult charges of conspiracy to commit murder for plotting a massacre at their middle school that would "kill more people than Columbine."

Disposition

If the court makes a finding of delinquency the judge will schedule a dispositional hearing to decide what action should be taken. Typically, the judge receives a pre-dispositional report prepared by a probation officer before passing sentence. Similar to a presentence report, this report contains information about the child's background, factors surrounding the delinquent event, and reports from social workers or psychiatrists. The report's purpose is to assist the judge in deciding the disposition that is in the best interests of the child and is consistent with the treatment plan developed by the probation officer.

Few juveniles are found by the court to be not delinquent at trial, because the intake and pretrial processes normally filter out cases in which a law violation cannot be proved. Besides dismissal, four other choices are available: (1) probation (2) alternative dispositions (3) custodial care, and (4) community treatment.

The traditional belief of juvenile court advocates was that rehabilitation was the only goal of the sanction imposed on young people. For most of the twentieth century, judges have sentenced juveniles to indeterminate sentences so that correctional administrators could decide when release was appropriate. As in the adult criminal justice system, indeterminate sentences and unbridled discretion in juvenile justice have been under attack during the last three decades. A number of states have tightened the sentencing discretion of judges, especially with regard to serious offenses. The state of Washington, for example, has adopted a determinate sentencing law for juveniles. In other states, a youth may be transferred more readily to the adult court for adjudication and sentencing. Jurisdictions such as the District of Columbia, Colorado, Florida, and Virginia have passed laws requiring mandatory sentences for certain offenses committed by juveniles.

Corrections

Many aspects of juvenile corrections are similar to those of adult corrections. Both systems, for example, mix rehabilitative and retributive sanctions. However, juvenile corrections differs in many respects from the adult system. Some of the differences flow from the *parens patriae* concept and the youthful, seemingly innocent persons with whom the system deals. At times, the differences are expressed in formal operational policies, such as contracting for residential treatment; at other times, the differences are apparent only in the style and culture of an operation, as in juvenile probation.

One predominant aim of juvenile corrections is to avoid unnecessary incarceration. When children are removed from their homes, they are inevitably damaged emotionally, even when the home life is harsh and abusive, for they are forced to abandon the only environment they know. Further, placing children in institutions has labeling effects; the children begin to perceive themselves as "bad" because they have received punitive treatment, and children who see themselves as bad are likely to behave that way. Finally, treatment is believed to be more effective when the child is living in a normal, supportive home environment. For these reasons, noninstitutional forms of corrections are seen as highly desirable in juvenile justice and have proliferated in recent years.

Probation

In more than half (53 percent) of cases the juvenile delinquent is placed on probation and released to the custody of a parent or guardian. Often the judge orders that the delinquent undergo some form of education or counseling. The delinquent can also be required to pay a fine or make restitution while on probation.

Juvenile probation operates in much the same way as adult probation, and it is sometimes carried out by the same agency. In two respects, however, juvenile probation can differ markedly from adult probation. First, juvenile probation has traditionally been better funded, so that officers have had smaller caseloads. Second, the juvenile probation officer is often infused with the sense that the offender is worthwhile and can change, and that the job is valuable and enjoyable. Such attitudes make for greater creativity than is possible with adult probation. For example, a young offender can be paired with a "big brother" or "big sister" from the community.

Alternative Dispositions

Although probation and commitment to an institution are the major dispositional options, intermediate sanctions served in the community now account for 15 percent of adjudicated juvenile cases. Judges have wide discretion to warn, to fine, to arrange for restitution, to refer a juvenile for treatment at either a public or a private community agency, or to withhold judgment.

A Question of Ethics

Residents of the Lovelock Home had been committed by the juvenile court because they were either delinquent or neglected. All twenty-five boys, aged 12 to 16, were streetwise, tough, and interested only in getting out. The institution had a staff of social services professionals who tried to deal with the educational and psychological needs of the residents. Because state funding was short, these services looked better in the annual report than to an observer visiting Lovelock. Most of the time the residents watched television, played basketball in the backyard, or just hung out in one another's rooms.

Joe Klegg, the night supervisor, was tired from the eight-hour shift that he had just completed on his second job as a daytime convenience-store manager. The boys were watching television when he arrived at seven. Everything seemed calm. It should have been, because Joe had placed a tough 15-year-old, Randy Marshall, in charge. Joe had told Randy to keep the younger boys in line. Randy used his muscle and physical presence to intimidate the other residents. He knew that if the home was quiet and there was no trouble, he would be rewarded with special privileges such as a "pass" to go see his girlfriend. Joe wanted no hassles and a quiet house so that he could doze off when the boys went to sleep.

■ Does the situation at Lovelock Home raise ethical questions, or does it merely raise questions of poor management practices? What are the potential consequences for the residents? For Joe Klegg? What is the state's responsibility?

Judges sometimes suspend judgment, or continue cases without a finding, when they wish to put a youth under supervision but are reluctant to apply the label "delinquent." The judge holds off on giving a definitive judgment for possible use should a youth misbehave while under the informal supervision of a probation officer or parents.

Custodial Care

Twenty-nine percent of delinquents are placed in either nonsecure facilities (foster homes; group homes; camp, ranch, or school) operated by public or private agencies or in secure facilities. The nonsecure placement includes a significant number of nonoffenders: youths referred for abuse, neglect, or emotional disturbance.

Secure facilities such as reform schools and training schools deal with juveniles who have committed serious violations of the law and have serious personal problems. Most secure juvenile facilities are small, designed to hold forty or fewer residents. However, many states have at least one facility holding two hundred or more hard-core delinquents who are allowed limited freedom. Because the residents are younger and somewhat more volatile than adults, behavioral control is often an everyday issue; fights and aggression are common. Poor management practices, such as those described in A Question of Ethics can lead to difficult situations.

As with adult corrections the number of boot camps for juvenile offenders has grown. By 1997, more than twenty-seven thousand teenagers were passing through fifty-four camps in thirty-four states annually. However, as with boot camps for adults, the results are not promising. A national study showed that recidivism among boot camp attendees ranged from 64 percent to 75 percent, slightly higher than for youths sentences to adult prisons (*New York Times,* January 2, 2000:WK3). After a series of hard-hitting exposés of physical abuse of participants by boot camp officers, the governor of Maryland suspended

At the Mount View Youth Service Center in Denver, juveniles in custody for various offenses line up for lunch. Nationally, almost 98,000 youths are held in institutional care, usually for six months. What lies ahead for these delinquents?

the paramilitary trappings and removed the five top juvenile justice executives (*Baltimore Sun,* December 16, 1999:1).

A national survey of public custodial institutions showed that 39 percent of juveniles were incarcerated for violent offenses, 60 percent used drugs regularly, and 50 percent said that a family member had been in prison at some time in the past. Also, 88 percent of the residents were male, only 30 percent had grown up in a household with both parents, and the percentages of African Americans (40 percent) and Hispanic Americans (18 percent) were greater than the percentage of those groups in the general population (OJJDP, 1999:195). The Close-Up (p. 598) tells the story of Fernando, whose background matches this profile. Figure 17.5 shows the types of offenses for the placement of juveniles in public correctional facilities.

Institutional Programs

Because of the emphasis on rehabilitation that has dominated juvenile justice for much of the past fifty years, a wide variety of treatment programs has been used. Counseling, education, vocational training, and an assortment of psychotherapy methods have been incorporated into the juvenile correctional programs of most states. Unfortunately, incarceration in a juvenile training institution primarily seems to prepare many offenders for entry into adult corrections. Research has raised many questions about the effectiveness of rehabilitation programs in the juvenile corrections setting. John Irwin's concept of the state-raised youth is a useful way of looking at children who come in contact with institutional life at an early age, lack family relationships and structure, become accustomed to living in a correctional facility, and are unable to function in other environments (Irwin, 1970).

Community Treatment

In the past decade, treatment in community-based facilities has become much more common. Today there are more private, nonprofit agencies that contract with states to provide services for troubled youths. Community-based options include foster homes in which juvenile offenders live with families, usually for a short period of time, and group homes, often privately run facilities for groups of twelve to twenty juvenile offenders. Each group home has several staff personnel who work as counselors or houseparents on eight- or twenty-hour shifts. Group home placements can allow juveniles to attend local schools, provide individual and group counseling, and offer a more structured life than most of the residents received in their own homes. However, critics suggest that group homes often are mismanaged and may do little more than "warehouse" youths.

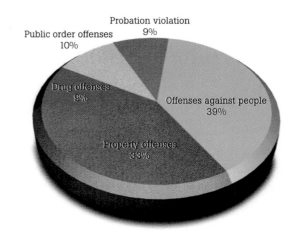

FIGURE 17.5 Juvenile delinquents in public custodial facilities: types of offenses

Public order offenses 10%
Probation violation 9%
Drug offenses 9%
Offenses against people 39%
Property offenses 33%

SOURCE: U.S. Department of Justice, Office of Juvenile Justice and Delinquency Prevention, *Juvenile Offenders and Victims: 1999 National Report* (Washington, D.C.:Government Printing Office, 1999), 188.

CHECK POINT

⑨ **What three discretionary decisions are made by the police with regard to processing of juveniles?**

⑩ **What five factors influence the police in deciding disposition of a case?**

⑪ **What is the purpose of diversion?**

⑫ **What are five sentencing dispositions available to the judge?**

CLOSE  up

Fernando, 16, Finds a Sanctuary in Crime

Fernando Morales was glad to discuss his life as a 16-year-old drug dealer, but he had one stipulation owing to his status as a fugitive. He explained that he had recently escaped from Long Lane School, a state correctional institution that became his home after he was caught with $1,100 worth of heroin known as P.

"The Five O caught me right here with the bundles of P," he said, referring to a police officer, as he stood in front of a boarded-up house on Bridgeport's East Side. "They sentenced me to eighteen months, but I jetted after four. Three of us got out a bathroom window. We ran through the woods and stole a car. Then we got back here and the Five O's came to my apartment, and I had to jump out the side window on the second floor."

WHAT FUTURE?

Since his escape in December, Fernando had been on the run for weeks. He still went to the weekly meetings of his gang, but he was afraid to go back to his apartment, afraid even to go to a friend's place to pick up the three guns he had stashed away. "I would love to get my baby, Uzi, but it's too hot now."

"Could you bring a photographer here?" he asked. "I want my picture in the newspaper. I'd love to have me holding a bundle right there on the front page so the cops can see it. They're going to bug out."

The other dealers on the corner looked on with a certain admiration. They realized that a publicity campaign might not be the smartest long-term career move for a fugitive drug dealer—"Man, you be the one bugging out," another dealer told him—but they also recognized the logic in Fernando's attitude. He was living his life according to a common assumption on these streets: There is no future.

When you ask the Hispanic teenagers selling drugs here what they expect to be doing in five years, you tend to get a lot of bored shrugs. Occasionally they'll talk about being back in school or being a retired drug dealer in a Porsche. But the most common answer is the one that Fernando gave without hesitation or emotion: "Dead or in jail."

The story of how Fernando got that way is a particularly sad one, but the basic elements are fairly typical in the lives of drug dealers and gang members in any urban ghetto. He has grown up amid tenements, housing projects, torched buildings, and abandoned factories. His role models have been adults who use "the city" and "the state" primarily as terms for the different types of welfare checks. His neighborhood is a place where 13-year-olds know by heart the visiting hours at local prisons.

THE FAMILY: A MOTHER LEAVES, A FATHER DRINKS

Fernando Morales was born in Bridgeport, Connecticut, and a few months after his birth his mother moved out. Since then he has occasionally run into her on the street. Neither he nor his relatives can say exactly why she left—or why she didn't take Fernando and her other son with her—but the general assumption is that she was tired of being hit by their father.

The father, Bernabe Morales, who was 24 years old and had emigrated from Puerto Rico as a teenager, moved the two boys in with his mother at the P. T. Barnum public housing project. Fernando lived there until the age of 8, when his grandmother died. . . .

After that Fernando and his brother Bernard lived sometimes with their father and his current girlfriend, sometimes with relatives in Bridgeport or Puerto Rico. They eventually settled with their father's cousin, Monserrate Bruno, who already had ten children living in her two-bedroom apartment. . . .

His father, by all accounts, was a charming, generous man when sober but something else altogether when drinking or doing drugs. He was arrested more than two dozen times, usually for fighting or drugs, and spent five years in jail while Fernando was growing up. He lived on welfare, odd jobs, and money from selling drugs, a trade that was taken up by both his sons.

THE "INDUSTRY": MOVING UP IN THE DRUG TRADE

Fernando's school days ended two years ago, when he dropped out of ninth grade. "School was corny," he explained. "I was smart, I learned quick, but I got bored. I was just learning things when I could be out making money."

Fernando might have found other opportunities—he had relatives working in fast-food restaurants and repair shops, and one cousin tried to interest him in a job distributing bread that might pay $700 a week—but nothing with such quick rewards as the drug business flourishing on the East Side.

He had friends and relatives in the business, and he started as one of the runners on the street corner making sales or directing buyers to another runner holding the marijuana, cocaine, crack, or heroin. The runners on each block buy their drugs—paying, for instance, $200 for fifty bags of crack that sell for $250—from the block's lieutenant, who supervises them and takes the money to the absentee dealer called the owner of the block.

By this winter Fernando had moved up slightly on the corporate ladder. "I'm not the block lieutenant yet, but I have some runners selling for me," he explained as he sat in a bar near the block. Another teenager came in with money for him, which he proudly added to a thick wad in his pocket. "You see? I make money while they work for me."

Fernando still worked the block himself, too, standing on the corner watching for cars slowing down, shouting "You want P?" or responding to veteran customers for crack who asked, "Got any slab, man?" Fernando said he usually made between $100 and $300 a day, and that the money usually went as quickly as it came.

He had recently bought a car for $500 and wrecked it making a fast turn [and running] into a telephone pole. He spent money on gold chains with crucifixes, rings, Nike sneakers, Timberland boots, an assortment of Russell hooded sweatshirts called hoodies, gang dues, trips to New York City and his 23-year-old girlfriend.

His dream was to get out of Bridgeport. "I'd be living fat somewhere. I'd go to somewhere hot, Florida or Puerto Rico or somewhere, buy me a house, get six blazing girls with dope bodies."

In the meantime, he tried not to think about what his product was doing to his customers.

"Sometimes it bothers me. But see, I'm a hustler. I got to look out for myself. I got to be making money. Forget them. If you put that in your head, you're going to be caught out. You going to be a sucker. You going to be like them." He said he had used marijuana, cocaine, and angel dust himself, but made a point of never using crack or heroin, the drugs that plagued the last years of his father's life. . . .

THE GANGS: "LIKE A FAMILY" OF DRUG DEALERS

"I cried a little, that's it," was all that Fernando would say about his father's death. But he did allow that it had something to do with his subsequent decision to join a Hispanic gang named Neta. He went with friends to a meeting, answered questions during an initiation ceremony, and began wearing its colors, a necklace of red, white, and blue beads.

"It's like a family, and you need that if you've lost your own family," he said. "At the meetings we talk about having heart, trust, and all that. We don't disrespect nobody. If we need money, we get it. If I need anything they're right there to help me."

Neta is allied with Bridgeport's most notorious gang, the Latin Kings, and both claim to be peaceful Hispanic cultural organizations opposed to drug use. But they are financed at least indirectly by the drug trade, because many members like Fernando work independently in drug operations, and the drug dealers' disputes can turn into gang wars. . . .

"I like guns, I like stealing cars, I like selling drugs, and I like money," he said. "I got to go to the block. That's where I get my spirit at. When I die, my spirit's going to be at the block, still making money. Booming." . . .

"I'll be selling till I get my act together. I'm just a little kid. Nothing runs through my head. All I think about is doing crazy things. But when I be big, I know I need education. If I get caught and do a couple of years, I'll come out and go back to school. But I don't have that in my head yet. I'll have my little fun while I'm out."

SOURCE: John Tierney, *New York Times*, April 13, 1993, pp. Al, B6. Copyright © 1993 by The New York Times Company. Reprinted by permission.

Problems and Perspectives

Much criticism of juvenile justice has emphasized the disparity between the treatment ideal and the institutionalized practices of an ongoing bureaucratic system. Commentators have focused on how the language of social reformers has disguised the day-to-day operations in which elements of due process are lacking and custodial incarceration is all too frequent. Other criticisms have emphasized that the juvenile justice system is apparently unable to control juvenile crime.

The juvenile court, in both theory and practice, is a remarkably complex institution that must perform a wide variety of functions. The juvenile justice system is charged with playing such a range of roles that it is inevitable that goals and values will collide. In many states the same judges, probation officers, and social workers are asked to deal with both neglected children and young criminals. Although departments of social services may deal primarily with cases of neglect, the distinction between the criminal and the neglected child is often not maintained.

In addition to recognizing that the juvenile system has organizational problems, society must acknowledge that only a limited understanding has been gained of the causes of delinquency and its prevention or treatment. Over the years, various social and behavioral theories have been advanced to explain delinquency. One generation looked to slum conditions as the cause of juvenile crime, and another points to the affluence of the suburbs. Psychologists may stress masculine insecurity in a matriarchal family structure, and some sociologists note the peer group pressures of the gang. The array of theories has led to an array of proposed—and often contradictory—treatments. In such confusion, those interested in the problems of youth may despair. What is clear is that additional research is needed to give insights into the causes of delinquency and the treatment of juvenile offenders.

The serious repeat offender who continues a life of crime as an adult is still a great concern. One key issue is the unavailability of juvenile court records to judges in the adult courts, which means that persons who have already served time on probation and in juvenile institutions are thought to be first offenders when they reach adulthood. Many believe juvenile records should be made available and young criminals should be treated more severely to deter them from committing future crimes.

What trends may foretell the future of juvenile justice? Many of the same trends that are found in the adult criminal justice system can be seen in the juvenile system. However, there is often a delay between reform of the adult system and that of the juvenile system. For instance, the restriction of the discretion of judges and parole boards, a major thrust of the 1970s, surfaced in juvenile justice in the 1990s. The toughening of sentencing standards and increases in the time served in adult prisons are also becoming part of the juvenile system. Youthful-offender laws have brought many delinquents to the adult system for adjudication and correction.

Although the future of juvenile justice may reflect the more conservative attitudes of the 1990s, the reforms of the 1970s have had an important impact. These changes have been referred to as the "Big D's" of juvenile justice: diversion, decriminalization, deinstitutionalization, and due process (Finckenauer, 1984:190). The Big D's have left a lasting mark on juvenile justice. Lawyers are routinely present at court hearings and other stages of the process, adding a formality that was not present twenty years ago. Status offenders now are seldom placed in secure, punitive environments such as training schools. The juvenile justice system looks more like the adult justice system than it formerly did, but it is still less formal. Its stated intention is also less harsh: to keep juveniles in the community whenever possible.

Barry Krisberg has added a fifth "D"—disarray. He believes that the conservative crime control policies that have hit the adult criminal justice system—with their emphasis on deterrence, retribution, and getting tough—have influenced juvenile justice. He points to growing levels of overcrowding in juvenile institutions, increased litigation challenging the abuse of children in training schools and detention centers, and higher rates of minority youth incarceration. All of these problems have emerged during a period of declining youth populations and fewer arrests of juveniles. With the demographic trend now reversing and the increased concern about drugs, Krisberg (1988) sees a surge of adolescents going through their criminally high-risk years in a system and community unable to cope with them.

Summary

- Crimes committed by juveniles have increased since 1980.
- The history of juvenile justice comprises five periods: Puritan, House of Refuge, juvenile court, juvenile rights, and crime control.
- Creation of the juvenile court in 1899 established a separate juvenile justice system dealing with delinquency, neglected children, and dependent children.
- The *In re Gault* decision by the U.S. Supreme Court in 1967 brought due process to the juvenile justice system.
- Decisions by police officers and juvenile intake officers dispose of a large portion of cases that are never referred to the court.
- In juvenile court most cases are settled through a plea agreement.
- After conviction or plea, a disposition hearing is held. The judge reviews the offense and the juvenile's social history before passing sentence.
- Possible dispositions of a juvenile case include suspended judgment, probation, community treatment, or institutional care.
- Juvenile court jurisdiction is increasingly being waived so that youths may be tried in the adult criminal justice system.

Questions for Review

❶ What are the major historical periods of juvenile justice in the United States?

❷ What is the jurisdiction of the juvenile court system?

❸ What are the major processes in the juvenile justice system?

❹ What are the sentencing and institutional alternatives for juveniles who are judged delinquent?

❺ What due process rights do juveniles have?

Key Terms and Cases

delinquent (p. 587)

dependent child (p. 588)

detention hearing (p. 591)

diversion (p. 591)

neglected child (p. 587)

parens patriae (p. 577)

PINS (p. 587)

status offense (p. 580)

waive (p. 592)

Breed v. Jones (1975) (p. 581)

Fare v. Michael C. (1979) (p. 590)

In re Gault (1967) (p. 581)

In re Winship (1970) (p. 581)

McKiever v. Pennsylvania (1971) (p. 581)

New Jersey v. T.L.O. (1985) (p. 591)

Schall v. Martin (1984) (p. 582)

For Further Reading

Ayers, William. *A Kind and Just Parent: The Children of Juvenile Court.* Boston: Beacon Press, 1997. Examination of the lives of offenders in the Chicago juvenile court system through the eyes of one of their teachers.

Decker, Scott H., and Barick Van Winkle. *Life in the Gang: Families, Friends, and Violence.* New York: Cambridge University Press, 1996. Follows the life of a juvenile gang in St. Louis for a year, documenting its trouble with the law. Examines juvenile justice efforts to deal with family and community problems.

Klein, Malcolm W. *The American Street Gang: Its Nature, Prevalence, and Control.* New York: Oxford, 1996. A study of street gangs in the American city. Argues for investment in jobs, schools, and social services to serve the needs of the poor and to discourage the growth of gangs.

Kotlowitz, Alex. *There Are No Children Here: The Story of Two Boys Growing Up in the Other America.* New York: Anchor, 1992. True story of two boys growing up in a Chicago housing project surrounded by street gangs, gunfire, violence, and drugs.

Matza, David. *Delinquency and Drift.* New York: Viking, 1974. A classic examination of the role of the juvenile court. Describes the influence of "kadi" justice (in which the judge exercises great discretion) on the system.

Platt, Anthony. *The Child Savers: The Invention of Delinquency.* Chicago: University of Chicago Press, 1970. A history of the Progressive child-saver movement.

Going Online

❶ Using the Internet, go to the federal government's web site concerning juvenile justice: ojjdp.ncjrs.org/ojstatbb/index.html. Read about juvenile corrections. What are the trends in juveniles being held in custody? Can you tell from data available at the web site whether these trends are caused by changes in the crime rates or by changes in custody policies?

❷ Using the Internet, go to Florida's web page: www.djj.state.fl.us/boards1.html#question1. Read about Florida's County Juvenile Councils and District Juvenile Justice Boards. Do these organizations appear to be good mechanisms for dealing with juvenile justice problems? How well would they work in your community?

❸ **Using InfoTrac College Edition,** search for the subject "juvenile delinquency." Click on "juvenile detention facilities" and read several articles that will help you answer the question "Should juveniles ever be held in adult jails or prisons?"

CHECK POINT ANSWERS

❶ There will be a greater number of youths in the crime-prone 14–18 age cohort.

❷ Age 7.

❸ Chancery courts had protective jurisdiction over children, especially those involved in issues of dependency, neglect, and property.

❹ The state acting as parent and guardian.

❺ To provide an environment where neglected children could learn good work and study habits, live in a disciplined and healthy environment, and develop character.

❻ A separate court for delinquent, dependent, and neglected children; special legal procedures that were less adversarial than in the adult system; separation of children from adults throughout the system; programs of probation to assist judges in deciding what is in the best interest of the state and the child.

❼ Procedural rights for juveniles, including notice of charges, right to counsel, right to confront and cross-examine witnesses, and protection against self-incrimination.

❽ The age of the juvenile: usually under 16 or 18; and the type of case: delinquency, status offense, neglect, or dependency.

❾ (1) Whether to take the child into custody, (2) whether to request that the child be detained, (3) whether to refer the child to court.

❿ The seriousness of the offense, the willingness of the parents to cooperate, the child's behavioral history, the extent to which the child and the parents insist on a formal court hearing, and local political and social norms.

⓫ To avoid formal proceedings when the child's best interests can be served by treatment in the community.

⓬ Suspended judgment, probation, community treatment, institutional care, judicial waiver to an adult court.

Should Juvenile Offenders Be Tried as Adults?

One Sunday afternoon, shots were fired at two groups of children playing on the south side of Chicago. Two boys were wounded and a 14-year-old girl, Shavon Dean, was killed as she stood a few feet away from her house. She had come out of the house to tell her brother, one of the boys who was fired upon, that it was time to stop playing and come inside. At that moment, a seemingly random shooting cut short her young life.

Using descriptions from witnesses, the police mounted a citywide manhunt for Robert "Yummy" Sandifur. Sandifur apparently chose the boys as random targets for a gang initiation shooting.

Although any homicide is disturbing, the national news media had little interest in the story of yet another inner-city youngster gunned down in senseless violence until they learned that the suspect was only 11 years old and that he had already been prosecuted for eight felonies—including robbery, car theft, arson, and burglary—committed between the ages of 9 and 11. He was not yet five feet tall and weighed less than seventy pounds.

Sandifur had been the victim of serious child abuse as a 3-year-old. An investigation by the Illinois Department of Children and Family Services had found scars on his face, cordlike marks on his abdomen, and cigarette burns on his buttocks. At the time of the shooting, he was in the temporary custody of his grandmother while the state tried to find a place for him in a secure juvenile detention center.

With the national news media following their every move, the Chicago police looked for Sandifur for several days. The following Thursday, they found him—lying dead in a pool of blood beneath a railroad overpass with two bullets in his head. He had probably been executed by older members of his own gang for generating too much "heat" from the police. The police arrested 16-year-old Cragg Hardaway and an unnamed juvenile for the killing of Robert Sandifur.

Arrests of juveniles for violent crimes—homicide, rape, robbery, and aggravated assault—more than doubled between 1988 and 1994. During this period the homicide arrest rate for teenagers aged 14–17 increased 41 percent. Since their peak in 1994 juvenile violent crime arrests have slowly declined, yet they still remain more than 40 percent above the 1988 level. Youths are also the primary victims of violent crime. Persons age 12–19 are about twice as likely as persons 25–34 and about three times as likely as persons age 35–49 to be victims of violent crime. The availability of guns, the prevalence of urban youth gangs, and the problem of drugs are cited by experts as the causes of violent youth crimes.

Of particular relevance for policy makers concerned about future crime-prevention strategies is the size of the current teenage population. In the midst of this great increase in youth violence, the number of juveniles in the 14–17 age group today is the smallest it has been in almost forty years. By contrast, the cohort of children aged 5–12—those who will be moving into the crime-prone ages in the near future—is much larger. By 2005 the number in that group will have increased by 20 percent and will continue to grow.

But the size of this population is not the whole story. Nearly all of the social factors that contribute to youth crime—single-parent households, child abuse, poor schools, and lack of parental supervision—are getting worse. John J. DiIulio Jr. warns of an enormous new generation of juvenile "superpredators" who will commit violent crimes.

Since the juvenile justice system was created a hundred years ago, a basic assumption has been that child offenders should not go through the adult criminal justice system. The juvenile courts were to handle children with more flexibility and on the basis of their youth instead of their offenses. Treatment and guidance were to be emphasized more than punishment.

With crimes such as those involving Robert Sandifur and the schoolyard shootings that shocked the nation in the late 1990s getting greater media attention, the public has loudly called for "getting tough with these young hoods." Politicians and criminal justice planners have urged that steps be taken to ensure that juveniles who are accused of serious crimes be dealt with in the adult system. In some states judges can waive jurisdiction and transfer juvenile offenders to adult courts. Some states have recently passed laws to make it easier to try certain youthful offenders as adults; other states have considered measures to automatically transfer children as young as 13 to the adult system if they are accused of certain crimes.

For Trying Juveniles as Adults

Supporters of making it easier to try juveniles as adults point not only to the increased violence but also to the heinous nature of some crimes committed by youths. They see the juvenile courts as "coddling" these young predators. Often, only when a youth is transferred to the adult system is his long record of felonies revealed—felonies for which little punishment was ordered by the juvenile court. They also point out that in some states the waiver process is complex and rarely used. The current high level of violence by juveniles requires that the offenders be dealt with swiftly and quickly so as to deter the upcoming generation from following in the footsteps of their older brothers.

To summarize the arguments for trying serious juvenile offenders in the adult criminal justice system:

- Violence by juveniles is increasing and must be dealt with in a swift and certain manner.
- Juvenile courts have not been effective in stemming the tide of violence by young people.
- Procedures for waiving juvenile jurisdiction are cumbersome in many states.
- Justice demands that heinous crimes, regardless of the age of the accused, be dealt with to the full extent the law provides.

Against Trying Juveniles as Adults

Although they recognize that serious youth crime is a problem, many experts believe that trying juveniles as adults only makes things worse. They point out that treating adolescents as adults ignores the fact that they are at a different stage of social and emotional development. The concept of *mens rea,* they argue, requires that children not be held to the same standards as adults. To prevent youth crime, the child's environment must be changed. In an increasingly violent world, children need help to navigate the temptations and threats of adolescence. The prosecutors and judges of the adult system are not trained or able to deal with these children.

To summarize the arguments against trying serious juvenile offenders in the adult criminal justice system:

- The juvenile justice system is better able to deal with the social and emotional problems of young offenders.
- The basic foundations of criminal law recognize that children have diminished responsibility for their acts.
- Punishing juveniles in adult institutions robs them of their childhood and threatens their future.
- The problem of violent crime by juveniles must be dealt with by changing the environment within which they live.

What Should U.S. Policy Be?

Under pressure to "do something" about violent juvenile crime, legislators have proposed that the age of adulthood be lowered and that the cases of serious offenders be tried in the adult criminal justice system. Is this the best way to protect community safety—to punish youthful offenders in the adult criminal justice system? Is the juvenile corrections system equipped to treat and guide juvenile offenders in a way that will return them to their communities as productive people? How should the juvenile justice system deal with the coming generation of crime-prone youths?

Constitution of the United States

Criminal Justice Amendments

The first ten amendments to the Constitution, known as the Bill of Rights, became effective on December 15, 1791.

IV. The right of the people to be secure in their persons, houses, papers, and effects, against unreasonable searches and seizures, shall not be violated, and no warrants shall issue but upon probable cause, supported by oath or affirmation, and particularly describing the place to be searched, and the persons or things to be seized.

V. No person shall be held to answer for a capital or otherwise infamous crime, unless on a presentment or indictment of a grand jury, except in cases arising in the land or naval forces or in the militia when in actual service in time of war or public danger; nor shall any person be subject for the same offense to be twice put in jeopardy of life or limb; nor shall be compelled in any criminal case to be a witness against himself, nor be deprived of life, liberty, or property, without due process of law; nor shall private property be taken for public use without just compensation.

VI. In all criminal prosecutions the accused shall enjoy the right to a speedy and public trial, by an impartial jury of the State and district wherein the crime shall have been committed, which district shall have been previously ascertained by law, and to be informed of the nature and cause of the accusation; to be confronted with the witnesses against him; to have compulsory process for obtaining witnesses in his favor, and to have the assistance of counsel for his defense.

VIII. Excessive bail shall not be required, nor excessive fines imposed, nor cruel and unusual punishments inflicted.

The Fourteenth Amendment became effective on July 28, 1868.

XIV. SECTION 1. All persons born or naturalized in the United States, and subject to the jurisdiction thereof, are citizens of the United States and of the State wherein they reside. No State shall make or enforce any law which shall abridge the privileges or immunities of citizens of the United States; nor shall any State deprive any person of life, liberty, or property, without due process of law; nor deny to any person within its jurisdiction the equal protection of the laws.

Understanding and Using Criminal Justice Data

When it comes to numbers, criminal justice is somewhat like baseball. Both require a wealth of quantitative data to answer a variety of questions. Casual baseball fans want to know who has the highest batting average in the league or how many runs a certain pitcher gives up per game. More serious fans might want information that can help them judge whether statistics on various events (home runs, stolen bases, sacrifice bunts) support one or more of the manager's strategies. Similarly, people interested in criminal justice need quantitative data to describe events as well as to make inferences about trends or about the impact of different policies. They want to know, for example, how much crime there is; whether crime is on the increase and which types of crimes are increasing or decreasing; whether strong gun control laws are linked to a decrease in violent crime; or what effects correctional policies have on the likelihood that criminals will break the law in the future.

Researchers constantly gather, analyze, and disseminate quantitative information that fosters an understanding of the dimensions of crime and the workings of the criminal justice system. As a student in this course and as an informed citizen, you need to be able to read about these data intelligently and to make valid inferences about them.

In this text, as in most criminal justice books and articles, quantitative data often are reported in graphs and tables that organize the information and highlight certain aspects of it. The way the information is presented reflects the writer's choices about what is important in the raw data that underlie the graphic display. So that you can better interpret and use quantitative information, this appendix provides some pointers on reading graphic presentations and on interpreting raw data.

Reading Graphs and Tables

Writers use graphs and tables to organize information so that key factors stand out. Although it is tempting to try to take in the meaning of such displays in a quick glance, you will need to *analyze* what is being presented so that you do not misinterpret the material.

To begin, read the title and descriptive caption carefully to find out what the data do and do not represent. For example, consider the title of Figure B.1: Violent crime trends measured by UCR and NCVS. The title tells you that the data presented pertain to *violent* crime (not all crime) and that the *sources* of the information are reports to police *(Uniform Crime Reports)* and victimization surveys (National Crime Victimization Survey). Knowing where the data come from is important, because different means of data collection have their own strengths and weaknesses. So what this figure presents is not a directly observed picture of crime trends, but a picture that has been filtered through two distinct methods of measuring crime. (These measures of crime are described in Chapter 2.) In general, always note the sources of the data before drawing conclusions from a graphic display.

After reading the title and caption, study the figure itself. In Figure B.1, you will note that the graph compares the number of crimes from 1973 to 1992 as reported by the two types of surveys. As indicated in the caption, the data are presented in terms of the *number* of victimizations, not the relative *frequency* of crime (a crime rate). For this reason you need to be cautious in making inferences about what the data show about crime trends. In baseball,

a graph showing an increase in the number of home runs hit over a certain period would not prove that home runs were becoming more common if during the same period new teams were added to the league. More teams and more games being played would naturally lead to an increase in the total number of home runs. Similarly, given the increases in the U.S. population over the twenty-year period of the data, part of the increase in the number of crimes can be attributed to the greater number of Americans.

Also note that the data show what has happened over the past two decades. Even though the lines in the graph depict trends during that period, they do not in themselves forecast the future. There are statistical procedures that could be used to predict future trends based on certain assumptions, but such projections are not a part of this figure.

A final caution about graphic display in general: the form in which data are presented can affect or even distort your perception of the content. For example, a graph showing incarceration rates in the United States from 1940 to 1998 could be drawn with a shorter or longer time line (see Figure B.2). Figure B.2a shows the graph in normal proportions. If the time line is made shorter in relation to the incarceration rate scale, as in Figure B.2b, the changes in incarceration rates will appear to be more drastic than if the line is longer, as in Figure B.2c. By the same token, the height chosen for the vertical axis affects the appearance of the data and can influence the way the data are interpreted. How does your impression of the same data change when you compare Figure B.2d with Figure B.2e?

F I G U R E **B.1** **Violent crime trends measured by UCR and NCVS**

Note that these data are for the number of violent victimizations reported, not for the victimization rate from 1973 to 1992.

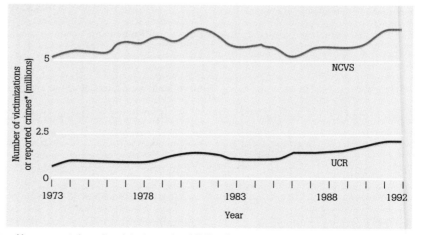

*Includes National Crime Victimization Survey (NCVS) violent crimes of rape, robbery, aggravated assault, and simple assault and *Uniform Crime Reports* (UCR) violent crimes of murder and nonnegligent manslaughter, forcible rape, robbery, and aggravated assault

SOURCE: U.S. Department of Justice, Bureau of Justice Statistics, *Highlights from Twenty Years of Surveying Crime Victims* (August 1993), 4.

FIGURE

B.2   Incarceration rates in the United States, 1940–1998

The panels of this graph are intentionally distorted to show the effects of varying the dimensions of graphs.

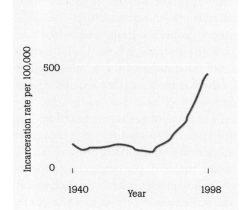

a

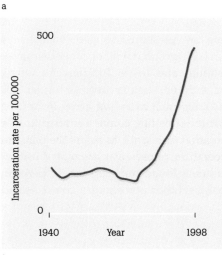

b

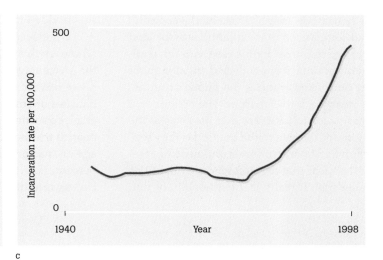

c

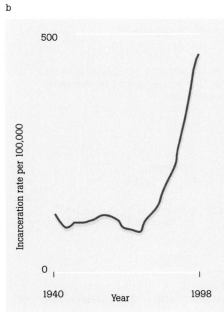

d

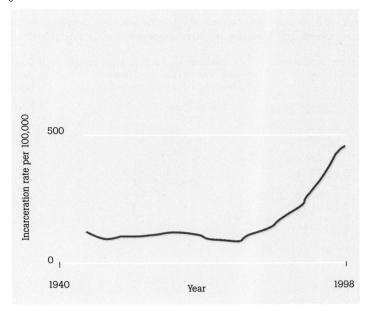

e

SOURCE: U.S. Department of Justice, Bureau of Justice Statistics, *Bulletin* (August 1996, June 1997, August 1998, August 1999).

Although much more could be said about interpreting graphical displays, these brief comments alert you to the need to carefully review data presented in graphic form. In criminal justice, as in baseball, you need to actively question and think about the information you encounter to become a serious student of the game.

Three Types of Graphs

You will find three types of graphs in this book: bar graphs, pie graphs (or pie charts), and line graphs. All three are represented in Figure B.3. Each graph displays information concerning public opinion about crime.

Figure B.3a is a bar graph. Bar graphs compare quantities organized in different categories. In this case, each bar represents the percentage of poll respondents ranking the indicated problem as "the most important problem facing this country today." The lengths of the bars (or their heights, when a bar graph is oriented vertically) allow for a visual comparison of the quantities associated with each category of response. In this case, you can readily see that when the data were collected in September 1993, health care outranked crime as the public's number one concern by nearly a 2 to 1 margin. The creator of a graph of this type needs to take care that the sizes of the bars are visually proportionate to the quantities they represent. A bar graph that is drawn unscrupulously or carelessly can make it appear that the difference in quantities is larger or smaller than it really is. Intentionally or not,

graphs that appear in the mass media often exaggerate some effect in this way. The lesson here is to go beyond looking at the shape of the graph. Use the scales provided on the axes to directly compare the numbers being depicted and verify your visual impression.

Figure B.3b is a pie graph. Pie graphs show the relative sizes of the parts of a single whole. Usually these sizes are reported as percentages. In this case, respondents were asked if there is more, less, or about the same amount of violence as there was five years ago. The whole consists of all the responses taken together, and the portions of the "pie" represent the percentage of respondents who chose each option. The pie graph indicates that a substantial majority (86 percent) of respondents in the survey believe that violence has increased. The same data could have been reported in a bar graph, but it would not have been as clear that a single whole was divided into parts.

Whenever data are presented as percentages of a whole—whether in a pie graph, table, or other display—the percentages should add up to 100 percent. Often, however, the sum may be slightly over or under 100 because of what is known as rounding error. Rounding error can occur when percentages are rounded to the nearest whole number. For instance, suppose the percentage of "more violence" responses was calculated as 86.7 percent. The figure might be reported as 87 percent. Unless rounding of the other percentages compensated

---

FIGURE B.3   Crime: in the nation, in our neighborhood

Crime remains one of the most important problems facing Americans. More than 8 in 10 people surveyed believed society is more violent than five years ago. A plurality say there is more crime in their neighborhood than a year ago.

A. Question: What do you think is the most important problem facing this country today?

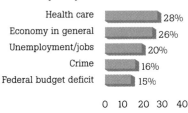

B. Question: Do you think there is more, less, or about the same amount of violence as there was five years ago?

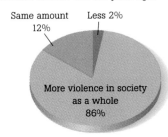

C. Question: In the past year, do you feel the crime rate in your area has been increasing, has been decreasing, or has remained the same?

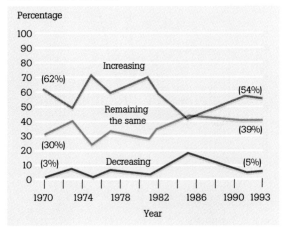

SOURCE: Public Opinion and Demographic Report," *The Public Perspective 5* (November/December 1993), 78.

for the error, the total of the reported percentages would sum to 101 percent. Where rounding error occurs, the figure or table will usually have a note indicating this fact.

Figure B.3c is a line graph. Line graphs show the relationship between two variables. The variables in question are indicated by the labels on the vertical axis and the longitudinal (horizontal) axis of the graph. In this case, the variable on the vertical axis is the percentage of people who say that crime has been increasing, decreasing, or staying about the same in the past year. The variable on the longitudinal axis is time, reported as years when the survey question was asked. In 1970, for instance, 62 percent of respondents said that crime had been increasing in the past year. Drawing a line through the points that show the percentage associated with each response for each year allows for a graphic presentation of how opinions have changed over time. The same data could have been presented in a table, but it would have been harder to see the direction of change in opinion. Line graphs are especially well suited to showing data about trends.

Analyzing Tables

All these points about graphic presentations in general apply also to tables. When you see a table, read the title and descriptive information carefully; note the source of the data; and be aware of how the presentation itself affects your perception of the content.

Tables relate two or more variables by organizing information in vertical columns and horizontal rows. In Table B.1, the columns give data about victimization rates for two categories of crime, violent crime and theft. The rows of the table show categories of victims organized by sex, age, race, ethnicity, and marital status by sex. Reading *down* a column allows for a comparison of information about theft, for example, for different types of victims. By inspecting each column in turn, you can see that

TABLE B.1

Who are the victims of personal crime?

National Crime Victimization Survey data help clarify the characteristics of crime victims.

	VICTIMS	RATE PER 1,000 PERSONS AGE 12 OR OVER			VICTIMS	RATE PER 1,000 PERSONS AGE 12 OR OVER	
		VIOLENCE	THEFT			VIOLENCE	THEFT
Sex	Male	40	65	**Family income**	Less than $7,500	59	62
	Female	23	58		$7,500–$9,999	42	61
					$10,000–$14,999	43	60
Age	12–15	63	101		$15,000–$24,999	31	57
	16–19	91	94		$25,000–$29,999	32	57
	20–24	75	115		$30,000–$49,999	25	60
	25–34	35	71		$50,000 or more	20	66
	35–49	20	56				
	50–64	10	35	**Education**	0–4 years	18	16
	65 and older	4	20		5–7 years	45	67
					8 years	28	49
Race	White	30	61		9–11 years	49	62
	African American	44	61		High school graduate	28	49
	Other	28	52		1–3 years college	36	83
					College graduate	18	68
Ethnicity	Hispanic	36	59				
	Non–Hispanic	31	61	**Residence**	Central city	44	75
					1,000,000 or more	39	76
Marital status	Males				500,000–999,999	50	80
by sex	Never married	80	97		250,000–499,999	54	70
	Divorced/separated	44	95		50,000–249,999	38	74
	Married	19	43		Suburban	26	61
	Widowed	*	23		Rural	25	44
	Females						
	Never married	43	90				
	Divorced/separated	45	74				
	Married	11	44				
	Widowed	6	22				

* Based on ten or fewer cases.

SOURCE: U.S. Department of Justice, Bureau of Justice Statistics, *Highlights of Twenty Years of Surveying Crime Victims* (August 1993), 18.

the rates for both types of crime victimization are higher for males than for females; for people aged 16–19 than for those in most other age groups; for African Americans than for whites or other racial groups; and so on. Reading across a row, for example, "males, never married," allows for a comparison of the different categories of crime victimization for the same type of victim. If you read across all the rows, you can see that nearly all types of crime victims report more incidents of theft than crimes of violence.

Like other types of data displays, tables often require close study beyond the particular information being highlighted by the writer. When you come across a table, read down the columns and across the rows to discover for yourself the shape of the information being reported. Be careful, however, to notice how the data are organized and to distinguish between the data themselves and any *inferences* you draw from them. In this case, for example, you might be struck by the lower victimization rates reported by males who are married compared with the rates reported by males who are not married. Before you speculate about why married men are less likely to be victims of crime, note that the data for marital status are not broken out by age. People under age 25 are more likely than those older to be victimized (see the data under "Age"). Because these younger males are far more likely than older males to be unmarried, the difference in victimization rates for married and unmarried males may be largely accounted for by age rather than by marital status. The table does not provide enough information to tell to what extent this might be the case.

In summary, data are presented in tables and graphs so they can be more easily grasped. But before you decide that you have truly understood the information, read the item and accompanying commentary attentively, and be aware of the ways the writer has chosen to organize and display the data. By working with graphic presentations and posing questions to yourself as you read them, you will also make the important information easier to remember.

Understanding Raw Data

Data that you see in graphs and tables have already been sifted and organized. As a student of criminal justice, you will also encounter raw (or "whole") data. For example, the *Sourcebook of Criminal Justice Statistics, 1998* reports that there were 11,475 arrests for murder in the United States in 1997. Measures of data may also be expressed in terms of percentage change over time. The number of murders in 1997 was a decrease of 12.4 percent over 1989. Finally, data often are expressed in terms of the rate at which an event occurs for a certain number of people in the population. The murder rate in 1997 was 6.8 murders per 100,000 people in the United States. The formula for determining the rate is

$$\frac{\text{Number of murders}}{\text{Total U.S. population}} \times 100{,}000 = \text{Rate per } 100{,}000$$

For some purposes, the total figures (the raw data) are needed; for other purposes, percentages are more informative; and for still other purposes, expressing data as a rate is most useful. To illustrate this point, consider the following example of data about incarceration in two different states.

On December 31, 1998, 32,227 offenders were held in the prisons of Louisiana and 31,121 in the prisons of New Jersey. How does incarceration in these states compare? Just knowing the number of prisoners does not allow many conclusions to be drawn about incarceration in these states. If, however, the numbers are expressed as a rate, the difference in the sizes of the two state populations would be taken into consideration and, thus, a much clearer picture would result. Although Louisiana has fewer prisoners than New Jersey, the incarceration rate in Louisiana (736 prisoners per 100,000 population) is considerably higher than in New Jersey (382 per 100,000). On a national basis, the number of incarcerated people in 1998 represented a rate of 461 prisoners for every 100,000 U.S. residents, so the rate in Louisiana is significantly higher than for the United States as a whole. In fact, Louisiana has the highest incarceration rate in the country.

Sources of Criminal Justice Data

To a large extent, criminal justice researchers are dependent on data collected and analyzed by agencies of government. You will see many of these sources cited throughout this book. In particular, the Bureau of Justice Statistics of the U.S. Department of Justice produces the *Sourcebook of Criminal Justice Statistics*, an annual compilation of data on most aspects of crime and justice (found on the Internet at www.albany.edu/sourcebook); the *Bulletin*, regularly published issues focusing on a single topic related to police, courts, and corrections; and the *Special Report*, a publication that presents findings from specific research projects (www.ojp.usdoj.gov/bjs/). The National Institute of Justice, also an arm of the U.S. Department of Justice, publishes *Research in Brief*, summary versions of major research studies (www.ojp.usdoj.gov/nij/). *Crime in the United States,* published each August by the Department of Justice, contains data collected through the FBI's *Uniform Crime Reports* system (www.fbi.gov).

The libraries of most colleges and universities hold these publications in the government documents or reference sections. Ask your librarian to help you find them. If you would like to get on the mailing list to receive the free publications of the Bureau of Justice Statistics, fill out the form on the last page of the *Bulletin*. You can also access most of these publications through the Internet. Go to the web site for the agencies as noted above.

References

Abadinsky, H. 1994. *Organized Crime.* Chicago: Nelson-Hall.

———. 1997. *Probation and Parole,* 6th ed. Upper Saddle River, N.J.: Prentice-Hall.

Acker, J. R., and C. S. Lanier. 1994. "In Fairness and Mercy: Statutory Mitigating Factors in Capital Punishment Cases." *Criminal Law Bulletin* 30:299–345.

———. 1995. "Matters of Life or Death: The Sentencing Provisions in Capital Punishment Statutes." *Criminal Law Bulletin* 31:3–18.

Acoca, L. 1997. "Hearts on the Ground: Violent Victimization and Other Themes in the Lives of Women Prisoners." *Corrections Management Quarterly* 1 (Spring):44–55.

———. 1998. "Defusing the Time Bomb: Understanding and Meeting the Growing Health Care Needs of Incarcerated Women in America." *Crime and Delinquency* 44 (January):49–69.

Adams, K. 1992. "Adjusting to Prison Life," *Crime and Justice: A Review of Research,* vol. 16, ed. M. Tonry. Chicago: University of Chicago Press, 275–359.

Adler, F. 1975. *Sisters in Crime: The Rise of the New Female Criminal.* New York: McGraw-Hill.

Adler, S. J. 1994. *The Jury: Disorder in the Court.* New York: Doubleday.

Administrative Office of the U.S. Courts. 1993. *Guide to Judiciary Policies and Procedures: Probation Manual,* vol. 10 (mimeo).

Ahern, J. F. 1972. *Police in Trouble.* New York: Hawthorne Books.

Alarid, L. F., J. M. Marquart, V. S. Burton Jr., and S. J. Cuvelier. 1996. "Women's Roles in Serious Offenses: A Study of Adult Felons." *Justice Quarterly* 13 (September):431–454.

Albanese, J. 1991. "Organized Crime: The Mafia Myth," *Criminology: A Contemporary Handbook,* ed. J. Sheley. Belmont, Calif.: Wadsworth, 201–218.

Alexander, R., Jr. 1993. "The Demise of State Prisoners' Access to Federal Habeas Corpus." *Criminal Justice Policy Review* 6:55–70.

Alschuler, A. 1968. "The Prosecutor's Role in Plea Bargaining." *University of Chicago Law Review* 35:54–65.

Amar, A. R. 1997. *The Constitution and Criminal Procedure: First Principles.* New Haven, Conn.: Yale University Press.

American Correctional Association. 1990. *The Female Offender: What Does the Future Hold?* Alexandria, Va.: Kirby Lithographic Company.

———. 1993. *Gangs in Correctional Facilities: A National Assessment.* Laurel, Md.: American Correctional Association.

———. 1996. *Juvenile and Adult Correctional Facilities Directory.* College Park, Md.: American Correctional Association.

Anderson, L. 1999. "Attacks Spur Call to Force Medications." *Chicago Tribune,* June 1, p. 1.

Anderson, M. M. 1989. *Policing the World: Interpol and the Politics of International Police Cooperation.* Oxford, England: Clarendon Press.

Andrews, D. A., and J. Bonta. 1994. *The Psychology of Criminal Behavior.* Cincinnati: Anderson.

Andrews, D. A., I. Zinger, R. D. Hoge, J. Bonta, P. Gendreau, and F. T. Cullen. 1990. "Does Correctional Treatment Work? A Clinically Relevant and Psychologically Informed Meta-Analysis." *Criminology* 28:369–404.

Applegate, B. K., F. T. Cullen, and B. S. Fisher. 1997. "Public Support for Correctional Treatment: The Continuing Appeal of the Rehabilitative Ideal." *The Prison Journal* 77:237–258.

Armstrong, K., and S. Mills. 1999 "Death Row Justice Derailed." *Chicago Tribune,* November 14, 15, p. 1.

Aspin, L. T., and W. K. Hall. 1996. "Campaigning for Retention in Illinois." *Judicature* 80:84–87.

Auerhahn, K. 1999. "Selective Incapacitation and the Problem of Prediction." *Criminology* 37:703–734.

Austin, J. 1997. "The Impact of Truth-in-Sentencing on Prison Classification Systems." *Correctional Management Quarterly* (Spring):54–55.

Austin, J., and R. Lawson. 1998. *Assessment of California Parole Violations and Recommended Intermediate Programs and Policies.* San Francisco: National Council on Crime and Delinquency.

Baldus, D. C., G. Woodworth, and C. A. Pulaski. 1994. *Equal Justice and the Death Penalty: A Legal and Empirical Analysis.* Boston: Northeastern University Press.

Baltimore Sun. December 16, 1999:1.

Bandy, D. 1991. "$1.2 Million to Be Paid in Stray-Bullet Death." *Akron Beacon Journal,* December 3, p. B6.

Barber, J. W. 1994. "The Jury Is Still Out: The Role of Jury Science in the Modern American Courtroom." *American Criminal Law Review* 31:1225–1252.

Barkan, S. E., and S. E. Cohn. 1998. "Racial Prejudice and Support by Whites for Police Use of Force: A Research Note." *Justice Quarterly* 15 (December): 743–753.

Barnes, C. W., and R. Kingsnorth. 1996. "Race, Drug, and Criminal Sentencing: Hidden Effects of the Criminal Law." *Journal of Criminal Justice* 24:39–55.

Basemore, G., and M. S. Umbreit. 1994. *Balanced and Restorative Justice: Program Summary.* Washington, D.C.: Office of Juvenile Justice and Delinquency Prevention, foreword.

Bast, C. M. 1995. "Publication of the Name of a Sexual Assault Victim: The Collision of Privacy and Freedom of the Press." *Criminal Law Bulletin* 31:379–399.

Baunach, P. J. 1985. *Mothers in Prison.* New Brunswick, N.J.: Transaction Books.

Bayley, D. H. 1986. "The Tactical Choice of Police Patrol Officers." *Journal of Criminal Justice* 14:329–348.

———. 1994. *Police for the Future.* New York: Oxford University Press.

———. 1998. *What Works in Policing?* New York: Oxford University Press.

Beck, A. 1997. "Growth, Change, and Stability in the U.S. Prison Population, 1980–1995." *Corrections Management Quarterly* 8 (January):1–14.

Becker, Howard S. 1963. *Outsiders: Studies in the Sociology of Deviance.* New York: Free Press.

Bell, D. 1967. *The End of Ideology,* 2d. rev. ed. New York: Collier.

Berns, W., and J. Bessette. 1998. "Why the Death Penalty Is Fair." *Wall Street Journal,* January 1, p. A16.

Bershard, L. 1985. "Discriminatory Treatment of the Female Offender in the Criminal Justice System." *Boston College Law Review* 26:389–438.

Biderman, A. D., and J. P. Lynch. 1991. *Understanding Crime Incidence Statistics.* New York: Springer-Verlag.

Biderman, A. D., L. A. Johnson, J. McIntyre, and A. W. Weit. 1967. *Report on a Pilot Study in the District of Columbia on Victimization and Attitudes toward Law Enforcement.* Washington, D.C.: Government Printing Office.

BJA (Bureau of Justice Assistance). 1998. *1996 National Survey of State Sentencing Structures.* Washington, D.C.: Government Printing Office.

BJS (Bureau of Justice Statistics). 1988. *Report to the Nation on Crime and Justice,* 2d ed. Washington, D.C.: Government Printing Office.

———. 1989. *Special Report* (April).

———. 1993a. *Law Enforcement Management and Administration Statistics (LEMAS) Survey.* Washington, D.C.: Government Printing Office.

———. 1993b. *Survey of State Prison Inmates.* Washington, D.C.: Government Printing Office.

———. 1995a. *Bulletin* (April).

———. 1995b. *Sourcebook of Criminal Justice Statistics, 1994.* Washington, D.C.: Government Printing Office.

———. 1995c. *Special Report* (August).

———. 1997a. *Bulletin* (December).

———. 1997b. *Correctional Population in the United States, 1995.* Washington, D.C.: Government Printing Office.

———. 1997c. *Police Use of Force.* Washington, D.C.: Government Printing Office.

———. 1997d. Press release, November 22.

———. 1997e. *Selected Findings,* March.

———. 1998a. *Bulletin* (January).

———. 1998b. *Bulletin* (June).

———. 1998c. *Bulletin* (August).

———. 1998d. *Bulletin* (December).

———. 1998e. *Crime and Justice in the United States and in England and Wales, 1981–1996.* Washington, D.C.: Government Printing Office.

———. 1998f. Press release, August 16.

———. 1998g. *Sourcebook of Criminal Justice Statistics, 1997.* Washington, D.C.: Government Printing Office.

———. 1998h. *Special Report* (September).

———. 1998i. *Violence by Intimates.* Washington, D.C.: Government Printing Office.

———. 1999a. *American Indians and Crime.* Washington, D.C.: Government Printing Office.

———. 1999b. *Bulletin* (January).

———. 1999c. *Bulletin* (August).

———. 1999d. *Correctional Populations in the United States, 1996.* Washington, D.C.: Government Printing Office.

———. 1999e. Press release, July 18.

———. 1999f. Press release, October 29.

———. 1999g. Press release, December 5.

———. 1999h. Press release, December 12.

———. 1999j. *Special Report* (January).

———. 1999k. *Special Report* (July).

———. 1999l. *Sourcebook of Criminal Justice Statistics, 1998.* Washington, D.C.: Government Printing Office.

Blankenship, M., J. Luginbuhl, F. Cullen, and W. Redick. 1997. "Juror's Comprehension of Sentencing Instructions: A Test of the Death Penalty Process in Tennessee." *Justice Quarterly* 14: 325–351.

Blomberg, T. G., and K. Lucken. 1993. "Intermediate Punishments and the Piling Up of Sanctions," *Criminal Justice: Law and Politics,* 6th ed., ed. G. F. Cole. Belmont, Calif.: Wadsworth, 470–482.

Bloch, P., and D. Anderson, 1974. *Policewomen on Patrol: First Report.* Washington, D.C.: Police Foundation.

Blumberg, A. 1967. "The Practice of Law as a Confidence Game." *Law and Society Review* 1:11–39.

Blumberg, M. 1989. "Controlling Police Use of Deadly Force: Assessing Two Decades of Progress," *Critical Issues in Policing,* ed. G. Dunham and G. Alpert. Prospect Heights, Ill.: Waveland Press.

Blumenson, E., and E. Nilsen. 1998. "The Drug War's Hidden Economic Agenda." *The Nation* (March 9):11.

Blumstein, A. 1996. "Youth Violence, Guns, and Illicit Drug Markets." *NIJ Research Preview.*

———. 1998. "U.S. Criminal Justice Conundrum: Rising Prison Populations and Stable Crime Rates." *Crime and Delinquency* 44 (January):129.

Blumstein, A., and A. J. Beck. 1999. "Population Growth in U.S. Prisons, 1980–1996," in *Prisons,* ed. M. Tonry and J. Petersilia, *Crime and Justice: A Review of Research,* vol. 26. Chicago: University of Chicago Press, 54–94.

Boland, B., E. Brady, H. Tyson, and J. Bassler. 1983. *The Prosecution of Felony Arrests.* Washington, D.C.: U.S. Department of Justice, Bureau of Justice Statistics.

Bonta, J., and P. Gendreau. 1995. "Reexamining the Cruel and Unusual Punishment of Prison Life," *Long-Term Imprisonment,* ed. T. J. Flanagan. Thousand Oaks, Calif.: Sage, 75–94.

Bourque, B. B., M. Han, and S. M. Hill. 1996. "A National Survey of Aftercare Provisions for Boot Camp Graduates." *Research in Brief.*

Bowker, L. H. 1982. "Victimizers and Victims in American Correctional Institutions," *Pains of Imprisonment,* ed. R. Johnson and H. Toch. Beverly Hills, Calif.: Sage.

Bradley, C. 1992. "Reforming the Criminal Trial." *Indiana Law Journal* 68:659–664.

Brandl, S. 1993. "The Impact of Case Characteristics of Detectives' Decision Making." *Justice Quarterly* 10 (September):395–415.

Brandl, S., and Frank, J. 1994. "The Relationship between Evidence, Detective Effort, and the Disposition of Burglary and Robbery Investigations." *American Journal of Police,* 13:149–168.

Brandon, K. 1999. "Legal Abortions Tied to Decline in Crime." *Hartford Courant,* August 8, p. A5.

Bray, K. 1992. "Reaching the Final Chapter in the Story of Peremptory Challenges." *U.C.L.A. Law Review* 40:517–555.

Brennan, P. A., S. A. Mednick, and J. Volavka. 1995. "Biomedical Factors in Crime," *Crime,* ed. J. Q. Wilson and J. Petersilia. San Francisco: ICS Press.

Brereton, D., and J. Casper. 1981–1982. "Does It Pay to Plead Guilty? Differential Sentencing and the Function of Criminal Courts." *Law and Society Review* 16:56–61.

Bright, S. B. 1994. "Counsel for the Poor: The Death Sentence Not for the Worst Crime But for the Worst Lawyer." *Yale Law Journal* 103:1850.

———. 1997. "Political Attacks on the Judiciary." *Judicature* 80:165–173.

Britton, D. M. 1997. "Perceptions of the Work Environment among Correctional Officers: Do Race and Sex Matter?" *Criminology* 35: 505–524.

Broeder, D. W. 1959. "The University of Chicago Jury Project." *Nebraska Law Review* 38:774–803.

Brown, J. R. 1999. "Drug Diversion Courts: Are They Needed and Will They Succeed in Breaking the Cycle of Drug-Related Crime," in *Criminal Courts for the 21st Century,* ed. L. Stolzenberg and S. D'Alessio. Saddle River, N.J.: Prentice-Hall.

Brown, L. A., and M. A. Wycoff. 1987. "Policing Houston: Reducing Fear and Improving Service." *Crime and Delinquency* 33 (January):71.

Brown, M. K. 1981. *Working the Street.* New York: Russell Sage Foundation.

Buchanan, J. 1989. "Police/Prosecutor Teams: Innovations in Several Jurisdictions." *NIJ Reports* (May/June).

Buentello, S. 1992. "Combating Gangs in Texas." *Corrections Today* 54 (July):58–60.

Burke, P. 1997. *Policy-Driven Responses to Probation and Parole Violations.* Washington, D.C.: National Institute of Corrections.

Burns, R., and J. Smith. 1999. "DNA: Fingerprint of the Future?" *ACJS Today* (November/December):1.

Butterfield, F. 1995a. "Idle Hands within the Devil's Own Playground." *New York Times,* July 16, p. E3.

———. 1995b. "More Blacks in Their 20's Have Trouble with the Law." *New York Times,* October 5, p. A18.

———.1996. "Three Strikes Rarely Invoked in Courtrooms." *New York Times,* September 10, p. A1.

———.1998a. "Decline in Violent Crimes Is Linked to Crack Market." *New York Times,* December 18, p. A16.

———. 1998b. "Police Accused of Altering Crime Data." *New York Times,* August 3, p. A1.

———. 1998c. "Prisons Replace Hospitals for the Nation's Mentally Ill." *New York Times,* March 5, p. A26.

———. 1999a. "Inmates Serving More Time, Justice Department Reports." *New York Times*, January 11, p. A10.

———. 1999b. "Rethinking the Strong Arm of the Law." *New York Times*, April 4, p. WK1.

———. 1999c. "Crime Fell 7 Percent in '98 Continuing a 7-Year Trend." *New York Times*, May 17, p. A12.

Buzawa, E. S., and C. G. Buzawa. 1990. *Domestic Violence: The Criminal Justice Response*. Newbury Park, Calif.: Sage.

Calhoun, F. 1990. *The Lawmen*. Washington, D.C.: Smithsonian Institution.

Call, J. E. 1995. "Prison Overcrowding Cases in the Aftermath of *Wilson v. Seiter*." *Prison Journal* 75 (September):390–405.

Callahan, L. A., M. A. McGreevy, C. Cirincione, and H. J. Steadman. 1992. "Measuring the Effects of the Guilty But Mentally Ill (GBMI) Verdict." *Law and Human Behavior* 16:447–462.

Camp, D. D. 1993. "Out of the Quagmire: After *Jacobson v. United States*: Toward a More Balanced Entrapment Standard." *Journal of Criminal Law and Criminology* 83:1055–1097.

Cannon, L. 1991. "Blue-Collar Judge on Washington State's Top Court." *Washington Post National Weekly Edition*, August 26-September 1, p. 15.

Cardozo, B. N. 1921. *The Nature of the Judicial Process*. New Haven, Conn.: Yale University Press.

Carelli, Richard. 1999. "*Miranda* Law May Face Test in Supreme Court." *Detroit News*, July 22, p. 4A.

Carlson, T. 1995. "Safety, Inc." *Policy Review* (Summer):67–73.

Carns, T. W., and J. Kruse. 1991. *Alaska's Plea Bargaining Ban: Re-Evaluated*. Anchorage: Alaska Judicial Council.

Carr, J. G. 1993. "Bail Bondsmen and the Federal Courts." *Federal Probation* 57 (March):9–14.

Carroll, L. 1974. *Hacks, Blacks, and Cons: Race Relations in a Maximum Security Prison*. Lexington, Mass.: Lexington Books.

Casey, M. 1999. "Defense Lawyers for Poor Clients May Get Pay Raise." *New York Times*, April 11, p. 5.

Casper, J. D. 1971. "Did You Have a Lawyer When You Went to Court? No, I Had a Public Defender." *Yale Review of Law and Social Change* 1:4–9.

Cassell, P. 1995. "How Many Criminals Has *Miranda* Set Free?" *Wall Street Journal*, March 1, p. A17.

Cassell, P., and R. Fowles. 1998. "Handcuffing the Cops? A Thirty-Year Perspective on *Miranda*'s Harmful Effects on Law Enforcement." *Stanford Law Review* 50:1055–1145.

Caulfield, S. L. 1994. "Life or Death Decision: Prosecutorial Power vs. Equality of Justice." *Journal of Contemporary Criminal Justice* 5:233–247.

Champagne, A., and K. Cheek. 1996. "PACs and Judicial Politics in Texas." *Judicature* 80:26–29.

Champion, D. J. 1989. "Private Counsels and Public Defenders: A Look at Weak Cases, Prior Records, and Leniency in Plea Bargaining." *Journal of Criminal Justice* 17:253–263.

Chapman, S. G. 1970. *Police Patrol Readings*, 2d ed. Springfield, Ill.: Charles C. Thomas.

Chapper, J. A., and R. A. Hanson. 1989. *Understanding Reversible Error in Criminal Appeals*. Williamsburg, Va.: National Center for State Courts.

———. 1990. *Intermediate Appellate Courts: Improving Case Processing*. Williamsburg, Va.: National Center for State Courts.

Cheesman, F., R. A. Hanson, and B. J. Ostrom. 1998. "To Augur Well: Future Prison Population and Prisoner Litigation." Paper presented at the Federal Judicial Center, Washington, D.C., May 20.

Chermak, S. M. 1995. *Victims in the News: Crime and the American News Media*. Boulder, Colo.: Westview Press.

Chilton, B. S. 1991. *Prisons under the Gavel: The Federal Court Takeover of Georgia Prisons*. Columbus, Ohio: Ohio State University Press.

Chiricos, T. G., and W. D. Bales. 1991. "Unemployment and Punishment: An Empirical Assessment." *Criminology* 29:701–724.

Chiricos, T. G., and C. Crawford. 1995. "Race and Imprisonment: A Contextual Assessment of the Evidence," *Ethnicity, Race, and Crime: Perspectives across Time and Place*, ed. D. F. Hawkins. Albany, N.Y.: State University of New York Press.

Chiricos, T. G., S. Escholz, and M. Gertz. 1997. "Crime, News, and Fear of Crime." *Social Problems* 44:342–357.

Christopher, R. L. 1994. "Mistake of Fact in the Objective Theory of Justification." *Journal of Criminal Law and Criminology* 85:295–332.

Church, T. W. 1985. "Examining Local Legal Culture." *American Bar Foundation Research Journal* (Summer):449.

Church, T. W., A. Carlson, J. Lee, and T. Tan. 1978. *Justice Delayed*. Williamsburg, Va.: National Center for State Courts.

Clear, T. R. 1994. *Harm in American Penology*. Albany, N.Y.: State University of New York Press.

———. 1996. "Mis-Truths in Sentencing." *Perspectives* 20:12–13.

Clear, T. R., and A. A. Braga. 1995. "Community Corrections," *Crime*, ed. J. Q. Wilson and J. Petersilia. San Francisco: ICS Press, 421–444.

Clear, T. R., and G. F. Cole. 1997. *American Corrections*, 4th ed. Belmont, Calif.: Wadsworth.

———. 2000. *American Corrections*, 5th ed. Belmont, Calif.: Wadsworth.

Clear, T. R., and D. R. Karp. 1999. *Community Justice: Preventing Crime and Achieving Justice*. Washington, D.C.: National Institute of Justice.

Clear, T. R., and P. L. Hardyman. 1990. "The New Intensive Supervision Movement." *Crime and Delinquency* 36:42.

Clear, T. R., and E. J. Latessa. 1993. "Surveillance vs. Control: Probation Officers' Roles in Intensive Supervision." *Justice Quarterly* 10:441.

Cohen, L. E., and M. Felson. 1979. "Social Change and Crime Rates: A Routine Activity Approach." *American Sociological Review* 44:588–608.

Cohen, M., and J. T. McEwen. 1984. "Handling Calls for Service: Alternatives to Traditional Policing." *NIJ Reports*, 4–8.

Cohen, M., T. R. Miller, and S. B. Rossman. 1990. "The Costs and Consequences of Violent Behavior in the United States." Paper prepared for the Panel on the Understanding and Control of Violent Behavior, National Research Council, National Academy of Sciences, Washington, D.C.

Commission on Accreditation for Law Enforcement Agencies.1989. *Standards for Law Enforcement Accreditation*. Fairfax, Va.: Commission on Accreditation for Law Enforcement Agencies.

Conley, J. A. 1980. "Prisons, Production, and Profit: Reconsidering the Importance of Prison Industries." *Journal of Social History* 14:257.

Connors, E., T. Lundregan, N. Miller, and T. McEwen. 1996. *Convicted by Juries, Exonerated by Science: Case Studies in the Use of DNA Evidence to Establish Innocence after Trial*. Washington, D.C.: National Institute of Justice.

Cook, P. J., and J. H. Laub. 1998. "The Unprecedented Epidemic in Youth Violence," *Youth Violence*, ed. M. Tonry and M. Moore. Chicago: University of Chicago Press, 27–64.

Cook, P. J., and D. B. Slawson with L. A. Gries. 1993. *The Cost of Processing Murder Cases in North Carolina*. Durham, N.C.: Terry Sanford Institute of Public Policy.

Cooney, M. 1994. "Evidence as Partisanship." *Law and Society Review* 28:833–858.

Corbett, R., and G. Marx. 1991. "Critique: No Soul in the New Machine: Technofallacies in the Electronic Monitoring Movement." *Justice Quarterly* 8:399–414.

Cordner, G. 1988. "A Problem-Oriented Approach to Community-Oriented Policing," *Community Policing: Rhetoric or Reality,* ed. J. Greene and S. Mastrofsky. New York: Praeger, 135–152.

Corrections Compendium. 1994. (March):5–6.

Constanzo, M. 1997. *Just Revenge.* New York: St. Martin's Press.

Cowan, C. C., W. C. Thompson, and P. C. Ellsworth. 1984. "The Effects of Death Qualification on Jurors' Predisposition to Convict and on the Quality of Deliberation." *Law and Human Behavior* 8:60.

Crew, B. K. 1991. "Race Differences in Felony Charging Sentencing: Toward an Integration of Decision-Making and Negotiation Models." *Journal of Crime and Justice* 14:99–122.

Criminal Justice Newsletter. 1994. (January 8):1.

Cripe, C. A. 1997. *Legal Aspects of Corrections Management.* Gaithersburg, Md.: Aspen Publishers.

Crocker, L. 1993. "Can the Exclusionary Rule Be Saved?" *Journal of Criminal Law and Criminology* 84:310–351.

Crouch, B. M., and J. M. Marquart. 1989. *An Appeal to Justice.* Austin: University of Texas Press.

Cullen, F. T., L. Cao, J. Frank, R. H. Langworthy, S. L. Browning, R. Kopache, and T. J. Stevenson. 1996. " 'Stop or I'll Shoot': Racial Differences in Support of Police Use of Deadly Force on Fleeing Felons." *American Behavioral Scientist* 39 (February):449.

Cullen, F. T., T. Leming, B. Link, and J. Wozniak. 1985. "The Impact of Social Supports in Police Stress." *Criminology* 23:503–522.

Cullen, F. T., E. J. Latessa, V. S. Burton Jr., and L. X. Lombardo. 1993. "The Correctional Orientation of Prison Wardens: Is the Rehabilitative Ideal Supported?" *Criminology* 31 (February):69–92.

Cullen, F. T., J. P. Wright, and B. K. Applegate. 1996. "Control in the Community: The Limits of Reform?" *Choosing Correctional Options That Work: Defining the Demand and Evaluating the Supply,* ed. A. T. Harland. Thousand Oaks, Calif.: Sage, 69–116.

Cuniff, M. 1987. *Sentencing Outcomes in Twenty-Eight Felony Courts.* Washington, D.C.: National Institute of Justice.

Cunningham, W. C., J. J. Strauchs, and C. W. Van Meter. 1990. *Private Security Trends, 1970 to the Year 2000.* Boston: Butterworth-Heinemann.

Daly, K. 1998. "Gender, Crime, and Criminology," *The Handbook of Crime and Punishment,* ed. M. Tonry. New York: Oxford University Press, 85–108.

Daly, K., and R. L. Bordt. 1995. "Sex Effects and Sentencing: An Analysis of the Statistical Literature." *Justice Quarterly* 12 (March):141–175.

Daly, K., and M. Chesney-Lind. 1988. "Feminism and Criminology." *Justice Quarterly* 5 (1988):497.

Daly, K., and M. Tonry. 1997. "Gender, Race, and Sentencing," *Crime and Justice: A Review of Research,* vol. 22, ed. M. Tonry. Chicago: University of Chicago Press, 201–252.

Davey, J. D. 1998. *The Politics of Prison Expansion.* Westport, Conn.: Praeger.

Davis, M., R. Lundman, and R. Martinez Jr. 1991. "Private Corporate Justice: Store Police, Shoplifters, and Civil Recovery." *Social Problems* 38:395–408.

Davis, R. C., and B. E. Smith. 1994. "The Effects of Victim Impact Statements on Sentencing Decisions: A Test in an Urban Setting." *Justice Quarterly* 11 (September):3.

Death Penalty Information Center. 2000. www.essential.org/dpic/.

Decker, S., R. Wright, A. Redfern, and D. Smith. 1993. "A Woman's Place Is in the Home: Females and Residential Burglary." *Justice Quarterly* 10 (March):142.

DeFrances, C. J., and G. W. Steadman. 1998. "Prosecutors in State Courts, 1996." *Bureau of Justice Statistics Bulletin.*

DeJong, C., and C. Smith. 2000. "Equal Protection, Gender, and Justice at the Dawn of a New Century." *Wisconsin Women's Law Journal.*

Diamond, S. S. 1990. "Scientific Jury Selection: What Social Scientists Know and Do Not Know." *Judicature* 73:178.

Diggs, D. W., and S. L. Peiper. 1994. "Using Day Reporting Centers as an Alternative to Jail." *Federal Probation* 58 (March):9–13.

DiIulio, J. J., Jr. 1987. *Governing Prisons.* New York: Free Press.

———. 1990a. *No Escape: The Future of American Corrections.* New York: Basic Books.

———. 1993a. "Rethinking the Criminal Justice System: Toward a New Paradigm," *Performance Measures for the Criminal Justice System.* Washington, D.C.: U.S. Department of Justice, Bureau of Justice Statistics.

———. 1993b. "Well-Governed Prisons Are Possible," *Criminal Justice: Law and Politics,* 6th ed., ed. G. F. Cole. Belmont, Calif: Wadsworth.

———. 1994. "The Question of Black Crime." *The Public Interest* (Fall):3–32.

———. 1999. "Two Million Prisoners Are Enough." *Wall Street Journal,* March 12, p. A18.

DiIulio, J. J., Jr., A. Piehl, and B. Useem. 1998. "New Estimates of the Criminality of Inmates from New York, Arizona, and New Mexico." Unpublished manuscript, Princeton University.

Dill, F. 1975. "Discretion, Exchange, and Social Control: Bail Bondsmen in Criminal Courts." *Law and Society Review* 9:644–674.

Dillehay, R. C., and M. R. Sandys. 1996. "Life under *Wainwright v. Witt:* Juror Dispositions and Death Qualification." *Law and Human Behavior* 20:147–165.

Donohue, J. J., and S. D. Levitt. 1998. "The Impact of Race on Policing, Arrest Patterns, and Crime." American Bar Foundation Working Paper #9705 (Revision).

Donziger, S. R., ed. 1996. *The Real War on Crime: The Report of the National Criminal Justice Commission.* New York: Harper Collins.

Drimmer, J. 1997. "America's Least Wanted: We Need New Rules to Stop Abuses." *Washington Post,* September 21, p. C6.

Dugdale, R. 1910. *The Jukes: Crime, Pauperism, Disease, and Heredity,* 4th ed. New York: Putnam.

Dumaine, B. 1998. "Beating Bolder Corporate Crooks." *Fortune* (April 25):193.

Earley, P. 1992. *The Hot House: Life inside Leavenworth Prison.* New York: Bantam Books.

Edna McConnell Clark Foundation. 1997. *Seeking Justice: Crime and Punishment in America.* New York: Edna McConnell Clark Foundation.

Egan, T. 1999a. "A Drug Ran Its Course, Then Hid with Its Users." *New York Times,* September 19, p. A1.

———. 1999b. "War on Crack Retreats, Still Taking Prisoners." *New York Times,* February 28, p. A1.

Eisenstein, J., R. B. Flemming, and P. F. Nardulli. 1988. *The Contours of Justice: Communities and Their Courts.* Boston: Little, Brown.

Eisenstein, J., and H. Jacob. 1977. *Felony Justice: An Organizational Analysis of Criminal Courts.* Boston: Little, Brown.

Emmelman, D. S. 1996. "Trial by Plea Bargain: Case Settlement as a Product of Recursive Decisionmaking." *Law and Society Review* 30:335–360.

Erez, E., and B. Thompson. 1990. "Rape in Sierra Leone: Conflict between the Sexes and Conflict of Laws." *International Journal of Comparative and Applied Criminal Justice* 14:201–210.

Eskridge, C. W. 1986. *Pretrial Release Programming.* New York: Clark Boardman.

Estrich, S. 1987. *Real Rape.* Cambridge, Mass.: Harvard University Press, 92.

———. 1998. *Getting Away with Murder: How Politics Is Destroying the Criminal Justice System.* Cambridge, Mass.: Harvard University Press.

Fabelo, T. 1999. *Biennial Report to the 76th Texas Legislature.* Austin, Texas: Criminal Justice Policy Council.

FBI (Federal Bureau of Investigation). 1999. *Crime in the United States—1998.* Washington, D.C.: Government Printing Office.

Federal Bureau of Prisons. 1998. *State of the Bureau: Accomplishments and Goals.* Washington, D.C.: Government Printing Office.

Feeley, M. M. 1979. *The Process Is the Punishment.* New York: Russell Sage Foundation.

———. 1982. "Plea Bargaining and the Structure of the Criminal Process." *Justice System Journal* 7:338–355.

———. 1983. *Court Reform on Trial.* New York: Basic Books.

Feeley, M. M., and R. A. Hanson. 1990. "The Impact of Judicial Intervention on Prisons and Jails: A Framework of Analysis and a Review of the Literature," *Courts, Corrections, and the Constitution,* ed. J. J. DiIulio Jr. New York: Oxford University Press.

Feeney, F. 1998. *German and American Prosecution: An Approach to Statistical Comparison.* Washington, D.C.: U.S. Department of Justice, Bureau of Justice Statistics.

Feld, B. C. 1993. "Criminalizing the American Juvenile Court," *Crime and Justice: A Review of Research,* vol. 17, ed. M. Tonry. Chicago: University of Chicago Press, 197–280.

Felice, J. D., and J. C. Kilwein. 1992. "Strike One, Strike Two . . .: The History and Prospect for Judicial Reform in Ohio." *Judicature* 75:193–200.

Fetzer, P. L. 1989. "Execution of the Mentally Retarded: A Punishment without Justification." *South Carolina Law Review* 40:419.

Finckenauer, J. O. 1984. *Juvenile Delinquency and Corrections: The Gap between Theory and Practice.* Orlando, Fla.: Academic Press.

Fine, R. A. 1986. *Escape of the Guilty.* New York: Dodd, Mead.

Fishbein, D. H. 1990. "Biological Perspectives in Criminology." *Criminology* 28:27.

Flanagan, T. J. 1991. "Adaptation and Adjustment among Long-Term Prisoners." *Federal Prison Journal* 2 (Spring):41–51.

———, ed. 1995. *Long-Term Imprisonment.* Thousand Oaks, Calif.: Sage.

Flanagan, T. J., and K. Maguire. 1993. "A Full Employment Policy for Prisons in the United States: Some Arguments, Estimates, and Implications." *Journal of Criminal Justice* 21:117–130.

Flango, V. E. 1994a. "Court Unification and the Quality of State Courts." *Justice System Journal* 16:33–55.

———. 1994b. *Habeas Corpus in State and Federal Courts.* Williamsburg, Va.: National Center for State Courts.

Fleisher, M. 1989. *Warehousing Violence.* Newbury Park, Calif.: Sage.

Fleisher, M., R. H. Rison, and D. W. Helman. 1997. "Female Inmates: A Growing Constituency in the Federal Bureau of Prisons." *Corrections Management Quarterly* 1:28–35.

Flemming, R. B. 1982. *Punishment before Trial.* New York: Longman.

Flemming, R. B., P. F. Nardulli, and J. Eisenstein. 1992. *The Craft of Justice: Politics and Work in Criminal Court Communities.* Philadelphia: University of Pennsylvania Press.

Forst, B. 1995. "Prosecution and Sentencing," *Crime,* ed. J. Q. Wilson and J. Petersilia. San Francisco: ICS Press.

Foucault, M. 1977. *Discipline and Punish,* trans. A. Sheridan. New York: Pantheon.

Fox, J. G. 1982. *Organizational and Racial Conflict in Maximum Security Prisons.* Lexington, Mass.: Lexington Books.

Foy, Paul. 1999. "Utah Liquor Laws Gaining Notoriety." *Lansing State Journal,* June 26, p. 5A.

Frank, J., S. G. Brandl, F. T. Cullen, and A. Stichman. 1996. "Reassessing the Impact of Race on Citizens' Attitudes toward the Police: A Research Note." *Justice Quarterly* 13 (June):320–334.

Friday, P. C., S. Metzger, and D. Walters. 1991. "Policing Domestic Violence: Perceptions, Experience, and Reality." *Criminal Justice Review* 16:198–213.

Fridell, L. 1990. "Decision Making of the District Attorney: Diverting or Prosecuting Intrafamilial Child Sexual Abuse Offenders." *Criminal Justice Policy Review* 4:249–267.

Fried, J. P. 1994. "Wide Use of Unelected Judges Prompts Voting Rights Inquiry." *New York Times,* July 19, pp. B1, B3.

Friedland, M., and K. Roach. 1997. "Borderline Justice: Choosing Juries in the Two Niagaras." *Israel Law Review* 31:120–157.

Friedman, L. M. 1993. *Crime and Punishment in American History.* New York: Basic Books.

Friedrichs, D. O. 1996. *Trusted Criminals: White-Collar Crime in Society.* Belmont, Calif.: Wadsworth.

Frohmann, L. 1997. "Convictability and Discordant Locales: Reproducing Race, Class, and Gender Ideologies in Prosecutorial Decisionmaking." *Law and Society Review* 31:531–556.

Fukurai, H. 1996. "Race, Social Class, and Jury Participation: New Dimensions for Evaluating Discrimination in Jury Service and Jury Selection." *Journal of Criminal Justice* 24:71–88.

Fyfe, J. 1993. "Police Use of Deadly Force: Research and Reform," *Criminal Justice: Law and Politics,* 6th ed, ed. G. F. Cole. Belmont, Calif.: Wadsworth.

Fyfe, J., D. A. Klinger, and J. M. Flavin, 1997. "Differential Policy Treatment of Male-on-Female Spousal Violence." *Criminology* 35 (August):454–473.

Gardner, M. A. 1993. "Section 1983 Actions under *Miranda:* A Critical View of the Right to Avoid Interrogation." *American Criminal Law Review* 30:1277–1328.

Garner, J. 1987. "Delay Reduction in the Federal Courts: Rule 50(b) and the Federal Speedy Trial Act of 1974." *Journal of Quantitative Criminology* 3:229–250.

Garner, J., and E. Clemmer. 1986. *Danger to Police in Domestic Disturbances—A New Look.* Washington, D.C.: U.S. Department of Justice, Bureau of Justice Statistics.

Garner J., T. Schade, J. Hepburn, and J. Buchanan. 1995. "Measuring the Continuum of Forced Used by and against the Police." *Criminal Justice Review* 20 (Autumn):146–168.

Garofalo, J., and M. McLeod. 1989. "The Structure and Operation of Neighborhood Watch Programs in the United States." *Crime and Delinquency* 35:326–344.

Geerken, M., and H. D. Hayes. 1993. "Probation and Parole: Public Risks and the Future of Incarceration Alternatives." *Criminology* 31 (November):549–564.

Geller, W. A., and Morris, N. 1992. "Relations between Federal and Local Police," *Modern Policing,* ed. M. Tonry and N. Morris. Chicago: University of Chicago Press, 231–348.

Gendreau, P., F. T. Cullen, and J. Bonta. 1994. "Intensive Rehabilitation Supervision: The Next Generation in Community Corrections?" *Federal Probation* 58:72–78.

Gershman, B. L. 1993. "Themes of Injustice: Wrongful Convictions, Racial Prejudice, and Lawyer Incompetence." *Criminal Law Bulletin* 29:502–515.

Gilboy, J. A., and J. R. Schmidt. 1979. "Replacing Lawyers: A Case Study of the Sequential Representation of Criminal Defendants." *Journal of Criminal Law and Criminology* 70:2.

Gill, M. S. 1997. "Cybercops Take a Byte out of Computer Crime." *Smithsonian* (May):114–124.

Girshick, L. B. 1999. *No Safe Haven: Stories of Women in Prison.* Boston: Northeastern University Press.

Gallup Poll. 1999. "Racial Attitudes towards the Police" (December 11), at www.Gallup.com.

Glick, R. M., and V. V. Neto. 1977. *National Study of Women's Correctional Programs.* Washington, D.C.: Government Printing Office.

Goddard, H. H. 1902. *The Kallikak Family.* New York: Macmillan.

Goldfarb, R. L. 1965. *Ransom: A Critique of the American Bail System.* New York: Harper & Row.

———. 1975. *Jails: The Ultimate Ghetto.* Garden City, N.Y.: Doubleday.

Goldfarb, R. L., and L. R. Singer. 1973. *After Conviction.* New York: Simon & Schuster.

Goldkamp, J. S. 1979. *Two Classes of Accused.* Cambridge, Mass.: Ballinger.

———. 1985. "Danger and Detention: A Second Generation of Bail Reform." *Journal of Criminal Law and Criminology* 76:1–75.

Goldkamp, J. S., and M. R. Gottfredson. 1985. *Policy Guidelines for Bail: An Experiment in Court Reform.* Philadelphia: Temple University Press.

Goldman, S., and Slotnick, E. 1999. "Clinton's Second Term Judiciary: Picking Judges under Fire." *Judicature* 82: 264–285.

Goldschmidt, J., and J. M. Shaman. 1996. "Judicial Disqualifications: What Do Judges Think?" *Judicature* 80:68–72.

Goldstein, H. 1977. *Policing a Free Society.* Cambridge, Mass.: Ballinger.

———. 1979. "Improving Policing: A Problem-Oriented Approach." Crime and *Delinquency* 25:236–257.

———. 1990. *Problem-Oriented Policing.* New York: McGraw-Hill.

Goodman, J. 1994. *Stories of Scottsboro.* New York: Random House.

Goodpaster, G. 1986. "The Adversary System, Advocacy, and Effective Assistance of Counsel in Criminal Cases." *New York University Review of Law and Social Change* 14:90.

Goolkasian, G. A., R. W. Geddes, and W. DeJong. 1989. "Coping with Police Stress," *Critical Issues in Policing,* ed. R. G. Dunham and G. P. Alpert. Prospect Heights, Ill.: Waveland Press, 489–507.

Gottfredson, M., and T. Hirschi. 1990. *A General Theory of Crime.* Stanford, Calif.: Stanford University Press.

Graham, B. L. 1995. "Judicial Recruitment and Racial Diversity on State Courts," *Courts and Justice,* ed. G. L. Mays and P. R. Gregware. Prospect Heights, Ill.: Waveland Press.

Green, G. S. 1990. *Occupational Crime.* Chicago: Nelson-Hall.

Greene, J. A. 1999. "Zero Tolerance: A Case Study of Police Policies and Practices in New York City." *Crime and Delinquency* 45 (April):171–187.

Greenhouse, L. 1999. "Supreme Court: The Justices Decide Who's in Charge." *New York Times,* June 27.

Greenwood, P., J. M. Chaiken, and J. Petersilia. 1977. *Criminal Investigation Process.* Lexington, Mass.: Lexington Books.

Griffin, A., and F. Rhee. 1999. "Twins, 11, Held in Gory Shooting of Parents, Sister." *Charlotte Observer,* April 3.

Griset, P. L. 1993. "Determinate Sentencing and the High Cost of Overblown Rhetoric: The New York Experience." *Crime and Delinquency* 39 (April):552.

———. 1995. "The Politics and Economics of Increased Correctional Discretion over Time Served: A New York Case Study." *Justice Quarterly* 12 (June):307.

Hagan, F. E. 1997. *Political Crime: Ideology and Criminality.* Needham Heights, Mass.: Allyn & Bacon.

Hagan, J., and R. D. Peterson. 1995. "Criminal Inequality in America: Patterns and Consequences," *Crime and Inequality,* ed. J. Hagan and R. D. Peterson. Stanford, Calif.: Stanford University Press, 14–36.

Haghighi, B., and J. Sorensen. 1996. "America's Fear of Crime," *Americans View Crime and Justice,* ed. T. Flanaghan and D. R. Longmire. Thousand Oaks, Calif.: Sage Publications, 16–30.

Halifax Chronicle Herald. July 22, 1999:1.

Halbfinger, D. 1999. "Guards Charged in Fatal Beating of Inmate at Nassau County Jail." *New York Times,* May 27, p. B1.

Hall, J. 1947. *General Principles of Criminal Law,* 2d ed. Indianapolis: Bobbs-Merrill.

Hall, M. G. 1995. "Justices as Representatives: Elections and Judicial Politics in the United States." *American Politics Quarterly* 23:485–503.

Hall, W. K., and L. T. Aspin. 1987. "What Twenty Years of Judicial Retention Elections Have Told Us." *Judicature* 70:340.

Hans, V., and N. Vidmar. 1986. *Judging the Jury.* New York: Plenum Press.

Hanson, R. A., and J. Chapper. 1991. *Indigent Defense Systems.* Williamsburg, Va.: National Center for State Courts.

Hanson, R. A., and H. W. K. Daley. 1995. *Challenging the Conditions of Prisons and Jails.* Williamsburg, Va.: National Center for State Courts.

Hartford Courant. February 18, 1997:A6.

———. December 27, 1998:A1.

———. April 7, 1999.

———. September 10, 1999:A22.

Hartman, M. J., H. S. Wallace, and C. Lyons. 1997. *Report of the Blue Ribbon Committee on Indigent Defense Services.* Washington, D.C.: National Legal Aid and Defender Association.

Hastie, R., S. Penrod, and N. Pennington. 1983. *Inside the Jury.* Cambridge, Mass.: Harvard University Press.

Hawkins, G. 1983. "Prison Labor and Prison Industries," *Crime and Justice,* ed. M. Tonry and N. Morris. Chicago: University of Chicago Press.

Heffernan, E. 1972. *Making It in Prison.* New York: Wiley.

Henning, P. J. 1993. "Precedents in a Vacuum: The Supreme Court Continues to Tinker with Double Jeopardy." *American Criminal Law Review* 31:1–72.

Hensley, T. R., and C. E. Smith. 1995. "Membership Change and Voting Change: An Analysis of the Rehnquist Court's 1986–1991 Terms." *Political Research Quarterly* 48:837–856.

Hepburn, J. R. 1985. "The Exercise of Power in Coercive Organizations: A Study of Prison Guards." *Criminology* 23:145–164.

Hepburn, J. R., and P. E. Knepper. 1993. "Correctional Officers as Human Services Workers: The Effect of Job Satisfaction." *Justice Quarterly* 10 (June):315.

Herbert, S. 1996. "Morality in Law Enforcement: Chasing 'Bad Guys' with the Los Angeles Police Department." *Law and Society Review* 30:799–818.

Herrnstein, R. J. 1995. "Criminogenic Traits," *Crime,* ed. J. Q. Wilson and J. Petersilia. San Francisco: ICS Press.

Heumann, M. 1978. *Plea Bargaining.* Chicago: University of Chicago Press.

Hickey, T. J. 1993. "Expanding the Use of Prior Act Evidence in Rape and Sexual Assault." *Criminal Law Bulletin* 29:195–218.

———. 1995. "A Double Jeopardy Analysis of the Medgar Evers Murder Case." *Journal of Criminal Justice* 23:41–51.

Hillsman, S. T., J. L. Sichel, and B. Mahoney. 1983. *Fines in Sentencing.* New York: Vera Institute of Justice.

Hirsch, A. J. 1992. *The Rise of the Penitentiary.* New Haven, Conn.: Yale University Press.

Hirschel, J. D., I. W. Hutchinson, C. W. Dean, and A. M. Mills. 1992. "Review Essay on the Law Enforcement Response to Spouse Abuse: Past, Present, and Future." *Justice Quarterly* 9:247–283.

Hirschi, T. 1969. *Causes of Delinquency.* Berkeley: University of California Press.

Ho, T. 1998. "Retardation, Criminality, and Competency to Stand Trial among Mentally Retarded Criminal Defendants: Violent Versus Non-Violent Defendants." *Journal of Crime and Justice* 21:57–70.

Hoffman, M. 1999. "Abolish Peremptory Challenges." *Judicature* 82:202–204.

Holmes, M. D., H. M. Hosch, H. C. Daudistel, D. A. Perez, and J. B. Graves. 1996. "Ethnicity, Legal Resources, and Felony Dispositions in Two Southwestern Jurisdictions." *Justice Quarterly* 13:11–29.

Holmes, O. W., Jr. 1881. *The Common Law*. Boston: Little, Brown.

Hoctor, M. 1997. "Domestic Violence as a Crime against the State." *California Law Review* 85 (May):643.

Horney, J., and C. Spohn. 1991. "Rape Law Reform and Instrumental Change in Six Urban Jurisdictions." *Law and Society Review* 25:117–153.

Houston, B., and J. Ewing. 1991. "Justice Jailed." *Hartford Courant*, June 16.

Howard, J. 1929. *The State of Prisons in England and Wales*. London, England: J. M. Dent.

Huff, C. R., and M. Meyer. 1997. "Managing Prison Gangs and Other Security Threat Groups." *Corrections Management Quarterly* 1 (Fall):11.

Hunt, G., S. Riegel, T. Morales, and D. Waldorf. 1993. "Changes in Prison Culture: Prison Gangs and the Case of the Pepsi Generation." *Social Problems* 40:398–409.

Ianni, F. A. J. 1973. *Ethnic Succession in Organized Crime*. Washington, D.C.: Government Printing Office.

Innes, C. A., and V. D. Verdeyen. 1997. "Conceptualizing the Management of Violent Inmates." *Corrections Management Quarterly* 1 (Fall):1–9.

Irwin, J. 1970. *The Felon*. Englewood Cliffs, N.J.: Prentice-Hall.

———. 1980. *Prisons in Turmoil*. Boston: Little, Brown.

Irwin, J., and D. Cressey. 1962. "Thieves, Convicts, and the Inmate Culture." *Social Problems* 10:142–155.

Italiano, L. 1999a. "Schizophrenia Splits Subway-Push Jury." *New York Post*, November 1.

———. 1999b. "Kendra's Kin Despair at Hung Jury." *New York Post*, November 3.

———. 1999c. "My Kendra Deserved Fair Trial, Says Mom." *New York Post*, November 5.

Ith, I. 1999. "Lawyer Says Ex-Infoseek Exec Is Innocent of Web Sex Charges." *Seattle Times*, October 1.

Jacob, H. 1973. *Urban Justice*. Boston: Little, Brown.

Jacob, H., Erhard Blankenburg, Herbert M. Kritzer, Doris Marie Provine, and Joseph Sanders. 1996. *Courts, Law, and Politics in Comparative Perspective*. New Haven, Conn.: Yale University Press.

Jacobs, J. B., C. Panarella, and J. Worthington. 1994. *Busting the Mob: United States v. Cosa Nostra*. New York: New York University Press.

———. 1995. "Judicial Impact on Prison Reform," *Punishment and Social Control*, ed. T. G. Blomberg and S. Cohen. New York: Aldine DeGruyter, 63–76.

Jacobs, J. B., and C. Panarella. 1998. "Organized Crime," *The Handbook of Crime and Punishment*, ed. M. Tonry. New York: Oxford University Press, 159–177.

Jacoby, J. 1979. "The Charging Policies of Prosecutors," *The Prosecutor*, ed. W. F. McDonald. Beverly Hills, Calif.: Sage.

———. 1995. "Pushing the Envelope: Leadership in Prosecution." *Justice System Journal* 17:291–307.

Janikowski, W. R., and D. Giacopassi. 1993. "Pyrrhic Images, Dancing Shadows, and Flights of Fancy: The Drug Courier Profile as Legal Fiction." *Journal of Contemporary Criminal Justice* 9:60–69.

Jenne, D. L., and R. C. Kersting. 1996. "Aggression and Women Correctional Officers in Male Prisons." *The Prison Journal* 76:442–460.

Johnson, D. T. 1998. "The Organization of Prosecution and the Possibility of Order." *Law and Society Review* 32:247–308.

Johnson, R. 1996. *Hard Time: Understanding and Reforming the Prison*, 2d ed. Belmont, Calif.: Wadsworth.

Jones, M. A., and J. Austin. 1995. "The 1995 NCCD National Prison Population Forecast: The Cost of Truth-in-Sentencing Laws." *NCCD Focus*.

Jones, P., and J. Goldkamp. 1991. "The Bail Guidelines Experiment in Dade County, Miami: A Case Study in the Development and Implementation of a Police Innovation." *Justice System Journal* 14:445–476.

Josephson, R. L., and M. Reiser. 1990. "Officer Suicide in the Los Angeles Police Department." *Journal of Police Science and Administration* 17:227–229.

Justice, R. 1996. "Irvin: No Contest to Drug Charge." *Washington Post*, July 16, p. E1.

Kairys, D., J. B. Kadane, and J. P. Lehoczky. 1977. "Jury Representativeness: A Mandate for Multiple Source Lists." *California Law Review* 65:776–827.

Kalinich, D. B. 1980. *Power, Stability, and Contraband*. Prospect Heights, Ill.: Waveland Press.

Kalven, H., and H. Zeisel. 1966. *The American Jury*. Boston: Little, Brown.

Kansas City Star, September 24, 1997:A2.

Kappeler, V. E., M. Blumberg, and G. W. Potter. 1996. *The Mythology of Crime and Criminal Justice*, 2d ed. Prospect Heights, Ill: Waveland Press.

Karmen, A. 1996. *Crime Victims*, 3d ed. Belmont, Calif.: Wadsworth.

Keil, T. J., and G. F. Vito. 1992. "The Effects of the *Furman* and *Gregg* Decisions on Black-White Execution Ratios in the South." *Journal of Criminal Justice* 20:217–226.

Kelling, G. L. 1985. "Order Maintenance, the Quality of Urban Life, and Police: A Line of Argument," *Police Leadership in America*, ed. W. A. Geller. New York: Praeger.

———. 1991. *Foot Patrol*. Washington, D.C.: National Institute of Justice.

———. 1992. "Measuring What Matters: A New Way of Thinking about Crime and Public Order." *City Journal* (Spring).

Kelling, G. L., and W. J. Bratton. 1993. "Implementing Community Policing: The Administrative Problem," *Perspectives on Policing*, no. 17. Washington, D.C.: National Institute of Justice.

Kelling, G. L., and C. M. Coles. 1996. *Fixing Broken Windows: Restoring and Reducing Crime in Our Communities*. New York: Free Press.

Kelling, G. L., and M. Moore. 1988. "The Evolving Strategy of Policing," *Perspectives on Policing*, no. 13. Washington, D.C.: National Institute of Justice.

Kelling, G. L., T. Pate, D. Dieckman, and C. E. Brown. 1974. *The Kansas City Preventive Patrol Experiments: A Summary Report*. Washington, D.C.: Police Foundation.

Kennedy, R. 1997. *Race, Crime, and the Law*. New York: Pantheon.

Kennedy, S., and K. Carlson. 1988. *Pretrial Release and Detention: The Bail Reform Act of 1984*. Washington, D.C.: U.S. Department of Justice, Bureau of Justice Statistics.

Kenney, D. J., and J. O. Finckenauer. 1995. *Organized Crime in America*. Belmont, Calif.: Wadsworth.

Kerry, J. S. 1997. *The New War*. New York: Simon & Schuster.

King, N. J. 1994. "The Effects of Race-Conscious Jury Selection on Public Confidence in the Fairness of Jury Proceedings: An Empirical Puzzle." *American Criminal Law Review* 31:1177–1202.

Kleinknecht, W. 1996. *The New Ethnic Mobs: The Changing Face of Organized Crime in America*. New York: Free Press.

Klinger, D. A. 1988. "The Guilty Plea Process in Three Small Pennsylvania Judicial Districts: An Inquiry into the Nature of Rural Criminal Justice." Unpublished masters essay, Department of Political Science, Pennsylvania State University (1983) [quoted in J. Eisenstein, R. B. Flemming, and P. F. Nardulli. 1988. *The Contours of Justice: Communities and Their Courts.* Boston: Little, Brown].

Klockars, C. B. 1985. "Order Maintenance, the Quality of Urban Life, and Police: A Different Line of Argument," *Police Leadership in America*, ed. W. A. Geller. New York: Praeger.

Klofas, J., and J. Yandrasits. 1989. " 'Guilty But Mentally Ill' and the Jury Trial: A Case Study." *Criminal Law Bulletin* 24:424.

Kolbert, E. 1999. "The Perils of Safety." *New Yorker*, March 22:50.

Koper, C. 1995. "Just Enough Police Presence: Reducing Crime and Disorderly Behavior by Optimizing Patrol Time in Crime Hot Spots." *Justice Quarterly* 12 (December):649–672.

Kotlowitz, A. 1994. "Their Crimes Don't Make Them Adults." *New York Times Magazine,* February 13, p. 40.

Kramer, G. P., and D. M. Koenig. 1990. "Do Jurors Understand Criminal Justice Instructions? Analyzing the Results of the Michigan Juror Comprehension Project." *University of Michigan Journal of Law Reform* 23:401–437.

Kramer, J. H., and J. T. Ulmer. 1996. "Sentencing Disparity and Departures from Guidelines." *Justice Quarterly* 13 (March):81.

Krauss, C. 1994. "No Crystal Ball Needed on Crime," *New York Times*, sec. 4, November 13:4.

Kridler, C. 1999. "Sergeant Friday, Where Are You?" *Newsweek*, May 17:14.

Krisberg, B. 1988. *The Juvenile Court: Reclaiming the Vision.* San Francisco: National Council on Crime and Delinquency.

Kruttschnitt, C., and S. Krmopotich. 1990. "Aggressive Behavior among Female Inmates: An Exploratory Study." *Justice Quarterly* 7 (June):71.

Kunen, J. S. 1995. "Teaching Prisoners a Lesson." *New Yorker,* July 10:34.

Kurtz, H. 1997. "The Crime Spree on Network News." *Washington Post,* August 12, p. 1.

Labaton, S. 1999. "House Approves Measure That Would Curb Government's Authority to Seize Property." *New York Times,* June 25.

Laffey, M. 1998. "Cop Diary." *New Yorker,* August 10:36–39.

———. 1999. "Cop Diary." *New Yorker,* February 1:29–32.

Langan, P. A. 1994. "Between Prison and Probation: Intermediate Sanctions." *Science* 264 (May):791–793.

Langan, P. A., and M. A. Cunniff. 1992. *Recidivism of Felons on Probation, 1986–89.* Washington, D.C.: U.S. Department of Justice, Bureau of Justice Statistics.

Langbein, J. H. 1992. "On the Myth of Written Constitutions: The Disappearance of the Criminal Jury Trial." *Harvard Journal of Law and Public Policy* 15:119–127.

Langworthy, R. H. 1989. "Do Stings Control Crime? An Evaluation of a Police Fencing Operation." *Justice Quarterly* 6 (March):27.

Lansing State Journal. September 9, 1999:8B.

———. October 3, 1999:6B.

Latessa, E. J., and L. F. Travis III. 1992. "Residential Community Correctional Programs," *Smart Sentencing: The Emergence of Intermediate Sanctions,* ed. J. M. Byrne, A. J. Lurigio, and J. Petersilia. Newbury Park, Calif.: Sage, 166.

Lave, T. R. 1998. "Equal before the Law." *Newsweek,* July 13:14.

Lear, E. T. 1995. "Contemplating the Successive Prosecution Phenomenon in the Federal System." *Journal of Criminal Law and Criminology* 85:625–675.

Leo, R. A. 1996a. "The Impact of *Miranda* Revisited." *Journal of Criminal Law and Criminology* 86:621–692.

———.1996b. "*Miranda*'s Revenge: Police Interrogation as a Confidence Game." *Law and Society Review* 30:259–288.

Levin, M. 1975. "Delay in Five Criminal Courts." *Journal of Legal Studies* 4:83–131.

———. 1998. "Urban Politics and Policy Outcomes: The Criminal Courts," *The Criminal Justice System, Politics and Politics,* 7th ed. ed. G. F. Cole and M. G. Gertz. Belmont, Calif.: Wadsworth.

Levine, J. P. 1992. *Juries and Politics.* Belmont, Calif.: Wadsworth.

———. 1996. "The Case Study as a Jury Research Methodology." *Journal of Criminal Justice* 24:351–360.

Levine, R. A. 1959. "Gusii Sex Offenses: A Study in Social Control." *American Anthropologist* 61:896–990.

Levy, S. 1997. "A Guru Goes Free." *Newsweek,* December 15.

Lewis, N. 1999. "Prosecutors Urged to Allow Appeals on DNA." *New York Times,* September 28, p. 14.

Lieb, R., V. Quinsey, and L. Berliner. 1998. "Sexual Predators and Social Policy," *Crime and Justice: A Review of Research,* vol. 23, ed. M. Tonry. Chicago: University of Chicago Press, 43–114.

Lilly, J. R. 1993. "The Corrections-Commercial Complex." *Crime and Delinquency* 39 (April):150.

Lim, M. 1987. "A Status Report on State Court Financing." *State Court Journal* 11 (Summer):7.

Logan, C. 1992. "Well Kept: Comparing Quality of Confinement in Private and Public Prisons." *Journal of Criminal Law and Criminology* 83 (Fall):577.

———. 1993. "Criminal Justice Performance Measures in Prisons." *Performance Measures for the Criminal Justice System.* Washington, D.C.: U.S. Department of Justice, Bureau of Justice Statistics, 19–60.

Logan, C., and J. J. DiIulio Jr. 1993. "Ten Deadly Myths about Crime and Punishment in the United States," *Criminal Justice: Law and Politics,* ed. G. F. Cole. Belmont, Calif.: Wadsworth, 486–502.

Lombroso, C. 1968. *Crime: Its Causes and Remedies.* Montclair, N.J.: Patterson Smith.

Loof, Susanna. 1999. "Both Side Argue over Boy's Confession." *Lansing State Journal,* January 7.

Los Angeles Times. November 23, 1997:A18.

———. January 4, 1998:1.

———. December 16, 1999:C–1.

Love, M., and S. Kuzma. 1996. *Civil Disabilities of Convicted Felons.* Washington, D.C.: Office of the Pardon Attorney.

Lovrich, N. P., and C. H. Sheldon. 1994. "Is Voting for State Judges a Flight of Fancy or a Reflection of Policy and Value Preferences?" *Justice System Journal* 16:57–71.

Lynch, D. 1999. "Perceived Judicial Hostility to Criminal Trials: Effects on Public Defenders in General and on Their Relationships with Clients and Prosecutors in Particular." *Criminal Justice and Behavior* 26:217–234.

Lynch, J. 1995. "Crime in International Perspective," *Crime,* ed. J. Q. Wilson and J. Petersilia. San Francisco: ICS Press, 11–38.

Lynch, M. 1998. "Waste Manager? New Penology, Crime Fighting, and the Parole Agent Identity." *Law and Society Review* 32:87.

MacCoun, R. J., A. Saiger, J. P. Kahan, and P. Reuter. 1993. "Drug Policies and Problems: The Promises and Pitfalls of Cross-National Comparisons," *Psychoactive Drugs and Human Harm Reduction: From Faith to Science,* ed. N. Heather, E. Nadelman, and P. O'Hare. London, England: Whurr Publications.

MacFarquhar, N. 1999. "A Rap Performer Is Charged with Assaulting a Producer." *New York Times,* April 17.

Mack, J. 1909. "The Juvenile Court." *Harvard Law Review* 1:119.

MacKenzie, D. L. 1995. "Boot Camp Prisons and Recidivism in Eight States." *Criminology* 33:327–358.

MacKenzie, D. L., and A. Piquero. 1994. "The Impact of Shock Incarceration Programs on Prison Crowding." *Crime and Delinquency* 40 (April):222–249.

Mahoney, B., L. Sipes, and J. Ito. 1985. *Implementing Delay Reduction and Delay Prevention Programs in Urban Trial Courts.* Williamsburg, Va.: National Center for State Courts.

Maitland, A. S., and R. D. Sluder. 1998."Victimization and Youthful Prison Inmates: An Empirical Analysis." *The Prison Journal* 78:55.

Maltese, J. A. 1998. *The Selling of Supreme Court Nominees.* Baltimore: Johns Hopkins University Press.

Mann, C. R. 1993. *Unequal Justice: A Question of Color.* Bloomington: Indiana University Press.

Manning, P. K. 1971. "The Police: Mandate, Strategies, and Appearances," *Crime and Justice in American Society,* ed. J. D. Douglas. Indianapolis: Bobbs-Merrill, 149–193.

_____. 1977. *Police Work.* Cambridge, Mass.: MIT Press.

Marsh, J. R. 1994. "Performing Pretrial Services: A Challenge in the Federal Criminal Justice System." *Federal Probation* 58 (December):3–10.

Martin, S. E. 1989. "Women in Policing: The Eighties and Beyond," *Police and Society,* ed. D. Kenney. New York: Praeger.

_____. 1991. "The Effectiveness of Affirmative Action." *Justice Quarterly* 8:489–504.

Martin, S. E., and L. W. Sherman. 1986. "Selective Apprehension: A Police Strategy for Repeat Offenders." *Criminology* 24 (February):155–173.

Martin, S. J., and S. Eckland-Olson. 1987. *Texas Prisons: The Walls Came Tumbling Down.* Austin: Texas Monthly Press.

Martinson, R. 1974. "What Works? Questions and Answers about Prison Reform." *The Public Interest* (Spring):25.

Marvell, T. B., and C. E. Moody. 1995. "The Impact of Enhanced Prison Terms for Felonies Committed with Guns." *Criminology* 33 (May):247–281.

Maschke, K. J. 1995. "Prosecutors as Crime Creators: The Case of Prenatal Drug Use." *Criminal Justice Review* 20:21–33.

Maudsley, H. 1974. *Responsibility in Mental Disease.* London, England: Macmillan.

Mauer, M., C. Potler, and R. Wolf. 1999. *Gender and Justice: Women, Drugs, and Sentencing Policy.* Washington, D.C.: The Sentencing Project.

Maxwell, S. R. 1999. "Examining the Congruence between Predictors of ROR and Failures to Appear." *Journal of Criminal Justice* 27:127–141.

Mayhew, P., and J. J. M. van Dijk. 1997. *Criminal Victimisation in Eleven Industrial Countries.* The Hague, Netherlands: Dutch Ministry of Justice.

Maynard, D. 1984. "The Structure of Discourse in Misdemeanor Plea Bargaining." *Law and Society Review* 18:81–87.

McConville, S. 1995. "Local Justice: The Jail," *The Oxford History of the Prison,* ed. N. Morris and D. J. Rothman. New York: Oxford University Press.

McCorkle, R. C. 1993. "Research Note: Punish and Rehabilitate? Public Attitudes toward Six Common Crimes." *Crime and Delinquency* 39 (April):240.

McCoy, C. 1986. "Policing the Homeless." *Criminal Law Bulletin* 22 (May/June):263.

_____. 1993. *Politics and Plea Bargaining: Victims' Rights in California.* Philadelphia: University of Pennsylvania Press.

_____. 1995. "Is the Trial Penalty Inevitable?" Paper presented at the annual meeting of the Law and Society Association, Phoenix, Arizona, June.

McDivitt, J., and R. Miliano. 1992. "Day Reporting Centers: An Innovative Concept in Intermediate Sanctions," *Smart Sentencing: The Emergence of Intermediate Sanctions,* ed. J. M. Byrne, A. J. Lurigio, and J. Petersilia. Newbury Park, Calif.: Sage, 152–165.

McDonald, D., J. Greene, and C. Worzella. 1992. *Day Fines in American Courts: The Staten Island and Milwaukee Experiments.* Washington, D.C.: National Institute of Justice.

McGabey, R. 1986. "Economic Conditions: Neighborhood Organizations and Urban Crime," *Crime and Justice,* vol. 8., ed. A. J. Reiss and M. Tonry. Chicago: University of Chicago Press.

McGee, R. A., G. Warner, and N. Harlow. 1998. "The Special Management Inmate," *Incarcerating Criminals,* ed. T. A. Flanagan, J. W. Marquart, and K. G. Adams. New York: Oxford University Press, 99–106.

McLeod, M. 1989. "Getting Free: Victim Participation in Parole Board Decisions." *Criminal Justice* 4.

Mears, T. 1998. "Place and Crime." *Chicago-Kent Law Review* 73:669.

Meier, R. F., and T. D. Miethe. 1993. "Understanding Theories of Criminal Victimization," *Crime and Justice: A Review of Research,* ed. M. Tonry. Chicago: University of Chicago Press.

Melekian, B. 1990. "Police and the Homeless." *FBI Law Enforcement Bulletin* 59:1–7.

Mentzer, A. 1996. "Policing in Indian Country: Understanding State Jurisdiction and Authority," *Law and Order* (June):24–29.

Merianos, D. E., J. W. Marquart, and K. Damphousse. 1997. "Examining HIV-Related Knowledge among Adults and Its Consequences for Institutionalized Populations." *Corrections Management Quarterly* 1 (Fall):84–87.

Messner, S. F., and R. Rosenfeld. 1994. *Crime and the American Dream.* Belmont, Calif.: Wadsworth.

Mickenberg, I., and H. S. Wallace. 1998. *National Survey of Indigent Defense Systems: Interim Report.* Washington, D.C.: National Legal Aid and Defender Association.

Miethe, T. D. 1995. "Fear and Withdrawal from Urban Life." *Annals of the American Academy of Political and Social Science* 539 (May):14–27.

Mileski, M. 1971. "Courtroom Encounters: An Observation Study of a Lower Criminal Court." *Law and Society Review* 5:524.

Miller, J. L., and J. J. Sloan. 1994. "A Study of Criminal Justice Discretion." *Journal of Criminal Justice* 22:107–123.

Miller, M., and M. Guggenheim. 1990. "Pretrial Detention and Punishment." *Minnesota Law Review* 75:335–426.

Monkkonen, E. H. 1981. *Police in Urban America, 1869–1920.* Cambridge, England: Cambridge University Press.

_____. 1992. "History of the Urban Police," *Modern Policing,* ed. M. Tonry and N. Morris. Chicago: University of Chicago Press.

Morash, M., R. N. Haarr, and L. Rucker. 1994. "A Comparison of Programming for Women and Men in the U.S. Prisons in the 1980s." *Crime and Delinquency* 40 (April):197.

Moore, M. 1992. "Problem-Solving and Community Policing," *Modern Policing,* ed. M. Tonry and N. Morris. Chicago: University of Chicago Press, 99–158.

Moore, M., and G. L. Kelling. 1983. "To Serve and to Protect: Learning from Police History." *The Public Interest* (Winter):55.

Moore, M., and M.Tonry. 1998. "Youth Violence in America," *Youth Violence,* ed. M. Tonry and M. Moore. Chicago: University of Chicago Press, 1–26.

Morris, N. 1982. *Madness and the Criminal Law.* Chicago: University of Chicago Press.

Morris, N., and D. J. Rothman, eds. 1995. *The Oxford History of the Prison.* New York: Oxford University Press, 1995.

Morris, N., and M. Tonry. 1990. *Between Prison and Probation: Intermediate Punishments in a Rational Sentencing System.* New York: Oxford University Press.

Murphy, P. V. 1992. "Organizing for Community Policing," *Issues in Policing: New Perspectives,* ed. J. W. Bizzack. Lexington, Ky: Autumn Press, 113–128.

NAACP Legal Defense and Educational Fund. 1999. *Death Row USA.* New York: NAACP Legal Defense and Educational Fund (Fall).

Nadelmann, E. A. 1993. *Cops across Borders: The Internationalization of U.S. Criminal Law Enforcement.* University Park, Penn.: Pennsylvania State University Press.

Nagel, R. F. 1990. "The Myth of the General Right to Bail." *The Public Interest* (Winter):84–97.

Nagin, D. S. 1998. "Criminal Deterrence Research at the Outset of the Twenty-First Century," *Crime and Justice,* vol. 23, ed. M. Tonry. Chicago: University of Chicago Press, 1–42.

Nardulli, P. F. 1983. "The Societal Costs of the Exclusionary Rule: An Empirical Assessment." *American Bar Foundation Journal*:585–690.

——. 1986. "Insider Justice: Defense Attorneys and the Handling of Felony Cases." *Journal of Criminal Law and Criminology* 79:416.

National Advisory Commission on Civil Disorders. 1968. *Report of the National Advisory Commission on Civil Disorders.* Washington, D.C.: Government Printing Office.

National Legal Aid and Defenders Association. 1999. "Full-Court Press on Federal CJA Rate Increase." Press release, April 21.

Neubauer, D. 1996. *America's Courts and the Criminal Justice System,* 5th ed. Belmont, Calif.: Wadsworth.

Neufeld, P. J., and N. Colman. 1990. "When Science Takes the Witness Stand." *Scientific American* 262 (May):46.

New York, Office of Justice Systems Analysis. 1991. *The Incarceration of Minority Defendant: An Identification of Disparity in New York State, 1985–1986.* Albany: New York: State Division of Criminal Justice Services.

New York Newsday. June 14, 1989:60.

New York Times. July 15, 1989:6.

——. June 27, 1990:A10.

——. November 1, 1992:A12.

——. November 30, 1992:30.

——. September 1, 1994:1.

——. April 17, 1995:1.

——. July 23, 1995:1.

——. November 1, 1995:A1.

——. November 7, 1995:1.

——. September 3, 1996:B1.

——. January 1, 1997:A12.

——. January 5, 1997.

——. January 20, 1997:1.

——. February 20, 1997:1.

——. March 30, 1997:12.

——. June 24, 1997:A19.

——. July 6, 1997:E4.

——. July 13, 1997:D5.

——. August 7, 1997:A35.

——. August 8, 1997:A16.

——. September 17, 1997:A33.

——. October 10, 1997:A12.

——. January 1, 1998:A16.

——. March 29, 1998:A1.

——. March 30, 1998:A1.

——. March 3, 1999:A1.

——. March 6, 1999:A15.

——. March 8, 1999:A14.

——. April 15,1999:A1.

——. May 10, 1999:A26.

——. May 23, 1999:A1.

——. September 9, 1999:A14.

——. September 26, 1999:26.

——. October 6, 1999:A1.

——. December 10, 1999:A1.

——. January 2, 2000:WK3.

New York Times Magazine. June 2, 1996:35.

Newman, T. C. 1996. "Fair Cross-Section and Good Intention: Representation in Federal Juries." *Justice System Journal* 18:211–232.

Newsweek. April 25, 1988:43.

——. April 26, 1993:52–53.

——. February 21, 1994:26.

——. September 26, 1994:58.

——. November 16, 1998:69.

——. May 3, 1999:25.

NIJ (National Institute of Justice). 1988. *Research in Action.* Washington, D.C.: Government Printing Office.

——. 1996. *Victim Costs and Consequences: A New Look.* Washington, D.C.: Government Printing Office.

——. 1997. *Research in Brief* (January).

Novak, V. 1999. "The Cost of Poor Advice." *Time,* July 5:38.

Ogletree, C. J., Jr., M. Prosser, A. Smith, and W. Talley Jr. 1995. *Beyond the Rodney King Story: An Investigation of Police Misconduct in Minority Communities.* Boston: Northeastern University Press.

OJJDP (Office of Juvenile Justice and Delinquency Prevention). 1998. *Trying Juveniles as Adults in Criminal Court: An Analysis of State Transfer Provisions.* Washington, D.C.: Government Printing Office.

——. 1999. *Juvenile Offenders and Victims: 1999 National Report.* Washington, D.C.: Government Printing Office.

Olivares, K., V. Burton, and F. Cullen. 1996. "The Collateral Consequences of a Felony Conviction: A National Study of State Legal Codes 10 Years Later." *Federal Probation* 60:10–18.

O'Reilly, G. W. 1997. "Opening Up Argentina's Courts." *Judicature* 80: 237–240.

Owen, B. 1998. *In the Mix: Struggle and Survival in a Woman's Prison.* Albany, N.Y.: State University of New York Press.

Owen, B., and B. Bloom. 1995. "Profiling Women Prisoners: Findings from National Surveys and a California Sample." *Prison Journal* 75 (June):165–185.

Packer, H. L. 1968. *The Limits of the Criminal Sanction.* Stanford, Calif.: Stanford University Press.

Palmer, T. 1992. *The Re-Emergence of Correctional Intervention.* Newbury Park, Calif.: Sage.

Parent, D. G. 1990. *Day Reporting Centers for Criminal Offenders: A Descriptive Analysis of Existing Programs.* Washington, D.C.: National Institute of Justice.

Pate, A. M., and E. H. Hamilton. 1991. *The Big Six: Policing America's Large Cities.* Washington, D.C.: Police Foundation.

Peoples, J. M. 1995. "Helping Pretrial Services Clients Find Jobs." *Federal Probation* 59 (March):14–18.

Perito, R. M. 1999. "Managing U.S. Participation in International Police Operations," *Civilian Police and Multinational Peacekeeping—A Workshop Series.* Washington, D.C.: National Institute of Justice, 9–11.

Perkins, C. A., J. J. Stephan, and A. J. Beck. 1995. "Jails and Jail Inmates 1993–94." *Bulletin* (April).

Perkins, D. B., and J. D. Jamieson. 1995. "Judicial Probable Cause Determinations after *County of Riverside v. McLaughlin.*" *Criminal Law Bulletin* 31:534–546.

Petersen, R. D., and D. J. Palumbo. 1997. "The Social Construction of Intermediate Punishments." *The Prison Journal* 77 (March):77–91.

Petersilia, J. 1990. "When Probation Becomes More Dreaded Than Prison." *Federal Probation* (March):24.

——. 1993. "Measuring the Performance of Community Corrections," *Performance Measures for the Criminal Justice System.* Washington, D.C.: U.S. Department of Justice, Bureau of Justice Statistics.

——. 1996. "A Crime Control Rationale for Reinvesting in Community Corrections." *Perspectives* 20 (Spring):21–29.

——. 1998. "Probation and Parole," *The Handbook of Crime and Punishment,* ed. M. Tonry. New York: Oxford University Press, 563–588.

——. 1999. "Parole and Prisoner Reentry in the United States," in *Prisons,* ed. M. Tonry and J. Petersilia, *Crime and Justice: A Review of Research,* vol. 26. Chicago: University of Chicago Press, 479–553.

Petersilia, J., and S. Turner. 1987. "Guideline-Based Justice Prediction and Racial Minorities," *Crime and Justice,* vol. 15, ed. N. Morris and M. Tonry. Chicago: University of Chicago Press.

———. 1989. "The Potential of Intermediate Sanctions." *State Government* (March/April):65.

———. 1990. *Intensive Supervision for High-Risk Probationers: Findings from Three California Experiments.* Santa Monica, Calif.: RAND Corporation.

———. 1993. "Intensive Probation and Parole," *Crime and Justice,* vol. 17, ed. M. Tonry. Chicago: University of Chicago Press.

Petersilia, J., J. Kahan, and J. Peterson. 1985. *Granting Felons Probation: Public Risks and Alternatives.* Santa Monica, Calif.: RAND Corporation.

Pfeiffer, C. 1998. "Juvenile Crime and Violence in Europe," *Crime and Justice: A Review of Research,* vol. 23, ed. M. Tonry. Chicago: University of Chicago Press, 255–328.

Phillips, C. 1999. "Rapper 'Puff Daddy' to Attend One-Day Class after Guilty Plea." *Los Angeles Times,* September 9:C–1.

Phillips, S. 1977. *No Heroes, No Villains.* New York: Random House.

Piliavin, I., and S. Briar. 1976. "Police Encounters with Juveniles," *Back on the Street,* ed. R. M. Carter and M. W. Klein. Englewood Cliffs, N.J.: Prentice-Hall, 197–206.

Pisciotta, A. W. 1994. *Benevolent Repression: Social Control and the American Reformatory-Prison Movement.* New York: New York University Press.

Platt, A. 1977. *The Child Savers,* 2d ed. Chicago: University of Chicago Press.

Pohlman, H. L. 1999. *The Whole Truth? A Case of Murder on the Appalachian Trail.* Amherst, Mass.: University of Massachusetts Press.

Pollock-Byrne, J. 1990. *Women, Prisons, and Crime.* Pacific Grove, Calif.: Brooks/Cole.

Possley, M., and T. Gregory. 1999. "DuPage 5 Win Acquittal." *Chicago Tribune,* June 5:1.

President's Commission on Law Enforcement and Administration of Justice, 1967. *The Challenge of Crime in a Free Society.* Washington, D.C.: Government Printing Office.

Propper, A. 1982. "Make Believe Families and Homosexuality among Imprisoned Girls." *Criminology* 20:127–139.

Proveda, T. 1990. *Lawlessness and Reform: The FBI in Transition.* Pacific Grove, Calif.: Brooks/Cole.

Pursley, R. D. 1995. "The Federal Habeas Corpus Process: Unraveling the Issues." *Criminal Justice Policy Review* 7 (June):115.

Radelet, M. L., H. A. Bedeau, and C. E. Putnam. 1992. *In Spite of Innocence.* Boston: Northeastern University Press.

Radelet, M. L., W. S. Lofquist, and H. A. Bedau. 1996. "Prisoners Released from Death Rows since 1970 Because of Doubts about Their Guilt." *Thomas M. Cooley Law Review* 13:907.

Rafter, N. H. 1983. "Prisons for Women, 1790–1980," *Crime and Justice,* 5th ed., ed. M. Tonry and N. Morris. Chicago: University of Chicago Press.

Reaves, B. A. 1992. *State and Local Police Departments, 1990.* Washington, D.C.: U.S. Department of Justice, Bureau of Justice Statistics.

———. 1998. *Felony Defendants in Large Urban Counties, 1994: State Court Processing Statistics.* Washington, D.C.: U.S. Department of Justice, Bureau of Justice Statistics.

Reaves, B. A., and T. C. Hart. 1999. *Felony Defendants in Large Urban Counties, 1996: State Court Case Processing Statistics.* Washington, D.C.: U.S. Department of Justice, Bureau of Justice Statistics.

Reaves, B. A., and J. Perez. 1994. "Pretrial Release of Felony Defendants, 1992." *Bulletin* (November).

Reaves, B. A., and P. Z. Smith. 1995. *Felony Defendants in Large Urban Counties, 1992.* Washington, D.C.: U.S. Department of Justice, Bureau of Justice Statistics.

Regoli, R. M., J. P. Crank, and R. G. Culbertson. 1987. "Rejoinder—Police Cynicism: Theory Development and Reconstruction." *Justice Quarterly* 4:281–286.

Regoli, R. M., and J. D. Hewitt. 1994. *Criminal Justice.* Englewood Cliffs, N.J.: Prentice-Hall.

Reibstein, L. 1997. "NYPD Black and Blue." *Newsweek,* June 2:66.

Reid, T. V. 1996. "PAC Participation in North Carolina Supreme Court Elections." *Judicature* 80:21–25.

Reichers, L. M., and R. R. Roberg. 1990. "Community Policing: A Critical Review of Underlying Assumptions." *Journal of Police Science and Administration* 17:105–114.

Reiman, J. . . . *And the Poor Get Prison: Economic Bias in American Criminal Justice.* 1996. Boston: Allyn & Bacon.

Reiss, A. J., Jr. 1988. *Private Employment of Public Police.* Washington, D.C.: National Institute of Justice.

———. 1992. "Police Organization in the Twentieth Century," *Crime and Justice: A Review of Research,* vol. 15, ed. M. Tonry and N. Morris. Chicago: University of Chicago Press, 51–97.

Reno, J. 1995. "A Federal Commitment to Tribal Justice Systems." *Judicature* 79: 113–117.

Renzema, M. 1992. "Home Confinement Programs: Development, Implementation, and Impact," *Smart Sentencing: The Emergence of Intermediate Sanctions,* ed. J. M. Byrne, A. J. Lurigio, and J. Petersilia. Newbury Park, Calif.: Sage, 41–53.

———. 1998. "Satellite Monitoring of Offenders: A Report from the Field." *Journal of Offender Monitoring* 11 (Spring):5–11.

Richardson, J. E. 1993. "It's Not Easy Being Green: The Scope of the Fifth Amendment Right to Counsel." *American Criminal Law Review* 31:145–167.

Rideau, W., and R. Wikberg. 1992. *Life Sentences: Rage and Survival in Prison.* New York: Times Books.

Robin, G. D. 1993. "Inquisitive Cops, Investigative Stops, and Drug Courier Hops: Returning to the Scene of the Crime." *Journal of Contemporary Criminal Justice* 9:41–59.

Robinson, P. H. 1993. "Foreword: The Criminal-Civil Distinction and Dangerous Blameless Offenders." *Journal of Criminal and Criminology* 83:693–717.

Rohde, D. 1999. "Rage against Women Said to Prompt Shove." *New York Times,* October 8, p. B3.

Roper, R., and V. Flango. 1983. "Trials before Judges and Juries." *Justice System Journal* 8:186–198.

Rosen, L. 1995. "The Creation of the Uniform Crime Report: The Role of Social Science." *Social Science History* 19 (Summer):215–238.

Rosenbaum, J. L. 1989. "Family Dysfunction and Female Delinquency." *Crime and Delinquency* 35:31.

Rosenbaum, R. 1989. "Too Young to Die?" *New York Times Magazine,* March 12, p. 60.

Rosencrance, J. 1988. "Maintaining the Myth of Individualized Justice: Probation Presentence Reports," *Justice Quarterly* 5:235.

Rosenman, S. I. 1964. "A Better Way to Select Judges." *Judicature* 48:64.

Rothman, D. J. 1971. *The Discovery of the Asylum: Social Order and Disorder in the New Republic.* Boston: Little, Brown.

———. 1980. *Conscience and Convenience.* Boston: Little, Brown.

———. 1994. "The Crime of Punishment." *New York Review of Books,* February 17:34–38.

Rothman, S., and S. Powers. 1994. "Execution by Quota?" *The Public Interest* (Summer):3–17.

Rousey, D. C. 1984. "Cops and Guns: Police Use of Deadly Force in Nineteenth-Century New Orleans." *American Journal of Legal History* 28:41–66.

Rubinstein, M. L., and T. J. White. 1979. "Alaska's Ban on Plea Bargaining." *Law and Society* 13:367–390.

Runda, J., E. Rhine, and R. Wetter. 1994. *The Practice of Parole Boards.* Lexington, Ky.: Association of Paroling Authorities.

Sacramento Bee. March 28, 1988:1.

————. March 31, 1996:A1ff.

Sampson, R. J., and J. L. Lauritsen. 1997. "Racial and Ethnic Disparities in Crime and Criminal Justice in the United States," *Crime and Justice,* vol. 21, ed. Michael Tonry. Chicago: University of Chicago Press, 311–374.

Samuelson, R. J. 1999. "Do We Care about Truth?" *Newsweek,* September 6:76.

San Francisco Chronicle. March 6, 1999:A3.

San Jose Mercury News. October 23, 1993.

Schmid, T. J., and R. S. Jones. 1991. "Suspended Identity: Identity Transformation in a Maximum Security Prison." *Symbolic Interaction* 14:415–432.

Schmidt, J., and E. H. Steury. 1989. "Prosecutorial Discretion in Filing Charges in Domestic Violence Cases." *Criminology* 27:487.

Scott, E. J. 1981. *Calls for Service: Citizen Demand and Initial Police Response.* Washington, D.C.: Government Printing Office.

Scott, T. 1985. "Pretrial Detention under the Bail Reform Act of 1984." *American Criminal Law Review* 21:21–34.

Sellin, T. 1970. "The Origin of the Pennsylvania System of Prison Discipline." *Prison Journal* 50 (Spring/Summer):15.

Sentencing Project. 1998. *Losing the Vote.* Washington, D.C.: The Sentencing Project.

Shapiro, B. 1997. "Sleeping Lawyer Syndrome." *The Nation* (April 7):27–29.

Sherman, A. 1994. *Wasting America's Future.* Boston: Beacon Press.

Sherman, L. W. 1983. "Patrol Strategies for Police," *Crime and Public Policy,* ed. J. Q. Wilson. San Francisco: ICS Press, 149–154.

————. 1990. "Police Crackdowns: Initial and Residual Deterrence," *Crime and Justice,* ed. M. Tonry and N. Morris. Chicago: University of Chicago Press, 1–48.

————. 1995. "The Police," *Crime,* ed. J. Q. Wilson and J. Petersilia. San Francisco: ICS Press, 327–348.

————. 1998. "Police," *The Handbook of Crime and Punishment,* ed. M. Tonry. New York: Oxford University Press, 429–456.

Sherman, L. W., and R. A. Berk. 1984. "The Specific Effects of Arrest for Domestic Assault." *American Sociological Review* 49:261–272.

Sherman, L. W., and E. G. Cohn. 1986. "Citizens Killed by Big City Police: 1970–84." Unpublished manuscript, Crime Control Institute, Washington, D.C., October.

Sherman, L. W., P. R. Gartin, and M. E. Buerger. 1989. "Hot Spots of Predatory Crime: Routine Activities and the Criminology of Place." *Criminology* 27:27–55.

Sherman, L. W., and D. P. Rogan. 1995a. "Effects of Gun Seizures on Gun Violence: 'Hot Spots' Patrol in Kansas City." *Justice Quarterly* 12 (December):673–693.

————. 1995b. "Deterrent Effects of Police Raids on Crack Houses: A Randomized Controlled Experiment." *Justice Quarterly* 12 (December):755–781.

Sherman, L. W., J. D. Schmidt, D. P. Rogan, P. R. Gartin, E. G. Cohn, D. J. Collins, and A. R. Bacich. 1991. "From Initial Deterrence to Long-Term Escalation: Short Custody Arrest for Poverty Ghetto Domestic Violence." *Criminology* 29:821–850.

Sherman, L. W., and D. A. Weisburd. 1995. "General Deterrent Effects of Police Patrol in Crime 'Hot Spots': A Randomized Controlled Trial." *Justice Quarterly* 12 (December):625–648.

Shichor, D. 1995. *Punishment for Profit: Private Prisons/Public Concerns.* Thousand Oaks, Calif.: Sage.

Shover, N. 1998. "White-Collar Crime," *The Handbook of Crime and Punishment,* ed. M. Tonry. New York: Oxford University Press, 133–158.

Sichel, J. 1978. *Women on Patrol.* Washington, D.C.: Government Printing Office.

Silberman, M. 1995. *A World of Violence.* Belmont, Calif.: Wadsworth.

Silverman, E. 1999. *NYPD Battles Crime.* Boston: Northeastern University Press.

Simon, L. M. S. 1993. "Prison Behavior and the Victim-Offender Relationships among Violent Offenders." *Justice Quarterly* 10 (September):263.

Simon, R. 1975. *Women and Crime.* Lexington, Mass.: D.C. Heath.

Skogan, W. G. 1990. *Disorder and Decline: Crime and the Spiral of Decay in America.* New York: Free Press.

————. 1995. "Crime and Racial Fears of White Americans." *Annals of the American Academy of Political and Social Science* 539 (May):59–71.

Skogan, W. G., and M. G. Maxfield. 1981. *Coping with Crime.* Newbury Park, Calif.: Sage.

Skolnick, J. H. 1966. *Justice without Trial: Law Enforcement in a Democratic Society.* New York: Wiley.

————. 1988. *Community Policing: Issues and Practices around the World.* Washington, D. C.: National Institute of Justice.

Skolnick, J. H., and J. J. Fyfe. 1993. *Above the Law: Police and Excessive Use of Force.* New York: Free Press.

Smeltz, J. R. 1995. *Analyzing the Growth of State-Local Corrections Spending.* Albany, N.Y.: Center for the Study of the States.

Smith, A. B., and H. Pollack. 1972. *Crimes and Justice in a Mass Society.* New York: Xerox Publishers.

Smith, C. E. 1990. *United States Magistrates in the Federal Courts: Subordinate Judges.* New York: Praeger.

————. 1993. "Black Muslims and the Development of Prisoners' Rights." *Journal of Black Studies* 24:131–146.

————. 1994. "Imagery, Politics, and Jury Reform." *Akron Law Review* 28:77–95.

————. 1995a. "The Constitution and Criminal Punishment: The Emerging Visions of Justices Scalia and Thomas." *Drake Law Review* 43:593–613.

————. 1995b. "Federal Habeas Corpus Reform: The State's Perspective." *Justice System Journal* 18:1–11.

————. 1995c. "Judicial Policy Making and Habeas Corpus Reform." *Criminal Justice Policy Review* 7:91–114.

————. 1997. *The Rehnquist Court and Criminal Punishment.* New York: Garland.

————. 1999a. "Criminal Justice and the 1997–98 U.S. Supreme Court Term." *Southern Illinois University Law Review* 23: 443–467.

————. 1999b. *Law and Contemporary Corrections.* Belmont, Calif.: Wadsworth.

————. 2000. "Criminal Justice and the 1998–99 U.S. Supreme Court Term." *Widener Journal of Public Law.*

Smith, C. E., and J. R. Hurst. 1996. "Law and Police Agencies' Policies: Perceptions of the Relative Impact of Constitutional Law Decisions and Civil Liability Decisions." Paper given at the annual meeting of the American Society of Criminology, Chicago.

Smith, C. E., and R. Ochoa. 1996. "The Peremptory Challenge in the Eyes of the Trial Judge." *Judicature* 79:185–189.

Smith, S. K., and C. J. DeFrances. 1996. "Indigent Defense." *Bureau of Justice Statistics Bulletin.*

Sorensen, J. R., J. M. Marquart, and D. E. Brock. 1993. "Factors Related to Killings of Felons by Police Officers: A Test of the Community Violence and Conflict Hypotheses." *Justice Quarterly* 10:417–440.

Sorenson, J. R., and D. H. Wallace. 1999. "Prosecutorial Discretion in Seeking Death: An Analysis of Racial Disparity in the Pretrial Stages of Case Processing in a Midwestern County." *Justice Quarterly* 16:561–578.

Sorin, M. 1984. "How to Make Bail Safer." *The Public Interest* 76:102–110.

Souryal, S. S., D. W. Potts, and A. I. Alobied. 1994. "The Penalty of Hand Amputation for Theft in Islamic Justice." *Journal of Criminal Justice* 22:249–265.

Spangenberg, R. L., and M. L. Beeman. 1995. "Indigent Defense Systems in the United States." *Law and Contemporary Problems* 58:31–49.

Sparrow, M. K., M. H. Moore, and D. M. Kennedy. 1990. *Beyond 911: A New Era for Policing.* New York: Basic Books.

Spears, J. W., and C. C. Spohn. 1997. "The Effect of Evidence Factors and Victim Characteristics on Prosecutors' Charging Decisions in Sexual Assault Cases." *Justice Quarterly* 14:501–524.

Spears, L. 1991. "Contract Counsel: A Different Way to Defend the Poor— How It's Working in North Dakota." *American Bar Association Journal on Criminal Justice* 6:24–31.

Spelman, W. G., and D. K. Brown. 1984. *Calling the Police: Citizen Reporting of Serious Crime.* Washington, D.C.: Police Executive Research Forum.

Spelman, W. G., and J. Eck. 1987. "Problem-Oriented Policing." *Research in Brief.*

Spitzer, S. 1975. "Toward a Marxian Theory of Deviance." *Social Problems* 22:639.

Spohn, C. 1992. "An Analysis of the 'Jury Trial Penalty' and Its Effect on Black and White Offenders." *The Justice Professional* 7:93–97.

Spohn, C., J. Gruhl, and S. Welch. 1987. "The Impact of the Ethnicity and Gender of Defendants on the Decision to Reject or Dismiss Felony Charges." *Criminology* 25:175–191.

Stafford, M. C., and M. Warr. 1993. "A Reconceptualization of General and Specific Deterrence." *Journal of Research in Crime and Delinquency* 30 (May):123.

Stahl, M. B. 1992. "Asset Forfeiture, Burden of Proof, and the War on Drugs." *Journal of Criminal Law and Criminology* 83:274–337.

Stanford, M. R., and B. L. Mowry. 1990. "Domestic Disturbance Danger Rate." *Journal of Police Science and Administration* 17:244–249.

Stanko, E. 1988. "The Impact of Victim Assessment on Prosecutors' Screening Decisions: The Case of the New York District Attorney's Office," *Criminal Justice: Law and Politics,* 5th ed., ed. G. F. Cole. Pacific Grove, Calif.: Brooks/Cole.

Steffensmeier, D., J. Kramer, and C. Streifel. 1993. "Gender and Imprisonment Decisions." *Criminology* 31:411–446.

Steinberg, J. 1999. "The Coming Crime Wave Is Washed Up." *New York Times,* January 3:4WK.

Steinman, M. 1988. "Anticipating Rank and File Police Reactions to Arrest Policies Regarding Spouse Abuse." *Criminal Justice Research Bulletin* 4:1–5.

Steury, E. 1993. "Criminal Defendants with Psychiatric Impairment: Prevalence, Probabilities, and Rates." *Journal of Criminal Law and Criminology* 84:352–376.

Steury, E., and N. Frank. 1990. "Gender Bias and Pretrial Release: More Pieces of the Puzzle." *Journal of Criminal Justice* 18:417–432.

Stith, K., and J. A. Cabranes. 1998. *Fear of Judging: Sentencing Guidelines in the Federal Courts.* Chicago: University of Chicago Press.

Stoddard, E. R. 1968. "The Informal 'Code' of Police Deviancy: A Group Approach to Blue-Coat Crime." *Journal of Criminal Law, Criminology, and Police Science* 59:204–211.

Stojkovic, S. 1990. "Accounts of Prison Work: Corrections Officers' Portrayals of Their Work Worlds." *Perspectives on Social Problems* 2:211–230.

Stolzenberg, L., and S. J. D'Alessio. 1994. "Sentencing and Unwarranted Disparity: An Empirical Assessment of the Long-Term Impact of Sentencing Guidelines in Minnesota." *Criminology* 32:301–310.

———. 1997. "Three Strikes and You're Out: The Impact of California's New Mandatory Sentencing Law on Serious Crime Rates." *Crime and Delinquency* 43:457.

Streib, V. L. 1998. "Executing Women, Children, and the Retarded: Second Class Citizens in Capital Punishment," *America's Experiment with Capital Punishment,* ed. J. R. Aker, R. M. Bohm, and C. S. Lanier. Durham, N.C.: Carolina Academic Press.

Strodtbeck, F., R. James, and G. Hawkins. 1957. "Social Status in Jury Deliberations." *American Sociological Review* 22:713–719.

Suffet, F. 1966. "Bail Setting: A Study of Courtroom Interaction." *Crime and Delinquency* 12 (October):318.

Sutherland, E. H. 1947. *Criminology,* 4th ed. Philadelphia: Lippincott.

———. 1949. *White-Collar Crime.* New York: Holt, Rinehart, and Winston.

———. 1950. "The Sexual Psychopath Laws." *Journal of Criminal Law and Criminology* 40 (January/February):543.

Sykes, G. M. 1958. *The Society of Captives.* Princeton, N.J.: Princeton University Press.

Talarico, S. M. 1988. "The Dilemmas of Parole Decision Making," *Criminal Justice: Law and Politics,* 5th ed., ed. G. F. Cole. Pacific Grove, Calif.: Brooks/Cole, 442–451.

Terry, C. 1997. "The Function of Humor for Prison Inmates." *Journal of Contemporary Criminal Justice* 13:26.

Terry, D. 1996. "After 18 Years in Prison, 3 Are Cleared of Murders." *New York Times,* July 3, p. A8.

Thomas, C. W. 2000. A "Real Time" Statistical Profile of Private Prisons for Adults Electronic Web Site (http://web.crim.ufl.edu/pcp/census).

Thomas, J. 1989. "The 'Reality' of Prisoner Litigation: Repackaging the Data." *New England Journal on Criminal and Civil Confinement* 15:27–53.

Thomas, J., D. Keeler, and K. Harris. 1986. "Issues and Misconceptions in Prisoner Litigation: A Critical View." *Criminology* 24:775–797.

Thomas, W. H., Jr. 1976. *Bail Reform in America.* Berkeley: University of California Press.

Timberg, C. 1999. "Mother in Oven Death to Be Tested." *Washington Post,* October 6, p. B2.

Toch, H. 1976. *Peacekeeping: Police, Prisons, and Violence.* Lexington, Mass.: Lexington Books.

Tonry, M. 1993. "Sentencing Commissions and Their Guidelines," *Crime and Justice,* vol. 17, ed. M. Tonry. Chicago: University of Chicago Press.

———. 1995. *Malign Neglect: Race, Crime, and Punishment in America.* New York: Oxford University Press.

———. 1996. *Sentencing Matters.* New York: Oxford University Press.

———. 1998a. "Intermediate Sanctions," *The Handbook of Crime and Punishment,* ed. M. Tonry. New York: Oxford University Press, 683–711.

———. 1998b. "Introduction," *The Handbook of Crime and Punishment,* ed. M. Tonry. New York: Oxford University Press, 22–23.

Tonry, M., and K. Hamilton, eds. 1995. *Intermediate Sanctions in Overcrowded Times.* Boston: Northeastern University Press.

Tonry, M., and M. Lynch. 1996. "Intermediate Sanctions," *Crime and Justice,* vol. 20, ed. M. Tonry. Chicago: University of Chicago Press, 99–144.

Traub, J. 1996. "The Criminals of Tomorrow." *New Yorker,* November 4:50–65.

Trout, C. 1992. "Taking a New Look at an Old Problem." *Corrections Today* (July):62–67.

Tucker, J. 1997. *May God Have Mercy.* New York: W. W. Norton.

Turner, M. G., J. L. Sundt, B. K. Applegate, and F. T. Cullen. 1995. "Three Strikes and You're Out Legislation: A National Assessment." *Federal Probation* (September):16–18.

Turner, S., and J. Petersilia. 1996. *Day Fines in Four U.S. Jurisdictions*. Santa Monica, Calif.: RAND Corporation.

Uchida, C., and T. Bynum. 1991. "Search Warrants, Motions to Suppress, and 'Lost Cases': The Effects of the Exclusionary Rule in Seven Jurisdictions." *Journal of Criminal Law and Criminology* 81:1034–1066.

Ugwuegbu, D. 1999. "Racial and Evidential Factors in Juror Attributions of Legal Responsibility," *The Social Organization of Law,* 2d ed., ed. M. P. Baumgartner. San Diego: Academic Press.

Uphoff, R. J. 1992. "The Criminal Defense Lawyer: Zealous Advocate, Double Agent, or Beleaguered Dealer?" *Criminal Law Bulletin* 28:419–456.

U.S. Deparment of Justice. 1980. *Principles of Prosecution.* Washington, D.C.: Government Printing Office.

USA Today. November 11, 1996:electronic edition at www.USAToday.com.

———. August 8, 1997:1.

Useem, B., and M. D. Reisig. 1999. "Collective Action in Prisons: Protests, Disturbances, and Riots." *Criminology* 37:735–760.

Utz, P. 1978. *Settling the Facts.* Lexington, Mass.: Lexington Books.

Van Dijk, J. J. M., and P. Mayhew. 1992. *Criminal Victimization in the Industrialized World.* The Hague, Netherlands: Ministry of Justice.

Vaughn, M. S., and R. del Carmen. 1997. "The Fourth Amendment as a Tool of Actuarial Justice: The 'Special Needs' Exception to the Warrant and Probable Cause Requirements." *Crime and Delinquency* 43:78–103.

Vera Institute of Justice. 1981. *Felony Arrests: Their Prosecution and Disposition in New York City's Courts.* New York: Longman.

———. 1992. *Felony Arrests,* rev. ed. New York: Longman.

Vicenti, C. N. 1995. "The Reemergence of Tribal Society and Traditional Justice Systems." *Judicature* 79:134–141.

Vitiello, M. 1997. "Three Strikes: Can We Return to Rationality?" *Journal of Criminal Law and Criminology* 87:395–463.

Vogel, M. 1999. "The Social Origins of Plea Bargaining: Conflict and the Law in the Process of State Formation, 1830–1860." *Law and Society Review* 33: 161–246.

von Hirsch, A. 1976. *Doing Justice.* New York: Hill and Wang.

Walker, P. 1998. "Felony and Misdemeanor Defendants Filed in the U.S. District Courts during Fiscal Years 1990–95: An Analysis of the Filings of Each Offense Level." *Journal of Criminal Justice* 26:503–511.

Walker, S. 1984. " 'Broken Windows' and Fractured History: The Use and Misuse of History in Recent Police Patrol Analysis." *Justice Quarterly* 1 (March):88.

———. 1993. *Taming the System: The Control of Discretion in Criminal Justice 1950–1990.* New York: Oxford University Press.

———. 1998. *Sense and Nonsense about Crime and Drugs,* 4th ed. Belmont, Calif.: Wadsworth.

———. 1999. *The Police in America,* 3d ed. New York: McGraw-Hill.

Walker, S., C. Spohn, and M. DeLone. 1996. *The Color of Justice.* Belmont, Calif.: Wadsworth.

Walker, S., and K. B. Turner. 1992. "A Decade of Modest Progress: Employment of Black and Hispanic Police Officers, 1983–1992." Department of Criminal Justice, University of Nebraska at Omaha.

Walker, S., and B. Wright. 1995. "Citizen Review of the Police, 1994: A National Survey." *Fresh Perspectives.* Washington, D.C.: Police Executive Research Forum.

Wallace, D. H. 1994. "The Eighth Amendment and Prison Deprivations: Historical Revisions." *Criminal Law Bulletin* 30:5–29.

Wall Street Journal. March 20, 2000:B8.

Walsh, W. 1989. "Private/Public Police Stereotypes: A Different Perspective." *Security Journal* 1:21–27.

Warr, M. 1993. "Fear of Victimization." *The Public Perspective* (November/December):25–28.

Washington Post. October 6, 1996.

Wasserman, D. T. 1990. *A Sword for the Convicted: Representing Indigent Defendants on Appeal.* New York: Greenwood Press.

Watson, G. 1999. "Prisons Struggling to Deal with Mental Illness." *Hartford Courant,* June 7, p. A8.

Watson, R. A., and R. G. Downing. 1969. *The Politics of the Bench and Bar: Judicial Selection under the Missouri Nonpartisan Court Plan.* New York: John Wiley & Sons.

Waunder, A. 1994. "Working for the Weekend: Prison Industries and Inmate Employees." *Correctional Compendium* (October):9–21.

Weinstein, J. B. 1992. "A Trial Judge's Second Impression of the Federal Sentencing Guidelines." *Southern California Law Review* 66:357.

Weisburd, D. A., and L. Green. 1995. "Measuring Immediate Spatial Displacement: Methodological Issues and Problems," *Crime and Place: Crime Prevention Studies,* vol. 4, ed. D. A. Weisburd and J. E. Eck. Monsey, N.Y.: Criminal Justice Press.

Weitekamp, E. 1995. "Restitution," *Intermediate Sanctions in Overcrowded Times,* ed. M. Tonry and K. Hamilton. Boston: Northeastern University Press, 65–68.

Welch, M. 1994. "Jail Overcrowding: Social Sanitation and the Warehousing of the Urban Underclass," *Critical Issues in Crime and Justice,* ed. A. Roberts. Thousand Oaks, Calif.: Sage, 249–274.

White, J. 2000. "Mother Found Fit for Trial in Son's Microwave Death." *Washington Post,* March 7, p.B3.

White, M. S. 1995. "The Nonverbal Behaviors in Jury Selection." *Criminal Law Bulletin* 31:414–445.

White, P. J. 1997. "An America without Judicial Independence." *Judicature* 80: 174–177.

Whitebread, C. H., and C. Slobogin. 1993. *Criminal Procedure: An Analysis of Cases and Concepts.* Westbury, N.Y.: Foundation Press.

Wice, P. B. 1978. *Criminal Lawyers: An Endangered Species.* Beverly Hills, Calif.: Sage.

———. 1995. "Court Reform and Judicial Leadership: A Theoretical Discussion." *Justice System Journal* 17:309–321.

Wigmore, J. H. 1937. "Roscoe Pound's St. Paul Address of 1906." *Journal of the American Judicature Society* 20:136–137.

Wilbanks, W. 1987. *The Myth of a Racist Criminal Justice System.* Pacific Grove, Calif.: Brooks/Cole.

Williams, H., and P. V. Murphy. 1990. "The Evolving Strategy of Police: A Minority View." *Perspectives on Policing,* no. 13. Washington, D.C.: National Institute of Justice.

Williams, H., and A. M. Pate. 1987. "Returning to First Principles: Reducing the Fear of Crime in Newark." *Crime and Delinquency* 33 (January):53–59.

Williams, V., and M. Fish. 1974. *Convicts, Codes, and Contraband.* Cambridge, Mass.: Ballinger.

Wilson, J. Q. 1968. *Varieties of Police Behavior.* Cambridge, Mass.: Harvard University Press.

———. 1994. "Just Take Away Their Guns." *New York Times Magazine,* March 20, p. 47.

Wilson, J. Q., and B. Boland. 1979. *The Effect of the Police on Crime.* Washington, D.C.: Government Printing Office.

Wilson, J. Q., and R. Herrnstein. 1985. *Crime and Human Nature.* New York: Simon & Schuster.

Wilson, J. Q., and G. L. Kelling. 1982. "Broken Windows: The Police and Neighborhood Safety." *Atlantic Monthly* (March):29–38.

Winerip, M. 1999a. "Bedlam Streets," *New York Times Magazine,* May 23, p. 42.

_____. 1999b. "The Juror's Dilemma." *New York Times Magazine,* November 21.

Winick, B. J. 1995. "Reforming Incompetency to Stand Trial and Plead Guilty." *Journal of Criminal Law and Criminology* 85:571–624.

Wolfgang, M. E., and F. Ferracuti. 1967. *The Subculture of Violence.* London, England: Tavistock.

Wooldredge, J. D., and K. Masters. 1993. "Confronting Problems Faced by Pregnant Inmates in State Prisons." *Crime and Delinquency* 39 (April):195.

Worden, A. P. 1991. "Privatizing Due Process: Issues in the Comparison of Assigned Counsel, Public Defenders, and Contracted Indigent Defense Counsel." *Justice System Journal* 15:390–418.

_____. 1993. "The Attitudes of Women and Men in Policing: Testing Conventional and Contemporary Wisdom." *Criminology* 31 (May):203–241.

_____. 1994. "Counsel for the Poor: An Evaluation of Contracting for Indigent Criminal Defense." *Justice Quarterly* 10:613–637.

_____. 1995. "The Judge's Role in Plea Bargaining: An Analysis of Judges' Agreement with Prosecutors' Sentencing Recommendations." *Justice Quarterly* 12:257–278.

Worden, R. 1993. "Toward Equity and Efficiency in Law Enforcement: Differential Police Response." *American Journal of Police* 12:1–32.

Wren, C. 1998. "Critics Say Rockefeller Drug Laws Pack the Prisons, Force Plea Deals, and Hit Small-Timers the Hardest." *New York Times,* January 18, p. B1.

Yang, S. S. 1990. "The Unique Treatment Needs of Female Substance Abusers: The Obligation of the Criminal Justice System to Provide Parity Services." *Medicine and Law* 9:1018–1027.

Zagaris, B. 1998. "U.S. International Cooperation against Transnational Organized Crime." *Wayne Law Review* 44 (Fall):1401–1464.

Zedner, L. 1995. "Wayward Sisters." *The Oxford History of Prisons,* ed. N. Morris and D. J. Rothman. New York: Oxford University Press, 329–361.

Zimbardo, P. G. 1994. *Transforming California's Prisons into Expensive Old Age Homes for Felons: Enormous Hidden Costs and Consequences for Taxpayers.* San Francisco: Center on Juvenile and Criminal Justice.

Zimmer, L. 1987 "Operation Pressure Point: The Disruption of Street-Level Trade on New York's Lower East Side." Occasional paper from the Center for Research in Crime and Justice, New York University School of Law.

Zimring, F. 1991. "The Treatment of Hard Cases in American Juvenile Justice: In Defense of Discretionary Waiver." *Notre Dame Journal of Law, Ethics, and Public Policy* 5:267.

Supreme Court Cases

Arizona v. Hicks, 480 U.S. 321 (1987)

Austin v. United States, 61 LW 4811 (1993)

Barron v. Baltimore, 32 U.S. 243 (1833)

Batson v. Kentucky, 476 U.S. 79 (1986)

Baxter v. Palmigiano, 425 U.S. 308 (1976)

Bennis v. Michigan, 116 S.Ct. 994 (1996)

Blackledge v. Allison, 431 U.S. 71 (1976)

Bordenkircher v. Hayes, 343 U.S. 357 (1978)

Boykin v. Alabama, 395 U.S. 238 (1969)

Breed v. Jones, 421 U.S. 519 (1975)

Brown v. Mississippi, 297 U.S. 281 (1936)

Burch v. Louisiana, 441 U.S. 130 (1979)

Chimel v. California, 395 U.S. 752 (1969)

Cooper v. Oklahoma, 116 S.Ct. 1373 (1996)

Cooper v. Pate, 378 U.S. 546 (1964)

Cruz v. Beto, 450 U.S. 319 (1972)

Daniels v. Williams, 474 U.S. 327 (1986)

Delaware v. Prouse, 440 U.S. 648 (1979)

Durham v. United States, 214 F.2d 862 (D.C. Cir. 1954)

Escobedo v. Illinois, 378 U.S. 347 (1964)

Ex parte Crouse, 4 Wharton (Pa.) 9 (1838)

Fare v. Michael C., 442 U.S. 707 (1979)

Felker v. Turpin, 116 S.Ct. 2333 (1996)

Ford v. Wainwright, 477 U.S. 399 (1985)

Furman v. Georgia, 408 U.S. 238 (1972)

Fulwood v. Clemmer, 206 F.Supp. 370 (D.C. Cir. 1962)

Gagnon v. Scarpelli, 411 U.S. 778 (1973)

Gideon v. Wainwright, 372 U.S. 335 (1963)

Graham v. Connor, 490 U.S. 396 (1989)

Gregg v. Georgia, 428 U.S. 153 (1976)

Griffin v. Wisconsin, 483 U.S. 868 (1987)

Hudson v. Palmer, 52 L.W. 5052 (1984)

Illinois v. Rodriguez, 110 S.Ct. 2793 (1990)

Illinois v. Wardlow, No. 98–1036 (2000)

In re Gault, 387 U.S. 9 (1967)

In re Winship, 397 U.S. 358 (1970)

Jacobson v. United States, 112 S.Ct. 1535 (1992)

J.E.B. v. Alabama ex rel.T.B., 511 U.S. 114 (1994)

Kansas v. Hendricks, 117 S.Ct. 2072 (1997)

Kent v. United States, 383 U.S. 541 (1966)

Knowles v. Iowa, 525 U.S. 113 (1998)

Lee v. Downs, 641 F.2d 318 (4th Cir. 1981)

Lee v. Washington, 390 U.S. 333 (1968)

Lewis v. Casey, 116 S.Ct. 2174 (1996)

Lewis v. United States, 116 S.Ct. 2163 (1996)

M'Naughten's Case, 8 Eng. Rep. 718 (1843)

Mapp v. Ohio, 367 U.S. 643 (1961)

Maryland v. Wilson, 117 S.Ct. 882 (1997)

McCleskey v. Kemp, 478 U.S. 1019 (1987)

McKeiver v. Pennsylvania, 403 U.S. 528 (1971)

Mempha v. Rhay, 389 U.S. 128 (1967)

Michigan Department of State Police v. Sitz, 496 U.S. 440 (1990)

Miller v. United States, 78 U.S. 268 (1871)

Miranda v. Arizona, 384 U.S. 436 (1966)

Monell v. Department of Social Services of the City of New York, 436 U.S. 658 (1978)

Montana v. Egelhoff, 116 S.Ct. 2013 (1996)

Moore v. Dempsey, 261 U.S. 86 (1923)

Morrisette v. United States, 142 U.S. 246 (1952)

Morrissey v. Brewer, 408 U.S. 471 (1972)

New York v. Class, 475 U.S. 321 (1986)

New York v. Quarles, 467 U.S. 649 (1984)

New Jersey v. T.L.O., 105 S. Ct. 733 (1985)

Nix v. Williams, 467 U.S. 431 (1984)

North Carolina v. Alford, 400 U.S. 25 (1970)

O'Lone v. Estate of Shabazz, 482 U.S. 342 (1987)

Pargo v. Elliott, 69 F.3d 280 (8th Cir.) (1995)

Penry v. Lynaugh, 492 U.S. 302 (1989)

People v. Clark, 183 Colo. 201 (1973)

Powell v. Alabama, 287 U.S. 45 (1932)

Procunier v. Martinez, 416 U.S. 396 (1974)

Purkett v. Elm, 115 S.Ct. 1769 (1995)

Queen v. Dudley and Stephens, 14 Q.B.D. 273 (1884)

R.A.V. v. City of St. Paul, 112 S.Ct. 2538 (1992)

Ricketts v. Adamson, 481 U.S. 1 (1987)

Robinson v. California, 370 U.S. 660 (1962)

Ross v. Moffitt, 417 U.S. 660 (1974)

Ruffin v. Commonwealth, 62 Va. 790 (1871)

Ruiz v. Estelle, 503 F.Supp. 1265 (S.D.Tex. 1980)

Santobello v. New York, 404 U.S. 260 (1971)

Schall v. Martin, 467 U.S. 253 (1984)

Scott v. Illinois, 440 U.S. 367 (1979)

Sitz v. Michigan Department of State Police, 506 N.W.2d209 (Mich. 1993)

Skinner v. Oklahoma, 316 U.S. 535 (1942).

Smith v. Fairman, 678 F.2d 52 (7th Cir. 1982)

Stanford v. Kentucky, 492 U.S. 361 (1989)

Strickland v. Washington, 466 U.S. 686 (1984)

Tennessee v. Garner, 471 U.S. 1 (1985)

Terry v. Ohio, 392 U.S. 1 (1968)

Thompson v. Oklahoma, 108 S.Ct. 1687 (1988)

Trop v. Dulles, 356 U.S. 86 (1958)

Turner v. Safley, 482 U.S. 78 (1987)

United States v. Bajakajian, 118 S.Ct. 2028 (1998)

United States v. Brawner, 471 F.2d 969 (D.C. Cir. 1972)

United States v. Cronic, 444 U.S. 654 (1984)

United States v. Dickerson, 116 F3d 667 (4th Cir. 1999)

United States v. Leon, 468 U.S. 897 (1984)

United States v. One Assortment of 89 Firearms, 465 U.S. 354 (1984)

United States v. One 1986 Chevrolet Van, 927 F.2d 39 (1st Cir. 1991)

United States v. Ross, 102 S.Ct. 2157 (1982)

United States v. Salerno and Cafero, 481 U.S. 739 (1987)

United States v. Ursery, 116 S.Ct. 2135 (1996)

Weeks v. United States, 232 U.S. 383 (1914)

Whren v. United States, 517 U.S. 806 (1996)

Wilkins v. Missouri, 492 U.S. 361 (1989)

Williams v. Florida, 399 U.S. 78 (1970)

Wilson v. Seiter, 111 S.Ct. 232 (1991)

Wisconsin v. Mitchell, 113 S.Ct. 2194 (1993)

Wolff v. McDonnell, 418 U.S. 539 (1974)

Wyoming v. Houghton, 119 S.Ct. 1297 (1999)

Glossary

accusatory process The series of events from the arrest of a suspect to the filing of a formal charge (through an indictment or information) with the court.

adjudication The process of determining the guilt or innocence of a defendant.

administrative regulations Rules made by governmental agencies to implement specific public policies in areas such as public health, environmental protection, and workplace safety.

admissible evidence Evidence that has been gathered by the police according to the law as specified in the Constitution, court decisions, and statutes.

adversary system Basis for the American legal system in which a passive judge and jury seek to find the truth by listening to opposing attorneys who vigorously advocate on behalf of their respective sides.

aggressive patrol A patrol strategy designed to maximize the number of police interventions and observations in the community.

anomie A breakdown in and disappearance of the rules of social behavior.

appeal A request to a higher court that it review actions taken in a completed trial.

appellate courts Courts that do not try criminal cases but hear appeals of decisions of lower courts.

arraignment The court appearance of an accused person in which the charges are read and the accused person, advised by a lawyer, pleads guilty or not guilty.

arrest The physical taking of a person into custody on the ground that probable cause exists to believe that he or she has committed a criminal offense. Police may use only reasonable physical force in making an arrest. The purpose of the arrest is to hold the accused for a court proceeding.

assigned counsel An attorney in private practice assigned by a court to represent an indigent. The attorney's fee is paid by the government with jurisdiction over the case.

attorney general Chief legal officer of a state responsible for both civil and criminal cases.

bail An amount of money specified by a judge to be paid as a condition of pretrial release to ensure that the accused will appear in court as required.

***Barron v. Baltimore* (1833)** The protections of the Bill of Rights apply only to actions of the federal government.

bench trial Trial conducted by a judge who acts as fact finder and determines issues of law. No jury participates.

biological explanations Explanations of crime that emphasize physiological and neurological factors that may predispose a person to commit crimes.

boot camp/shock incarceration A short-term institutional sentence, usually followed by probation, that puts the offender through a physical regimen designed to develop discipline and respect for authority.

***Bordenkircher v. Hayes* (1978)** A defendant's rights were not violated by a prosecutor who warned that declining to accept a guilty plea would result in a harsher sentence.

***Boykin v. Alabama* (1969)** Defendants must state that they are voluntarily making a plea of guilty.

***Breed v. Jones* (1975)** Juveniles cannot be found delinquent in juvenile court and then transferred to adult court without a hearing on the transfer; to do so violates the protection against double jeopardy.

case law Court decisions that have the status of law and serve as precedents for later decisions.

challenge for cause Removal of a prospective juror by showing that he or she has some bias or some other legal disability. The number of such challenges permitted to attorneys is unlimited.

circumstantial evidence Evidence provided by a witness from which a jury must infer a fact.

citation A written order or summons issued by a law enforcement officer directing an alleged offender to appear in court at a specified time to answer a criminal charge.

civil forfeiture The confiscation of property by the state as punishment for a crime. In recent years the police have used civil forfeiture to seize property that they believe was purchased with drug profits.

civil law Law regulating the relationships between or among individuals, usually involving property, contract, or business disputes.

classical criminology A school of criminology that views behavior as stemming from free will, demands responsibility and accountability of all perpetrators, and stresses the need for punishments severe enough to deter others.

classification The process of assigning an inmate to a category specifying his or her needs for security, treatment, education, work assignment, and readiness for release.

clearance rate The percentage of crimes known to the police that they believe they have solved through an arrest; a statistic used to measure a police department's productivity.

common law The Anglo-American system of uncodified law, in which judges follow precedents set by earlier decisions when they decide new but similar cases. The substantive and procedural criminal law was originally developed in this manner but was later codified—set down in codes—by state legislatures.

community correctional center An institution, usually in an urban area, that houses inmates soon to be released. Such centers are designed to help inmates establish community ties and thus promote their reintegration with society.

community corrections A model of corrections based on the goal of reintegrating the offender into the community.

community service A sentence requiring the offender to perform a certain amount of unpaid labor in the community.

conditions of release Restrictions on parolees' conduct that must be obeyed as a legally binding requirement of being released.

congregate system A penitentiary system, developed in Auburn, New York, in which each inmate was held in isolation during the night but worked and ate with fellow prisoners during the day under a rule of silence.

constitutions The basic laws of a country defining the structure of government and the relationship of citizens to that government.

continuance An adjournment of a scheduled case until a later date.

contract counsel   An attorney in private practice who contracts with the government to represent all indigent defendants in a county during a set period of time and for a specified dollar amount.

control theory   Theories holding that criminal behavior occurs when the bonds that tie an individual to society are broken or weakened.

Cooper v. Pate (1964)   Prisoners are entitled to the protection of the Civil Rights Act of 1871 and may challenge the conditions of their confinement in federal courts.

corrections   The variety of programs, services, facilities, and organizations responsible for the management of people who have been accused or convicted of criminal offenses.

count   Each separate offense of which a person is accused in an indictment or an information.

crime   A specific act of commission or omission in violation of the law, for which a punishment is prescribed.

crime control model   A model of the criminal justice system that assumes that freedom is so important that every effort must be made to repress crime; it emphasizes efficiency, speed, finality, and the capacity to apprehend, try, convict, and dispose of a high proportion of offenders.

crime control model of corrections   A model of corrections based on the assumption that criminal behavior can be controlled by more use of incarceration and other forms of strict supervision.

crimes without victims   Offenses involving a willing and private exchange of illegal goods or services that are in strong demand. Participants do not feel they are being harmed, but these crimes are prosecuted on the ground that society as a whole is being injured.

criminogenic   Factors thought to bring about criminal behavior in an individual.

Cruz v. Beto (1972)   Inmates whose faiths are not the conventional ones practiced in the United States should have reasonable opportunities to practice their faith.

custodial model   A model of incarceration that emphasizes security, discipline, and order.

cybercrime   An offense committed through the use of one or more computers.

dark figure of crime   A metaphor that emphasizes the dangerous dimension of crime that is never reported to the police.

day reporting center   A community correctional center where an offender reports each day to comply with elements of a sentence.

defense attorney   The lawyer who represents the accused and the convicted offender in their dealings with criminal justice officials.

delinquent   A child who has committed an act that if committed by an adult would be criminal.

demonstrative evidence   Evidence that is not based on witness testimony but that demonstrates information relevant to the crime, such as maps, X-rays, and photographs; includes real evidence involved in the crime.

dependent child   A child who has no parent or guardian or whose parents are unable to give proper care.

detention hearing   A hearing by the juvenile court to determine if a juvenile is to be detained or released prior to adjudication.

determinate sentence   A sentence that fixes the term of imprisonment at a specific period of time.

differential response   A patrol strategy that assigns priorities to calls for service and chooses the appropriate response.

direct evidence   Eyewitness accounts.

directed patrol   A proactive form of patrolling that directs resources to known high-crime areas.

discovery   A prosecutor's pretrial disclosure to the defense of facts and evidence to be introduced at trial.

discretion   The authority to make decisions without reference to specific rules or facts, using instead one's own judgment; allows for individualization and informality in the administration of justice.

discretionary release   The release of an inmate from prison to conditional supervision at the discretion of the parole board within the boundaries set by the sentence and the penal law.

discrimination   Differential treatment of individuals or groups based on race, ethnicity, gender, sexual orientation, or economic status, instead of on their behavior or qualifications.

disparity   The inequality of treatment of one group by the criminal justice system, compared with the treatment accorded other groups.

diversion   The process of screening children out of the juvenile justice system without a decision by the court.

double jeopardy   The subjecting of a person to prosecution more than once in the same jurisdiction for the same offense; prohibited by the Fifth Amendment.

dual court system   A system consisting of a separate judicial structure for each state in addition to a national structure. Each case is tried in a court of the same jurisdiction as that of the law or laws broken.

due process model   A model of the criminal justice system that assumes freedom is so important that every effort must be made to ensure that criminal justice decisions are based on reliable information; it emphasizes the adversarial process, the rights of defendants, and formal decision-making procedures.

Enlightenment   A movement during the eighteenth century in England and France, in which concepts of liberalism, rationalism, equality, and individualism dominated social and political thinking.

entrapment   The defense that the individual was induced by the police to commit the criminal act.

Escobedo v. Illinois **(1964)**   An attorney must be provided to suspects when they are taken into police custody.

exchange   A mutual transfer of resources; a balance of benefits and deficits that flow from behavior based on decisions about the values and costs of alternatives.

exclusionary rule   The principle that illegally obtained evidence must be excluded from a trial.

Fare v. Michael C. **(1979)**   By examining the totality of the circumstances, trial court judges must evaluate the voluntariness of juveniles' waiving their rights to an attorney and to protections against self-incrimination.

federalism   A system of government in which power is divided between a central (national) government and regional (state) governments.

felonies   Serious crimes usually carrying a penalty of death or incarceration for more than one year.

filtering process   A screening operation; a process by which criminal justice officials screen out some cases while advancing others to the next level of decision making.

fine   A sum of money to be paid to the state by a convicted person as punishment for an offense.

forfeiture   Seizure by the government of property and other assets derived from or used in criminal activity.

frankpledge   A system in old English law in which members of a tithing, a group of ten families, pledged to be responsible for keeping order and bringing violators of the law to court.

Fulwood v. Clemmer **(1962)** Black Muslims have the same right to worship and practice their religion that inmates of other faiths have.

fundamental fairness A legal doctrine supporting the idea that so long as a state's conduct maintains basic standards of fairness, the Constitution has not been violated.

furlough The temporary release of an inmate from a correctional institution for a brief period, usually one to three days, for a visit home. Such programs help maintain family ties and prepare inmates for release on parole.

Furman v. Georgia **(1972)** The death penalty, as administered, constituted cruel and unusual treatment.

Gagnon v. Scarpelli **(1973)** Before probation can be revoked, a two-stage hearing must be held and the offender provided with specific elements of due process.

general deterrence Punishment of criminals that is intended to be an example to the general public and to discourage the commission of offenses by others.

Gideon v. Wainwright **(1963)** Defendants have a right to counsel in felony cases. States must provide defense counsel in felony cases for those who cannot pay for it themselves.

going rate Local view of the appropriate sentence for the offense, the defendant's prior record, and other characteristics.

Gregg v. Georgia **(1976)** Death penalty laws are constitutional if they require judge and jury to consider certain mitigating and aggravating circumstances in deciding which convicted murderers should be sentenced to death.

grouping A collection of individuals who interact in the workplace, but because of shifting membership they do not develop into a workgroup.

habeas corpus A writ or judicial order requesting the release of a person being detained in a jail, prison, or mental hospital. If a judge finds the person is being held improperly, the writ may be granted and the person released.

halfway house A correctional facility housing convicted felons who spend a portion of their day at work in the community but reside in the halfway house during nonworking hours.

hands-off policy Judges should not interfere with the administration of correctional institutions.

home confinement A sentence requiring the offender to remain inside his or her home during specified periods.

Hudson v. Palmer **(1984)** Prison officials have a right to search cells and confiscate from inmates any materials found.

In re Gault **(1967)** Juveniles have the right to counsel, to confront and examine accusers, and to have adequate notice of charges when there is the possibility of confinement as a punishment.

In re Winship **(1970)** The standard of proof beyond a reasonable doubt applies to juvenile delinquency proceedings.

incapacitation Depriving an offender of the ability to commit crimes against society, usually by detaining the offender in prison.

inchoate offense Conduct that is criminal even though the harm that the law seeks to prevent has not been done but merely planned or attempted.

incident-driven policing A reactive approach to policing emphasizing a quick response to calls for service.

incorporation The extension of the due process clause of the Fourteenth Amendment to make binding on state governments the rights guaranteed in the first ten amendments to the U.S. Constitution (the Bill of Rights).

indeterminate sentence An indefinite period set by a judge that specifies a minimum and a maximum time served in prison. Sometime after the minimum, the offender may be eligible for parole. Because it is based on the idea that the time necessary for treatment cannot be set, the indeterminate sentence is closely associated with rehabilitation.

indictment A document returned by a grand jury as a "true bill" charging an individual with a specific crime on the basis of a determination of probable cause as presented by a prosecuting attorney.

information A document charging an individual with a specific crime. It is prepared by a prosecuting attorney and presented to a court at a preliminary hearing.

inmate code The values and norms of the prison social system that define the inmates' idea of the model prisoner.

inquisitorial system Basis for legal systems in Europe in which the judge takes an active role in investigating the case and asking questions of witnesses in court.

intensive supervision probation (ISP) Probation granted under conditions of strict reporting to a probation officer with a limited caseload.

intermediate sanctions A variety of punishments that are more restrictive than traditional probation but less severe and less costly than incarceration.

internal affairs unit A branch of a police department that receives and investigates complaints against officers alleging violation of rules and policies.

jurisdiction The geographic territory or legal boundaries within which control may be exercised; the range of a court's authority.

jury A panel of citizens selected according to law and sworn to determine matters of fact in a criminal case and to deliver a verdict of guilty or not guilty.

labeling theory Theories emphasizing that the causes of criminal behavior are not found in the individual but in the social process that labels certain acts as deviant or criminal.

law enforcement The police function of controlling crime by intervening in situations in which the law has clearly been violated and the police need to identify and apprehend the guilty person.

learning theories Theories that see criminal behavior as learned, just as legal behavior is learned.

legal sufficiency model The presence of the minimum legal elements necessary for prosecution of a case. When a prosecutor's decision to prosecute a case is customarily based on legal sufficiency, a great many cases are accepted for prosecution, but the majority of them are disposed of by plea bargaining or dismissal.

Lewis v. Casey **(1996)** Limits the power of federal judges to ensure that prisoners have adequate access to prison law libraries and other legal resources.

line functions Police components that directly perform field operations and carry out the basic functions of patrol, investigation, traffic, vice, juvenile, and so on.

local legal culture Norms shared by members of a court community as to how cases should be handled and how a participant should behave in the judicial process.

mala in se Offenses that are wrong by their very nature.

mala prohibita Offenses prohibited by law but not wrong in themselves.

mandatory release The required release of an inmate from incarceration to community supervision upon the expiration of a certain time period, as specified by a determinate sentencing law or parole guidelines.

mandatory sentence A sentence determined by statutes and requiring that a certain penalty be imposed and carried out for convicted offenders who meet certain criteria.

Mapp v. Ohio **(1961)** The Fourth Amendment protects citizens from unreasonable searches and seizures by state officials.

McCleskey v. Kemp **(1987)** Rejected a challenge of Georgia's death penalty on grounds of racial discrimination.

McKeiver v. Pennsylvania **(1971)** Juveniles do not have a constitutional right to a jury trial.

medical model A model of corrections based on the assumption that criminal behavior is caused by biological or psychological conditions that require treatment.

Mempa v. Rhay **(1967)** Probationers have the right to counsel at a revocation and sentencing hearing.

mens rea "Guilty mind" or blameworthy state of mind, necessary for legal responsibility for a criminal offense; criminal intent, as distinguished from innocent intent.

merit selection A reform plan by which judges are nominated by a commission and appointed by the governor for a given period. When the term expires, the voters are asked to approve or disapprove the judge for a succeeding term. If the judge is disapproved, the committee nominates a successor for the governor's appointment.

Miranda v. Arizona **(1966)** Confessions made by suspects who were not notified of their due process rights cannot be admitted as evidence.

misdemeanors Offenses less serious than felonies and usually punishable by incarceration of no more than a year, probation, or intermediate sanction.

money laundering Moving the proceeds of criminal activities through a maze of businesses, banks, and brokerage accounts so as to disguise their origin.

Morrissey v. Brewer **(1972)** Due process rights require a prompt, informal inquiry before an impartial hearing officer before parole may be revoked. The parolee may present relevant information and confront witnesses.

motion An application to a court requesting that an order be issued to bring about a specified action.

National Crime Victimization Survey (NCVS) Interviews of samples of the U.S. population conducted by the Bureau of Justice Statistics to determine the number and types of criminal victimizations and thus the extent of unreported as well as reported crime.

National Incident-Based Reporting System (NIBRS) A reporting system in which the police describe each offense in a crime incident, together with data describing the offender, victim, and property.

neglected child A child who is not receiving proper care because of some action or inaction of his or her parents.

net widening Process in which the new sentencing options increase instead of reduce control over the offenders' lives.

New Jersey v. T.L.O. **(1985)** School officials may search a student based on a reasonable suspicion that the search will produce evidence that a school or a criminal law has been violated.

nolle prosequi An entry made by a prosecutor on the record of a case and announced in court to indicate that the charges specified will not be prosecuted. In effect, the charges are thereby dismissed.

nonpartisan election An election in which candidates who are not endorsed by political parties are presented to voters for selection.

North Carolina v. Alford **(1970)** A plea of guilty may be accepted for the purpose of a lesser sentence by a defendant who maintains his or her innocence.

occupational crime Criminal offenses committed through opportunities created in a legal business or occupation.

order maintenance The police function of preventing behavior that disturbs or threatens to disturb the public peace or that involves face-to-face conflict among two or more persons. In such situations the police exercise discretion in deciding whether a law has been broken.

organized crime A framework for the perpetration of criminal acts—usually in fields such as gambling, drugs, and prostitution—providing illegal services that are in great demand.

pardon An action of the executive branch of state or federal government excusing an offense and absolving the offender from the consequences of the crime.

parens patriae The state as parent; the state as guardian and protector of all citizens (such as juveniles) who are unable to protect themselves.

parole The conditional release of an inmate from incarceration under supervision after part of the prison sentence has been served.

partisan election An election in which candidates endorsed by political parties are presented to voters for selection.

penitentiary An institution intended to punish criminals by isolating them from society and from one another so they can reflect on their past misdeeds, repent, and reform.

penology A branch of criminology dealing with the management of prisons and the treatment of offenders.

peremptory challenge Removal of a prospective juror without giving any reason. Attorneys are allowed a limited number of such challenges.

PINS Acronym for "person in need of supervision," a term that designates juveniles who are either status offenders or thought to be on the verge of trouble.

plea bargain A defendant's plea of guilty to a criminal charge with the reasonable expectation of receiving some consideration from the state for doing so, usually a reduction of the charge. The defendant's ultimate goal is a penalty lighter than the one formally warranted by the charged offense.

political crime An act that constitutes a threat against the state (such as treason, sedition, or espionage).

positivist criminology A school of criminology that views behavior as stemming from social, biological, and psychological factors. It argues that punishment should be tailored to the individual needs of the offender.

Powell v. Alabama **(1932)** An attorney must be provided to a defendant facing the death penalty.

presentence report Report prepared by probation officer, who investigates a convicted offender's background to help the judge select an appropriate sentence.

presumptive parole date The presumed release date stipulated by parole guidelines if the offender serves time without disciplinary or other incidents.

presumptive sentence A sentence for which the legislature or a commission sets a minimum and maximum range of months or years. Judges are to fix the length of the sentence within that range, allowing for special circumstances.

preventive detention Holding a defendant for trial based on a judge's finding that, if the defendant were released on bail, he or she would endanger the safety of any other person and the community or would flee.

preventive patrol Making the police presence known, to deter crime and to make officers available to respond quickly to calls.

proactive Acting in anticipation, such as an active search for offenders initiated by the police without waiting for a crime to be reported. Arrests for crimes without victims are usually proactive.

probable cause The criterion for deciding whether evidence is strong enough to uphold an arrest or to support issuing an arrest or search warrant. Also, the facts upholding the belief that a crime has been committed and that the accused committed the offense.

probation A sentence that the offender is allowed to serve in the community under supervision.

problem-oriented policing An approach to policing in which officers routinely seek to identify, analyze, and respond to the circumstances underlying the incidents that prompt citizens to call the police.

procedural criminal law Law defining the procedures that criminal justice officials must follow in enforcement, adjudication, and correction.

procedural due process The constitutional requirement that all persons be treated fairly and justly by government officials. An accused person can be arrested, prosecuted, tried, and punished only in accordance with procedures prescribed by law.

prosecuting attorney A legal representative of the state with sole responsibility for bringing criminal charges. In some states referred to as district attorney, state's attorney, or county attorney.

psychological explanations Explanations of crime that emphasize mental processes and behavior.

public defender An attorney employed on a full-time, salaried basis by the government to represent indigents.

reactive Occurring in response, such as police activity in response to notification that a crime has been committed.

real evidence Physical evidence such as a weapon, records, fingerprints, stolen property—objects involved in the crime.

reasonable doubt The standard used by a juror to decide if the prosecution has provided enough evidence for conviction. Jurors should vote for acquittal if they think there is a reasonable doubt.

recidivism A return to criminal behavior.

reformatory An institution for young offenders emphasizing training, a mark system of classification, indeterminate sentences, and parole.

rehabilitation The goal of restoring a convicted offender to a constructive place in society through some form of vocational or educational training or therapy.

rehabilitation model A model of corrections that emphasizes the need to restore a convicted offender to a constructive place in society through some form of vocational or educational training or therapy.

reintegration model A model of a correctional institution that emphasizes maintaining the offender's ties to family and community as a method of reform, recognizing that the offender will be returning to society.

release on recognizance (ROR) Pretrial release granted on the defendant's promise to appear in court because the judge believes that the defendant's ties in the community guarantee that he or she will appear.

restitution Repayment—in the form of money or service—by an offender to a victim who has suffered some financial loss from the offense.

restoration Punishment designed to repair the damage done to the victim and community by an offender's criminal act.

retribution Punishment inflicted on a person who has violated a criminal law and so deserves to be penalized. The severity of the sanction should fit the seriousness of the crime.

Ricketts v. Adamson **(1987)** Defendants must uphold the plea agreement or suffer the consequences.

Ruffin v. Commonwealth **(1871)** By committing a crime, the prisoner has become a slave of the state and has forfeited all personal rights.

Ruiz v. Estelle **(1980)** Conditions of confinement in the Texas prison system were unconstitutional.

Santobello v. New York **(1971)** When a guilty plea rests on a promise of a prosecutor, it must be fulfilled.

Schall v. Martin **(1984)** Juveniles can be held in preventive detention if there is concern that they may commit additional crimes while awaiting court action.

search warrant An order of a judge that allows a police officer to search a designated place for specific persons or items to be seized.

selective incapacitation Making the best use of expensive and limited prison space by targeting for incarceration those individuals whose incapacity will do the most to reduce crime in society.

self-incrimination The act of exposing oneself to prosecution by being forced to respond to questions whose answers may reveal that one has committed a crime. The Fifth Amendment protects defendants against self-incrimination. In any criminal proceeding the prosecution must prove the charges by means of evidence other than the testimony of the accused.

sentencing guidelines A mechanism to indicate to judges the expected sanction for certain offenses, to reduce disparities in sentencing.

separate confinement A penitentiary system, developed in Pennsylvania, in which each inmate was held in isolation from other inmates. All activities, including craft work, took place in the cells.

service The police function of providing assistance to the public, usually in matters unrelated to crime.

shock probation A sentence in which the offender is released after a short incarceration and resentenced to probation.

social conflict theories Theories that assume criminal law and the criminal justice system are primarily a means of controlling the poor and the have-nots.

social process theories Theories that see criminality as normal behavior. Everyone has the potential to become a criminal, depending on the influences that impel one toward or away from crime and also how one is regarded by others.

social structure theories Theories that blame crime on the existence of a powerless lower class that lives with poverty and deprivation and often turns to crime in response.

socialization The process by which the rules, symbols, and values of a group or subculture are learned by its members.

sociological explanations Explanations of crime that emphasize the social conditions that bear on the individual as causes of criminal behavior.

special deterrence Punishment that is inflicted on criminals to discourage them from committing any future crimes.

status offense Any act committed by a juvenile that is considered unacceptable for a child, such as truancy or running away from home, but that would not be a crime if it were committed by an adult.

statutes Laws passed by legislatures. Statutory definitions of criminal offenses are found in penal codes.

strict liability An obligation or duty that when broken is an offense that can be judged criminal without a showing of *mens rea,* or criminal intent; usually applied to regulatory offenses involving health and safety.

subculture The symbols, beliefs, and values shared by members of a subgroup within the larger society.

substantive criminal law Law defining the acts that are subject to punishment, and specifying the punishments for such offenses.

sworn officers Police employees who have taken an oath and been given powers by the state to make arrests and use necessary force, in accordance with their duties.

system A complex whole consisting of interdependent parts whose operations are directed toward goals and are influenced by the environment within which they function.

system efficiency model   Policy of the prosecutor's office that encourages speedy and early disposition of cases in response to caseload pressures. Weak cases are screened out at intake, and other nontrial alternatives are used as primary means of disposition.

Tennessee v. Garner (1985)   Deadly force may not be used against an unarmed and fleeing suspect unless necessary to prevent the escape and unless the officer has probable cause to believe that the suspect poses a significant threat of death or serious injury to the officers or others.

Terry v. Ohio (1968)   A police officer may stop and frisk an individual if it is reasonable to suspect that a crime has been committed.

testimony   Oral evidence provided by a legally competent witness.

theory of differential association   Theories that people become criminals because they encounter more influences that view criminal behavior as normal and acceptable than influences that are hostile to criminal behavior.

trial courts of general jurisdiction   Criminal courts with jurisdiction over all offenses, including felonies. In some states these courts may also hear appeals.

trial courts of limited jurisdiction   Criminal courts with trial jurisdiction over misdemeanor cases and preliminary matters in felony cases. Sometimes these courts hold felony trials that may result in penalties below a specified limit.

trial sufficiency model   The presence of sufficient legal elements to ensure successful prosecution of a case. When a prosecutor's decision to prosecute a case is customarily based on trial sufficiency, only cases that seem certain to result in conviction at trial are accepted for prosecution. Use of plea bargaining is minimal; good police work and court capacity to go to trial are required.

unconditional release   The release of an inmate from incarceration without any further correctional supervision; the inmate cannot be returned to prison for any remaining portion of the sentence for the current offense.

Uniform Crime Reports (UCR)   An annually published statistical summary of crimes reported to the police, based on voluntary reports to the FBI by local, state, and federal law enforcement agencies.

United States attorney   Officials responsible for the prosecution of crimes that violate the laws of the United States. Appointed by the president and assigned to a U.S. district court jurisdiction.

United States v. Leon (1984)   Evidence seized using a warrant that is later found to be defective is valid if the officer was acting in good faith.

United States v. Salerno and Cafero (1987)   Preventive detention provisions of the Bail Reform Act of 1984 are upheld as a legitimate use of governmental power designed to prevent people from committing crimes while on bail.

victimology   A field of criminology that examines the role the victim plays in precipitating a criminal incident.

visible crime   Offenses against persons and property committed primarily by members of the lower class. Often referred to as "street crimes" or "ordinary crimes," these offenses are most upsetting to the public.

voir dire   A questioning of prospective jurors to screen out persons the attorneys think might be biased or incapable of delivering a fair verdict.

waive   Procedure by which the juvenile court waives its jurisdiction and transfers a juvenile case to the adult criminal court.

warrant   A court order authorizing police officials to take certain actions; for example, to arrest suspects or to search premises.

Williams v. Florida (1970)   Juries of fewer than twelve members are constitutional.

Wilson v. Seiter (1991)   The standard of review of official conduct is whether state policies or actions by correctional officers constitute "deliberate indifference" to constitutional rights.

Wolff v. McDonnell (1974)   Basic elements of procedural due process must be present when decisions are made about the disciplining of an inmate.

work and educational release   The daytime release of inmates from correctional institutions so they can work or attend school.

workgroup   A collection of individuals who interact in the workplace on a continuing basis, share goals, develop norms regarding how activities should be carried out, and eventually establish a network of roles that differentiates the group from others.

working personality   A set of emotional and behavioral characteristics developed by a member of an occupational group in response to the work situation and environmental influences.

Name Index

Subject Index

Photo Credits